# Legal Reasoning, Writing, and Persuasive Argument

ROBIN S. WELLFORD
Director, Legal Research and Writing
Chapman University School of Law

LexisNexis™

Library of Congress Control Number: 2002105781

ISBN#: 0-82055-389-1

Editorial Offices
744 Broad Street, Newark, NJ 07102 (973) 820-2000
201 Mission St., San Francisco, CA 94105-1831 (415) 908-3200
701 East Water Street, Charlottesville, VA 22902-7587 (804) 972-7600
www.lexis.com

Pub. 3166

*This book is dedicated to my family, for whom words are inadequate. I am so grateful for your unwavering support, guidance and love. I am truly blessed.*

# *ACKNOWLEDGMENTS*

I would like to thank my students at both Washington University and Chapman University, without whom this book would not have been possible. It is through their questions, challenges and break-throughs that I am inspired to try new approaches and become a more effective educator. I would also like to express my gratitude to numerous former and present colleagues who were the source of ideas that appear as exercises in this book and who provided editorial support and constructive criticism. They include, Jacline Evered, Jeff Hanslick, Jo Ellen Lewis, Tomea Mayer, Ann Shields, and Dana Underwood. I would also like to thank and acknowledge New York University School of Law and their Moot Court Casebook, whose hypothetical problems inspired the appellate and trial court brief examples that appear in the Appendices.

I am blessed to be a part of the national legal writing community, a community in which colleagues so generously share their innovative ideas and expertise. Many of these ideas have inspired teaching approaches, exercises and examples that appear in this book. I also owe a debt of gratitude to so many people in the legal writing field for their encouragement and support as I grow as a teacher, writer and human being. I am also so appreciative of the Deans and faculty at Chapman University School of Law. They have fully supported my efforts and created a work environment in which it is a true pleasure to teach and write. Finally, to the legal writing faculty, Nancy Schultz and Jacline Evered, and to our wonderful adjunct professors of legal writing, thank you for helping make this work fun and exciting.

# *PREFACE*

Evaluating a client's legal problem and communicating that analysis to the client is the heart and soul of any attorney's practice. Day in and day out, in every field of law, you will have the opportunity to practice and master these skills. Legal Reasoning, Writing, and Persuasive Argument is designed to help you develop these fundamental lawyering skills. Legal writing is challenging, in part, because the clarity and effectiveness of the final product depends on the clarity of the underlying legal reasoning. Thus, this book teaches and illustrates the underlying skills of legal reasoning and analysis that are integral components of effective legal writing. The forms of written communication in legal writing are also new and challenging. In fact, even though you have been writing most of your life, the legal writing terrain is deceptively challenging for that very reason. To become a skilled legal writer, you must be willing to abandon writing techniques that have worked well in other disciplines, and be open to learning new ways of expressing yourself. Therefore, this book is also designed to help you become a skilled writer by teaching and illustrating effective templates for written legal analysis and argument. It is my hope that you will not only find this book to be a valuable learning guide during law school, but that it will also serve as a useful resource to you as you begin practicing law.

Like learning to play a musical instrument, you will become expert at legal writing by practicing—the more you practice, the more accomplished you will become. To help you learn and then master the skills of legal reasoning and writing, this book emphasizes the *process* of legal reasoning and writing, from the reading and thinking stages, through the outlining and drafting stages, to the final written product itself. Taking the musical analogy a step further, no one would expect a novice musician to master Beethoven's Ninth Symphony without first having practiced and mastered more basic musical scores. Similarly, law students learn legal writing most easily by first mastering basic skills, and then building gradually towards mastery of more complex skills. Therefore, the chapters incorporate a building block approach, demonstrating how to evaluate a single case before evaluating how to synthesize a group of cases, and how to draft a simple memo based on one case before drafting a more complex memo based on multiple cases.

Because illustrations are a critically important component of the learning process, this book liberally illustrates every step of the process, from reading a case, to evaluating how a case affects a client's problem, to synthesizing a group of cases, to outlining a template for your written product, to the drafting process itself. Comments are inserted alongside each illustration to help you understand the reasoning, logic and drafting decisions that underlie each part of the illustration. To help you evaluate the illustrations at a deeply comprehensive level, the book uses several repeating hypothetical problems to illustrate each pre-drafting and drafting step. These illustrations are also linked to the sample office memos and court briefs illustrated in the Appendices. Thus, you will have the opportunity not just to review sample documents, but to study the underlying analysis, logic, and choices that influence drafting decisions in the final products.

# *TABLE OF CONTENTS*

# INTRODUCTION TO LEGAL ANALYSIS AND WRITING

The skills of evaluating and solving a client problem, and communicating that analysis in writing, are the cornerstones of an attorney's practice. This book describes and illustrates the basic problem-solving and writing skills that will enable you to advise prospective clients of their legal rights and duties and to advocate your clients' interests. Because of the importance of learning by example, each chapter liberally illustrates each of the pre-drafting and drafting steps required in evaluating a client problem and in representing that client.

 ## I  ROLES OF THE ATTORNEY

### A.  Attorneys as Problem-Solvers

You cannot advise a client or persuade an opponent or judge without first understanding the factual and legal issues involved. Before communicating your analysis or argument to a client, opposing attorney, or judge, you must first engage in some preliminary problem-solving, carefully studying the law and evaluating how it affects your client. Chapters 3–7 of this book discuss the basic skills involved in evaluating client problems.

### 1.  The Basic Inquiry: Identifying Rules of Law and Issues

When you meet with a client, your client will relay to you a factual story and ask for your legal advice. Before you can begin to advise your client, you will need to study statutes and cases and determine the rules of law that may affect your client. From these rules of law, you will then identify the legal issue or issues these rules may raise for your client. In order to spot legal issues, you will need to consider the myriad of facts that pertain to your client's situation and how they relate to relevant rules of law. As you do so, you will find that some of the client's facts will not be relevant at all to the rules of law you are evaluating. Other facts may trigger questions about whether, and how, the law might affect the client. These facts, together with the requirements of the rule of law you are evaluating, pose what are called *legal issues* for your client. In Chapters 4 and 5, you will learn how to evaluate rules of law. You will also learn how to distinguish "legally significant" facts from those facts that are not relevant from a legal perspective.

## 2.   *Fact-Centered Issues*

### (a)  *Analogical Reasoning*

As a first-year law student, you will be reading cases in all of your courses. However, in your introductory legal research and writing course, or basic lawyering skills course, you will learn to read cases from a slightly different perspective—from the perspective of an attorney who represents a client's interests. As an attorney representing a client's interests, you will read cases both to predict what the law would have to say about your client's situation (your role as an advisor) and to argue, if possible, why the law favors your client (your role as an advocate).To help you learn how to assume those roles effectively, Chapter 6 describes the process of reasoning by analogy to earlier cases. This process of *analogical reasoning* simply means that, as you study and evaluate a case, you will compare and distinguish the facts of that case to your client's facts. Based on the factual similarities, or distinctions, you will be able to predict whether your client's situation should turn out the same way as the earlier case, or in a different way.

### (b)  *Case Synthesis*

Usually when you evaluate a client's problem, you will find that there is more than one precedent case in your jurisdiction that can help you solve your client's problem. As you read the relevant cases, you will likely find that, even though the courts interpreted the same rule of law, in some cases the plaintiff won and in other cases the defendant won. Why is this so? The facts in each case were different enough that they merited different results when the courts applied the same rule of law to the unique set of facts involved in the different disputes. In order to advise and represent your client's interests competently, you will need to make some sense of the earlier cases by synthesizing and reconciling them. In Chapter 7, you will learn how to synthesize and reconcile a group of cases.

### 3. Law-Centered Issues

Sometimes when attorneys research the law, they dispute what the law itself means, independently of any factual controversy. As an example, when Congress enacted the federal wiretap statute, it required the government to obtain the protection of an immediate judicial seal after it obtained wiretap evidence. The purpose of the sealing requirement is to safeguard the evidence from tampering. Should the government fail to obtain an immediate judicial seal, the statute requires the government to provide a "satisfactory explanation" for its sealing delay. What does the term "satisfactory explanation" actually mean? Before a court could resolve the factual question of whether the government had supplied a satisfactory explanation in a particular case, the court would first have to resolve the preliminary legal question. Chapters 20 and 21 discuss the strategies involved in arguing law-centered issues.

## B. Attorneys as Advisors

When a client asks you for legal advice, you will counsel your clients by responding to concerns they have raised. These concerns may range from questions about whether a client can lawfully take a certain action, to legal advice on a corporate merger, to representing a client in a lawsuit. In your role as advisor, you will review the law fairly and impartially, considering the ambiguities in the law that both favor your client and disfavor your client. As an advisor, your goal is to predict what the law will have to say about your client's situation.

After you have studied relevant statutes and cases, you will convey your analysis to the client. Attorneys usually advise their clients of the results of their research verbally, in a telephone call or meeting. Commonly, however, they also reduce their analysis to written form. By reducing their analysis to written form they preserve their thinking and research results for future reference. One of the most common documents attorneys draft in their role as advisor is an internal memorandum that will be reviewed only by other members of the legal team. This written form of communication is called an office memorandum. Because of the importance of this type of written communication, it is discussed in depth in Chapters 8–17 of this book.

Another common way in which attorneys reduce their legal analysis to writing is, not surprisingly, by writing client letters. Client advisory letters are usually not as detailed or technical as office memos; however, they are also an important means of written communication. Chapter 18 describes the various considerations involved in drafting client letters.

## C.  *Attorneys as Advocates*

The other role you will assume when you practice law is the role of an advocate. Based on what we read in the news and view on television, most non-lawyers tend to think of the role of advocate as limited to the courtroom. However, in most areas of the law, attorneys routinely assume an advocacy role. For example, attorneys negotiating a real estate transaction for a client advocate why their client is entitled to favorable terms. Tax attorneys advocate their clients' interests when seeking a favorable outcome from the Internal Revenue Service. Copyright attorneys not only help their clients gain the protection of a copyright, but assume an advocacy role when a competitor attempts to circumvent the copyright laws.

As in their advisory role, attorneys commonly reduce their persuasive arguments into written form. These written arguments are often included in letters to opposing counsel, and in documents submitted to judges and to other adjudicators. Chapters 19–24 describe the basic persuasive argument strategies and constructs that are used in all arguments, irrespective of the forum. Because attorneys commonly submit arguments to courts, and because such arguments are an effective vehicle for you to learn basic persuasive skills, Chapters 25–28 describe the particular nuances of drafting arguments to trial and appellate courts. Chapter 29 discusses how to engage in an oral argument before a court. Not surprisingly, attorneys also communicate with opposing counsel in writing. Chapter 30 discusses the special considerations involved in drafting demand and settlement letters to opposing counsel.

## D.  *A Suggestion*

As you may have guessed by now, the process of analyzing a legal problem and conveying that analysis to a third party likely differs from anything you have ever experienced before. Legal analysis and writing differs from the writing you performed as an undergraduate, and differs from the narrative writing to which you are exposed when reading a novel or the newspaper. If you try to cling to the writing practices that have worked so well for you in other disciplines, you will likely experience some difficulty and frustration when learning these new skills. Instead, this book invites you to suspend all judgment of what has worked for you in the past, and stay open to learning new analytical skills and new ways of communicating information.

## ◆ II ◆ *EMPLOYERS' EXPECTATIONS*

You will soon be swept up in the law school experience and all of the attendant excitement and anxiety. Burdened with seemingly limitless demands on your time and faced with the prospect of final exams, it is easy to lose perspective of why you decided to go to law school. Most law students come to law school for training in how to become competent, ethical attorneys. Of course, you will develop and polish the legal skills involved in representing a client throughout your legal career. You cannot possibly become an expert at these skills in your first year of law school, and employers do not expect to hire "experts." However, the following survey conducted by the American Bar Foundation does provide some perspective.

In a survey conducted by the American Bar Foundation, over 100 hiring attorneys were interviewed in the Chicago, Illinois legal market.[1] The hiring partners were asked to identify the skills they demanded that new attorneys bring with them to their firms and/or corporations, and those skills they expected new attorneys to develop "on the job." The survey reflects the reality in today's legal market that most employers expect new law school graduates to begin their new careers already possessing a certain level of competence in the basic legal skills you will learn in this course. As you review the following excerpts from that survey, you may be surprised to see that the fundamental skills you will learn in this course are the top five ranked skills that employers will expect you to know when you walk in the door.

---

[1] Bryant B. Garth & Joanne Martin, *Law Schools and the Construction of Competence*, 43 J. of Leg. Educ. 469, 490 (1993).

| SKILLS | BRING | DEVELOP |
|---|---|---|
| **Oral communication** | **91%** | **9%** |
| **Written communication** | **90** | **10** |
| **Library legal research** | **92** | **9** |
| **Computer legal research** | **84** | **16** |
| **Ability in legal analysis and legal reasoning** | **81** | **19** |
| Instilling others' confidence in you | 52 | 48 |
| Knowledge of procedural law | 28 | 72 |
| Understanding and conducting litigation | 6 | 94 |
| Negotiation | 4 | 96 |
| Counseling | 9 | 91 |
| Organization and management of legal work | 33 | 67 |
| Sensitivity to professional ethical concerns | 74 | 25 |
| Ability to diagnose and plan solutions for legal problems | 41 | 59 |
| Ability to obtain and keep clients | 8 | 92 |
| Fact gathering | 47 | 53 |

## III  *TIME LINE OF DOCUMENTS ATTORNEYS ROUTINELY PREPARE*

As an attorney, you will draft office memos, client letters and letters to other attorneys through-out the entire time you represent a particular client, whether or not any lawsuit has been filed. Even when you represent a client in a law-suit, you will continue to memorialize the results of your research and analysis by drafting office memos and letters. Therefore, on the graph on the following page, the arrow flowing from the top box reflects the on-going process of ad-vising clients and drafting letters, continuing through-out the stages of a law-suit. You may find the diagram useful because it will provide you with an un-derlying context as you are asked to draft documents in this course. In addition, because most of the cases in your casebooks arise from a lawsuit, the diagram should provide you with a framework for understanding the proce-dural context of the cases in your casebooks as well.

| **Factual/Procedural Context for Drafting Documents** | | **Documents Attorneys Draft** |
|---|---|---|
| Client seeks attorney's advice. A lawsuit may or may not ensue. A lawsuit may or may not be ongoing. | ⇨ | Office Memorandum Client Advisory/Opinion Letter Demand/Settlement Letter |

**Courthouse**

| | | |
|---|---|---|
| Plaintiff begins lawsuit by filing a "complaint" in the courthouse. | ⇨ | Complaint or ("Petition") |
| Defendant responds, often with a motion and an accompanying "brief." | ⇨ | Answer, or Motion to Dismiss, or Motion to Remove, or Motion for More Definite Statement |
| If the lawsuit survives the defendant's motions, the parties engage in "discovery" to obtain information about each other. | ⇨ | Interrogatories Request for Documents Motion to Compel Motion for Sanctions |
| Either party may ask the judge to enter judgment in its favor without going to trial. | ⇨ | Motion for Summary Judgment |

**Factual/Procedural Context
for Drafting Documents**

**Documents
Attorneys Draft**

During the trial, parties may ask the judge to grant a variety of different requests, or "motions."

Motion to Suppress
Motion in Limine
Motion for Directed Verdict

After the trial, the losing party may ask the trial court to reverse the verdict and then may file an appeal to a higher court. The winning party responds to the appeal.

Post-Trial Brief
Motion for New Trial
Motion for J.N.O.V.

Appellant's Brief
Appellee's Brief

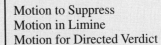

# 2

# INTRODUCTION TO AMERICAN LEGAL SYSTEM

When evaluating a client's legal problem, you will research and analyze "the law." Most lay people think of the law as traffic laws and criminal laws, which are simply types of statutes. However, the sources of law extend beyond statutes, and the different federal and state legal systems complicate matters even further. This chapter provides a basic introduction to our legal system.

##  INTRODUCTION

### A.  Two Basic Court Systems

The federal government and each individual state have their own laws and hierarchy of courts within their court systems. Both federal and state legal systems operate simultaneously. In general, federal laws govern everyone who resides in the United States or who has certain minimal contacts within the United States. Each state also has its own set of laws that govern the people who reside within that state as well as people who have certain minimal contacts within that state. Therefore, if you practiced law in Los Angeles, California, you would consider how both federal laws and California state laws might affect a client's conduct. Similarly, a lawyer practicing law in Chicago, Illinois would consider Illinois state laws as well as federal laws when advising a client. As a general rule, legal issues that arise from federal law are interpreted by federal courts and agencies. Legal disputes that arise from a state source of law are generally resolved by state courts and agencies.[1]

---

[1] As you will learn in your civil procedure class, there are a few exceptions. Even though the federal and state court systems are separate legal systems, federal courts, in limited circumstances, sometimes hear disputes that arise

## B. Sources of Law

Both the federal and state legal systems have three primary sources of law that may affect a client: the constitution, statutes, and common law.

### 1. Constitutions

Most lay people are aware of the United States Constitution; however, each state has also ratified its own constitution. A state constitution may be even more protective of the rights of its citizens than the United States Constitution. For example, a police search potentially might not violate a person's federal constitutional right against an "unreasonable search and seizure," but might violate a particular state's more restrictive constitutional provisions.

### 2. Statutes & Administrative Regulations

In both systems, the legislative branch has the primary law-making power, enacting statutes that govern the rights and duties of the people who have the requisite minimum contacts within that jurisdiction. It is entirely possible that a client's actions would be governed by both a state statute and a federal statute. For example, Congress has passed Title VII, a comprehensive statute that prohibits employers from discriminating against their employees on the basis of race, color, religion, sex, or national origin. However, most states also have their own statutes prohibiting employers within their states from engaging in similar discriminatory acts. How does this affect you as an attorney? If you represented an employer in such a matter, you would want to ensure that your client complied with both sets of statutes. When representing an individual employee who has complained of discriminatory practices at work, you would carefully evaluate both sets of statutes before helping your client decide on a course of action.

Although legislatures enact statutes, they also delegate law-making power to the executive branch by authorizing agencies to issue regulations that will implement the statutes. Thus, the Equal Employment Opportunity Commission (the EEOC) has implemented regulations and guidelines that help interpret Title VII and give it practical effect. Depending upon whether Congress has given an administrative agency rule-making authority, an agency's regulations may or may not have the binding force of law. Regulations that have the force of law may in a sense be considered a fourth source of law, even though their authority is derived from legislation.

---

from state laws. Similarly, state courts sometimes consider federal laws, assuming certain jurisdictional issues are satisfied.

### 3.  Common Law

Some laws do not have their source in a constitution or statute. Instead, these laws evolve solely from court decisions, and are called the "common law." How did common law evolve? Judges started from a few basic ideas that seemed to be universally accepted in medieval society. As new factual controversies arose, the judges expanded on and refined their interpretations of the common law by focusing on the similarities to and distinctions from previous cases. Although the common law originated in England, it was brought to the United States by British colonists, eventually becoming each state's original body of law.[2] Today, legislative bodies have enacted statutes that have replaced a fair amount of the common law. However, the common law still exists today. As importantly, the common law method of reasoning by analogy is still the primary means by which attorneys evaluate cases and predict what the law might say about their clients' conduct.

## EXERCISE 1:
## NATURE OF THE LAW

Sometime in the future, as a result of some catastrophe, life as we know it no longer exists.[3] A group of survivors congregate and form a new society, Gilligan's Island. As the society evolves, the citizens elect a seven-member council and an administrator, who is authorized to institute and administer any rules the council may adopt. The council recognizes that the haphazard system of farming that previously existed is inefficient, and they divide the land into equal plots. Each able-bodied member of the society gets a plot. The Howells and Ginger are fortunate enough to have a creek bisect their plots. The Howells are savvy, unscrupulous business people, and they divert the creek's water wholly for their own use. Ginger objects to this diversion. The Howells and Ginger squabble. At the height of one of their confrontations, Ginger strikes Mr. Thurston Howell, III over the head with a shovel, killing him.

The council elects a judge and directs the judge to empanel a group of citizens to try Ginger for killing Mr. Howell. Brought before the judge, Ginger admits that she killed Mr. Howell, but claims that she has broken no law because the island does not have a law that forbids killing.

---

[2] Richard K. Neumann, Jr., *Legal Reasoning and Legal Writing: Structure, Strategy, and Style* 5 (4th ed. Aspen L. & Bus. 2001).

[3] The ideas for Exercises 1–3 were inspired by James E. Moliterno & Fredric I. Lederer, *An Introduction to Law, Law Study, and the Lawyer's Role*, Ch. 3 (1991).

You are the judge in Ginger's case. You clearly have delegated power to hear the case, i.e., you have jurisdiction. However, before you can proceed with Ginger's trial, you must decide if killing is against the law on the island. Deciding whether killing is against the law on the island requires you to think about the question of what "law" is. Does law consist only of positive, affirmative declarations? That is, must someone or something with recognized authority enact a rule for there to be law that can be enforced? If that definition of law is too narrow, from where else might "law" be derived? From religious doctrine? From societal mores? From natural law? If so, what are the limits of this approach?

Typically, in the Anglo-American legal system, the judge decides what the "law" is. As judge, what is your decision in Ginger's case? What value judgments does your decision embody?

## C.   Interplay Between Branches of Government

Although each source of law stands on its own, there is also significant interplay between the three branches of government. Constitutions and statutes are generally future-oriented. Therefore, they are written in broad, general terms in order to encompass a range of future conduct that might fall within their ambit. Inevitably, when the broad language of a statute or constitution is applied to a specific factual situation, questions arise. Does this specific conduct fall within the ambit of that law? Is this particular individual the type of person the legislature intended to cover? As these questions arise in individual cases, judges are required to interpret the meaning of specific statutes and constitutions. By giving texture and additional substance to the law, judges play an active role in the evolving interpretation of what a law means, even when the source of law is statutory or constitutional.

Sometimes during the process of judicial interpretation, legislatures disagree with the courts' interpretation of a particular statute. If the legislature does not like the manner in which a statute has been interpreted, the legislature can, in turn, amend the statutory language to clarify its meaning. In the process, the new legislation invalidates earlier court decisions that interpreted the statute in a different manner. For example, in 1991, Congress amended the Civil Rights Act of 1964 so as to nullify a series of Supreme Court cases that interpreted that Act in a manner with which Congress disagreed.

## EXERCISE 2:
### NATURE OF THE LAW

Review the facts from Exercise 1, and assume that, following Ginger's case, the council quickly and without debate enacts the following statute:

> Any person who kills another shall be guilty of murder and the jury shall sentence such person either to death or to life imprisonment.

Some months later, Gilligan and the Skipper get into an argument in their hut. The two men had a history of conflict. Apparently, Gilligan clumsily broke a conch that was near and dear to the Skipper. Enraged, the Skipper approached Gilligan swinging a club and vowing to kill him. Frightened, Gilligan grabbed a sharpened bamboo shoot, and, as the Skipper lunged toward him, Gilligan plunged the shoot into the Skipper's ample gut, killing him.

The island constable arrests Gilligan and brings him before you for trial on murder charges. Gilligan admits he killed the Skipper, but claims that the killing was not against the law because it was in self-defense.

The judge must decide the contextual meaning of the statute. When interpreting a statute, judges typically begin with the literal text of the statute and look for the statute's plain meaning. Sometimes, when the language is ambiguous or when the plain meaning would lead to an absurd or unreasonable result, judges go beyond the literal text of the statute and look for legislative intent by examining the statute's legislative history. Here, however, there is no legislative history, as the council passed the statute quickly and without debate.

What is your decision in Gilligan's case? Do you apply the plain meaning of the statute? Do you go beyond the plain meaning and conclude that the council surely would have exempted killing in self-defense had it thought of it? What are the consequences of your decision?

## II. *STARE DECISIS—MANDATORY & PERSUASIVE PRECEDENT*

In our legal system, the meaning of each of the sources of law evolves through a process of judicial interpretation known as *stare decisis*. Judges face the continuing challenge of interpreting how a particular law should be applied to a specific factual dispute before the court. In that sense, the result in a particular case is dependent on the specific facts of that case. At the same time, our system of government favors predictability and consistency. It would be difficult to advise clients about their rights and duties under the law if attorneys had no idea how a particular court might interpret that rule of law. Therefore, judges look to the decisions of prior courts for guidance in interpreting a source of law so that their decision in a particular case is consistent with prior case law in their jurisdiction.

In evaluating cases under our system of stare decisis, judges consider two different kinds of precedent, *mandatory* and *persuasive* authority. As the names imply, courts are required to follow only the rules of law established in earlier cases that are considered to be mandatory authority. Courts may or may not be persuaded to follow earlier cases that are only persuasive authority. As a future attorney who will advise clients of their legal rights, it is of course critical that you know how to tell the difference between mandatory and persuasive authority.

Whether a case is mandatory or persuasive authority depends on the jurisdiction within which the case arose and the hierarchal level of that court within the jurisdiction. A previous case is binding on a court only: (1) if it arose within the *same jurisdiction* as the dispute presently before the court, and (2) the earlier decision was rendered by a *higher level court* within that jurisdiction. For example, a Missouri state trial court judge who is interpreting a state law would not be bound by an earlier decision of the Eighth Circuit Court of Appeals, even if the Eighth Circuit had interpreted the same Missouri state law. Even though the Eighth Circuit Court of Appeals is a higher level court than a trial court, the two cases are not within the same jurisdiction. Recall that the federal and state court systems are two parallel, and separate, legal systems. As another example, an earlier decision of the Missouri Court of Appeals would never be binding on the Missouri Supreme Court. Why? Even though the courts are within the same jurisdiction, the Missouri Court of Appeals is not a higher level court.

## EXERCISE 3:
## NATURE OF THE LAW

Whatever your actual decision in Exercise 2, assume for present purposes that you decided to apply probable legislative intent rather than the plain meaning of the statute. Therefore, you instructed the jury, in the form of a written decision, that self-defense is an absolute defense to the charge of murder. After deliberating, the jury acquitted Gilligan. Some members of the council vocally criticized the judge for "creating" law in this manner, arguing that only the council should have the ability to create law. Despite such criticism, the council does not change the statute. The judge retires, and the council selects a replacement.

Six months later, another killing occurs. Having argued, Marianne advanced on Mrs. Lovey Howell brandishing a large club and announcing that she was going to kill Lovey. Lovey was standing about fifty feet from the society's constable and was armed with a small, snub-nosed pistol. She easily and safely could have retreated to the protection of the constable. She did not. Instead, she shot Marianne in the chest, killing her. The constable arrests Lovey and brings her before you, as the new judge, for trial on murder charges. Lovey admits to killing Marianne, but claims that the killing was not against the law because it was in self-defense.

As the new judge, you must first decide whether to recognize self-defense at all. In other words, is the new judge bound to follow the prior judge's interpretation of the statute?

Assume that the Anglo-American system of stare decisis applies and that the new case is in the same court as the earlier Gilligan case. Is the Gilligan case binding, mandatory authority? As the new judge in the Lovey case, are you required to follow the Gilligan case? Assuming that you wanted your decision to be consistent with Gilligan, are the facts in this new case close enough to the facts of Gilligan's case as to require the same result?

What is your decision in Lovey's case? What if the judge in Gilligan's case had added to the opinion: "However, Lovey would not be able to invoke self-defense as a defense to her murder charge if she could have easily and safely retreated."? Assuming for present purposes that the Gilligan case was mandatory authority, would you be required to follow that portion of the opinion? Would that language make your present dilemma any easier? More difficult?

## A.  Impact of Jurisdiction on Stare Decisis

As discussed above, an earlier case is not binding on a judge unless the earlier case falls within the same jurisdiction as the new case. This section describes in greater detail the impact of jurisdiction on stare decisis within the federal and state court systems in our country.

### 1.  Federal Courts

Federal courts have jurisdiction to resolve disputes that involve the United States Constitution, federal statutes, and federal regulations. In addition, federal courts have jurisdiction to resolve disputes that involve state laws if the parties satisfy other jurisdictional requirements (i.e., diversity of citizenship; pendent jurisdiction). Unlike the differing state laws, federal laws are, by definition, national in scope and apply irrespective of whether conduct covered by the law arises within the State of New York, the State of Florida, or the State of Illinois.

Because our nation is so vast and the volume of lawsuits so expansive, for practical reasons Congress has divided the country into thirteen federal judicial circuits. There are eleven numbered circuits, such as the United States Court of Appeals for the First Circuit, the Second Circuit, and so on. In addition to the eleven numbered circuits, there is also the United States Court of Appeals for the District of Columbia and the United States Court of Appeals for the Federal Circuit. The Federal Circuit resolves disputes involving patents, certain international trade disputes, and some cases involving damage claims against the United States government. Take a look at the accompanying map of the thirteen judicial circuits to gain a sense of how the country is divided into separate regions. Note that each numbered federal judicial circuit encompasses a number of different states. As you review the map, recall, however, that the jurisdiction of a federal judicial circuit extends only to acts within those states that affect a *federal* law. In what federal circuit do you reside?

How do the different federal judicial circuits affect the doctrine of stare decisis? An earlier case is mandatory, or binding, authority only with respect to new federal court cases that arise within the same judicial circuit. For example, a decision issued by the United States Court of Appeals for the First Circuit is binding only on future cases that arise within the First Circuit. That decision does not carry any binding weight within any other circuit. A judge or panel of judges within the Second Circuit is free to agree or disagree with the manner in which the First Circuit Court of Appeals interprets a federal law.

## 2.   *State Courts*

Each individual state has its own laws and court system. State court judges have sole jurisdiction to resolve controversies involving their state's constitution, statutes, and common law. Therefore, earlier cases have binding effect only on future disputes that arise within that same state. Conversely, a case from one state has no binding effect on a judge in another state. As an example, a judge in the State of Illinois interpreting Illinois' burglary statute would not be required to follow a Wisconsin judge's interpretation of a similar Wisconsin statute. As a practical matter, the judge in Illinois would likely not even find the Wisconsin case persuasive; unlike the sources of federal law, which apply nationwide, each state's laws are different from the laws in other states and result from a unique balancing of interests and public policy within that state.

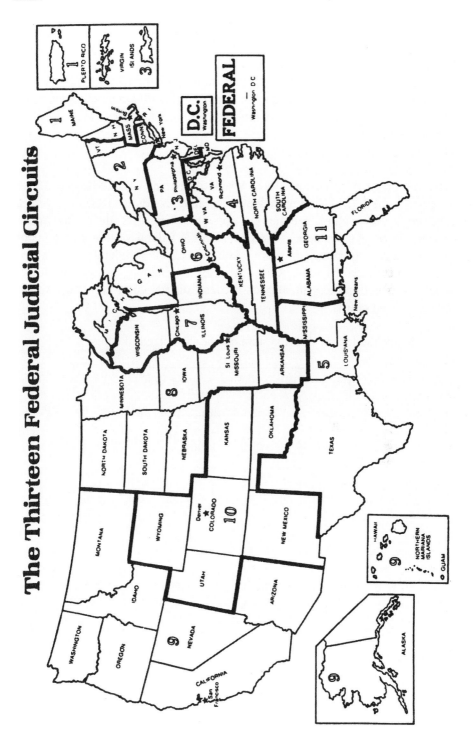

The Thirteen Federal Judicial Circuits

## B. *Impact of Court Hierarchy on Stare Decisis*

In order for an earlier case to have mandatory precedential effect, the earlier case must not only arise within the same jurisdiction as the new case, but the earlier case must be decided by a higher level court within that jurisdiction. The federal government, the District of Columbia, and each individual state have their own hierarchy of courts within their court systems. Again, within each jurisdictional system, higher level courts are binding on lower level courts. Lower level courts are never binding on higher level courts.

### 1. *Federal Court System*

The federal court system has three levels of courts: (1) the trial court level (*District Courts*); (2) the intermediate appellate court level (*United States Courts of Appeal*); and (3) and the final appellate court level (the *United States Supreme Court*). As the highest level court in the federal system, decisions of the United States Supreme Court are binding on all other federal courts. Decisions of each United States Court of Appeals are binding only on the lower federal courts within their jurisdiction. Federal district court decisions are not binding on other courts.

Graphically, the federal court system can be visualized like this:

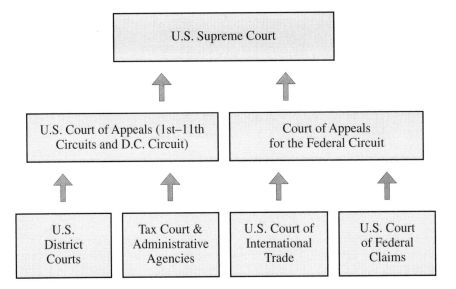

### (a) *Federal District Courts*

If you were to file a lawsuit that involved a federal law, you would file the lawsuit in a federal district court, which is the trial level court within the fed-

eral judiciary system.[4] Each of the twelve federal circuits (the eleven numbered circuits and the District of Columbia), has a number of district courts
within their jurisdiction. The size and number of federal district courts within a
particular circuit depends upon the size and caseload of that district. For example, the Ninth Circuit includes the states of Alaska, Arizona, California,
Hawaii, Idaho, Montana, Nevada, Oregon, and Washington. Depending upon
the size of their caseloads, each of those states has at least one, and possibly
more, federal district courts. Because federal courts in California hear a significant number of cases, California has four federal districts, including the
Northern, Southern, Eastern, and Central Districts. Thus, if you were to practice law in the geographic area designated as the Southern District of California, you would file that lawsuit in the District Court for the Southern District
of California.

Additionally, each federal district court is typically comprised of more than
one judge. The Central District of California has had as many as twenty-one
(21) active district court judges, all of whom, at any one time, could be trying
cases and speaking for the court.

### (b)   United States Courts of Appeal

The United States courts of appeal are the intermediate courts of appeal in
the federal system. Therefore, if your client did not prevail at the trial court
level, you would have the opportunity to appeal the district judge's ruling to
the applicable United States court of appeal. In California, you would appeal
the decision of the district court judge to the United States Court of Appeals
for the Ninth Circuit. The number of judges that sit on a particular circuit court
of appeals differs from circuit to circuit, depending upon caseload. For example, approximately twenty-five (25) active judges presently sit on the Ninth
Circuit Court of Appeals, whereas only a dozen or so active judges sit on the
Fifth Circuit Court of Appeals.

All active judges on a federal court of appeals do not hear every case that
comes before that court. Instead, cases are heard by three-judge panels during
one week of the month. Additionally, more than one three-judge panel is active
at one time. For example, because the Ninth Circuit has twenty-five (25) active
judges, that court might have nine panels of judges hearing cases at one time.
All active judges on a federal court of appeals hear a case together only when
the court is sitting *en banc*.

---

[4] For present purposes, assume that the legal matter you are handling does
not involve a specialized issue that would be addressed by the United States
Tax Court, the Court of Federal Claims, or the Court of International Trade.

### (c)   United States Supreme Court

The United States Supreme Court, the highest level of court in the land, is comprised of nine justices, one of whom acts as chief justice. Out of thousands of petitions for appeal every year, the Supreme Court consents to hear only 100 to 200 per year. Generally, it agrees to hear only those cases that are of exceptional constitutional or statutory magnitude, or those cases upon which lower courts have disagreed in their interpretation of federal law, i.e., where two or more federal circuit courts of appeal have disagreed. When the Supreme Court declines to hear an appeal, the technical term is that it has *denied certiorari*. This term is abbreviated for citation purposes. Thus, when you see the phrase *"cert. denied"* following the citation of a case, that means that the attorneys in that case appealed the case to the United States Supreme Court and that the Supreme Court declined to hear the appeal.

## 2.   State Court Systems

Like the federal court system, many, but not all, states have three levels of courts—trial level courts, intermediate appellate level courts, and a final appellate level court. (Most states also have courts of limited jurisdiction, such as small claims courts or municipal courts.) However, some states have only two levels of courts. To complicate matters even further, some states name their final appeals court the "Supreme Court," while other states name their final appeals court the "Appellate Court." Attorneys who practice law in a particular state quickly become familiar with the courts in their state. As law students, the *Bluebook* and the *ALWD Manual* can be helpful in unraveling a particular state's court system. Appendix 1 of the ALWD Citation Manual, and Table 1 of the Bluebook, list each state alphabetically and designate each state's appellate court structure.[5] Ignoring the courts of very limited jurisdiction, such as small claims and municipal courts, a typical state court system such as Missouri would look like this:

---

[5] The ALWD Citation Manual and the Bluebook only list those state courts from which decisions are actually published. In most states, intermediate appellate court and final appellate court decisions are published and are therefore denoted in the ALWD Citation Manual and the Bluebook. However, most states do not publish their trial court opinions. For example, the State of Missouri does not publish trial court opinions. Thus, the citation manuals do not list Missouri's trial level courts. (*See, e.g.,* ALWD Citation Manual, at 355, and Bluebook, at 212 of the 17th edition).

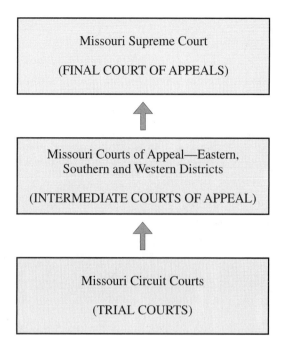

Like the federal court system, in a state system, the highest level of appellate court binds all lower level courts. Intermediate level appellate courts bind all trial level courts within all districts within the state. For example, an earlier case decided by the Court of Appeals for the Western District of Missouri would bind all state trial courts within the state, even those trial courts that sit within the Eastern District of Missouri.

However, because court decisions do not bind other courts of the same level, it is possible for different intermediate appellate courts within a state to conflict. Thus, it is possible for the Court of Appeals for the Western District of Missouri to disagree with a decision of the Court of Appeals for the Eastern District of Missouri. Under those circumstances, the trial court must follow the higher level court that sits within its district. Accordingly, a trial court within the western district would follow that district's appellate court decision, while a trial court within the eastern district would follow the earlier decision of the eastern district court of appeals.

## C.  *Illustration of the Federal and State Court Structures*

The illustration on the following page reflects, in practical terms, the two parallel court systems, how the source of law affects whether attorneys litigate a dispute in federal or state court, and the appeals process.

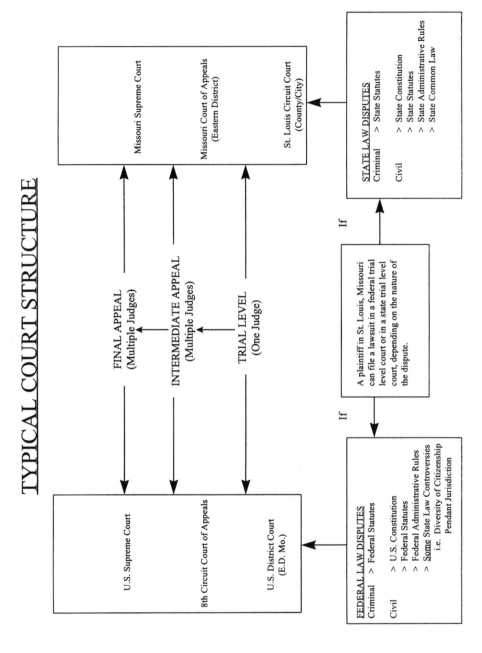

# TYPICAL COURT STRUCTURE

**FINAL APPEAL** (Multiple Judges)

**INTERMEDIATE APPEAL** (Multiple Judges)

**TRIAL LEVEL** (One Judge)

Missouri Supreme Court

Missouri Court of Appeals (Eastern District)

St. Louis Circuit Court (County/City)

STATE LAW DISPUTES
Criminal    >    State Statutes

Civil       >    State Constitution
            >    State Statutes
            >    State Administrative Rules
            >    State Common Law

If

A plaintiff in St. Louis, Missouri can file a lawsuit in a federal trial level court or in a state trial level court, depending on the nature of the dispute.

If

U.S. Supreme Court

8th Circuit Court of Appeals

U.S. District Court (E.D. Mo.)

FEDERAL LAW DISPUTES
Criminal   >    Federal Statutes

Civil      >    U.S. Constitution
           >    Federal Statutes
           >    Federal Administrative Rules
           >    Some State Law Controversies
                 i.e.  Diversity of Citizenship
                        Pendant Jurisdiction

## EXERCISE 4:
### MANDATORY AND PERSUASIVE PRECEDENT

*Factual Situation:* Assume that you are practicing law in Los Angeles, California. California is in the Ninth Circuit of the federal court of appeals. You represent Tim Jones, who has asked for your advice concerning a potential lawsuit against his former employer, Rainmaid. After a lengthy discussion, you discovered the following facts. Jones is a member of a religious sect that worships the sun. When the sun shines, the religion requires its followers to frolic in the sun on Wednesday afternoons and worship the sun god. The religious doctrine strictly forbids its members from engaging in any kind of work on such afternoons. Rainmaid recently fired Jones for refusing to work on one such Wednesday afternoon. Jones has informed you that he told Rainmaid at the time he was hired that his religion would require him to miss work on certain Wednesday afternoons. Jones claims that he and his employer verbally agreed that Jones would compensate for the lost time by working Wednesday evenings instead. Jones has given you a copy of his employment contract, which states that Rainmaid would not fire Jones except "for good cause." Jones is a data processor. His job duties included inputting data about Rainmaid's customers into a computer and then generating invoices for the customers.

Jones is worried about the expenses of a lawsuit and the time involved. Depending upon the results of your research, you agreed that you might be willing to accept the case on a contingency fee basis (i.e., if you win the lawsuit, you take 1/3 of the judgment as your legal fees; if you lose, you take nothing). Jones was also amenable to the idea of at least considering paying you on an hourly basis. You and he agreed that, before you actually filed any lawsuit on his behalf, you would let him know the likelihood of success of such a lawsuit. You agreed to forward to him a legal memorandum that would educate him about the relevant law and the likelihood of success.

***Possible Legal Claims:*** After talking to your client, you have pursued the possibility of filing a lawsuit on Jones' behalf alleging two separate claims for relief. One such claim would allege that Rainmaid breached the employment contract by firing Jones without good cause.

The second claim would seek damages against Rainmaid for religious discrimination in violation of Title VII, a statute. Title VII makes it an unlawful employment practice for an employer "to discharge any individual . . . because of such individual's . . . religion. . . ." 42 U.S.C. § 2000(e)-2 (1994).

### Consider the following questions concerning the Title VII claim:

(1)   Is this claim based on constitutional, statutory or common law?

(2)   Is this a civil or a criminal lawsuit?

(3)   In what court would you file this lawsuit?

(4) You conducted some initial research to investigate the viability of your client's claims. You found a July, 2000 case in which a federal appeals court in the Tenth Circuit held that another member of this same religious sect had a Title VII cause of action against her employer when her employer fired her for missing work on Wednesday afternoons.

   (a) Is this case mandatory or persuasive authority?

   (b) Based on this case, should you go ahead and file a lawsuit against Tim's employer under the Title VII claim?

   (c) What additional information would you want to know before filing a Title VII lawsuit?

      (i) About the case itself?

      (ii) About other cases?

(5) After more exhaustive research, you were able to find only one other case in the country that involved a claim by a member of this sect against a former employer. In this second case, a 1996 case, a federal appeals court in Oregon held that the plaintiff did not state a valid claim under Title VII because the employer had a valid business reason for firing the plaintiff for failing to work Wednesday afternoons.

   (a) Is the federal appellate court case that originated in an Oregon district court mandatory or persuasive authority?

(6) Which of the two cases is more important, the Tenth Circuit case decided in 2000, or the 1996 case?

(7) Are either of the two cases irrelevant to your client's Title VII claim?

(8) In light of the Oregon case, should you forget about filing a Title VII claim against Rainmaid?

(9) What other facts would you want to know about the cases in order to assess the value of your client's Title VII claim?

   (a) What additional facts might help your client?

   (b) What additional facts might hurt your client?

(10) Should you tell your client about both cases, or just the case that has the favorable holding?

***Consider the following questions concerning the breach of contract claim:***

(1)  Is this claim based on constitutional, statutory or common law?

(2)  Is this a civil or a criminal lawsuit?

The 1996 federal appellate court case that held the plaintiff did not have a cause of action under Title VII also considered the plaintiff's claim that the employer breached the employment contract by firing him. In this Ninth Circuit case, the court held that the plaintiff did not state a valid claim for breach of an employment contract because the employer had "good cause" to fire the employee.

(3)  Is the Ninth Circuit case that originated in an Oregon district court mandatory or persuasive authority?

(4)  In light of this Ninth Circuit case, should you forget about filing a breach of contract claim against Jones' employer?

(5)  Assume there are no other cases in the country that have addressed these issues with respect to this religious sect. What other kinds of cases might prove to be helpful as you investigate your client's potential claims? Consider:

　　(a)  the legal issue involved in the cases;

　　(b)  the nature of the relationship between the plaintiff and the defendant; and

　　(c)  the nature of the dispute between the plaintiff and the defendant.

(6)  As you research the issue further, in what jurisdiction would you focus your research efforts?

# 3

# READING AND BRIEFING CASES: THE BASICS

 **I   COMPONENTS OF A COURT OPINION**

## A.  Introduction

During law school and throughout your legal career, you will read cases to help you understand the law and advise your client of his or her rights or obligations under the law. In the beginning, reading cases can seem daunting. As you read a case, how can you distinguish the relevant from the irrelevant information in the case? How can you decipher from the often obscure language within a case what the professor wants you to learn? How can you use a case as a tool to help you predict what the law might have to say about your client's situation? This chapter discusses the nuts and bolts of reading cases and lays the groundwork for the more advanced skill of reading cases in your role as a legal advisor to your clients (discussed in Chapter 5).

Before discussing the components of a court opinion, it is important first to understand the underlying context in which court opinions arise. Most of the cases you will read in your case books are appellate court opinions. In other words, such cases involve disputes that have already been resolved at the trial court level, either following a trial on its merits or following one of the parties' successful motions for the judge to enter judgment on its behalf. During the course of a trial, attorneys ask the judge to rule on a wide range of legal issues. These issues might include objections to the admission of a document into evidence, to objections to the testimony of a witness, to the language in the jury instructions, and so on. The party who loses the case at the trial court level has the option of filing an appeal. Typically, when a losing party files an appeal, the attorney attacks the trial court's rulings on any number of issues. However, many of the issues raised on appeal will have absolutely nothing to do with the reason you have been asked to study the case for a particular course.

The authors of your law school case books usually redact much of the language that is not relevant to the specific reason you are studying each case. Nevertheless, some language in the cases you read will unavoidably be irrelevant to the reason you are studying them. And, as you begin to use the library to research cases, you will read cases that address a range of different issues. However, only one of the issues discussed within a case might be relevant to you. Therefore, before you begin to read a case, take a moment and think about why you are studying the case. For example, in a contracts course, one very basic piece of information to keep in mind is that you will be reading the case to learn about the law of contracts. Thus, an issue on appeal addressing the ineffective assistance of counsel will not be relevant to your analysis. You may find it useful to take a look at the table of contents in your case books to locate the cases you are reviewing. Where do the cases fall within the table of contents? For example, a typical contracts course covers such basic legal concepts as how parties form contracts, how parties might break ("breach") a contract, and the types of damages or other relief a party might recover when a contract has been breached. Knowing that a case falls within the contract formation part of the case book will signal to you why the case is important to you as a law student—the case will contain important information about how parties form, or fail to form, a valid contract.

After you have a general idea about why you have been asked to read a case in a law school class, you then face the challenge of understanding why the case is important. Understanding the various components of a case will help make this process easier. Cases share some general characteristics, or components. Court opinions typically include most of the following components:

1.   The *facts* of the case, including:
     (a)   procedural facts, and
     (b)   evidentiary facts;

2.   The original *rule or rules of law* the court evaluates, which
     might arise from:
     (a)   a statute,
     (b)   a constitution, or
     (c)   the common law;

3.   The *issue or issues* presented to the court to resolve, which may
     include:
     (a)   law-centered issues, and
     (b)   fact-centered issues;

4.   A summary of the various *arguments* raised by the attorneys in
     the case;

5.   The court's *holding* on each issue;

6.   The court's *rationale* that supports its holding, which may in-
     clude:
     (a)   interpretations or definitions of the original rule of law,
     (b)   public policy implications of the rule of law, and
     (c)   gratuitous dicta suggesting how different facts might com-
           pel a different outcome;

7.   The court's *judgment*.

## B.   Individual Components of a Case

### 1.   Case Facts

#### (a)  Procedural Facts

Procedural facts are the procedural events that occur *after* a lawsuit has been
filed. They include such facts as who is being sued? by whom? for what? and
in which court? On appeal, the procedural facts include such information as
who lost in the trial court and why. Often, you will find the procedural facts at
the beginning of a court opinion because they set the context for the issues the
judge will address in the opinion. The time line of a lawsuit depicted in Chap-

ter 1 describes the various procedural contexts from which legal issues arise. For example, a party may appeal the granting of an opponent's motion for summary judgment. When an appellate court notes that fact in its opinion, you would describe that fact as a "procedural fact." Many procedural facts are cloaked in legal terminology and will probably seem confusing at first. However, over time the legal terminology will become more familiar and easier to decipher.

### *(b)  Evidentiary Facts*

Evidentiary facts are also called "historical" or "substantive" facts. These facts describe the factual story underlying the parties' dispute. Thus, they describe what happened *before* the parties ended up in court and explain why the parties are in court. Some of the facts described in a court's narrative may have profound legal significance, because the judge's holding hinged on the existence of those facts. Other facts may provide helpful background so that you can better understand the factual story of the case, but they are not legally significant in themselves. When reading a case, the goal is to hone in on the facts that are legally significant, and focus on background facts only to the extent they help you understand what happened.

How can you tell the difference between important, legally significant facts and those facts that are not important? You will not be able to make this determination until after you have read the court's holding and rationale. A fact is critical if, had that fact not been present, the court would have reached a different decision. In that sense, a critical fact is *outcome determinative*—it determines the outcome of the case. Other facts, although perhaps not outcome determinative, are nevertheless important enough that they contributed to the court's ultimate decision. In the following example, the court describes within its rationale those facts that were important to its holding. Depending upon how you read the opinion as a whole, the presence or absence of any of these important facts might or might not be outcome determinative.

> We hold that the defendant was not so intoxicated as to lack the reasoning necessary to form the specific intent to commit murder. There is an abundance of evidence to support this conclusion. The defendant was later able to recall the conversation he had with the victim immediately prior to the shooting, including the victim's threats to call the police. The defendant had the presence of mind to call a friend to obtain an alibi and to remove his fingerprints from the telephone. The defendant had the necessary motor skills to drive the ten mile route to his home.

In the above example, the court justified its holding by very clearly articulating the facts that were important to the holding. Sometimes, however, courts do not clearly identify the facts that were important to the holding and you will have to deduce from the opinion as a whole those facts you think were *probably* important or necessary to the court's holding. In the *Nelson v. Lewis* case illustrated later in this chapter, the descriptive comments to the right of the court opinion reflect how you would identify facts that are critical or important to the court's holding.

## 2.   *Issues*

Issues are the legal questions a court must answer to resolve the dispute between the parties in a particular case. Courts address and resolve two kinds of issues: (a) *law-centered issues*, when the court must interpret what a particular law means; and (b) *fact-centered issues*, when the court must apply a rule of law to the factual dispute between the parties. In a particular case, the court may be asked to resolve a law-centered issue, a fact-centered issue, or both.

### (a)  *Law-Centered Issues*

Sometimes judges are asked to decide the *meaning* of a particular rule of law, separate and apart from the specific factual controversy before the judge. Such issues are law-centered because the judge's determination is not dependent on the facts in the case before it. The *Nelson v. Lewis* case illustrated later in this chapter contains a law-centered issue. In Illinois, a state statute protects dog owners from liability if the dog had "provocation" to attack a person.[1] Courts had interpreted the term "provocation" to include any intentional act

---

[1] 510 Ill. Comp. Stat. § 55/1 (1996).

that incites a dog's attack. However, the *Nelson* court was asked to resolve a new question—whether the statutory term "provocation" includes even unintentional acts that might incite a dog to attack. This issue is law-centered because the court's interpretation of the statute does not depend on the specific type of unintentional act that occurred in the factual situation before the court.

### (b) Fact-Centered Issues

Courts are also asked to decide how a rule of law should *apply* to a particular factual controversy. In *Nelson v. Lewis*, the appellate court was also asked to resolve a fact-centered issue—whether, in the particular situation before the court, a child's unintentional act of stepping on a dog's tail was an unintentional act that provoked the dog to bite. Notice that, in contrast to the law-centered question, here the court was asked to apply the rule of law to the very specific facts of the case before it: the unintentional act of stepping on a dog's tail.

## 3. Holdings

A holding is the court's answer to an issue. Accordingly, the number of holdings in a case is dictated by the number of issues the attorneys raised before the court. You may find only a single holding in a case, or numerous holdings. The issues before the court also dictate whether the holding is law-centered or fact-centered. In *Nelson v. Lewis*, the court responded to the law-centered issue by holding that even unintentional acts of children can constitute provocation under Illinois' dog-bite statute. The court responded to the fact-centered issue by holding that, under the specific facts of the case before it, the child's act of stepping on the dog's tail provoked the dog under Illinois' dog-bite statute.

It is tempting as a new law student to search for clear, concrete, immovable answers to questions. However, what makes law so fascinating, and challenging, are the ambiguities and questions that courts leave unresolved. Holdings are not static, rigid rules of law. Rather, they are fluid and capable of being interpreted narrowly or broadly. As a law student, your professors will ask you hypothetical questions in class designed, in part, to help stimulate you to consider just how narrowly or broadly you might construe a court's holding.

As an advocate who represents your clients' interests, you will face the same challenge. For example, assume that you represent a client in the State of Illinois who was attacked by a dog after she screamed in fright upon seeing the dog. The dog's owner has claimed that, under *Nelson v. Lewis*, your client's unintentional act of screaming provoked the dog's attack. The dog's owner has adopted a broad interpretation of the *Nelson* court's holding, arguing that the holding encompasses any unintentional act that ultimately provokes a dog. In contrast, you would construe the *Nelson* court's holding more narrowly, arguing that the holding was restricted to the specific factual situation before the court—stepping on a dog's tail when the dog was chewing on a bone. You would then argue that the act of screaming is different enough from the act of stepping on a dog's tail that the result for your client should be different than the result in *Nelson*. The trial court judge before whom you have brought this dispute might ultimately agree with your opponent's broad interpretation of the *Nelson* court's holding, or your narrow interpretation of the *Nelson* court's holding, or arrive at an interpretation that is somewhere in between. Chapter 5 discusses this process in greater detail.

### 4.  *Rationale*

Courts usually state the reasoning, or *rationale*, that justify their holdings. Unfortunately, sometimes courts do not clearly explain why they held the way they did, and you must try to discern the unstated, or implied, reasons that support the holding. Rationale often appears directly after a court's statement of its holding. However, rationale may be scattered through-out the opinion. To identify the court's rationale, consider the original source of law the court has been asked to interpret and how the court has defined or applied that rule of law to the factual controversy before the court. For fact-centered issues, consider which facts seem to support the court's holding and interpretation of the original rule of law. When interpreting a statute, courts are likely to discuss how the language of the statute and the purpose of the statute support the holding. Courts sometimes discuss how public policy supports the holding. All of these statements that justify a court's holding are important parts of the court's rationale.

A court's rationale sometimes includes dicta. Dicta is simply gratuitous rationale that is not necessary to support the court's holding or to resolve the legal issues before the court. Although dicta is not direct justification for a court's holding, dicta can offer helpful guidance as to the parameters of the court's holding. Dicta can suggest how broadly or narrowly the court's holding should properly be interpreted. For example, the *Nelson v. Lewis* case contains dicta implying that the court's holding is fairly narrow. In that case, the court stated: "the present appeal does not involve a vicious attack which was out of all proportion to the unintentional acts involved." By that statement, the court implied that a different fact pattern might merit a different result—an unintentional act may not constitute "provocation" under the statute if the dog's attack is out of proportion to the unintentional act.

## 5.  *Judgment*

The court's judgment is that part of the opinion in which the court indicates the formal action, if any, that is to be taken now that the court has resolved (the "holding") the legal "issues" before it. The court may affirm, reverse, remand, or vacate a lower court. The court may award damages, or equitable relief, or it may order that something be done (e.g., declaratory relief).

## ◆ II ▶  *ILLUSTRATION OF A COURT OPINION*

The *Nelson v. Lewis* case illustrated below contains all seven components of a court opinion.[2] The annotations on the right-hand column signal each component of the opinion and how an attorney might interpret the opinion. While reading *Nelson v. Lewis*, keep in mind that the court resolved both a law-centered issue (can unintentional acts provoke a dog?) and a fact-centered issue (did this particular act of falling on the dog's tail provoke the dog?). The court jumped back and forth between the two issues and its rationale for each issue, making the opinion a bit difficult to follow. While reading the case, look for three reasons the court used to justify its law-centered holding, and the key facts the court emphasized when justifying its fact-centered holding.

---

**JO ANN NELSON**, a Minor, by Eric D. Nelson, her Father and Next Friend, Plaintiff-Appellant,
**v. GEORGE N. LEWIS**,
Defendant-Appellee
No. 75-432
Appellate Court of Illinois, Fifth District
36 Ill. App. 3d 130; 344 N.E.2d 268
March 3, 1976, Filed

MR. PRESIDING JUSTICE KARNS delivered the opinion of the court. JONES and G.J. MORAN, JJ., concur. Plaintiff, by her father and next friend, brought an action under the Illinois "dog-bite" statute (Ill. Rev. Stat. 1973, ch. 8, par. 366)] for injuries inflicted upon her by defendant's dog. From judgment entered on a jury verdict for the defendant, she appeals.

This paragraph describes the *procedural* facts—what happened procedurally *after* the plaintiff filed the lawsuit.

---

[2] *Nelson v. Lewis*, 344 N.E.2d 268 (Ill. App. Ct. 1976). The idea of using the Dog Bite Statute and *Nelson v. Lewis* was inspired by Diana V. Pratt, *Legal Writing: A Systematic Approach* (West 1989).

On the date of her injury, plaintiff Jo Ann Nelson, a 2½-year-old, was playing "crack-the-whip" in defendant's backyard with his daughter and other children. Jo Ann was on the end of the "whip." The testimony shows that after she had been thrown off the whip, Jo Ann fell or stepped on the dog's tail while the dog was chewing a bone. The dog, a large Dalmatian, reacted by scratching the plaintiff in her left eye. There was no evidence that plaintiff or anyone else had teased or aggravated the dog before the incident, nor was there evidence that the dog had ever scratched, bitten, or attacked anyone else. According to its owner, the dog had not appeared agitated either before or after the incident. As a result of her injuries, Jo Ann incurred permanent damage to a tear duct in her left eye. It was established that Jo Ann's left eye will overflow with tears more frequently and as a result of less irritation than normal, but that her vision in the eye was not affected.

Our statute pertaining to liability of an owner of a dog attacking or injuring persons provides:

"If a dog or other animal, without provocation, attacks or injures any person who is peacefully conducting himself in any place where he may lawfully be, the owner of such dog or other animal is liable in damages to such person for the full amount of the injury sustained." (Ill. Rev. Stat. 1973, ch. 8, par. 366.)

Under this statute there are four elements that must be proved: injury caused by a dog owned or harbored by the defendant; lack of provocation; peaceable conduct of the person injured; and the presence of the person injured in a place where he has a legal right to be.

(*Siewerth v. Charleston*, 89 Ill. App. 2d 64, 231 N.E.2d 644 (1967); *Messa v. Sullivan*, 61 Ill. App. 2d 386, 209 N.E.2d 872 (1965); *Beckert v. Risberg*, 50 Ill.App. 2d 100, 199 N.E.2d 811 (1964) *rev'd on other grounds*, 33 Ill. 2d 44, 210 N.E.2d 207 (1965).) There is no dispute but that the dog caused the plaintiff's injury; the defendant owned the dog; the plaintiff's conduct was peaceable; and she was injured in a place where she had a legal right to be. The issue presented is whether plaintiff's unintentional act constitutes "provocation" within the meaning of the statute.

---

This paragraph describes the *evidentiary* facts (also called the *substantive* or *historical* facts). Even though these facts were elicited during the trial itself, the narrative tells the story, or the history, of the incident that triggered the lawsuit. An attorney would pay careful attention to the facts that describe the child's act of falling on the dog's tail, what the dog was doing at the time, and the resulting attack and injuries.

Here, the court quotes the statute

and then analyzes the statute, finding that the statute has four elements.

The court provides a useful road map for attorneys by:

(1) eliminating those elements that do not present an issue for the court under the facts presented; and (2) identifying the is-

It appears that this issue has not been passed upon by an Illinois court. The statute does not distinguish between intentional and unintentional acts of provocation and thus, defendant argues, an unintentional act, so long as it provokes an animal or dog, may constitute provocation. Defendant's position, that the mental state of the actor who provokes a dog is irrelevant, is consistent with the commonly understood meaning of provocation. Provocation is defined as an act or process of provoking, stimulation or incitement. (Webster's Third New International Dictionary 1827 (1961).) Thus it would appear that an unintentional act can constitute provocation within the plain meaning of the statute.

*sue the court will resolve.*

*Because no earlier Illinois cases have addressed the issue, the court can not rely on statutory interpretations, or rules of law, established by earlier courts.*

*Rationale #1 for law-centered issue: court accepts attorney's argument.*

In the present case, it was admitted that the plaintiff jumped or fell on the dog's tail; that the dog was of a peaceful and quiet temperament; and that the dog was gnawing on a bone when the incident occurred. Under these circumstances, we believe that the Dalmatian was provoked, although the provocation was not intentional.

*Rationale for fact-centered issue: critical facts that support the holding.*
*Holding for fact-centered issue.*

Plaintiff argues that since her act was unintentional, or that because she was of an age at which she could not be charged with scienter, she did not provoke the dog within the meaning of the act. Although her counsel presents a strong argument for interpreting the instant statute to impose essentially strict liability upon a dog owner for injuries caused to a child of tender years, we cannot agree that the public policy of this State compels the adoption of such a standard.

*Attorney's argument for law-centered issue.*

*Holding for law-centered issue.*

[T]his act was apparently drawn to eliminate as much as possible any inquiry into subjective considerations. Whether the injured person was attacked or injured while conducting himself in a peaceful manner in a place where he could lawfully be are all matters which require no inquiry into a person's intent. We believe that the determination of "provocation" should also be made inde-

*Rationale #2 for law-centered issue: legislative intent drawn from other statutory elements that do not require intent.*

pendently of such considerations. A determination of provocation does not require consideration of the degree of willfulness which motivates the provoking cause.

Had the legislature intended only intentional provocation to be a bar to recovery we think it would have so specified. Its conclusion apparently was that an owner or keeper of a dog who would attack or injure someone without provocation should be liable. This implies that the intent of the plaintiff is immaterial.

*Rationale #3* for law-centered issue: legislative intent derived from absence of plain language in statute requiring intent.

Although we believe that the instant statute does not impose liability upon a dog owner whose animal merely reacts to an unintentionally provocative act, the present appeal does not involve a vicious attack which was out of all proportion to the unintentional acts involved. *E.g., Messa v. Sullivan, supra.* The Dalmatian here apparently only struck and scratched plaintiff with a forepaw in response to the plaintiff's stepping or falling on its tail while it was gnawing on a bone, an act which scarcely can be described as vicious.

*Dicta*: court implies result might be different under different set of facts.

*Rationale* for fact-centered holding.

Therefore we hold that "provocation" within the meaning of the instant statute means either intentional or unintentional provocation; that the defendant's dog was provoked by the plaintiff's unintentional acts and did not viciously react to these acts; and that no reversible error was committed in the trial court.

*Law-centered holding.*

*Fact-centered holding.*

For the foregoing reasons, the judgment of the Circuit Court of St. Clair County is affirmed.

The court's *judgment.*

*Affirmed.*

# III ▸ *BRIEFING A CASE*

## A. *What is a Case Brief?*

The word "brief" has two different meanings in the law. The written arguments attorneys submit to courts and other adjudicators are generically referred to as briefs. Later in this book, when you learn how to draft persuasive arguments, you will read more about the types of briefs attorneys file with courts. However, for present purposes, the term case brief simply refers to your own written notes about a case. Although a case brief is simply your personal notes about a case, most briefs follow a fairly structured format that is different than the type of notes you may have taken in the past.

There are three good reasons to brief cases. First, briefing a case will help prepare you for class. Taking written notes about a case allows you to sharpen your analysis about a case. It is all too easy when passively reading a case to presume you understand it when in fact there may be gaps in your understanding or ambiguities in the case that merit evaluation. The process of writing helps identify any gaps in understanding and reduces the risk of inadvertently missing a key component of the case.

Second, case briefs will serve as an important resource tool for you during class discussion. Most law students find law school classes to be rigorous and challenging. Professors ask students questions designed to probe their understanding of the assigned cases and to lead students to a more sophisticated understanding of the law. Without a written case brief, many students report that they leave class frustrated and confused because they had no reference point to help them follow the seemingly endless stream of questions. A case brief can serve as an important anchor during class discussion. In class, the professor will simply help you build a more sophisticated structure from the basic foundation of your case brief.

Third, case briefs will help prepare you for final examinations. You will study an enormous number of cases throughout the semester. Imagine yourself at the end of the term looking back at the hundreds of cases you studied during the semester. Without written case briefs, it would be almost impossible to recall all of the myriad details and important rules of law you gleaned from the wide range of cases you studied. Your case briefs will help you organize each course into a study outline as you prepare for exams.

## B.  The Components of a Case Brief

There are a variety of ways in which you can brief cases. Because you will draft case briefs for your personal benefit, choose a style that will be most helpful for you to evaluate a case and, months later, recall why the case was significant. With that said, a few professors have strong style preferences about case briefing and provide their students with detailed instructions for briefing cases in their courses. In those courses, you should follow your professors' instructions when briefing cases. Generally, however, case briefs describe, on a separate sheet of paper: (1) the name of the case; (2) the relevant facts of the case; (3) the issues involved; (4) the holdings in the case; (5) the court's rationale; (6) the court's dicta, if any; and (7) the court's judgment.

 *ILLUSTRATION: Nelson v. Lewis*

---

### *Nelson v. Lewis*, 344 N.E.2d 268 (Ill. App. Ct. 1976)

*FACTS*: **Evidentiary**—Plaintiff is a minor child who was injured when a dog bit her while she was playing "crack the whip" in a friend's yard. While playing, the plaintiff either fell or stepped on the dog's tail while the dog was chewing a bone. The dog reacted by scratching the plaintiff in her eye. The dog had not appeared agitated before the incident and had never attacked anyone before.
**Procedural**—Plaintiff sued the dog's owner for damages under the Illinois Dog Bite Statute. Plaintiff appeals a jury verdict for defendant.

*ISSUE I:* **(Law-Centered Issue)** Can a person's unintentional act constitute "provocation" within the meaning of the Dog Bite Statute when the act triggers a response from a dog that is in proportion to the unintentional act?

*HOLDING:* Yes, unintentional acts directed towards a dog can "provoke" the dog within the meaning of the Dog Bite Statute when the resulting attack is in proportion to the unintentional act.

*RATIONALE:*
(1) Webster's Dictionary definition of provocation, a commonly understand definition, does not require intent.
(2) The other statutory elements also ignore the plaintiff's state of mind or intent; therefore the legislature must have not been concerned with intent.
(3) The plain language of the statute does not contain any restrictive language modifying the statutory term "provocation." Had the legislature intended unintentional provocation to bar recovery, it would have modified the term "provocation."

> ***ISSUE II***: **(Fact-Centered Issue)** Does the act of unintentionally falling on a dog's tail constitute "provocation" within the meaning of the Dog Bite Statute when the dog's response is in proportion to the inciting act?
>
> ***HOLDING***: Yes, the unintentional act of stepping on a dog's tail while the dog is chewing on a bone constitutes "provocation" within the meaning of the Dog Bite Statute, when the dog's response is in proportion to the inciting act.
>
> ***RATIONALE***:
> (1) The child unintentionally stepped on the dog's tail while the dog was chewing a bone.
> (2) The dog was of a peaceable temperament with no violent past; the dog responded by merely swiping its paw at the plaintiff.
>
> **DICTA**: Court emphasized that the dog's response was proportional to the plaintiff's act of provocation; court implied that a vicious attack that is out of proportion to the child's unintentional act may not be protected under the statute.
>
> **JUDGMENT**: Affirmed.

## C. Suggestions for Drafting Case Briefs

### 1. Case Facts: Evidentiary Facts

When describing "what happened" in the case, the goal is to include only those facts that you believe are legally significant, and the basic background facts that will help provide context for the factual story. Legally significant facts are those facts the court expressly found to be significant, as well as those facts you think were probably relevant to the court, even though the court did not expressly so state. Because you will not know what facts are legally significant until after you have studied the court's holding and rationale, you will need to wait until after you have read a case in its entirety before describing the case facts. In the *Nelson* sample case brief, the factual statement contains not just the specific facts the court expressly found relevant, but also the facts that the dog had not previously been violent and did not appear agitated before the incident. Common sense would suggest that these latter facts may also have been relevant to the court—if the dog had a known violent temperament and was already visibly agitated just prior to the incident, the defendant would probably have had more difficulty convincing the court that the child's act of stepping on its tail was the inciting cause of the attack.

## 2. Issues

Clearly identifying the issues a court addresses is one of the more challenging aspects of writing a case brief and takes time and practice to master. Do not become discouraged if the issues you draft as a new law student are not perfect models of clarity. Most law students begin drafting issues by either framing the issue too broadly or too narrowly. If your statement of an issue is too broad and general, it will be difficult for you to use your brief later for study purposes because you will not be able to recall exactly why the case was important. On the other hand, an issue that is too narrow and detailed will not capture the essential reason why the case is relevant. As you draft briefs, consider the following guidelines. First, refer to the original rule of law that is in dispute, and, if applicable, the specific element of the rule of law the court is evaluating. For example, in the *Nelson* case, the source of the original rule of law is Illinois' Dog Bite Statute. The specific element of the statute the court evaluated was the provocation element. Therefore, both the Illinois Dog Bite Statute and the provocation element should be mentioned in the statement of the issue. Second, if the issue is fact-centered, include enough of the critical facts to help you identify what it is about this particular case that is unique and valuable.

Using the *Nelson* case as an example, consider the following broad description of the fact-centered issue:

> ### Example 1:
> *Issue*: Did plaintiff provoke defendant's dog under the statute?

Example 1 is too broad and general. First, the issue fails to identify the relevant statute in dispute or the key statutory term that is at issue: the element of provocation under Illinois' dog bite statute. Second, the issue fails to identify the critical facts that framed the issue. This broad, general statement would not be very helpful to you as a reference guide during class. As importantly, imagine yourself trying to use this as a study guide three months later while preparing for final exams. This broad, vague statement of the issue would likely not trigger your memory as to why the case was unique and valuable or where the case fits within the broader scheme of the course.

At the opposite end of the spectrum, consider the following very detailed description of the issue:

> **Example 2:**
> *Issue*: Did Jo Ann Nelson, a 2 and a half year old child, provoke a dog to swipe her with its paw, scratching her eye, when she fell on the dog's tail while playing the game of crack-the-whip in her backyard while the dog was peacefully chewing on a bone, and the dog had not previously been violent?

In Example 2, it would be easy to lose sight of the truly significant facts within the numerous factual details. In addition, the detailed facts would make it more difficult for you to see how this case applies to a wide range of cases whose facts may vary somewhat from the facts in *Nelson*.

The following illustration strikes the appropriate balance between being too broad and too narrow. Note that the issue includes the source of law and element at issue, and the facts the court found critical when evaluating the issue.

> **Example 3:**
> *Issue:* Does the act of unintentionally falling on a dog's tail constitute "provocation" within the meaning of the Dog Bite Statute when the dog's response is in proportion to the inciting act?

### 3.   Holdings

The term "holding" is somewhat ambiguous. In one sense, a court's holding is the rule of law the case illustrates. In the *Nelson* case, there are two rules of law that make the case important: first, that unintentional acts can provoke dogs under the dog bite statute; and second, that an unintentional act of falling on a dog's tail will provoke a dog's response under the statute, so long as the response is proportional to the inciting act. In a narrower sense, a holding is simply the court's answer to the issue. In the *Nelson* case, the court responded "yes" to both issues. Of course, without a well-crafted statement of the issue, a simple "yes" or "no" in a case brief would not be useful to you. Because you read cases to learn about the various rules of law the cases illustrate, the relevant rules of law should appear somewhere in your case brief.

If you crafted your statement of an issue carefully, so that the issue itself contains the important rule of law the case illustrates, you may wish to state your holding as a simple yes or no answer. In the *Nelson* case, the following statement of the issue and holding would be effective:

> *ISSUE:* Does the act of unintentionally falling on a dog's tail when the dog is chewing on a bone constitute "provocation" within the meaning of the Dog Bite Statute when the dog's response is in proportion to the inciting act?
> *HOLDING:* Yes.

In the above example, you can identify the important rule of law the case illustrates by reading your statement of the issue. Many students prefer, however, to broaden the holding so that it restates the important rule of law in a clear, declarative statement. Framing the rule of law in a declarative statement may make it easier for you to absorb at a glance why a case is important. The following example illustrates this method of drafting holdings.

> *ISSUE*: Does the act of unintentionally falling on a dog's tail constitute "provocation" within the meaning of the Dog Bite Statute when the dog's response is in proportion to the inciting act?
> *HOLDING*: Yes, the unintentional act of stepping on a dog's tail while the dog is chewing on a bone constitutes "provocation" under the Dog Bite Statute, when the dog's response is in proportion to the inciting act.

## 4. Rationale

When stating the court's rationale, strive to encapsulate the key reasons the court held as it did. Avoid simply rewriting large portions of the court's opinion; that would not only be tedious but your brief would not be a very effective summary of the case. At the same time, an effective case brief should not omit any of the key reasons that support the court's holding. The court's rationale may be scattered through-out the opinion, requiring you to read the case very carefully. For example, in the *Nelson* case, the court's rationale not only appeared in various places throughout the opinion, but the opinion also jumped back and forth between the reasons that supported its law-centered holding and the reasons that supported its fact-centered holding. Although dicta can also be considered part of the court's rationale, you may wish to summarize the dicta under a separate heading in your case brief. Dicta differs from other rationale because it is gratuitous—dicta does not directly support a court's holding. However, dicta can be important because it may indicate how the court might resolve the same issue under slightly different factual circumstances.

## 5.  *Judgment*

Conclude your case brief with a description of how the court disposed of the case as a result of its holding. For example, a court might affirm the lower court, reverse the lower court, reverse and remand the case, or deny a motion.

 **EXERCISE 1: BRIEFING A CASE**

Brief the following case:

State v. Haley
Court of Appeals, 1983.
64 Or. App. 209, 667 P.2d 560.

GILLETTE, Presiding Judge.

Defendant seeks reversal of his convictions for driving while suspended (ORS 487.560(1)) and driving under the influence of intoxicants (ORS 487.540), contending that the trial court erred by withdrawing his affirmative defense of necessity from the jury. Because defendant offered no evidence to support one of the two elements of that defense, the trial court's ruling was not reversible error. We therefore affirm.

Prior to trial, defendant stipulated that he was driving a motor vehicle on the night of his arrest, that his driver's license was suspended and that he was under the influence of intoxicants. Despite these stipulations, defendant pleaded not guilty to the charge of driving while suspended and raised a "necessity" defense under ORS 487.560(2)(a). That statute states:

"(2) In a prosecution [for the crime of 'driving while suspended'] * * * it is an affirmative defense that:
"(a) An injury or immediate threat of injury to human or animal life and the urgency of the circumstances made it necessary for the defendant to drive a motor vehicle at the time and place in question; * * * "

In support of his defense, defendant introduced evidence that his father had fallen from a bar stool and broken his ankle and that he, defendant, was driving his father to the hospital when the police officer stopped their car. The state asked the court to withdraw the necessity defense from the jury; the court granted the motion. This appeal followed.

. . . .

Defendant next contends that the trial court erroneously interpreted ORS 487.560(2)(a) by requiring defendant to show that his father's injury was "life-threatening." The trial court's oral ruling on the state's withdrawal motion demonstrates that the court interpreted the statutory phrase "injury or threat of injury to human or animal life" to mean "life-threatening injury" and granted the motion in part because defendant had failed to produce evidence of a life-threatening injury.[4] The state

---

[4] The state, arguing its motion for withdrawal, said:

" * * * [W]hat I am saying is [that defendant had] not shown that there was an *immediate life threatening situation.* * * * Neither [has defendant] shown that it was necessary for [defendant] to drive rather than calling an ambulance; rather than seeking aid from other people in the bar; rather than calling the police; rather than having two people who were examined by another police officer who were found not to be under the influence of intoxicants. Have them drive. * * *"

The trial judge then made the following findings and statements in his oral ruling:

* * * "Certainly there is no evidence at all that there was a *life threatening situation* here. * * *
" * * * [T]here is no evidence in the case that there was *a threat of injury to life,* and so I will withdraw the emergency defense.
" * * * I find that there was no *threat of injury to* the defendant's father's *life* and that there was no urgency or [of] circumstances that made it necessary for the defendant to drive a vehicle at the time and place in question * * *.
" * * * There was no evidence in the case at all that it appeared to the defendant that there was a *life threatening* situation. * * *
" * * * [The] injury had already taken place [and] there is nothing to indicate that the defendant's father's injury would have been worsened or that he could have been further injured had the defendant not driven him to the hospital. * * * " (Emphasis supplied.)

agrees with the trial court's interpretation. Defendant, on the other hand, contends that the statute does not require such evidence. We are thus called on to decide for the first time whether ORS 487.560(2)(a) requires proof of an injury of "life-threatening" severity.[5]

As noted, the statute requires a defendant to show "an injury or threat of injury to human or animal life." This phrase could mean either: (1) actual or threatened harm to a human being or an animal, as opposed to other, inanimate property, or (2) actual or threatened harm severe enough to cause the death of a human being or an animal. Neither the remainder of the statute nor its commentary resolves this ambiguity. We are convinced, however, that the legislature intended the statute to have the former meaning.

First, a comparison of the "necessity" defense at issue here and the more general "choice of evils" defense in ORS 161.200 suggests that the reference to "human or animal life" in ORS 487.560(2)(a) is simply intended to make the "necessity" defense unavailable when the "injury or threat of injury" is to real or personal *property* rather than a living creature. By contrast, the "choice of evils" statute provides:

> "(1) Unless inconsistent with * * * some other provision of law, conduct which would otherwise constitute an offense is justifiable and not criminal when:
> "(a) That conduct is necessary as an emergency measure to avoid an imminent public or private injury; and
> "(b) The threatened injury is of such gravity that, according to ordinary standards of intelligence and morality, the desirability and urgency of avoiding the injury clearly outweigh the desir-

---

[5] The state contends that we answered this question in the affirmative in *State v. Peters*, *supra*. The defendant in *Peters* alleged that his mother's illness required him to drive her to the hospital. The severity of the defendant's mother's illness was not in issue, but we noted in passing that "the jury could have found [from the evidence] that the situation appeared to defendant to be life-threatening." The state argues that this language establishes a requirement that defendants prove "life-threatening" injury in order to establish a necessity defense. The state is mistaken. As noted above, a defendant asserting a necessity defense must prove two elements: (1) actual or threatened injury and (2) urgent circumstances. The issue in *Peters* involved the second element. Our brief discussion of the "injury" element was therefore dictum rather than a considered interpretation of the pertinent statutory language.

ability of avoiding the injury sought to be prevented by the statute defining the offense in issue.
" * * * "

This language and the Official Commentary to the 1971 Oregon
Criminal Code, at 20, demonstrate that the choice of evils defense may
be invoked by a defendant who has acted unlawfully in order to prevent
the destruction of inanimate property. The necessity defense is similar
in nature to the choice of evils defense but narrower: it will only shelter
a defendant whose illegal action was intended to remedy or prevent injury to human or animal *life.* This difference in the scope of the two defenses was achieved by the legislature's use of the phrase "human or
animal life" in ORS 487.560(2)(a). We think it is fair to assume that the
creation of that distinction was the only purpose of the phrase "human
or animal life."

Second, the imposition of a "life-threatening" standard could have un-
reasonably harsh effects in certain circumstances. For example, suppose that a suspended driver and another person travel 30 miles by
motor vehicle to a remote area in order to camp and hike. In the course
of a hike, the suspended driver's companion breaks his leg. It is clear to
the suspended driver that his companion is not in danger of dying, although he is in pain. The driver is faced with a choice: he can violate
ORS 487.560(1) and drive 30 miles for help, or he can *hike* that distance. The state's construction of subsection (2)(a) would compel the
latter decision, but we think it unlikely that the legislature intended such
a harsh result. We have often held that we "presume the legislature did
not intend harsh results that literal application of statutory terms would
cause." *State ex rel Juv. Dept. v. Gates,* 56 Or.App. 694, 699, 642 P.2d
1200 (1982); *Mallon v. Emp. Div.,* 41 Or.App. 479, 484, 599 P.2d 1164
(1979). *A fortiori,* we are not inclined to read into *ambiguous* language
a meaning with the potential to produce such results.

Third, there is no harm in omitting a "life-threatening" requirement
from the defense. If the state is concerned that, absent such a requirement, suspended drivers will use passengers' minor cuts and pulled
muscles to establish the defense, the state's fear is unfounded. In addition to proving the existence or threat of an injury, a defendant must
demonstrate that the "urgency of the circumstances" compelled him to
drive. The circumstances attending most minor injuries will not be "urgent" enough to aid in the establishment of a necessity defense.

Finally, we note that, as a general rule of statutory construction, we are to resolve doubts about legislative intent in favor of criminal defendants. *State v. Linthwaite,* 52 Or.App. 511, 523 n. 12, 628 P.2d 1250 (1981), *rev'd and rem'd on other grounds,*295 Or. 162, 665 P.2d 863 (1983); *see State v. Cloutier,* 286 Or. 579, 587–88, 596 P.2d 1278 (1979). In the absence of clear legislative intent or other reasons why we should read a requirement of "life-threatening" injury into the ambiguous language of ORS 487.560(2)(a), we decline to do so. To the extent that the trial court imposed such a requirement on defendant, the court erred.

Our refusal to apply a "life-threatening" standard does not, however, require reversal. As the findings quoted, *supra,* n. 4, demonstrate, the trial court found no evidence that "the urgency [of] the circumstances made it necessary" for defendant to drive his father to the hospital. This finding was based on evidence that defendant made no attempt to telephone an ambulance, the police or other emergency services, although he knew such services existed in the vicinity, and did not request the driving assistance of other individuals at the bar who were both sober and licensed. Defendant offered no explanation for his failure to secure an alternative form of transportation for his father, and he points to no other evidence which could support an inference that the "urgency of the circumstances" compelled *him* to drive his injured parent to the hospital. The language of ORS 487.560(2)(a) makes it clear that a defendant seeking to establish a necessity defense must prove *both* injury and urgent circumstances. Defendant's failure to offer evidence to establish the latter element justified the trial court's decision to withdraw the necessity defense from the jury. *State v. Peters, supra.*

Affirmed.

# 4

# *EVALUATING RULES OF LAW*

 **I** **WHAT ARE RULES OF LAW?**

Rules of law are not that different from the rules we encounter on a daily basis—from the "12 item limit" in the express checkout lane of the grocery store to a required attendance policy in class. Like rules imposed by private individuals and businesses, legislatures and courts also impose rules of law that regulate the conduct of the government and its citizens. As most commonly understood, a rule of law is a broad legal rule that grants rights, prohibits conduct, or mandates compliance with its provisions. However, the term "rule of law" is a relatively generic term that can refer both to the broad legal rules set forth in statutes and constitutions, and to judicial interpretations of such rules of law. For purposes of clarity, this textbook separately refers to the former type of rules as "original" rules of law, and to judicial interpretations of such rules as "processed" rules of law.[1] Because original rules of law are the starting point for every legal inquiry, the remainder of this chapter discusses original rules of law. In Chapter 5, you will learn more about processed rules of law and how courts interpret and refine original rules of law through their decision-making process.

## A. *Original Rules of Law*

Original rules of law stem from the original three sources of law—constitutions, statutes, and common law—and are intended to govern behavior following their enactment or creation.[2] In other words, they are forward-directed.

---

[1] The term "processed" rule of law was coined in: Linda Holdeman Edwards, *Legal Writing: Process, Analysis, and Organization*, Ch. 4 (2d ed. Aspen L. & B. 1999).

[2] A few statutes are applied retroactively. However, these statutes are the exception and not the general rule.

Because original rules of law are intended to apply prospectively to a large number of people, they are usually written in fairly broad, general language.

Today, statutes are the most common sources for original rules of law. Both federal and state legislatures have enacted countless statutes that govern our behavior. Although statutes are the most common source of original rules of law, constitutions and the common law are also sources. As an example of an original source of law emanating from a constitutional source, the First Amendment to the United States Constitution prohibits Congress, among other things, from enacting any law "abridging the freedom of speech."[3] This law that prohibits Congress from engaging in certain conduct defined by the First Amendment is an original rule of law.

The common law elements of a contract illustrate an original rule of law that arises from the common law. To create a valid contract, there must be an offer, an acceptance, and consideration for the contract. This statement of the law sets out in general terms the required elements of a common law contract and is also an original rule of law.

## B.  *The Structure of Original Rules of Law*

Original rules of law have the following components[4]:

| |
|---|
| 1.  (a)  An element or set of elements *or* <br> (b)  Guidelines or factors; and |
| 2.  A word or phrase that indicates whether the rule is mandatory, prohibitory, or discretionary; and |
| 3.  A result that occurs after evaluating the elements or factors. |
| In addition, some rules of law also contain: |
| 4.  An exception or group of exceptions. |

---

[3] U.S. Const. Amend. I.

[4] Adapted from Richard K. Neumann, Jr., *Legal Reasoning and Legal Writing* 16 (4th ed. Aspen L. & Bus. 2001).

## 1.  Elements and Guidelines

Elements are simply a set of requirements that, if proven, compel a particular result. If each of the elements is proven, the rule of law mandates a specific result. To illustrate, if a plaintiff proves the common law elements of (1) offer (2) acceptance and (3) consideration, the result is a binding contract (assuming there are no defenses that might invalidate the contract). This type of rule, with elements that mandate a result, is by far the most common type of original rule of law. Although some rules have only a single element, original rules of law more typically have two or more elements. Some rules of law clearly set out the separate elements that must be satisfied. More often, however, rules of law are not models of clarity. As an attorney, you will be required to study vague rules of law and to decipher the rules' separate components.

Although the most common rule structure is a rule with elements, legislatures have also enacted some statutes that provide judges with guidelines and factors to consider when interpreting legal rules. This type of rule either identifies factors or criteria to guide judges in their decision-making process, or sets out competing factors for judges to balance when arriving at a decision. Unlike the set of elements rule structure, statutes with guidelines or factors provide judges with discretion to arrive at a result that seems fair and equitable.

Both types of rules of law contain the conjunctive term "and" and the disjunctive term "or" to signal the relationship between different elements or factors. When elements are separated by the conjunctive term "and," each element must be satisfied. To illustrate, Illinois' kidnapping statute states that a person must "knowingly *and* secretly confine another against his will" in order to be guilty of kidnapping.[5] Under this statute, the state must prove both that the defendant knowingly confined another against his will, and that the confinement was secret.

In contrast, the term "or" signals that either one of two or more elements may satisfy the statute. For example, a Texas statute states that a person commits arson "if he starts a fire *or* causes an explosion with intent to destroy *or* damage" certain defined properties.[6] Thus, under this statute, a person would be guilty of arson if he either started a fire or caused an explosion on certain property with the intention of either destroying or damaging the property.

---

[5] 720 Ill. Comp. Stat. 5/10-1 (West 1993) (emphasis added).
[6] Tex. Arson Code Ann. § 28.02 (1994) (emphasis added).

## 2.   *Terms Reflecting the Type of Rule and Result*

When evaluating a client's rights or obligations under a statute, it is important to identify whether the rule is mandatory, prohibitory, or merely discre\*tionary. Mandatory and prohibitory rules require a specific result if the elements are satisfied. In contrast, discretionary rules merely provide options, guidelines or factors for judges to consider when arriving at an equitable result. Rules of law commonly use specific causal terms to indicate the mandatory, prohibitory or discretionary nature of the rule.

The words "shall" and "shall not" are terms commonly used to indicate that a rule requires a specific result. The word "shall" mandates compliance with specific requirements. For example, the federal tax code mandates that all tax returns based on the calendar year "*shall* be filed on or before the 15th day of April."[7] The term "shall not" prohibits specific conduct. The Fourth Amendment to the United States Constitution illustrates a prohibitory rule of law: "The right of the people to be secure in their persons, houses, papers, and effects, against unreasonable searches and seizures, *shall not* be violated." (emphasis added).[8] Here, the Constitution prohibits the government from engaging in unreasonable searches and seizures. Although these are the most commonly used terms to indicate a rule's mandatory or prohibitory nature, other terms are also used. The phrase "it is necessary" also denotes a mandatory rule. Even the phrase "may not" can signal a mandatory rule if the phrase is linked to other language that suggests that result. Thus, a state statute declares that: "A married person, not lawfully separated from the person's spouse, *may not* adopt a child *without* the consent of the spouse . . ." (emphasis added).[9] Taken in its entirety, the language suggests a mandatory prohibition.

The term "may" is commonly used to indicate that a rule is discretionary. For example, should an employer discriminate against an employee in violation of a federal statute, the statute provides that "the court, in its *discretion, may* allow the prevailing party . . . a reasonable attorney's fee."[10] Here, the discretionary nature of the statute is clear not only from the explicit phrase "in its discretion," but from the use of the word "may."

---

[7] 26 U.S.C. § 6072 (1989) (emphasis added).
[8] U.S. Const. Amend. IV.
[9] Cal. Fam. Code § 8603 (West 1994).
[10] 42 U.S.C. § 2000e-5(k)(1994) (emphasis added).

**II** *OUTLINING RULES OF LAW*

## A. Outlining Rules of Law with Elements

### 1. Elements

Outlining the separate elements of a rule of law is the essential starting point of any legal inquiry. An outline allows you to understand each component of the original rule of law and, from there, to evaluate how the rule will affect your client. When outlining a rule of law, it is important to isolate each separate element of the rule of law. Only by separately identifying each element of the rule of law can you accurately identify all of the relevant issues that might affect a client.

For purposes of illustration, assume that you are a state prosecutor and that you have been asked whether you can charge a thief with burglary under Illinois' residential burglary statute.[11] Illinois' residential burglary statute is a typical example of a rule in which the elements are not separately and clearly delineated. That statute states:

> A person commits residential burglary who knowingly and without authority enters the dwelling place of another with the intent to commit therein a felony or theft.

It would be almost impossible to evaluate the meaning of this rule of law and to determine whether the thief could be charged under this statute without first outlining its structure. An outline of the residential burglary statute would look like this:

---

[11] 720 Ill. Comp. Stat. § 5/19-3 (1993).

A person commits residential burglary who:

1.  knowingly and
2.  without authority
3.  enters
4.  the dwelling place
5.  of another
6.  with the intent to commit therein a:
    (a)  felony, or
    (b)  theft.

The above outline clarifies that, in order to be convicted of residential burglary, the state would have to prove that all six elements of the statute were present. How would you determine from the single statutory sentence that the statute has six separate elements? When evaluating a rule statement, look for separate words or phrases that relate to a single, important idea. Each separate idea becomes an element of the rule. After you have jotted down an outline of each of the elements, carefully evaluate each element and ask yourself the following question: Is it possible for someone to satisfy some word or phrase within the proposed element but not satisfy another word or phrase within the element? If so, then break down the element even further, until you are confident that each element expresses only a single idea.

For example, in the above outline, suppose you initially identified the phrase "enters the dwelling place of another" as a single element. Superficially, the phrase seems to embody a single idea. However, is it possible for someone to satisfy the "dwelling place" component of the proposed element but not the "of another" component? Yes, it is possible for someone to enter his own dwelling place. Therefore, the phrase "of another" should be grouped separately from the term "dwelling place." In addition, it is possible to envision a scenario in which a would-be thief opens an unlocked door of another person's dwelling place, but is deterred by a guard dog before he actually crosses the threshold of the residence. Although the home is clearly a "dwelling place" "of another," a court may or may not conclude that the act of opening an unlocked door satisfies the "enters" requirement. Again, because it is possible for someone to satisfy some language in the proposed element (dwelling place of another) while potentially failing to satisfy other language (enters), the proposed element should be further sub-divided.

## 2. *Result*

The residential burglary statute clearly states the result that occurs when the six elements are present—a person commits residential burglary. By considering the verb "commits" in conjunction with the result ("residential burglary"), it is clear that this statute requires a finding of residential burglary should the state prove all six elements of the statute.

## B. *Outlining Rules of Law with Factors*

You will use the same principles to outline a discretionary rule as you will for the more traditional rule that has required elements. Again, it is important to list separately each criterion or factor identified in the rule of law. Consider the following language:

> In determining the amount to be ordered for support, the court shall consider the following circumstances of each party: (a) Earning capacity and needs. (b) Obligations and assets. (c) Age and health. (d) Standard of living. (e) Other factors the court deems just and equitable.

In the above example, the term "shall" signals that the judge is required to consider the enumerated guidelines. However, the weight the judge gives to each factor is within the judge's discretion. The judge has the discretion to decide that certain factors are more important than other factors, and therefore weigh them more heavily when deciding an appropriate monetary amount for support payments. In addition, the statute specifically authorizes the judge to consider any other factors the judge believes may be relevant when determining the amount of the award for monetary support. Note how the judge's discretion differs from rules of law in which the decision-maker must find that all of the required elements exist.

Because factors are only guidelines and not required elements, you may outline the factors in any manner that seems logical and reasonable to you, being careful not to omit any enumerated factor. Thus, in the above illustration, you might decide to change the order in which the factors were enumerated in the statute in order to make it easier for you to evaluate the law. You might outline the rule of law as follows:

In determining the amount to be ordered for support, the court must consider each party's:
1.   earning capacity
2.   assets
3.   needs
4.   financial obligations
5.   standard of living
6.   age
7.   health
8.   other factors the court deems just and equitable

The above outline re-organizes the factors, beginning with factors that relate to financial resources, then detailing factors that relate to liabilities and expenses, and finally, listing those factors that relate to physical conditions. Another logical way to outline the above rule of law would be to clarify the different conceptual categories, like this:

In determining the amount to be ordered for support, the court must consider each party's:
A.   Financial resources, including:
    1.   earning capacity
    2.   assets
B.   Liabilities, including:
    1.   present and future needs
    2.   financial obligations
    3.   standard of living
C.   Physical Conditions, including:
    1.   age
    2.   health
D.   Other factors the court deems just and equitable

The above outline merely clarifies the writer's conceptualization of the different types of factors courts evaluate when considering an award of financial support. There is no single "right" way to outline a discretionary rule of law. However, when outlining a discretionary rule of law, be careful to include every enumerated factor in your outline, including the generic "other factors" criterion that many discretionary rules of law include.

## III ▸ *EXERCISES IN OUTLINING RULES OF LAW*

The following exercises include both the more traditional type of rule structure with a set of elements and a discretionary rule structure. Carefully review each rule below, identify the type of rule structure the rule of law illustrates, and then outline each rule. When outlining a rule structure with a set of elements, remember that it is important to identify each separate element of the rule, even when the statute itself does not clearly reflect the separate elements. When outlining discretionary rules, there are often a number of ways in which they can be outlined. You may or may not decide to change the order in which factors are enumerated. You may or may not decide to add subsections that conceptualize different criteria for you, or to reorganize any subsections that already appear in the rule of law.

 ## EXERCISE 1

> Or. Rev. Stat. § 163.212(1)—Unlawful use of an electrical
> stun gun, tear gas or mace in the second degree.

A person commits the crime of unlawful use of an electrical stun gun, tear gas or mace in the second degree if the person recklessly discharges an electrical stun gun, tear gas weapon, mace, tear gas, pepper mace or any similar deleterious agent against another person.

 ## EXERCISE 2

> 42 U.S.C. § 2000e-2—Unlawful Employment Practices.

It shall be an unlawful employment practice for an employer—

(1) to fail or refuse to hire or to discharge any individual, or otherwise to discriminate against any individual with respect to his compensation, terms, conditions, or privileges of employment, because of such individual's race, color, religion, sex, or national origin; or

(2) to limit, segregate, or classify his employees or applicants for employment in any way which would deprive or tend to deprive any individual of employment opportunities or otherwise adversely affect his

status as an employee, because of such individual's race, color, religion, sex, or national origin.

 **EXERCISE 3**

N.Y. Ment. Hyg. § 9.61(e)(2)—Criteria for involuntary outpatient treatment

A court may order the involuntary administration of psychotropic drugs as part of an involuntary outpatient treatment program if the court finds the hospital has shown by clear and convincing evidence that the patient lacks the capacity to make a treatment decision as a result of mental illness and the proposed treatment is narrowly tailored to give substantive effect to the patient's liberty interest in refusing medication, taking into consideration all relevant circumstances, including the patient's best interest, the benefits to be gained from the treatment, the adverse side effects associated with the treatment and any less intrusive alternative treatments. Such order shall specify the type and amount of such psychotropic drugs and the duration of such involuntary administration.

 **EXERCISE 4**

N.J. Stat. Ann. § 2C:12-1.2(a)—Endangering an injured victim

A person is guilty of endangering an injured victim if he causes bodily injury to any person or solicits, aids, encourages, or attempts or agrees to aid another, who causes bodily injury to any person, and leaves the scene of the injury knowing or reasonably believing that the injured person is physically helpless, mentally incapacitated or otherwise unable to care for himself.

##  IV ▸ *IDENTIFYING ISSUES FROM RULES OF LAW*

After you have evaluated and outlined a rule of law, the next step in evaluating a client's problem is to identify the issues and potential issues the rule of law raises for your client. Next to each separate element of the rule of law, make a note of the specific client facts that seemingly satisfy or fail to satisfy the element. From this initial evaluation, identify those elements that, on their face, are potential issues that might merit further research and analysis. These potential issues will guide your research and, ultimately, your written analysis of the law.

Be very careful before setting aside the elements you do not believe merit further analysis under the facts as you know them; you do not want to ignore an element only to find out later that the element was important. Therefore, keep an open mind and consider every client fact that might possibly present a potential issue under any possible interpretation of the language of each element. If you are uncertain whether an element merits further analysis, identify that element as a potential issue. It is far better to be over-inclusive rather than under-inclusive in your research and analysis.

### ILLUSTRATION:
### *Residential Burglary Problem*

Assume that you represent the State of Illinois and have been asked to address whether the state can charge an individual with residential burglary. From the preliminary facts you received, you know a man identified as Gerry Arnold has been apprehended for breaking into a garage owned by the Stripe family. One-third of the Stripe family garage is used to store the family car, while the remaining two/thirds of the garage is used as a get-a-way by Michael Stripe, the couple's college-age son. A wall separates the two different areas of the garage. Michael Stripe's get-a-way has its own separate entry through a door. He spends two to three evenings a week and his free time on weekends in the garage, writing music. He also sometimes sleeps in the garage on a futon in a loft area. The garage is physically separated from the Stripes' home.

You also know that Arnold was apprehended with a bass guitar belonging to Michael Stripe and tools that would allow him to forcibly enter the garage. Michael Stripe claims that he left the guitar in his get-a-way earlier that day. Arnold has confessed that he entered the garage and took Michael Stripe's guitar. Arnold has also admitted that he does not know the Stripe family and did not have their permission to enter the garage. The Stripes would like the state to press charges.

Recall the residential burglary statute outlined earlier in this chapter. The outline reflects six elements the state has to prove in order to convict Mr. Arnold of residential burglary. Therefore, as the state's attorney, you would carefully consider each element and make a note of the facts that seemingly satisfy or fail to satisfy that element. Your notes would look like this:

A person commits residential burglary who:

| | | |
|---|---|---|
| 1. | knowingly | Likely non-issue. No facts at this point to suggest unknowingly. Element likely satisfied. |
| 2. | and without authority | Non-issue. Arnold admits he did not have permission to enter the Stripe family garage. Element satisfied. |
| 3. | enters | Non-issue. Arnold was apprehended with a guitar Michael Stripe has identified as his guitar; Arnold had tools capable of forcing entry into the garage and admits he entered the garage. Element satisfied. |
| 4. | the dwelling place | ✔ Issue. Unclear whether the 2/3's of the garage used as a get-a-way could be a "dwelling place" under the statute. |
| 5. | of another | Non-issue. Garage clearly belongs to the Stripes. |
| 6. | with the intent to commit (a) felony, or (b) theft. | Non-issue under present facts. Arnold had tools to break and enter. He admits the guitar does not belong to him and that he took it from the garage. |

## EXERCISE 5:
## THE SELF-DEFENSE PROBLEM

Assume you have received a memo from a senior attorney in your law firm that asks you to work on the Jeffrey Bing matter. The memo is dated September 1, 2001 and is set forth in Appendix F. After reading the memo, outline the self-defense statute described within the memo in accordance with the memo's instructions. Alternatively, review the fact pattern and rule of law assigned by your professor. Do not read any of the cases in Appendix F. At this point you need only evaluate the fact pattern and memo.

5

# EVALUATING A CASE

 **I** ## HOW COURTS PROCESS ORIGINAL RULES OF LAW

## A. *Evolution of Rule Enactment and Refinement*

Because original rules of law are broad and general, questions and disputes inevitably arise when attorneys attempt to evaluate how the law affects a client's unique factual situation. Attorneys bring these disputes to courts, asking courts to resolve what the law itself means (law-centered issues) and how the broad rule of law applies to a specific factual situation (fact-centered issues).[1] When a court interprets or applies an original rule of law, it does not create a new rule of law. Instead, you might visualize the court's legal interpretation of an original rule of law as a sub-rule of the original rule. For example, when a court is asked to consider whether a person's verbal statement constitutes an "offer" that would create a legally binding contract, the court's interpretation of the term "offer" does not create a new law. Rather, the interpretation merely illuminates the meaning of an "offer." To help distinguish this type of legal rule from original sources of law, judicial interpretations of original sources of law will be referred to as *processed* rules of law.

As an example of this continuous evolution of rule enactment and refinement, consider the federal wiretap statute. Congress enacted the wiretap statute in part to curb perceived abuses of governmental wiretapping. One procedural limitation was designed to protect wiretap evidence from tampering during the time frame before trial. That section of the statute requires the government "immediately" to obtain the safeguard of a judicial seal after retrieving wiretap evidence. Should the government fail to obtain a judicial seal immediately, the statute provides the government with only one alternative: it must provide a

---

[1] Review Chapter 3 for a more extended discussion of law-centered and fact-centered issues.

"satisfactory explanation" for its failure to do so.[2] This original rule of law leaves many questions unresolved. What exactly is a satisfactory explanation? Does a satisfactory explanation require that the government prove there was no possibility of tampering during the delay, or must the defendant prove tampering was possible? Is a mere mistake a satisfactory explanation, or must the government prove that it had a legitimate law enforcement reason for the delay?

These unresolved questions require courts to define in more concrete terms what a "satisfactory explanation" means—a law-centered issue. Even with a more concrete definition, courts also have to determine whether specific types of explanations satisfy the new legal definition—fact-centered issues.

## 1.  Processed Rules of Law: Law-Centered Definitions & Interpretations

When a court resolves what an original rule of law actually means, its interpretation of the law effectively changes how the original rule will be applied. Where once the law was silent, a court has now supplied a definition that will, in itself, become a test for litigants to satisfy. Using the federal wiretapping statute as an example, a court was asked to define the term "satisfactory explanation." In resolving the question, the *Gigante* court held that a satisfactory explanation requires proof that the government acted with "reasonable diligence" to obtain the required judicial seal.[3] This new definition is a processed rule of law. It is not an original rule of law because the court merely interpreted the original rule—the statutory term "satisfactory explanation"—and gave it further definition. However, although the *Gigante* court only interpreted an original rule of law, the processed rule effectively changed how the original rule would be applied by setting factual standards for the government to satisfy. Where once the rule of law was silent, the *Gigante* court clarified that, at least within the Second Circuit, the statutorily mandated "satisfactory explanation" requires the government to prove that it acted with reasonable diligence.

## 2.  Processed Rules of Law: Fact-Centered Holdings

Even judicial interpretations of original rules of law leave many questions unanswered as attorneys evaluate how a newly defined rule affects their clients' unique factual situations. For example, even the "reasonable diligence" standard is vague. What set of facts might satisfy this standard? The *Gigante*

---

[2] 18 U.S.C. § 2518(8)(a) (2000).
[3] *United States v. Gigante*, 538 F.2d 502 (2d Cir. 1976).

court resolved only the specific factual question before the court—whether an innocent mistake might constitute a satisfactory explanation. The *Gigante* court held that a mere mistake is not a satisfactory explanation because it does not satisfy the "reasonable diligence" standard. This fact-centered holding is also a processed rule of law. By holding that governmental mistake does not satisfy the new standard, the court provided additional meaning to the original rule of law. We now know that innocent mistakes do not constitute satisfactory explanations within the Second Circuit.

Even the *Gigante* court's fact-centered holding generates questions as courts face new fact patterns. For example, what if the government's delay was caused by something other than an innocent mistake? What if the delay was caused by the government's need to transcribe the tapes from Spanish to English, and the government faced a limited budget, equipment failure and limited personnel? In *Vazquez*, a later court in the Second Circuit applied the "reasonable diligence" standard to this new set of facts. The *Vazquez* court held that the government satisfied the reasonable diligence standard because the government worked around the clock to minimize the sealing delay.[4] By applying the original rule of law, as previously interpreted by the *Gigante* court, to a new set of facts a rule of law also emerged from the *Vazquez* case. The rule of law emerging from the *Vazquez* case might be expressed as: the government acts with reasonable diligence when the delay is caused by a legitimate governmental purpose and the government makes reasonable efforts to minimize the delay.

To summarize, when a court interprets and defines an original rule of law, it creates a processed rule of law. Thus, the *Gigante* court interpreted the term "satisfactory explanation" to require that the government act with reasonable diligence. When a court applies a rule of law to a specific factual situation, its holding also creates a processed rule of law. The rule of law that emerges from the *Gigante* case is that an innocent mistake does not rise to the level of reasonable diligence. The rule of law that emerges from the *Vazquez* case is that the government acts with reasonable diligence when the delay is caused by a legitimate governmental purpose and the government makes reasonable efforts to minimize the delay.

The creation and refinement of a rule of a law can be illustrated as follows:

---

[4] *United States v. Vazquez*, 605 F.2d 1269 (2d Cir. 1979).

---

ORIGINAL RULE OF LAW

*E.g.,* Government must provide a "satis-factory explanation" for sealing delays.

---

PROCESSED BY COURTS

---

PROCESSED RULE OF LAW:
LAW-CENTERED ISSUE

*E.g., Gigante*: A satisfactory explanation requires "reasonable diligence."

---

---

PROCESSED RULE OF LAW:
FACT-CENTERED ISSUE

*E.g., Gigante*: A mere mistake does not constitute reasonable diligence and is therefore not a satisfactory explanation.

PROCESSED RULE OF LAW:
FACT-CENTERED ISSUE

*E.g., Vazquez*: The government acts with reasonable diligence when the delay is caused by a legitimate governmental purpose and the government makes reasonable efforts to minimize the delay.

## II  *EVALUATING CASES IN YOUR ROLE AS AN ATTORNEY*

In Chapter 3, you learned about the different components of a court opinion and how to brief cases for law school classes. As you read and study cases for class, your purpose is to learn about different legal doctrines, such as contracts and torts. In your role as an attorney, you must not only be able to read and understand cases in the abstract, but also understand how the cases affect a client. Therefore, as an attorney representing a client, your evaluation of cases will be affected by your client's unique factual situation. From a group of cases that address an issue you are researching, you will focus only on those cases that contain helpful interpretations of the original rule of law and/or facts that are analogous to your client's factual situation. Essentially, you will read cases to identify how courts define and interpret original rules of law that present an issue for your clients. For fact-centered issues, you will also read cases to evaluate how courts have applied the rule of law to fact patterns analogous to your clients' factual situations and how the courts' holdings express unique rules of law. The remainder of this chapter describes how you will read and evaluate cases in your role as an attorney, using the hypothetical residential burglary problem for purposes of illustration.

### ILLUSTRATION: Residential Burglary Problem
### People v. Thomas

Recall the residential burglary illustration from Chapter 4. You were asked to assume the role of a young prosecutor for the State of Illinois who was evaluating whether the state could charge Gerry Arnold with residential burglary. Mr. Arnold had broken into a garage that was sometimes used as a retreat by the owners' son. After outlining the residential burglary statute, it became clear that the "dwelling" element posed an issue for further research. Specifically, the issue became whether a garage can be a "dwelling" under the statute. Assume that you have researched Illinois law and found the *Thomas* case, a case interpreting the residential burglary statute. In *Thomas*, the Illinois Supreme Court held that the garage in that case was not a dwelling under the statute. *People v. Thomas*, 561 N.E.2d 57 (Ill. 1990).

As you read the text of the *Thomas* case below, look for definitions or interpretations of the term "dwelling" and carefully consider how the facts in that case support the court's legal interpretations and its holding. The comments on the right hand column reflect how an attorney might read the case, and the questions and steps the attorney would choose to pursue having read the case.

| People v. Thomas<br>137 Ill.2d 500, 148 Ill. Dec. 751,<br>561 N.E.2d 57 (1990) | *Attorney's*<br>*Thoughts While*<br>*Reading the Case:* |
|---|---|
| Justice Ryan delivered the opinion of the court: | |
| Defendant, Walter Thomas, was indicted by a Du Page County grand jury on four counts of murder (Ill. Rev. Stat. 1985, ch. 38, par. 9-1) [note], two counts of burglary (Ill. Rev. Stat. 1985, ch. 38, par. 19-1(a)), two counts of arson (Ill. Rev. Stat. 1985, ch. 38, par. 2 I(a)) and one count of aggravated arson (Ill. Rev. Stat. 1985, ch. 38, par. 20-1.1). A jury found defendant guilty of each defense. After separate hearings concerning the question of whether to impose the death penalty, the same jury found that Thomas was eligible for the death penalty | Procedural history—will skim through and see if any of the history is relevant to my issue.<br><br>Skimming through rest of procedural history—again, |

and found that there were not sufficient mitigating factors to preclude imposing the death sentence (Ill. Rev. Stat. 1985, ch. 38, par. 9-1). The trial court then sentenced Thomas to death.

*nothing relevant to my issue—can ignore.*

The trial court also sentenced defendant to prison terms of seven years for burglary and 50 years for aggravated arson. The arson charge merged with the aggravated arson count. Defendant's death sentence was stayed (107 Ill.2d R. 609(a)) pending direct appeal to this court (107 Ill.2d R. 603). We affirm the convictions and the sentences.

*Court affirmed the lower court.*

## Facts

The facts are essentially as follows. On the morning of November 26, 1986, Detective James Davis of the Aurora police department investigated the scene of an apparent murder and arson at 302 Windstream in Aurora. There he found the body of Sophie Darlene Dudek on the floor of her garage. He observed fire damage in the rear of the garage and in the car that was parked there. He also found a broken perfume bottle. The perfume was used as an accelerant in the fire.

*These facts are not relevant to "dwelling" issue. Can skim and ignore.*

Detective Davis then spoke with Allen Albus, who stated that earlier that morning he saw a black man, wearing a gray hooded sweat shirt, walking in front of Dudek's garage. Albus stated that several minutes later he saw smoke coming from the garage. Donnie Moore, who was defendant's employer, later informed Detective Davis that defendant was the leader of a cleaning crew that was working at Dudek's building on the day of the murder, and that defendant was wearing a gray hooded sweat shirt on that day.

Detective Davis, along with several other officers, later contacted Thomas, brought him to the Aurora police station and questioned him extensively. Defendant was again questioned on a different day. During the second day of interrogation, Thomas orally confessed and then signed a written statement in which he admitted committing the crimes with which he was charged.

Thomas stated in his confession that he had entered Dudek's garage, where she stored a large quantity of perfume that she was in the business of selling. Defendant stated that he opened a bottle of perfume, which he planned to remove from the garage, and that it fell on the floor, at which time Dudek entered the garage. Thomas stated that he tried to leave the garage but Dudek grabbed the back of his sweat shirt and began to scream. Defendant then, according to his written statement, removed a butterfly knife from his pocket and stabbed Dudek repeatedly. One of the stab wounds severed her spinal cord, killing her instantly. Thomas stated that he then poured perfume throughout the garage, in the car and on decedent's body, set it on fire with the hope of concealing the murder, and then left, later disposing of the knife. Based on this confession, and on other physical evidence, the indictments were forthcoming.

*Skim and ignore—facts re: body and confession are not relevant to the dwelling issue.*

At trial, the State called Albus and Moore. It also called several law enforcement officials who testified generally as to the condition of the crime scene and decedent's body, and the circumstances surrounding defendant's confession. Following the presentation of the State's and the defendant's evidence, the jury returned guilty verdicts for all the crimes charged.

*Skim and ignore.*

Burglary Conviction

Defendant's third point of error involves his burglary conviction. He contends that the facts, as presented by the State, establish that he committed, if anything, residential burglary rather than burglary. As such, he argues, he was improperly charged and convicted. We reject this argument.

*Good—here's the gist of the issue—was it burglary or residential burglary? Court holds not residential burglary.*

The decedent's body was found in her garage. This garage is part of a multi-unit structure. All of the living units and garage units are attached and are under the same roof. Decedent stored perfume products in her garage, which provided defendant with the incentive to enter it.

*These facts may be important—take note:*
*1. garage is attached to multi-unit structure;*
*2. perfume stored in garage;*
*3. perfume gave Def. incentive to enter the garage.*

Given these facts, the prosecution chose to charge defendant with burglary, rather than residential burglary.

*History of burglary statute—I can just*

The crime of residential burglary was severed from the burglary statute in 1982 to create a four year mandatory sentence for those convicted of entering the dwelling place of another without authority to do so. We held, in People v. Bales, (1985), 108 Ill.2d 182, 91 Ill.Dec. 171, 483 N.E.2d 517, that the residential burglary statute is constitutional because it is distinct from the crime of burglary and, therefore, it does not confer unbridled discretion upon the State to choose which crime to charge. Defendant argues in the present case that, because he entered decedent's attached garage, he committed residential burglary. Therefore, defendant argues, to allow the State to charge him with burglary illustrates an instance in which the State has acted arbitrarily. We disagree.

*skim through this to make sure court doesn't say anything about dwellings.*

*This is my issue—focus on what court says...*

We hold here that an attached garage is not necessarily a "dwelling" within the meaning of the residential burglary statute. In Bales, we stated that a dwelling is a structure that is "used by another as a residence or living quarters in which the owners or occupants actually reside." (108 Ill.2d at 191, 91 Ill. Dec. 171, 483 N.E.2d 517.) This definition was later essentially codified by the legislature in the statute defining "dwelling." (Ill. Rev. Stat. 1987, ch. 38, par. 2-6(b).)

*Great—a definition of dwelling! Wait a minute—that definition is now part of the statute itself.*

*Note: ✓ out that statutory section.*

A garage, at least in this instance, whether attached to the various living units or not, cannot be deemed a residence or living quarters. As such, the prosecution, armed with the residential burglary statute (Ill. Rev. Stat. 1985, ch. 38, par. 19-3) and Bales appropriately determined that defendant Thomas should be charged with burglary. Ill. Rev. Stat. 1985, ch. 38 par. 19-1.

*Bingo! Key language. I wonder what the court means by: "at least in this instance." Does that mean that in other instances a garage* might *be a residence?*

*Also, the court says "whether attached ... or not"— does that imply that a* detached *garage could maybe be a residence?*

*✓ and see whether there is other lan-*

We understand that the conclusion in this case is contrary to that in People v. Dawson, (1983), 116 Ill. App. 3d 672, 72 Ill. Dec 260, 452 N.E.2d 385, which involved essentially the same facts, and held that one who enters another person's attached garage commits residential burglary. Dawson, however, was decided before this court decided Bales and before the legislature adopted the new definition of "dwelling." Our decision today is not, therefore, necessarily inconsistent with the reasoning in Dawson. We leave to another day the question of whether the entry of an unoccupied portion of the second floor (People v. Suane (1987), 164 Ill. App. 3d 997, 115 Ill.Dec 933, 518 N.E.2d 458) or the porch (People v. Wile (1988), 169 Ill. App. 3d 140, 120 Ill.Dec. 433, 523 N.E.2d 1344) of a house constitutes the unlawful entry of a residence.

guage in the case that answers these questions. Also ✓ to see whether other cases clarify this language.

✓ out the *Dawson* case because there a garage was a dwelling.

✓ out the *Bales* case and see how it changed the law. Is *Dawson* still good law after *Bales*? ✓ this out.

Shepardize *Thomas*— ✓ to see whether any of these questions have been answered post-*Thomas*.

## A. Identify Useful Interpretations of the Original Rule of Law

As in the *Thomas* case, courts often provide useful commentary about what an original rule of law means. This commentary might range from a valuable definition buried within a single sentence in the opinion, to the law's impact on public policy, to a survey of earlier court decisions that have interpreted the original rule of law. Each of these judicial pronouncements can loosely be described as rules of law, albeit not original sources of law.

When you research and read cases, keep in mind that courts often address and evaluate many different issues within the body of a single opinion. Only those aspects of a case that relate to the precise issue you are researching will be helpful to you as you evaluate your client's problem. In the above illustration, note how the attorney skimmed through the judge's commentary on legal elements that did not concern the issue the attorney was researching. In contrast, the attorney focused very intently on the parts of the court's opinion that analyzed the issue relevant to whether a structure is a dwelling. Note how the attorney paused and considered various questions the court's language inspired.

Again using the *Thomas* decision for purposes of illustration, consider the court's commentary regarding the residential burglary statute:

> We held in *People v. Bales* that the residential burglary statute is constitutional because it is distinct from the crime of burglary and, therefore, it does not confer unbridled discretion upon the State to choose which crime to charge.

The above statement is clearly a judicial comment about the residential burglary statute. You might even find the statement interesting because you learned something new about the residential burglary statute. However, that statement is totally irrelevant to the issue being researched—whether a garage can be a dwelling under the statute. Therefore, you would not jot down this statement in your notes about the case; it would only distract you from your goal of finding language that clarifies the meaning of the statutory term "dwelling."

Although the above commentary is not helpful, the *Thomas* court did make two relevant statements about the "dwelling" element. Your notes on how the *Thomas* court interpreted the dwelling element might look like this:

> 1.  "[A]n attached garage is not necessarily a dwelling."
>
>     *Question*: What does the word "necessarily" mean? Could it mean that a garage *may* be a dwelling under the residential burglary statute with the right set of facts? Or maybe it means that only *attached* garages might be a dwelling with the right set of facts? Check this out.
>
> 2.  "A dwelling is a structure used . . . as a residence or living quarters."
>
>     Note to me: Court seems to be emphasizing the use of a structure as an important factor. This definition was incorporated into the statute. Check the statute to verify.

As the above notes illustrate, a court's interpretations and definitions of an original rule of law often prompt additional questions and the need for additional inquiry. For example, the meaning of the word "necessarily" can be properly understood only by scouring the rest of the court's opinion for facts and language that might provide added insight.

## B.  Identify How the Court Applied the Rule of Law to Facts

### 1.  Identify the Fact-Centered Holding

To identify the court's holding, look for a statement that answers the legal question presented to the court. In *Thomas,* the question was whether the garage in that case was a dwelling. The court's statement that "a garage is not necessarily a dwelling" under the statute does not answer that question. The court merely concluded that a garage may or may not be a dwelling. A few sentences later, the court answers the question before it: "A garage, at least in this instance, whether attached to the various living units or not, cannot be deemed a residence or living quarters." Your notes might look like this:

> *Holding:*  "A garage, at least in this instance, whether attached to the various living units or not, cannot be deemed a residence or living quarters."
>
> *Note to me:* Will want to verify all of the facts that support this holding—e.g., how the owner used the garage—why it wasn't a residence or living quarters
>
> *Another note to me*: Check out significance of phrase "whether attached or not"—any language or facts to support the inference that physical attachment or detachment isn't important to court?

### 2.  Identify Relevant Case Facts and Factors

Before arriving at any firm conclusion, make an initial list of every fact you think may have been relevant to the court. If the court described specific facts when it defended its holding, these facts are clearly significant and should be identified in your notes. However, some facts may not be so obvious. Review again the court's description of the factual story underlying the case and look for facts that might support the court's holding and its legal interpretations of the original rule of law. In *Thomas*, the court did not clearly identify the specific facts that supported its holding. However, by carefully reviewing the factual story underlying the case, the following facts may have been relevant to the *Thomas* court:

1. Owner used the garage to store perfume products for her business.
2. Perfume gave defendant an incentive to enter the garage.
3. Garage is attached to multi-unit structure.
4. Living units and garage units are under the same roof.

From this list of potentially relevant facts, carefully examine each fact's relationship to the court's holding and any statements interpreting or defining the law. Next to your notes of the court's holding and interpretative statements, write down the facts that support or illustrate each statement. Then review the facts that do not clearly seem to support any of the court's statements. However, before discarding any fact as irrelevant, consider whether the fact may have been implicitly important to the court. Your decisions about these facts will often be judgment calls over which reasonable attorneys may differ.

Using the *Thomas* case for purposes of illustration, the court made three relevant statements about the original rule of law: (1) that "an attached garage is not necessarily a dwelling;" (2) that "a dwelling is a structure used . . . as a residence or living quarters;" and (3) that "a garage, at least in this instance, whether attached to the various living units or not, cannot be deemed a residence or living quarters." Separately considering each statement and potentially relevant facts, your notes might look like this:

1) *"Dwelling"*    "An attached garage is not necessarily a dwelling."
   *element*
   *interpreted*:

   *Relevant Facts*    Can't tell from this statement—too vague.
   *or Factors*?

   ---

2) *"Dwelling"*    "A dwelling is a structure used . . . as a residence or
   *element*       living quarters."
   *defined*:

   *Relevant Factor*? Use of the structure as a residence or living quarters seems to be the critical factor.

| | |
|---|---|
| *Relevant Facts*? | None. No facts here to indicate residential use. No dictum that suggests specific facts that might indicate residential use. |

| | |
|---|---|
| 3) *Holding*: | "*A garage, at least in this instance*, whether attached to the various living units or not, *cannot be deemed a residence or living quarters.*" |
| *Relevant Facts*? | Critical fact → Garage was used to store perfume for commercial purposes. |
| *My reasoning*: | This fact supports the holding and is consistent with the court's definition of a dwelling as a structure used as a residence or living quarters. Storing commercial products is not a residential use. Therefore, this fact is critical. |

| | |
|---|---|
| 3) *Holding*: | "A garage, at least in this instance, *whether attached to the various living units or not*, cannot be deemed a residence or living quarters." |
| *Relevant Facts*? | Seemingly non-critical facts → garage was attached to multi-unit structure and shared the same roof with living units. |
| *My reasoning*: | By stating "whether attached . . . or not," the court implies that attachment vs. detachment to the residence isn't very important—particularly when coupled with the court's emphasis on the *type of use* as the dispositive factor. However, I'm not sure whether I should totally discount this fact. What if the court merely meant that an attached garage is not automatically part of the dwelling? |

## 3. A Word About Factors and Standards

### (a) Factors

Whether consciously or subconsciously, we weigh factors in every decision we make. For example, when deciding whether to purchase a car, we might weigh such factors as the *cost* of the car, the *performance* and *appearance* of the car, along with the car's *age* and *reliability*. Factors guide our decisions. Similarly, when a court determines how a law should be applied to a specific factual situation before it, the court weighs different factors as well. In some cases, courts explicitly state the factors that guide them in their decision-making process. More often, however, the guiding factors are implicit and attorneys must deduce the guiding factors by carefully evaluating the facts, holding and rationale of a case.

Why are factors important? They provide the analytical links between case law and the legal problems of clients. For example, suppose you were to conclude only that the *Thomas* case illustrates that a garage used to store perfume is not a dwelling. Your narrow fact-specific evaluation of *Thomas* would not be very helpful to you in evaluating other structures in which the owners did not store perfume. By identifying "type of use" as an important factor in evaluating whether a structure is a dwelling, the *Thomas* case would now help you evaluate a client's situation that is similar, but not identical, to the facts of the *Thomas* case. For instance, assume that, as a young prosecutor for the State of Illinois, you are also evaluating whether you can prosecute someone under the residential burglary statute for breaking into a country cottage used by the owners as a weekend retreat. The *Thomas* court's "type of use" factor would help you evaluate whether the country cottage satisfies the dwelling requirement of the statute. Using that factor as a guideline, you would then compare and contrast the specific facts in *Thomas* that reflected the garage's use (storage of perfume for commercial purposes) to the specific facts in the new situation that reflected the cottage's use (living in the cottage on weekends).

### (b) Standards

A standard is a requirement that must be satisfied under the rule of law. In *Thomas*, the court defined a dwelling as a "living quarters" in which the owners or occupants must "actually reside." This standard, later codified in the statute, is a legal requirement that must be satisfied for a structure to be considered a dwelling. Some standards are concrete and narrow enough that the standard itself can serve as a useful evaluative tool without the necessity of identifying underlying factors. After reading the *Thomas* case, you might appropriately conclude that the "living quarters" standard serves as a useful evaluative tool, in and of itself, without the need to identify any underlying factors.

However, sometimes you can clarify even fairly narrow, concrete standards by illuminating the underlying factors that seemed to guide courts as they consider whether a standard is satisfied. For example, even though the statutory definition of a dwelling might be an appropriate evaluative tool to explain the

*Thomas* case, you may find that the "type of use" factor helps you clarify your analysis. Although this factor may seem obvious from reading the *Thomas* case in isolation, the use of factors may help you later as you review other cases that evaluate the dwelling issue and as you synthesize the cases.

## C. *Formulate the Rule of Law the Holding Expresses*

When a court resolves a law-centered issue, its holding is usually expressed as a clear rule of law. For example, when the *Gigante* court interpreted the federal wiretap statute, it expressed its law-centered holding in a rule format: A satisfactory explanation requires the government to prove that it acted with reasonable diligence. This law-centered holding, stated as a rule of law, reflects an important rule of law the case illustrates.

However, when expressing fact-centered holdings, courts are usually not so artful or clear. Very few courts express their holdings as rules of law that perfectly and clearly reflect why the courts held as they did. For example, the *Thomas* court held only that "a garage, at least in this instance, whether attached to the various living units or not, cannot be deemed a residence or living quarters." In one sense, this statement can be said to express the court's holding. However, this holding does not really capture why *Thomas* is important and unique. Why wasn't the garage "in this instance" a dwelling under the statute?

Your goal is to answer this question in a manner that will reflect how the *Thomas* court's holding expresses a unique rule of law based on the unique set of facts in *Thomas*. In your role as an advisor to a client, you will strive to express the rule of law in a manner that most accurately expresses the result in the case. At the same time, the ambiguities inherent in most court's fact-centered holdings will also create opportunities for you in your role as an advocate. The ambiguous nature of a court's holding provides advocates with a fair degree of latitude to express the holding as a broad or narrow rule of law, depending upon which rule statement most effectively supports the client's interests. Thus, the unique rule of law a court's fact-centered holding expresses is not rigid but fluid. For example, in the *Thomas* case, the rule of law that embodies the court's holding might be expressed in any of the following ways:

> 1.  An attached garage used to store perfume for business purposes is not a dwelling under the residential burglary statute.
>
> 2.  An attached garage used solely to store commercial products is not a dwelling under the residential burglary statute.
>
> 3.  A garage used solely to store commercial products is not a dwelling under the residential burglary statute.
>
> 4.  A structure used solely to store commercial products is not a dwelling under the residential burglary statute.
>
> 5.  A structure used primarily to store commercial products is not a dwelling under the residential burglary statute.
>
> 6.  A structure used to store commercial products is not a dwelling under the residential burglary statute.

The first rule statement illustrated above is narrowly linked to the case facts. Under this statement, the *Thomas* rule is restricted not only to an "attached garage" but one used to "store perfume for business purposes." Under this statement of the *Thomas* rule, the court's holding would not extend to any structure other than an attached garage or to any use other than the storage of perfume. Under this very narrow rule statement, the *Thomas* court's holding would not extend to an attached garage used to store whippets rather than perfume. A later court would almost certainly not interpret *Thomas* this narrowly because the rule statement does not reflect the concerns and rationale underlying the court's holding.

The second rule statement is somewhat broader, expanding the definition of impermissible use from perfume storage to one used "solely to store commercial products." Under this rule statement, any attached garage used for the sole purpose of storing commercial products would not be a dwelling. This rule statement would be a reasonable expression of the rule of law established in *Thomas*. Under this rule statement, an attached garage used only to store whippets would not be a dwelling under the statute.

The third rule statement is even more expansive, expanding the rule to all garages, both attached and detached. Under this rule statement, any garage used only to store whippets would not be a dwelling under the statute, regardless of whether the garage is attached or detached. Again, this rule statement appears to be a reasonable expression of the rule of law established in *Thomas*.

The fourth rule statement is more expansive yet, expanding the *Thomas* rule to all structures, not just garages. Under this rule statement, any structure used only to store commercial products would not be a dwelling under the statute. Thus, a warehouse used to store whippets would not be a dwelling. A porch attached to a home would also not be a dwelling if the porch was used only to store whippets. Again, this rule statement appears to be a reasonable expression of the rule of law established in *Thomas*. In fact, advocates might reasonably differ as to whether this rule statement more accurately reflects the *Thomas* case than the previous two rule statements.

The fifth rule statement is even more expansive, expanding the definition of impermissible use from a structure used solely to store commercial products to a structure used *primarily* to store commercial products. Under this interpretation of the *Thomas* holding, a porch attached to a home would not be a dwelling if the porch was used primarily to store whippets, even though the porch might have other uses as well. Again, this rule statement appears to be a reasonable expression of the rule of law established in *Thomas*.

The sixth rule statement is more expansive yet, expanding the definition of impermissible use from a structure used primarily to store commercial products to a structure that stores *any* commercial products. Under this interpretation of *Thomas*, the *Thomas* court's holding would extend even to an attached sun porch used by a family for eating and sitting, so long as the owners stored a single box of commercial products in the corner of the sun porch. After considering the *Thomas* court's underlying concerns and the facts it emphasized in the opinion, a later court would probably reject this rule statement as being too broad.

At this point, you should have a sense of the fluidity of rules of law and of the latitude you will have as an advocate to interpret case law. At the same time, the above rule statements also illustrate the limits of that latitude. A later court will not interpret an earlier court's holding in a manner that would create an absurd or unfair result.

## EXERCISE 1:
## THE SELF-DEFENSE PROBLEM

Recall the Bing problem you evaluated in Chapter 4, Exercise 5. In that exercise, you evaluated the self-defense statute to determine whether it might provide Jeffrey Bing with a defense to murder. Review again the September 1ˢᵗ memo set forth in Appendix F. Assume that you have found the *People v. S.M.* case, a case that interprets the self-defense statute. Read the *People v. S.M.* case in Appendix F. After reading *People v. S.M.*, fully evaluate the case and identify: (1) any helpful interpretations or definitions of the self-defense statute; (2) the court's holding; (3) the relevant facts that support the court's holding; (4) the factors that guided the court's decision; and (4) the rule of law the court's holding illustrates.

Alternatively, read the case your professor has assigned for you to review and prepare written notes that evaluate that case, considering the above-listed components.

# 6

# EVALUATING HOW AN EARLIER CASE AFFECTS YOUR CLIENT

After you have thoroughly studied a precedent case, you are ready to assess how the case might be helpful to you in evaluating your client's situation. At this point, assume that the case you have studied discusses the relevant issue you are researching; otherwise, you would not have spent your valuable time evaluating the case. From your evaluation of relevant cases, you will have already identified helpful aspects of each case. A case might be helpful to you because it clearly interpreted or defined the original rule of law, or explored the policy implications of a rule of law. That same case might also have analogous facts that will help you predict what the law would have to say about your client's situation. Some cases might contain useful interpretations of the law but have no analogous facts. Other cases might have facts that closely resemble your client's situation but no helpful rationale. In this chapter, we will begin by evaluating how a single case might affect a client. Later, in Chapter 7, you will learn how to synthesize a group of relevant cases, and, in Chapter 9, how to select and prioritize case law for use in an office memorandum.

##  I. EVALUATING CASES WITH ANALOGOUS FACTS

### A. Comparing Case Facts to the Client's Facts

When an earlier case's facts appear analogous to your client's situation, your goal is to evaluate how the factual analogies might dictate the outcome in your client's situation. Using your notes from the precedent case to guide you, separately consider each factor that guided the earlier court. For each factor, list the case facts that fall within the umbrella of that factor and then create a parallel list of any client facts that relate to that factor. Do not be concerned if only one of several factors in an earlier case applies to your client's situation. Unlike elements of a rule of law, factors are only guidelines to be weighed and evaluated. All of the factors do not have to be present in order to evaluate whether an element has been satisfied. However, the absence of a factor may affect how you evaluate the strength of your client's case when compared to the precedent case.

As you took notes from the earlier case, you may have determined that the court articulated a concrete, narrow standard or definition that guided its decision. Recall that concrete, narrow standards serve the same purpose as factors—they provide the court, and you, with concrete concepts that serve as evaluative tools. If you have decided that the legal standard or definition itself is so clear and specific that factors are not necessary analytical tools for your analysis, use the standard or definition instead. Simply list the case facts that fall within the umbrella of that standard or definition and then create a parallel list of client facts.

After you have created parallel lists of facts, you will compare and evaluate how your client's facts compare to the precedent case facts. If you determine that your client's facts are similar enough to the case facts to merit the same result, then you would conclude that your client's situation would likely be resolved in the same manner as the precedent case. On the other hand, if you determine that your client's facts are distinguishable from the case facts, then you would conclude that your client's situation would likely be resolved differently than the precedent case.

 ### ILLUSTRATION: *Residential Burglary Problem* *People v. Thomas and the Stripe Garage*

We will continue to use the residential burglary problem for purposes of illustration. Assuming the role of a prosecutor for the State of Illinois, you evaluated the *Thomas* case in Chapter 5. In *Thomas*, the court held that a garage used to store perfume for commercial use was not a dwelling under the residential burglary statute. After evaluating how the court interpreted the term "dwelling," we concluded that the garage's "type of use" was the critical factor that guided the court's ultimate holding. The court emphasized a structure's "use" by defining a dwelling as a "living quarters" in which the owner "actually resides." (This definition was codified and is now a part of the statutory language.) The *Thomas* court reasoned that a garage used to store perfume did not satisfy this definition. Equipped with that information, you are ready to assess how the *Thomas* case would help you decide whether to charge Mr. Arnold with residential burglary for breaking into the Stripe family's garage.

At this point, you have the following information about your case: Gerry Arnold has been apprehended for breaking into a garage owned by the Stripe family. The garage is physically separated from the Stripe's home. One-third of the Stripe family garage is used to store the family car while the remaining two/thirds of the garage is used as a get-a-way by Michael Stripe, the couple's college-age son. A wall separates the two different areas of the garage. Michael Stripe's get-a-way has its own separate entry through a door.

The son, Michael Stripe, spends two to three evenings a week and his free time on weekends in the garage, writing and listening to music on his stereo system. Michael is the lead singer in a band, R.E.N., that plays once a month in clubs around town. The band practices in the garage most Sunday mornings, and stores some equipment in the garage. Michael has an expensive sound system in his get-a-way section of the garage. He also keeps a portable five-inch T.V. in the garage and a mini-refrigerator that stores soda and beer. The garage has electricity and a space heater, but no running water or heat. During the summer and fall when his parents are in town, Michael sleeps in the garage on a futon in a loft area. When his parents travel to Florida during the winter and spring, Michael sleeps in the house in the bedroom in which he was raised.

You also know that Arnold was apprehended with a bass guitar belonging to Michael Stripe and tools that would allow him to forcibly enter the garage. Michael Stripe claims that he left the guitar in his get-a-way earlier that day. Arnold has also confessed that he entered the garage and took Michael Stripe's guitar, and that he does not know the Stripe family and did not have their permission to enter the garage. The Stripes would like the state to press charges.

Your notes evaluating how *Thomas* might affect your ability to prosecute Mr. Arnold for residential burglary would look like this:

| Factor: Type of Use *Thomas Case* | Factor: Type of Use Client's Case | Compare Type of Use Factor Per Court's Rationale |
| --- | --- | --- |
| *Why decided this was important*: *Thomas* definition: dwelling must be used as a residence or living quarters <br><br> *Thomas Facts:* <br><br> * Stored perfume to sell in business | *Client Facts*: <br><br> * Used as get-a-way to: <br><br> (1) Play music <br> (2) Listen to music <br> (3) Sleep ½ the year <br> (4) Relaxing, snacking, watching T.V. | Unlike the act of storing perfume to sell for business purposes, Michael Stripe used the garage for living-type activities—these activities seem to be the type of activities with which the *Thomas* court was concerned. <br><br> Is it a problem that Michael's band practices in the garage and the band makes money playing around town—a commercial activity? Probably not. This activity seems secondary to its use as a part-time living quarters. Check out whether there are other cases in which occupant used structure for both residential and commercial use. |

Based on the "type of use" factor, your ability to prosecute Mr. Arnold under the residential burglary statute seems fairly promising. In other words, you have determined that the facts in your case are distinguishable from the *Thomas* case facts in a legally significant way. Michael Stripe used the garage for living type purposes while the victim in *Thomas* used the garage only for commercial storage purposes. However, before arriving at a definitive conclusion, you would also address a potentially troubling distinction you noticed when comparing your case to *Thomas*. Recall that the *Thomas* court mentioned, on two occasions, that the garage in *Thomas* was attached to the multi-unit apartment building. You do not know for sure what the court was thinking when it noted the garage was attached. Perhaps it meant that a structure's physical attachment or detachment to a primary residence is irrelevant. However, suppose it merely meant that an attached garage is not automatically a dwelling because it is attached to a home. This ambiguity becomes problematic because, unlike the garage in *Thomas*, the garage you are evaluating is detached from the owner's home. Is it possible that an attached garage is more likely to be considered part of the dwelling than a detached garage? Thus, you should evaluate this factor as well:

| Factor: Proximity to Home *Thomas* Case | Factor: Proximity to Home Client's Case | Compare Proximity Factor Per Court's Rationale |
|---|---|---|
| *Why potentially important*: <br><br> 2 statements <br><br> "An attached garage is not necessarily a dwelling." <br><br> "A garage, at least in this instance, whether attached to the various living units or not, cannot be deemed a residence or living quarters." <br><br> *Thomas Facts*: <br><br> * Attached to a multi-unit apartment dwelling. | *Client Facts*: <br><br> * 30 feet behind the Stripe family home | Potentially troubling distinction. A garage physically removed from the principal dwelling could be considered less likely to be a part of the dwelling than an attached garage. <br><br> However, given the court's emphasis on the *use* of the garage, and the fact that the Stripe's garage was sometimes used as a living quarters, I do not think this distinction would change my initial conclusion that the Stripe's garage is a living quarters. In other words, the garage could be considered a living quarters in and of itself. I am not trying to make the argument that, merely because of its proximity/attachment to the primary home, by extension, it is also part of the home. |

## EXERCISE 1:
## SOCIAL HOST LIABILITY

To:       Summer Law Clerk
From:     Senior Attorney
Date:     [Date exercise is assigned]
Re:       Social Host Liability

Recently, a client named Ben Smith came to our firm to sue and hopefully recover money damages from John Havanother. Havanother had recently hosted a poker night and Smith feels that Havanother was directly responsible for severe injuries Smith suffered in a fight.

Havanother hosted this strictly social Friday night poker party several months ago. Philip Douglas attended the party, as did Ben Smith. Havanother served three alcoholic drinks to Douglas, although he definitely appeared past the point of intoxication. Smith did not drink.

Douglas and Smith began to drive home at the same time in separate cars. At the end of Havanother's driveway, Douglas' car hit Smith's car at a very slow speed, causing little damage. Despite the small amount of damage, Douglas started a fight on Havanother's front lawn. Witnesses will testify that Douglas began to "lose it," ranting and raving and beating Smith brutally. Smith will probably incur medical expenses for rehabilitative physical therapy for the rest of his life.

Douglas was found to have a blood alcohol level of .172 at the time of the fight. This level indicated acute alcohol intoxication of at least nine drinks.

A summary of a relevant case, *Linn v. Rand*, 356 A.2d 15 (N.J. 1976), follows. Evaluate the similarities and distinctions between the client's facts and the facts of *Linn*, and assess the strengths and weaknesses of your client's claim in light of *Linn*.

*Linn v. Rand*: The plaintiff charged the defendant with negligence in serving an excessive amount of alcoholic beverages to Rand, a minor, while she was a guest at the defendant's home. The plaintiff further charged that the defendant negligently permitted Rand to drive her car from defendant's home just prior to Rand's running down and seriously injuring the plaintiff. The trial court granted summary judgment in favor of the defendant, concluding that liability in negligence for the sale or serving of alcoholic beverages to intoxicated persons is specifically limited to tavern keepers and to those in a strictly business setting. The appellate court reversed, rejecting the defendant's claim that social hosts were immune from liability in negligence for the serving of alcoholic beverages to intoxicated persons. The court concluded that the defendant's potential liability was a jury question. Specifically, the court stated that "a jury might well determine that a social host who serves excessive amounts of alcoholic beverages to a visibly intoxicated minor, knowing the minor was about to drive a car on the public highways, could reasonably foresee or anticipate an accident or injury as a reasonably foreseeable consequence of his negligence in serving the minor." The court further pointed out that "[t]his becomes devastatingly apparent in view of the ever-increasing incidence of serious automobile accidents resulting from drunken driving."

## B.   When Case Facts and Client Facts Do Not Seem Analogous

Sometimes you may not easily be able to identify how an earlier case's facts might be useful to you as the basis for comparison. For example, in Chapter 7 you will read the *People v. McIntyre* case, another case that interprets the residential burglary statute. In that case, the court evaluated whether the burglary of a porch attached to a home was a dwelling within the meaning of the statute. At first blush, the burglary of a porch does not seem to be analogous to the burglary of a garage located thirty feet behind a residence. Before discarding the case as a potentially useful case, you would first try broadening the level of generalization to find a common characteristic between the two groups of facts.

From a narrow interpretation of the facts, the facts in *McIntyre* do not seem to share a common characteristic with the Stripe family's garage. A porch attached to a home is not "like" a garage located thirty feet behind a building. However, by broadening the level of generalization, we can find a common characteristic that both facts share—they are both "structures" measured in part by their closeness to or distance from the main residence. This common characteristic becomes a helpful factor, or analytical tool, when evaluating how the *McIntyre* case affects the Stripe family's garage—a structure's proximity to the primary dwelling.

Of course, not all cases will be helpful to you as the basis for factual analogy. If you are forced to broaden the level of generalization to a point that the common characteristic does not make any sense, then the case would not be helpful as the basis of comparison or distinction.

## EXERCISE 2: FINDING AN ANALOGY BETWEEN DISSIMILAR FACT PATTERNS

Assume you represent a client who was injured in an automobile accident. The other driver, an employee of a "deep-pocket" employer, was clearly at fault. During your investigation, you discover the following facts. The other driver was a traveling salesman and his job required him to drive thousands of miles a year. When the employer hired the salesman, it did not check his driving record. In fact, the salesman had numerous speeding tickets. When researching whether your client can sue the employer for negligently hiring the employee, you discover the following rule of law: an employer is liable for negligently hiring an employee if the employer knew or should have known of the employee's dangerous proclivities.

Assume that you are unable to find any case that involves an accident caused by an employee's speeding. You cannot even find a single case that involves an accident caused by an employee's negligent acts. In fact, the only cases you can find are cases involving intentional torts or actual crimes committed by an employee. Consider how you might use the following such case as a basis of comparison to your client's situation:

> In case X, an employee assaulted a customer on the work premises during working hours. The employee's job duties required him to circulate among the customers. When the employer hired the employee, it did not check his criminal record, which would have disclosed a prior assault conviction. In case X, the court held that the employer negligently hired the employee, reasoning that the employer knew or should have known of the employee's dangerous proclivities because of the employee's criminal record.

What common characteristic do these two factual scenarios share? How might you use this common characteristic to argue that the employer in your case negligently hired the traveling salesman?

 ## II   *EVALUATING POLICY STATEMENTS*

Some cases openly discuss the policy implications of a particular rule of law. Such policy implications can help you evaluate how the rule of law would be applied to a client's factual situation. Even the implicit policy concerns underlying a court's analysis of a rule of law can be helpful as you evaluate how the rule applies to a client. If a particular outcome would further the policy underlying the rule, a court is more likely to rule in a manner consistent with that outcome. On the other hand, if a particular outcome would thwart the policy underlying the rule of law, a court is more likely to rule in a manner that would not promote that outcome.

 **ILLUSTRATION: *Residential Burglary Problem***
***People v. Silva and the Stripe Garage***

As the *Thomas* court noted, the legislature amended the residential burglary statute to incorporate the *Thomas* court's definition of dwelling into the statute. The statute now defines a dwelling as "a living quarters in which at the time of the alleged offense the owners or occupants actually reside or in their absence intend within a reasonable period of time to reside." Following *Thomas*, the *Silva* court was asked to interpret the codified definition of the term "dwelling." The court reviewed the legislative purpose underlying the statutory amendment and quoted the following statement of Senator Sangmeister during the Senate Proceedings:

> Yes, it was even brought to our attention by the Illinois Supreme Court in a number of cases that *** there should be a better definition to the dwelling house. We are having people prosecuted for residential burglary for breaking into *** unoccupied buildings such as garages. Therefore, very simply, we have redefined dwelling to mean a house, apartment, mobile home, trailer, or other living quarters in which at the time of the alleged offense the owners or occupants actually reside in or *** in their absence intend within a reasonable period of time to reside. So that still covers, in my opinion, the vacation home; you intend to reside in that and if you burglarize that, you would still be committing residential burglary, but it tightens up some of these cases where we got old abandoned buildings around our garages and stuff that *** would not be residential burglary.[1]

If you were evaluating whether to charge Gerry Arnold with residential burglary for breaking into the Stripe's garage, this policy statement would at least be relevant to your decision. Superficially, the statement seems problematic— Senator Sangmeister implied that people could not be prosecuted for breaking into garages. However, consider that the penalty for breaking into a residence is more severe than the penalty for breaking into a warehouse. What underlying policy concerns might be implied from reading the *Silva* court's examination of the legislative history? You might argue that Senator Sangmeister's own

---

[1] *People v. Silva*, 628 N.E.2d 948, 951 (Ill. App. Ct. 1993).

statement reflects the legislative concern with protecting human life. The senator was concerned that people were being prosecuted under the statute for breaking into "unoccupied buildings"—buildings where no living-type activities take place. Because Michael Stripe uses the Stripe's garage as a retreat and frequent living quarters, its very occupancy as a living quarters addresses the legislative concern for human life. Therefore, the garage is arguably more like a living quarters than an unoccupied garage.

 ## EXERCISE 3:
## THE SELF-DEFENSE PROBLEM

Recall the self-defense problem involving Jeffrey Bing that you evaluated in Chapter 4 (Exercise 5) and in Chapter 5 (Exercise 1). Review again the September 1st memo and the *People v. S.M.* case in Appendix F. Prepare written notes comparing the facts and reasoning of *People v. S.M.* to the facts of the hypothetical situation involving Jeffrey Bing. After evaluating the factual comparisons and distinctions, conclude whether you believe the outcome in the Bing situation would likely be the same as in the *S.M.* case (facts are similar enough to merit the same outcome) or different from the *S.M.* case (facts are distinguishable enough to merit a different outcome).

Alternatively, review the case and fact pattern your professor has assigned for you to evaluate. Prepare written notes comparing the facts of the case to the fact pattern you have been assigned. Conclude by noting whether you believe the outcome in the assigned fact pattern would likely be the same as or different from the precedent case.

# 7

# EVALUATING MULTIPLE CASES

 **I** ▷ *CASE SYNTHESIS*

When you research a legal issue you will usually find that more than one court has already addressed the issue. When you find more than one case that addresses a legal issue, you must "synthesize" the diverse case facts and results into workable rules of law and common factors that explain the different results. For example, assume you find three cases that address an issue you are researching. It is highly unlikely that any of these three cases will be identical to the client's factual situation or even to one another. In some cases, the plaintiff won; in other cases, the defendant won. In each of the cases, what happened between the plaintiff and the defendant will be different. Your ultimate goal is to take these diverse case results and case facts and advise your client how these cases, as a group, affect the client.

The first step in synthesizing cases is to review the notes you have taken from each individual case you have already evaluated. Your notes for each case should reflect the rule of law the holding illustrates, together with any relevant factors that guided the court's decision and the facts that illustrate each factor. To synthesize these cases, you would take the individual rules of law and factors you extracted from each case and formulate a common rule of law and factors that explain the cases as a group.

When evaluating an individual case, you engage in a process of *inductive* reasoning. The process of inductive reasoning requires that you examine specific facts to form broad conclusions. Thus, you reason inductively as you process a myriad of facts and details in an individual case into a broad rule of law that expresses the court's holding. Case synthesis involves a similar inductive reasoning process. From numerous cases that interpret and apply a rule of law, you will formulate a broad rule of law that synthesizes the cases as a group. The inductive reasoning process can be visualized like this:

| Case 1 | Case 2 | Case 3 |
|---|---|---|
| 1) Useful interpretation of rule of law<br>2) Holding  | 1) No useful interpreta-tion of rule of law<br>2) Holding  | 1) Useful definition of rule of law<br>2) Holding  |
| 3) Factors A & B seemed to guide court's holding  | 3) Factors B & C seemed to guide court's holding  | 3) Definition of rule of law is standard that guided court's holding  |
| 4) Relevant facts that illustrate factors A & B  | 4) Relevant facts that illustrate factors B & C  | 4) Relevant facts that support legal definition  |
| 5) Rule of law the holding expresses | 5) Rule of law the holding expresses | 5) Rule of law the holding expresses |

Verify accuracy of factors

Synthesize legal definition in Case 3 with factors in Cases 1 & 2

Formulate rule of law that illustrates cases as a group

***ILLUSTRATION: Residential Burglary Problem***
***Thomas, McIntyre and Silva Cases***

## 1.   *People v. McIntyre Case*

After having read the *Thomas* case, assume that you next evaluated the *People v. McIntyre* case. As you read the attorney's notes to the right of the court opinion, notice how the attorney reads *McIntyre* from two perspectives: the *McIntyre* case as an opinion that stands on its own, and the *McIntyre* case as it relates to *Thomas*—the case the attorney has already evaluated.

### *(a)   Court Opinion*

***People v. McIntyre***
**218 Ill. Dec. 187, 578 N.E.2d 314 (1991)**

JUSTICE KNECHT delivered the opinion of the court:

Defendant Bruce McIntyre was convicted of residential burglary (ILL. REV. STAT. 1989, ch. 38, par. 19-3) after a bench trial in the circuit court of Macon County. He was sentenced to a six-year term of imprisonment and now appeals, alleging he was not proved guilty of residential burglary beyond a reasonable doubt. We disagree and affirm.

Betty Houser of 3930 Bayview Drive, Decatur, was on vacation. While away, she asked her daughter, Jana Chisenall, and Jana's husband, Gary, to check on her house. On the evening of May 8, 1990, the Chisenalls checked the house and noticed nothing unusual. After leaving the house, they decided to drive around the block and go by the house again. On doing so they observed a white Dodge station wagon parked adjacent to the Houser property.

As they approached, they observed two men running from the backyard of the Houser property toward the white car. Gary observed two men get into the wagon but, as he and Jana pulled up in their car and looked inside, they saw only one person, whom they identified as defendant.

Jana asked the defendant if he needed help, but he

*Attorney's Thoughts While Reading Case*

Residential burglary as issue— good. Is the dwelling element the issue or something else? Check it out.

Peruse these irrelevant facts until get to facts that deal with my issue—the type of structure that was burglarized.

only stared at them and sped off. They recorded the license-plate number. They then discovered a large gas grill in the middle of the Hauser backyard about 10 feet away from where they had seen the men running. The gas grill was always kept on the screened-in porch attached to the Houser residence. They called the police, who discovered the screen near the porch door had been torn, and the porch door had been unlocked and was open.

At trial, defendant testified he made two trips to the Houser residence on the evening of May 8, because he was in the company of Michael Houser, who was checking his parents' residence while they vacationed. Michael Houser was also charged with residential burglary as a result of the incident. Defendant knew Michael socially, and had a vehicle for sale which Michael came to his residence to see. Because Michael had no vehicle, as a favor defendant drove him to his parents' home to check on the house. After arriving there, Michael remembered he had forgotten the house keys and defendant then drove Michael back to Michael's apartment to get them. They returned to the Houser residence, and Michael approached the house while defendant waited in his vehicle.

Shortly thereafter, the Chisenalls' van pulled up and Michael returned from the house and entered defendant's vehicle. Michael told defendant the woman in the van was his sister and to just drive away. Defendant did so without responding to the woman.
Defendant denied knowing Michael Houser intended to steal anything and denied seeing a gas grill. He also testified a prior serious injury and spinal operation prevented him from running or carrying heavy objects. Defendant's two prior felony convictions were admitted into evidence for impeachment purposes. The trial judge rejected defendant's version of the incident, and stated he did not believe his testimony. The finding of guilty was based primarily on the Chisenalls' testimony regarding two men running in the Houser backyard, their proximity to the gas grill that had been removed from the porch, and the identification of defendant as the driver of the vehicle that sped away.

Defendant raises two issues on appeal. First, he contends the State failed to prove a residential burglary

Still skimming...

Still haven't found any facts that relate to my issue.

Finally—my issue: The structure was

because any entry that did occur was only to a screened porch attached to a house. Defendant argues the supreme court's decision in People v. Thomas, (1990), 137 Ill.2d 500, 148 Ill. Dec. 751, 561 N.E.2d 57, cert. denied (1991), ___ U.S. ___ , 111 S.Ct. 1092, 112 L.Ed.2d 1196, and the definition of dwelling in section 2-6(b) of the Criminal Code of 1961 (Code) (ILL. REV. STAT. 1989, ch. 38, par. 2-6(b)) require us to conclude a screened porch attached to a house is not part of a dwelling. We disagree.

a screened porch attached to a house.

And yes—this case deals with the right issue—whether it was a dwelling.

Holding = this porch was part of the dwelling. Now I need to focus—I wonder why this porch was a dwelling and the garage wasn't?

Thomas held, for our purposes here, that an attached garage is not necessarily a dwelling within the meaning of the residential burglary statute. Our supreme court also stated it would wait until some future date to decide whether the unlawful entry of the porch of a house may constitute the unlawful entry of a residence. We need not decide whether every porch is part of a dwelling. We are satisfied this porch was a part of the Housers' living quarters.

Was my conclusion that the Thomas court was more interested in "use" than in "attachment" correct? I wonder if the type of structure is important—will a porch be treated the same way as a garage?

The enclosed porch in this case is a wood frame structure with a wooden floor and dimensions of 8 by 10 or 12 feet. The porch includes both solid walls to a height of three feet and screen from that height to a roof. The floor, walls, and roof are all attached to the house. The porch has a metal door with glass inset and a lock to provide access to the backyard. A wooden door with glass inset and three locks connects the porch to the utility room of the house.

Court is describing the porch's physical dimensions—important?

Court notes there was a lock between the house and the porch—important?

The Housers furnished the porch with a metal table, chairs, a wrought iron love seat, a small table and a large gas grill. The furniture was always kept on the porch regardless of the season.

Court is describing how the porch is furnished.

The Housers used the porch in the summer for most of their meals, and in the winter cooked on the porch four or five times per week.

Now court is describing how the owners used the porch and how often—this is like the "type of use" factor in *Thomas*.

If "type of use" is relevant to this court, maybe that's why the court described the furnishings—they are evidence of the way in which the owners used the porch.

The Code defines "dwelling" for purposes of the residential burglary as "a house, apartment, mobile home, trailer, or other living quarters in which at the time of the alleged offense the owners or occupants actually reside or in their absence intend within a reasonable period of time to reside." (ILL. REV. STAT. 1989, ch. 38, par. 2-6(b).) In our view, the porch here is a part of the house.

Court's definition of dwelling—quote pulled right out of the statute. Court restates holding—porch is part of the house.

It is attached, enclosed, and used for sitting, eating, and cooking. These activities make the porch part of the living quarters of the house. This conclusion is not inconsistent with Thomas.

Affirmed.

Court reasons: it is "attached"—is attachment important? Rethink in light of *Thomas*. Court also emphasizes the activities of sitting, eating, and cooking— court states that it is "these activities" that make the porch part of the living quarters. This would clearly fit with *Thomas*.

### (b)  Notes from <u>McIntyre</u> Case

After carefully reviewing the *McIntyre* case and writing down some "thinking notes," your notes would reflect the following important information:

---

1.  Court's holding was fact-specific—e.g., held only that this porch was a dwelling under the statute.

2.  Court emphasized the following facts and factors:

(a)  *Factor #1*:      <u>Type of activities on porch</u>

   *Facts that support*: Sitting, eating, drinking and cooking meals

   *Language that supports*: "The porch here is a part of the house. It is . . . used for sitting, eating, and cooking."

(b)  *Factor #1(a)*: <u>Amount of time spent on porch</u>

   *Facts that support*: 4–5 times a week

(c)  *Factor #1(b)*: <u>Evidence of living-type activities</u>

   *Facts that support*: Gas grill, metal table, chairs, wrought iron love seat and small table

(d)  *Factor #2*:      <u>Physical proximity & characteristics of structure</u>

   *Facts that support*: Porch with solid wall and screen
                         Attached to home by wooden door with 3 locks

   *Language that supports*: "The porch here is a part of the house. It is attached, enclosed . . ."

---

3. My evaluation of factors:

The <u>type of activities</u> that occurred on the porch, as reflected by the <u>frequency</u> of these activities (amount of time spent on porch) and <u>evidence of these activities</u> (furnishings) seemed to be critical. The porch's <u>attachment</u> to the house & maybe its <u>physical</u> characteristics as part of the house were also important to the court.

Case support for my conclusion: When supporting its holding, the court observed: "The porch is *attached, enclosed . . .*" and the court also stated that "these activities make the porch part of the living quarters of the house."

4. Rule of Law the Holding Expresses:

An attached porch frequently used for residential activities is part of the living quarters of a home.

## 2. *People v. Silva Case*

After reading *Thomas* and *McIntyre*, assume that you next discovered the *People v. Silva* case. Having read that case, you determined that the facts in *Silva* were not particularly helpful as a basis of analogy to the Stripe garage. However, the court did engage in an interesting policy discussion of legislative intent and also interpreted the *Thomas* case. Only the relevant portions of the Silva case have been reproduced below. As you read the *Silva* case, note how it enhances our understanding of *Thomas* and *McIntyre*, even though the case is not helpful as a basis of factual analogy:

### (a) *Court Opinion*

| | *Attorney's Thoughts While Reading Case* |
|---|---|
| . . . . <br> During legislative debates, Senator Sangmeister explained the intent of the amendment as follows: <br><br> "Yes, it was even brought to our attention by the Illinois Supreme Court in a number of cases that * * * there should be a better definition to the dwelling house. We are having people prosecuted for residential burglary for breaking into * * * unoccupied buildings such as garages. Therefore, very simply, we have redefined dwell- | Legislative intent discussed—maybe this will help clarify my questions. This is not good— implies here that |

ing to mean a house, apartment, mobile home, trailer or other living quarters in which at the time of the alleged offense the owners or occupants actually reside in or * * * in their absence intend within a reasonable period of time to reside. So that still covers, in my opinion, the vacation home; you intend to reside in that and if you burglarize that, you would still be committing residential burglary, but it tightens up some of these cases where we got old abandoned buildings around our garages and stuff that * * * would not be residential burglary. . . ." 84th Ill.Gen.Assem., Senate Proceedings, June 18, 1986, at 66-67 (statements of Senator Sangmeister).

garages are not dwellings.

But wait a minute—the distinction seems to be abandoned, vacant buildings vs. occupied homes— Stripe garage isn't abandoned so maybe we are fine.

Burglary is a Class 2 felony with a statutory penalty range of not less than three years' nor more than seven years' imprisonment. (Ill.Rev.Stat.1991, ch. 38, pars. 19-1(b), 1005-8-1(a)(5); now codified as 720 ILCS 5/19-1(b) 730 ILCS 5/5-8-1(a)(5) (West 1992).) Residential burglary is a Class 1 felony with a statutory penalty range of not less than four years' nor more than 15 years' imprisonment. (Ill.Rev.Stat. 1991, ch. 38, pars. 19-3(b), 1005-8-1(a)(4); now codified as 720 ILCS 5/19-3(b); 730 ILCS 5/5-8-1(a)(4) (West 1992).) "The overall legislative scheme evidences an intent to make clear that an offender may not be charged with residential burglary—a crime with a more severe penalty—when he unlawfully entered a structure that was not a 'dwelling place of another.'" *Edgeston*, 243 Ill.App.3d at 10, 183 Ill.Dec. 196, 611 N.E.2d 49.

Court notes the difference in penalties between burglary and resid'l burglary.

Residential burglary carries the more severe penalty.

The residential burglary statute is designed to protect the "privacy and sanctity of the home," with a view toward the "greater danger and potential for serious harm from burglary of a home as opposed to burglary of a business." *Edgeston*, 243 Ill.App.3d at 10, 183 Ill.Dec. 196, 611 N.E.2d 49.

Here is why the penalty is more severe: 1) protect sanctity of home; & 2) greater potential for serious harm to home than to business.

The [structure] implicated the concerns for privacy, sanctity of the home, and the potential for serious harm which are addressed by the residential burglary statute. . . .

Great—court is evaluating how the structure's *use* implicates the public policy concerns underlying statute—not "attachment."

*Thomas* did not hold that a garage *per se* is not a dwelling within the meaning of the residential burglary statute; rather, *Thomas* held that the particular garage involved in that case was not a dwelling.

The judgment of the circuit court is affirmed.
Affirmed.

Even better—court interprets *Thomas* just like I did!

### (b)   Notes from *People v. Silva* Case

After carefully reviewing the *Silva* case and writing down some "thinking notes," your notes would reflect the following important information:

1.   Legislative intent: to prosecute people for residential burglary when they break into occupied residences and places used as living quarters, but not to prosecute for residential burglary when the structure is an abandoned or vacant building.

2.   Public policy reflected in legislative intent:

(a)   To protect the privacy and sanctity of the home.

(b)   To deter burglary of homes because of the greater danger posed to human life in homes.

3.   My evaluation of policy statements & court's interpretation of *Thomas*:

Court supports my interpretation of Thomas—a garage can, under appropriate circumstances, be a dwelling.

Court clarifies the policy underlying the statute—the concern for increased danger to homes as opposed to businesses (or, more clearly, vacant buildings and garages). This policy is consistent with the emphasis in both *Thomas* and in *McIntyre* re: the manner in which the owners use the structure is critical in determining whether it is a living quarters.

> I can argue that Michael Stripes' frequent use of the garage as a living quarters is consistent with the policy concerns underlying the statute—a place used as a private retreat & living quarters poses an increased danger to human life. Also—to protect the sanctity of the home.

### 3.   Synthesis of _Thomas_, _McIntyre_, and _Silva_ Cases

As you read the _Thomas, McIntyre_ and _Silva_ cases, notice how you did not read the cases in isolation. Although you will separately evaluate and make tentative conclusions about each case you read, other cases you have reviewed do affect your evaluation of each individual case. As you read each case, you cannot help but engage in an informal synthesis as your mind continually seeks to make sense of the wealth of information it is evaluating. Therefore, at this stage of your analysis, you will likely have arrived at some informal, tentative conclusions about the cases you have reviewed. Before solidifying your conclusions and drafting a written analysis of your findings, first verify whether your initial assumptions about the cases are valid in light of all of the cases you may have reviewed. It is very important to keep an open mind about each case and to be prepared to change some of your initial assumptions.

#### (a)   Synthesize Interpretations of the Original Rule of Law

Sometimes courts simply quote the original rule of law and do not attempt to define the rule further. However, as you learned in Chapter 5, courts often interpret an original rule of law by explaining what they think the rule of law means. When reviewing several cases that contain definitions and explanations of an original rule of law, it may seem at first that each case has defined the original rule of law in a different way. Before concluding that the definitions are different and not reconcilable, consider whether the courts are merely using slightly different language to make the same point. If so, synthesize the various statements into one or more definitions or explanations that embody the ideas expressed in each of the cases. If one of the cases clearly and cogently expresses the rule of law in a manner that is consistent with each case, make note of that language, as you may decide to quote that language when you draft your memo.

Using the residential burglary problem as an example, the _Thomas_ court defined dwelling as a "living quarters" in which the owners or occupants "actually reside." The legislature codified this definition and it is now part of the original rule of law—the statute. The _McIntyre_ court chose not to define the term "dwelling" any further and instead simply quoted the statutory definition of a living quarters. Thus, these two cases do not provide any interesting new interpretations of the original rule of law. However, the *Silva* court considered the purpose underlying the statute and reasoned that the statute was designed to protect the "privacy and sanctity of the home" because of the "greater danger and potential for serious harm from burglary of a home as opposed to burglary of a business." This new interpretation of the statute is relevant because it would affect your analysis of whether the Stripe family garage is a living quarters under the statute. This interpretation would also help you evaluate the *Thomas* and *McIntyre* cases. In other words, the legislative concerns expressed in *Silva* would affect your analysis of the relative importance of such potential factors as the type of structure and its attachment to or detachment from the primary residence. If the legislative concern is to protect privacy and to reduce the potential for serious harm to human life, then the manner in which a structure is used, including the type of use and frequency of use of that structure, is far more important than the structure's attachment to a primary residence. Therefore, even when a structure such as the Stripe family's garage is not a complete residence in and of itself, its use as a part-time living quarters may be dispositive.

### (b) Synthesize Factors and Standards

If you identified a narrow legal standard or definition that guided a specific court decision, consider how that standard is reconcilable with any factors you may have identified from reading other cases. If you identified factors that guided the court decisions, consider whether the factors you identified from each case are still viable when you study the cases as a group. As you evaluate the various factors that guide various court opinions, consider whether any factors appear to be more or less important than other factors.

In the residential burglary problem, the statutory definition of "dwelling" is a relatively narrow legal standard: a dwelling is a "living quarters" in which the owners or occupants "actually reside." Reviewing the cases as a group, the "type of use" factor illustrates and supports the standard itself. Obviously, when determining whether a structure is a "living quarters," one must look at the manner in which the structure is used. The sub-factors identified from the *McIntyre* case also support the standard—the "frequency of use" and "evidence of use."

In addition, the different case results would also support your initial tentative conclusion that the "type of use" factor is more important than the structure's physical attachment to the primary residence. In *Thomas*, the structure was not a living quarters when the owner used the garage only to store commercial products. In *McIntyre*, the structure was a living quarters when the owners frequently used the structure for such living-type activities as "sitting, eating, and cooking." In both cases, the structures were attached to the primary residence. Thus, to explain the diverse results, the manner in which the structures were used seems to be the definitive factor. The structure's attachment to the primary residence did not compel a positive outcome in the *Thomas* case. However, because the *McIntyre* court also emphasized the porch's physical attachment to the residence, this factor can not be totally discounted, even though it may not be as important a factor.

### (c)  Synthesize the Rules of Law

When evaluating each case, you formulated a rule of law that embodied the court's holding. From these individual rules of law expressed in each case, formulate one or more general rules of law that accurately reflects the group of cases as a whole. If the cases do not appear to be reconcilable after your initial comparison, you would need to evaluate the cases further to determine whether they are in fact reconcilable. You will learn more about reconciling cases later in this chapter. However, assuming that the cases are reconcilable, you will use the common threads that run through-out the cases and synthesize them into broad principles that accurately depict the cases as a group.

In the residential burglary problem, your notes might look like this:

---

*Rules of law I formulated from each case:*

    *Thomas*:        An attached garage used primarily to store commercial products is not a dwelling under the residential burglary statute.

    *McIntyre*:    An attached porch frequently used for residential activities is part of the living quarters of a home.

*General rules of law that depict the holdings & rationale from both cases:*

A structure is a living quarters when the owners frequently use the structure for activities that occur in a living quarters, and the furnishings reflect that use.

Although a structure's attachment to the main residence is also relevant, physical attachment to the primary residence is not necessary.

---

## ◆ II ◆ *CASE RECONCILIATION*

On occasion, you may read cases within the same jurisdiction that seemingly conflict with each. In our system of jurisprudence, courts within the same jurisdiction are supposed to follow the rules of law adopted by higher level courts within their jurisdiction. Therefore, before concluding that the cases are irreconcilable, review again the language in each case and consider whether the courts have simply used different language to describe the same rule of law. Also consider whether there might be a relationship between the seemingly different standards that reconciles them. For example, one standard might express the general rule in the jurisdiction, while another standard might express an exception to the general rule. Also consider whether the differing standards are intended to apply to different factual situations. If after carefully re-evaluating the cases you still can not reconcile them, you might wish to review secondary sources to determine whether a legal scholar has addressed the issue. Legal periodicals and the American Law Reports often discuss issues that are the subject of splits of authority. Such articles typically catalog the various court decisions that discuss the legal point and discuss the competing policy interests that affect the different courts' analyses. By surveying the law and synthesizing the different cases, secondary authorities can save you a significant amount of time.

If you conclude that the cases truly are not reconcilable, first consider the level of court adopting the different rules of law. If the highest level court in a jurisdiction adopts a rule of law that differs from a lower level court decision, the higher court's rule is controlling over the lower level decision. Occasionally you may find a split of authority within courts of the same level, such as within the intermediate courts of appeal. As an example, in the state of Missouri, the Court of Appeals for the Eastern District of Missouri might adopt a different interpretation of an original rule of law than the Court of Appeals for the Western District of Missouri. In that event, follow the rule of law adopted by the courts within the district that governs your client's legal problem. In the event of a split of authority between different intermediate level appellate courts, the court that oversees your district is controlling.

If the split of authority cannot be resolved by either of the above methods, consider the dates of the conflicting opinions. You might conclude that, over time, the policy in a given jurisdiction has changed, suggesting that the more recent cases would serve a more valuable function in predicting the outcome of the client's situation. Also consider whether any of the cases discusses the policy considerations underlying the adoption of a rule of law. You might then be able to use the policy considerations to help evaluate the client's situation.

Chapters 21 and 24 discuss in greater detail the argument strategies that can be used in such situations.

 ## EXERCISE 1:
## SOCIAL HOST LIABILITY

   This exercise builds on Exercise 1 in Chapter 6. First review the fact pattern in that exercise. Then analyze and synthesize the following case notes, formulating general rules of law that accurately depict the group of cases, and the relevant factors that guide the courts' decisions.

## *Case Notes*

*Rappaport v. Nichols* (1959): A tavern owner served alcoholic beverages to a minor, who became intoxicated. The minor later drove and caused a car crash, killing the other driver. The plaintiff sued the tavern owner under a negligence theory. The court decided that if a jury found that the tavern owner knew the patron was a minor, or if the tavern owner was on notice that the patron was intoxicated, then in either case the tavern owner could be responsible under a negligence theory.

*Soronen v. Olde Milford Inn, Inc.* (1966): A tavern owner served five drinks of alcohol to an adult patron who rose from his barstool, took several steps and fell, striking his head on a steel column. He later died. A doctor arrived quickly on the scene and later testified that there was "a very very profuse, profound odor of alcohol" from the body and opined that he must have been in a state of acute alcoholism for at least two hours. The court decided that if a jury could find that the decedent was visibly intoxicated, then the tavern owner was liable to the decedent, despite the fact that the decedent played a large role in his own death. The court reasoned that the liquor licensee's duty not to serve intoxicated persons is for the protection of the individual patron as well as the public.

*Linn v. Rand* (1976): A friend served a minor alcoholic beverages in the friend's home. The minor subsequently drove a car and hurt a pedestrian who sued the driver's friend. The court decided that the jury should decide whether the host knew the minor would be driving, and thus, whether the host should be responsible in a negligence suit. The court declined to give social hosts any broad kind of immunity, and the court cited the public policy of curtailing "the ever-increasing incidence of serious automobile accidents resulting from drunken driving."

*Kelly v. Gwinnell* (1984): A friend (host) served liquor to an adult guest, knowing the guest would have to drive home. The host continued to serve drinks even after the guest was visibly intoxicated. The guest drove negligently and injured a third party. The court held that the host was liable to the third party under these facts, reasoning that the injury was reasonably foreseeable.

*Griesenbeck v. Walker* (1985): A father served two drinks to his adult daughter, who left in her car about midnight to drive three miles home. By 1:20 a.m., a blazing fire in her home killed the daughter, her husband, and one of her two children. The fire was caused by the daughter's cigarette left smoldering in a sofa. The expert toxicology report indicated acute alcohol intoxication (at least nine drinks). The child of the adult daughter sued her grandfather for negligence, on the theory that he served his daughter when she was visibly intoxicated and permitted her to go home impaired by alcohol, where she was so intoxicated that she caused the fire and was unable to save herself or help evacuate her other family members. The court held that the father was not liable because the fire was not a foreseeable or probable harm.

## EXERCISE 2:
## THE SELF-DEFENSE PROBLEM

Review again the September 1ˢᵗ memo describing the Jeffrey Bing fact pattern, and the *People v. S.M.* case reproduced in Appendix F. For this exercise, review the September 15ᵗʰ memo describing additional facts for this exercise, and the *People v. Moore* and *People v. Shipp* cases. Fully evaluate each case and identify for each case: (1) any helpful interpretations or definitions of the self-defense statute; (2) the court's holding; (3) the relevant facts that support the court's holding; (4) the factors that guided the court's decision; and (4) the rule of law the court's holding illustrates. Finally, reviewing your notes from *S.M., Moore* and *Shipp*, synthesize the cases, noting: (1) the relevant factors that guided the courts' decisions; (2) relevant interpretations or definitions of the original rule of law; and (3) rules of law that accurately depict the three cases as a group.

Alternatively, review the cases your professor has assigned for you to evaluate and respond to each of the foregoing questions with respect to such cases.

# 8

# THE OFFICE MEMORANDUM: AN OVERVIEW

## I INTRODUCTION

Attorneys in a law office regularly convey legal analysis in an internal document that is called an office memorandum. Office memoranda are internal in-house documents that are typically drafted by more junior attorneys in response to legal questions senior attorneys have asked them to research and analyze. The context in which office memoranda are drafted will help you better understand the purpose and structure of an office memorandum.

In a typical situation, a client asks the senior attorney for advice, such as whether it can lawfully take XYZ action, whether it can sue ABC corporation, or whether it has a lawful defense to a lawsuit filed against it. Senior attorneys have a significant number of clients and files over which they have responsibility. The number of client matters often exceeds 100. In short, senior attorneys usually work on numerous client matters at any given time. Instead of researching and analyzing every legal question presented by every client, senior attorneys routinely delegate many research issues to more junior attorneys.

When you practice law and a senior attorney asks you to draft an office memo, you will become the expert on that particular area of the law. You will be expected to research, analyze and then communicate to the senior attorney how the subtleties of complex laws affect a client's legal question. Because legal analysis is often complex and detailed, you will typically relay your analysis to senior attorneys in written form, in a document known as an office memorandum. In the office memo, you will analyze the legal problem and answer the question or questions presented by the client situation. Typically, you will sum up your analysis by either advising whether the client can lawfully engage in specific conduct, or predicting how a decision-maker is likely to rule on the client's existing legal problem.

Because your intended readers will be trained attorneys, they will expect the information within the memo to conform to the ways in which attorneys evaluate the law. Thus, they will expect to review first the relevant rule or rules of law, followed by an identification of the issue or issues presented by the rule of law, followed by an exploration of previous cases that have interpreted and applied the rule of law, followed by an examination of how the rule of law and previous cases impact the client's situation. You will want to conform to these expectations when writing legal memos. This section of the book provides you with basic guidelines that reflect commonly understood writing practices within the legal community.

 ## II  *INFORMATION CONVEYED IN AN OFFICE MEMO*

A good office memo should evaluate every significant aspect of the relevant rules of law and issues, the previous cases that have interpreted the law, and the effect of the rules of law and courts' interpretations on the client's factual situation. The information in the office memo should be so thorough that the reviewing senior attorney would understand the nuances of how the law affects the client's situation without having to read the relevant cases discussed in the memo. The office memo should be so thorough that the senior attorney would be able to sit down with you and discuss your interpretation of a case cited in the memo without personally having to read the case. The office memo should be so thorough that the senior attorney would feel comfortable giving the client advice based on the legal analysis contained in your memo.

The most common mistake first-year law students make when drafting office memos is "bottom-lining" their analysis—conveying only a summary of their conclusions. Students often say that they do so out of the belief that, because a senior attorney is an expert in the law, they would insult the senior attorney's intelligence by divulging too much information. They fear that a senior attorney might be insulted by the presumption that he or she did not already know the details of the law. This fear is misplaced for three reasons. First, even an expert in a particular area of the law cannot possibly maintain a thorough knowledge of every nuance in the law. A tax attorney may be an expert on tax law. However, numerous volumes of books contain the tax code, and literally hundreds of thousands of cases interpret the code. Only a handful of these will be helpful in resolving a client's specific factual problem.

Second, even when the senior attorney understands what the law requires or permits in the abstract, that attorney cannot be expected to know, from thousands of cases, the details of the specific applicable cases that might be helpful in resolving the client's problem. Therefore, even though the senior attorney may understand the general requirements of a particular law, that attorney will expect *you* to become the expert on how the law would affect a client's very specific problem.

Third, even though a senior attorney might understand the general elements of a particular rule of law you are researching, the office memo should be a self-contained document. It should contain the relevant content of every rule of law and court opinion that helped you arrive at your legal conclusion. The reviewing attorney will expect to see the logical links of your analysis within the body of the office memo itself. You do not want to force the reviewing attorney to have to go to the library and read the original rule of law and cases that interpret it.

 ## III THE PREDICTIVE FUNCTION OF THE OFFICE MEMO

Office memos explore the relevant rules of law and then predict how the law would apply to a client's factual situation. The senior attorney who reviews an office memorandum will make recommendations to the client about future conduct based on the analysis contained in your memo. Therefore, you want to evaluate very carefully every aspect of the legal problem, including the legal arguments an opponent might make. Recall that the office memo is reviewed only by members of your own law office. You need not be concerned that your exploration of weaknesses in the client's position might be exposed to opposing counsel. Instead, the reviewing partner and client need to know the potential risks involved if the client takes or fails to take certain actions. Failure to evaluate the risks could ultimately result in losing the client or facing a malpractice claim filed by the client. Therefore, office memos describe all of the legal arguments that support the client's conduct, as well as all of the legal arguments that do not favor the client.

 ## IV THE STRUCTURAL FORMAT OF THE OFFICE MEMO

Office memos generally follow a standard format that most attorneys find to be the clearest means of communicating legal analysis. The general format of the typical office memorandum is premised on two notions. First, because senior attorneys are presumably very busy, the over-all format of a standard office memo allows reviewing attorney first to obtain a quick and insightful overview of the legal problem (the Question Presented and Short Answer) followed by a more thorough analysis of the details of the problem (the Fact and Discussion sections).

Second, the over-all format of an office memo reflects the fact that readers automatically search for context when reading new material. Because legal analysis is often extremely complex, the need for context is particularly important in documents that evaluate the law. Therefore, an office memo provides the reviewing attorney with general context before analyzing the specific details of the legal problem. This format of providing context before details begins with the very first component of the typical memorandum—the Question Presented, and continues through the heart of the memorandum itself—the Discussion section.

Although office memos generally reflect a common pattern of analysis, some law offices have their own internal formats the attorneys in that office are expected to follow. For example, they may refer to certain sections of the office memo by specific titles that differ somewhat from the titles used in this book. When you begin practicing law, you will of course follow the preferred format that exists within your law office. Any such variations in format will be primarily cosmetic and easy to pick up as you begin practicing law.

A typical office memo follows the basic structure illustrated below:

---

### MEMORANDUM

To:      Senior Attorney
From:    Junior Attorney
Date:     [Date memo is submitted]
Re:      XYZ Client Matter

### QUESTION PRESENTED

This is the section that identifies the legal question or questions the memo will evaluate. (Chapter 14 discusses the Question Presented in greater detail.)

---

## SHORT ANSWER

After identifying the legal question, this section provides a brief answer to the question. As the name implies, the Short Answer simply answers the Question Presented and provides a very brief summary of the reasons that support the answer. (Chapter 14 discusses the Short Answer in greater detail.)

## STATEMENT OF FACTS

The Statement of Facts section of the memo simply tells the client's factual story. Included within the description of that story are all of the legally relevant facts and any background facts that help tie the story together. This section includes relevant facts that are favorable to the client as well as any relevant facts that are unfavorable to the client. (Chapter 14 discusses the Statement of Facts in greater detail.)

## DISCUSSION

The Discussion section is the heart of the office memorandum, where the relevant law is evaluated and then applied to the facts of the client's situation. Because the Discussion section can be fairly lengthy and complex, this section of the memo is further comprised of the following components:

- An overview paragraph that lays the foundation for the discussion;
- A thesis paragraph that summarizes the issue;
- Paragraphs that explain and evaluate the law concerning the issue (Rule Explanation);
- Paragraphs that apply the law to the client's factual situation (Rule Application); and
- A conclusion.

(Chapters 11–13 discuss the Discussion section of an office memo in greater detail.)

At this point, you may wish to take a look at Sample Memo A in Appendix A to see how the residential burglary problem and the Stripe garage was evaluated in a memo.

# 9

# SELECTING CASES FOR THE MEMO

 **I** ❖ *ASSESSING THE VALUE OF EACH CASE*

When you have found a number of cases that address a legal issue you are evaluating, your goal is to incorporate into your memo only those cases that help explain what the law means and help predict how a judge, administrative agency or other adjudicator might apply the law to your client's factual situation. From that group of cases, you must assess each case's relative importance and the specific reasons why that case is important to your analysis before you can begin to outline or draft your analysis.

Not all cases are factually analogous enough to merit a thorough evaluation of their facts, holding and rationale. As Chapter 5 explained, a case may be relevant in several ways. A specific case may interpret the original rule of law in a manner that helps you understand what the law means. For example, the court may define the rule of law or may express a standard or factors that should be used when evaluating the rule of law. A case may include a useful discussion of the purpose underlying the rule of law, or the public policy considerations the law was designed to address. Finally, the factual scenario in a case may be analogous to your client's factual situation, allowing you to use the case as a vehicle for factual comparisons or distinctions.

With these ideas in mind, consider each case you think may be potentially helpful to you in drafting your analysis of the law. For each case, identify the different ways in which the case may be helpful.

Does the case contain:

1.  Any helpful definitions or explanations about what the law means?

2.  A helpful discussion about the underlying purpose of the rule of law or public policy considerations?

3.  Analogous case facts that can serve as the basis of comparison to or distinction from the client's facts?

After you have carefully considered the different ways in which each case is useful to you, you are now ready to decide how you might incorporate each case in your memo. Some cases may be relevant in all three of the basic ways in which a case might be useful. These cases will obviously assume a significant role in your written analysis of the law. However, other cases may be useful for only a discrete point, meriting only a brief mention.

## A.  Cases With Useful Definitions or Interpretations of the Law

A case may be important to you solely because it contains a sentence or two that beautifully defines the original rule of law. The court's interpretation of the law may include a standard by which the rule of law must be measured or the factors which courts must consider when evaluating the rule of law. In some cases, a court's interpretation or definition of the law may be so important in the jurisdiction that it becomes what is known as a "landmark" decision—a case to which later courts routinely refer when evaluating the law. Unless such a case is also valuable to you for other reasons (i.e., an analogous fact pattern or policy discussion), you would likely refer only briefly to the case itself, simply quoting or paraphrasing the definition, standard or factors.

Because definitions, standards and factors provide a foundation, or context, for a detailed legal analysis, such ideas are usually included within a roadmap paragraph that introduces the discussion. For example, a thesis paragraph often contains such general interpretations. If the court's definition or other interpretation is clearly and cogently expressed, you would quote the statement and then cite to the case to show the origins of the quote. If, however, the definition or interpretation is not very clearly expressed, and you can not find any other case that makes the point more clearly, you should instead paraphrase in your own words the court's statement. Again, you should follow the statement with a citation that tells the reader the origin of your idea.

To illustrate, the following cases are used to support a specific interpretation of the rule of law. The courts' interpretations are paraphrased rather than quoted because the language in each case was not particularly clear.

> When evaluating whether a condition is a hidden danger, or trap, courts consider the inherent dangerousness of the condition and the age of the injured child. A condition constitutes a hidden danger, or trap, if its dangerous condition would be hidden to a child because of the child's age and immaturity. *Ansin v. Thurston*, 98 So. 2d 87, 88 (Fla. Dist. Ct. App. 1957). In addition, the dangerous condition that injures the child must have a connection with the object that initially attracts the child onto the property, such that the two conditions jointly contribute to the child's injury. *Starling v. Saha*, 451 So. 2d 516, 518–19 (Fla. Dist. Ct. App. 1984).

## B. Cases That Describe the Underlying Purpose or Policy of the Law

Some cases may be useful because they describe the underlying purpose of the law or the law's effect on public policy. In the case of a statutory rule of law, the court may comment on the legislative history and even incorporate relevant parts of the legislative history, such as congressional testimony or reports. If the underlying purpose of a rule of law is relevant because it provides a useful backdrop for your general analysis, you might incorporate such comments in a roadmap paragraph. Sometimes, however, a court's policy discussion may affect a specific argument you wish to evaluate in the memo. Under those circumstances, you would incorporate the case discussion into the section of your analysis in which you evaluate that argument.

As an example, consider the residential burglary problem and the *Silva* case. In that case, the court remarked on the statute's purpose and included relevant legislative history within that discussion. Recall that the legislative history directly relates to an argument the drafting attorney needed to evaluate—whether the legislature intended to exclude garages as potential dwellings under the statute. Therefore, the drafting attorney waited to address the case until the section of the memo that addressed the statutory purpose argument. In the following example excerpted from Sample Memo A in Appendix A, note how the drafting attorney only referred to that part of the *Silva* case that relates to the legislative history and purpose of the statute. Because the case facts are not analogous, the case facts and holding were omitted from the case discussion.

Defendant might also argue that the legislative history suggests that the legislators did not intend for the statute to cover structures such as garages. As the court noted in *People v. Silva*, 629 N.E.2d 948 (Ill. App. Ct. 1993), the legislature amended the statute in 1986 to clarify and to narrow the meaning of the term "dwelling." The court quoted the following statement of Senator Sangmeister made during legislative hearings: "It was even brought to our attention by the Illinois Supreme Court in a number of cases that . . . there should be a better definition to the dwelling house. We are having people prosecuted for residential burglary for breaking into . . . unoccupied buildings *such as garages*." *Id*. at 951(emphasis added).

This argument lacks merit. The *Silva* court noted that "[t]he residential burglary statute is designed to protect the 'privacy and sanctity of the home,' with a view toward the 'greater danger and potential for serious harm from burglary of a home as opposed to burglary of a business.'" 629 N.E.2d at 951, *quoting, People v. Edgesto*, 611 N.E.2d 49 (Ill. App. Ct. 1993). Senator Sangmeister's concern that people are being prosecuted for breaking into "unoccupied buildings" is consistent with the general legislative purpose to deter residential burglary because of its potential for serious harm. An occupied garage used as a living quarters invokes the same legislative concerns for the sanctity of the home and the increased risk of harm that result from an invasion of that home. Moreover, the Illinois Supreme Court decided the *Thomas* case only a few years after the amendment. In *Thomas*, the court suggested that a garage used as a living quarters would be a dwelling under the statute.

## C. Cases With Analogous Facts

Some cases may be useful because the court has evaluated how the original rule of law affects a factual situation that is analogous to the client situation you are evaluating. If you have more than one factually analogous case to consider, you may not discuss each of these cases in depth. Instead, you may decide to discuss a few of the cases in depth and refer only briefly to other cases. When deciding which cases to emphasize and which cases to omit or to incorporate only tangentially, consider the following:

## *1.   Consider the Standard or Factors That Guide Each Case*

First, consider the various standards or factors that guided the courts' decisions. If you did not already do so when you synthesized the cases, you may
find it helpful to make a list of each of the standards or factors you will incorporate into your memo. Next to each standard or factor, note the cases in
which that idea helped guide the decision. (Not every case will necessarily explore every factor you have identified as important because the fact pattern in a
particular case may not be relevant to certain factors.)

After you have identified the cases that can potentially illustrate each standard or factor, you are ready to make preliminary decisions about the cases
you will incorporate into your office memo. If you discover that only one case
illustrates a particular factor or standard, your choice is clear—you will definitely want to include that case in your memo because the case will be your
only means of illustrating that idea. If, however, several cases each illustrate
the same standard or factor, the decision becomes a bit more complex. If two
or more cases are guided by the same standard or factors, consider the results
in the cases. If two cases were guided by the same standard or factors but the
different fact patterns yielded two different results, you may want to discuss
both cases in detail. The cases can then illustrate how far the rule of law or
standard extends in each direction.

Suppose, however, that two or more cases each evaluate the same standard
or factors and the court in each case arrived at the same result. In that situation,
consider whether the cases bring out different nuances of the law that may be
helpful as you evaluate how the cases affect the client. If so, you may decide to
address both cases in your memo. However, unless each case brings out a different nuance of the law you would like to explore in depth, you may not want
to engage in a full and detailed discussion of each case. Instead, you might
discuss one case in depth and refer only tangentially to the other case.

In the follow example excerpted from Sample Memo D in Appendix A, the
drafting attorney discusses the *Ansin* and *Allen* cases. Prior to drafting the
memo, the attorney evaluated the relative importance of each case and decided
that, while each case was factually analogous, the *Ansin* case provided a
stronger basis for factual analogies. In addition, the attorney concluded that the
*Allen* case did not bring out any nuance of the law not already expressed in the
*Ansin* case. Therefore, the attorney elected to fully discuss the facts, holding
and rationale of the *Ansin* case and to use the *Allen* case only as supplemental
support. The following example is excerpted from the "rule explanation" section of the first issue:

> It is foreseeable that children will trespass on property when the property is attractive and alluring to children and the landowner has actual knowledge that children have previously trespassed on the property. *Ansin v. Thurston*, 98 So. 2d 87, 88 (Fla. Dist. Ct. App. 1957). In *Ansin*, the defendant's property contained an artificial pond with white sand banks, a floating dock, and a raft. *Id.* at 88. A child drowned in the pond after playing on the raft. The court upheld a jury's finding that the presence of child trespassers was reasonably foreseeable, holding that it was "certain that children would be attracted to such a place. . . ." *Id.* The court reasoned that the pond was both visible and accessible to children, as it was close to well-traveled streets and homes. Moreover, the property was seven blocks from an elementary school. Finally, the owner knew that children had used the pond for swimming. *Id. See also Allen v. William P. McDonald_Corp.*, 42 So. 2d 706, 707 (Fla. 1949) (holding that white sand banks adjacent to a pond were sufficiently alluring and attractive to children to entice them to trespass).

## 2.   *Consider Which Cases Serve a More Useful Predictive Function*

### (a)   *General Rule of Thumb*

Assuming you have more than one case that illustrates a particular standard or factor, you should also consider which cases serve a more useful predictive purpose in evaluating your client's factual situation. Generally, a case grows increasingly more useful as a predictive tool the more closely it matches your client's factual situation. Thus, if two cases serve the same purpose (i.e., illustrate the same factors or standard with the same result), the case that more closely matches your client's situation would be more useful as a predictive tool. In making that decision, you may find it helpful to create a graph of the cases. The following graph uses the residential burglary example to illustrate how you might create a graph to assess the relative importance of different cases in terms of their predictive function:

| Not a Dwelling | | | | Dwelling |
|---|---|---|---|---|
| ⟸  &#124;  &#124; | &#124; | &#124; | &#124; | &#124;  ⟹ |
| Case 1: | Case 2: | Stripe garage | Case 3: | Case 4: |
| Empty ware-house in indus-trial district | Garage used to store perfume and attached to a dwelling | Detached garage used as a get-a-way | Attached porch used for sitting, eating & cooking | Vacation home |
| *Not a dwelling* | *Not a dwelling* | *?* | *Dwelling* | *Dwelling* |

In the above example, the Stripe garage falls somewhere between Case 2 and Case 3. Because Case 2 and Case 3 yield different results, each case may be useful in evaluating whether the Stripe garage is a dwelling. The discussion would evaluate whether the Stripe garage is more like the facts in Case 2 or the facts in Case 3. In contrast, the facts in Case 1 and Case 4 do not serve as useful a predictive function because there are other cases with facts that are more closely analogous to the client. Therefore, these cases would either be omitted from the discussion or brought in only tangentially to illustrate a specific point.

### (b) When Case With Less Desirable Facts Produces a Favorable Result

At times your client's factual situation may fall somewhere between two cases that illustrate the same factors or standard and that have the same favorable result. In such circumstances, the case that produces a favorable result with less desirable facts would serve the most useful predictive function. Thus, in the illustration below, Case 2 would serve a more useful predictive function than Case 3. The attorney could argue that, if a case with less desirable facts produces the desirable result the client seeks, then the court should hold in the same manner with the client's more desirable facts. The case then becomes helpful because of the favorable distinctions you might make between the case and your client's factual situation

| Not a Dwelling | | | | Dwelling |
|---|---|---|---|---|
| ⟸  &#124;  &#124; | &#124; | &#124; | &#124; | &#124;  ⟹ |
| Case 1: | Case 2: | Stripe garage | Case 3: | Case 4: |
| Empty ware-house in indus-trial district | Detached garage sometimes used as an artist studio by the owner | Detached garage used as a get-a-way | Attached porch regularly used for sitting, eating & cooking | Vacation home |
| *Not a dwelling* | *Dwelling* | *?* | *Dwelling* | *Dwelling* |

## EXERCISE 1

Assume that you represent a client who is being prosecuted for kidnapping. One of the elements of the state kidnapping statute is that the confinement must be "secret." You know the following facts: Your client, Mr. Tate, confined Mr. Campbell to a chair in Mr. Campbell's living room. Mr. Campbell's home is a large, renovated, two-story brownstone. The living room is on the first floor of the home. The first floor is primarily a glass picture window (a large, uninterrupted pane of glass), with a small amount of brick surrounding the entrance and providing support at the exterior wall of the home. The picture window is not tinted or coated in any way to affect its transparency. The confinement took place in the evening; your client left a light on in the living room that evening. Your client did not close the drapes to obscure the view into the living room. The lot on which the home is situated is level, and the front door to the home is only two steps up from the sidewalk that leads to the home. The front door is solid wood with no window. The home sits back only twenty feet from the street. The street in front of Mr. Campbell's home is classified by the police as "moderately traveled" and is open to both commercial and residential traffic. A neighbor claims that she can see into the home at night when the lights are on, although she did not look into the home that particular evening.

In researching whether the confinement was "secret" under the kidnapping statute, assume you discovered the following four cases:

1.  *Case A*—In this case the court held that the confinement was secret when the defendant confined the victim in a basement apartment. The confinement took place at night; the drapes were closed and a friend trying to find the victim peered in through the window of the apartment and could not see anything.

2.  *Case B*—The court held that the confinement was not secret when an enraged defendant, holding a gun, dragged the victim from the victim's private office into the lobby of the office building. A security guard was present in the lobby and the enraged defendant caught the security guard's attention when he shouted that he would kill the victim unless the victim complied with his demands.

3.  *Case C*—In this case, the court held that the confinement was secret. The defendant hid in the victim's garage one evening. The garage was attached to the victim's home and the garage door was closed. When the victim left her home to enter her car, the defendant forced the victim to climb into the trunk of the car. The defendant drove the car to a deserted

landfill when he finally removed the victim from the trunk of the car. No one saw the victim at any time during this abduction.

4. *Case D*—The court held that the confinement was not secret when the defendant confined the victim in a small vestibule of an apartment building. The vestibule was a few steps up from a busy street and took place during morning rush hour. A driver on the street saw the defendant holding the victim against her will and honked his horn.

After evaluating the above cases:

(1) List those cases that would serve the most useful predictive function for your client.

(2) List those cases that would serve the least useful predictive function for your client.

(3) Explain your choices.

### 3.  *Consider the Rationale in Each Case*

The depth of the court's rationale is another factor to consider when deciding which cases to discuss in a memo. A case with analogous facts becomes more valuable when the court justifies its holding with an in-depth discussion of why it applied the law to the case facts in the manner that it did. Thus, all other things being equal, a case with a thorough explanation of its holding is more useful than a case in which the rationale is fairly superficial. If a case with weak rationale has a specific point you would like to bring out, you might make that point by referring to the case in passing without necessarily discussing the case in detail.

## D.  *Consider the Level of Court*

When selecting cases for a memo, also consider the level of court that rendered each decision. A case decided by the highest level court in a jurisdiction has greater weight in the jurisdiction than a case decided by a lower level court. However, do not disregard lower level cases solely because you may have a case decided by a higher court. The case decided by the lower court may be more valuable to you if, for example, the facts of that case are more analogous to your client.

## E.  *Consider the Date of Decision*

Finally, also consider the dates of the cases you are evaluating. All other things being equal, a recent case is more valuable than an older case, particularly when there is a wide difference in time. For example, a case decided in 2001 would potentially carry greater weight than a case decided in 1950, even though the 1950 case might still be "good law." This is particularly true in areas of the law where the law has undergone some transformation due to changing policy considerations. *Caveat:* An older case might still be an effective choice if it contains analogous facts or useful rationale.

 **EXERCISE 2**

You represent Chester Tate and are defending him with respect to attempted murder charges filed by the State of Illinois. Another associate in the law firm has previously worked on Chester Tate's defense to *kidnapping* charges filed by the State in connection with the same incident. To acquaint yourself with the factual and legal background underlying your representation:

A.   Review the Sample Office Memo that analyzes a potential defense to kidnapping charges (Sample Memo B in Appendix A); and

B.   Review the memo in Appendix G. That memo is from a senior attorney and provides additional factual details that may be relevant to an attempted murder defense.

C.   Carefully evaluate the cases in Appendix G and consider their relative importance and usefulness in analyzing the viability of Mr. Tate's intoxication defense to attempted murder.

After carefully evaluating and taking notes from each case:

1.   Select the cases that you would emphasize as cases of "primary" emphasis in a memo that assesses the viability of an intoxication defense. Primary emphasis cases are those analogous cases that are of such primary relevance that they would merit a complete case discussion in an office memo, including a discussion of case facts, holding, and rationale. For each such case of primary emphasis, note:

   (a)   the case facts that you would use as a basis of comparison to or distinction from the client's facts; and

(b) the important rationale from the court's decision.

2. Select those cases that you would use as "tangential" cases in assessing the viability of an intoxication defense. Tangential cases are those cases that have some relevance to the client's problem but, because they are not as important as primary emphasis cases, they do not merit an extended discussion in an office memo. Sample Memo D in Appendix A reflects the use of tangential cases (*see, e.g.,* the use of the *Allen, Bathey* and *Newby* cases referenced in that memo). For each such tangential case, note:

   (a) The specific purpose for which you would use such case in an office memorandum (*e.g.,* does it contain a good statement of a rule of law? A valuable interpretation of public policy? Would a few case facts be helpful in a parenthetical to support a factual analogy made by a primary case?); and

   (b) State the specific language or case facts that you would select from the case to serve such purpose.

3. Identify those cases that you would not mention in an office memo at all (*e.g.,* because they have no relevance to the client's problem or because other cases reflect the same points more clearly).

# 10

# THE DISCUSSION SECTION: THE BASIC TEMPLATE FOR ANALYSIS

 **CHAPTER IN FOCUS**

MEMORANDUM

To:      [Senior Attorney]
From:    [Junior Attorney]
Date:    [Date of Submission of Memo]
Re:      [XYZ Client Matter]

QUESTION PRESENTED

. . .

SHORT ANSWER

. . .

STATEMENT OF FACTS

. . .

DISCUSSION

## II    *THE DEDUCTIVE WRITING PATTERN*

### A.   *The Shift From Inductive to Deductive Analysis*

After you have fully evaluated a rule of law and the cases that interpret the rule of law, you are ready to begin the drafting process. The drafting process can be challenging, and even frustrating at times, because the writing process tends to illuminate the complexity and ambiguities inherent in ideas that often seem so clear in the abstract. In addition, the very nature of the pre-drafting analytical thought process presents an additional challenge during the shift from the pre-drafting to the drafting process. When you evaluate rules of law and cases, you separately examine each court's holding, reasoning and numerous case facts to identify any underlying factors or principles that guided the court, and to formulate a rule of law that captures the essence of the case. After separately evaluating each case, you then evaluate the cases as a group to formulate rules of law that accurately express the cases as a group. This analytical process of examining specific facts and reasoning to identify broad rules of law is *inductive*. The inductive process involves the examination of specific details to arrive at general principles.

Although the inductive reasoning process makes sense in the pre-drafting stage, a written analysis patterned on the same inductive process would be extremely confusing for a reader to follow. Imagine forcing a reader to meander through the same lengthy, winding path you traveled when evaluating the law. Imagine the reader's mounting frustration as the reader reviews case after case, all the while wondering where the path is leading and why the details of various cases will ultimately become important. To avoid that result, when drafting a legal discussion you must totally reverse your pre-drafting analytical process to a *deductive* analytical pattern. The deductive writing pattern is premised on the notion that readers can absorb information more easily if they understand its significance as soon as they see it. The best way to assure immediate understanding is to present the context of an idea before describing its details.[1] The context provides a basis, or "foundation," for understanding the details that will follow. Therefore, a deductive analytical pattern is one that progresses from a broad conclusion to narrow, specific illustrations of why the conclusion is sound.

---

[1] Stephen V. Armstrong & Timothy P. Terrell, *Thinking Like a Writer, A Lawyer's Guide to Effective Writing and Editing*, 3-3 through 3-5 (Clark, Boardman, Callaghan 1992).

To appreciate the importance of the deductive writing pattern, compare the following set of instructions.

---

(1)  After you have turned onto Highway 170 South, take Forest Parkway East.

Before that you will have to take the appropriate exit from Highway 70 going east.

Look for Big Bend Boulevard. You will not turn at that street but continue going straight until you see the law school.

At that point, you will be on Millbrook, which you will have arrived at having followed Forest Parkway to its conclusion.

---

(2)  To get from the airport to the law school, take Highway 70 East to Highway 170 South.

From Highway 170 South, take the "Forest Parkway East" exit.

Take Forest Parkway East for about two miles until it becomes Millbrook Avenue.

Go straight on Millbrook through one stoplight (Big Bend is the cross street).

After going past that intersection, the law school will be on your right. Turn right into the law school parking lot.

---

As you read the first set of instructions, you were probably frustrated trying to understand what you were reading. Even though the second set of instructions conveyed the same substantive information, this set was easier to follow. Why was the second set of instructions clearer? First, the information was presented to you in an order with which you are familiar when receiving travel instructions (from the beginning of the journey to the end). Second, you were given the appropriate context for the set of instructions at the very beginning of the second set of instructions. Thus, you knew at the beginning that you would be reading instructions from an airport to a law school.

## B.  The Deductive Pattern in Legal Analysis

In the legal setting, a deductive analytical pattern is equally as important. In the discussion section of an office memo, a written legal analysis begins by describing the original rule of law upon which the analysis rests, and the writer's conclusion as to how the original rule of law affects the client's situation. The remainder of the discussion illustrates and proves why the conclusion is sound. In organizing the "proof," the deductive drafting pattern begins by providing a broad overview of the element of the rule of law at issue, followed by a more detailed evaluation of the law, finally leading to an explanation of how the law applies to the client's factual situation.

The broad framework of a written legal analysis might be visualized as follows:

*Overview Paragraph*:
Outline the Rule of Law
Identify Issues/Conclusion
↓
For each issue:
Prove your Conclusion:
↙ ↙ ↘ ↘
*Thesis Paragraph*: Summarize the
issue and the analysis that will follow
↙ ↙ ↘ ↘
*Rule Explanation*: Examine the rule of law in
detail, with case law and/or statutory interpretation
↙ ↙ ↘ ↘
*Rule Application*:  Favorably apply the rule to client's
factual situation and then evaluate any opposing arguments
↓
Restate the *Conclusion*

In the above diagram, note how the deductive analytical pattern resembles a pattern with which you may be familiar from other courses in law school— IRAC, an acronym for: Issue → Rule → Apply Rule → Conclusion. In a very general sense, the deductive pattern of analysis follows a pattern similar to IRAC. However, as the discussions in Chapters 12 and 13 reflect, the organizational structure of a legal discussion is somewhat more complicated, and fluid, than a literal adherence to IRAC might otherwise suggest.

## III   *ORIGINAL RULE OF LAW AS THE TEMPLATE*

Drafting a discussion that reflects legal analysis is not unlike formulating a mathematical equation. Like a mathematical equation, each piece of your analysis should logically build from an earlier section of the analysis and logically lead to the section that will follow. Because the structure of your analysis is in a sense formulaic, you must have a basic grasp of the "formula" your memo will follow before you begin writing. The formula of each memo is based on the original rule of law that is the subject of evaluation. Thus, the original rule of law you are evaluating serves as the template for the discussion.

If you determine that the original rule of law has a number of elements, but only one element presents an issue that merits discussion, your memo would discuss in depth only one issue. Therefore, you would follow the template for a single-issue memo outlined below. If, however, you determine that two or more elements of a rule of law merit discussion, the structure of your memo would of necessity have to accommodate each issue. Adding another issue to the equation is not complicated because the basic template for each separate issue does not vary. Instead, the template for a single issue discussion is duplicated (for a two-issue memo), tripled (for a three-issue memo), and so on. The following very broad outlines illustrate the macro template of a single-issue discussion and a multiple issue discussion.

## A.  *Outline of the Single-Issue Memo*

---

### Discussion

1. <u>Lay the Foundation</u> (*Overview Paragraph*):

If the original rule of law has more than one element or factor, it is generally good practice to begin your analysis with an overview of the original rule of law. This paragraph lays the foundation for the analysis by stating the conclusion, outlining the elements (or factors) of the original rule of law, identifying those elements that are not issues, and identifying the element that will be discussed—the "issue." Chapter 11 discusses the components of the overview paragraph in greater detail.

2. <u>Summarize the Issue</u> (*Thesis Paragraph*):

Unlike the more general framework provided in the overview paragraph, the thesis paragraph provides a focused roadmap of the specific legal issue that will be discussed in the memo. This paragraph summarizes the analysis that will follow by stating what the rule of law means and by describing any relevant factors that guide courts in evaluating the issue. Chapter 11 discusses the components of the thesis paragraph in greater detail.

### Prove Your Conclusion:

3. <u>Explain the Law</u> (*Rule Explanation*):

Because this section of the memo evaluates in detail the element of the rule of law that presents an issue, this section may span pages of your memo. Your evaluation of the law may include an analysis of how earlier cases have interpreted and applied the rule of law and, in the case of a statutory rule of law, may also include statutory interpretation and an examination of legislative history. Chapters 12 and 13 discuss in detail this section of the memo and the different formatting options that relate to this specific section of the memo.

---

4. Apply the Law to the Client's Factual Situation
(*Rule Application*):

This section evaluates how the standard or factors that were explained in the rule explanation section affect the client's situation. Like the rule explanation section of the memo, this section may also span a number of pages. Chapters 12 and 13 discuss in detail this section of the memo and the different formatting options that relate to this specific section of the memo.

(a) *Favorable Rule Application*:

If a standard or factor merits a favorable explanation of the law's impact on a client, attorneys typically evaluate how the law supports the client's position before addressing unfavorable rule application.

(b) *Unfavorable Rule Application*:

After evaluating the ways in which the law favors the client with respect to a specific idea, the discussion then evaluates any counter-arguments that relate to that same idea. This section of the memo is very important. In your role as an advisor to the client, you have a responsibility to advise the client about unfavorable arguments as well as arguments that favor the client.

5. Conclusion

Most memos end with a brief conclusion that again answers the issue. Depending upon the complexity and length of the memo, the conclusion might appear within the body of the discussion section itself, or may appear under a separate heading—the "Conclusion."

## B. *Template of the Multi-Issue Memo*

If you determine that two or more elements of a rule of law present issues that merit discussion, you will need to adjust the template of your discussion to accommodate both issues. With a two or more issue discussion, the pattern of analysis for each individual issue does not change from that of the single issue memo. You will simply duplicate the template for a one-issue memo and add headings to serve as visual signposts for the reader.

Headings that serve as visual signposts are often called "point-headings." In order for point-headings to be useful to a reader, they should be very clear and relatively short. Simply by glancing at the point-heading your reader should be able to grasp the direction in which the memo is headed. Some attorneys prefer simply to identify the issue with a short word or phrase. For example, assume in the residential burglary hypothetical problem that the prosecutor has identified two issues that merit analysis: whether the Stripe garage is a dwelling, and whether Mr. Arnold had the requisite intent to commit a theft. The two point-headings might be identified as:

> I.     The Stripe garage as a dwelling.
>
> II.    Intent to commit a theft.

Other attorneys prefer to state their conclusion about the issue within the point-heading itself. Stated as conclusions, the two point-headings would be described as follows:

> I.     The Stripe garage is a dwelling under the statute.
>
> II.    Mr. Arnold had the requisite intent to commit a theft.

When drafting point-headings for multi-issue memos, follow the preference of your professor or the attorney who asked you to draft the memo.

The basic template of the multi-issue memo is as follows:

> **DISCUSSION**
>
> Lay the Foundation (*Overview paragraph*):
>
> Identifies the separate elements of the rule of law and the two or more elements that are issues to be evaluated in the memo.
>
>     I. **Issue One Heading** (e.g., "The Stripe garage is a dwelling.")
>
> 1.   Summarize Issue 1 (*Thesis paragraph*): Provides a roadmap for Issue 1.

Prove Your Conclusion for Issue 1:

2. Explain the Rule (*Rule Explanation*): Examines previous cases that interpret Issue 1, and any relevant statutory interpretation.

3. Apply the Rule of the Client's Factual Situation (*Rule Application*):

   (a) *Favorable Rule Application*: If there are favorable arguments that can be made, examines how the rule of law for this issue favorably affects the client's factual situation.

   (b) *Unfavorable Rule Application*: Identifies and evaluates any unfavorable arguments from the rule of law for Issue 1 (if applicable).

4. Conclusion: Restates the answer to Issue 1.

   **I. Issue Two Heading** (e.g., "Mr. Arnold had the intent to commit a theft.")

1. Summarize Issue 2 (*Thesis paragraph*): Provides a roadmap for Issue 2.

Prove Your Conclusion for Issue 2:

2. Explain the Rule (*Rule Explanation*): Examines previous cases that interpret Issue 2, and any relevant statutory interpretation.

3. Apply the Rule to the Client's Factual Situation (*Rule Application*):

   (a) *Favorable Rule Application*: If there are favorable arguments that can be made, examines how the rule of law for this issue favorably affects the client's factual situation.

   (b) *Unfavorable Rule Application*: Identifies and evaluates any unfavorable arguments from the rule of law for Issue 2 (if applicable).

4. Conclusion: Restates the answer to Issue 2.

> ### Conclusion
>
> Depending on the length of the memo and the preferences of your professor or assigning attorney, you may provide a short conclusion that summarizes each of the issues that have been separately evaluated in the memo.

## C.  Template of the Multi-Claim Memo

Sometimes when researching a problem on behalf of a client, you will conclude that you must not only address several issues, but that several different original rules of law affect the client. For example, assume you represented a client who was terminated from her employment. After researching a number of potential claims she might have against her employer, suppose you concluded that she might have a viable claim for breach of her employment contract, and might also have a viable claim for sexual discrimination under Title VII of the United States Code. Like the addition of another issue, adding another claim to the equation is not complicated. You would simply follow the discussion of the first claim with a discussion of the second claim, with appropriate point-headings to guide the reader through the analysis. The outline of a multi-claim memo resembles two separate memos combined in a single document. The format for discussion of each individual claim and each individual issue conforms to the templates illustrated above.

The following macro-outline presumes that the first claim (breach of contract) involves two issues, while the second claim (sexual discrimination) involves only a single issue.

> ### DISCUSSION
>
> *Introductory Paragraph*: Because the memo will address two separate claims, many attorneys insert a brief introductory paragraph prior to the first point-heading. The paragraph provides a roadmap for the entire discussion by separately identifying each of the claims that will be discussed in the memo.

**I.    Claim One Heading** (e.g., "I. Breach of Contract")

*Overview Paragraph*: Depending on the complexity of the claim, you may wish to include an overview paragraph that provides a roadmap for the discussion of the first claim. This roadmap outlines the elements of the original rule of law and identifies the elements to be discussed (the "issues").

**A.    Issue One Heading** (e.g., "A. Terms of the Offer")

1.    *Thesis paragraph*: Provides a roadmap for Issue 1.

2.    *Rule Explanation*: Examines previous cases that interpret Issue 1 and any relevant statutory interpretation.

3.    *Rule Application*:

(a) *Favorable Rule Application*: If there are favorable arguments that can be made, examines how the rule of law for this issue favorably affects the client's factual situation.

(b) *Unfavorable Rule Application*: Identifies and evaluates any unfavorable arguments from the rule of law for Issue 1 (if applicable).

4.    *Conclusion*: Restates the conclusion for Issue 1.

**B.    Issue Two Heading** (e.g., "B. Breach of Contract")

1.    *Thesis paragraph*: Provides a roadmap for Issue 2.

2.    *Rule Explanation*: Examines previous cases that interpret Issue 2 and any relevant statutory interpretation.

3.    *Rule Application*:

(a) *Favorable Rule Application*: If there are favorable arguments that can be made, examines how the rule of law for this issue favorably affects the client's factual situation.

(b) *Unfavorable Rule Application*: Identifies and evaluates any unfavorable arguments from the rule of law for Issue 2 (if applicable).

4. *Conclusion*: Answers the Question Presented for Issue 2.

## II. Claim Two Heading (e.g., "II. Sexual Discrimination under Title VII")

*Overview Paragraph*: Depending on the complexity of the claim, you may wish to include an overview paragraph that provides a roadmap for the discussion of the second claim. This roadmap would outline the elements of the original rule of law and identify the element that will be discussed (the "issue").

1. *Thesis paragraph*: Provides a focused roadmap of the issue that will be discussed.

2. *Rule Explanation*: Examines previous cases that interpret the issue and any relevant statutory interpretation.

3. *Rule Application*:

   (a) *Favorable Rule Application*: If there are favorable arguments that can be made, examines how the rule of law for this issue favorably affects the client's factual situation.

   (b) *Unfavorable Rule Application*: Identifies and evaluates any unfavorable arguments that relate to this issue (if applicable).

4. *Conclusion*: Restates the conclusion for this claim.

### CONCLUSION

Multi-claim memos often conclude with a separate section that summarizes the conclusions of each claim discussed in the memo.

# THE DISCUSSION SECTION:
## DRAFTING ROADMAP PARAGRAPHS

 **CHAPTER IN FOCUS**

MEMORANDUM

To:     [Senior Attorney]
From:   [Junior Attorney]
Date:   [Date of Submission of Memo]
Re:     [XYZ Client Matter]

QUESTION PRESENTED

. . .

SHORT ANSWER

. . .

STATEMENT OF FACTS

. . .

DISCUSSION

*Overview Paragraph*
*Thesis Paragraph*

Rule Explanation
Rule Application
Conclusion

**II** ▸ *DRAFTING THE OVERVIEW PARAGRAPH*

## A.  The Overview Paragraph

The deductive writing pattern satisfies the reader's curiosity right away by stating the writer's ultimate conclusion and by providing a roadmap of the analysis that will follow. Imagine yourself as a reader and, for a moment, assume the role of a senior attorney who has asked a more junior attorney to evaluate a legal problem. Using the hypothetical residential burglary problem as an example, assume that you have not read any of the cases that discuss the circumstances under which a structure would be a dwelling under that statute. Instead, assume that you asked another attorney in your office to determine whether you can prosecute someone for residential burglary of a detached garage. What information would you like to read first? If the first paragraph you reviewed described the specific facts and holding of the *Thomas* case, you would likely be confused. Without a foundation, or context, for the analysis, you would not understand why the specific details of the *Thomas* case might be important. Therefore, a written analysis of the law begins with a roadmap that provides a foundation for the detailed analysis that will follow.

Because a legal analysis is based on a rule of law, a description of the rule of law is the logical place to build the foundation for the analysis that will follow. Thus, in your overview paragraph, describe the separate elements or factors of the original rule of law that is being evaluated. After outlining the elements of the original rule of law, next identify those elements which do not present an issue under the unique factual situation being evaluated, and then identify those elements which merit further discussion and evaluation. Finally, satisfy the reader's curiosity by responding to the ultimate question paramount in the reader's mind—how the original rule of law affects the client.

## B.  When an Overview Paragraph is Unnecessary

Some original rules of law contain only a single element. As such, the reader will not need to peruse an outline of the rule of law's components. Under these circumstances, an overview paragraph is usually unnecessary. Instead, you can describe the rule of law in a thesis paragraph instead. The thesis paragraph then becomes the single roadmap paragraph for the discussion that follows. However, when the original rule of law being evaluated has more than one element or factor, it is usually good practice to describe the rule's components in a separate overview paragraph. The overview paragraph sets the stage for the detailed discussion of the issues that will follow.

## C.  Structural Format of an Overview Paragraph

The same deductive writing pattern that guides the over-all organization of a legal discussion also guides the organizational structure of individual paragraphs. Within the context of an overview paragraph, it would be confusing for a reader to read about the issues that will be discussed in the memo before the reader has first had the opportunity to review the original rule of law itself. The elements of the rule of law provide the foundation, or context, for a discussion of the elements that do and do not present issues for the client. Therefore, describe the elements of the rule of law before identifying those elements that are non-issues and those elements that present issues that merit discussion. Depending on the preference of your professor or the assigning attorney, state the ultimate conclusion in either the first or final sentence of the overview paragraph. Some attorneys prefer to begin the overview paragraph with the conclusion in order to satisfy the reader's curiosity immediately. Other attorneys prefer to wait until the end of the paragraph because the rule of law provides context for the reader to understand the basis for the conclusion. In a multi-issue memo with point-headings, the conclusion might also be stated within the point-heading (e.g., "A. <u>The Stripe garage is a dwelling under the residential burglary statute</u>.")

### The Overview Paragraph Checklist

---

1.  State your conclusion (or, alternatively, wait until the end of the paragraph).

2.  Describe the elements or components of the original rule of law.

3.  Identify the elements that do not present issues under the client's unique factual situation (i.e., non-issues).

4.  Identify the elements that are at issue and merit further discussion.

---

 **ILLUSTRATION: Residential Burglary Problem**
**An Overview Paragraph**

In the following illustration, two statutory sections are described in the overview paragraph. The first section describes the elements of residential burglary. The second section further defines one of the elements of the residential burglary statute—the dwelling element. When two or more sections of a statutory rule of law affect a problem you are evaluating, first discuss the statutory section that provides the foundation for understanding other statutory sections. In the residential burglary example, the elements of the residential burglary statute provide the foundation, or context, for the definition of one of its elements. Thus, that section is described first.

| | |
|---|---|
| The Stripe garage is a dwelling under Illinois' Residential Burglary Statute (the "Statute"). To prosecute Arnold successfully under the Statute, the State must prove that Arnold "knowingly and without authority enter[ed] the dwelling place of another." 720 Ill. Comp. Stat. 5/19-3 (West 1993) (emphasis added). There is no real dispute that Arnold "knowingly" entered the Stripe garage or that his entry was "without authority." Whether the garage is a "dwelling place" is more problematic. The Statute defines a dwelling as "a house, apartment, mobile home, trailer or other living quarters in which . . . the owners or occupants actually reside . . . ." 720 Ill. Comp. Stat. 5/2-6(b) (1993)(emphasis added). This memorandum addresses whether the Stripe garage is a "living quarters" in which Michael Stripe "actually resides." | 1. *Conclusion.*<br><br>2. The *original rule of law*.<br><br>3. Elements *not in dispute*.<br><br>4. The element that presents an *issue* for discussion, as defined by the statute. |

## EXERCISE 1:
### THE SELF-DEFENSE PROBLEM

Review again the materials contained in Appendix F, including the two memos from a senior attorney and the *People v. S.M.*, *People v. Moore*, and *People v. Shipp* cases. Draft an overview paragraph that describes the original rule of law, dispenses with any non-issues and identifies the issues. Alternatively, draft an overview paragraph for a memo assigned by your professor.

## III    *DRAFTING THE THESIS PARAGRAPH*

Even though the thesis paragraph physically appears in the memo before the discussion of relevant cases and their application to the client's situation, you may wish to delay writing the thesis paragraph until after you have drafted the rest of the discussion. Some attorneys find this approach to be time-efficient because drafting a thesis paragraph requires a sophisticated understanding of the law and how the law affects the client's situation. Ideally, you would have acquired the requisite level of understanding during the pre-drafting process as you evaluated the rule of law and cases that interpret the rule of law. However, the writing process itself often reveals that some ideas that seemed so clear in the abstract are in fact only partially-formed. Therefore, even when you believe you have a solid grasp of the cases from your pre-drafting analysis, the writing process not infrequently reveals unanticipated gaps in thinking. Because this is a fairly common experience, many attorneys choose to wait until after they have drafted the remainder of the discussion section before drafting a thesis paragraph.

## A.  Content of the Thesis Paragraph

Like overview paragraphs, thesis paragraphs also serve as roadmaps. However, while overview paragraphs merely provide a roadmap of the original rule of law, thesis paragraphs are more focused and specific. They only summarize the specific element of the original rule of law that presents an issue for discussion. Thus, in the residential burglary example, the overview paragraph described the basic components of the residential burglary statute. In contrast, the thesis paragraph focuses on the specific issue being evaluated, e.g., whether the Stripes' garage is a "living quarters" in which Michael Stripe "actually resides."

Because the thesis paragraph serves as a roadmap for the legal discussion of a specific issue, it summarizes the most important points that will be explored in the discussion that follows. If your memo does not include an overview paragraph that has already identified the issue to be discussed, begin the thesis paragraph by identifying the issue you will discuss. The thesis paragraph then states the conclusion as to how the issue affects your client's situation, followed by a brief summary of the reasons why your conclusion is sound.

In proving why the conclusion is sound, summarize the rules of law expressed in the case law, including any standards or factors that courts consider when interpreting and applying the original rule of law. These rules of law, standards and factors serve as guideposts that will help lead the reviewing senior attorney through the discussion that follows. Finally, to the extent the complexity of the memo requires, conclude the thesis paragraph by briefly summarizing how the rules of law, factors and/or guidelines apply to the client's facts, thereby justifying the conclusion.

## B.   When a Thesis Paragraph is Necessary

Because thesis paragraphs summarize the law pertaining to a specific issue, as a general rule, each issue discussed in a memo merits a separate thesis paragraph. Thus, a one-issue memo would contain a single thesis paragraph, a two-issue memo would contain two thesis paragraphs, and so on. (*See, e.g.,* the templates of one-issue, multi-issue and multi-claim memos illustrated in Chapter 10). However, like overview paragraphs, in some circumstances you may not find it necessary to draft a thesis paragraph for an issue. If you are evaluating a relatively minor issue that can be thoroughly addressed in a few paragraphs, a full thesis paragraph may be unnecessary. In that case, you might instead simply introduce a summary of the rule of law in a thesis sentence introducing your first case discussion. However, when an issue is substantive enough to merit a discussion of any length, it is good practice to introduce that discussion with a thesis paragraph.

## C.   Organizational Format of a Thesis Paragraph

The same deductive writing pattern that dictates that context should be introduced before details also applies to the internal structure of the thesis paragraph. Therefore, if your memo does not have an overview paragraph that identifies the issue to be discussed, begin the thesis paragraph by identifying the issue under discussion. The issue provides the framework for the standards, factors and general rules of law that help explain the issue. In turn, the standards, factors and general rules of law provide the context, or foundation, for a summary of how they affect the client's facts. As with the overview paragraph, some attorneys prefer to begin the thesis paragraph with the writer's conclusion, while other attorneys prefer to end the thesis paragraph with the conclusion.

### *The Thesis Paragraph Checklist*

1.  Describe the *original rule of law* and *issue* (if not already explained in the overview paragraph).

2.  *Conclude* how the law affects the client's factual situation (or, alternatively, wait until the end of the paragraph).

3.  Identify any *factors or standards* that guide courts as they apply the rule of law.

4.  Summarize the *general rules of law* expressed in the case law.

5.  *Briefly apply* the factors or standards to the client's factual situation, showing how they support the conclusion.

 ***ILLUSTRATION: Residential Burglary Problem***
***A Thesis Paragraph***

The Stripe's garage is a "living quarters" in which Michael Stripe "actually resides." When determining whether a structure is a living quarters, courts evaluate the type of activities for which the owners use the structure, as well as the frequency of those activities and physical evidence of those activities. A structure is considered a living quarters when the owners frequently use the structure for activities that occur in a living quarters, and the furnishings reflect that use. *People v. McIntyre*, 578 N.E.2d 314 (Ill. App. Ct. 1991). Although a structure's attachment to the main residence is also relevant, physical attachment to the primary residence is not necessary. *See People v. Thomas*, 561 N.E.2d 57 (Ill. 1990). Therefore, a structure used as an extension of the home's living quarters may be a dwelling even though it is not physically connected to the primary residence. Because Michael Stripe frequently and regularly uses the Stripe garage as a living quarters, it satisfies the statutory definition of "dwelling."

1. *Conclusion.*

2. *Factors* courts consider.

3. *Rules of Law* the cases express.

4. *Brief application* of factors to client's factual situation.

### EXERCISE 2:
### THE SELF-DEFENSE PROBLEM

Review again the materials contained in Appendix F, including the two memos from a senior attorney and the *People v. S.M.*, *People v. Moore*, and *People v. Shipp* cases. Draft a thesis paragraph for each issue you will discuss in your memo, and for each issue: describe any standard or factors courts consider, any general rules of law that accurately express the cases as a group, and briefly conclude how the standards or factors affect the client. Alternatively, draft a thesis paragraph for a memo assigned by your professor.

### EXERCISE 3:
### THE SOCIAL HOST PROBLEM

This exercise builds on Exercise 1 in Chapters 6 and 7. First review the fact pattern in that exercise (Exercise 1 in Chapter 6). Then review the cases that were summarized in Exercise 1 in Chapter 7 and your notes from that exercise. Draft a thesis paragraph that: (1) identifies the issue; (2) describes a rule or rules of law that accurately expresses the group of cases; (3) incorporates any relevant standards or factors that guided the courts; (4) briefly summarizes how the standards or factors affect the client; and (5) concludes.

# 12

# THE DISCUSSION SECTION: DRAFTING THE ANALYSIS (Single Case)

 **I  CHAPTER IN FOCUS**

---

### MEMORANDUM

To:     [Senior Attorney]
From:   [Junior Attorney]
Date:   [Date of Submission of Memo]
Re:     [XYZ Client Matter]

### QUESTION PRESENTED

. . .

### SHORT ANSWER

. . .

### STATEMENT OF FACTS

. . .

### DISCUSSION

Overview Paragraph
Thesis Paragraph

*Rule Explanation*
*Rule Application*

Conclusion

---

## II    *SINGLE CASE/SINGLE ISSUE MEMO*

When only one element or component of an original rule of law merits discussion, you would draft a single issue memo. Because the drafting process is deductive in nature, you would begin your analysis by describing the original rule of law. The original rule of law serves as the foundation for the analysis that follows. In Chapter 11, you learned how roadmap paragraphs serve the purposes of outlining the original rule of law, identifying the issue to be discussed in the memo and summarizing the law respecting the issue. At this point, you are ready to draft a detailed analysis of the issue. Under the deductive drafting pattern, you would first explain the rule of law in detail ("rule explanation") before evaluating how the rule of law affects the client's unique factual situation ("rule application"). The explanation of the rule provides the necessary context for the reader to evaluate how the rule of law affects the client.

### A.   *Drafting the Rule Explanation*

When describing a case that has interpreted the original rule of law, it is usually safe to assume that the senior attorney who asked you to draft the memo has not reviewed the case or evaluated the original rule of law. Even if the senior attorney has previously read the case, he or she presumably has not thoroughly evaluated the case; otherwise you would not have been assigned to draft a memo that evaluates the issue. Given these assumptions, your goal is to convey every important aspect of the case without distracting the reviewing attorney with irrelevant information. After the reviewing attorney has read your case discussion, he or she should possess as much relevant information about the case as you possess. In short, you will transform your pre-drafting notes into a written discussion. In your pre-drafting notes, you identified facts that were relevant to the court in its evaluation of the rule of law, the court's holding, and its rationale. You also formulated a rule of law that accurately expressed the court's holding. Your explanation of the case should describe each of these important components of the court's decision.

### 1.   *A Typical Format for Discussing a Factually Analogous Case*

#### (a)   *The Thesis Sentence*

Your discussion of the case should begin with a thesis sentence that describes a rule of law that expresses the court's holding. The rule of law should identify the legal standard or important factors that guided the court in its decision, thereby providing the foundation for the case discussion that follows. An ideal thesis sentence should alert the reviewing attorney to the crux of why the case is important and why the attorney will be reading that case discussion. For example, consider the *McIntyre* case and its interpretation of the "dwelling" element of the residential burglary statute. That case, and the attorney's "thinking notes" from that case, are reproduced in Chapter 7. In the attorney's written notes of the *McIntyre* case, the attorney formulated the following rule of law that expresses the *McIntyre* court's holding: An attached porch frequently used for residential activities is part of the living quarters of a home. That rule statement can easily become the thesis sentence that introduces the discussion of that case:

| An attached porch frequently used for residential activities is part of the living quarters of a home. *People v. McIntyre*, 578 N.E.2d 314 (Ill. App. Ct. 1991). | 1. Thesis Sentence. |
|---|---|

### (b)  The Relevant Case Facts

Although there are several ways you can format your discussion of a case, one of the easiest ways to structure your case discussion is to follow the thesis sentence with a description of the case facts you determined were relevant to the court. If the case facts have a chronological order, describe the facts chronologically to make it easier for the reader to absorb the factual story underlying the case. The case facts will then provide the reader with a foundation, or context, from which the reviewing attorney can understand the significance of the court's holding and rationale. It is important to keep in mind that in this section of the memo you are not describing any of the facts of your *client's* factual situation. It would be too difficult for a reader to absorb the factual story of a precedent case while simultaneously attempting to decipher analogies to the client. In the rule explanation section of your memo, you are only describing the facts of the relevant case. Again using the *McIntyre* case for purposes of illustration, the thesis sentence is followed by a description of the relevant case facts:

In *McIntyre*, the owners used an attached, screened porch for "sitting, eating and cooking." *Id.* at 315. They ate most of their meals on the porch in the summer and cooked meals there four or five times a week in the winter. The owners furnished the porch with wrought-iron furniture and a barbecue grill that reflected its use. The porch was enclosed and attached to the home, although three locks separated the porch from the home. *Id.*

2. Description of the relevant case facts.

### (c)  The Court's Holding & Rationale

The thesis sentence and the factual story of the case provide a foundation for the court's holding, or answer to the issue. When stating the holding, simply identify how the court answered the legal question before the court. For example, if the court evaluated whether an attached porch was a living quarters under the residential burglary statute, the holding would simply identify the court's answer to that specific question (i.e., "The court held the porch was a living quarters under the statute.").

The holding, in turn, provides context for the reviewing attorney to understand how the court justified its holding (the rationale). When describing the court's rationale, do not simply restate all of the facts you described earlier in the case discussion. Instead, the rationale should link the legal standard or factors described in the thesis sentence to a summary of the facts that illustrate how the court applied the standard or factors. The following example excerpted from Sample Memo A in Appendix A illustrates how the holding and rationale in the *McIntyre* case were described:

The court held that, under these facts, the porch was a "living quarters" under the Statute. *Id.* The court reasoned that the owners used the porch as part of their living quarters by engaging in such activities as "sitting, eating, and cooking." *Id.* In addition, the owners regularly used the porch in this manner and furnished the porch with furniture and a grill that reflected such use. The court also observed that the porch was enclosed and attached to the house, indicating that the porch's physical attachment to the house was a relevant factor. However, the court emphasized that it was the activities of "sitting, eating, and cooking" that "make the porch part of the living quarters of the house." *Id.*

3. Holding.
4. Rationale:
(a) *Type of use* linked to key facts.

(b) *Frequency & evidence of use.*

(c) *Physical attachment* factor.

## 2. An Alternative Format for Discussing a Factually Analogous Case

An alternative way of discussing a case is to weave the factual story of the case into a description of the court's rationale. This can be an effective format, particularly when the case facts are not very complex and lengthy. When the factual story is fairly complex and lengthy, it is more difficult to weave the factual story into the rationale in a manner that will not be confusing to the reader. The goal is to keep the factual story clear while also explaining the relevance of different facts. This approach is a bit more challenging to accomplish, but can be very effective when done well. The following example illustrates how the *McIntyre* case might be described under this alternative format:

| | |
|---|---|
| An enclosed, attached porch frequently used as part of the home's living quarters is a dwelling under the residential burglary statute. *People v. McIntyre*, 578 N.E.2d 314 (Ill. App. Ct. 1991). In *McIntyre*, the court held that an attached porch was a dwelling because the owners used the porch as a living quarters. The court observed that the activities of "sitting, eating and cooking" made the porch part of the living quarters of the home. *Id.* at 315. The court also noted that the owners regularly used the porch in this manner. They ate most of their meals on the porch in the summer and cooked meals there four or five times a week in the winter. In addition, the owners furnished the porch with wrought-iron furniture and a barbecue grill that reflected its use. Finally, the court observed that the porch was enclosed and attached to the house, indicating that the porch's physical attachment to the house was a relevant factor. However, the court emphasized that it was the activities of "sitting, eating, and cooking" that "make the porch part of the living quarters of the house." *Id.* | 1. Thesis sentence: rule of law.<br><br>2. Holding.<br>3. Rationale/Facts:<br>(a) *Type of use* linked to facts.<br>(b) *Frequency of use* linked to facts.<br><br>(c) *Evidence of use* linked to facts.<br>(d) *Physical attachment* linked to facts. |

## B. Rule Application

After describing all of the relevant aspects of the case precedent, you are now ready to inform the reviewing attorney about how the case affects the factual situation you are evaluating on behalf of your client. In the rule explanation section of the memo, you identified the important standard or factors that guided the court in its decision. In the rule application section of the memo, you will evaluate how the standard or each factor affects the client's factual situation. Each such standard or factor will be used as an analytical tool to evaluate the client situation.

## 1.  Outlining the Framework for Analysis

Before you begin drafting your analysis of how the law affects a client situation, you will first need to outline at least the basic framework of your analysis. Each standard or factor you previously identified as important will become the topic of a separate paragraph or group of paragraphs. Therefore, you must consider the relative importance of each such standard or factor and decide the order in which you will discuss them. Sometimes you may find that there is a logical order in which ideas should be discussed. If there is no logical order for discussion, begin with the most important standard or factor, followed by the second most important idea, and so on. If each standard or factors seems equally important, begin with the idea that has the most favorable application to the client's situation. When two or more factors are inter-related, discuss the factors one after the other, rather than inserting an unrelated factor in the middle of the analysis.

Using the residential burglary problem and the *McIntyre* case for purposes of illustration, a template for the rule application section would look like this:

---

1.  Type of Use (the most important factor)

2.  Evidence of Use (sub-factor of the first factor and therefore logically related to the first factor)

3.  Frequency of Use (sub-factor of the first factor and therefore logically related to the first factor)

4.  Proximity of the structure to the residence (arguably the least important factor and also the least favorable factor)

---

## 2.  Filling in the Framework for Analysis

Some attorneys find it time efficient to fill in their framework for analysis with further details before beginning the drafting process. They do so to avoid drafting mistakes that may arise when they have failed to consider in advance the specific details of each argument. Other attorneys prefer to begin the drafting process at this point, reasoning that the writing process helps trigger the creative process. At first, you may wish to experiment with a more detailed outline so you can determine whether such a process might be helpful to you.

To fill in the framework for your analysis, list the client facts and case facts that fall within the umbrella of each standard or factor. Under each standard or factor, make a note of the favorable and unfavorable arguments you will evaluate. As a practical matter, because you are an attorney representing a client's interests, you will usually evaluate any favorable arguments that can be made before evaluating any unfavorable arguments. Again using the residential burglary problem and the *McIntyre* case for purposes of illustration, a more detailed outline of the rule application section would look like this:

---

1.  <u>Type of Use factor</u>

*Thesis* = As in *McIntyre*, Michael Stripe ("M.S.") uses garage as a living quarters

*Proof of thesis* =

- M.S. uses garage to play and listen to music, for snacking, sleeping, watching T.V.—like *McIntyre* acts of "sitting, eating and cooking"
- Sleeping seems even more residential than in *McIntyre*

2.  <u>Evidence of Use</u>

*Thesis* = Furnishings reflect its use as a living quarters

Proof of thesis =

- Futon, T.V., mini-refrigerator, sound system—like *McIntyre* grill, wrought-iron chairs and table

3.  <u>Frequency of Use</u>

*Thesis* = Frequency of use is similar to the use in *McIntyre*

Proof of thesis =

- M.S. spends 2–3 evenings a week and weekends—like *McIntyre*, where used 4 to 5 times a week
- M.S. sleeps there during summer and fall—which is even greater frequency than in *McIntyre*

---

---

4.    Proximity to Residence (factor that will be raised by opponent)

*Basis for opponent's argument* = the garage's detachment from the Stripe home prevents it from being a living quarters

*Proof of opponent's thesis* =

- *McIntyre* porch was attached; court noted its attachment to the residence in its rationale

*My conclusion re: opponent's argument* = lacks merit

*My proof*:

- It was more important to the court that the owners used the porch as a living quarters than it was that the porch was attached—quote from court opinion to illustrate
- Porch was separated from home by 3 locks—not an open part of the primary residence; therefore not really that different from M.S. separate living quarters

---

### 3. *Drafting the Rule Application*

#### (a) *Introduce Each New Idea with a Thesis Sentence*

As the above outline reflects, each standard or factor you will evaluate becomes an analytical tool that leads a paragraph or group of paragraphs. Begin your evaluation of each new standard or factor by stating your premise about that idea. In other words, state your conclusion about how the client's situation relates to the standard or factor. When evaluating factors, be careful not to slide into an analysis of whether the client facts "satisfy" a factor. Remember, factors are only guidelines, not standards to be satisfied. Compare the following two illustrations:

---

*Not:*     Michael Stripe's use of the garage satisfies the "type of use" factor.

*Instead:*     Like the porch in *McIntyre*, Michael Stripe uses the garage for activities associated with a living quarters.

---

The second illustration correctly states the writer's premise about the type of use factor—Michael Stripe used the garage for activities associated with a living quarters. Although you should introduce each *new* idea with a thesis sentence, when your discussion of a standard or factor spans more than one paragraph, you can use transition sentences to continue the analysis in later paragraphs.

### (b)  Prove Each Premise

After stating the premise, the remainder of the paragraph proves why the premise is sound. To prove a premise, describe the client's facts that illustrate the premise and, when appropriate, make concrete, direct comparisons to and distinctions from the precedent case's facts. As a novice writer, it is very easy to fall into the habit of making comparison after comparison without letting the reader know why the comparisons are legally significant. Therefore, make sure that you spell out the legal significance of the client facts and comparisons you are making. Consider the following example:

---

### Example 1:

Michael Stripe's use of the Stripe's garage is like *McIntyre*. In *McIntyre*, the owners engaged in eating, sitting and cooking activities. In our case, Michael Stripe played and listened to music and watched television. Eating snacks is like the *McIntyre* activity of eating meals on the porch. Michael Stripe also sleeps in his garage retreat, which is an even stronger argument than the *McIntyre* activities of cooking, eating and sitting.

---

While the facts and comparisons in the above example are accurate, the legal significance of each fact is only implied, forcing the reader to stop and consider why the comparisons are important. The paragraph is structured as "this is what happened in the precedent case" and "the case facts are like the client facts." The reader is left wondering why the factual similarities are important. By focusing on the *premise* that is being proved rather than on simple factual similarities, the legal significance becomes clear. Thus, a more effective evaluation of the same facts and ideas is illustrated below. The statements that clarify the legal significance of facts and comparisons are underlined so that you can easily identify the few changes that enhance the clarity of the analysis. Note how each added explanation simply spells out why specific facts and analogies are important to the issue being evaluated.

---

*Example 2:*

Like the porch in *McIntyre*, Michael Stripe used the Stripe's garage for <u>activities commonly associated with a living quarters</u>. Like the activities of "sitting, eating and cooking" in *McIntyre*, Michael Stripe's use of the garage for playing and listening to music, watching television, and eating snacks <u>are uses commonly associated with a living quarters</u>. In addition, <u>Michael Stripe's use of the garage as a sleeping quarters</u> during the summer and fall only <u>strengthens the argument that the garage is a dwelling under the Statute</u>. Unlike the *McIntyre* activities of barbecuing, eating and sitting, <u>which can occur outside of a dwelling, sleeping is an activity uniquely associated with a living quarters</u>.

---

### 4.   *Rule Application Checklist*

Each section of analysis that discusses a standard or factor should have the following components:

---

A.   Begin with a thesis sentence that:

   1.   Identifies the standard or factor to be evaluated; and

   2.   States a premise about that standard or factor.

B.   Prove the premise by:

   1.   Elaborating on client facts that support the thesis;

   2.   Weaving in concrete comparisons to & distinctions from case law where applicable; and

   3.   Clarifying the legal significance of the facts and analogies.

---

## ILLUSTRATION:
### Residential Burglary Problem

The following example illustrates the rule explanation and rule application sections of a memo discussing the residential burglary statute, the *McIntyre* case and the Stripe garage.

| | |
|---|---|
| An enclosed, attached porch frequently used as part of the home's living quarters is a dwelling under the residential burglary statute. *People v. McIntyre*, 578 N.E.2d 314 (Ill. App. Ct. 1991). In *McIntyre*, the owners used an attached, screened porch for "sitting, eating and cooking." *Id.* at 315. They ate most of their meals on the porch in the summer and cooked meals there four or five times a week in the winter. The owners furnished the porch with wrought-iron furniture and a barbecue grill that reflected its use. The porch was enclosed, locked, and attached to the home. *Id.* The court held that, under these facts, the porch was a "living quarters" under the Statute. *Id.* | Rule Explanation:<br>1. Rule of law case illustrates.<br><br><br>2. Case facts.<br><br><br><br><br><br>3. Holding. |
| The court reasoned that the owners used the porch as part of their living quarters by engaging in such activities as "sitting, eating, and cooking." *Id.* In addition, the owners regularly used the porch in this manner and furnished the porch with furniture and a grill that reflected such use. The court also observed that the porch was enclosed and attached to the house, indicating that the porch's physical attachment to the house was a relevant factor. However, the court emphasized that it was the activities of "sitting, eating, and cooking" that "make the porch part of the living quarters of the house." *Id.* | 4. Rationale, identifying each factor court considered & the key facts that illustrate the factor. |
| Like the porch in *McIntyre*, Michael Stripe used the Stripe's garage for activities commonly associated with a living quarters. Like the activities of "sitting, eating and cooking" in *McIntyre*, Michael Stripe's use of the garage for playing and listening to music, watching television, and eating snacks are uses commonly associated with a living quarters. In addition, Michael Stripe's use of the garage as a sleeping quarters during the summer and fall only strengthens the argument that the garage is a dwelling under the Statute. Unlike the *McIntyre* activities of barbecuing, eating and sitting, which can occur outside of a dwelling, sleeping is an activity uniquely associated with a living quarters. | *Rule Application*:<br>1. Premise for type of use factor.<br>2. Facts & analogies that prove the premise. |

In addition, like the owners in *McIntyre*, Michael Stripe furnished the garage in a manner that reflects its use as a living quarters. Like the grill and wrought-iron furniture in *McIntyre*, Michael Stripe's sound system, small t.v., mini-refrigerator, and futon reflect that he uses the garage for activities typically associated with a living quarters.

1. Premise for evidence of use factor.

2. Facts & analogies that prove the premise.

Finally, the frequency of Michael's use of the garage as a living quarters is also similar to the use of the porch in *McIntyre*. Michael spends at least two to three evenings a week and his spare time on weekends in his get-a-way. During the summer and fall, he sleeps there seven nights a week. During those months, Michael's frequency of use even exceeded that of the owners in *McIntyre*, who used the porch only four to five times a week.

1. Premise for frequency of use factor.

2. Facts that prove the premise.

Defendant may argue that, despite Michael Stripe's frequent use of the garage for activities associated with a living quarters, the garage's physical detachment from the Stripe's home prevents it from being a "living quarters" in which the owners "reside." Under this theory, the defendant would argue that the garage, standing alone, is not a living quarters in which anyone resides. The garage has no running water, bathroom facilities or heat. Thus, the garage's status as a dwelling is dependent upon whether it can reasonably be viewed as an extension of the Stripe family's living quarters within the home itself. The defendant would argue that the fact that the *McIntyre* porch was physically attached to the family's home was essential to the court's holding. Only because it was physically attached to the home could the porch reasonably be viewed as an extension of the family's living quarters. In contrast, the Stripes' garage stands thirty feet away from their residence.

1. Premise for opposing argument re: proximity factor.

2. Examination of opponent's "proof" of such a premise.

While having some merit, this argument should fail. Although the *McIntyre* court did note that the porch was physically "attached and enclosed," it concluded that it was the owners' "activities" and *use* of the porch that made the porch "part of the living quarters of the house." 578 N.E.2d at 314. Thus, the court implied that the activities for which the porch was used were more important than the porch's attachment to the home. Moreover, the fact that the porch was separated from the utility room of the owners' home by a door with "three locks" lends less significance to the attached/detached distinction. The presence of three locks implies that the porch area was not an open part of the main residence, but was in-

1. Writer's premise (conclusion) re: opposing argument.

2. Proof of writer's premise.

> stead physically separate from the main residence. Like the physically separate porch in *McIntyre*, the Stripe garage is used as an extension of the Stripe family's living quarters.

# III ▸ *SINGLE CASE/MULTI-ISSUE MEMO*

The rule explanation and rule application sections of a multi-issue memo do not differ from the analysis of a single-issue memo. In a multi-issue memo, your pre-drafting analysis would have revealed that there were two or more issues from the original rule of law that merit discussion. For a multi-issue memo, simply repeat the same outlining and drafting steps you performed for the first issue. For example, assume that the hypothetical residential burglary fact pattern revealed a second issue: whether Mr. Arnold had the requisite "intent to commit theft." Your template for the analysis of this second issue would be identical to your template for the analysis of the first issue. For the second issue, you would again discuss the case that interpreted the "intent to commit theft" element of the statute (rule explanation), followed by a discussion of how the standards or factors for this issue affect the client situation (rule application).

Using the same precedent case to explore each issue in a multi-issue memo presents only one additional drafting challenge. When you describe the case for each issue, include *only* the case facts, holding and rationale that relate to that issue. Do not confuse the discussion by weaving in information about the case that relates to the other issue. For example, assume that the *McIntyre* court evaluated both the "dwelling" and "intent to commit theft" elements of the statute. In your discussion of the *McIntyre* case for the dwelling issue, you would describe only those case facts, holding and rationale that pertained to whether the porch was a dwelling. In your later discussion of the *McIntyre* case for the intent to commit theft issue, you would bring out for the first time those facts, holding and rationale that pertained to whether the thief in *McIntyre* intended to commit theft. In every other respect, drafting a multi-issue memo is the same as drafting a single issue memo.

## EXERCISE 1:
## THE SELF-DEFENSE PROBLEM

Review the facts and cases in Appendix F (the Jeffrey Bing problem). Draft your explanation of *People v. S.M.* (rule explanation) and your analysis of how the standards and/or factors in that case affect your client, Jeffrey Bing (rule application). When drafting the discussion, you may assume that the senior attorney is fairly confident that your law office can show that Mr. Bing personally believed he had to use deadly force to prevent his own death or great bodily harm. Therefore, you need not address or evaluate the issue of whether Mr. Bing subjectively believed he had to use deadly force to prevent his own death or great bodily harm. Instead, you may assume that the senior attorney has asked you to address only whether Mr. Bing's belief was reasonable.

Alternatively, draft the rule explanation and rule application sections of a memo previously assigned by your professor.

# 13

# THE DISCUSSION SECTION
## DRAFTING THE ANALYSIS (Multiple Cases)

 **CHAPTER IN FOCUS**

---

MEMORANDUM

To:      [Senior Attorney]
From:    [Junior Attorney]
Date:    [Date of Submission of Memo]
Re:      [XYZ Client Matter]

QUESTION PRESENTED
. . .

SHORT ANSWER
. . .

STATEMENT OF FACTS
. . .

DISCUSSION

Overview Paragraph
Thesis Paragraph

*Rule Explanation*
*Rule Application*

Conclusion

---

**II** *MULTIPLE CASES/SINGLE ISSUE MEMO*

## A.  Similarity to Single Case Memo

The same general writing principles described in Chapter 12 apply to memos that explore more than one case. In other words, the macro-organization of the discussion still follows the same general deductive writing pattern: you will explain the rule of law (rule explanation) before applying the rule of law to the client's factual situation (rule application). In addition, the micro-organization of each paragraph also follows the same deductive writing pattern: (1) each paragraph begins with a thesis sentence that expresses the thesis, or premise, of the paragraph; and (2) the remainder of the paragraph illustrates the thesis. Finally, the content of each paragraph also follows the same principles described in Chapter 12. A discussion of an important analogous case still describes for the reader each of the important aspects of the case (e.g., the rule of law the case illustrates, the relevant case facts, the holding, and the rationale). Your analysis of how the rule of law affects the client's situation also stays the same, with each paragraph evaluating how a standard or factor affects the client's unique factual situation.

## B.  Deductive Analytical Pattern Becomes Fluid

When addressing more than one case in a memo, however, your pre-drafting and drafting choices become a bit more complex. Before drafting a memo that addresses more than one case, you must assess the relative importance of each case you uncovered in your research and decide the specific purpose or purposes for which you will use each case. As Chapter 9 discussed, not all cases will require an extensive evaluation of their facts, holding and rationale. This chapter discusses the drafting choices involved in a multi-case memo. In a multi-case memo, the interplay between the "rule explanation" and "rule application" sections of your memo will become more fluid. Therefore, you must select a template for your discussion that will most clearly convey your analysis to the reader.

Recall from Chapter 12 that under the deductive drafting pattern, you must first explain and examine a rule of law (rule explanation) before evaluating how the rule of law affects the client's unique factual situation (rule application). When discussing only a single case that interprets the rule of law, the pattern of rule explanation to rule application is fairly straight-forward. However, assume you want to discuss in detail four different cases that address a single issue. You can imagine how confusing it might be for a reader to read detailed discussions of four different cases before reading how each of the cases applies to the client problem. Alternatively, assume you followed a discussion of each separate case with a discussion of how that case affected the client. If you were using two or more cases to illustrate the same point, this format might prove to be unnecessarily repetitive as you evaluated how the same client facts related to each of the cases.

Instead of arbitrarily deciding to format your discussion according to either one of these alternatives, instead think of the interplay between the rule explanation and rule application sections as fluid. You will either insert a rule application paragraph or paragraphs following a case discussion, or wait to insert the rule application paragraphs, depending on the particular cases and points being addressed. The following guidelines will help you outline and draft an analysis that involves the discussion of more than one case. These guidelines are helpful in terms of structuring the analysis of analogous cases of primary emphasis; cases that are of secondary importance can be woven into the discussion wherever they relate.

## 1.  Option 1: Grouping Cases

Some analogous cases illustrate the same factors and will generate factual comparisons to or distinctions from the same client facts. In some instances, you might elect to discuss only one of these cases in detail and refer to similar cases only parenthetically to lend further support to your primary case discussion. Assume, however, that two cases were guided by the same standard or factors but the different fact patterns yielded two different results. You may wish to explore each of the cases in detail because they may help you predict the result in your client's situation—are the client facts more like Case 1 in legally significant ways, or more like Case 2? The *McIntyre* and *Thomas* cases in the residential burglary memo are grouped together for that reason (Sample Memo A in the Appendix A). Alternatively, perhaps two cases illustrate the same factors and will generate factual comparisons to or distinctions from the same client facts, but, nevertheless, each case brings out a slightly different nuance of the law.

Under such circumstances, group the cases by discussing each case (rule explanation) before evaluating how the cases, as a group, affect the client (rule application). Note that the term "grouping cases" does not mean that each of the cases would be discussed in a single paragraph, or that the case discussions themselves would be intermingled. Instead, the term simply means that you will thoroughly evaluate each case before evaluating how the cases, as a group, affect the client. Thus:

Group two or more analogous cases when each case:

(1)  Illustrates the *SAME* key factors or ideas; AND

(2)  Generates factual comparisons to or distinctions from the *SAME* client facts.

---

***Rule Explanation:***

¶     Case #1—discuss facts/holding/rationale—illustrating factors A & B

¶     Case #2—discuss facts/holding/rationale—illustrating factors A & B

***Rule Application*:**

¶     Apply Factor A to client facts (analogizing to both Cases 1 & 2)

¶     Apply Factor B to client facts (analogizing to both Cases 1 & 2)

---

Note that with this formatting option, each of the factors that guided a court are discussed within the same case discussion. Thus, if a court was guided by three factors, each of the factors would be identified within the discussion of that court's rationale. However, each different factor described in the case discussion later serves as a separate analytical tool to evaluate how that factor affects the client. In short, the case discussions themselves may explore several different factors, while each rule *application* paragraph is organized by a separate standard or factor.

*Test for Viability of Option 1:* After completing your first draft, critically review your analysis from the perspective of a reader who is not familiar with the cases. Is the discussion clear and distinct or is it confusing? If you think the discussion is confusing, consider why it might be confusing. This formatting option can be confusing for any of the following reasons:

(1)  Do the cases you discuss illustrate a different standard that evolves from the same rule of law?

(2)   Do the cases illustrate different factors? (Although the cases do not have to share every factor in common, cases that are grouped together should illustrate several common factors.)

(3)   Even if the cases illustrate common factors, do the factors engender comparisons to and distinctions from different client facts? You might wish to review your pre-drafting notes. Are you analogizing the same or different client facts to each of the cases?

If you responded affirmatively to any of these questions, either Option 2 or 3 would be a more effective formatting choice.

## 2.   Option 2: Separating Cases

When cases illustrate *different* factors or standards, each case should be separately discussed and used as a separate analytical tool to evaluate how the factors or standard affect the client. Even when two cases illustrate the same standard or factors, they should also be used as separate analytical tools when you will use them to generate analogies to *different* client facts. For example, review the sample kidnapping memo illustrated as Sample Memo B in Appendix A. In that memo, even though the *Enoch* case discusses the same factors as the *Lamkey* and *Franzen* cases, it is separately discussed and applied to the client facts because it generates analogies to a different group of client facts than the other two cases. In contrast, *Lamkey* and *Franzen* are grouped together (Option 1) because they not only illustrate the same factors but generate factual comparisons to and distinctions from the same client facts. Thus:

Separate a case or group of cases with "rule application" paragraphs when the cases:

(1)   Illustrate DIFFERENT factors or standards; OR

(2)   Illustrate the same factors or standards but generate factual comparisons to or distinctions from DIFFERENT client facts.

*Illustration*:

---

**Rule Explanation:**

¶     Case #1—discuss facts/holding/rationale—illustrating factors A & B

¶     Case #2—discuss facts/holding/rationale—illustrating factor B

**Rule Application:**

¶     Apply Factor A to client facts (analogizing to Case 1)

¶     Apply Factor B to client facts (analogizing to Cases 1 & 2)

**Rule Explanation:**

¶     Case #3—discuss facts/holding/rationale—illustrating factor C

**Rule Application:**

¶     Apply Factor C to client facts (analogizing to Case 3)

---

*Test for Viability of Option 2:* After you complete your first draft, critically review your discussion and evaluate how easily a reader would be able to follow the analysis. Do the rule application paragraphs seem repetitive? Alternatively, do the rule application paragraphs seem very vague and general? When two cases serve the same analytical purpose and therefore should be grouped together (Option 1), repetitive rule application paragraphs are a red flag. The repetition simply signals that you have unnecessarily separated two cases that should instead be discussed and then, as a group, applied to the client facts. Alternatively, watch for broad, general, vague language in your rule application paragraphs. To avoid unnecessary repetition, you may have drafted one of the rule application sections in very general, vague terms. Again, such vague, general language can be a red flag that you have separated two or more cases that should instead be grouped together. This formatting option can be repetitive or vague when:

(1)   Do the cases explore the same standard or factors? AND

(2)   Do the cases engender factual comparisons to and distinctions from the same client facts?

If the answer to both questions is "yes," then Option 1 is a clearer formatting option. If you have difficulty responding to these questions, you might wish to review your pre-drafting notes and consider again which factors each case illustrates, and the client facts you will analogize to each case.

### 3.  Option 3: Organizing Rule Explanation by Factors

In Options 1 and 2, each of the factors that guided a court are evaluated within that particular case discussion. The individual factors described in the case discussion later serve as separate analytical tools to evaluate how each separate factor affects the client in the rule application paragraphs. Thus, under Options 1 and 2, only the rule application sections are organized around individual factors. However, there is another way in which you can format a legal analysis. Under this approach, the entire discussion (both rule explanation and rule application sections) are organized around the factors, rather than just the rule application section. This approach can be very effective, although it is significantly more difficult for a novice legal writer to draft effectively.

One reason this formatting option can be difficult to draft is that you must strike a fine balance when conveying information in a particular case discussion. The goal is to divulge only the specific information about a case that relates to the *specific factor* under discussion, while also including enough information to give the reader sufficient context to understand the case. For example, suppose a court considered and weighed three factors when it evaluated a rule of law. Under Option 3, your rule explanation paragraph would include only the specific parts of the case facts, holding and rationale that relate to that factor. Thus, specific, discrete aspects of that case would be discussed three different times—once for each relevant factor. Although that sounds easy enough, recall that your reader has likely not read the cases that are the subject of discussion in your memo. Therefore, you must include enough information about the case the first time you discuss it for the reader to be able to absorb the over-all context within which a specific factor was evaluated. At the same time, you do not want to confuse the reader by incorporating too much information that, while providing context, relates to another factor.

Another reason this formatting option can be difficult to draft effectively is that some factors are so inter-related that it is very difficult to discuss what happened in a case without describing each of the inter-related factors that guided the court's decision. In addition, inter-related factors may also generate a discussion of the same client facts. Under those circumstances, a discussion formatted under Option 3 would likely be repetitive.

Finally, you must be very careful in the manner in which you frame the relevant factors. Sometimes courts weigh the same underlying idea, or factor, in arriving at their decisions although they use different language to describe their reasoning process. If you mistakenly decide that two courts are evaluating two separate factors, and structure your analysis accordingly, the analysis will reflect that confusion.

Although challenging to strike the right balance, this approach is often used very effectively by experienced writers. Sample Memo C in Appendix A illustrates how the residential burglary problem can also be formatted using Option 3.

*Illustration*:

---

### *Factor A:*

#### *Rule Explanation:*

¶ Examine Factor A, as illustrated by Case #1—(discuss only those facts/holding/rationale that relate to Factor A)

¶ Examine Factor A, as illustrated by Case #2 & perhaps Case #3 (again discussing only those components of each case that illustrate Factor A)

#### *Rule Application*:

¶ Apply Factor A to client facts (analogizing to Cases 1, 2 & 3)

### *Factor B:*

#### *Rule Explanation:*

¶ Examine Factor B, as illustrated by Case #1—(discuss only those facts/holding/rationale that relate to Factor B)

¶ Examine Factor B, as illustrated by Case #2 (again discussing only those components of each case that illustrate Factor B)

#### *Rule Application*:

¶ Apply Factor B to client facts (analogizing to Cases 1 & 2)

---

> **Factor C:**
>
> **Rule Explanation:**
>
> ¶ Examine Factor C, as illustrated by Case #1—(discuss only those facts/holding/rationale that relate to Factor C)
>
> ¶ Examine Factor C, as illustrated by Case #2 & perhaps Cases #3 & #4 (discussing only those components of each case that illustrate Factor C)
>
> **Rule Application:**
>
> ¶ Apply Factor C to client facts (analogizing to Cases 1, 2, 3 & 4)

*Test for Viability of Option 3:* After completing the first draft of your memo, critically review the discussion from a reader's perspective. Is the analysis clear or is it repetitive or confusing? If the discussion is repetitive or confusing, consider the reasons why that may be so.

If the discussion is repetitive:

(1) Are the factors you have selected truly independent factors, or are they just different ways to state the same point?

(2) Even if the factors are independent, do they generate a discussion of the same client facts?

If the discussion is confusing:

(1) Are the factors, although independent, so interwoven in the courts' reasoning that it is difficult to analyze the courts' holdings/rationale without examining all of the factors together?

(2) Did you provide enough background information about each important precedent case the first time you discussed it for the reviewing attorney to grasp how the factor relates to the case as a whole?

## EXERCISE 1:
## FORMATTING OPTION EXERCISE

This example evaluates an issue that often arises when an employee injures someone. The injured party, seeking the deeper pocket of the employer, seeks to hold the employer liable under a theory of "respondeat superior." Under that theory, an employer may be liable for an employee's behavior if the particular activity was "within the scope" of the employee's employment. Assume that an insurance salesman injured someone while playing for the company softball team. Assume that in a roadmap paragraph, the drafting attorney indicated that the following factors were important in determining whether an employee's conduct occurred while the employee was acting within the scope of his or her employment: (1) whether the employer specifically authorized the conduct; (2) whether the employer repeatedly approved of the conduct; (3) whether other similarly situated employees engaged in similar conduct; and (4) whether the employee previously had engaged in similar conduct.

Review the following discussion based on these four factors and evaluate whether Option 3 has been drafted effectively. Specifically, consider:

(1)  Is each factor truly different from the other factors, or just another way to state the same point?

(2)  Does each factor generate a discussion of the same, or different, client facts from those used to evaluate the other factors? *Query:* If a factor generates a discussion of the same client facts as those used to evaluate another factor, which formatting option would be a more effective selection?

(3)  Has the writer provided enough information in each case law paragraph for you to assess how the factor relates to the case as a whole?

### DISCUSSION

### [Examine "Specific Authorization" Factor]

Where an employer specifically authorizes the conduct in which the employee is engaged, the employee is acting within the scope of his or her employment. In *Riviello v. Waldron*, the owner of a restaurant specifically authorized his chef to visit with the patrons in the dining room of the restaurant and to perform knife tricks while doing so. 391 N.E.2d 1278, 1280 (N.Y. 1979). On one occasion, the chef mishandled the knife while tossing it in the air, and a restaurant patron was injured when the knife struck her in the eye.

*Id.* Under these facts, the court held that the chef was acting within the scope of his employment while tossing the knife. *Id.* The court reasoned that the owner of the restaurant had specifically authorized and approved of the conduct that resulted in the patron's injury. The court noted that the employer hired the chef based on the chef's ability to perform the knife tricks and frequently asked the chef to go "perform" in the dining room among the patrons. *Id.*

[Apply "Specific Authorization" Factor to Client's Facts]

Similarly, the employer specifically authorized Mr. Henderson to participate in the conduct that resulted in the client's injury. The insurance company both sponsored the softball team and allowed its employees in the Albany office to leave early on Thursdays to participate in the team's games. Under *Riviello*, Mr. Henderson was acting within the scope of his employment when he injured the client.

[Examine "Repeated Approval" Factor]

Additionally, where an employer repeatedly approves of the conduct in which the employee is engaged, the employee is acting within the scope of employment. In *Riviello*, in concluding that the chef was acting within the scope of his employment while tossing the knife, in addition to looking at whether the owner of the restaurant specifically authorized the chef's knife tossing, the court pointed out that the owner had also repeatedly approved of the conduct that resulted in the patron's injury by frequently visiting the kitchen and asking the chef to go "perform" in the dining room among the patrons. *Id.*

[Apply "Repeated Approval" Factor to Client's Facts]

Similarly, the employer repeatedly approved of Mr. Henderson's participation in the conduct that resulted in the client's injury. The insurance company both sponsored the softball team and allowed its employees in the Albany office to leave early on Thursdays to participate in the team's games. Under *Riviello*, Mr. Henderson was acting within the scope of his employment when he injured the client.

[Examine "Previous Conduct" Factor]

Additionally, where the employee previously had engaged in the same or similar conduct as that which resulted in injury, the employee is acting within the scope of employment. In *Lundberg v. State*, the court held that an employee broker was acting within the scope of his employment when he negligently struck another member of an aerobics class in the eye. 255 N.E.2d 177, 179 (N.Y. 1969). The court reasoned that "the broker here involved was a routine and regular participant in the class." *Id.* at 182.

[Apply "Previous Conduct" Factor to Client's Facts]

Similarly, Mr. Henderson was a "routine and regular participant" in the softball games. Under *Lundberg*, this "routine and regular" participation brings the games within the scope of his employment. Similarly, Mr. Henderson was a "routine and regular participant" in the softball games. Under *Lundberg*, this "routine and regular" participation brings the games within the scope of his employment.

[Examine "Acts of Other Employees" Factor]

Finally, where other similarly situated employees within the company engaged in substantially similar conduct as that which resulted in injury, the employee is acting within the scope of his employment. In *Lundberg*, the owner of a brokerage house encouraged all of his employees to participate in a noontime aerobics class to reduce stress. The class occurred in the gymnasium on the premises of the brokerage house. 255 N.E.2d at 179. The court held that a broker was acting within the scope of his employment when he negligently struck another member of the class in the eye. The court reasoned that "all eight of the brokers in the brokerage house participated in the noontime aerobics class at the prompting of their employer." *Id.* at 181 (emphasis added).

[Apply "Acts of Other Employees" Factor to Client's Facts]

Similarly, all six of the insurance salesman in the company's Albany office played for the company-sponsored softball team. In fact, the salesmen here perceived the contact with the clients at the games as a necessity for advancement within the company, whereas there was no mention in *Lundberg* that the brokers felt similarly. Accordingly, this case is an even stronger case for liability than *Lundberg*.

## EXERCISE 2:
## THE SELF-DEFENSE PROBLEM

Review the facts and cases in Appendix F (the Jeffrey Bing problem). Draft your explanation of *People v. S.M.*, *People v. Moore, and People v. Shipp* (rule explanation) and your analysis of how the standards and/or factors in that case affect your client, Jeffrey Bing (rule application). When drafting the discussion, you may assume that the senior attorney is fairly confident that your law office can show that Mr. Bing personally believed he had to use deadly force to prevent his own death or great bodily harm. Therefore, you need not address or evaluate the issue of whether Mr. Bing subjectively believed he had to use deadly force to prevent his own death or great bodily harm. Instead, you may assume that the senior attorney has asked you to address only whether Mr. Bing's belief was reasonable.

Alternatively, draft the rule explanation and rule application sections of a memo assigned by your professor.

# 14

# DRAFTING AN OFFICE MEMO: COMPLETING THE DRAFT

## I CHAPTER IN FOCUS

### MEMORANDUM

To:         Senior Attorney
From:       Junior Attorney
Date:       Date of Submission of Memo
Re:         XYZ Client Matter

### QUESTION PRESENTED

### SHORT ANSWER

### STATEMENT OF FACTS

### DISCUSSION

Overview Paragraph
Thesis Paragraph
Rule Explanation
Rule Application
Conclusion

## II   *DRAFTING THE HEADING*

Now that you have completed a draft of the Discussion section of your memo, you are in a position to add the remaining sections. Drafting the heading is fairly straight-forward. The centered "<u>MEMORANDUM</u>" title informs the reader that the document is an office memorandum. In the remaining portions of the heading, include the name of the person to whom you are writing the memo (the "To" designation), your own name (the "From" designation), and the date you submitted the memo (the "Date" designation). The date is very important because it represents that your analysis is accurate as of the date you submitted the memo. Should you or another attorney later decide to revisit the issue evaluated in the memo, the date serves as a reminder that the analysis is complete only as of the date designated on the memo and that the research will need to be updated. The "Re:" designation refers to the client matter that is the subject of the memo. Because many clients have numerous matters that are pending within a law office, include enough information about the client matter and file so that other attorneys in your office will be able to identify easily the client matter that is the subject of the memo.

## III   *DRAFTING THE QUESTION PRESENTED*

### A.  *Purpose*

Following the heading, the next section identifies for the reviewing attorney the issue or issues that will be discussed in the memo. The issue statement is commonly called the Question Presented, although some law offices label the issue statement as the "Issue" or the "Issue Presented." You should follow the format preferred by your professor or the law office in which you work. The purpose of the Question Presented is to frame the legal questions that will be evaluated in the memo. The Question Presented should provide the reviewing attorney with an accurate, focused overview of the issue or issues the memo will discuss, including the component of the rule of law that is at issue and the critical client facts that present an issue under that rule of law. As you might imagine, it can be quite challenging to draft a clear, succinct Question Presented that accomplishes such goals. Therefore, although the Question Presented is the first section of the memo itself, many attorneys wait until after they have drafted the Discussion section before drafting the Question Presented. Like the thesis paragraph, drafting an effective Question Presented requires a sophisticated understanding of the law and how the law affects the client's situation.

## B.  The Question Presented in a One-Issue Memo

### 1.  Content

Unless you have been informed otherwise, you should presume that the senior attorney who will read your memo does not understand the intricacies of the specific client facts that pose a legal problem and why they pose a legal problem. If the senior attorney understood the intricacies of the client problem at that depth you probably would not have been asked to research the law and draft a memo on the matter. Therefore, your Question Presented should (1) inform the reviewing attorney of the component of the legal rule that presents the issue for the client, and (2) summarize the critical client facts that create the issue. It is important to summarize not only the critical client facts that support your ultimate conclusion but also any critical client facts that are particularly problematic. Your goal is to capture the essence of the issue that will be addressed; therefore, you should incorporate a summary of all critical client facts.

### 2.  Format

Recall that readers need to know the context of what they are reading before they can understand details. The same principle is true when reading Questions Presented. Therefore, the most effective format is one that first identifies the component of the rule of law that presents the issue before summarizing the critical client facts. The rule of law presents the context for the issue itself. The format follows this form:

> "Can . . . [identify the component of the rule of law that presents an issue] . . . when [summarize the critical client facts that present the issue] . . . ?

A typical Question Presented would look like this:

---

#### QUESTION PRESENTED

Is a detached garage a "living quarters" in which the owners "actually reside" under Illinois' Residential Burglary Statute, when it has been converted into a retreat for the owners' college-age son, who uses it on a weekly basis as a get-a-way and sleeps there half the year, although the retreat does not have plumbing facilities?

---

The above illustration begins with the word "is," followed by the question. Other common verbs that follow this format are: "Was . . . ?" or "Can . . . ?" or "May . . . ?"

Instead of forming a question within the Question Presented, some attorneys prefer to begin the Question Presented with the word "whether" rather than with a verb that signals a question. This format follows the same sequence as the above illustration—the rule of law followed by a summary of the critical facts. However, the Question Presented ends with a period rather than question mark. Thus, the Question Presented illustrated above could also be framed like this:

---

### QUESTION PRESENTED

Whether a detached garage a "living quarters" in which the owners "actually reside" under Illinois' Residential Burglary Statute, when it has been converted into a retreat for the owners' college-age son, who uses it on a weekly basis as a get-a-way and sleeps there half the year, although the retreat does not have plumbing facilities.

---

### 3.  Avoiding a Common Trap

It is easy when drafting a Question Presented to fall into the trap of including your conclusion within the statement of the issue itself. For example, the issue illustrated above could be erroneously drafted as follows:

---

### QUESTION PRESENTED

*Incorrect:*     Whether a detached garage is a dwelling when it is a living quarters in which the owners' son resides on a weekly basis.

---

Note how the above example contains the legal conclusion within the issue statement itself—it presumes that the detached garage is a "living quarters." There can only be one answer to a question that presumes that a structure is a living quarters. Instead, carefully review your draft to ensure that you have not crafted a question that inadvertently contains the legal conclusion itself.

### 4. Personalizing the Question Presented

There are several schools of thought as to whether it is preferable to personalize the Question Presented or to refer to the client by a more abstract characterization. Attorneys who prefer to personalize the issue statement reason that the memo involves a specific client; thus, the Question Presented itself should also refer to the client by name. In the residential burglary example, the issue statement would refer to the "Stripe garage" rather than to the more generic label of "a detached garage." Other attorneys prefer instead to characterize the client by a generic label, reasoning that other attorneys who review the memo will more easily be able to identify the characterizations rather than specific party names. For example, a reviewing attorney who is not intimately familiar with the facts of a specific client problem may find it easier to understand the significance of labels such as "landowner" or "child trespasser" rather than by the specific names of the parties involved in a controversy. As with other formatting issues that involve individual preferences, follow the formatting preference of your professor or of the senior attorney who asked you to draft the memo.

## C. The Question Presented in a Multi-Issue Memo

In a multi-issue memo, it can be challenging to draft a single Question Presented that identifies the original rule of law, the separate issues, and the critical facts that relate to each separate issue. Often in a multi-issue memo, attorneys add an "umbrella" question that (1) contains the over-all question the memo will address and (2) the elements of the rule of law that present issues for discussion. Underneath that umbrella question, each issue becomes a separate Question Presented. Each separate issue is drafted just like a Question Presented in a one-issue memo. The following example is excerpted from Sample Memo D in Appendix A:

| | |
|---|---|
| QUESTION PRESENTED | The *"Umbrella" question* that identifies: |
| Does our client have a valid claim against landowners under Florida's attractive nuisance doctrine, which requires proof that: (a) the landowners could reasonably foresee the presence of trespassing children on their property, (b) the property contained a hidden danger, and (c) the landowners failed to exercise reasonable care to protect the child from injury? | 1. The ultimate question; and the 2. Elements of the rule of law. |
| A. *Is the presence of trespassing children reasonably foreseeable when* the property is located next to an elemen- | *1ˢᵗ issue*: 1. *The element of* |

> tary school, a pond on the property contains inner-tubes, ducks, and fish, and the landowners had previously discovered school children trespassing?

*the rule of law &*
2. Key facts under that element.

B.  *Is a dock a hidden danger to a six-year-old child when* it is covered by moss and algae, provides the only means of access to the pond, and is so deteriorated that it collapsed under the weight of the child?

*2nd issue:*
1. *The element of the rule of law &*
2. Key facts.

C.  *Do landowners fail to exercise reasonable care to protect children from foreseeable injury when* they do not lock the gate to the property, repair the dock, or post warning signs of the deteriorating condition of the dock, although they erected a chain link fence around the property and posted a "Do Not Climb Fence" sign on the fence?

*3rd issue:*
1. *The element of the rule of law &*
2. Key facts.

## EXERCISE 1:
## THE SELF-DEFENSE PROBLEM

Review the materials in Appendix F and your draft of the Discussion section of the Bing memo. Draft a Question Presented section for an office memo evaluating the Bing self-defense problem. Alternatively, draft a Question Presented for an office memo assigned by your professor.

# IV   *DRAFTING THE SHORT ANSWER*

## A.   *The Short Answer in a One-Issue Memo*

After identifying for the reader the issue or issues the memo will address, the memo next provides an answer to the Question Presented. The Short Answer both (1) answers the question itself, and (2) provides a brief, succinct summary of the key reasons that justify the answer.

Many attorneys prefer that the Short Answer begin with a simple responsive statement, such as "yes" or "no." However, unless you are comfortable that your analysis supports a conclusion such as "yes" or "no," it is perfectly acceptable to allow your conclusion to reflect any uncertainty you may have. Therefore, conclusions that state "probably" or "probably not" are also common means of answering the Question Presented. Another way of framing the conclusion is to begin the Short Answer with a declarative sentence that expresses your opinion as to the strength or validity of the client's claim or defense. Thus, instead of framing the conclusion with a "probably," you might state: "The client has a *strong* claim (or defense) . . ." A more tentative favorable conclusion might be framed as: "The client has a *viable* claim (or defense), although . . ." Avoid, however, responding to the Question Presented with a term such as "possibly" or "it is possible." Anything in life is "possible;" your conclusion should provide the reviewing attorney with more direction than a "anything in life is possible" response.

After stating your conclusion, next provide the reviewing attorney with a brief summary of the most important reasons that support your conclusion. If you have identified a legal standard or factors that guide courts as they interpret the rule of law, incorporating the relevant standard or factors into the Short Answer is often a clear way to summarize your reasons. However, do not cite to cases or statutes in this section of the memo. This section of the memo should be very brief, allowing the reviewing attorney to absorb the essence of your conclusion without being weighed down by an extensive evaluation of the law or client facts.

The following illustration reflects a Short Answer that begins with a simple direct response to the question. It also stays consistent with the drafting choice reflected in the Question Presented to refer to the owners and their garage generically rather than by their names.

---

### SHORT ANSWER

Yes. A detached garage used as a retreat and seasonal sleeping place is a "living quarters" under the statute. The owner frequently and regularly uses the garage for activities typically associated with a living quarters. The garage is furnished to reflect that use.

---

The following Short Answer illustrates another way to draft the Short Answer. This example begins by stating the answer in a declarative sentence rather than a simple "yes." It also presumes that the Question Presented referred to the client by name, instead of by generic classification.

---

### SHORT ANSWER

The Stripe's detached garage used as a retreat and seasonal sleeping place is probably a "living quarters" under the statute. The Stripe's son frequently and regularly uses the garage for activities typically associated with a living quarters. The garage is furnished to reflect that use.

---

## B.  The Short Answer in a Multi-Issue Memo

In a multi-issue memo, the Short Answer should track the Question Presented section. Thus, it begins with an answer to the over-all question the memo will address (the question identified in the "umbrella" question). The Short Answer should then separately respond to each separate Question Presented in the preceding section. Thus, if the Question Presented contains two separate questions, the Short Answer section would contain two separate answers. The content of each Short Answer is no different than a Short Answer in a single-issue memo. The following example is excerpted from Sample Memo D in Appendix A:

---

### SHORT ANSWER

| | |
|---|---|
| Yes, our clients have a strong claim against the landowners for injuries sustained by her child under the doctrine of attractive nuisance. | *The answer to the ultimate question.* |
| A.  First, their child's presence on the property was reasonably foreseeable because the landowners' property is both visible and accessible from an area that young children frequent, it contains objects or conditions that attract children, and the landowners had previously discovered school children trespassing on their property. | *1st issue:* 1. Answers the issue; and 2. Identifies the general factors that support the answer. |
| B.  Second, the deteriorating dock was a hidden danger because a six-year-old child is too young to appreciate its dangerous condition. | *2nd issue:* 1. Answers the issue; and 2. Supports the answer. |
| C.  Finally, the landowners failed to exercise reasonable care to protect trespassing children from the danger of the dock be- | *3rd issue:* 1. Answers the is- |

cause the burden of taking reasonable precautionary measures was slight when compared to the risk of harm to foreseeable child trespassers.

sue; and
2. Supports the answer with legal standard relevant to the issue.

## EXERCISE 2:
## THE SELF-DEFENSE PROBLEM

Review the materials in Appendix F and your draft of the Discussion section of the Bing memo. Draft a Short Answer for an office memo evaluating the Bing self-defense problem. Alternatively, draft a Short Answer for an office memo assigned by your professor.

## EXERCISES 3–6

Review the Statement of Facts and thesis paragraph for the kidnapping memo illustrated in Appendix A as Sample Memorandum B. Compare the following examples and consider their respective appeal to a busy partner. For each exercise, respond to the following questions:

1.  Does the Question Presented:

    (a)  Identify the element of the rule of law that is at issue?

    (b)  Clearly and succinctly summarize for the reviewing attorney the key client facts? If not, how might the facts be more effectively presented?

    (c)  Follow a format that provides the reader with context before details? If not, how might the Question Presented be restructured?

2.  Does the Short Answer:

    (a)  Answer the question?

    (b)  Identify the element of the rule of law that frames the answer?

    (c)  Inform the reviewing attorney of the reasons that support the answer?

**EXERCISE 3**

---

### QUESTION PRESENTED

Does a defendant have a viable defense under Illinois' Aggravated Kidnapping Statute when he confined a friend to a chair in his living room?

### SHORT ANSWER

He may have a viable defense under the Aggravated Kidnapping Statute.

---

 **EXERCISE 4**

---

### QUESTION PRESENTED

If a defendant ties a friend to his chair in the living room of his home, and the living room is on the first floor of his home, which is primarily surrounded by a large picture window with a small amount of brick surrounding the entrance, and the home is twenty feet from a moderately-traveled road, and the front door is two steps up from the sidewalk, making it visible to passers-by, but he does not answer the telephone or doorbell, does he have a viable defense under Illinois' Aggravated Kidnapping Statute that he did not "secretly" confine his friend under the statute?

### SHORT ANSWER

Yes. He has a viable defense that he did not "secretly" confine his friend.

---

## EXERCISE 5

### QUESTION PRESENTED

Does a defendant have a viable defense under Illinois' Aggravated Kidnapping Statute that he did not "secretly" confine another under the statute, when he confined a victim in the victim's home in front of a large picture window visible to neighbors and passers-by and made no effort to conceal the victim, although he failed to answer the telephone or doorbell?

### SHORT ANSWER

Yes, a defendant has a viable defense that he did not secretly confine another under the statute. The defendant selected a visible location near a public area from which witnesses were likely to view the confinement, and made no effort to conceal the victim in a less visible location. In view of the location's visibility to potential witnesses, the fact that the defendant failed to answer the telephone or doorbell should not make the confinement "secret."

## EXERCISE 6

### QUESTION PRESENTED

Does a defendant have a viable defense under Illinois' Aggravated Kidnapping Statute that he did not "secretly" confine another under the statute, when he confined a victim in front of a large picture window visible to neighbors and passers-by?

### SHORT ANSWER

Yes, a defendant has a viable defense that he did not secretly confine another under the statute. The defendant selected a visible location near a public area from which witnesses were likely to view the confinement.

#  V  *DRAFTING THE STATEMENT OF FACTS*

## A.  *Purpose*

The Statement of Facts simply tells the factual story of the client's situation. In this section of the memo, you will simply describe the facts and refrain from making legal conclusions about the facts. Save any legal conclusions about the facts for the legal analysis that will follow in the Discussion section of your memo.

The Statement of Facts serves several purposes. First, the factual story serves as context for the legal analysis in the Discussion section of the memo. Just as with every other section of the memo, your reader will appreciate understanding the underlying context of the client's situation before focusing on the aspects of the client situation that create an issue under the relevant rule of law.

Second, including a thorough factual statement within your memo gives the reviewing attorney the opportunity to correct any misunderstandings. It is not uncommon for a senior attorney to relate the facts to a junior attorney during an office conference that is subject to telephone calls and other interruptions. As a practical matter, a senior attorney may inadvertently neglect to inform you of a fact that may prove to be legally significant. On other occasions, you and the senior attorney may both be present during a client meeting; however, you may each leave the meeting with two different impressions of certain facts. Therefore, the factual statement provides an opportunity to correct any misunderstandings that may have arisen.

Third, because your analysis and legal conclusions will be based on the existence of certain facts, the Statement of Facts protects you. Should additional facts later be revealed, it will be clear from the memo itself that your conclusion in that memo is premised on a specific set of facts and might be different in light of any additional facts.

Finally, an office memo is a self-contained document. Should other attorneys in the office review your memo at a later date, or should you decide to refer to the memo as you research a related matter, it is important that all of the relevant information be contained within a single document.

## B.  Content

The Statement of Facts section of an office memo contains two different types of facts: (1) those facts that are legally significant; and (2) those helpful backgrounds facts that provide context for the factual story. Legally significant facts are those facts that are significant to your analysis of how the law affects the client's situation. You will not know which facts are legally significant until after you have researched the law, carefully evaluated the cases, and analogized and compared their facts to the client's situation. In fact, as you research the law you may change your mind a number of times as to which facts are significant and how they are significant. It is important to include the legally significant facts that do not favor your ultimate legal conclusion as well as those facts that support your ultimate conclusion. Because the senior attorney and client will rely on your analysis of the law in making future decisions, it is important that you fully apprise them of all of the legally significant facts, unfavorable as well as favorable.

Every legally significant fact that appears in your Statement of Facts should also appear somewhere in your Discussion section. Thus, your Statement of Facts can serve as a useful editing tool when you revise and finalize your memo. After completing the Statement of Facts, check to make sure that every legally significant fact is incorporated in the Discussion section as well. Although this may seem repetitive to you as the writer, the reader will not view it as such. Because the Statement of Facts serves a different purpose than the Discussion section of the memo, the facts will be presented differently. In the Statement of Facts, the reader learns all about the factual story, including what the client did or did not do and what happened to the client. There are no legal conclusions that might distract the reader from understanding "what happened." In the Discussion section, the client's facts are presented and evaluated for their legal significance. Thus, they are presented to illustrate how they support a particular premise, including how they are similar to or distinguishable from the facts in precedent cases.

## C.  Format

Like the roadmap paragraphs in the Discussion section of the memo, begin the Statement of Facts with a sentence or two that will provide context for the factual story that follows. Depending on the complexity of the case, these contextual facts may absorb a paragraph or may only require a single sentence. You may also wish to include in the opening paragraph a brief description of the procedural posture of the case. However, although some attorneys prefer to include a brief statement of the procedural posture in the first paragraph, other attorneys prefer to wait until the end of the Statement of Facts. You should follow the format preferred by your professor or assigning attorney. The following introductory paragraph is excerpted from Sample Memo A in Appendix A:

> On August 20, 2001, Defendant, Gerry Arnold, broke into Carl and Rita Stripe's two-car detached garage and removed some of their personal property. The State has charged Arnold under the Residential Burglary Statute. Arnold's attorney has moved to dismiss the charge, contending that the Stripe's garage is not a "dwelling" within which the Stripes "reside," as required by the statute.

The remaining paragraphs of the Statement of Facts can be organized chronologically, or by issue, or by a combination of both approaches.

## 1.   Chronological Order

Because readers are accustomed to absorbing facts chronologically, detailing the factual events in chronological sequence can be a clear and effective means of telling the story. In fact, if the factual situation you are describing lends itself to a chronology of events, a reader would have difficulty understanding the factual story if it were to be told out of sequence. Consider the following example:

> **Example 1:**
> On August 20, 2001, when a police officer stopped Mr. Arnold, he noticed the stolen equipment in the back seat of the car, and arrested Mr. Arnold. The police officer observed Mr. Arnold driving erratically. Gerry Arnold had broken into the Stripe's garage by breaking a window. After breaking a window in the garage, Mr. Arnold then unlocked the door and made three trips to his car, carrying with him Michael Stripe's guitar, a sound system, and a T.V.

In the above illustration, you probably found it difficult to absorb what happened without going back and rereading certain sentences. Without the context that a chronological sequence would provide, it is difficult to follow the story. For example, the first sentence in Example 1 describes a police officer stopping Mr. Arnold and arresting him because of stolen equipment in the back seat of the car. Without knowing that Mr. Arnold had earlier broken into the Stripes' garage and taken away certain equipment, that part of the factual story lacks context. In addition, the story describes the police officer's search of the car before disclosing why the police officer stopped the car in the first place. Assuming such facts were relevant to the issue to be evaluated in the memo, the following example describes the factual story in chronological sequence, making it easier for the reader to follow.

---

***Example 2:***

   On August 20, 2001, Gerry Arnold broke into the Stripe's garage by breaking a window. Mr. Arnold then unlocked the door and made three trips to his car, carrying with him Michael Stripe's guitar, a sound system, and a T.V. While fleeing from the scene, a police officer observed Mr. Arnold driving erratically. When the police officer stopped Mr. Arnold, he noticed the stolen equipment in the back seat of the car, and arrested Mr. Arnold.

---

## 2.   *Grouping Facts Per Issue or Factor*

Sometimes facts do not have a chronological order. Instead, they simply describe an object or person or general events. For example, in the residential burglary problem, the facts relating to whether the Stripe family garage is a dwelling do not have a chronological order. When facts do not lend themselves to a chronological sequence of events, group the facts according to the common issue to which they relate. Thus, if courts are guided by A, B and C factors when interpreting a rule of law, you might tell the factual story by separately grouping the client facts that relate to each factor. For example, consider the following paragraph excerpted from the Statement of Facts for the residential burglary memo (Sample Memo A in Appendix A):

---

   The Stripe's garage is equipped to accommodate Michael Stripe's interests. In addition to a futon, the garage contains an expensive sound system, a portable five-inch television, and a mini-refrigerator. The garage has electricity and a space heater, but no running water or heat.

---

In the above example, this factual paragraph groups together all of the facts that describe the manner in which the Stripe's garage was furnished, a factor relevant to courts in determining whether a garage is a "living quarters" under the residential burglary statute. As the sample memo reflects, each of the remaining paragraphs in the Statement of Facts is also grouped by issue. The paragraphs separately describe the physical characteristics of the garage, Michael Stripe's use of the garage and the frequency of Michael's use of the garage.

### 3.   Combining the Two Formatting Strategies

Often, a client's story involves some facts that have a chronological order and other facts that do not. Under such circumstances, you will likely want to use a combination of both formatting strategies. When combining the two strategies, try and structure the story so that paragraphs relating to specific issues do not interrupt the chronology of events. Therefore, when possible to do so, place the paragraphs that are grouped according to an issue or factor so that they either *precede* or *follow* the paragraphs describing the chronological flow of events. For example, in the Statement of Facts for the residential burglary memo, the paragraphs describing the Stripe's garage and its uses and structure (issue grouping paragraphs) follow a paragraph describing the events that happened on August 20th (chronology of events paragraph).

## D.   Deducing Inferences from Facts

Clients do not usually provide their attorneys with all of the facts that may be relevant to their legal problem. Even though clients try to provide their attorneys all of the relevant information concerning their legal problem, clients are typically not trained to deduce important inferences from facts. The skill of deducing inferences from facts is an important skill that you will learn and practice in law school. Essentially, the art of deduction involves examining the facts that you know are true. From those facts you know to be true, deduce the existence of other facts that must also be true. For example, if a client were to walk in the door with snow sprinkled over her winter coat, you would deduce that it is snowing outside. Such inferences will be valuable to you as you evaluate client problems.

The following example illustrates this process of deductive reasoning. In this example, assume that the attorney who drafted the following Statement of Facts represents a defendant who has been charged with a crime. The government's case against the defendant rests solely on transcripts of wiretap tapes the government intercepted from the defendant's home telephone. The government lost the tapes for a period of two months. Because the government lost the tapes, and cannot assure the court that the tapes were not altered during that time period, the attorney will evaluate in a memo whether a judge would "suppress" the tapes, thereby depriving the government of the ability to introduce the tapes into evidence during trial.

Assume that prior to drafting the Statement of Facts, the drafting attorney had the following information concerning the government's loss of the wiretap tapes: (1) Agent Friday placed the tapes in a cardboard box on Sept. 7 and states she placed a label on the box indicating it was to go to the courthouse for the court to "seal" the tapes; (2) Agent Friday states that she sealed the box of tapes; (3) her office of 5,000 people moved offices on Sept. 8th; (4) a janitor saw the box of tapes in an office supply room at the new location but did not realize what it was—the box of tapes was not labeled and "was open. You could look right in and see what was inside."; (5) until Agent Friday discovered the tapes two months later in the storage room, the government was not aware the tapes were missing; (6) the government can not explain why the box of tapes was open when it was found; and (7) this case was Agent Friday's only responsibility during the relevant time period.

Keeping that background in mind, review the following Statement of Facts. The facts that have been inferred from known facts are <u>underlined</u> to help you identify them. As you consider the facts that have been inferred, identify the known fact that is the source of the inference.

---

Our client, Mr. Joseph Hart, has been indicted with . . . [e.g., statutory violation]. Wiretap tapes the government obtained from a wiretap on Mr. Hart's home are the sole basis of the government indictment. On September 6th and 7th, the government obtained the tapes they are using as the sole basis for Mr. Hart's indictment.

On September 7, 2001, Agent T. Friday removed the tapes from the surveillance van parked near Mr. Hart's home and took them to the investigating bureau's office. <u>Although Agent Friday had to have been aware</u> that the Bureau was moving offices the next day, she dropped the tapes in a plain cardboard box <u>that was identical to the thousands of cardboard boxes used for the move.</u> Although Agent Friday testified that she placed a label on the box indicating that the box was to be transported to the courthouse, the building janitor testified that no label appeared on the box of tapes. Although Agent Friday testified that she sealed the box of tapes, the building janitor testified that the box of tapes "was open. You could look right in and see what was inside." (R. at 14.) The government has not explained these factual discrepancies.

> After the Bureau moved offices, Agent Friday never telephoned or appeared at the courthouse to ensure the tapes arrived for sealing. Agent Friday never asked the court clerk to confirm whether a judge had sealed the tapes. And, despite the fact that Agent Friday had no responsibilities other than this case during the entire period of August to November, 2001, Agent Friday apparently did not make a single attempt to locate her only evidence in this case.
>
> On or about November 8, 2001, Agent Friday finally found the missing tapes while looking for party decorations. (R. at 12.) The government speculates that the tapes sat exposed in an open box in the unlocked office supply room for over two months. (R. at 12.) The exposed tapes sat in the busy supply room amidst note pads, pencils, office supplies and party decorations, open to the 5,000 occupants of the building who frequent the room for coffee and office supplies.

Note the factual discrepancies between Agent Friday's testimony and the janitor's testimony. From the factual discrepancies identified in the Statement of Facts, the attorney would then argue in the Discussion section how such discrepancies are legally significant. Thus, the attorney would later explore the legal consequences of the inferences raised from such discrepancies—either an unknown individual later removed the tapes from a box that Agent Friday sealed, or Agent Friday did not originally place the tapes in sealed envelopes or seal the box itself. Either inference would have legal ramifications.

## EXERCISE 7:
## FACTUAL INFERENCES

Assume that your client was sued for stealing trade secrets from her former employer and selling them to a competitor with whom she is now employed. During the lawsuit, the plaintiff (former employer) asked the court to dismiss the lawsuit after it discovered that your client was not, in fact, the culpable party. Your client seeks monetary sanctions against her former employer for filing a lawsuit that was not "well-grounded in fact" after a "reasonable investigation." The applicable court rules require attorneys to conduct a "reasonable investigation" before filing a lawsuit to ensure that the factual basis for the lawsuit is "well-grounded in fact." Your job is to evaluate whether you should file a request for sanctions on the ground that the former employer did not reasonably investigate its claim before filing suit.

During the discovery process, the plaintiff described all of the information it had available that indicated your client was culpable, and all of the steps it took to investigate the matter before filing the lawsuit: (1) your client had access to and used the trade secret information while employed by the plaintiff; (2) your client became employed by the competitor immediately after leaving the plaintiff's employ; (3) approximately six months after your client began working for the competitor, the competitor began marketing technology based on trade secret information; (4) the employer's employment records reflected that your client was the only employee who left its employment to become employed by the competitor; and (5) the plaintiff asked each of its ten present employees who have access to the trade secrets to take a lie detector test; all passed the test.

At least superficially, the plaintiff appears to have taken reasonable steps to investigate the claim. Nevertheless, your job is to infer from the known facts the existence of other facts that might reveal that the investigation was, in fact, superficial in scope and not reasonable. For this exercise, you can assume that the plaintiff failed to take any potential investigative step not described above.

As you evaluate the facts, consider the following:

(1) ***Factual possibilities the plaintiff failed to consider:*** List other groups of culprits, or alternative explanations, the plaintiff failed to consider while pursuing its investigation.

(2) ***Steps the plaintiff failed to take:*** List any other steps the plaintiff could have taken when investigating this matter.

(3) ***Faulty inferences from the facts it had available:*** Consider whether the plaintiff's incorrect conclusion that your client was the culpable party was based on any faulty inferences from the facts it had available. List any faulty inferences the plaintiff made.

 **EXERCISE 8:**
**THE SELF-DEFENSE PROBLEM**

Draft a Statement of Facts for the Bing memo. Alternatively, draft a Statement of Facts for the memo previously assigned to you by your professor.

# 15

# REVISING AND FINALIZING THE MEMO: CONTENT & ORGANIZATIONAL STRUCTURE

 ## THE IMPORTANCE OF THE REVISION PROCESS

Prior to law school, you may not have had much practice in reviewing, editing and finalizing your written work. However, in the practice of law, it is common for attorneys to go through many drafts of their written work before submitting it to other attorneys or to their clients or judges. Clear and persuasive legal writing requires two, three, and even four or more rewrites. The process of revising and finalizing written work is extraordinarily important. Although a first draft is a necessary first step in the drafting process, it would be a mistake to view the first draft as a work product that would be satisfactory in a legal setting.

The following excerpts from a letter forwarded by a corporate employer to a law school dean provide a graphic illustration of the value of the revision process. The corporate employer forwarded this letter to the law school dean following that employer's experience interviewing law students for employment.

***Excerpts from a corporate employer's letter:***

> Dear _____ :
>
> The Office of Legal Counsel of . . . has concluded a successful recruiting season. We are writing to express our gratitude for your assistance.

We have hired four second-year students for our Summer Intern Program. The successful candidates are. . . .

Our pleasure with these fine recruits is tempered, however, by concern and disappointment in the quality of the writing samples submitted by applicants for summer positions. We have enclosed a representative sample from one of your students. *The sample's flaws include sloppy editing, poor organization, significant grammatical and syntactical errors, as well as poor logic, reasoning and analysis.* (emphasis added)

Our concern is multifaceted. First, the writing sample a student submits should be representative of the student's writing ability. If the enclosed writing sample is truly typical, these students lack a vital skill required for success. If not typical, the students displayed poor judgment in submitting such samples to prospective employers. Second, submission of writing samples like the enclosed example reflects a basic misunderstanding about the significance of writing samples. If students believe that recruiters do not scrutinize the samples carefully, they are sorely mistaken. In our office, each writing sample is read and evaluated by a minimum of three attorneys. Many students who were well regarded after the office interviews were deleted from our 'potential hire' list or moved several places down the list because of the poor quality of the writing sample. . . .

A law school should counsel its students on the importance of quality communication (both oral and written) and on the importance of the writing samples that students provide on their career opportunities. We wanted to alert you to the problems we perceived this year and over the last few years. If you share our concern, will you please inform your students of the importance attached to their writing ability and choice of writing samples.

[Signature]

As the above letter illustrates, whether submitting your written work to a professor, a potential employer, or a senior attorney in a law office, submitting a first draft as a final draft can lead to unfortunate consequences. Because the revision process is so important, this textbook devotes two chapters to discussing the reflection and revision strategies that will help you become an effective editor of your own work.

After drafting the first draft of your memo, it is important to keep an open mind about the draft itself. When reviewing our own work, it is very easy to become invested in what we have written, particularly when we have spent a significant amount of time thinking through the analysis, organizing the analysis, and finding the right words to express our thinking. After all of that time and effort, our egos tend to want to defend the written work product. However, it is so very important to review initial drafts from the perspective of a detached observer, a challenging prospect. The passage of time makes it easier to see the draft from the fresh perspective of the intended reader. Therefore, whenever possible, allow time within your drafting schedule to put the draft away for a few days.

 ## II    *REVIEWING THE SUBSTANTIVE CONTENT*

As you review your draft, first consider the substantive content of your analysis. Openly question whether you have provided enough information to the reader about the rule of law and the relevant cases that interpret the rule of law. If the reader had not studied the original rule of law or any of the cases that have interpreted the law, would the reader understand every relevant aspect about the law? Next consider whether you have adequately informed the reader about the law's effect on the client's factual situation. Have you evaluated the impact of each standard or factor on the client's situation? Consider whether you have thoroughly elaborated on the significance of each legally significant fact from the client's situation, including the unfavorable as well as the favorable arguments that can be made. Review again your Statement of Facts to ensure that each legally significant fact described in your factual statement is evaluated within the Discussion section as well. As you carefully review your draft, consider whether any of the substantive content is unnecessary or repetitive and should be deleted. You may realize at this point that some of the information originally included in your analysis was not ultimately legally significant.

***Content Checklist:***

Have you:

1.    Identified the components of the original rule of law?
      (a)   The components that are not at issue?
      (b)   The issue or issues?
      (Chapter 11—Drafting Overview Paragraphs)

2. Summarized the meaning of the rule of law, including:
   (a) The rules of law the cases as a group express?
   (b) Any definitions, standards or factors that guide courts when evaluating the rule of law?
   (Chapter 11—Drafting Thesis Paragraphs)

3. Explained how courts have interpreted the rule of law?
   For each case, if relevant for that case, have you identified:
   (a) The rule of law expressed by the case?
   (b) The important facts of the case?
   (c) The holding of the case?
   (d) The court's rationale, including the application of a standard or factors to the case facts, or statutory interpretation?
   (Chapters 12 & 13—Drafting the Analysis)

4. Applied the rule of law to the client's factual situation?
   For each standard or factor to be evaluated, have you:
   (a) Elaborated on client facts that illustrate how the law favorably affects the client?
   (b) Made concrete, specific analogies to facts in cases that help bolster your analysis?
   (c) Explained the legal significance of client facts and analogies to cases?
   (d) Evaluated arguments on the opposing side?
   (Chapters 12 & 13—Drafting the Analysis)

5. If applicable, identified additional facts to elicit from the client?

6. Stated a conclusion?

 ## III　*EVALUATING THE ORGANIZATIONAL STRUCTURE*

### A. *Macro-Organization of the Discussion*

On a large scale perspective, consider whether you are satisfied with the order in which you have presented the various issues. If the issues have a logical order, have you structured the presentation of issues in a manner that follows a logical format? For each separate issue evaluated in your memo, review the effectiveness of the organizational format you selected for the first draft. Are the most important standards or factors presented first? Recall that when evaluating more than one case, the boundaries between the rule explanation and rule application sections become fluid. Carefully review the format you have selected to discuss the rule explanation and rule application sections of the memo. Drafting a legal discussion is a fluid, on-going process. Often, attorneys end up trying different formatting options in later drafts, sometimes ultimately deciding to stay with their initial decisions, and sometimes deciding to adopt a different organizational format. Therefore, consider whether your organizational format allows for a clear evaluation of the law and its effect on the client. If you conclude that at least part of the discussion seems confusing or repetitive, review again the three basic formatting options discussed in Chapter 13 that reflect the interplay between the rule explanation and rule application sections of a memo.

As you consider the effectiveness and clarity of the organizational structure you selected, review again your thesis and transition sentences. You may wish to copy and paste each thesis and transition sentence in the Discussion section onto a separate document so that you can more easily see the framework of your analysis. Reviewing the flow of your thesis and transition sentences will help you identify any gaps in your analysis and any unnecessary repetition.

## B.  *The Micro-Format of Each Paragraph*

Under the deductive writing pattern, roadmap paragraphs provide the context for the details that will follow in the Discussion section of the memo. Even on the smaller scale of an *individual paragraph*, the paragraph itself should follow a deductive analytical format, transitioning the reader from old information to new information. On the smaller scale of a paragraph, thesis and transition sentences provide the context that transitions a reader from old information to the new information that will follow within a particular paragraph.

The thesis or transition sentence in a paragraph identifies the broad thesis or premise the paragraph will explore and illustrate. The remaining information in the paragraph illustrates and proves with supporting details why the broad thesis or premise is sound. Therefore, each paragraph also follows a deductive format, with the thesis sentence reflecting the paragraph's broad premise and providing the context for the details that will illustrate the premise.

### 1.  *Thesis and Transition Sentences*

At this stage of the reflection process, consider whether each thesis and transition sentence clearly serves the purpose for which it is intended. Thesis and transition sentences serve as visual "sign posts" that guide a reader through a discussion. Thesis and transition sentences assume a critical role in legal analysis because of the very complexity of legal analysis. The more complex the substantive content, the more difficult it is for a reader to follow the train of analysis. To serve as effective sign posts, thesis and transition sentences should both:

    (1)   *relate back* to information the reviewing attorney has already read; and

    (2)   *signal forward* to the essence of the new information that will follow.

By both relating back to old information and signaling forward to new information, thesis and transition sentences serve as valuable links that allow a reader to follow the logical flow of the analysis.

### (a)  *Thesis Sentences*

Whenever you introduce a new idea in a legal discussion, a thesis sentence should alert the reader to the introduction of the new idea. Because a thesis sentence introduces a new idea, and because readers understand information best if they understand the relationship of the new idea to old information, an effective thesis sentence should both state the paragraph's thesis, or premise, (the "new information") and its relationship to the entire document (the "old information"). An effective way to accomplish this goal is to use the roadmap paragraphs as the *source* for thesis sentences. Recall that roadmap paragraphs summarize for the reader the rules of law and any legal standards or factors that guide courts when they interpret the law. Restating the relevant parts of that same information in a thesis sentence effectively: (1) reminds the reviewing attorney of the "old information" from the roadmap paragraphs; and (2) alerts the attorney that the "new information" to be discussed in the upcoming paragraph will elaborate on a particular aspect of the old information.

### (i)  *Thesis Sentences Introducing a Case Discussion*

When discussing a relevant case, the thesis sentence usually states the rule of law the case illustrates, including any relevant factors that help frame the rule of law. When possible, use the same language used in the roadmap paragraphs to describe standards or factors. By using the same language, the paragraph's connection to the over-all analysis is instantly clear to the reader. Unlike a typical undergraduate essay, varying the language to avoid presumed boredom will not excite the reader! Instead, using different language to describe the same idea can confuse the reviewing attorney. In your roadmap paragraphs, you assigned specific legal meaning to certain language. Varying the language could imply that the new language has a different *legal meaning* than the old language.

Using the residential burglary memo as the basis of illustration, the following thesis sentence is excerpted from Sample Memo A in Appendix A. In the thesis paragraph of that memo, the following factors were identified as important guiding factors: (1) type of use, including the frequency and evidence of use; and (2) the structure's proximity to the home. The rule of law that captures the essence of the *McIntyre* case reflects how the court applied both factors in that case. The thesis sentence is illustrated as follows:

> An enclosed, attached porch frequently used as part of the home's living quarters is a dwelling under the residential burglary statute. *People v. McIntyre*, 578 N.E.2d 314 (Ill. App. Ct. 1991).

### (ii) Thesis Sentences Introducing Rule Application

When applying law to a client's factual problem, the thesis sentence should state the conclusion, or premise, the paragraph will reach as it applies the law to the client's facts. In that manner, the thesis sentence both relates back to old information (the law as previously evaluated) and alerts the reviewing attorney to the essence of the new information that will follow (how the law affects the client). Thesis sentences incorporate both: (1) the standard or factor that will be the subject of the analysis; and (2) the paragraph's premise concerning how the standard or factor relates to the client. Again using the residential burglary memo as the basis of illustration, the following thesis sentence is excerpted from Sample Memo A in Appendix A.

> Like the porch in *McIntyre*, Michael Stripe used the Stripe's garage for activities commonly associated with a living quarters.

The above thesis sentence states the premise of the paragraph (that the use of the garage is similar to the use in *McIntyre*), and identifies the factor that will be discussed in the paragraph (the "type of use" factor). As you evaluate each thesis sentence introducing a rule application paragraph, consider whether the thesis sentence relates to the client or to the case law. In the above illustration, note that the premise of the thesis sentence relates to the *client*, not to case law. The paragraph's premise is that Michael Stripe used the garage for activities associated with a living quarters. It does not restate the thesis from the *McIntyre* case (e.g., "The *McIntyre* court observed that the use of a structure is important in determining whether it is a living quarters."). By framing the thesis around the client, the sentence accurately signals that this will be a paragraph of rule application rather than rule explanation.

### (b)   Transition Sentences

Transition sentences serve the same function as thesis sentences insofar as they help orient a reader to the relationship between old information and new information. In contrast to thesis sentences, however, transition sentences signal the continuation of a discussion of the same general idea. Transition sentences show readers the connection between information in a previous paragraph and in a new paragraph that explores the same general idea.

The following sentences are also excerpted from the residential burglary memo illustrated as Sample Memo A in Appendix A. One argument the writer explores is a potential opposing argument that a garage can never be a dwelling under the residential burglary statute. In the previous paragraph, the writer explored the state's rebuttal to this argument by examining the language and reasoning in the *McIntyre* case. In the illustration below, the first sentence is the final sentence in that previous paragraph. The final sentence of that paragraph reflects the writer's conclusion that, even though the Stripe garage is detached, it is still an extension of the family's living quarters. The transition sentence that follows signals to the reader that the *Thomas* case bolsters the conclusion reached in the previous paragraph.

> . . . . Like the physically separate porch in *McIntyre*, the Stripe garage is used as an extension of the Stripe family's living quarters.
>
> *People v. Thomas* lends further support to this conclusion. . . .

## 2.   Remainder of Each Paragraph: Illustrating the Thesis

### (a)   Rule Explanation Paragraphs

As Chapter 12 discusses, there are several ways in which you can organize the discussion of a factually analogous case that will be discussed in depth (e.g., that you will discuss for its factual significance, holding and rationale). The thesis sentence should serve as the context for the specific details that will follow. As you re-examine each paragraph of rule explanation, verify that you have adequately laid a foundation for each sentence of the paragraph. Consider whether you have omitted to tell the reader any background information that will help the reader understand the significance of your analysis. When describing the factual story of a case that lends itself to a chronological description of the events, consider whether there are any confusing lapses in the chronology.

## EXERCISE 1:
## THE MICRO-ORGANIZATION OF A PARAGRAPH

The following illustration reflects the importance of providing context within each paragraph. This case discussion contains the four components of an analogous case of primary importance: a rule statement; holding; relevant case facts; and rationale. While reading this example discussion of the *McIntyre* case, identify each sentence that does not have the necessary foundation for a reader to understand easily its significance. Note how the order in which the four different components are presented interferes with clarity.

---

In *People v. McIntyre*, 578 N.E.2d 314 (Ill. App. Ct. 1991), the owners furnished the porch with wrought-iron furniture and a barbecue grill that reflected its use. They ate most of their meals on the porch in the summer and cooked meals there four or five times a week in the winter. The porch was enclosed, locked, and attached to the home. They used an attached, screened porch for "sitting, eating and cooking." *Id.* at 315.

The court observed that the porch was enclosed and attached to the house, indicating that the porch's physical attachment to the house was a relevant factor. The court reasoned that the owners used the porch as part of their living quarters by engaging in such activities as "sitting, eating, and cooking." *Id.* The court held that, under these facts, the porch was a "living quarters" under the Statute. *Id.* In addition, the owners regularly used the porch in this manner and furnished the porch with furniture and a grill that reflected such use. However, the court emphasized that it was the activities of "sitting, eating, and cooking" that "make the porch part of the living quarters of the house." *Id.* An enclosed, attached porch frequently used as part of the home's living quarters is a dwelling under the residential burglary statute.

---

At this point, you are already familiar with the *McIntyre* case and have even read the case. Nevertheless, you probably had some difficulty following the train of analysis in the above illustration. Imagine the difficulty a reader would have who had never read the *McIntyre* case.

## EXERCISE 2:
## THE SELF-DEFENSE PROBLEM

Consider the *People v. Shipp* case illustrated in Appendix F and the memo you are drafting on behalf of Mr. Bing. Following a deductive analytical format:

(1) Reorganize and renumber the following information into a format that would more clearly describe the *Shipp* case.

(2) Rewrite a case discussion of the *Shipp* case to enhance the clarity of the case discussion.

---

1. Decedent threatened to "take care of" the defendant and friend
2. Decedent was previously convicted of attempting to kill the defendant
3. Decedent continued to advance on and cornered the defendant in an upstairs bedroom after she pointed the revolver at him
4. Decedent brutally assaulted the defendant on a number of occasions
5. Decedent threatened to kill the defendant if he found her with another man
6. A description of the court's holding
7. Decedent made numerous threats against the defendant's life
8. Defendant left the bar with a man she had propositioned
9. Defendant shot the decedent after pleading with him not to "come any closer"
10. A description of the factors you will incorporate into the *Shipp* case discussion
11. A description of the rule of law you have formulated from the Shipp case
12. The Shipp court's rationale

### (b) Rule Application Paragraphs

The detailed information in each paragraph of rule application should illustrate the premise described in the thesis sentence of that paragraph (or in the thesis sentence of a previous paragraph if the analysis of a premise continues beyond a paragraph). Therefore, carefully review each paragraph of analysis to ensure that the information in the paragraph illustrates only the major idea reflected in the thesis sentence. The detailed information in the paragraph should illustrate why the premise is sound.

If you are discussing a factor that contains several different sub-factors, you may or may not decide to include a discussion of the different sub-factors in the same paragraph. If each sub-factor is of a complexity that a discussion of the sub-factor merits a separate paragraph, then review your draft to ensure that you have restricted each such paragraph only to that sub-factor. Sometimes, however, different sub-factors are minor enough that they can be adequately discussed within a single paragraph. If you have selected this alternative, review your draft to ensure that you have fully evaluated and concluded your discussion about one sub-factor before moving on to the next. It is difficult for a reader to absorb the logical flow of an analysis when the discussion itself jumps back and forth between different sub-factors. When discussing a factor that brings out several different sub-factors, check to see whether you can clarify your analysis by introducing each sub-factor with a new premise. Again, the premise for each sub-factor provides the necessary context for the reader to understand the factual details that illustrate the premise.

For example, in the residential burglary problem, the "type of use" factor has several inter-related sub-factors: frequency of use and evidence of use. The discussion of each sub-factor is complex enough that they should be discussed in separate paragraphs. Assume, however, that while drafting a memo based on this problem, your first draft evaluated both sub-factors within the same paragraph. As you review each example, consider the comments to the right that identify the organizational format of each paragraph.

| | |
|---|---|
| ***Example 1:*** In addition, like the owners in *McIntyre*, Michael Stripe frequently uses the garage as a living quarters and has furnished the garage in a manner that reflects such use. Like the grill and wrought-iron furniture in *McIntyre*, Michael Stripe's sound system, small t.v., mini-refrigerator, and futon reflect that he uses the garage for activities typically associated with a living quarters. Michael spends at least two to three evenings a week and his spare time on weekends in his get-a-way. During the summer and fall, he sleeps there seven | 1. Thesis sentence introduces both sub-factors. 2. Stripe facts re: <u>evidence of use</u> & cf. to *McIntyre*. 3. Stripe facts re: <u>frequency of use</u>. |

| | |
|---|---|
| nights a week. In fact, in August when the garage was burglarized, Michael's frequency of use even exceeded that of the owners in *McIntyre*, who used the porch only four to five times a week. Therefore, the frequency of Michael's use of the garage as a living quarters is also similar to the use of the porch in *McIntyre*. In addition, the furnishings are a far cry from the garage in *Thomas*, which housed only the owner's car and boxes of commercial products for sale. Michael's regular and frequent use far exceeds the owner's limited, occasional use of the garage in *Thomas* to retrieve her car or perfume products from storage. | 4. Cf. to *McIntyre* re: <u>frequency of use</u>.<br>5. Premise re: <u>frequency of use</u>.<br>6. Cf. to *Thomas* re: <u>evidence of use</u>.<br>7. Cf. to *Thomas* re: <u>frequency of use</u>. |

In Example 1 above, note how several organizational problems impeded the clarity of the analysis. First, the writer jumped back and forth between an analysis of each sub-factor. Second, the writer jumped from facts describing the "evidence of use" sub-factor to facts describing the "frequency of use" sub-factor, without inserting a premise that would introduce the new sub-factor. Instead, the writer waited until *after* describing the new facts before stating a premise about those facts. This organizational format can be confusing because it describes facts that do not have a context, thereby forcing the reader to wonder why such facts are important.

Compare the previous example to the following revised version:

| | |
|---|---|
| ***Example 2:***    In addition, like the owners in *McIntyre*, Michael Stripe frequently uses the garage as a living quarters and has furnished the garage in a manner that reflects such use. Like the grill and wrought-iron furniture in *McIntyre*, Michael Stripe's sound system, small t.v., mini-refrigerator, and futon reflect that he uses the garage for activities typically associated with a living quarters. These furnishings are a far cry from the garage in *Thomas*, which housed only the owner's car and boxes of commercial products for sale. In addition, the frequency of Michael's use of the garage as a living quarters even exceeded that of the owners in *McIntyre*. In *McIntyre*, the owners used the porch only four to five times a week, while Michael sleeps in his get-a-way seven nights a week during the summer and fall. Moreover, he spends at least two to three evenings a week and his spare time on weekends in his get-a-way. Michael's regular and frequent use far exceeds the owner's limited, occasional use of the garage in *Thomas* to retrieve her car or perfume products from storage. | 1. Thesis sentence introduces both sub-factors.<br><br>2. Stripe facts re: <u>evidence of use</u> & cf. to both *McIntyre* and *Thomas*.<br>3. Premise re: frequency of use.<br>4. Cf. to both *McIntyre* and *Thomas* re: frequency of use. |

In Example 2 above, the writer has clarified the analysis by introducing each sub-factor with a premise and then fully evaluating that sub-factor before moving on to a new idea. Thus, the facts relating to the "evidence of use" factor are fully discussed and analogized to the precedent cases before the writer introduces the premise and facts relating to the "frequency of use" factor.

# 16

# REVISING & FINALIZING THE MEMO: SENTENCE STRUCTURE & WORD CHOICE

 **I** **SENTENCE STRUCTURE**

At this stage in the drafting process, when you are fairly confident that the content and format of your analysis will not change, you are now in a position to consider how you might modify the structure of each sentence and clarify your word choices so that they more clearly express your analysis. Effective legal writing is not legalese or long, contorted sentences that would take a devoted and willing senior attorney hours to decipher. Most senior attorneys, clients and judges do not have the time or inclination to puzzle over convoluted sentences to discern their meaning. Instead, your goal is to take complex legal issues and communicate them in a manner that appears to be simple and straightforward.

## A. Use "Micro" Road Maps Within Sentences to Transition Reader

As is true on the larger scale, readers understand information more easily if each sentence shows its link to old information before it conveys new information. In order to achieve this, each sentence begins with old information and ends with new information. You might picture each sentence in a paragraph as follows: (Old ⇨ New) ⇨ (Old ⇨ New) ⇨ (Old ⇨ New). Note: A reader's knowledge base is "old" information.

## 1.   Writing Tips

### (a)   Repeat Part of the Prior Sentence's Content

At or near the beginning of a sentence, repeat part of the preceding sentence's content, using the same words or easily recognizable synonyms. Consider how the following example excerpted from Sample Memo A in Appendix A transitions the reader from "old" to "new" information. To help you identify the transitions, the old information is *italicized* and the repetition of that information is underlined.

> Moreover, the fact that the porch in *McIntyre* was separated from the utility room of the owners' home by a *door with "three locks"* lends less significance to the attached/detached distinction. The presence of three locks implies that the porch area was not an open part of the main residence, but was instead physically kept separate from the main residence.

### (b)   Use Transitional Words and Phrases

At or near the beginning of a sentence, use a word or phrase of transition that shows the sentence's logical connection to the previous paragraph or sentence—does it qualify it? add to it? rephrase its point? Transitional expressions are a wonderful means of showing the logical relationship between "old" and "new" information. They can enhance the clarity of any idea, including ideas expressed in a thesis or transition sentence. However, use care when selecting a transitional expression. Use of an inappropriate transition can mislead and confuse the reader, making it more difficult for the reader to follow the train of analysis.

## 2.   Examples of Transitional Expressions[1]

(1)   To add a new point:

---

[1] Transitional expressions adapted from Laurel C. Oates, et al., *The Legal Writing Handbook* (Aspen L. & Bus. 1993); Helen S. Shapo, et al., *Writing and Analysis in the Law* 147–48 (3d ed. Found. Press 1995).

| | |
|---|---|
| and | further |
| also | furthermore |
| in addition | moreover |
| in fact | next |
| finally | second, third, etc. |

(2)   To indicate a difference:

| | |
|---|---|
| alternatively | in contrast |
| but | on the other hand |
| contrary to | rather than |
| conversely | to the contrary |
| however | |

(3)   To indicate a similarity:

| | |
|---|---|
| also | likewise |
| as | similarly |
| like | |

(4)   To illustrate or explain an idea:

| | |
|---|---|
| after all | in other words |
| as an example | simply put |
| for example | specifically |
| for instance | to illustrate |
| in fact | under such circumstances |
| in particular | |

(5) To conclude:

|                |             |
| -------------- | ----------- |
| accordingly    | in summary  |
| as a result    | therefore   |
| consequently   | thus        |
| in conclusion  |             |

In the following example excerpted from Sample Memo A in Appendix A, transitional words and phrases are used through-out the paragraph, beginning with the thesis sentence and continuing through-out the discussion. To help you identify the transitions, the transitional words are <u>underlined</u>.

> <u>Finally</u>, the frequency of Michael's use of the garage <u>also</u> is similar to the use of the porch in *McIntyre*. Michael spends at least two to three evenings a week and his spare time on weekends in his getaway. <u>Moreover</u>, during the summer and fall, he sleeps there seven nights a week. Michael's regular and frequent use far exceeds the owner's limited, occasional use of the garage in *Thomas* to retrieve perfume products from storage. <u>In fact</u>, in August when the garage was burglarized, Michael's frequency of use even exceeded that of the owners in *McIntyre*, who used the porch only four to five times a week.

 **EXERCISE 1:**
**USING INTERNAL ROADMAPS**

Assume that you represent a client who was injured in a softball game by a player on the opposing team. The members of the opposing team are all employed by Ajax Cleaning & Plumbing ("Ajax"). You are evaluating whether you can sue the employer, Ajax Cleaning & Plumbing, under a theory of "respondeat superior." Under that theory, an employer may be liable for an employee's behavior if the particular activity was "within the scope" of the employee's employment. Assume that you have drafted the following rule explanation paragraph:

Where an employer specifically authorizes the conduct in which the employee is engaged, the employee is acting within the scope of his employment. In *Riviello v. Waldron*, the owner of a restaurant specifically authorized his chef to visit with the patrons in the dining room of the restaurant and to perform knife tricks while doing so. 391 N.E.2d 1278, 1280 (N.Y. 1979). On one occasion, the chef mishandled the knife while tossing it in the air, and a restaurant patron was injured when the knife struck her in the eye. *Id.* Under these facts, the court held that the chef was acting within the scope of his employment while tossing the knife. *Id.* The court reasoned that the owner of the restaurant had specifically authorized and approved of the conduct that resulted in the patron's injury. The court noted that the employer hired the chef based on the chef's ability to perform the knife tricks and frequently asked the chef to go "perform" in the dining room among the patrons. *Id.*"

In the following rule application paragraph, add transitions that clearly link old information to new information. Consider: (1) repeating key language within the beginning of a new sentence that might help link the new information in that sentence to old information; and (2) adding transitional words and phrases that might help link new information to old information.

Ajax specifically authorized Mike Jones to play softball as part of his job duties. Ajax hired Mr. Jones as a salesperson. Ajax selected Mr. Jones over other qualified applicants in part because of his reputation as a softball player. Ajax prides itself on winning the Division I title every year. Its star catcher resigned last year. Ajax actively sought to hire someone who would be a strong replacement. Ajax provides its team members with shirts that bear the Ajax logo. It allows its employees to leave work early when necessary in order to compete in softball games that require the team to travel.

## B. Use the Active Voice

When reading, a reader's eyes automatically search for "who did what to whom?" Sentences written in the active voice easily and clearly satisfy the reader's natural curiosity because they describe an actor (the subject) ⇒ acting upon ⇒ the object. In other words, the sentence structure is as follows: subject ⇒ acts upon ⇒ an object.

In contrast, the passive voice forces the reader to work harder to discover "who did what to whom." In a passive voice sentence, the writer states: this object ⇒ was acted upon ⇒ by this actor. This structural format satisfies the writer's curiosity in reverse order, forcing the reader to "think backwards." The reader has to wait until the end of the sentence to find the actor, or subject, and then has to review the sentence again to determine the action in which the actor engaged. This problem becomes even more pronounced when the writer hides the actor entirely. This writing style problem, called the "truncated" passive voice, requires the reader to consider as well the identity of the missing subject. In addition to forcing the reader to think harder, passive voice sentences usually require more words to make the same point. Therefore, as a general rule, write in the active voice.

## 1.   *Example of Passive Voice That Hides the Actor*

Compare the clarity of the following two sentences:

| |
|---|
| **Original:**   Two to three evenings a week and free time on weekends are spent in the get-a-way writing, listening to music, and watching television.<br><br>**Revised:**   Michael spends two to three evenings a week and his free time on weekends in the get-a-way writing, listening to music, and watching television. |

Who is writing, listening & watching t.v.?

## 2.   *Example of How Passive Voice Requires More Words*

Compare the clarity and wordiness of the following very simple sentence:

| |
|---|
| **Original:**   A futon in a loft area of the garage is used by Michael to sleep. [15 words]<br><br>**Revised:**   Michael sleeps in the garage on a futon in a loft area. [12 words] |

Object ⇒ Verb ⇒ Subject

Subject ⇒ Verb ⇒ Object

## 3.    When Passive Voice Is Appropriate

As a general rule, use the passive voice only in the following three situations: (1) when the object of the sentence is more important than the identity of the actor/subject; (2) when using the passive voice clarifies the relationship/transition between "old" and "new" information within a paragraph; or (3) when, for persuasive argument purposes, you want to de-emphasize the link between an actor and favorable or unfavorable actions (discussed and illustrated later in Chapter 19).

### (a)    When the Object of the Sentence is Most Important

The following example is excerpted from Sample Memo A in Appendix A. This sentence is excerpted from a paragraph that evaluates how the Stripe garage's furnishings reflect its use as a living quarters. Because the furnishings are more important than the identity of the subject (the actor who supplied the furnishings), the object of the sentence is stated first:

> The furnishings are a far cry from the garage in *Thomas*, which housed only the owner's car and boxes of commercial products for sale.

### (b)    When Passive Voice Links "Old" Information to "New" Information

| | |
|---|---|
| In <u>People v. Lamkey</u>, the defendant confined the victim in the vestibule of an apartment building that had commercial space on the first floor. | *1ˢᵗ sentence*: Defendant confined victim in a vestibule. |
| The vestibule was two steps up from one of Chicago's busiest streets and was separated from the sidewalk by a glass door. | *2ⁿᵈ sentence*: Vestibule (object) links the information from the 1ˢᵗ sentence to new information. |

✔ *Editing Tips:*

(1)   Check for forms of the verb "to be"—these verb forms often reflect passive voice (e.g., is, are, was, were, has been)

(2)   Ask: who is the actor in this sentence, and where is the actor placed? Does the actor "act" (active voice), or does the verb act upon the actor (passive voice)?

## C.  Keep Sentences Relatively Short

Because readers automatically search for "who did what to whom" when reading a sentence, they generally expect to find a single actor, verb, and object within a single sentence. When several ideas are combined within a single sentence, the reader's eye will often skim over the second and third ideas and miss their significance entirely. Therefore, in legal writing, where every expressed idea is important to the writer's understanding of the legal analysis, generally restrict each sentence to one main idea. However, incorporating several *interrelated* ideas within a single sentence can be effective. As a general rule of thumb, most sentences should have approximately twenty-five (25) words. Sentences that run significantly longer than that risk confusing the reader. Sentences that run significantly less than twenty-five words may appear less fluid and choppy. Use the following techniques to help transform run-on-sentences into sentences of a more manageable length.

### 1.  Make Dependent Clauses "Independent"

Dependent clauses are clauses that do not stand on their own because they are introduced with words that depend on another clause to complete their thought (e.g., although, even though). Run-on-sentences often contain one or more dependent clauses that either begin the sentence, or interrupt the sentence in the middle somewhere. One way of simplifying the sentence is to remove the dependent clause from the run-on sentence and create two sentences from the original sentence.

To clarify the link between the two newly created sentences, use a transitional word to introduce the second sentence. The transitional word should incorporate the *same transitional idea* as the word that introduced the original dependent clause. In the following example, the transitional word "however" in the second illustration reflects the same transitional idea as the word "although" in the original sentence.

| | |
|---|---|
| **Original:** | Although a structure's proximity to the main residence is a relevant factor, a structure that is not physically connected to the primary residence may still constitute a living quarters because the owner's use of the structure is a more important factor. **(41 words)** |

> **Revised:**   A structure's proximity to the main residence is a relevant factor. **[11 words]** However, a structure that is not physically connected to the primary residence may still constitute a living quarters because the owner's use of the structure is a more important factor. **[30 words]**

✔*Editing Tip:*

When reviewing an overly lengthy sentence, check for dependent clauses that you might remove and incorporate into a separate sentence. To find dependent clauses, look for the following words that often introduce dependent clauses:

| | |
|---|---|
| Although | Rather than |
| Because | Since |
| Before | Though |
| Despite | Unless |
| Even if | While |
| Even though | |

### 2.   *Eliminate Superfluous Statements*

Superfluous statements purport to alert the reader of why a sentence is important without really adding any new meaning to the sentence itself. They are often called "throat-clearing" statements. They can introduce a sentence (*"You should note that . . ."*), or can appear in the middle of a sentence following a dependent clause ("Although the court held x,y,z, *it is important to point out that . . ."*). Because such superfluous statements unnecessarily clutter the purpose of the sentence, check your writing for such phrases and then remove them as you edit your work.

> **Original:**   It is important to note that the proximity of the structure to the main residence is also relevant.
>
> **Revised:**   The proximity of the structure to the main residence is also relevant.

The following example illustrates a slightly less obvious form of the super-fluous statement.

| | |
|---|---|
| **Original:** | In *People v. McIntyre*, the court <u>addressed the dwelling issue</u>, holding that an attached porch was a living quarters under the statute. |
| **Revised:** | In *People v. McIntyre*, the court held that an attached porch was a living quarters under the statute. |

In the above example, the fact that the *McIntyre* court addressed the dwelling issue is already obvious because the entire memo discusses that issue. Thus, the underlined phrase in the original example is superfluous.

✔*Editing Tip:*

The following phrases are typical examples of "throat-clearing:"

> It is interesting to note that . . .
> Another important point that . . .
> Here it should be pointed out that . . .
> I should emphasize that . . .
> Please note that . . .
> It is significant that . . .

## D.  Keep the Actor, Verb, and Object Together

Recall that readers automatically seek to find the subject, verb, and object in each sentence (e.g., who did what to whom?). Dependent clauses (e.g., "although . . .") can confuse a reader when they separate the subject from the verb or the verb from the object. By separating key components of the sentence they interrupt the reader's natural focus on "who did what to whom." To eliminate the problem of dependent clauses that break up the actor, verb, object sequence, either move the dependent clause to the beginning or end of the sentence, or break the sentence into two sentences.

## 1.  *Example of Moving the Dependent Clause*

| | |
|---|---|
| **Original:** | Moreover, the <u>court</u>, by limiting the holding to the specific facts before it, <u>left open</u> the possibility that a garage could, given the appropriate use, constitute a living quarters under the Statute. |
| **Revised:** | Moreover, by limiting the holding to the specific facts before it, the <u>court left open</u> the possibility that a garage could, given the appropriate use, constitute a living quarters under the Statute. |

## 2.  *Example of Breaking the Sentence Into Two Sentences*

| | |
|---|---|
| **Original:** | Moreover, the <u>court</u>, by limiting the holding to the specific facts before it, <u>left open</u> the possibility that a garage could, given the appropriate use, constitute a living quarters under the Statute. |
| **Revised:** | Moreover, the <u>court limited</u> the holding to the specific facts before it. Thus, the <u>court left open</u> the possibility that a garage could, given the appropriate use, constitute a living quarters under the Statute. |

## E.  *Use Parallel Structure*

When you express two or more ideas of a similar nature, express them in parallel form. For example, if the first verb in a sequence ends with the letters "ing," the remaining verbs in the sentence that continue the sequential description should also end with the letters "ing."

| | |
|---|---|
| **Original:** | He learned <u>to swim</u>, <u>to play</u> tennis, and horseback <u>riding</u>. |
| **Revised:** | He learned <u>to swim</u>, <u>to play</u> tennis, and <u>to ride</u> horses. |

| | |
|---|---|
| **Original:** | At camp, they enjoyed such activities as <u>swimming</u> and horseback <u>riding</u> and <u>played</u> tennis. |
| **Revised:** | At camp, they enjoyed such activities as <u>swimming</u>, horseback <u>riding</u>, and <u>playing</u> tennis. |

## II ▷ *CLARITY OF WORD CHOICE*

### A. *Substitute Simple Words for Longer Words*

Many law students have the mistaken impression that, as an attorney, they should use sophisticated, formalistic language. To the contrary, effective attorneys take complex ideas and communicate them in simple, concrete, clear language. In the following illustration, notice how much easier it is to grasp the purpose of the sentence in the revised example:

| | |
|---|---|
| **Original:** | Defendant may <u>set forth the proposition</u> that, despite the <u>usage</u> of the garage by Michael as a getaway, the <u>edifice's</u> physical detachment from the Stripes' <u>principal place of habitation</u> prevents it from being a living quarters. |
| **Revised:** | Defendant may <u>argue</u> that, despite Michael's <u>use</u> of the garage as a getaway, the <u>garage's</u> physical detachment from the Stripes' <u>home</u> prevents it from being a living quarters. |

### B. *Use Active Verbs, Not Nominalizations*

As readers subconsciously search for "who did what to whom," they automatically think in terms of short, concrete active verbs. By writing in the active voice and using short active verbs that reflect exactly "who did what to whom," you will easily satisfy the reader's natural curiosity. To emphasize people and what they do, place the action in the sentence in the verb itself. As you review your writing for clarity, check to see whether you have inadvertently converted verbs into nouns. A verb that has been converted into a noun is called a "nominalization." Nominalizations obscure the action in a sentence—the action verb becomes a noun, while the remaining verb within the sentence often becomes a detached abstraction.

### *Example of How Nominalizations Obscure Clarity*

| | |
|---|---|
| **Original:** | Michael *engages in* <u>sleeping</u> *activities* on a futon in a loft area of the garage. |
| **Revised:** | Michael <u>sleeps</u> on a futon in a loft area of the garage. |

In the above example, the action verb "sleeps" becomes the noun "sleeping" in the original sentence. To replace the verb "sleeps," the writer necessarily has to use another verb. The replacement verb, "engages," is a detached abstraction that does not convey the action in the sentence.

### ✔ *Editing Tip:*

When reviewing your writing, ask yourself what the actor in the sentence is really doing.[2] In the above example, is Michael Stripe "sleeping" or is he "engaging?" As you consider whether you have inadvertently converted a verb into a noun, watch for words with the following endings:

| | | |
|---|---|---|
| ⇒ | tion | (e.g., *violation vs* violate) |
| ⇒ | sion | (e.g., *decision vs* decide) |
| ⇒ | ence | (e.g., *deterrence vs* deter) |
| ⇒ | ance | (e.g., *assistance vs* assist) |
| ⇒ | edge | (e.g., *knowledge vs* know) |
| ⇒ | ment | (e.g., *statement vs* state) |

## C.  Use Concrete, Specific Words Rather Than Vague, Abstract Language

Perhaps more so than in any other form of written communication, legal analysis must be communicated in specific language that clearly conveys the attorney's thinking. First, legal analysis often requires the reader to follow and absorb complex ideas that may have taken the drafting attorney literally days

---

[2] Laurel C. Oates, Anne Enquist & Kelly Kunsch, *The Legal Writing Handbook: Analysis, Research, and Writing* 644 (2d ed., Aspen L. & Bus. 1998).

or weeks to evaluate and analyze. Using concrete, specific words that have a definite meaning helps the reader readily absorb the complex analysis. Second, many words have specific legal significance. Thus, your choice of words can have tremendous ramifications. Loose, vague language could potentially propel your client into a lawsuit or cost the client significant sums of money.

First drafts often contain vague language, in part because ideas are often not fully crystallized until the drafting process itself reveals gaps in the writer's understanding. In short, vague language often reflects thinking that has not been fully developed. Therefore, as you review your early drafts it is very important to ask yourself probing questions: "What exactly do I mean by this statement?" "What exactly is the purpose of this paragraph?" You may find it helpful even to verbalize your questions. The goal is to find areas in your analysis that are not fully developed and clarify the written expression of your thinking.

In the following example, the vague language in the original illustration obscures the clarity of the writer's analysis. The revisions simply clarify the writer's thinking. Upon reviewing the first draft, the writer would have prompted the revision by asking: "what exact point do I want to make about the *Thomas* case? What exact point about the *Thomas* court's discussion of the garage am I trying to make here?"

---

**Original:**     In *Thomas*, the court discussed the garage . . .

**Revised:**     In *Thomas*, the court minimized the importance of the garage's physical attachment to the main residence.

---

## D.  Use the Proper Tense

It is important to use the proper tense when evaluating the law so that the reader can properly assess the sequence of events and the present status of factual events and the law. The present tense refers to facts or rules of law that exist as of the moment you are drafting a memo. The past tense refers to facts and events that are in the past—they happened before you began drafting the memo.

### 1.  Client's Factual Situation

When discussing a client's factual situation, use the past tense to refer to events that have already occurred, and use the present tense to refer to conditions that presently exist. Thus, in the following example, because the event that occurred on August 20<sup>th</sup> is in the past, the drafting attorney uses the past tense to refer to that event. In contrast, because the Stripe garage still exists today, the description of the garage is in the present tense.

---

On August 20, 2001, Defendant, Gerry Arnold, <u>forcibly entered</u> Carl and Rita Stripes' two-car detached garage and <u>removed</u> personal property belonging to them. The garage <u>is</u> located approximately thirty feet behind the Stripes' home.

---

## 2. Discussion of Precedent Case

The actual events that occurred and were reported in a case all occurred in the past. Therefore, use the past tense to describe the factual events of a case. Because the court's holding and reasoning also occurred in the past, refer to the court's holding and rationale in the past tense. However, when describing a rule of law that presently exists as you draft your memo, refer to the rule of law in the present tense.

### (a) Description of Actual Case "Events"—Past Tense

---

In *McIntyre*, the owners <u>used</u> the porch for such activities as "sitting, eating and cooking." . . . The court <u>held</u> that the attached porch was part of the living quarters of the home. The court <u>reasoned</u> that the owners used the porch as part of their living quarters by engaging in such activities as "sitting, eating, and cooking." . . .

---

### (b) Description of Rule of Law that Presently Exists—Present Tense

---

An enclosed, attached porch frequently used as part of a home's living quarters <u>is</u> a dwelling under the residential burglary statute.

---

## E. Strike the Appropriate Tone of Formality

Because legal analysis concerns matters that are important and serious to the client, your writing should avoid the informality of colloquialisms, or jargon. Moreover, unless the client is a minor, avoid referring to an individual client by first name, instead respectfully referring to the client by last name. Finally, avoid extensive use of the first person when drafting a legal document. As with colloquialisms and first names, extensive use of the first person implies a level of informality that is not appropriate in most legal writing.

## 1.   Eliminate Colloquialisms and Jargon

| | |
|---|---|
| **Original:** | During the summer and fall when his <u>folks</u> are in town, Mike <u>crashes</u> on a futon in the loft. |
| **Revised:** | During the summer and fall when his <u>parents</u> are in town, Michael Stripe <u>sleeps</u> on a futon in the loft area of the garage. |

## 2.   Refer to Adults by Last Names

| | |
|---|---|
| **Original:** | <u>Carl</u> and <u>Rita's</u> garage is located thirty feet behind their home. |
| **Revised:** | The Stripes' garage is located thirty feet behind their home. |
| **Or revised:** | Mr. and Mrs. Stripes' garage . . . |

## 3.   Avoid Using the First Person

| | |
|---|---|
| **Original:** | In <u>my opinion</u>, <u>we</u> can successfully prosecute Mr. Arnold under the Residential Burglary Statute. |
| **Revised:** | <u>The State</u> can successfully prosecute Mr. Arnold under the Residential Burglary Statute. |

In the above example, one of the first person references is also an example of "throat-clearing." Unless otherwise indicated, readers presume that the opinions expressed in a memo are the writer's opinion.

## F.  Avoid Sexist Language

In today's society, sexist language has the potential to offend a reviewing attorney, client, or adjudicator. Of course, if you are referring to a specific person who happens to be male, then you would refer to that person by the pronoun "he." For example, if you are referring to a specific defendant in a case who happens to be a male, use a pronoun that reflects his male gender. If, however, you are referring to people in general, rather than to a specific person, avoid using language that presumes the hypothetical person is a male. Because the English language has not evolved to the point where commonly-used gender-neutral phrases have replaced sexist phrases, avoiding sexist language skillfully and artfully takes some practice. The following examples illustrate different ways you can avoid using sexist language.

### 1.  Avoid the Generic Use of the Pronoun "He"

The most common way in which sexist language appears in the English language is through variations of the pronoun "he." Instead, try any of the following alternatives: (1) use the plural form rather than the singular form; (2) substitute other pronouns for the pronoun "he"; (3) omit pronouns altogether by rewriting the sentence to make the pronoun unnecessary; (4) substitute articles for the pronoun "he"; (5) repeat the original noun rather than refer to the pronoun "he"; or (6) if all else fails, refer generically to each gender—"he or she."[3]

#### (a)  Use the Plural Form

When converting a sentence from the singular to the plural form, check to make sure that you have also made the subject of the sentence plural. The subject, pronoun and verb must all reflect the same form.

---

[3] Ideas adapted from Linda H. Edwards, *Legal Writing: Process, Analysis and Organization* 223–224 (Aspen L. & Bus. 1996); Helene S. Shapo, *Writing and Analysis in the Law* 173 (3rd ed. Foundation Press 1993) (adapting recommendations from the "Guidelines for the Nonsexist Use of Language" written for the American Philosophical Association by Virginia L. Warren, published in 59 Proceedings and Addresses of American Philosophical Association, No. 3 (Feb. 1988)).

| | |
|---|---|
| **Original:** | Skilled writers know that a reader understands information best when <u>he is</u> presented with context before details. |
| **Revised:** | Skilled writers know that <u>readers</u> understand information best when <u>they are</u> presented with context before details. |
| **Not:** | Skilled writers know that a <u>reader</u> understands information best when <u>they are</u> presented with context before details. |

### (b)   Substitute Another Pronoun

| | |
|---|---|
| **Original:** | <u>He</u> should carefully evaluate every aspect of the legal problem in an office memorandum. |
| **Revised:** | <u>One</u> should carefully evaluate every aspect of the legal problem in an office memorandum. |

### (c)   Omit Pronouns Altogether

If the pronoun itself is not important, you can avoid sexist language by omitting the pronoun altogether.

| | |
|---|---|
| **Original:** | A skilled writer knows that a reader understands information best <u>when he is presented</u> with context before details. |
| **Revised:** | A skilled writer knows that a reader understands information best <u>when presented</u> with context before details. |

### (d)   Substitute Articles or Nouns for the Pronoun

| | |
|---|---|
| **Original:** | In an office memo, the writer should make sure that <u>he</u> carefully evaluates every aspect of the legal problem. |
| **Revised:** | <u>An office memo</u> should carefully evaluate every aspect of the legal problem. |

### (e)   Repeat the Original Name

| | |
|---|---|
| **Original:** | When preparing to draft an office memorandum, an attorney has two primary decisions to make. First, <u>he</u> must consider the actual substantive content of the memo. |
| **Revised:** | When preparing to draft an office memorandum, an attorney has two primary decisions to make. First, <u>the attorney</u> must consider the actual substantive content of the memo. |

### (f)   Refer Generically to Each Gender

| | |
|---|---|
| **Original:** | The Question Presented and Short Answer provide the reviewing attorney with a quick overview of the legal problem. The Discussion section provides the reviewing attorney with a more thorough analysis of the law when <u>he</u> has more time to consider a detailed analysis of the problem. |
| **Revised:** | The Question Presented and Short Answer provide the reviewing attorney with a quick overview of the legal problem. The Discussion section provides the reviewing attorney with a more thorough analysis of the law when <u>he or she</u> has more time to consider a detailed analysis of the problem. |

## 2.  *Avoid Generic Use of Gender-Specific Nouns*

Another common example of how the English language embraces sexist phrases is through the use of gender-specific nouns (e.g., "chairman"). To avoid this, whenever possible replace the gender-specific noun ("man") with a gender-neutral term ("person"). The following are some common examples of gender-specific nouns and their gender-neutral counterparts.

***Examples:***

| | | |
|---|---|---|
| Brother/sister | ⇒ | Sibling |
| Chairman | ⇒ | Chair or Chairperson |
| Fireman | ⇒ | Firefighter |
| Husband/wife | ⇒ | Spouse |
| Maid | ⇒ | Housekeeper |
| Mailman | ⇒ | Mail Carrier |
| Man, woman | ⇒ | Person |
| Newsman | ⇒ | News reporter |
| Policeman | ⇒ | Police Officer |
| Stewardess | ⇒ | Flight attendant |

## EXERCISE 2:
## CLARITY OF WORDS & SENTENCES

For each of the following sentences:

(1)  Identify and label each writing style problem that detracts from clarity and simplicity.

(2)  Rewrite each sentence to improve its clarity.

1.  A person who reasonably fears for his life has been held to be justified in killing the aggressor.

2.  The focus of the court will lie on whether Bing reasonably feared for his life.

3.  Having given chase to the defendant, the defendant was then surrounded by the four older boys.

4. The defendant in *People v. S.M.*, after waving a gun at the four older boys, and being chased by them until he was backed against a fence, and warning them that he would shoot them if they did not stop and/or fired a warning shot into the air, finally shot each of them while they charged at him.

5. The state questioned the validity of the defendant's fear, but the court upheld the jury's finding heretofore entered that his defense under the justification statute was valid.

6. The issue in this case revolves around the Illinois Justification statute and what constitutes reasonableness under the statute.

7. More closely analogous to this case would be the decision in *People v. S.M.*, a case involving the shooting of four boys by a defendant, which was determined to be in self-defense under the justification statute.

8. Prosecution of Bing has commenced under the homicide and manslaughter statutes.

9. There is sufficient proof allowing one to logically conclude that Bing acted consistently with the justification statute, that being; acting with a reasonable belief that such force was necessary to prevent imminent death or great bodily harm to himself.

10. The court's reasoning places strong emphasis on the defendant's efforts to avoid.

11. Newton, a friend who also witnessed the first part of the attack, was slashed in the arm when he was in the process of pulling Geller off of Bing.

12. A criminal complaint has been filed against Bing to prosecute him for homicide and manslaughter.

13. Like the defendant in *S.M.*, Bing tried to fend off his aggressor by waving a gun, but the aggressor would not be deterred but kept charging Bing, and Bing tried to warn Geller that he would have to shoot him, but Geller replied that "only one of us is going to walk out of here alive," such that Bing was forced to shoot Geller.

## III   *EFFECTIVE USE OF QUOTATIONS*

Because it is critical to convey the law accurately, the use of quotations is very important in legal writing. Nevertheless, novice legal writers often rely too heavily on case quotations. A blind reliance on quotations can create several problems. First, many statutes and court decisions are not models of clarity. Although judges may admonish attorneys to write clearly, many judges do not follow their own advice. Thus, quoting a poorly-written sentence from a case would not serve your goal of clear communication. Second, by relying heavily on quotations you may be tempted to neglect your own careful predrafting synthesis of the relevant cases. Third, you will refer to legal standards and factors by specific language; that specific language will assume legal significance to the reader. If a court has not used that identical language when referring to the legal standard or factor, the reader may fail to see the link between the legally significant information in a roadmap paragraph and the information from a case. Finally, every writer has a unique style. It can be disconcerting to a reader to jump frequently from your style to the various writing styles of different judges or legislation. Therefore, your goal is to find the proper balance between a blind reliance on quotations and a failure to use quotations at all.

### A.   *Quotations from Cases*

Effective attorneys use case quotations sparingly and with purpose, quoting only vitally important components of a relevant case whose meaning might otherwise be lost if paraphrased. Therefore, you might quote critical parts of a court's reasoning. In quoting critical language from a court decision, you need not quote an entire sentence. Instead, the most effective case quotations often reflect only a single critical word or phrase from a decision. You should quote an entire paragraph only in very limited circumstances when the court has so clearly and beautifully articulated a critical point that any attempt to paraphrase would not capture the meaning of the quoted language. Whether quoting language or paraphrasing ideas, you must *always* cite to the source of your quotation.

### 1.   *Example of Effective Case Quotations*

In the following example, the drafting attorney quotes select critical phrases from the court's holding and reasoning, and then comments on the significance of the quoted language.

> The court held that the attached garage, "at least in this instance," was not a living quarters. *Id.* The court reasoned that "an attached garage is *not necessarily* a 'dwelling' within the meaning of the residential burglary statute." *Id.* (emphasis added). By that statement, the court implied that the owner's use of the structure is more important than its proximity to the main residence.

### 2.   *Example of Ineffective Case Quotations*

In the following example, note how the writer has quoted the court's observations about the facts of the case, as well as the entire holding and stated rationale. This approach of "throwing in the kitchen sink" is not effective. Rarely does the manner in which the court states the facts merit a direct quote (unless the court has quoted a witness whose testimony the attorney would like to emphasize). Moreover, by quoting the court's holding and reasoning in its entirety, the significance of the truly critical language is all but lost (i.e., "these activities make the porch part of the living quarters of the house.").

> In *McIntyre*, the court was "satisfied this porch was a part of the Houser's living quarters." 578 N.E.2d at 315. In *McIntyre*, the owners used an attached porch "in the summer for most of their meals, and in the winter cooked on the porch four or five times per week." *Id.* "The Housers furnished the porch with a metal table, chairs, a wrought iron love seat, a small table and a large gas grill." *Id.* The court held that, "in our view, the porch here is a part of the house. It is attached, enclosed, and used for sitting, eating, and cooking. These activities make the porch part of the living quarters of the house. This conclusion is not inconsistent with *Thomas*." *Id.*

## B.   *Quotations from Statutes*

When discussing statutory issues, you should quote the critical language from the statute because it is the source of law under evaluation. However, if a statute is poorly written and difficult to follow, paraphrase the non-critical language of the statute, quoting only the specific statutory words or phrases at issue. Alternatively, you might quote most of the statutory language but insert transitional words between the elements to make the language more readable. When there are a number of different statutory elements, you might use numbers as transitions, numbering each separate element for clarity.

### 1.  Example of Paraphrasing & Quoting Statutory Language

Under the Dog Bite Statute, the plaintiff must prove that: (1) he was "peaceably conducting himself" (2) in a "place where he may lawfully be" (3) when, "without provocation," a dog owned by the defendant (4) "attacked or injured" him. 510 Ill. Comp. Stat. § 5/16 (1993).

### 2.  Example of Quoting the Statutory Language

The State must prove that the defendant "knowingly and without authority enter[ed] the *dwelling place* of another." 720 Ill. Comp. Stat. § 5/19-3 (1993) (emphasis added). The statute defines a dwelling as "a house, apartment, mobile home, trailer or *other living quarters* in which . . . the owners or occupants *actually reside. . . .*" 720 Ill. Comp. Stat. § 5/2-6(b) (1993)(emphasis added).

# 17

# FINALIZING THE MEMO: CITATION FORM

 **I ▷ LEGAL CITATION**

## A. The Basics of Legal Citation

### 1. Citations as a Means of Finding Law

The sources of law and the court opinions that interpret them are all reported in books and on-line. These reporting services would not be helpful to you if you did not know how to locate specific rules of law and the cases that are reported within the books and on-line. Legal citations provide the means of locating statutes, constitutions, cases and articles that are written about the law.

Obviously the legal citation system must be published and the rules must be fairly uniform so that attorneys and judges can follow and understand the significance of a particular citation. Two books publish the rules of citation that are most commonly followed by attorneys and judges: the ALWD Citation Manual and the Bluebook. You will likely use one of these books to learn about citation rules, or your professor may have assigned both books for you to use as reference guides. Both books address the same citation issues and generally teach the same citation rules. Thus, as a practicing attorney, whether you use the ALWD Citation Manual or the Bluebook should result in the same citations. The minor variations in citation between the ALWD Manual and the Bluebook are no more significant than the minor variations between the seventeen editions of the Bluebook.

The most significant difference between the ALWD Citation Manual and the Bluebook is their treatment of legal citations that appear in law review articles. The Bluebook contains specialized typeface rules for legal citations that appear in law review articles, while the ALWD Manual does not make such a distinction. However, that distinction for law review articles will not affect the legal citations you draft in your legal writing course. In a legal writing course, you will be drafting the types of documents that practicing attorneys draft, not law review articles.

### 2.   Citations as a Means of Showing Support for Your Analysis

Legal citations will also be important to you in your drafting role. Each of the ideas and arguments expressed in your written work must be properly supported by citation. You likely already know that you must cite to an authority when you have quoted from that authority or have paraphrased language from an authority. However, in the practice of law, you must also cite to a source whenever you have taken an *idea* from a source. In addition, it is good practice to acknowledge your source when your own analysis or conclusion builds on that source. Citing to an authority enhances the persuasive appeal of your arguments. You have informed the reader that this idea is not only your own, but that an author or court also agrees with that idea. Within the legal community, it is considered plagiarism to fail to attribute a source from whom you have taken an idea. And, of course, it is also considered plagiarism to fail to attribute the sources of any quoted language or paraphrased language. Later in this chapter, you will learn how to cite to authority within your own writing.

## B.   ALWD Citation Manual

If you are using the ALWD Manual, continue reading this *Section B*. If you are reading the Bluebook, skip to *Section C*. Before learning the nuts and bolts of legal citation, it is important to become acquainted with the ALWD Manual itself. As you read this section, pick up your ALWD Manual and find the different sections that are discussed.

1.   Open your ALWD Manual and turn to the inside front and back covers. The inside front cover contains a "Fast Format Locator" for different topics. For example, if you wanted to know how to cite to a case, the front cover instructs you to turn to page 57 of the book. The inside back cover of the book contains a "Short Citation Locator" for common sources. As you will discover later in this chapter, you will not always cite to a source in its full form; sometimes you will take a shortcut and refer to the source in an abbreviated form. The inside back cover simply informs you of the exact rule numbers to which you can refer if you want to use an abbreviated citation form.

2.  Following the Table of Contents, Part 1 of the ALWD Manual contains such introductory material as the purpose and use of citations and how to use this book

3.  Part 2 of the ALWD Manual provides the basic citation rules that govern all sources, including typeface for citations, the basic rules for citing to pages, sections and paragraphs in a source, and an introduction to full and short citation formats. The first page of Part 2 contains a list of the rules that are covered within Part 2, including the rule numbers and the pages on which you can find each rule.

4.  Turn to the first page of Part 3 of the ALWD Manual. As the title for Part 3 reflects, Part 3 contains the citation rules for specific print sources. Again, the first page of Part 3 provides a list of the rules covered in Part 3, including the rule numbers and the pages on which you can find each rule. Because there are numerous print sources, this section of the book is fairly lengthy. However, the citation rules for cases and statutes are two of the rules you will use most frequently.

    (a)  *Case citations*: Turn to Rule 12, the rule that governs case citations. Note that Rule 12 (like every other rule in Part 3) contains an initial page of "Fast Formats." As you peruse the Fast Formats, notice that this page illustrates the common citation forms for federal and state cases in both print and electronic form. Turning the page, note that Rule 12.1 illustrates the various components of a full case citation. Particularly in the beginning, you may find it helpful to refer to this illustration as well as the illustrations in the Fast Formats.

         As you peruse the rest of Rule 12, note the "Sidebars" that contain helpful explanations of certain aspects of case citations. For example, Sidebar 12.3 explains commonly used phrases and terms (page 67). Rule 12 also contains helpful charts. For example, turn to Chart 12.1, at page 68, which illustrates the abbreviations for the reporters that report cases.

    (b)  *Statutory citations*: Next turn to Rule 14, which covers the citation rules for statutory codes, session laws and slip laws. Notice, again, that the introductory page to Rule 14 contains Fast Formats that illustrate the common citation forms for federal and state states statutes, session laws and slip laws (page 101). Again, as with each rule section, this section of the ALWD Manual contains Sidebars that explain certain information that might not otherwise be clear to you.

(c)   As you peruse the book, turn to Rule 29, at page 231. As the intro-
      ductory page to Rule 29 indicates, this rule informs you of the cita-
      tion rules that apply to court documents, transcripts and appellate re-
      cords. The Fast Formats illustrate how you would cite to such
      common court documents as an affidavit, a hearing transcript or a
      discovery document.

5.   Part 4 of the ALWD Manual contains the citation rules for electronic
     sources and neutral citations. You may from time to time cite to sources
     you find on Lexis or Westlaw or on the Web. At page 272, Sidebar 38.1
     discusses the instances in which you might cite to an electronic source
     rather than a print source and the practical considerations involved in
     your decision.

6.   Part 5 of the ALWD Manual contains the citation rules for incorporating
     citations into your written work. The rules within Part 5 inform you of
     how to incorporate case citations into a legal document (Rule 44), how to
     use introductory signals (Rule 45), how to order your citations if you are
     citing more than one source to support an idea (Rule 46), and how to use
     parentheticals to explain why a citation is relevant (Rule 47).

7.   Part 6 of the ALWD Manual contains the citation rules that govern the
     use of quotations, including how to cite to a source when you have altered
     the quoted material (Rule 49).

8.   Finally, turn to the Appendices towards the back of the book. Appendix 1
     contains citation information about the court systems, reporters and
     statutory compilations for each jurisdiction within the United States. The
     jurisdictions are organized alphabetically, beginning with state jurisdic-
     tions (from Alabama to Wyoming) and ending with federal materials.
     Appendix 2 contains local citation rules or preferences issued by each
     state jurisdiction. Again, the jurisdictions are organized alphabetically.
     Appendices 3, 4 and 5 describe the basic abbreviations for common
     terms, courts and legal periodicals. Finally, Appendix 6 illustrates how
     the citation rules would be incorporated into a sample office memo.

## C.  The Bluebook

If you are using the Bluebook, continue reading this *Section C*. If you are
using the ALWD Citation Manual, skip this section and review instead *Section
B*. The Bluebook is published by several law review associations. Before
learning the nuts and bolts of legal citation, it is important to become ac-

quainted with the Bluebook itself. As you read this section, pick up your Bluebook and find the different sections that are discussed.

1.  Open your Bluebook and turn to the inside front and back covers. The inside front cover illustrates common citation forms for law review articles; the inside back cover illustrates common citation forms for court documents and legal memoranda. The covers are an easy means of finding more detailed discussions of citation rules—each citation contains a reference to the rule that governs that citation. In addition, the outside back cover of the Bluebook provides a thumbnail sketch of the rules that govern different sources.

2.  Turn to the white pages in the very beginning of the Bluebook. This Introduction explains and illustrates the basic rules of citation.

3.  Next turn to the blue pages in the very front of the Bluebook that follow the introductory section. These pages contain the citation rules that apply to practicing attorneys (Practitioners' Notes). In this course you will be learning how to cite to the law as a practicing attorney. Therefore, this section will be of particular importance to you.

4.  The white pages that follow the blue Practitioners' Notes contain general rules of citation and style. Be careful, however, because some of the typeface requirements and other rules relate specifically to the citation form used in law review articles and do not apply to practitioners.

    (a)  *Case citations*: Turn to Rule 10 of the Bluebook. You will refer to this rule frequently because it contains the citation rules for cases. The first page of Rule 10 illustrates the various components of a case citation.

    (b)  *Statutory citations*: Rules 11, 12, 13 and 14 of the Bluebook contain the rules of citation for constitutions, statutes, and legislative, administrative and executive materials. Again, the first page of each rule contains illustrations of legal citations for the various sources. These illustrations can be an easy reference tool to use when you want to verify the accuracy of your citation form.

5.  The blue pages in the middle of the book contain descriptions of the courts, reporters and statutory sources in every jurisdiction, and their proper abbreviations. Table 1 is arranged alphabetically, beginning with the United States, and then by state, beginning with Alabama and ending with Wyoming.

6.   Tables 5 through 17, also located within the blue pages in the middle of the book, contain the citation rules for abbreviating various case and court names and other terms.

7.   Turn to the Index at the back of the Bluebook to familiarize yourself with its content. The Index is very detailed and can often be a helpful resource in finding specific citation rules that govern a source you would like to cite. For example, if you wished to review the rules on how to cite to a secondary authority, the Index lists the different secondary authorities and the pages that discuss them under "Secondary authorities."

## D.  Basic Citation Forms

There are three basic ways of citing to legal authority: (1) in the full citation format that is required whenever an authority is cited for the first time in a legal document (e.g., *People v. McIntyre*, 578 N.E.2d 314 (Ill. App. Ct. 1991)); (2) in an abbreviated version after the authority has already been cited in full form (e.g., *Id.* at 315); and (3) in a broad textual reference to an authority that has already been discussed (e.g., "Like the porch in *McIntyre*, the Stripes' garage was used as a living quarters"). This chapter will explain each way of citing to legal authority.

### 1.  Citation to Statutes

A statutory citation contains four basic components that are cited in the following order:

---

1. The *title or chapter number* (if the code has them);

2. The name of the *code* in which the statute is contained;

3. Within the code book, the particular *section* of the statute; and

4. The *date* of the code book.


The citation rules for statutes are described in:

*ALWD Rules 14.2 & 14.4* and *Appendix 1*
*Bluebook Rules 12.1, 12.2 & 12.3* and *Table 1*

---

### (a)  Illustration of Federal Statutory Citation (the United States Code):

> (1)  (2)       (3)       (4)
> Title Code   Section   Date
> ⇓   ⇓         ⇓         ⇓
> 18 U.S.C. § 1962(a) (2000).

### (b)  Illustration of State Statutory Citation:

> (2)              (3)     (4)
> Code           Section  Date
> ⇓               ⇓        ⇓
> Mich Comp. Laws. § 37.203 (1985).

### (c)  Pathfinder to Statutory Citations:

The first time you cite to a statute in a written document you must cite it in full, mindful of the applicable citation rules that you must follow. Both the ALWD Manual and the Bluebook provide an easy way to map out a citation for specific statutes. Simply turn to Table 1 (ALWD Manual) or Appendix 1 (Bluebook) and find the jurisdiction of the statute you are interested in citing. For example, assume you are researching the law in Wisconsin on hazardous waste and want to cite a statute that describes the penalties for violating the statute. You have the section number, 289.96, and you know that the code book containing section 289.96 was published in 1999. To find out how to cite to this section of Wisconsin's statutes, turn to the Wisconsin section of Table 1 or Appendix 1. Under the Wisconsin heading, note the references to "Statutory Compilations" within that jurisdiction. Under that heading, both the ALWD Manual and the Bluebook illustrate the manner in which Wisconsin statutes should be cited. You need only copy the format and insert the specific section number and year into your citation. Thus, your citation would read as follows:

Wis. Stat. § 289.96 (1999).

*Caveat*: Remember that the Bluebook illustrates citations that would appear in a law review article. However, as Practitioner's Note 1 reflects, in ordinary legal memos and court documents, you should use ordinary typeface rather than the specialized typeface that appears in law review articles (e.g., large and small capped letters). Therefore, in following the illustration in Appendix 1 of the Bluebook, you would ignore the large and small capped letters and instead use ordinary typeface. Because the ALWD Manual makes no typeface distinction for citations that appear in legal periodicals and citations that practitioners use, your citation should follow the format and typeface of the ALWD illustrations.

## 2.  *Citation to Cases*

A full case citation includes five basic pieces of information, which appear in the following order:

---

1. The *name of the parties* in the case, properly abbreviated;

2. Where the case can be found, including:

   (a)  The *volume number* of the reporter that reports the case,
   (b)  The abbreviated *name* of that reporter, and
   (c)  The first *page* of the reporter in which the case can be found;

3. The *court* that decided the case, properly abbreviated;

4. The *year* the court decided the case; and

5. If relevant, the case's *later history* (e.g., whether it was affirmed or reversed).

The citation rules for cases are described in:

*ALWD Rule 12* and *Appendices 1 & 3*
*Bluebook Rule 10* and *Tables 1 & 6*

---

## (a)  *Illustration of Federal Court Case*

---

*(1) Name of Parties   (2) Reporter   (3) Court   (4) Date*
⇓                    ⇓             ⇓           ⇓
*United States v. Mora*, 821 F.2d 837 (5th Cir. 1975).

---

### (b)  Illustration of State Court Case

> (1) Name of Parties    (2) Reporter    (3) Court  (4) Date
> ⇓                  ⇓                ⇓         ⇓
> *People v. Lamkey*, 608 N.E.2d 406 (Ill. App. Ct. 1993).

### (c)  Citing to a Specific Page of a Case

When you cite to a case as your source for a specific idea that is contained within a particular page of the opinion, you must include that specific page within your citation. In a full case citation, simply insert the specific page of the case immediately following the first page of the case opinion. Separate the first page and the relevant page of the case with a comma. For example, suppose you wanted to refer to page 408 of the *Lamkey* decision. Your case citation would look like this:

> Specific Pg.
> ⇓
> *People v. Lamkey*, 608 N.E.2d 406, 408 (Ill. App. Ct. 1993).
> ⇑
> Initial Pg.
> of Case

### (d)  Pathfinder to Case Citation

Until you become familiar with the rules of case citation, citing cases is a bit more challenging than citing to statutes because you can not turn to Table 1 or Appendix 1 and find an easy map to follow for each jurisdiction. Instead, take careful note of the format for case citations. The format in which citation information is presented does not change from jurisdiction to jurisdiction (other than for United States Supreme Court decisions, in which the court's name is not included within the citation). Think of the citation format as a set formula that you will fill in with specific information about the case you are citing. The formula looks like this:

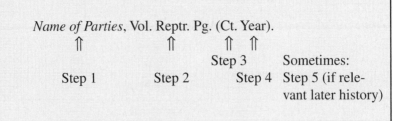

*Name of Parties*, Vol. Reptr. Pg. (Ct. Year).
    ⇑                    ⇑          ⇑  ⇑
                              Step 3      Sometimes:
        Step 1           Step 2      Step 4   Step 5 (if rele-
                                              vant later history)

### (i)  Filling in the Formula Using the ALWD Manual

| | |
|---|---|
| Step 1: Filling in the *Party Names* | ⇒ Review Rule 12.2 and then review Appendix 3 to find the appropriate abbreviations for any party names. |
| Step 2: Filling in the *Reporter* | ⇒ Turn to Appendix 1 and find the jurisdiction of the case you are citing (e.g., Wisconsin). Find the appropriate abbreviation for the reporter you are citing (*e.g.*, N.W.2d). Conforming to the formula above, insert the volume number of the reporter before the reporter abbreviation and the page number following the reporter abbreviation. Review Rule 12.4 for a detailed explanation. |
| Step 3: Filling in the *Court* | ⇒ You have already opened the ALWD Manual to Appendix 1 and the jurisdiction you are citing. Within that jurisdiction, find the court that decided the case you are citing (e.g., Wisconsin Supreme Court). Table 1 indicates the proper abbreviation for the court's name by indicating the name within a parenthetical following the court's name (*e.g.*, Wis.). Review Rule 12.6 for a detailed explanation. |
| Step 4: Filling in the *Date* | ⇒ Fill in the year the court decided the case following the abbreviated designation for the court that decided the case, and within the same parenthetical. Review Rule 12.7 for a detailed explanation. |

| Step 5: Filling in *Later History* | ⇒ If the case was later affirmed or reversed, you will also need to include that information within the cite. In certain cases, you should indicate whether an appeal was denied. If your case has later history, review Rule 12.8. That rule both describes when you must include later history and illustrates how to include later history within a citation. |
|---|---|
| If you are submitting a document to a court | ⇒ Turn to Appendix 2 and find the jurisdiction of the case you are citing. Make note of any local court rules of which you should be aware (*e.g.*, requiring parallel citations or references to specific reporters). |

### (ii)  Filling in the Formula Using the Bluebook

| Step 1: Filling in the *Party Names* | ⇒ Review Rule 10.2 and Practitioners' Note 1(a) and then review Table 6 to find the appropriate abbreviations for any party names. |
|---|---|
| Step 2: Filling in the *Reporter* | ⇒ Turn to Table 1 and find the jurisdiction of the case you are citing (*e.g.*, Wisconsin). Find the appropriate abbreviation for the reporter you are citing (*e.g.*, N.W.2d). Conforming to the formula above, insert the volume number of the reporter before the reporter abbreviation and the page number following the reporter abbreviation. Review Rule 10.3 for a detailed explanation. |
| Step 3: Filling in the *Court* | ⇒ You have already opened the Bluebook to Table 1 and the jurisdiction you are citing. Within that jurisdiction, find the court that decided the case you are citing (e.g., Wisconsin Supreme Court). Table 1 indicates the proper abbreviation for the court's name by indicating the name within a parenthetical following the court's name (*e.g.*, Wis.). Review Rule 10.4 for a detailed explanation. |

| Step 4: Filling in the *Date* | ⇒ Fill in the year the court decided the case following your abbreviated designation for the court that decided the case, and within the same parenthetical. Review Rule 10.5 for a detailed explanation. |
|---|---|
| Step 5: Filling in *Later History* | ⇒ If the case was later affirmed or reversed, you will also need to include that information within the cite. In certain cases, you should indicate whether an appeal was denied. If your case has later history, review Rules 10.6, 10.7 and Practitioners' Note 1(d). These rules describe when you must include later history and illustrate how to include later history within a citation. |
| If you are submitting a document to a court | ⇒ The Bluebook does not reference local court rules. However, if you are submitting a document to a court, you should check to see whether there are any local court rules with which you must also comply (*e.g.*, requiring parallel citation, references to specific reporters). |

## 3.  Acceptable Abbreviated Versions of Citations

When you draft legal documents, you will often cite to a particular case or statute many times within a single document. Your citation task would be very burdensome if you were required to cite the case or statute in full citation form each time you cited it. Repeatedly referring to the same case or statute in full citation form would also add unnecessary length to your document. Therefore, after you have cited a case or statute in full, both the ALWD Manual and the Bluebook allow you to take a short-cut when you later refer to the same source. There are four acceptable ways of citing to an authority in an abbreviated version. An abbreviated version of a legal citation is commonly called a "short-form" citation. When selecting an appropriate short-form citation, your paramount concern should be your reader. Always consider the reader's perspective and the form that would be easiest for the reader to follow. The four ways of referring to an authority in short-form are:

1.  *Lamkey*, 608 N.E.2d at 409.
    This form is generally used when the previous citation to the case was on an earlier page of the discussion.

2.  608 N.E.2d at 409.
    This form is generally used when the case name, or part of the case name, is included in the textual sentence preceding the citation.

3.  *Id.* at 409.
    This form is used when *Lamkey* was the case cited *immediately* before this reference. The term "*Id.*" means simply: refer to the immediately preceding cite. If *Lamkey* was the immediate previous cite, use "*Id.*" rather than options 1 or 2.

4.  *Id.*
    This form is used when *page 409* of *Lamkey* was cited immediately before this reference and the immediate reference is also to page 409. Because the immediate citation also referred to page 409, no specific page reference is necessary. Again, do not use options 1 or 2 when *Id.* is appropriate.

*ALWD Rule 12.21.*
*Bluebook Practitioners' Note 4.*

### 4.  *Broad Textual References by Name Only*

At times, you will want to refer to a statute or case only in very general terms. Under appropriate circumstances, it is also acceptable to make textual references to a case or statute by simply referring to the authority by name (e.g., "As in *Lamkey*, the client . . ."). If you have already discussed a case and simply wish to make a general reference back to the case, it is acceptable to refer to the case by its name, or by one of the parties' names. If citing to just one of the parties' names, cite to the plaintiff's name unless that name is so common that its reference would cause confusion. For example, the full name of the *Lamkey* case is *People v. Lamkey*. Because the name "*People*" would cause confusion, the defendant's name is used instead. (ALWD Rule 12.21(c)).

Referring back to a case in general terms often occurs in the rule application section of a memo. Assume you have already discussed a case and want to refer to the case again to indicate a factual analogy to a client's situation. You might simply state:

> Like the owners in *McIntyre*, Michael Stripe also used his garage get-a-way as part of the home's living quarters.

## E.   When and How Often to Cite

As the beginning of this chapter discussed, you must cite to your source any time you: (1) quote from an authority; (2) paraphrase from an authority; (3) take an idea from an authority; or (4) any time your analysis or conclusion builds on an authority. Therefore, you should provide the reader with a specific citation that supports each new idea you introduce.

How does this rule of citation fit within the context of an office memo or persuasive argument? Consider for a moment the rule explanation section of a memo. If you take an idea from a case, you must cite to the case as your authority. Your citation would look like this:

> A structure is considered a living quarters when the owners frequently use the structure for activities that occur in a living quarters, and the furnishings reflect that use. *People v. McIntyre*, 578 N.E.2d 314 (Ill. App. Ct. 1991). Although a structure's attachment to the main residence is also relevant, physical attachment to the primary residence is not necessary. *People v. Thomas*, 561 N.E.2d 57 (Ill. 1990).

Assume, however, that you wish to discuss an important case at some length, describing not only the relevant rule of law it expresses, but its case facts, holding and rationale. Most attorneys do not provide a separate page cite following each sentence of the case discussion. That would be distracting to the reader. Instead, a good rule of thumb is to insert page cites: (1) at the end of each paragraph of the case discussion; *and* (2) following any quoted text from the case; *and* (3) when the page or section of the cited material changes. (ALWD Rule 44.2). Your citations in a lengthy case discussion would look like this:

An enclosed, attached porch frequently used as part of the home's living quarters is a dwelling under the residential burglary statute. *People v. McIntyre*, 578 N.E.2d 314 (Ill. App. Ct. 1991). In *McIntyre*, the owners used an attached, screened porch for "sitting, eating and cooking." *Id*. at 315. They ate most of their meals on the porch in the summer and cooked meals there four or five times a week in the winter. The owners furnished the porch with wrought-iron furniture and a barbecue grill that reflected its use. The porch was enclosed, locked, and attached to the home. The court held that, under these facts, the porch was a "living quarters" under the Statute. *Id*.

* 1ˢᵗ time case is cited: full cite.

* Following quoted text, *Id*. is proper. Because the page differs, it becomes: *Id*. at 315.

* *Id*. at end of paragraph.

The court reasoned that the owners used the porch as part of their living quarters by engaging in such activities as "sitting, eating, and cooking." *Id*. In addition, the owners regularly used the porch in this manner and furnished the porch with furniture and a grill that reflected such use. The court also observed that the porch was enclosed and attached to the house, indicating that the porch's physical attachment to the house was a relevant factor. However, the court emphasized that it was the activities of "sitting, eating, and cooking" that "make the porch part of the living quarters of the house." *Id*.

* *Id*. following quote. Because page remains the same, the signal is simply: "*Id*."

* *Id*. following quote & at end of paragraph.

## F.   *Where to Insert Citations in Sentences*

### 1.   *When the Cite Supports the Entire Sentence*

When an authority supports an entire sentence, insert the citation after the sentence, making the citation itself its own sentence. By inserting the citation after the sentence rather than within the sentence, you will avoid cluttering the ideas expressed in your sentence with detailed citation information. A citation that supports an entire sentence looks like this:

A structure is considered a living quarters when the owners frequently use the structure for activities that occur in a living quarters, and the furnishings reflect that use. *People v. McIntyre*, 578 N.E.2d 314 (Ill. App. Ct. 1991).

## 2.   When the Cite Supports Only Part of the Sentence

Sometimes an authority supports only part of a sentence. In that case, insert the citation immediately after the text it concerns. If the citation is within the middle of the sentence, set off the citation with commas. If the citation is at the end of the sentence, follow the citation with a period rather than a comma. (ALWD Rule 44.1(b) and Bluebook Practitioner's Note 2). The following example is excerpted from Rule 44.1(b) of the ALWD Manual:

---

Although the Fourth Amendment prohibits unreasonable searches and seizures, *Elkins v. United States*, 364 U.S. 206, 222 (1960), each case must be decided on its own facts and circumstances, *Harris v. United States*, 331 U.S. 145, 150 (1947).

---

The above citation format is perfectly acceptable. However, even in this very simple sentence, notice how the citation within the middle of the sentence interferes a bit with the flow of ideas. Therefore, if you are attempting to insert citations into a fairly lengthy, complex sentence, consider separating the sentence into two sentences. In that manner, the citations themselves can be relegated to the end of each separate sentence. Although the above sentence is short enough that it does not need to be separated, it could be separated by removing the "although" and creating two sentences, as follows:

---

The Fourth Amendment prohibits unreasonable searches and seizures. *Elkins v. United States*, 364 U.S. 206, 222 (1960). However, each case must be decided on its own facts and circumstances. *Harris v. United States*, 331 U.S. 145, 150 (1947).

---

## G.   Using Explanatory Parentheticals

There will be instances in which you will want to cite to a case or other authority for a very specific purpose that does not require a lengthy textual discussion. For example, a case might contain a very specific idea that bolsters your analysis of another case or argument, yet the citation, standing alone, would not adequately convey the significance of the case citation. Under such circumstances, an explanatory parenthetical can be an effective means of conveying the information. (*See* ALWD Rule 47 and Bluebook Rule 1.5 for a discussion of explanatory parentheticals). In deciding whether to include an explanatory parenthetical, consider whether the information you want to convey in a parenthetical is simplistic and concrete enough for a parenthetical reference. If the information you want to convey will require some explanation in order for the reader to understand its importance, discuss the case in a textual discussion rather than in a parenthetical.

The key to using an explanatory parenthetical effectively is to be very clear about the purpose of the parenthetical. Before even attempting to draft the parenthetical, identify first in your own mind the specific way in which the case supports your analysis. A poorly drafted explanatory parenthetical only ends up confusing the reader. Consider the following two examples of an explanatory parenthetical following a citation to the *Allen* case:

---

**Example 1:** It is foreseeable that children will trespass on property when the property contains a pond that is attractive and alluring to children and is both visible and accessible from an area that children frequent. *Ansin v. Thurston*, 98 So. 2d 87 (Fla. Dist. Ct. App. 1957). In *Ansin*, the defendant's property contained an artificial pond with white sand banks, a floating dock, and a raft. A child drowned in the pond after playing on the raft. The court upheld a jury's finding that the presence of child trespassers was reasonably foreseeable, holding that it was "certain that children would be attracted to such a place. . . ." *Id.* at 88. The court reasoned that the pond was both visible and accessible to children, as it was close to well-traveled streets and homes. Moreover, the property was seven blocks from an elementary school. *Id. See also Allen v. William P. McDonald Corp.*, 42 So. 2d 706, 707 (Fla. 1949) (holding that the owner should have foreseen the presence of trespassing children).

---

In Example 1 above, the explanatory parenthetical at the end of the paragraph fails to provide any additional useful information to the reader. There is not enough factual information within the parenthetical for the reader to understand the way in which the *Allen* case bolsters the writer's analysis of the *Ansin* case. The fact that the *Allen* case has a similar holding to the *Ansin* case is not enough to merit a parenthetical. Removing the parenthetical would not eliminate the confusion. The citation, standing alone, would make the reader question why the case has been cited as all. Does the *Allen* case also involve children trespassing on property that is seven blocks from an elementary school? Therefore, the solution is not merely to remove the parenthetical but to reconsider why the *Allen* case has been cited at all. Upon further reflection, the writer decided that the court's holding about trespassing children, together with a few key facts that supported the holding, bolstered the writer's analysis of the *Ansin* case. Consider the added clarity of the revised explanatory parenthetical below:

> **Example 2:** . . . *See also Allen v. William P. McDonald Corp.*, 42 So. 2d 706, 707 (Fla. 1949) (holding that white sand banks adjacent to a pond were sufficiently alluring and attractive to children to entice them to trespass).

## H. Using Introductory Signals

When citing a case merely to show support for a line of analysis, sometimes an introductory signal can clarify the reason you are citing the case. For example, the *Allen* case illustrated in the above example is introduced with the signal "*See also.*" This signal indicates that the *Allen* case supports the preceding analysis. (ALWD Rule 45 and Bluebook Rules 1.2 and 1.3 discuss the purpose of introductory signals and how to use them.) Do not use signals when: (1) the purpose of your citation is otherwise clear; (2) the citation simply identifies the source of a quotation; or (3) the citation directly supports the preceding statement. (ALWD Rule 45.2; Bluebook Rule 1.2(a)). Thus, most of your citations should not require introductory signals. In fact, because of the ambiguity surrounding the meaning of certain introductory signals, try and use introductory signals sparingly. Since 1947, every edition of the Bluebook changed the definitions of signals in some way.[1] The changes made in the 16th edition were particularly troublesome, as that edition reversed the previous meaning of the signal "*see.*" After being uniformly criticized, the 17th edition reverted to the earlier definition of *see* that was contained within the 15th edition. As a consequence, certain introductory signals may mean different things to different attorneys and judges, depending on the version of the Bluebook they use. Nevertheless, there are still situations when an introductory signal is appropriate. For example, a signal should be used to introduce a citation that contains an explanatory parenthetical because the signal helps clarify the purpose of the explanatory parenthetical.

 **EXERCISE 1**

In the overview paragraph below, assume that the applicable statute can be found in chapter 720 of the Illinois statutes. The quoted statutory section is

---

[1] Richard K. Neumann, Jr., *Legal Reasoning and Legal Writing: Structure, Strategy, and Style* 243 (Aspen L. & Bus. 4th ed. 2001).

contained within section 5/10-1. The volume that reports this statute was published in 1993.

Rewrite the overview paragraph below to incorporate the appropriate citations.

---

For the State to prosecute Mr. Tate for aggravated kidnapping, it must prove that Mr. Tate "knowingly . . . and secretly confined another against his will . . . while armed with a dangerous weapon." There is no real dispute that Mr. Tate "confined another against his will" or that he was armed with a "dangerous weapon" because he tied Mr. Campbell to a chair and shot him with a gun. While the "knowingly" requirement might possibly be an issue due to Mr. Tate's apparent intoxication, you have requested that this memorandum focus only on whether Mr. Tate's actions satisfy the "secretly" requirement.

---

  **EXERCISE 2**

In the thesis paragraph below, assume that the definition of the term "secretly," was derived from the *People v. Franzen* case. Assume that the factors and the rule of law were derived from both the *People v. Lamkey* case and the *People v. Franzen* case. Each case evaluated all of the cited factors. The holding in *Lamkey* directly supports the rule of law described in the thesis paragraph. The holding in *Franzen* supports the rule of law; however, due to the factual scenario in that case, the *Franzen* court held that the confinement was secret.

Assume that an appellate court in Illinois decided the *People v. Franzen* case in 1993. That case is reported in the second series of the Northeastern reporter system, within volume 622. The first page of the case appears on page 877 of that volume. The court's definition of the term "secretly" appears on page 887. The court's analysis of the relevant factors and the rule of law derived from that case also appear on page 887. Certiorari was denied in the *Franzen* case in 1994. The denial of certiorari is reported in volume 631 of the second series of the Northeastern reporter system at page 712.

Assume that the *People v. Lamkey* case was decided in 1993 by an appellate court in Illinois. The case is reported in the second series of the Northeastern reporter system, within volume 608. The first page of the case appears on page

406 of that volume. The court's analysis of the relevant factors and the rule of law derived from that case appear on page 409.

1.   Draft a full-form citation for the *People v. Franzen* case. In drafting your citation, consider whether you need to include a reference to the denial of certiorari.

2.   Draft a full-form citation for the *People v. Lamkey* case.

3.   Redraft the thesis paragraph below by incorporating the proper citations. As you do so, consider both the placement of the citations and the appropriate shortened citation form for each case after each such case has been cited in its full citation form.

> Illinois courts have defined "secretly" to mean "concealed; hidden; not made public. . . ." When considering whether a confinement is "secret," courts evaluate the visibility of the location of the confinement, as evidenced by its proximity to a public area and by whether there were, or could have been, witnesses, and the defendant's attempts to conceal the victim from the knowledge of others. When a defendant confines a person in a location clearly visible to witnesses, and makes no attempt to conceal the person, the confinement is not secret. Because Mr. Tate confined Mr. Campbell in front of a large window visible to potential witnesses, and did not attempt to conceal Mr. Campbell from the knowledge of others, the confinement was not secret.

## EXERCISE 3

Redraft the following paragraph that discusses the *People v. Lamkey* case, inserting appropriate citations within the paragraph. Assume that you have previously cited to the *Lamkey* in full within the preceding thesis paragraph.

An appellate court in Illinois decided the *People v. Lamkey* case in 1993. The case is reported in the second series of the Northeastern reporter system, within volume 608. The first page of the case appears on page 406 of that volume. The case facts appear on page 408. The court's holding and rationale appear on page 409.

When the defendant confines the victim in a location close to a public area that is visible to potential witnesses, and makes no attempt to conceal the victim, the confinement is not secret. In *Lamkey*, the defendant confined the victim in the vestibule of an apartment building that had commercial space on the first floor. The vestibule was two steps up from one of Chicago's busiest streets and was separated from the sidewalk by a glass door. From within the vestibule, the victim was able to see cars and passers-by. Moreover, a passing motorist witnessed and interrupted the assault. On these facts, the court held that the confinement was not "secret" and overturned the defendant's conviction. The court reasoned that the attempted assault occurred "within public view . . . in an area clearly visible to anyone walking or driving down the street." Moreover, the court found it "significant" that the defendant made no attempt to conceal the victim by moving her to a more concealed location within the building.

# 18

# DRAFTING CLIENT LETTERS

 **I TYPES OF CLIENT LETTERS**

Letter writing is the bread-and-butter of an attorney's practice. Attorneys routinely communicate with their clients by letter. In fact, the typical attorney drafts more letters than any other type of legal document. Client letters can be grouped into three basic types. The first type of letter does not involve legal analysis and resembles the typical letter most of us are used to receiving in other contexts. Such letters convey "non-legal" information, such as confirming a meeting, summarizing a telephone conversation, notifying a client of the status of the client's legal matter, or forwarding a document to the client. When a document is enclosed within the letter, the letter is commonly called a "transmittal letter."

In addition to such commonplace letters, attorneys also convey legal analysis in letter form. The first type of letter conveying legal analysis is formally called an "opinion letter." Opinion letters state the law firm's conclusion that the client's actions comply or do not comply with the law. These letters are highly specialized, formal documents. They express the legal opinion of the law firm as to the *legal validity* of a client's proposed action. The potential legal ramifications from these letters can be enormous. If the client relies on the attorney's opinion letter and is later sued or criminally sanctioned because of those actions, the attorney's law firm could be vulnerable to liability in a malpractice action. Because of these legal ramifications, many law firms will not issue an opinion letter until at least two law partners have reviewed the letter and "signed off" on it, representing that the firm has complied with certain due diligence procedures.

The "advisory letter" is by far the more common type of client letter that conveys legal analysis. This type of letter is similar to an office memo insofar as the letter presents a well-balanced analysis of the law. In these letters, attorneys generally analyze a legal problem and advise the client about the merits of alternative courses of action. Because the advisory letter is the type of letter you can expect to draft on a fairly routine basis, the remainder of this chapter discusses the nuts and bolts of drafting advisory letters.

## II ◆ CLIENT ADVISORY LETTERS

An advisory letter typically has four basic sections. Like any letter, an advisory letter begins with an introductory paragraph that introduces the purpose of the letter. Next, the advisory letter contains a summary of the relevant client facts that relate to the issue under discussion. Following the factual summary, the letter evaluates the law. This section is akin to an abbreviated version of the rule explanation and rule application sections of an office memo. Finally, the letter concludes by summarizing the attorney's legal analysis and recommending courses of action to the client.

### A.  Introductory Paragraph

An introductory paragraph accomplishes the following three purposes:

(1)   It states the issues or questions the letter will address;

(2)   It briefly answers the questions; and

(3)   It sets the proper tone of the letter.

#### 1.  Setting the Tone

Because the introductory paragraph is the very first paragraph the client reviews, it is important to set an appropriate tone. Before you begin to draft a letter, stop and consider your client. Although every client advisory letter should be professional in tone, your client's preferences may dictate a slightly more formal or informal tone. An extremely formal letter written to a client who prefers informality may not establish the kind of rapport you ultimately want to develop with the client. In contrast, a letter that is too informal in tone may convey a lack of professionalism and consideration for what is, to the client, a very serious matter. Also consider your client's educational level and relative sophistication. Does your client have a high school education or an advanced degree? Is your client a blue-collar worker or an executive of a major corporation? Your goal is to convey information in language the client will readily understand and in a manner that will inspire trust and confidence.

In setting the appropriate tone, consider not only the client's background and personal preferences, but also the particular circumstances that have brought the client to your office and the information you will convey in the letter. For example, when writing to a client who has retained you to represent the client in a wrongful death suit following the loss of a spouse, your language should convey your sensitivity to the client's loss. To illustrate, consider the following example:

---

*Example 1:*

Dear Mr. and Mrs. McClean,

It was great meeting with you. After our meeting, I checked out the law regarding "attractive nuisance" and I have some good news. We have a very good shot at collecting money against the Hurts' insurance company in the death of your son! The upshot of my research is that the Hurts probably violated the law by leaving the gate to their pool open in which your son was drowned.

---

In the above example, the phrases "great meeting with you" and "good news" reflect the attorney's insensitivity to the tragedy the clients have endured. The informality of the words "checked out," "good shot" and "upshot of my research" belie the seriousness of the matter and could be viewed as insulting by the clients. Finally, the attorneys' insensitivity to the client is further reflected by the exclamation mark following the reference to the death of the clients' son. Grieving clients would be left with the impression that the attorney cavalierly expects them to rejoice that they have a "good shot at collecting money" from the insurance company. Now consider the different tone reflected in Example 2 below:

---

***Example 2:***

Dear Mr. and Mrs. McClean,

I enjoyed meeting with you, although I am sorry that it was under such sad circumstances. Following our meeting, I researched the law of negligence in our state and confirmed that property owners who own pools are generally responsible for any death of a young child who gains access to the pool through an unlocked gate. From my research, I believe that we have a very strong legal cause of action against the Hurts.

---

## 2. *Stating the Issue and Answering the Question*

Introduce the purpose of the letter by reminding the client of the legal question you have been asked to address. In identifying the precise question you have been asked to address, be careful to use language the client will easily understand.

After stating the legal question the letter addresses, attorneys *usually* provide a short, succinct answer to the question. It is easy to answer the question with good news. However, because clients deserve a realistic appraisal of their legal problems, you will not always be able to give your clients the answers they want to hear. When the answer is unfavorable, attorneys differ as to whether to include the answer within the introductory paragraph or whether to wait until later in the letter. Some attorneys favor conveying the unfavorable news within the introductory paragraph, contending that the client deserves to know the "bottom-line" immediately. They reason that the client has requested an answer, has paid for an answer, and is anxious to know the bottom-line without sifting through a lengthy analysis of the legal problem. However, other attorneys prefer to wait until later in the letter to deliver unfavorable news. They reason that the client will view the answer more favorably after they have walked the client through the legal analysis.

You should follow your own inclination in any given situation, based on your knowledge of the client and your own beliefs. In either event, when you must provide the client with an unfavorable answer, it is very important to strike an appropriate tone that will serve to strengthen your future relationship with the client. For example, in the illustration below, the word "unfortunately" conveys a sense of regret and alliance with the client's interests. The following introductory paragraph is excerpted from the sample letter in Appendix B.

| | |
|---|---|
| Dear Mr. and Mrs. Jones:<br><br>As you requested, I have analyzed the viability of a legal claim against your landlord to recover for the injuries you suffered when you fell on an icy sidewalk at your apartment complex. This letter summarizes the facts as I understand them and my analysis of Missouri law concerning a landlord's duty to keep common walkways free from snow and ice. Our legal option is to sue your landlord for negligence. Unfortunately, we face significant legal hurdles in recovering damages against your landlord. | 1. Identifies the issue & purpose of letter.<br><br><br><br><br>2. States the conclusion. |

## B. Factual Statement

Although a client is presumably aware of the facts (because they involve the client), it is important to include a factual statement in an advisory letter. The factual statement is important because your advice, or legal recommendation, will be based on facts you believe to exist. If the facts differ from your understanding, the additional facts might change your legal analysis and advice. Clients often fail to inform their attorneys of relevant facts, not because they wish to deceive their attorneys, but because they are not aware that the facts are legally important. Thus, incorporating the relevant facts in the advisory letter serves two purposes. First, it provides the client with an opportunity to review the factual story and to inform you if the facts are incomplete or inaccurate. Second, by incorporating the legally relevant facts into an advisory letter and then limiting your legal advice to those facts, you will avoid misunderstandings and limit any potential exposure to malpractice.

In drafting the factual statement, include all facts you believe are legally relevant to the issue you are evaluating, as well as any helpful background facts that provide fluidity to the factual story. Your goal is to achieve a tone that portrays the facts objectively and respectfully, yet reflects empathy for the client. The following paragraph is excerpted from the sample letter in Appendix B.

Under the facts as I understand them, on December 18, 2000, Mr. Johnson slipped and fell on an icy patch of the sidewalk that leads to several different apartments at your apartment complex. You advised me that the sidewalk was icy and that the landlord had not shoveled the walkway or placed any salt on the sidewalk. You have discussed the incident with your landlord and he has denied all responsibility for your accident. Your landlord claims that if the tenants wish to have walkways free from snow and ice, they are welcome to shovel the walkways themselves. The landlord insists that he has never agreed to assume that responsibility. However, because the landlord mowed the lawn in the summer, you assumed that he would also shovel the common sidewalks in the winter. I have examined your lease and it does not address which party is responsible for keeping the common walkways safe from weather hazards.

## C.  Discussion of the Law

Before drafting your legal analysis, first consider the degree of detail your client seeks and your client's knowledge base. Some clients have a strong desire to know every detail of the legal analysis and are willing to pay for the time it will take to convey detailed information to them in writing. For such clients, you would present a more thorough, formal analysis of the law. Other clients may prefer to know only the broader perspective and would appreciate a simplified analysis of the law. Such clients would not be interested in sifting through a complex legal analysis replete with legal citations. The sample letter in Appendix B illustrates a relatively lengthy client letter.

Consider as well the client's presumed knowledge base. Your client might be the in-house legal counsel of a major corporation. If your client happens to be an attorney, you can presume that the client has a basic understanding of the law and understands legal citations. When writing to a non-lawyer, however, you may need to explain certain basic legal concepts within the body of the letter. Non-lawyers may not understand legal citations and may not wish to be burdened with an endless stream of supporting citations.

Whether your discussion is a lengthy analysis of the law or a more abbreviated version of that analysis, your legal discussion will follow the same deductive writing pattern as a legal discussion in an office memo. The legal discussion should begin with a roadmap paragraph, followed by a discussion of relevant law (rule explanation), followed by a discussion of how the law affects the client's facts (rule application), followed by a conclusion and recommendation.

## 1.  Roadmap Paragraph(s)

As in an office memo, provide a foundation for the legal discussion by beginning the analysis with a roadmap paragraph or paragraphs. Depending upon the complexity and length of the letter, you may begin the legal analysis with an overview paragraph or a thesis paragraph, or perhaps both.

In the following example, because the legal discussion is somewhat complex, the attorney uses three roadmap paragraphs to set the proper framework for the discussion. The first paragraph is akin to an overview paragraph, providing the client with general background information about the law of negligence, as well as the conclusion. The next paragraph provides a more detailed explanation of the law of negligence and explains why the law does not favor the client. Note that the tone is professional and straightforward while also being empathetic (e.g., "you cannot recover compensation *for even the severe injuries you suffered* unless the law first finds . . . ;" "unfortunately"). The tone also serves to strengthen the attorney/client relationship by reminding the client that the attorney and client are a team (e.g., "*Our* legal option . . ." "*We* would argue . . ."). The third roadmap paragraph summarizes the basis for potential success against the back-drop of unfavorable law.

| | |
|---|---|
| Although we have a legitimate cause of action, we face significant legal hurdles to recovery of damages. Our legal option is to sue your landlord for negligence. We would argue that your landlord was "negligent" by breaking his duty to keep the common premises safe from your foreseeable injuries. | *Overview paragraph*: 1. States conclusion; and 2. Identifies legal option. |
| Under the law of "negligence," you cannot recover compensation for even the severe injuries you suffered unless the law first finds that your landlord violated some "duty" he owed you under the law. The courts impose a duty on landlords to keep an apartment building's "common" areas safe from permanent hazards. Although the walkway is part of the "common" area, unfortunately, Missouri courts have distinguished cases where the danger in the common areas is caused by a temporary weather hazard, such as snow. When the danger is caused by snow, courts have not imposed a duty upon landlords to shovel the snow from common walkways. Courts justify this rule by noting that the duty to remove snow would | *Thesis paragraphs*: Summarizes rule of law, including: 1. General rule of law; and 2. Summary of how courts have processed the rule of law; and |

> "subject the landlord to an unreasonable burden of vigilance and care."
>
> A trend in landlord/tenant court decisions does offer a ray of hope. The last reported Missouri opinion that decided the issue of snow removal is over thirty years old. Even in that thirty-two year old decision, the court noted that the more "modern" rule adopted in other states imposed a duty on landlords to shovel snow from their common walkways. We could argue that more recent Missouri Supreme Court opinions reflect this State's willingness to follow a national trend to protect tenants' rights to a greater degree than they have been protected in the past. The Missouri Supreme Court has implied that landlords have a broad duty to keep common areas safe from all dangers of which the landlords have "reasonable notice."

3. Summary of recent developments in the law that provide the basis for a potential legal claim

## 2. *Discuss the Relevant Law: Rule Explanation*

If your client only desires a summary of the legal problem, the roadmap paragraphs illustrated above might represent your entire legal discussion—the abbreviated rule explanation and rule application appearing in the roadmap paragraphs apprise the client of the legal problem. In other words, you would omit detailed rule explanation and rule application sections and proceed directly to the conclusion. However, assuming that you decide to discuss the law in more depth, again consider your client when evaluating the relative formality and tone of the extended legal analysis. Consider carefully the client's education, vocabulary and familiarity with the law. For example, does the client know what "negligence" is? An artful analysis of the law is useless if the client does not understand the basic rule of law on which your analysis is based, or legal vernacular. In addition, consider whether the client really wishes to pay the legal fees a ten-page in-depth analysis of the legal issue would require.

At the same time, it is important that you provide the client with enough information about the law for the client to understand how the law supports your conclusion. The cases might be summarized into the broad rules of law and factors they represent, with select facts excerpted where appropriate. In a longer letter, you might inform the client of the relevant facts, holdings, and rationale of the most important cases. In addition, if there is case law that supports a *contrary* conclusion, you would discuss those cases as well, and illustrate why they are not dispositive. When a client decides to take action based on your recommendations, it is critical that the client know the legal risks involved in taking that action. Moreover, should the client decide to take a risky course of action, and ultimately find itself in legal trouble, your written communication to the client informing the client of such risk will be important.

The sample letter in Appendix B is an example of a client letter that provides the client with a fairly extensive analysis of the law. In the following paragraph excerpted from that letter, the attorney evaluates the law by discussing two cases. The attorney decides here to omit citations to the cases because the clients are not lawyers and are not accustomed to reading legal analysis. The attorney also avoids using terms of art, such as "holding" or "held," instead using language that is more commonly understood by lay people ("found").

| | |
|---|---|
| Fifteen years ago, the Missouri Supreme Court imposed a "duty" on a landlord to place speed bumps in the parking lot of an apartment building. In this case, a child was injured on the parking lot of the landlord's apartment complex when a speeding bicycle struck her. The Supreme Court affirmed a jury verdict for the child, finding that the landlord should have taken the precaution of installing speed bumps on the parking lot. The court reasoned that, "as strongly emphasized in recent cases," the landlord owes a duty to its tenants to make common areas of leased property reasonably safe. A couple of years later, the Missouri Supreme Court found that a landlord had a duty to relocate the fire escape on an apartment building so that criminal intruders could not use the fire escape to break into a tenant's apartment. | Thesis Sentence: the rule of law the case expresses. Key case facts. Holding.<br><br>Rationale.<br><br><br>Holding of 2nd case. |

### 3.    Apply the Relevant Law to the Client's Facts: Rule Application

After informing the client of the relevant law, then explain how the law affects the client's factual situation. If there are arguments that support the client, explore those arguments before evaluating any opposing arguments. The following paragraph of rule application immediately follows the rule explanation paragraph in the previous illustration.

| | |
|---|---|
| Under the broad language and shifts in policy reflected in the more recent Supreme Court opinions, we can argue that the landlord owed you a duty to keep the sidewalk free from ice because the landlord had "reasonable notice" of the danger. The landlord had actual notice that snowy and icy conditions existed, as public and private schools in the City of St. Louis were closed for two days prior to your injury. Given the | 1. Thesis sentence: Premise for client argument.<br><br>2. Explores facts that support the premise. |

known snow and ice conditions, the landlord arguably had "reasonable notice" that a tenant might slip and fall on the icy sidewalk. Under this argument, by failing to keep the sidewalk safe, the landlord breached his duty to you under the law. If a court were to adopt this interpretation of the law, the law would permit you to recover damages for injuries you suffered as a result of the landlord's breach of duty.

If there are any reasonable arguments that the law does not favor the client, it is important to explore those arguments as well. Again, you have a duty to apprise the client of all of the realistic advantages and risks inherent in taking or failing to take a specific action. In the sample letter in Appendix B, therefore, the attorney continues the rule application section by evaluating the weaknesses in the client's position.

| | |
|---|---|
| Unfortunately, these recent Missouri Supreme Court cases did not have the opportunity to address whether the older "temporary hazard" cases involving snowy conditions are still valid in this State. The Supreme Court did not address that issue because the "hazards" involved in the recent cases were permanent hazards, not temporary conditions. Thus, the Supreme Court did not have to decide whether the earlier cases involving temporary hazards were still good law. Therefore, despite a policy trend that favors tenants, and broad policy language that favors us, the latest Supreme Court decisions do not explicitly reject any of the older cases that absolve landlords from liability involving temporary conditions such as snow. Because the older cases are the only higher level court cases that address the landlord's responsibility to protect against temporary hazards, the trial court will probably follow these older cases. (A trial court judge has to follow the law announced by higher level courts.) Realistically, our best chance to prevail in such a lawsuit would be before a higher court, most likely the Missouri Supreme Court. | 1. Thesis sentence: identifies the weakness in the client's position.<br><br>2. Explains more fully the basis of the problem, including:<br><br><br><br><br><br><br><br><br>the nuances of our legal system. |

### 4.  Conclusion and Recommendation

Conclude your letter by:

    (1)  Restating your conclusion;

    (2)  Making recommendations; and

(3)   Identifying a proposed course of action for the client.

Begin the concluding paragraph by restating your legal conclusion. When making recommendations, keep in mind the distinction between *legal* recommendations and *business* decisions. When making a legal recommendation, your task is clear—you will recommend the action you deem to be in the client's best legal interests (*e.g.*, whether to file a lawsuit or comply with a governmental regulation). On the other hand, when the ultimate decision is essentially a business decision, your client will decide the ultimate course of action. It is not your role to tell the client what business action to take. Instead, describe the different possible courses of action the client could take and the potential consequences from each possible course of action.[1] When stating the potential consequences, consider both the possible legal consequences and the practical consequences to the client (*e.g.*, costs involved).

Clients routinely report that one of the major sources of their dissatisfaction with their attorneys is their attorneys' failure to communicate and to keep them informed. You can minimize the potential for misunderstandings that cause communication lapses by concluding each advisory letter with a proposed course of action. Without an explicit course of action, misunderstandings can all too easily arise. For example, you might legitimately believe that, by sending the client a letter, the client will initiate the next round of communications. The client, however, might legitimately believe that, as the attorney, you will assume the lead role and initiate the next round of communications. The resulting lapse in communication could foster the impression that you do not believe the client's problem is important enough to merit your continuing attention.

To avoid any potential for misunderstanding, end any client letter with a proposed course of action that: (1) clearly informs the client of the steps the *client* should take (e.g., telephone the attorney; write a letter; wait for the attorney to contact the client); and (2) clearly informs the client of the steps *you* intend to take (e.g., file a lawsuit; wait to hear from the client; contact the client again). The sample letter in Appendix B concludes as follows:

---

[1] Charles R. Calleros, *Legal Method and Writing* 460 (2d ed. Aspen L. & Bus. 1994).

| | |
|---|---|
| In sum, Missouri law does not provide us with a promising opportunity to prevail at the trial court level. I do believe we have a reasonable chance of succeeding at a higher court level. However, that option will likely take a number of years and involve significant legal fees. In light of the present state of the law in Missouri, and your desire to resolve this dispute quickly, I recommend that we contact the landlord to negotiate the best possible settlement under the circumstances. Although the landlord may not be willing to offer you money that would fully compensate you for your medical bills and lost wages, the landlord may be willing to settle this dispute if it would mean avoiding lengthy litigation. | 1. Legal conclusion and practical effect on client.<br><br>2. Recommendation to client. |
| After you have had an opportunity to digest and consider this letter, please give me a call and let me know the course of action you want me to pursue. I will wait to hear from you before I take any further action. | 3. Proposed course of action. |

## EXERCISE 1:
## DRAFTING A CLIENT LETTER

Review Sample Memo B in Appendix A that discusses a potential defense to a kidnapping charge. Assume that you represent Mr. Tate. Draft a letter to your client advising him of how the "secretly" element of the statute might provide him with a defense to the kidnapping charges that have been filed against him.

# 19

# PERSUASIVE WRITING STYLE STRATEGIES

In persuasive argument, effective advocates seek a balance between strident advocacy and a predictive analysis of the law. Strident advocacy is not a particularly effective technique for several reasons. First, language that too obviously reflects the advocate's underlying strategy loses its persuasive appeal because the reader recognizes the strategy and subconsciously resists it. The goal is to paint a very *subtle* persuasive picture without the adjudicator or opposing counsel being consciously aware of the underlying strategy. Second, an advocate whose language is too strident risks losing credibility. In law, as elsewhere, attorneys who appear emotionally overwrought and prone to overstatement do not seem as credible as persons who simply appear to be stating a professional, objective analysis of the law. Third, strident language may offend an adjudicator. At the very least, it does not convey the degree of respect most adjudicators expect from attorneys who appear before them.

At the opposite end of the spectrum, it is equally unpersuasive to adopt an objective tone typical of a legal analysis found in an office memo or client advisory letter. In your role as an advocate, you have a responsibility to champion the client's legal position, not to present an objective, neutral recitation of the law. Therefore, the goal is to achieve a balance between the two extremes—persuasively arguing why the law compels a favorable outcome for the client while also appearing objective and reasonable. The following writing strategies illustrate effective persuasive techniques that will also help you achieve the proper persuasive tone.

**PERSUADE THROUGH WORD CHOICE**

Many words have both explicit and implicit meanings. In persuasive writing, advocates select words not only on the basis of their explicit meaning, but on their implicit meaning as well.

## A. Verbs and Adverbs

Verbs and adverbs are wonderful tools used by advocates to present the law and factual events in a light most favorable to their clients. For example, in the following sentence, compare the use of the adverb and verb "finally stumbled" to the verb "found." In which example does Agent Friday appear more careless?

---

(1) Agent Friday *found* the missing tapes while looking for party decorations.

vs.

(2) Agent Friday *finally stumbled* upon the missing tapes while looking for party decorations.

---

In which of the following statements do the police appear reasonable? Unreasonable?

---

(1) The police *warned* the defendant.

vs.

(2) The police *threatened* the defendant.

---

Consider the following word pairings and their connotations. In each pairing, which example is a more powerful statement for the defendant? Why?

(1)  (a)  The plaintiff *stated* that. . . .

vs.

(b)  The plaintiff *conceded* that. . . .

(2)  (a)  The witness *remembers* the defendant outside the liquor store.

vs.

(b)  The witness *claims* the defendant was outside the liquor store.

(3)  (a)  The plaintiff *failed to act* with reasonable diligence.

vs.

(b)  The plaintiff *did not act* with reasonable diligence.

## B.  Nouns and Adjectives

Nouns and adjectives can also be effective persuasive techniques. In the following example, the noun/adjective "home telephone" implies an invasiveness that the noun "telephone" alone does not capture.

(a)  The Government wiretapped Defendant's *home telephone*.

vs.

(b)  The Government wiretapped Defendant's *telephone*.

## C.  Use Verbs and Nouns With Subtlety

Your goal as an advocate is to use verbs and nouns with such subtlety that the opposing counsel or adjudicator is unaware of your strategy. If your underlying strategy is obvious, at best the strategy will provide the reader with amusement; at worst, the reader will resist your strategy and lose confidence in your credibility. Consider how the subtlety of "home telephone" in the above example loses its persuasive appeal in the following example:

> The Government wiretapped one of Defendant's most personal possessions, a possession he uses to discuss his private yearnings and dreams, his home telephone.

 **EXERCISE 1**

Using stronger verbs and/or nouns, rewrite the following sentences to be more persuasive for the advocate.

(a)  *Advocate for a health clinic against abortion protestors*: "The protestors illegally entered the health clinic, taking and harming the clinic's property."

(b)  *Advocate for a health clinic against abortion protestors*: "The protestors stated to the media that their actions made the health clinic close!"

(c)  *Advocate for abortion protestors against a health clinic*: "The health clinic did not tell the public that it was terminating pregnancies."

 **II**  *PERSUADE THROUGH ACTIVE/PASSIVE VOICE AND ACTION VERBS*

Advocates use the *active voice and action verbs* to bind an actor visually with an action. For example, a prosecutor might write: "Tim Jones snatched the purse from the arm of a seventy-year-old woman." (Sentence structure: Actor (Subject) ⇒ action verb ⇒ object) In contrast, advocates use the *passive voice and non-action verbs* when they want to distance their client from their client's actions. For example, a defense attorney representing Tim Jones might write: "The purse was taken from the complainant by the defendant." (Sentence structure: Object $\Rightarrow$ non-action verb $\Rightarrow$ actor (subject))

## EXERCISE 2

Using active/passive voice, and action/non-action verbs, rewrite the following sentences as an advocate representing the *opposing* party.

(a) *Advocate for the defendant writes*: "The document was not produced to Plaintiff in April, as the result of an oversight by a legal assistant. As soon as we discovered the error in June, Defendant promptly produced the document."

Redraft as an advocate for the plaintiff.

(b) *Advocate for the defendant writes*: "The death of the victim resulted from a stab wound allegedly caused by Defendant."

Redraft as an advocate for the prosecution.

## III PERSUADE BY USING CONCLUSIVE, RATHER THAN "OPINION" STATEMENTS

Effective advocates use forceful, conclusive statements in their writing rather than statements that appear to be only opinions over which reasonable people might differ. Advocates use conclusive statements as topic or thesis sentences to state favorable conclusions. However, conclusive statements appear through-out persuasive writing. When reviewing your writing, evaluate how you can eliminate unnecessary introductory clauses and tentative language to transform "opinion" language into more forceful "conclusive" language.

In each of the following examples, select the statement from each pairing that appears more like an affirmative "truth" and, therefore, more persuasive. Under what circumstances, if any, would you use the statement that appears more like an opinion?

(1)  (a)  *It is our contention that* Plaintiff's complaint is meritless.

vs.

(b)  Plaintiff's complaint is meritless.

(2)  (a)  *It has been argued that* the officers violated Defendant's Constitutional right to privacy.

vs.

(b)  The officers violated Defendant's Constitutional right to privacy.

(3)  (a)  *One court has held that* when the Government fails to obtain an immediate judicial seal, its alternative "satisfactory explanation" must provide the same level of protection as a judicial seal. *United States v. Johnson,* [citation]

vs.

(b)  When the Government fails to obtain an immediate judicial seal, its alternative "satisfactory explanation" must provide the same level of protection as a judicial seal. *United States v. Johnson,* [citation]

## EXERCISE 3

Rewrite the following sentences to make them appear as "truths" rather than opinions.

(a) "Two courts have interpreted the legislative history to mean that the statute does not cover activities such as political protests. [citations]"

(b) "This Court can find that the employer's conduct rises to the level of racial harassment under Title VII."

##  PERSUADE BY USING AFFIRMATIVE, RATHER THAN DEFENSIVE STATEMENTS

The tone of persuasive writing is one that *affirms* the client's position rather than one that denies an opponent's position. By simply denying the opponent's position, you run the risk of appearing defensive and unsure of your client's legal position. In addition, any time you directly rebut the opponent's position and argue why that position is unsound, the adjudicator continues to view the law and facts from within the context of your *opponent's* framework, and to question whether that position is correct or incorrect. Instead, you would prefer that the adjudicator view the law and facts from within the context of your own favorable argument.

At times it is necessary to rebut directly an opponent's argument (for example, when responding to arguments the opponent has raised in a court brief). However, even then it is more persuasive to argue first why your client's position is sound, framing the issues in a manner that favors your client. Having first persuaded the adjudicator of the brilliance of your client's position, your direct rebuttal will be even more compelling. An opponent's argument loses much of its persuasive appeal when you have already convinced the adjudicator to view the problem from your client's perspective.

In the following example, an advocate for the defendant, Mr. Hart, seeks to suppress wiretap evidence the government obtained from Mr. Hart's telephone. The wiretap statute requires that, in order for the evidence to be admissible in court, the government must either obtain an "immediate" judicial seal safeguarding the evidence, or provide a "satisfactory explanation" for its failure to do so. The government did not immediately secure the integrity of the wiretap evidence by obtaining a judge's seal. Hart's attorney seeks to convince the court that the government also failed to provide the required alternative—a "satisfactory explanation." Compare the persuasive appeal of the following two examples of Hart's argument.

(1) The government incorrectly contends that the wiretap tapes are admissible as evidence during trial. The federal wiretap statute requires that the government either obtain the protection of an "immediate" judicial seal to safeguard the integrity of wiretap evidence, or provide a "satisfactory explanation" for its delay. The government argues that, even though it did not obtain an immediate judicial seal, it had a "satisfactory explanation" because it did not know the tapes were not sealed. The government points out that, as soon as it discovered its mistake, it obtained a judicial seal. However, the government's argument should be rejected. Although the government was unaware the tapes were not immediately sealed, it stored the tapes in an open box and misplaced them for over two months. Thus, its explanation was not "satisfactory."

*Defending against opponent*: "opponent incorrectly contends"

and stating the basis of the opposing argument.

Finally, the *advocate's premise*: opponent's argument should be rejected, and why.

(2) The wiretap tapes the government obtained from tapping Mr. Hart's home telephone are not admissible at trial. The evidence is inadmissable because the government failed to comply with the requirements of the federal wiretap statute. The wiretap statute requires the government to safeguard the integrity of wiretap tapes by obtaining an "immediate" judicial seal, or by providing a "satisfactory explanation" for its failure to do so. By waiting for over two months, the government failed "immediately" to obtain the protection of a judicial seal. The government also failed to provide a "satisfactory explanation" for its failure to do so. Instead, the government lost this sensitive evidence as it allegedly sat exposed in an open box in a busy, unlocked storage room for over two months. By failing either to store the tapes in a manner that affords the same level of protection as an immediate judicial seal, or to act with reasonable diligence, the government failed to offer a "satisfactory explanation" for its lengthy delay.

*Advocate's thesis*: tapes are not admissible.

*Proof of thesis*:

Hart's favorable standard and why the government has failed to satisfy the favorable standard.

 **EXERCISE 4**

Assume you represent a plaintiff who has sued her former employer for damages, alleging that the former employer violated Title VII. Rewrite the following statement on behalf of the plaintiff to shift from an objective observation about the law to a persuasive declaration that affirms your client's position.

(a) "In a Title VII suit, the plaintiff must prove that the employer unlawfully discriminated against an "individual with respect to his terms, conditions or privileges of employment because of such individual's . . . race.""

Assume you represent the state in a criminal action against a man accused of murdering his spouse. You seek to admit into evidence the defendant's communications with his psychotherapist, in which he indicated his intent to murder his wife. The defendant's attorney has filed a motion to suppress the evidence, arguing that the communications are protected by the patient/psychotherapist privilege. As the state's attorney, rewrite the following sentences into declarations that affirm the state's position.

(b) "Communications between the defendant and his psychotherapist are not privileged communications and should not be withheld from the jury."

(c) "The *Dixon* court `assumed, without deciding, that such a privilege does exist.' However, that case was a civil case, not a criminal case. The court also noted that the plaintiff had advanced no policy interests in that case that might justify disclosure. Therefore, the *Dixon* case is not controlling and this Court should not base its decision on *Dixon*."

#  V  *PERSUADE BY USING JUXTAPOSITION AND PARRALLELISM*

## A.  *To Attack Opponent's Credibility or Legal Theory*

Juxtaposing conflicting statements can be a very effective persuasive tool. Advocates use this technique to discredit their opponent's factual story or legal theory without sounding strident or obviously biased. Thus, instead of passionately arguing that the opponent's story is absurd, or that the opponent is lying, juxtapose conflicting statements so that the reader can draw the obvious conclusions from the discrepancy.

Compare the persuasive appeal of the following examples:

(1) Agent Friday testified that she placed a label on the box of tapes indicating the box was to be transported to the courthouse. However, Agent Friday must be lying to this Court because there was no label on the box two months later!

vs.

(2) Although Agent Friday testified that she placed a label on the box indicating that it was to be transported to the courthouse, the building janitor testified that no label appeared on the box of tapes. The government has not explained this factual discrepancy.

## B.  To Emphasize Similarities to Precedent Cases

Advocates also use juxtaposition and parallelism as a technique to make a client's facts appear to be more analogous to the facts of a precedent case. By placing the client's facts immediately following a case discussion, and using identical language to emphasize the similarities, the reader easily sees the parallels.

Compare the persuasive appeal of the following examples:

(1)  . . . In allowing the plaintiff to recover damages for his injury, the *Porter* court reasoned: "Under the pleadings, the defendants did not say the plaintiff was a bad check writer; they only caused him to appear to be one . . . to injure him in his reputation." *Id.* at 272.

Similarly, in the present case, the company attempted to imply that Martin received a $250,000 kickback in an effort to harm him.

In the above illustration, does the Martin situation seem to parallel the *Porter* case? Yes, perhaps in some ways. However, one cannot help but notice the distinctions as well. The *Porter* case deals with a bad check writer while Martin allegedly received a $250,000 kickback. Now consider the subtle writing style strategies that make the two cases appear more similar.

> (2)   . . . In allowing the plaintiff to recover damages for his injury, the *Porter* court reasoned: "Under the pleadings, the defendants did not *say* the plaintiff was a bad check writer; they only caused him to *appear* to be one . . . to injure him in his reputation." *Id.* at 272 (emphasis added).
>
> Similarly, in the present case, the company did not *say* that Martin was fired because he received a $250,000 kick-back. However, the company certainly caused him to *appear* that way in an effort to injure Martin's reputation.

In the second example, the words "say" and "appear" are not emphasized by the court in the original opinion. However, the advocate enhanced the similarity between the case and the client's facts by adding the emphasis in the case discussion, and then paralleling the *same words* and *emphasis* when analogizing the case to the client's factual situation. Although this technique can be wonderfully effective, use it selectively. If used with every case discussion, the technique becomes obvious and loses its persuasive appeal.

## VI   *PERSUADE BY DE-EMPHASIZING NEGATIVE INFORMATION*

Sometimes, a broad argument or precedent case that generally favors a client also contains within it information that is not as favorable to the client. Under those circumstances, you can use several persuasive writing techniques to de-emphasize the negative information. Be careful not to confuse this technique with the strategy of saving direct rebuttal to the end of your argument. Instead, this technique refers to instances in which you wish to de-emphasize certain language within the body of an otherwise favorable argument.

### A.  *Make Negative Information Implicit*

Sometimes it is possible to make "negative" information implicit rather than explicit. For example, assume you want to persuade a court to adopt a position taken by the Equal Employment Opportunity Commission ("EEOC"). However, the court is not required to adopt the EEOC's position, because the EEOC regulations are merely persuasive, not mandatory authority. Consider the difference in persuasive appeal when the "negative" information is made implicit rather than explicit.

> (1) While the EEOC Guidelines are interpretive regulations only and are not binding on courts, the United States Supreme Court has given courts the authority to look to the Guidelines as persuasive guidance when interpreting Title VII.
>
> vs.
>
> (2) The United States Supreme Court has instructed lower courts to look to the EEOC Guidelines as persuasive guidance when interpreting Title VII.

## B.  *"Bury" Negative Information*

Sometimes "negative" information cannot be made implicit. However, you may either be ethically obligated to disclose the information or may elect to disclose it to avoid losing credibility. Under these circumstances, you can minimize the information's impact by "burying" unfavorable information in the middle of a sentence and/or paragraph.

For example, assume you represent Adams, a client who seeks to recover punitive damages for the defendant's gross negligence. You know that punitive damages are very rarely rewarded in such cases, yet believe that you would lose credibility if you were to ignore that point.[1] Compare the following two examples and consider the difference in persuasive appeal when the negative information is buried in a dependent clause in the middle of the paragraph.

> (1) *It is true that punitive damages for negligence are not often awarded.* However, Adams is entitled to punitive damages in this exceptional case because the defendant was grossly negligent in failing to repair the hole in the sidewalk even after three small children injured themselves by falling into the hole.
>
> vs.

---

[1] *See, e.g.*, Charles R. Calleros, *Legal Method and Writing*, 311 (2d ed. Aspen L. & Bus. 1994).

> (2) Adams is entitled to punitive damages for the defendant's gross negligence in this exceptional case, *even though such awards are not typically awarded in negligence actions*, because the defendant failed to repair the hole in the sidewalk even after three small children injured themselves by falling into the hole.

## EXERCISE 5

Again, assume that you represent the state in a criminal action against a man accused of murdering his spouse. After researching whether communications between the defendant and his psychotherapist are privileged, assume that you discover the *Burtrum* case. In that case, the court held that, due to the compelling state interests in *child abuse* cases, there was no psychotherapist and patient privilege. This is the first and only case in this jurisdiction in which a court has considered whether a privilege exists in a criminal case. Rewrite the following sentence to de-emphasize the distinction between child abuse cases and homicide.

"Although it is true that *Burtrum* involved the abuse of a minor child, the court's holding that the psychotherapist patient privilege does not exist should apply to these criminal proceedings for murder as well."

## EXERCISE 6

Judge Cardozo wrote the following statement of facts in the famous *Palsgraf* case. The court ultimately held that the defendant railroad company was not negligent because the acts of its employees were not the "proximate cause" of the plaintiff's injuries. Judge Cardozo wrote the statement of facts in *Palsgraf* from a defendant's perspective, creating a visual picture that weakens the connection between the defendant's employees' actions and the plaintiff's injuries.[2]

For this writing exercise: (1) note the different persuasive style strategies Cardozo used in drafting this factual statement; and (2) redraft the following paragraph of facts from a perspective that favors the plaintiff.

---

[2] *See* Diana V. Pratt, *Legal Writing: A Systematic Approach* 290 (2d ed. West 1993) (describing the writing style techniques used by Justice Cardozo in crafting the factual statement).

CARDOZO:

Plaintiff was standing on a platform of defendant's railroad after buying a ticket to go to Rockaway Beach. A train stopped at the station, bound for another place. Two men ran forward to catch it. One of the men reached the platform of the car without mishap, though the train was moving. The other man, carrying a package, jumped aboard the car, but seemed unsteady as if about to fall. A guard on the car, who had held the door open, reached forward to help him in, and another guard on the platform pushed him from behind. In this act, the package was dislodged, and fell upon the rails. It was a package of small size, about fifteen inches long, and covered with newspaper. In fact it contained fireworks, but there was nothing in its appearance to give notice of its contents. The fireworks when they fell exploded. The shock of the explosion threw down some scales at the other end of the platform many feet away. The scales struck the plaintiff causing injuries for which she sues.

# LAW-CENTERED ARGUMENTS: BASED ON STATUTORY CONSTRUCTION

 ## FRAMING FAVORABLE INTERPRETATIONS OF THE LAW

As an attorney, you will sometimes address legal issues in which the meaning of the law itself is unclear, separate and apart from how the law might affect the client's factual situation. Statutes, in particular, often give rise to disputes about what the law means because their broad, general language is susceptible to a myriad of different interpretations. Consider the federal wiretap statute that was introduced in Chapter 5. Congress enacted the wiretap statute in part to curb perceived abuses of governmental wiretapping. One procedural limitation was designed to protect wiretap evidence from tampering during the time frame before trial. That section of the statute requires that the government "immediately" obtain the safeguard of a judicial seal after retrieving wiretap evidence. Should the government fail to obtain a judicial seal immediately, the statute provides the government with only one alternative: it must provide a "satisfactory explanation" for its failure to do so.[1] This original rule of law left many questions unresolved. What exactly is a satisfactory explanation? Does a satisfactory explanation require that the government prove there was no possibility of tampering during the delay, or must the defendant prove that tampering actually occurred? Is a mere mistake a satisfactory explanation or must the government prove that it had a legitimate law enforcement reason for the delay?

The statute's vague language and the resulting questions that inevitably arise require courts to define in more concrete terms what a "satisfactory explanation" means—a law-centered issue. If a higher level court in a jurisdiction had already clearly resolved these questions, attorneys would not be disputing the

---

[1] 18 U.S.C. § 2518(8)(a) (2000).

law's meaning—a lower court judge would be compelled to follow such precedent. Thus, this chapter discusses how to construct a statutory law-centered argument when no clear mandatory precedent exists. When no mandatory precedent exists, advocates have room to argue that the vague language should be interpreted in a manner that advances their clients' interests.

## A.  Preliminary Assessment of the Statute

When a statute is the original source of law, you must convince the adjudicator that the statutory scheme itself supports the favorable legal interpretation you are advocating. Even if an adjudicator might agree that your legal interpretation best serves public policy, the adjudicator will not adopt your theory unless the source of law—the statute—permits that interpretation. Therefore, when interpreting statutory language, first carefully evaluate and outline the separate statutory elements, as discussed in Chapter 4. As you consider the statute's language, it is important to verify your preliminary assessment by looking beyond the exact section of the statute you are evaluating. Many statutes have sections that contain definitions of the significant language used elsewhere in the statute.

When considering the meaning of the statutory language, also review the statutory scheme as a whole. An adjudicator is not likely to interpret a section of the statute in a manner that would make the statute internally inconsistent or that would thwart the purpose of the statute as revealed by the statutory scheme. Reviewing the statutory scheme in its entirety may not only help you interpret the statutory language at issue, but also help you determine whether any other statutory provisions may be relevant in evaluating the client's legal problem. Therefore, when considering the meaning of the statute's plain language, carefully evaluate: (1) the language of the statutory section that is at issue; (2) the definitions contained elsewhere in the statute, if applicable; and (3) the entire statutory scheme. You are now in a position to consider the potential meaning of the statutory language and how you might use the statutory language to advance your client's interests.

During this process, research the law in other jurisdictions to determine how other courts have interpreted the statute. Although these cases do not have the force of mandatory authority, they serve two purposes. First, persuasive authority cases can provide you with ideas that will help you formulate a favorable interpretation of the law for your client. Second, the persuasive authority cases will also serve a purpose in the argument you ultimately draft. Citing to such cases in your argument will provide you with supplemental authority to support the argument.

As you consider how to formulate a favorable rule of law from ambiguous statutory language, consider first your client's factual situation and what you will need to prove in order to prevail. Your goal is to formulate an interpretation of the rule of law from which your client will ultimately prevail. Then consider how the statute's ambiguous language might help you formulate a winning interpretation.

## B. *Framing a Favorable Standard*

The elements of a statute commonly create standards that must be satisfied in order to fall within the rubric of the statute. For example, the federal wiretap statute created a standard, albeit a vague one, by requiring the government to provide a "satisfactory explanation" when it does not immediately submit tapes to a judge for sealing. When evaluating a vague legal standard, any interpretation you advocate must be a good faith and reasonable interpretation of the statute. However, with that in mind, there is usually room for reasonable people to differ. Therefore, first consider whether you want to set a high bar that would be very difficult to satisfy, or, alternatively, set a low bar that could easily be met. How high you want to set the bar depends on who you represent and the factual situation before you. If your client must satisfy a standard to avail itself of privileges under a statute, you would advocate an interpretation of the standard that your client could easily satisfy. If, on the other hand, your client must satisfy a standard before being *penalized* under a statute, you would advocate an interpretation of the statute that your client would not satisfy. The same strategies apply when the opposing party must satisfy a standard. If your client's interests dictate that the opposing party not satisfy the standard, then you would consider how you might define the standard in a manner that would be difficult to satisfy. Alternatively, if your client's interests dictate that the opposing party satisfy the standard, then you would consider how you might define the standard in a manner that would be easy to satisfy.

Using the federal wiretap statute as an example, consider the two parties' differing interpretations of the term "satisfactory explanation." In the fact pattern for the sample brief in Appendix D, the government did not immediately obtain a judicial seal that would safeguard sensitive wiretap evidence. The government's explanation for its delay is that the tapes were lost during an office move. The tapes were missing for two months and were finally discovered in an open box in an office supply room. Immediately upon discovering the tapes, the government took them to a judge for sealing. Assume you represent the government in this case. Under this set of facts, you recognize that the government would have great difficulty in satisfying a standard that sets a high bar. For instance, an easily avoidable mistake would likely not satisfy a standard that would require the government to act with reasonable diligence.

Therefore, you would urge the court to adopt a low standard that could easily be satisfied. You might argue, for example, that the government supplies a "satisfactory explanation" any time it has a "good faith" explanation for the delay in sealing. Even an easily avoidable mistake could be deemed to be in "good faith." In fact, under that interpretation, almost all governmental explanations would be deemed satisfactory unless the defendant's attorney could produce evidence that the government acted in bad faith to alter the evidence.

Now assume that you represent the defendant, Mr. Hart, and want to argue that the government's explanation was not "satisfactory." As an advocate representing Mr. Hart, you would urge the court to adopt a very stringent standard that would be difficult for the government to satisfy. As you consider the fact pattern, you recognize that the government has two problems. First, the government was not very diligent—the mistake easily could have been avoided because the government agents knew the bureau was moving offices the next day. To avoid the mistake, the government could easily have arranged for a courier to deliver the tapes to the courthouse rather than putting the tapes in a box that was identical to thousands of moving boxes. Second, the government can not account for the tapes' whereabouts for two months. Although the box of tapes was ultimately discovered in an office supply room, the tapes could have been anywhere during the two-month delay. Therefore, as an advocate representing Mr. Hart, you would urge the court to adopt a very stringent standard the government could not satisfy.

As Mr. Hart's attorney, you would have researched case law in other jurisdictions and found cases in which courts have imposed very stringent standards on the government. Adopting the standards imposed by these courts, you would argue that a governmental explanation is not "satisfactory" unless the government can prove both: (1) that prior to judicial sealing the government stored the tapes in a manner that safeguarded them from any *possibility* of tampering; and (2) that the government acted with "reasonable diligence" to obtain the required judicial seal. This interpretation of the statute would compel the government to satisfy a significantly higher legal standard, making it impossible for the government to prove that it complied with the statute.

## C.  Framing a Favorable Definition

Statutes also identify the type of person or conduct or object that is subject to the statute. In some cases, there will be no dispute as to whether the person, conduct or object falls within the umbrella of the statute. For example, in the federal wiretap hypothetical problem, the government is clearly the government and the object of the dispute—wiretap tapes—is clearly the subject of that statute. Sometimes, however, the answers are not so clear. Recall the residential burglary problem illustrated in Sample Memo A in Appendix A. In that case, the issue turned on whether a garage could possibly be a dwelling under the residential burglary statute. Whether you interpreted the term "dwelling" broadly or narrowly would depend on whether you represented the State of Illinois or the defendant.

## ◆ II ◆ *CONSTRUCTING PROOF*

Formulating a favorable rule from a statute is just the first step in the process. You must also convince an adjudicator to adopt your favorable interpretation of the statute. The fact that other courts in other jurisdictions agree with your interpretation, while perhaps persuasive, would not convince an adjudicator to adopt your interpretation. When a statute is the original source of law, you must convince the adjudicator that the statute itself supports the favorable legal interpretation you are advocating. When interpreting a statute's meaning, adjudicators consider some or all of the following:

1. The *plain language* of the statutory section at issue;
2. The *statutory scheme* as a whole, including:
   (a) Any *definition sections* of the statute that define key language;
   (b) The *title* or any *preamble* that might indicate the statute's purpose;
   (c) The *remaining sections* of the statute to evaluate how the sections might interrelate;
3. The *legislative history*, if any, to determine the legislative purpose;
4. Any *canons of construction* that might help the court interpret the statutory language;
5. The *equities*, to ensure an equitable and fair result to the parties;
6. The *public policy* ramifications of its decision;
7. *Prudential concerns* about the decision's impact on the judicial system; and
8. The interpretations adopted by *other courts and legal scholars*.

Each of these tools of statutory construction can be used not only to advance an argument illustrating why your interpretation of the statute is sound, but to argue why your opponent's interpretation of the statute is unsound. Therefore, as you consider each of these tools of statutory construction, evaluate them from two perspectives. First, consider how each tool of statutory construction might be used to advance an argument that favors your interpretation. Second, consider how the same tool of construction might be used to attack your opponent's argument.

## A.  *Language of the Statute*

The statute's language is the starting point. Does the language either compel or support your favorable interpretation of the statute? Sometimes, of course, the statutory language is itself so vague and unclear that it is not really susceptible to any "plain language" argument. For example, the term "satisfactory explanation" in the federal wiretap statute is not defined within the statutory scheme itself and the term is so broad and vague that it does not lend itself to an argument based on the language of the statute. The vague term "satisfactory explanation" would permit the judge to render any reasonable interpretation of that language. With such broad, vague language, your argument would not contain a "plain language" argument. Often, however, the language of the statute either clearly supports a particular interpretation or at least lends itself to an argument based on the statutory language. In such cases, the language of the statute would be the cornerstone of your argument.

 *ILLUSTRATION: Title VII Problem*

As an example, consider the Title VII problem that is the basis of Sample Brief A in Appendix C. *The background*: Title VII prohibits employers from discriminating against employees on the basis of their sex, among other protected classifications. The statute prohibits any "employer" from discriminating against its employees, and defines the term "employer" to include "any agent" of the employer. The term "agent" lends itself to an argument based on the statute's language. Prior to 1991, when Title VII was amended, some attorneys argued that the term "agent" merely incorporated *respondeat superior* liability into the statute, with the employer thereby liable for the acts of its agents. Other attorneys argued that the term "agent" made supervisory employees liable. However, prior to 1991 the conflicting interpretations had little practical effect on the outcome because plaintiffs could recover only injunctive relief, reinstatement or hiring, or up to two years of back-pay.[2] These remedies are available only against an employer, not individual employees.

---

[2] 42 U.S.C. § 2000e-5(g) (1994).

In 1991, Congress amended Title VII to allow plaintiffs to recover compensatory and punitive damages.[3] The expanded remedies intensified the debate. Following the amendment, some attorneys argued that, by expanding the available remedies, Congress also expanded the group of potential defendants to include individual employees who were supervisors. They argued that the term "agent," together with the expanded remedies available to plaintiff, made certain supervisory employees personally liable for both compensatory and punitive damages. Other attorneys argued that when Congress amended Title VII in 1991, it intended only to increase the monetary award plaintiffs could recover. These attorneys argued that the amendments did not also expand the class of potential defendants from employers to supervisory employees. They argued that the term "agent" merely incorporated *respondeat superior* liability into the statute, with the employer thereby liable in compensatory and punitive damages for the acts of its agents.

### 1. Example of Argument Based on Statutory Language— Plaintiff:

The plaintiff claims that a former supervisor sexually harassed her in violation of Title VII. She seeks to recover damages not only from her former employer but also from her former supervisor. Therefore, her attorney advocates a broad definition of the term "agent" that would hold the former supervisor personally liable. In the following example, note how the language of the statute is the engine that drives the argument. The underlying purpose of the statute is woven into the argument to bolster the plaintiff's interpretation of the statutory language.

| | |
|---|---|
| The statute's plain language could not be any clearer. Title VII prohibits any "*employer*" from "discriminat[ing] against any individual with respect to his compensation, terms, conditions, or privileges of employment, because of such individual's . . . sex . . . ." 42 U.S.C. § 2000e-2(a) (1994) (emphasis added). Title VII broadly defines the term "employer" to include "a person engaged in an industry affecting commerce who has fifteen or more employees . . . and *any agent* of such a person . . . ." 42 U.S.C. § 2000e(b) (1994) (emphasis added). Thus, the statutory language, on its face, encompasses "any agent" of the employer. | *Broad premise*: Plain language supports plaintiff. *Proof*: Exact language from the Definition Section is quoted. Key language is *emphasized* |
| In interpreting the scope of agency, Title VII must "be accorded a liberal interpretation in order to effectuate the pur- | Plaintiff urges broad interpreta- |

---

[3] 42 U.S.C. § 1981a (1994).

| | |
|---|---|
| pose of Congress to eliminate the inconvenience, unfairness, and humiliation of ethnic discrimination." *Rodgers v. E.E.O.C.*, 454 F.2d 234, 238 (5th Cir. 1972). Thus, a person is properly an agent under Title VII when "he participates in the decision-making process that forms the basis of the discrimination." *Jones v. Metro. Denver Sewage Disposal Dist.*, 537 F. Supp. 966, 970 (D. Colo. 1982). Any other interpretation "would encourage supervisory personnel to believe that they may violate Title VII with impunity." *Hamilton v. Rodgers*, 791 F.2d 439 (5th Cir. 1986). | tion of statute to set up a favorable rule. States the favorable rule. Argues that the opponent's rule would thwart the statutory purpose. |

In the above illustration, the plaintiff's attorney not only argues how the plain language of the statute supports the plaintiff's favorable interpretation, but how the opponent's interpretation would thwart the statutory purpose.

## 2.   *Example of Argument Based on Statutory Language—Defendant:*

In the factual scenario involving Title VII, the defendant wants to avoid personal liability. He would argue that the term "agent" must be read narrowly to mean only that an employer is liable for the acts of its agents. The following argument is excerpted from the defendant's argument that appears in Sample Brief A in Appendix C:

| | |
|---|---|
| When prohibiting employers from discriminating against their employees, Title VII narrowly defines employer as "a person engaged in an industry affecting commerce who has fifteen or more employees . . . and any agent of such a person. . ." 42 U.S.C. § 2000e(b) (1994). By defining employer as a "person . . . who has fifteen or more employees . . . and any agent of such a person," Congress codified its intention to exclude individuals in their individual capacities from liability for violations of Title VII. First, individuals in their individual capacities do not qualify as "person[s] . . . who ha[ve] fifteen or more employees." Individuals do not have employees, employers do. | *Broad Premise*: Statutory language narrowly defines the term "employer." The defendant's favorable rule. *Proof*: 1st argument that supports Def's interpretation. |
| Second, interpreting the statutory language to include individuals in their individual capacities would produce an absurd result. The conjunctive term "and" links the term "any agent" to the phrase "person . . . who has fifteen or more employees." Thus, as an "agent" of an employer, an individual employee's liability would depend on whether the employer employed | 2nd argument: opponent's interpretation would create internal inconsistency within the statutory scheme. |

> fifteen or more employees. Individuals who are "agents" of employers with fewer than fifteen employees would be exempt from liability—as an agent of an employer with fewer than fifteen employees, they would fall within the statutory exemption. In contrast, individuals who are "agents" of employers with fifteen or more employees would be liable in their individual capacities. Because their employer would not fall within the exemption, they would similarly not be exempt. Congress could not have intended this result. *Hudson v. Soft Sheen Prods.*, 873 F. Supp. 132, 135 n.2 (N.D. Ill. 1995).

2nd argument continues—Congress could not have intended this result.

Again, in the above example, the defendant not only argues why a favorable interpretation is sound, but attacks the opponent's theory as being inconsistent with the statutory scheme and as creating an absurd result that Congress could not possibly have intended.

## B. The Statutory Scheme as a Whole

When evaluating statutory language, the entire statutory scheme often provides guidance as to the meaning of a particular section of a statute. The statutory scheme may reveal what the legislature intended when it enacted the statute, thereby shedding light on the meaning of the disputed language. When considering the statutory scheme, check first to see whether the statute begins with a preamble or policy statement that identifies the legislature's policy concerns and the reasons it enacted the statute. These statements can usually be found at the beginning of the over-all statute. Next, peruse the statutory scheme as a whole to gain a clearer perspective of the legislature's broad purpose in enacting the statutory scheme. Then consider how the specific purpose of the particular section with which you are concerned might help effectuate the broad statutory purpose. Reviewing the statutory scheme in its entirety will also help you determine whether any additional statutory provisions may be potentially relevant in evaluating the client's legal problem. Finally, courts are reluctant to construe a specific statutory section in a manner that would create an inconsistent or absurd result when viewed in conjunction with other statutory sections.

### Example of Argument Based on Statutory Scheme

To illustrate, consider again the Title VII problem and the defendant employee's argument. The defendant, a supervisory employee, urges the court to adopt a narrow interpretation of the statutory term "agent." The defendant argues that the term "agent" does not impose personal liability on individual employees. The defendant has already argued that the specific statutory language itself supports his interpretation. However, he also uses other sections within the statutory scheme to argue that Congress could not have intended this result. The defendant uses the damages provisions within the 1991 Amendments to bolster his argument that the term "agent" does not impose individual liability.

| | |
|---|---|
| The elaborate liability scheme of the 1991 Amendments confirms that Congress intended to preserve Title VII's provision of exclusive employer liability. In expanding the scope of remedies available to victims of Title VII violations to include compensatory and punitive damages, Congress also carefully limited the damages to which an employer could be subjected depending upon the number of employees employed by the employer. For example, on the low end, Congress subjected an employer who employs between fourteen and 101 employees to no more than $50,000 in compensatory and punitive damages. 42 U.S.C. § 1981a(b)(3)(A) (1994). On the high end, Congress subjected an employer who employs more than 500 employees to no more than $300,000 in compensatory and punitive damages. *Id.* § 1981a(b)(3)(D). Congress' failure to include a damage cap for individuals reflects that it did not contemplate individual liability for compensatory and punitive damages under the Amendments. *See Hudson*, 873 F. Supp. at 135 ("[I]f Congress had envisioned individual liability under Title VII for compensatory and punitive damages, it would have included *individuals* in this litany of limitations. . .") (quoting *Miller*, 991 F.2d at 588 n.2). | *Premise*: Statutory scheme supports Def's interpretation. <br><br> *Proof*: <br> Def. points to the provisions in another section of the statute that limit liability for employers. <br><br><br> Def. argues that the absence of damage limits for individuals means that Congress did not intend to make individuals liable. |

## C. *Legislative Purpose*

The legislative purpose underlying a statute's enactment is also relevant when interpreting a statute. Adjudicators strive to interpret statutory language in a manner that will further the underlying statutory purpose. Conversely, they are reluctant to interpret statutory language in a manner that would thwart the statutory purpose. As the above examples illustrate, the statutory purpose can be gleaned from the statutory scheme as a whole. Indeed, the statutory purpose can be woven into a "plain language" or "statutory scheme" argument to enhance the persuasive appeal of such arguments.

You can also discover the probable purpose of a statute by examining the statute's legislative history, if any. Federal statutes, and some state statutes, contain legislative history that can be helpful in identifying the statute's underlying purpose. A statute's legislative history may contain committee reports

and hearing transcripts that reflect the reasons the legislature enacted the statute. Note, however, that legislative history is generated by legislators and ad-
ministrators who are usually invested in the outcome of a particular piece of
legislation. Therefore, portions of the legislative history may contain statements that might not accurately reflect the consensus of the legislative body
that enacted the statute. A legislative body votes on statutes as they are written,
not on the committee reports and hearing transcripts. For these reasons, if an
adjudicator determines that the plain language of a statute differs from the
legislative intent as revealed in the statute's legislative history, the adjudicator
will often (although not always) interpret the statute according to its plain language. Adjudicators reason that their responsibility is to interpret statutes as
they were written and enacted, not as some members of the legislature may
have wished the statute was written.

As you consider the purpose underlying the statute, and its legislative history, keep in mind that some portions of the legislative history might benefit
your interpretation of the statute while other portions of the legislative history
might benefit your opponent's interpretation. There are often a number of different purposes underlying a statute, as the legislature attempts to strike a reasonable balance between competing interests. Again using the Title VII problem for purposes of illustration, the defendant argues that, in 1991, Congress
intended only to expand the scope of remedies available to plaintiffs and did
not intend to expand the class of potential defendants.

### *Example of Argument Based on Legislative History*

| | |
|---|---|
| The legislative history to the 1991 Amendments also con-firms that Congress intended only to expand the scope of remedies available, not to expand the class of defendants against whom victims of Title VII violations could proceed. None of the Committee Reports, including the House Reports on the 1991 Amendments and the Senate Reports on the pre-cursor bill to the 1991 Amendments, even mention individual liability. *See Hudson*, 873 F. Supp. at 136 (detailing the failure of the legislative history to mention individual liability). In-stead, the legislative history is replete with references to *em-ployer* compensation and the possibility of *employer* deter-rence. For example, Congress focused on the need for employers to compensate wronged employees. The House Reports reflect Congress' intent to prevent "employers who intentionally discriminate [from avoiding] any meaningful li-ability." H.R. Rep. No. 41, 102nd Cong., 1st Sess., pt. 2, at 4 (1991). The Senate Reports addressed the need to make "em-ployers liable for all losses—economic or otherwise—[that] | *Premise*: legisla-tive history sup-ports Def's inter-pretation. *Proof*: Absence of history for individual li-ability is signif. Instead: replete with references to *employer* liability. |
| | Def. weaves in legislative purpose |

are incurred as a consequence of prohibited discrimination." *Id.* at 5.

    The legislative concern with deterrence also focused on employers, not on individual employees. The Senate Reports noted that employers must provide "punitive damages . . . in cases of intentional discrimination if the employer acted with 'malice' . . . ." *Id.* The reports also observed that employer liability "will serve as a necessary deterrent to future acts of discrimination . . . " *Id.* Even the suggested mechanisms for deterrence are restricted to mechanisms an employer might implement, not an individual. Congress hoped to "encourage employers to design and implement complaint structures [that] encourage victims to come forward by overcoming fear of retaliation and fear of loss of privacy . . . . Data suggests that employers do indeed implement measures to interrupt and prevent employment discrimination when they perceive that there is increased liability." *Id.* at 18 (statement of Dr. Klein).

    Moreover, the vocal dissenters to the Amendment failed to mention individual liability in their complaints. Had they considered individual liability even a remote possibility, they would have objected.

    [T]he dissenters supplied exhaustive, thoughtful, and even caustic responses to the Amendments. On such issues as the cost of business, number of litigants, and remuneration of lawyers, [Congress] apparently thought of every conceivable negative outcome and shouted it from the rooftops . . . [H]ad they considered individual liability a conceivable outcome, they would also have considered it a negative one and denounced it in a similar fashion. Yet they never mentioned it.

*Hudson,* 837 F. Supp. at 138.

*Side annotations:*

argument—that dual purposes of compensation and deterrence are adequately fulfilled by employer liability.

Def. argues that Congressional silence supports the Def's interpretation.
Def. quotes a compelling argument from a persuasive authority case to bolster the argument.

## D. Canons of Construction

    Canons of construction are guidelines that suggest possible ways to interpret statutory language and can also be useful tools of statutory interpretation. However, canons of construction are often criticized because their use may not actually promote the legislative purpose. No court will apply a canon of construction if it defeats the purpose of the statute. Nevertheless, effective advocates often employ canons of construction to argue why statutory language should be interpreted in a manner that benefits the client's position. In fact, because they are only broad guidelines, two different canons of construction can sometimes suggest two totally different interpretations of statutory language. Because canons of construction do not necessarily provide accurate guidance of legislative intent, judges may use canons of construction more to justify their decisions rather than to assist them in interpreting statutory language.[4] The following are a few of the better-known and often used canons of construction.

### 1.  *Criminal Statutes Narrowly Construed*

One of the more widely-known canons of construction is that criminal statutes should be interpreted narrowly in favor of the criminal defendant. The broad policy underlying this canon is that, in our society, people should not be punished for conduct unless they have reasonable notice that the conduct is prohibited. Therefore, when the language of a criminal statute does not expressly and clearly prohibit or apply to a particular defendant's conduct, you might use this canon to argue that the statute should be interpreted narrowly in favor of the criminal defendant.

### 2.  *Remedial Statutes Broadly Construed*

Another popular canon of construction advocates that remedial statutes should be broadly interpreted in favor of the plaintiff who seeks to recover remedies under the statute. The policy underlying this canon is that when the legislature seeks to compensate a class of individuals, the statute should be broadly construed to ensure that the intended victims will have redress under the statute. Examples of remedial statutes are workers' compensation laws, which provide money damages to employees who are injured while at work, and Title VII, which provides relief to persons who have been discriminated against in the terms of their employment due to race, sex, religion, color or national origin.

### 3.  *Ejusdem Generis*

Under the canon of *ejusdem generis*, when a statute mentions specific items to which it applies, followed by a general, sweeping phrase, the general phrase should be narrowly interpreted to include only those items that have the same characteristics as the specific items that were previously mentioned. Consider how this canon of construction might be applied to a residential burglary statute. An Illinois residential burglary statute prohibits the burglary of "dwell-

---

[4] Richard K. Neumann, Jr., *Legal Reasoning and Legal Writing: Structure, Strategy & Style* 161 (4th ed. Aspen L. & Bus. 2001), citing Karl N. Llewellyn, *The Common Law Tradition* 521–35 (Little, Brown & Co. 1960).

ings," and defines a "dwelling" as: "a house, apartment, mobile home, trailer or *other living quarters* in which at the time of the alleged offense the owners or occupants actually reside. . . ." Using this canon of construction, the term "other living quarters" might be narrowly interpreted to include those living quarters that share the same physical characteristics as a house, apartment, mobile home or trailer.

### 4. *Expressio Unius*

Under this canon of construction, when a statute expressly lists the conduct or items that it covers, any conduct or items not explicitly mentioned is thereby excluded.

## E. *The Equities*

When determining a statute's meaning, courts also want to arrive at a judgment that will be fair and equitable to the parties before the court. Therefore, consider how your favorable rule would result in a fair and just outcome to the parties. For example, in the federal wiretap problem illustrated in Appendix D, the government lost its wiretap evidence for two months before it submitted the tapes to a judge for sealing. In that case, it was the government's mistake in losing the wiretap evidence that created the problem before the court. Therefore, the defendant's attorney uses that mistake to an advantage, as follows:

| | |
|---|---|
| Finally, fairness mandates that the government bear this burden. "Inasmuch as a need for a 'satisfactory explanation' only arises when those in charge of the wiretap operation fail to do their homework and to present the tapes for immediate sealing, any doubts about the integrity of the evidence should be laid at law enforcement's doorstep." *United States v. Mora*, 821 F.2d at 868. | Defendant appeals to judge's fairness. Any doubts should favor the Def. because it was the government's mistake that caused the problem. |

## F. *Public Policy*

Courts also consider the public policy ramifications of their decisions. With statutes as the source of law, public policy considerations are usually linked to the legislative purpose. Courts strive to interpret statutes in a manner that will further the underlying purpose of the statute and have a positive impact on society. Conversely, they are reluctant to interpret statutes in a manner that would have a negative impact on society. Therefore, if possible, strengthen your argument by illustrating how your interpretation of the statute will advance the purposes of the statute and will positively affect society.

You can strengthen your argument even further if you identify the negative policy implications of the opponent's interpretation. When arguing why the opponent's interpretation would have negative policy implications, advocates often use a "slippery slopes" argument that leads to a "parade of horribles." To make such an argument, consider the logical consequences of your opponent's theory if taken to an absurd extreme. In fact, you have already had an opportunity to witness such an approach first-hand in your law school classes. Law professors often lead students down a slippery slope to an absurd extreme (the parade of horribles) as a means of teaching students how to think critically and how to draw reasonable lines.

### 1.  Example Illustrating Positive Effect on Public Policy

The following example is excerpted from Sample Brief A in Appendix C (the Title VII brief) and illustrates just one of the several policy arguments that appear in that brief.

| | |
|---|---|
| Additionally, restricting liability to employers, as Congress intended, adequately serves the deterrent purpose of the 1991 Amendments. By imposing liability on employers, Congress ensured that employers would police their workplaces and workforces. "A company that risks liability for the discriminatory acts of its agents will police its employees and institute disciplinary measures to deter discriminatory acts." *Haltek*, 864 F. Supp. at 805-06. No employer would permit its employees to violate Title VII when the employer is liable for the Title VII violation. "An employer that has incurred civil damages because one of its employees believes he can violate Title VII with impunity will quickly correct that employee's erroneous belief." *Miller*, 991 F. 2d at 586. | *Premise*: Def's interpretation serves the deterrent purpose of Title VII. *Proof*: 1st argument: employers will discipline employees. |
| Moreover, individuals face deterrents outside of Title VII that promote the Congressional goal of deterring future discrimination. For example, individuals face both professional and social sanctions in the form of demotion or firing and disapproval. They face "a loss of employment status, defense fees, and social approval." *Hudson*, 873 F. Supp. at 136. In addition, any conduct that violates Title VII also subjects an individual to civil liability for, among other things, assault, battery, and intentional infliction of emotional distress, or criminal liability for criminal sexual assault. Thus, individual | 2nd argument: individuals face outside deterrents. Arguments lead to conclusion: individual liability is unnecessary, redundant & unfair. |

liability under Title VII is unnecessary. It would be redundant as a deterrent and would unfairly expose individuals to double or triple punishment.

## 2. *Example Illustrating Negative Effect on Public Policy*

The following example is also excerpted from the Title VII brief illustrated in Appendix C. In the following paragraphs, the advocate argues that the opponent's interpretation (imposing individual liability) would thwart the legislative purpose and have a negative effect on public policy. The advocate argues why the opponent's interpretation of the statute is inconsistent with the statutory scheme and would thereby create unfair results. An argument attacking an opponent's position generally follows a favorable argument regarding the same idea. Because the opposing argument illustrated below relates to the damages provisions of the 1991 Amendments, this opposing argument follows a favorable argument regarding the damages provisions of the 1991 Amendments.

| | |
|---|---|
| Moreover, reading individual liability into the statute would mean that individuals would be subjected either to unlimited liability or to liability that depends upon the size of the employer for whom they work. Neither of these alternatives makes sense. First, subjecting employees to unlimited individual liability is simply inconsistent with Congress' careful efforts to prescribe the parameters of employer liability. "It is unreasonable to think that Congress would protect small entities from the costs associated with litigating discrimination claims and limit the available compensatory and punitive damages based on the size of the . . . employer, but subject an individual supervisory employee to unlimited liability." *Haltek*, 864 F. Supp. at 805. This result would cavalierly subject individuals to the vagaries of juries while protecting employer liability. Such a result would not only be manifestly unfair to individual employees but would thwart Congress' carefully calibrated scheme of damages. | *Broad Premise*: opponent's interpretation would create 1 of 2 absurd results. *Premise*: 1st result is inconsistent with legislative purpose.<br><br><br><br><br>*Proof*: 1st result is unfair to individuals and would thwart Congress' statutory scheme. |
| Second, imposing individual liability depending upon the size of the employer for whom the individual works is equally as nonsensical and unfair. Under this scenario, individuals who work for an employer with fewer than fifteen employees would not be subject to liability at all, while individuals who work for employers with fifteen or more employees would be subject to liability. In other words, it would create an incentive for potential violators of Title VII to work for small employers | *Premise*: 2nd result is equally as unfair.<br><br>*Proof*: Absurd results. |

to ensure that they could escape liability. Congress could not have intended this result. *Hudson*, 873 F. Supp. at 135.

Moreover, the damage caps reflect an employer's ability to pay, not an individual's ability to pay. In enacting the damage caps, Congress carefully calibrated the caps to consider an employer's ability to pay and the amount necessary to "punish" the offending employer, i.e., "to make it hurt." Thus, the calibrated damages caps reflect Congress' intention not to bankrupt an employer or punish an employer beyond the amount necessary to "make it hurt." Imposing an employer's damages cap on its individual employees would create unfair results that Congress could not possibly have intended. The calibrated damage caps do not similarly reflect an individual's ability to pay or the amount necessary to "punish" an individual. An individual who works for a large company does not necessarily have the ability to pay up to $300,000 in compensatory and punitive damages for violating Title VII, nor is that amount necessary to punish the individual. In fact, that penalty would easily bankrupt many employees and would thwart the legislative intent to avoid that prospect. Thus, the damages caps make sense only in the context of exclusive employer liability.

*Premise*: 2nd result would also thwart legislative intent.

*Proof*: Explores the purpose underlying the damage caps, and then

illustrates the unfair result to individuals that would thwart the statutory purpose.

## G. *Prudential Concerns*

When evaluating the meaning of rules of law, courts are also concerned with the impact their judgments might have on the court system, or "prudential concerns." As an example, courts are reluctant to interpret a statute in a manner that might "open the floodgates" of litigation. Thus, by invoking a "slippery slopes" argument, you might argue that the unfortunate result of the opponent's interpretation would be to open the floodgates of litigation, creating an unmanageable case load within the court system. Courts are also understandably concerned with judgments that might impede the ability of courts to manage their case loads efficiently. For example, a judge might be concerned about interpreting a statute in a manner that would require courts to engage in costly and time-consuming fact-finding inquiries. An appeal to the court's prudential concerns is illustrated in the sample wiretapping brief in Appendix D. An appeal to the court's prudential concerns is subtly buried within a paragraph, as follows:

> ... Congress carefully incorporated external safeguards within the statute to avoid the costly, time-consuming and inconclusive expert inquiries that inevitably result from fact-finding expeditions. By proving it held the tapes in a manner that ensures their integrity remained inviolate, the government's satisfactory explanation not only affords the level of protection of an immediate seal but avoids the problems Congress sought to avoid.

## H.  Persuasive Authority

When there is no mandatory authority that has interpreted a statutory provision and thereby resolved the dispute, the law-centered argument is not based on case law but, instead, on statutory interpretation. Persuasive authority cases are woven into the argument only to show their support for your ideas. Your ideas will be the engine that runs the argument, not persuasive authority cases.

Carefully review the examples within this chapter to observe how the advocate weaves persuasive authority into the argument. Notice that the advocate does not attempt to persuade the judge by out-right appeals to follow another court's decision. For example, the advocate does not argue: "Title VII does not impose individual liability because the Fifth Circuit Court of Appeals said so." This argument is not persuasive because an adjudicator's responsibility is to interpret the *statute*, not to follow courts in other jurisdictions. Thus, the argument focuses on the statute and what Congress intended, not on what other courts have decided. Nevertheless, the fact that other courts have interpreted the statute in a manner favorable to the advocate does have some persuasive appeal. Therefore, the cases are woven into the argument only as they illustrate specific points from the argument itself.

Some cases are woven into the argument because they contain persuasive language that can be quoted. For example:

> "It is unreasonable to think that Congress would protect small entities from the costs associated with litigating discrimination claims and limit the available compensatory and punitive damages based on the size of the ... employer, but subject an individual supervisory employee to unlimited liability." *Haltek*, 864 F. Supp. at 805.

Other cases simply provide support for an idea that is explored in the argument.

> In other words, it would create an incentive for potential violators of Title VII to work for small employers to ensure that they could escape liability. Congress could not have intended this result. *Hudson*, 873 F. Supp. at 135.

However, when the identity of a court has particular persuasive appeal, advocates sometimes emphasize the court itself. For example, you might find a favorable idea or quote from a decision of the United States Supreme Court or of a higher level court within your jurisdiction. These decisions of course would not have resolved the issue you are exploring. If they had, you would not be arguing what the statute means. Although these decisions may not have resolved the issue you are exploring, they may, nevertheless, contain general policy language that supports your underlying argument. The following hypothetical example illustrates how to draw the judge's attention to the court itself:

> As the United States Supreme Court observed, [statement follows]. . . . *Brown v. Bd. of Educ.*, 349 U.S. 294, 297 (1955).

## III  ▸ *DRAFTING THE ARGUMENT*

### A.  *Your Favorable Interpretations of the Law as the Focal Point*

You are now familiar with the types of arguments available to you when you draft arguments based on statutes. How might you organize the various arguments into a persuasive, coherent argument? A good focal point is the favorable interpretation of the law you want to persuade the adjudicator to adopt. Your over-all goal is to convince the adjudicator to adopt your interpretation of the statute. As you outline and then draft your argument, keep your focus on this goal. Every paragraph should help lead the reader to the conclusion that your interpretation of the statute is superior to any other interpretation and should, therefore, be adopted. Thus, every paragraph should help prove why the statutory language supports your interpretation, or why the statutory scheme supports your interpretation, or how your interpretation furthers the underlying purpose of the statute, or why your interpretation is most equitable, or how your interpretation favorably affects public policy. As you advance these arguments, you should weave in arguments that illustrate how your opponent's interpretation fails to accomplish these goals. Keeping your focus on the ultimate goal can also help you edit and polish your initial drafts. As you review your initial drafts, make margin notes describing the premise of each paragraph. If the paragraph does not serve any of these purposes, then it does not belong in a persuasive argument.

## B.  Begin With Your Strongest Arguments

Consider the various arguments you have identified from reading the statute and persuasive authority cases. In drafting a persuasive argument, begin with your strongest argument, followed by the next strongest argument, and so on. When a statute is the source of law, the statute's plain language is the first step of any court's inquiry into a statute's meaning. After all, the statutory language itself is the strongest proof of the statute's meaning. If the statutory language supports your conclusion, begin your argument by arguing why the statutory language compels or at least supports your interpretation. The statutory language of the specific section at issue may support your argument, and/or the statutory scheme as a whole may support your argument. As you argue why the statutory language or statutory scheme supports your favorable interpretation, you might also weave in the legislative purpose of the statute where appropriate. Sometimes policy arguments can enhance the persuasive appeal of an argument based on statutory language or a statutory scheme.

Recall, however, that not every statute lends itself to such an argument. For example, the term "satisfactory explanation" in the federal wiretap statute is so broad and vague that it does not lend itself to an argument based on the language of the statute. Therefore, include this argument only if it makes sense to do so with the statutory language you are interpreting.

Following any statutory language argument, the outline of your argument will vary depending upon the relative strength of different arguments that support your interpretation. Generally, however, after the statute itself, the next best evidence of the statute's meaning is the underlying purpose of the statute. Again, the structure of your argument should be dictated by the strengths of the various arguments you have available. Save the weaker arguments until the end. Omit entirely any arguments that are so weak that they might dilute the strength of other arguments or weaken your credibility. Include only those arguments that a reasonable person would find persuasive in evaluating the meaning of the statute.

## C.   Outlining Your Argument

After you have prioritized your arguments by their relative strength, you are in a position to sketch a template of your argument. Recall the deductive writing pattern of an office memo. The deductive writing pattern begins with broad principles and then illustrates the broad principles with specific information. You will use the same deductive writing pattern when structuring an argument based on statutory interpretation. However, the deductive pattern will be focused on achieving your ultimate goal—to persuade an adjudicator to give your client the relief the client desires. The most effective way to achieve that goal is by using an organizational structure that is so logical and reasonable that the reader cannot help but agree with your conclusion. As Judge Aldisert, Senior United States Circuit Judge for the Third Circuit Court of Appeals, notes:

> Your objective . . . should be to start with a proposition that the court—whatever its bent—must accept; then reason, logically, step by step, to your conclusion. If you do this well, you will arrive at your destination with the court right beside you. Your conclusion will make sense, not just because you say so, but because the court will have reasoned along with you.[5]

### 1.   Create a Skeleton Outline of Your Argument

How might you achieve this goal of logically, step by step, leading an adjudicator to your conclusion? First, write down the ultimate conclusion you want the adjudicator to reach—your favorable interpretation of the statute. Next, fill in the essential, major points you will need to make in order to prove why your interpretation is sound (*"major premises"*). These major premises provide the skeleton outline of your argument. Using the Title VII argument for purposes of illustration, a skeleton outline of the defendant's argument would look like this:

---

[5] Ruggero J. Aldisert, *Winning on Appeal: Better Briefs & Oral Argument* 146 (NITA 1992).

> *Ultimate conclusion to prove*: Title VII, including the 1991 Amendments, imposes liability only on employers, not individual employees.
>
> *Major premises*:
>
> I.    The plain language of Title VII imposes liability only on employers.
>
> II.   The 1991 Amendments expanded only the scope of remedies and did not expand the class of defendants.
>
> III.  Exclusive employer liability adequately furthers the dual purposes of Title VII to compensate and deter.

## 2.  Fill in the Basic Premises that Prove Each of the Major Premises

After you have drafted the major premises you will use to prove your conclusion, next consider the arguments that support each of the major premises. You might visualize the process as an unfolding accordion, with the broad skeleton outline as a closed accordion. The accordion begins to unfold in this step, as you begin to fill in the skeleton outline, as follows:

> *Ultimate conclusion to prove*: Title VII, including the 1991 Amendments, imposes liability only on employers, not individual employees.
>
> I.    *1ˢᵗ Major Premise*: The plain language of Title VII imposes liability only on employers.
>
>   1. Title VII's definition of "employer" provides for exclusive liability.
>   2. Original remedies under Title VII confirms that liability is imposed only on employers.

II.   *2ⁿᵈ Major Premise*: The 1991 Amendments expanded only the scope of remedies and did not expand the class of defendants

    1.   The original definition of "employer" and "agent" was left undisturbed.

    2.   The new damages provisions reflect exclusive employer liability.

    3.   Legislative history under the 1991 Amendments reflects exclusive employer liability.

III.  *3ʳᵈ Major Premise*: Exclusive employer liability adequately furthers the dual purposes of Title VII to compensate and deter.

    1.   1991 Amendments ensure adequate compensation from the entity best able to provide compensation.

    2.   1991 Amendments serve deterrent purpose because employers now have incentive to police their workplaces.

    3.   Individual employees are already adequately deterred.

### 3.   Fill in the "Proof" for Each Basic Premise

Before beginning the drafting process, many attorneys create an even more detailed outline, filling in the structure of the "proof" that will support each basic premise. They reason that the outlining process ultimately saves them time while drafting the argument because they can begin the drafting process with a clear idea of each of the arguments they will need to make. Other attorneys prefer to begin drafting at this point, reasoning that they can think more clearly as they draft. They reason that, after drafting the argument, they can cut and paste various sections of the argument to ensure that the final draft is logical and persuasive. Choose the process that works most effectively for you. However, whether you further fill in the details of your outline or begin drafting at this point, the template of your final draft should resemble a fully opened accordion that clearly lays out each step of your analysis.

### (a)   Template of the Argument

The template of a completed argument should look like this:

I.    Ultimate Conclusion

    A.    First major premise that proves the conclusion

        1.    First basic premise that proves the major premise
            (a)   $1^{st}$ supporting proof for first basic premise
            (b)   $2^{nd}$ supporting proof for first basic premise
            (c)   And so on

        2.    Second basic premise that proves the major premise
            (a)   $1^{st}$ supporting proof for second basic premise
            (b)   $2^{nd}$ supporting proof for second basic premise
            (c)   And so on

        3.    And so on
    B.    Second major premise that proves the conclusion

        1.    First basic premise that proves the second major
           premise
            (a)   $1^{st}$ supporting proof for first basic premise
            (b)   $2^{nd}$ supporting proof for first basic premise
            (c)   And so on

        2.    Second basic premise that proves the second major
           premise
            (a)   $1^{st}$ supporting proof for second basic premise
            (b)   $2^{nd}$ supporting proof for second basic premise
            (c)   And so on

        3.    And so on

    C.    Third major premise that proves the conclusion

    And so on . . .

*(b)   Illustration of Detailed Outline for the Title VII Argument:*

Ultimate conclusion to prove: Title VII, including the 1991 Amendments, impose liability only on employers, not individual employees.

I.   *1ˢᵗ major premise*: The plain language of Title VII imposes liability only on employers.

    1.   Title VII's definition of "employer" provides for exclusive liability.

       (a)   Only employers can have 15 or more employees.

       (b)   Because the statute links the word "agent" to the "employer," imposing individual liability would create absurd result—individual liability would be dependent on whether the employer had more than 15 employees.

       (c)   Imposing liability on individuals would thwart Congress' purpose in shielding entities with limited resources.

    2.   Original remedies under Title VII confirm that liability is imposed only on employers.

       (a)   Original remedies are restricted to remedies only an employer can provide.

II.   *2ⁿᵈ major premise*: The 1991 Amendments expanded only the scope of remedies and did not expand the class of defendants.

    1.   The original definition of "employer" and "agent" was left undisturbed.

       (a)   If Congress had wanted to change the definition, it would have done so.

    2.   The new damages provisions reflect exclusive employer liability.

       (a)   Congress calibrated the damage caps based only on employer size, not individuals.

       (b)   Imposing individual liability would create absurd results, either:

          (i)   Unlimited individual liability, or

          (ii)   Individual liability tied to the size of the employer.

    3.   Legislative history under the 1991 Amendments reflects exclusive employer liability.

       (a)   Congress focused exclusively on employers, both in terms of:

          (i)   Compensation, and

(ii)  Deterrence.
    (b)  Legislative history is silent re: individuals.

III.  *3rd major premise*: Exclusive employer liability adequately furthers the dual purposes of Title VII to compensate and deter.

    1.  1991 Amendments ensure adequate compensation from the entity best able to provide compensation.

    2.  1991 Amendments serve deterrent purpose because employers now have incentive to police their workplaces.
    3.  Individual employees are already adequately deterred:
        (a)  Professional and social sanctions
        (b)  Civil and criminal liability

## EXERCISE 1

Carefully review the sample brief in Appendix D that evaluates the federal wiretap statute. Then draft an outline of the law-centered argument (the argument following the first point-heading: I. AS PART OF ITS "SATISFACTORY EXPLANATION" THE GOVERNMENT MUST PROVE THAT ITS PRE-SEALING PROCEDURES PROTECTED THE WIRETAP TAPES FROM ANY POSSIBILITY OF TAMPERING).

In your outline, begin with the conclusion the advocate wants the judge to adopt. Following that conclusion, outline the template of that argument, including: (1) the major premise or premises that support the conclusion; (2) the basic premises that support each major premise; and (3) the proof that supports each basic premise.

# 21

# LAW-CENTERED ARGUMENTS: BASED ON CASES

 ## I  CASE JUSTIFICATION

Law-centered issues are those issues in which the meaning of the law itself is unclear. Chapter 20 discusses the construct of a law-centered argument when there is no mandatory precedent in the jurisdiction. Sometimes, however, higher level courts in a jurisdiction have arguably addressed the disputed legal issue. Of course, if the previous cases were crystal clear, you and your opposing counsel would not be disputing the law's meaning—a court would be compelled to follow such precedent. The fact that you and your opposing counsel are actually disputing the significance of legal precedent in your jurisdiction means that the precedent is less than clear. For example, it may be unclear whether a precedent case actually resolved the issue at all. Alternatively, perhaps there are several cases in a jurisdiction that seemingly conflict.

When previous higher level courts in your jurisdiction have left the meaning of the law unclear, you must convince the court that it has the *legal authority* to adopt your legal interpretation. Recall that, under our legal system of stare decisis, courts must follow the previous legal interpretations of higher level courts within the relevant jurisdiction ("mandatory authority"). Therefore, you must not only convince the judge that the original rule of law itself supports your interpretation, but that mandatory precedent gives the judge the legal authority to adopt your interpretation. To distinguish this type of law-centered argument from other types of arguments, we will refer to this type of law-centered argument as a *"case justification"* argument. A case justification argument illustrates how prior mandatory case law justifies a favorable decision.

## A.  *Options When Evaluating Each Individual Case*

When the meaning of a mandatory case precedent is ambiguous, the case can potentially be construed in one of three ways. First, after careful consideration of the prior case's language, you might argue that the court actually interpreted the rule of law in a manner favorable to your client. As an advocate, this is the most favorable option—if mandatory case precedent actually adopts your favorable rule, our system of stare decisis would *compel* the judge to adopt your legal interpretation.

Second, you might argue that the prior case failed to resolve the legal issue at all. If no prior higher level court in the jurisdiction has definitively resolved the legal question, the issue is actually one of first impression. Therefore, the judge would be justified in interpreting the rule of law in whatever manner the judge deems appropriate.

Finally, you might conclude that the court did indeed adopt your opponent's unfavorable interpretation of the rule of law. Of course, you would not be constructing such an argument unless there were other more favorable cases in the jurisdiction that at least arguably conflicted with the adverse case—you would not be attempting to convince an judge to adopt a position that is flatly inconsistent with mandatory precedent. Therefore, under this scenario, you would argue that, because previous case law is inconsistent, the judge is justified in interpreting the legal rule in either manner.

### *The Options at a Glance:*

| | |
|---|---|
| *Option 1:* | Prior case adopts your favorable interpretation of the rule of law. |
| *Option 2:* | Prior case does not resolve the issue. |
| *Option 3:* | Prior case adopts your opponent's interpretation of the rule of law. |
| | (You would concede an unfavorable interpretation only if there were other cases in the jurisdiction that conflict with the adverse case.) |

## 1. Arguing that a Prior Mandatory Case Has Adopted Your Favorable Rule Interpretations

Before arguing that a higher level court in your jurisdiction has already resolved the issue in a manner favorable to your legal position, review the previous court decision with an excruciatingly precise attention to detail. Carefully review each and every word of the case, including the footnotes, noting the specific quoted language that supports your argument. Consider all of the reasons underlying the previous court's decision, both expressed and implied. To successfully persuade a judge that a previous higher level court has already resolved the issue, your argument concerning that individual case would look like this:

---

*Thesis Sentence*:  State your conclusion—that the case has adopted your favorable interpretation.

*Prove why your conclusion is sound*:

1.  Highlight and quote specific language in the opinion that supports your conclusion;

2.  Emphasize how the court's over-all holding supports your conclusion; and, if possible,

3.  Describe how logic or policy considerations support your conclusion that the court adopted your favorable legal interpretation.

---

 **ILLUSTRATION: Fifth Amendment Problem**

As an example, consider the Fifth Amendment problem that is the basis of Sample Brief B in Appendix C. *Background*: In that hypothetical problem, the government is prosecuting the defendant, Mr. Browne, for unlawful distribution of drugs. The government has issued a subpoena to obtain Mr. Browne's personal diary. The government contends that the diary contains entries that reflect Mr. Browne's illegal drug activities. Rather than turning over the diary to the government, Browne's attorney has filed a Motion to Quash the subpoena. Browne's attorney argues that Mr. Browne's personal diary is protected by the Fifth Amendment of the United States Constitution. The Fifth Amendment protects people from self-incrimination. However, the language is vague and general, leaving courts to resolve specific issues as to the Amendment's meaning. The Amendment states that: "No person . . . shall be compelled in any criminal case to be a witness against himself. . . ." U.S. Const. amend. V.

The government's attorney argues that the Fifth Amendment should be narrowly construed only to protect persons from incriminating themselves with their *oral* testimony. The government argues that the Fifth Amendment does not also protect persons from incriminating themselves with their *written* documents. Browne's attorney argues, however, that the Fifth Amendment should be broadly construed to protect persons from incriminating themselves with their written documents as well as their oral testimony. Browne has a favorable Supreme Court case that has adopted this position. As we will see later, however, this Supreme Court case is an old case and its holding has been eroded over the years. Nevertheless, Browne must use the old case to persuade the judge that mandatory authority has adopted Browne's broad interpretation of the Fifth Amendment. Thus, Browne's attorney argues:

| | |
|---|---|
| The Supreme Court has long held that the Fifth Amendment protects personal papers as well as oral testimony. *See United States v. Boyd*, 116 U.S. 616 (1886). | *Premise*: Mandatory case adopts favorable rule. |
| In *Boyd*, the Court equated seizing a person's personal documents as evidence against him with compelling that person to be a witness against himself: "And we have been unable to perceive that the seizure of a man's private books and papers to be used in evidence against him is substantially different from compelling him to be a witness against himself." *Id.* Additionally, the Court admonished that "any forcible and compulsory extortion of a man's own testimony or of his private papers . . . is within the condemnation of [the Fifth Amendment]," *id.* at 630, and "contrary to the principles of a free government." *Id.* at 635–36. | *Proof*: Policy reason why court adopted broad rule. |
| | Exact language is quoted to illustrate the broad holding. |

### 2.  Arguing that a Prior Mandatory Case Failed to Resolve the Legal Issue at All

As with the preceding option, before arguing that a higher level court in your jurisdiction has failed to resolve a legal issue, carefully review the previous court decision with a painstaking attention to detail. Carefully review each and every word of the case, including the footnotes, noting the specific quoted language that supports your argument that the court did not resolve the issue.

To successfully persuade a judge that a previous higher level court failed to resolve the issue, your argument concerning that case would look like this:

---

*Thesis Sentence*:    State your conclusion—that the case failed to resolve the legal issue.

*Prove why your conclusion is sound*:

1.    Highlight and quote *specific language* in the opinion that supports your conclusion;

2.    Emphasize how the court's *holding* was extremely narrow, resolving only the precise narrow issue in dispute in that case (i.e., an issue that differs from the issue you are disputing); and, if possible,

3.    Emphasize how *logic or policy considerations* compel the conclusion that the court intended a very narrow holding; and, if possible,

4.    Emphasize how *logic or policy* considerations compel the conclusion that the court could not possibly have intended to resolve the present disputed issue.

---

Again using the Fifth Amendment problem as an example, the defendant's attorney also had to address several other Supreme Court cases that are more recent than the century old *Boyd* case. *Boyd* has been criticized by more recent Supreme Court decisions and its present viability has been questioned. Therefore, in order to convince the court that it is compelled to follow *Boyd*, Browne's attorney must also persuade the court that the recent Supreme Court cases (*Fisher* and *Doe*) did not actually address the narrow legal issue before the court—whether a written personal document is protected by the Fifth Amendment. Because the recent Supreme Court cases held that business records are not protected by the Fifth Amendment, Browne's attorney must make a distinction between business records and personal documents. If the court accepts Browne's argument that *Fisher* and *Doe* did not resolve the narrow question of personal documents, the court would be compelled to follow the earlier *Boyd* case—the *Boyd* case would be the only mandatory precedent that actually resolved the precise issue before the court. In the following example excerpted from Sample Brief B in Appendix C, the defendant argues that two recent Supreme Court cases did not actually resolve the question before the court:

| | |
|---|---|
| Although the Supreme Court recently concluded that *Boyd* does not protect *business* documents, it has preserved *Boyd*'s protection of personal papers. *See Doe*, 465 U.S. at 610; *Fisher*, 425 U.S. at 403. In *Fisher*, the Court held that the Fifth Amendment does not protect the contents of tax records prepared by the defendant's accountant. *Id.* at 393. The Court based this holding on the fact that business documents do not implicate the privacy interests of personal papers: "special problems of privacy [that] might be presented by subpoena of a personal diary are not involved here." *Id.* at 407 n.7. | *Premise*: Recent cases did not resolve issue. *Proof*: 1$^{st}$ case: Narrow holding— only tax records. Public policy illustrates narrow holding. |
| Additionally, the Court preserved *Boyd*'s protection of personal papers by emphasizing that "[w]hether the Fifth Amendment would shield the taxpayer from producing his own tax records . . . is a question not involved here; for the papers demanded here are not his 'private papers.'" *Id.* at 414. | Quotes exact language that illustrates narrow holding. |
| Similarly, *Doe* preserved *Boyd*'s protection of personal papers. In *Doe*, the Court held that the Fifth Amendment did not protect the contents of business records in the possession of the owner of a sole proprietorship. *Doe*, 465 U.S. at 617. However, the *Doe* Court preserved *Boyd*'s protection of personal papers by premising its holding on the corporate nature of the documents. The Court carefully noted that "each of the documents sought here pertained to [the defendant's] business." *Id.* at 610 n.7. | *Premise*: Case 2 does not resolve issue. *Proof*: Narrow holding—only business records. Exact language that emphasizes narrow holding. |

## B.  Constructing an Argument Strategy for a Group of Cases

If your research reveals only one mandatory authority case that has arguably addressed the disputed legal issue, the preceding discussion illustrates two straight-forward options. You might argue that the case resolves the issue in a manner favorable to your client, or argue that the case fails to resolve the issue at all. However, when your research reveals two or more mandatory authority cases within your jurisdiction that have arguably addressed the legal issue you are disputing, your argument strategy is more challenging. Under such circumstances, you must not only decide how you want to interpret each individual case's holding, but must also look at the cases as a collective group.

When dealing with more than one mandatory authority case, you must be careful to ensure that your treatment of each individual case within the group is consistent with your over-all goal. Your goal is to frame each court's holding in such a way that the group of cases, collectively, supports your legal argument. When viewed collectively, all of the individual case's outcomes must either *compel* the judge to adopt your favorable interpretation of the rule of law or *allow* the judge to adopt that interpretation. Consider the consequences if you failed to include each relevant case within your argument construct. If, for example, Browne's attorney in the Fifth Amendment problem had relied only on the favorable *Boyd* case, the attorney might well have lost the ultimate argument. Without Browne's artful advocacy, the government might have been able to convince the judge that the two recent Supreme Court decisions resolved the question and implicitly overruled *Boyd*. Therefore, when evaluating more than one prior case, you must construct an argument strategy that helps ensure that your client will ultimately prevail.

In considering the cases as a collective group, there are four possible ways to structure your argument. First, you might argue that each case within the collective group has adopted your favorable interpretation of the rule of law. Second, you might argue that one or more cases within the collective group has adopted your favorable interpretation of the rule of law, while the remaining cases have not resolved the legal issue at all. Third, you might argue that none of the cases within the collective group has actually resolved the legal issue. Finally, you might argue that one or more cases within the collective group has adopted your favorable interpretation of the rule of law, while one or more of the remaining cases has adopted an unfavorable interpretation of the rule of law (i.e., a split of authority within the jurisdiction).

## 1.  Each Case Within the Group Has Adopted Your Favorable Interpretation

Assuming the cases in your jurisdiction can reasonably be construed as having adopted your favorable legal interpretation, this is a highly favorable argument construct—if each of the higher level courts within the jurisdiction has already adopted your favorable rule, the judge would be compelled to adopt that legal interpretation. Assuming there are two such cases that have adopted your favorable rule, the template of your case justification argument would look like this:

| | |
|---|---|
| *Ultimate Conclusion & Consequences* | Mandatory precedent has adopted your favorable interpretation of the rule of law. Therefore, the court is compelled to adopt your favorable interpretation. |
| | *Proof of Ultimate Conclusion*: |
| Case 1:    Premise: | Adopts your favorable interpretation of the rule of law. |
| Proof: | Highlight and quote *specific language*, the favorable *holding* and, if possible, the *logic or policy considerations* that support your conclusion. |
| Case 2:    Premise: | Adopts your favorable interpretation of the rule of law. |
| Proof: | Highlight and quote *specific language*, the favorable *holding* and, if possible, the *logic or policy considerations* that support your conclusion. |
| *Restate conclusion & ultimate consequences* | Because Cases 1 & 2 have adopted your favorable interpretation of the law, the court is compelled to follow Cases 1 & 2. |

## 2.   Some Cases Adopt Your Favorable Interpretation & Remaining Cases Fail to Resolve

| | |
|---|---|
| *Ultimate Conclusion & Consequences* | Mandatory precedent has adopted your favorable interpretation of the rule of law. Therefore, the court is compelled to adopt your favorable interpretation. |

|  | | *Proof of Ultimate Conclusion*: |
|---|---|---|
| <u>Case 1</u>: | Premise: | Adopts your favorable interpretation of the rule of law. |
| | Proof: | Highlight and quote *specific language*, the favorable *holding* and, if possible, the *logic or policy considerations* that support your conclusion. |
| <u>Case 2</u>: | Premise: | Fails to resolve the issue at all. |
| | Proof: | Highlight and quote *specific language*, the *narrow holding* and, if possible, the *logic or policy considerations* that support your conclusion. |
| <u>*Restate conclusion & ultimate consequences*</u>: | | Because Case 1 has adopted your favorable interpretation of the law, and Case 2 has failed to resolve the issue, the court is compelled to follow Case 1. |

The Fifth Amendment brief illustrates this type of argument construct. In the Motion to Quash, Browne's attorney argued that *Boyd* adopted the favorable rule interpretation (the Fifth Amendment protects personal papers from compelled disclosure), and that remaining mandatory authority failed to address the issue at all (*Fischer* and *Doe* narrowly addressed the compelled disclosure of business records but did not address private papers).

### 3.   No Case Within the Collective Group Has Resolved the Issue

After carefully reviewing each precedent case, you might conclude that none of the cases actually addresses or resolves the narrow question you are disputing. If no prior case in the jurisdiction has definitively resolved the legal question, the issue becomes one of "first impression." When a court addresses an issue of first impression, the court is justified in interpreting the rule of law in whatever manner the court deems appropriate. Assuming again there are two cases within the jurisdiction that are the subject of your inquiry, the template of your case justification argument would look like this:

| | |
|---|---|
| *Ultimate Conclusion & Consequences*: | Mandatory precedent has not addressed or resolved the issue before the court. Therefore, the court is justified in adopting your favorable interpretation.<br><br>*Proof of Ultimate Conclusion*: |
| Case 1:   Premise | Failed to resolve the issue at all. |
|         Proof: | Highlight and quote *specific language,* the *narrow holding* and, if possible, the *logic or policy considerations* that support your conclusion. |
| Case 2:   Premise: | Failed to resolve the issue at all. |
|         Proof: | Highlight and quote *specific language,* the *narrow holding* and, if possible, the *logic or policy considerations* that support your conclusion. |
| *Restate conclusion & ultimate consequences*: | Because Cases 1 & 2 failed to address or resolve the issue, the court is justified in adopting your favorable interpretation. |

Using the Fifth Amendment problem as an example, if the *Boyd* case did not exist, Browne's attorney would argue that, because neither *Fischer* or *Doe* definitively resolved the issue, the court would be justified in adopting the defendant's broad interpretation of the Fifth Amendment.

## 4.   *The Cases Conflict*

The fourth argument construct is the least desirable option. It not only allows the court to adopt either your favorable interpretation of the rule of law or your opponent's unfavorable interpretation, but you must convince the judge to reject the unfavorable law. Under this argument construct, you would argue that one or more mandatory cases have adopted your favorable interpretation of the law and that one or more mandatory cases adopted your opponent's unfavorable interpretation of the law. You must also motivate the court to follow the favorable cases and reject the unfavorable cases. For purposes of clarity, we will refer to the latter type of arguments as "motivating" arguments. Motivating argument strategies are discussed below in Section II. Setting the details of motivating arguments aside for the moment, when structuring a case justification argument, argue the favorable case first. Thus, the general template of your case justification argument would look like this:

| | |
|---|---|
| _Ultimate Conclusion &_ _Consequences_: | Mandatory precedent has adopted your favorable interpretation. The favorable precedent should be followed because . . . . Unfavorable mandatory precedent should be ignored because . . . |
| | _Proof of Ultimate Conclusion_: |
| Case 1:   Premise: | Case has adopted your favorable interpretation of the rule of law. |
| Proof: | Highlight and quote _specific language_, the favorable _holding_ and, if possible, the _logic or policy considerations_ that support your conclusion. |
| Case 2:   Premise: | Case incorrectly interpreted the rule of law and should be ignored. |
| Proof: | Argue why the case _incorrectly interpreted_ the rule of law, and/or how the court's unfavorable holding would have _adverse policy ramifications_. |
| _Restate conclusion &_ _ultimate consequences_: | Because Case 1 correctly interpreted the rule of law, and Case 2 incorrectly interpreted the law, the court should follow Case 1. |

# II   *MOTIVATING ARGUMENTS*

## A.  *Motivate the Judge to Adopt Your Interpretation*

### 1.  *Argue the Favorable Implications of Your Interpretation*

Rarely is an advocate so convinced of the merits of the case justification argument that the advocate summarily ends the argument there. If mandatory
precedent was so clearly one-sided, two attorneys would not be disputing the
meaning of that precedent. Therefore, it is good practice to also convince the
judge why the favorable cases are reasonable and just. In other words, your
goal is to motivate the judge to approve of your favorable interpretation of the
law. Like most people, judges strive to "do the right thing." If you and an opposing counsel each argue that the same case should be interpreted in two conflicting ways, a judge is more likely to climb out on a limb and accept your argument if the judge believes that your interpretation of the mandatory case law
would produce better law.

How might you persuade a court that your favorable interpretation of the
rule of law is better law? You would employ the arguments described in
Chapter 20 to argue how the favorable interpretation best effectuates the purposes of the rule of law. For example, you might argue how your interpretation
of the mandatory precedent would ensure an equitable and fair result to the
parties (the *equities* argument from Chapter 20). You might also argue how
your favorable interpretation would have positive public policy ramifications
(the *public policy* argument from Chapter 20). You might also argue how your
favorable interpretation addresses any prudential concerns the court might
have (the *prudential concerns* argument from Chapter 20). If the source of the
law is statutory, you would also argue how the statutory language and the
statutory scheme support your favorable interpretation (the *plain language* and
*statutory scheme* arguments from Chapter 20).

### 2.  *Incorporating Motivating Arguments into the Argument*
###     *Structure*

As you consider how to incorporate motivating arguments into your argument structure, you have two basic formatting options and a hybrid of the two
basic options. First, you can weave the motivating arguments into the case justification argument, arguing not only what the precedent court held, but why
the court's holding is sound policy. Second, you can argue the justification and
motivating arguments separately, first arguing one type of argument and then
arguing the other type of argument. Finally, you can format your argument

based on a hybrid of the two other alternatives, weaving some motivating arguments into your case justification arguments but also including a separate section that explores the motivating arguments in greater detail.

### (a)   Weave the Motivating Arguments Into the Case Justification Argument

Often, the two arguments relate to each—the precedent court ostensibly adopted your favorable interpretation of the rule of law because of sound policy reasons. Under such circumstances, it is very effective to weave the motivating arguments into the justification arguments—any argument appears more reasonable when supported by policy and logic. You may find it helpful to outline the case justification argument first, and then weave into the outline specific motivating arguments that support a particular point. Then, if there are some motivating arguments that do not dovetail into the justification argument, they can be incorporated into the beginning and/or end of the argument (the hybrid option).

Again using the Fifth Amendment problem for purposes of illustration, Sample Brief B illustrates the hybrid option. Recall that Browne's attorney seeks to quash the subpoena of the client's personal diary, arguing that the diary is protected from compelled disclosure by the Fifth Amendment. In the first and second paragraphs illustrated below, Browne's attorney introduces the argument with the strong public policy interests that underlie the Fifth Amendment (motivating arguments). In the third and fourth paragraphs, Browne's attorney argues how mandatory precedent has adopted a favorable, expansive interpretation of the Fifth Amendment (case justification arguments). Through-out the case justification arguments, Browne's attorney also weaves in motivating arguments.

| | |
|---|---|
| The privilege against compulsory self-incrimination derives from the Fifth Amendment's "'respect [for] a private inner sanctum of individual feeling and thought' . . . that necessarily includes an individual's papers." *Bellis*, 417 U.S. at 91. In particular, it recognizes that "compelling self-accusation . . . would be both cruel and unjust." *Boyd*, 116 U.S. at 629. While the privilege may at times protect the guilty, the Supreme Court has admonished that "the evils of compelling self-disclosure transcends any difficulties . . . in the detection and prosecution of crime." *United States v. White*, 322 U.S. 694, 698 (1944). These evils include subjecting people to "iniquitous methods of prosecution," *id.*, betraying "the inviolability of the human personality," risking | Browne begins the argument by emphasizing the broad policy that underlies the Fifth Amendment.

These policy concerns set up the favorable conclusion that the protections of the Fifth Amendment |

encroachment on the basic liberties of all citizens, and undermining the adversarial system. *Murphy*, 378 U.S. at 55. Accordingly, the Fifth Amendment proscribes invasion into "the privacies of life." *Boyd*, 116 U.S. at 630.

must be broadly construed to protect personal papers.

Personal papers are part of "the privacies of life." Failure to protect personal papers would thwart their development, thus inhibiting creativity and suppressing expression. Moreover, failure to protect personal documents would adversely affect the innocent as well as the guilty. *Boyd*, 116 U.S. at 629. Finally, failing to protect personal documents would create an artificial distinction between an individual's oral testimony and writings, even if the two are substantively identical. The Fifth Amendment does not contemplate such an anomalous result.

Policy reasons why personal papers should be protected under the Fifth Amendment.

Accordingly, the Supreme Court has long held that the Fifth Amendment protects personal papers as well as oral testimony. *See Boyd*, 116 U.S. at 633. In *Boyd*, the Court equated seizing a person's documents as evidence against him with compelling that person to be a witness against himself: "And we have been unable to perceive that the seizure of a man's private books and papers to be used in evidence against him is substantially different from compelling him to be a witness against himself." *Id.* Additionally, the Court admonished that "any forcible and compulsory extortion of a man's own testimony or of his private papers . . . is within the condemnation of [the Fifth Amendment]," *id.* at 630, and "contrary to the principals of a free government." *Id.* at 635–36.

The previous policy reasons set up Browne's favorable interpretation of *Boyd*. Even in this case justification paragraph, policy is woven into the argument to show why the court's holding is good policy.

Since *Boyd*, the Supreme Court has reiterated *Boyd's* protection of personal papers. For example, in *Bellis*, the Supreme Court acknowledged that "[i]t has long been established . . . that the Fifth Amendment . . . protects an individual from compelled production of his personal papers." 417 U.S. at 87. And, in *White*, the Supreme Court observed that it is the Fifth Amendment's "historic function [to protect an individual] from compulsory incrimination through his own testimony or personal records." 322 U.S. at 701. In each of these cases, the Supreme Court could not have been clearer; the Fifth Amendment protects individuals from the compelled production of their personal papers.

Browne bolsters the case justification argument with two additional Supreme Court cases that adopted the favorable interpretation of the 5th Amendment.

### (b)  Argue Case Justification and Motivating Arguments Separately

Sometimes motivating arguments do not neatly dovetail into a case justification argument. For example, if you argue that earlier mandatory cases have not addressed or resolved an issue, then presumably the courts did not consider the policy or other arguments that relate to the issue. It is still possible under this scenario to weave in motivating arguments. However, you might decide that such arguments would interfere with your ability to present your case justification argument clearly and effectively.

Should you choose to argue your case justification and motivating arguments separately, you can argue either type of argument first. Each choice has advantages and can be used effectively depending upon the legal issue in question. From a logical perspective, the case justification argument is the threshold issue. If a judge does not have the authority to adopt a particular interpretation of a rule of law, it does not matter how compelling the motivating arguments might be. The judge is bound by stare decisis to follow mandatory precedent. Therefore, if the justification argument is hotly disputed and will require a detailed, sophisticated argument, a judge would probably want to consider that argument first. Under this scenario, after advancing your case justification argument, you would then motivate the judge by elaborating on all of the sound reasons why your favorable interpretation is the better rule.

However, if your strongest arguments are motivating arguments, and your case justification argument is somewhat weak, it can be persuasive to argue the motivating arguments first. The convincing policy and other considerations in the motivating argument might enhance the likelihood that a judge would also accept your case justification argument. Nevertheless, if the case justification argument is so important that it really must be argued first, this option is not viable. Instead, you can choose an alternative format that accommodates the competing concerns—the hybrid option

### (c) The Hybrid Option

For the reasons stated above, you may sometimes conclude that the case justification argument should be argued first, even though it is the weaker of the two types of arguments. Under such circumstances, you can strengthen the case justification argument by expanding the roadmap paragraphs that introduce the body of the argument itself. In other words, you can set the stage for your case justification argument by enlarging and enhancing your introductory roadmap paragraphs so that they persuasively summarize the motivating arguments. Thus, when the judge begins reading the first argument—the case justification argument—the thrust of the motivating arguments will have already been laid out as a backdrop in the introductory paragraphs.

## B.   Motivate the Judge to Reject the Opponent's Case Law

What should you do when the mandatory cases in your jurisdiction arguably conflict, with one or more cases adopting your favorable interpretation and one or more cases adopting your opponent's unfavorable interpretation? Under such circumstances, you must not only convince the judge why sound policy and other reasons support your favorable cases but why the unfavorable cases should be rejected. Chapter 24 discusses in detail how to address and rebut unfavorable law. When convincing a judge to reject unfavorable mandatory precedent, you can either attack the unfavorable court's reasoning or argue that the unfavorable case is no longer "good law." Both of these strategies are discussed and illustrated in Chapter 24.

**22**

# FACT-CENTERED ARGUMENTS: PRE-DRAFTING STRATEGIES

 ### I ▸ FRAMING FAVORABLE INTERPRETATIONS OF THE LAW

Just as statutes often have vague, broad language that is susceptible to differing interpretations, the fact-centered holdings of courts are also susceptible to differing interpretations. When a court articulates why it held as it did under the unique fact pattern before the court, the court's reasoning usually provides advocates with a fair degree of latitude to express the holding as a broad or narrow rule of law, depending upon which rule statement supports the client's interests. Thus, the unique rule of law a court's fact-centered holding expresses is not rigid but fluid. As you consider how you might frame the rule of law a case or group of cases expresses, first evaluate your client's factual situation and what you will need to prove in order to prevail. Your goal is to formulate an interpretation of the rule of law from which your client will ultimately prevail. Then consider how the holding and rationale in a case or group of cases might help you formulate a winning argument.

As with statutory arguments, courts also impose standards that must be satisfied. If the issue involves a standard, consider whether you want to set a high bar that would be very difficult to satisfy, or, alternatively, set a low bar that could easily be met. How high you want to set the bar depends on who you represent and the factual situation before you. If your client must satisfy a standard to obtain favorable privileges under a rule of law, you would attempt to construe the case law as imposing a broad standard that your client could easily satisfy. If, on the other hand, your client would be penalized should the client satisfy a standard, you would attempt to construe the case law as imposing a narrow standard that your client would not be able to satisfy. The same strategies apply when the opposing party must satisfy a standard. If your client's interests dictate that the opposing party not satisfy the standard, then you would attempt to interpret case law as setting a standard that would be difficult to satisfy. Alternatively, if your client's interests dictate that the opposing party satisfy the standard, then you would attempt to interpret case law as setting a standard that would be easy to satisfy.

Courts often define the type of person or conduct or object that is subject to the law. If the issue is definitional, again consider the ultimate result you want to achieve. If your client's interests would be satisfied by falling within the definition, you would strive to construe the courts' definitional statements to embrace a broad group that would include your client. On the other hand, if your client's interests would be satisfied by falling outside the definition, you would strive to construe the courts' definitional statements to embrace a narrow group that would not include your client.

Although case law is susceptible to differing interpretations, it is important to keep in mind the parameters of ethical legal interpretation. Ethical rules of conduct prohibit attorneys from advancing legal theories or arguments that are "frivolous" or "unwarranted under existing law."[1] Although there is room for creative interpretation, you must not stray into frivolous territory. Not only would such an interpretation violate ethical rules of conduct, but it would negatively affect your credibility as well. Thus, your goal is to formulate the most favorable rules of law possible from case precedent while also retaining your credibility and honoring your ethical obligations to the court.

 **ILLUSTRATION: Federal Wiretap Problem**

As an example of how advocates formulate favorable rules from case law, consider the federal wiretap problem that is the basis of the sample brief in Appendix D. The federal wiretap statute requires the government to comply with certain wiretapping procedures designed to safeguard the integrity of wiretap evidence. After obtaining wiretap evidence the government must "immediately" obtain the protection of a judicial seal or provide a "satisfactory explanation" for its failure to do so. Congress enacted the judicial sealing requirement to protect wiretap evidence from tampering. In the hypothetical fact pattern that is the basis of the sample brief in Appendix D, the government's case against the defendant, Mr. Hart, rests solely on transcripts of wiretap tapes the government intercepted from the defendant's home telephone. However, the government delayed obtaining a judicial seal for a period of two months because the government lost the box of tapes during an office move.

---

[1] Model Code of Professional Responsibility, DR7-102(A)(2); Model Rules of Professional Conduct, Rule 3.1.

Hart's attorney seeks to convince the court that the government failed to provide a "satisfactory explanation" for its sealing delay. If the court finds that the government's explanation was not "satisfactory" under the statute, the tapes must be suppressed and cannot, therefore, be used as evidence against the defendant during a trial. As Hart's attorney reviews precedent cases that address the issue, the attorney recognizes that the holdings can be framed broadly or narrowly.

Consider one such case and how it might be construed. In *United States v. Mora*,[2] the court considered whether the government's explanation for its sealing delay was satisfactory under the following factual record. After obtaining the wiretap tapes, the government designated a Massachusetts State Police Officer as custodian of the tapes. The trooper placed the tapes in a cardboard box, closed the box, and signed it. He then sealed the box within a plastic bag. The trooper originally kept the bags at a listening post, which was staffed and guarded twenty-four hours a day. After two weeks, he removed the tapes and placed them in a locked vault that was accessible only to limited, authorized personnel. The vault was equipped with an alarm system. As the court considered the factual record, it could not find "any scintilla of evidence" that the tapes could have been tampered with, even after "scour[ing] the record, searching in vain for any intimation that the content of the tapes was compromised."

As Mr. Hart's advocate, what would be the most favorable construction of the rule of law the *Mora* case embodies? One interpretation of the fact-centered holding might produce this rule:

> The government's explanation is "satisfactory" when the government can prove that no one tampered with the tapes. *United States v. Mora*, 821 F.2d 860 (1ˢᵗ Cir. 1987).

The above rule would be a fair reading of the case—the court clearly "scoured" the factual record to determine whether there was any evidence of tampering. Finding that no such evidence existed, the court held that the government's explanation for its sealing delay was "satisfactory." However, place yourself in the role of Hart's attorney drafting the argument. Would this statement of the rule necessarily compel the conclusion that the government's explanation was not satisfactory when it lost the tapes for two months? Perhaps. As Hart's attorney, you would certainly argue that the government's proce-

---

[2] *United States v. Mora*, 821 F.2d 860 (1ˢᵗ Cir. 1987).

dures to safeguard the tapes fell far short of the procedures in *Mora*. Nevertheless, if you were to advocate a rule that requires the government to prove that no one tampered with the tapes, the government might be able to satisfy this burden of proof by other means. For example, even though the government lost the box of tapes for two months, the government could hire an expert to testify that the tapes were not in fact altered during the time they were missing. Therefore, although the above rule statement would allow you to distinguish the *Mora* case, it might not compel a favorable result for your client.

Because the above rule statement does not necessarily compel a favorable result for Hart, consider how the case might be construed even more favorably. Recall that the statute creates a standard the government must satisfy—the government must provide a "satisfactory explanation." Therefore, consider how you might construe the *Mora* case to set a standard that the government could not possibly satisfy. Although the government might be able to prove that the tapes were not altered, it can not prove that the manner in which it stored the tapes foreclosed any *possibility* of tampering. Thus, consider the following alternative interpretation of the fact-centered holding:

> The government's explanation is "satisfactory" only when the government can prove that its pre-sealing procedures protected the wiretap tapes from any possibility of tampering. *United States v. Mora*, 821 F.2d 860 (1ˢᵗ Cir. 1987).

If the court accepts that rule, it must rule in favor of Mr. Hart—because the government lost the tapes, it simply cannot satisfy the above standard. However, identifying a rule of law that compels a favorable ruling for your client is not the end of the inquiry. You must also consider whether this alternative rule is a reasonable and fair interpretation of the court's fact-centered holding. The fact pattern in *Mora* certainly satisfies this more restrictive rule because the government's pre-sealing procedures in *Mora* did in fact protect the wiretap tapes from any possibility of tampering. Next carefully review the court's rationale to ensure that the court's own language does not conflict with your restrictive standard. Finally, you would carefully evaluate other mandatory precedent to ensure that your favorable interpretation of the rule is not inconsistent with other mandatory precedent. Assuming there is no language within the case or group of mandatory authority cases that conflicts with your restrictive interpretation of the court's holding, you would formulate the rule of law as the more favorable rule.

# II ▸ *THE CASE SELECTION PROCESS*

## A. *Assessing the Relative Persuasive Appeal of Case Law*

From the numerous cases you might review and analyze, your goal is to select only the most favorable cases to incorporate into the argument. Of course, there are ethical and pragmatic considerations that might cause you to incorporate unfavorable case law into your argument. These considerations are discussed in Chapter 24. However, before you can even begin to consider whether you will incorporate an unfavorable case into your argument, you must first evaluate each case and make some preliminary determinations. After evaluating each case, determine whether the case is generally favorable or unfavorable, and the manner in which you might use the case to argue why your client should prevail. When evaluating the cases to incorporate into the argument, consider the following:

---

1.  Whether the case is *mandatory or persuasive* authority.

2.  The court's *holding under the specific facts* before the court.

3.  The *rationale* within the case.

4.  The *date* of the case.

5.  The *level of court* that decided the case.

---

### 1. *Mandatory or Persuasive Authority*

The most important preliminary consideration is whether the case is mandatory or persuasive authority. If there is solid mandatory case authority addressing a legal issue, judges are often reluctant to rely on cases outside the jurisdiction. Therefore, as you research case law, first focus on cases within your jurisdiction. If there is good law within your jurisdiction, you may not want to expand your research to cases outside the jurisdiction.

## 2.   Holding and Facts

### (a)   Favorable Result Cases

Next consider the relative value of each case's holding under the unique fact pattern before the court. Assuming you are evaluating cases that are all mandatory authority (or are all persuasive authority), prefer cases with favorable holdings. Of the cases with favorable holdings, the most persuasive cases have case facts that are less desirable than the client's facts. These cases provide wonderful fodder for a persuasive argument because you can highlight the point that, even with less desirable facts, the court nevertheless held in a manner favorable to your client. Then, as you apply the favorable case to the client's facts, your argument is relatively easy—if less desirable facts yielded a favorable holding, then the court should clearly rule in your favor on your client's more desirable facts.

The next most persuasive type of case with a favorable holding is a case in which the case facts are comparable to your client's facts. If you can convince the judge that a previous case is factually similar to your client's situation in every legally significant way, then the judge should apply the rule of law to your client's situation with the same result.

Somewhat less persuasive is the case with a favorable holding that has more desirable facts than your client's facts. When a precedent case has more desirable facts than in the client situation, an adjudicator might conclude that the factual distinctions are legally significant. If the factual distinctions are legally significant, then the adjudicator would apply the precedent case to your client's facts and arrive at a different result. Nevertheless, if the distinguishable facts are not legally significant enough to compel a different result, then the precedent case might still be persuasive.

### (b)   Unfavorable Result Cases

Cases with unfavorable holdings are generally less desirable precedent for the obvious reason that their holdings are unfavorable to the client. Moreover, it is sometimes difficult to distinguish the precedent case without appearing defensive. However, cases with unfavorable holdings can also be persuasive as precedent if they are clearly distinguishable, particularly if the precedent court's rationale would seemingly compel a different result under a fact pattern similar to your client's. Thus, even cases with unfavorable holdings can support the client's position and can thereby be used as favorable cases within an argument. For example, even though the court in *Mora* held the "wrong way,"

*Mora* is factually distinguishable enough that Hart's attorney used it as favorable precedent.

As a case grows less distinguishable from the client's factual situation, it becomes less favorable as precedent. Some cases with unfavorable holdings can not easily be transformed into favorable law. The ethical and pragmatic considerations involved in deciding whether to incorporate unfavorable law into the argument are discussed in Chapter 24.

*A cautionary note*: these considerations are only rules of thumb to consider when selecting cases for a persuasive argument. For example, unfavorable rationale in a otherwise favorable case might make the case an unwise selection for a persuasive argument. As another example, a very old case with a favorable holding and facts might be de-emphasized in favor of a more recent case with slightly less favorable facts.

### *Case Holdings and Facts at a Glance:*

---

A.   Prefer cases with favorable holdings in the following order:

    1.   Case facts that are less desirable than the client's facts.

    2.   Case facts of the same relative value as the client's facts.

    3.   Case facts that are more desirable than the client's facts, thereby not necessarily requiring a judge to reach the same result when evaluating the client's facts.

B.   Prefer cases with unfavorable holdings in the following order:

    1.   Case facts that are far less desirable than the client's facts, making the case easily distinguishable.

    2.   Case facts that are somewhat less desirable than the client's facts, making the case distinguishable.

    3.   Case facts that are of the same relative value as the client's facts (potentially unfavorable law to rebut).

---

### 3. Rationale

The reasoning within each case is also critically important as you consider whether to incorporate that case into a persuasive argument. Rationale might transform an otherwise borderline case into a highly favorable or unfavorable case. Consider how clearly each case illustrates the favorable rule of law you have formulated. Consider the specific language in each case that interprets and defines the law. Does the court interpret the meaning of the law in a manner that favors or damages your client's interests? Also consider any policy statements within a court opinion. Based on the court's policy statements, can you argue that the relief requested by your client will promote favorable public policy? Finally, consider the facts the court emphasized in justifying its holding. Although your client's situation may be similar to a precedent case, upon further examination you may find that the facts the court found most significant are distinguishable from your client. Do the distinctions help you advance your argument or hinder your ability to do so?

### 4. Date and Level of Court

The date of each precedent case and the level of court that decided each case are also relevant, although somewhat less important than the above factors. All other things being equal, a more recent case is more valuable than an older case, and a case decided by the highest level court in the jurisdiction is more valuable than a case decided by a lower level court. However, lower courts are compelled to follow decisions of higher level courts within the jurisdiction. Thus, an intermediate appellate court binds a trial court just as much as the highest appellate court. The level of court may have more relevance when the meaning of the law is unclear or the cases arguably conflict.

## B. Evaluating Cases with Unfavorable Holdings

It is rare to research an issue and find only cases that have favorable holdings. You may sometimes find yourself in the enviable position of having enough favorable result cases to make a persuasive, credible argument without even having to incorporate an unfavorable result case into the argument. Often, however, you must incorporate cases that have unfavorable holdings. Even cases with unfavorable holdings might still be used persuasively in an argument. A case with an unfavorable holding can effectively advance the client's interests if you can easily distinguish the case. In addition, any favorable policy statements or dicta within the case can enhance the case's persuasive appeal.

## 1.  Distinguish the Case on Its Facts

Often advocates transform seemingly unfavorable cases into favorable law by distinguishing such cases on their facts. In evaluating whether an unfavorable result case is distinguishable enough to be included in your argument, consider how narrowly you can realistically construe the court's holding. If you can plausibly argue that the court's holding is dependent upon certain facts that are distinguishable from your client's facts, then the case might have persuasive value.

As an example, consider again the federal wiretap problem that is the basis of the sample brief in Appendix D. In that problem, the government delayed obtaining a judicial seal for a period of two months because the government lost the box of tapes during an office move. Recall that the government must provide a "satisfactory explanation" for its sealing delay. During the defense counsel's review of cases, the attorney discovered the *Mora* case, discussed earlier in this chapter. Although the *Mora* case has an unfavorable holding, recall that the *Mora* case is supportive of the attorney's favorable rule interpretation—that the government must store the tapes in a manner that protected them from any possibility of tampering. Is the *Mora* case also factually distinguishable enough to be persuasive precedent? In *Mora*, the government sealed the box within a plastic bag and originally kept them at a listening post that was staffed and guarded twenty-four hours a day. After two weeks, the agent removed the tapes and placed them in a locked vault that was accessible only to limited, authorized personnel. The vault was equipped with an alarm system.

The precautions the government took in *Mora* are easily distinguishable from Hart's situation. In *Mora*, the government's precautions ensured that the tapes could not be compromised, while the government in Hart's situation lost the tapes for two months. Thus, the government's lack of precautions are easily distinguishable from the precautions taken in *Mora*. Assuming there were no better cases to illustrate the government's failure to implement necessary precautions, *Mora* would be a good candidate to incorporate into the argument.

## 2.  Consider Favorable Policy Statements

When evaluating a case with an unfavorable holding, also consider whether public policy might dictate a different result under the client's fact pattern. Strong policy statements within a court opinion can enhance the persuasive appeal of the factual distinctions. Again consider the federal wiretap problem. In the sample brief illustrated in Appendix D, Hart's attorney argues that the government must satisfy two standards in order for its explanation to be "satisfactory." The first standard, illustrated in *Mora*, requires the government to show that its procedures guaranteed the integrity of the tapes. Hart's attorney found a second standard and a favorable policy statement in the *Vazquez* case.[3] Although the *Vazquez* court held that the government provided a "satisfactory explanation," as in *Mora*, the case facts are easily distinguishable from Hart's situation, in which the government lost the tapes for two months. As importantly, the *Vazquez* court implicitly adopted a second standard the government must satisfy in order to supply a "satisfactory explanation" under the statute, and also made a highly favorable policy statement. The following passages are excerpted from the *Vazquez* case:

| | |
|---|---|
| In the circumstances of this case, where we discern on the government's part no bad faith, no lack of diligence, and no attempt to gain an advantage over the defendants, we believe that the government's lack of foresight regarding the actual scope of the investigation does not justify the exclusion of probative evidence lawfully obtained.<br><br>. . . | Hart's attorney finds 2nd favorable standard from this language—what is it? |
| However, in law as in life, today's satisfactory explanation may very well be tomorrow's lame excuse. As the federal and state case law in this area grows, the failure to foresee and, where possible, prevent sealing delays becomes less justifiable, as law enforcement officials must be expected to learn from their own experiences and those of others. As other courts have done: "We decline to allow the police to rely on their own failure to use proper equipment or to institute more efficient procedures as an excuse for delay." *People v. Washington*, 46 N.Y.2d 116, 124, 412 N.Y.S.2d 854, 859, 385 N.E.2d 593, 597 (1978). | Favorable policy statement Hart can use to argue that the government's careless mistake encourages inefficiency & carelessness. |
| The wiretapping statute imposes a duty on the judiciary as well as on the prosecutor. It is our role to exclude from evidence tapes not sealed in conformance with the law, and we are aware that by faithfully performing this statutory duty we encourage law enforcement officers to perform their duties in an equally rigorous manner. For this reason, we will continue to scrutinize wiretap cases with care, and will not hesitate to exclude evidence when exclusion is appropriate. | This statement appeals to the courts' duty to require compliance with the statute. |

---

[3] *United States v. Vazquez*, 605 F.2d 1269 (2[d] Cir. 1979).

The above excerpted passages are ripe with possibility for Hart's attorney. From the first paragraph illustrated above, Hart can formulate a second standard the government must satisfy—that a "satisfactory explanation" requires that the government act with "reasonable diligence." Like the first standard Hart's attorney identified from *Mora*, the government in the present case simply can not satisfy this standard. A foreseeable mistake that is not rectified for two months does not constitute reasonable diligence. Note that the *Vazquez* court also expresses a possible third standard—that the government act with good faith. However, Hart's attorney elects not to incorporate this standard into the argument because the government's actions in the Hart situation appear to be innocent, albeit careless. In short, the standard is irrelevant because the facts in Hart's situation do not present an issue of bad faith.

Turning to the favorable policy statements contained within the *Vazquez* opinion, Hart's attorney can use these policy statements to the client's advantage. Hart's attorney can argue that the government's careless mistake in the present case is precisely the type of danger with which the *Vazquez* court was so concerned. Thus, although the *Vazquez* case has an unfavorable result, the *Vazquez* case is actually very favorable upon close examination.

### 3. Consider Favorable Dicta

Favorable dicta can also enhance the persuasive appeal of an unfavorable result case. Sometimes courts imply that the result might be different under a different set of facts. If a client's factual situation is similar to the hypothetical facts implied within the dicta, the case might also be used as favorable case precedent. As you consider whether to incorporate such a case into your argument, evaluate how closely the client's factual situation seems to fit within the court's dicta and whether the case, as a whole, fits within the favorable argument you are constructing.

# 23

# FACT-CENTERED ARGUMENTS: THE ARGUMENT

 ## I ▷ THE TEMPLATE OF THE ARGUMENT

## A. The Persuasive Paradigm

After you have formulated a favorable rule or rules of law from the case law and have selected the cases you will emphasize in your argument, you are in a position to outline and draft the argument. As you consider your argument, stay focused on your over-all goal. Your over-all goal is to convince the adjudicator that the precedent cases, as applied to your client's factual situation, compel a ruling that favors your client. How might you structure the argument to compel the adjudicator to arrive at a favorable conclusion?

The structure of a persuasive argument paradigm leads the adjudicator, step by logical step, to the desired ultimate conclusion. The persuasive argument paradigm is a carefully constructed formula, with each step of the argument leading to the next inevitable step. Like the predictive analysis in office memos, arguments also follow a deductive writing pattern. Therefore, a persuasive argument begins with the ultimate conclusion the advocate wants the adjudicator to reach. Next, the advocate describes the favorable rule or rules of law that support the ultimate conclusion. Finally, the advocate applies each favorable rule of law to the client's factual situation, illustrating how the law, as applied to the client's facts, compels the ultimate conclusion. The following template illustrates the persuasive argument paradigm for a single issue argument.

1.   State the *ultimate conclusion* you want the judge to adopt.

2.   State the *favorable rule or rules of law* you have formulated from the case law. (The favorable rule or rules of law, when applied to the client facts, should result in an intermediate conclusion that compels the adjudicator to adopt the ultimate conclusion.)

3.   *Prove and explain* the favorable rule of law by examining favorable case precedent.

4.   *Favorably apply* the rule of law to the client's factual situation, by proving how each factual premise leads to the intermediate conclusion.

5.   Restate how the favorable rule of law, as applied to your client (the *intermediate conclusion*), compels the *ultimate conclusion*.

## B.   Creating a Template of Your Argument

Before drafting your argument, first sketch the basic template, or framework, of your argument. As you construct the framework, you will begin to identify any gaps in your thinking and ideas that need further clarification. In addition, sketching the framework of an argument before you begin the drafting process should also save you time in the end; the template will help you stay "on track" during the drafting process.

Prior to drafting the argument, first clarify in your own mind the ultimate conclusion you want the adjudicator to reach. Second, identify each favorable rule of law that, when applied to the client's facts, will compel the ultimate conclusion. Third, consider how you will prove and explain each favorable rule of law. Note the specific cases that will help you prove that your favorable rules are reasonable and sound, and/or that apply the favorable rules of law to fact patterns in a favorable manner, and/or that contain favorable policy statements. As you consider how to incorporate these cases into your argument, argue first the case that is most likely to convince the adjudicator to apply the law favorably to your client, then identify the next most persuasive case, and so on. Finally, consider how you will favorably apply the law to the client's factual situation in a manner that will result in the desired conclusion. When arguing how the precedent supports a favorable outcome for your client, consider each factual premise that will help you prove the conclusion. As you structure the factual premises, argue first the most persuasive factual premise, and then the second most persuasive premise, and so on.

 ## *ILLUSTRATION: Federal Wiretap Problem*

As an example, consider the federal wiretap problem illustrated in Appendix D. The federal wiretap statute requires the government to comply with certain wiretapping procedures designed to safeguard the integrity of wiretap evidence. After obtaining wiretap evidence the government must "immediately" obtain the protection of a judicial seal or provide a "satisfactory explanation" for its failure to do so. Congress enacted the judicial sealing requirement to protect wiretap evidence from tampering. In the hypothetical fact pattern that is the basis of the sample brief in Appendix D, the government's case against the defendant, Mr. Hart, rests solely on transcripts of wiretap tapes the government intercepted from the defendant's home telephone. However, the government delayed obtaining a judicial seal for a period of two months because the government lost the box of tapes during an office move.

Hart's attorney seeks to convince the court that the government failed to provide a "satisfactory explanation" for its sealing delay. If the court finds that the government's explanation was not "satisfactory" under the statute, the tapes must be suppressed and cannot, therefore, be used as evidence against the defendant during a trial. In Chapter 22, you learned how Hart's attorney formulated two favorable standards the government must satisfy in order to provide a "satisfactory explanation" under the federal wiretap statute.

*The First Argument*: From the *Mora* case, Hart's attorney formulated the following favorable rule of law: The government's explanation is "satisfactory" only when the government can prove that its pre-sealing procedures protected the wiretap tapes from any possibility of tampering. Because Hart argues that the government must satisfy that standard independently of the second standard, the first standard becomes the basis of the first fact-centered argument.

Step back a moment and consider the framework of the argument. Hart wants to convince the court to arrive at the following ultimate conclusion: "The government's explanation is not satisfactory." Hart has formulated a favorable rule of law that, when applied to the client's factual situation, will lead to the desired ultimate conclusion: "The government's pre-sealing procedures must protect the wiretap tapes from any possibility of tampering." This favorable rule of law, when applied to the client's facts, inevitably leads to the intermediate conclusion that the government failed to protect the tapes from any possibility of tampering. This intermediate conclusion, in turn, leads to the ultimate conclusion: "Therefore, the government's explanation is not satisfactory." Stripped to the essential components of the persuasive argument paradigm, Hart's argument for the first issue looks like this:

| | |
|---|---|
| 1. *Ultimate Conclusion*: | Government did not provide a satisfactory explanation. |
| 2. *Favorable Rule of Law*: | The government's pre-sealing procedures must protect the wiretap tapes from any possibility of tampering. |
| 3. *Prove and Explain the Favorable Rule of Law*: | *Mora, Diana, Johnson* cases prove the rule of law and explain how it is applied to distinguishable fact patterns. |
| 4. *Apply the Favorable Law to the Client*: | (a) *1ˢᵗ premise*: The complete lack of security measures did not safeguard the tapes. |
| | (b) *2ⁿᵈ premise*: Due to lack of security measures, tapes may well have been compromised. |
| | (Intermediate conclusions that compel the ultimate conclusion) |
| 5. *Restate the Conclusion*: | The government's explanation is not satisfactory because it did not protect the wiretap tapes from any possibility of tampering. |

*The Second Argument*: From the *Vazquez* case, Hart's attorney formulated the following favorable rule of law: The government's explanation is "satisfactory" only when the government acts with "reasonable diligence." From evaluating the case facts and holding within the *Vazquez* case, Hart's attorney also formulated the following favorable sub-rule: The government acts with reasonable diligence only when the delay is caused by a legitimate law enforcement purpose and the government acts diligently to minimize the delay. Again, because Hart argues that the government must satisfy this standard in addition to the first standard, the second standard becomes its own fact-centered argument (the argument following the second fact-centered point-heading in the sample brief illustrated in Appendix D).

Hart's attorney follows the same persuasive argument paradigm for this argument as for the first argument. Thus, Hart must lead the court to the following intermediate conclusion: The government failed to act with reasonable diligence because the delay was not caused by a legitimate law enforcement purpose and because the government did not act diligently to minimize the delay. Again, the intermediate conclusion inevitably leads to the ultimate conclusion: Therefore, the government's explanation is not satisfactory. In sketching in the rest of the template, Hart must argue how the case law supports the favorable rule of law and how the favorable rule of law, when applied to the client facts, supports the intermediate conclusion. Stripped to the essential components of the persuasive argument paradigm, Hart's argument for the second issue looks like this:

| | |
|---|---|
| 1. *Ultimate Conclusion*: | Government did not provide a satisfactory explanation. |
| 2. *Favorable Rule of Law*: | The government must act with reasonable diligence. |
| *Favorable sub-rule*: | The government acts with reasonable diligence only when the delay is caused by a legitimate law enforcement purpose <u>and</u> the government works diligently to minimize the delay. |
| 3. *Prove and Explain the Favorable Rule of Law*: | *Gigante & Vazquez* cases prove the rule of law and explain how it is applied to a similar and a distinguishable fact pattern. |
| 4. *Apply the Favorable Law to the Client*: | (a) *First Premise*: A mistake is not a legitimate law enforcement purpose<br>(b) *Second Premise*: Agent Friday failed to minimize the delay:<br>　(i) when she lost the tapes; and<br>　(ii) when she failed to locate the missing tapes in a timely manner.<br>(Intermediate conclusions that compel the ultimate conclusion). |

> 5. *Restate the Conclusion*: The government's explanation is not satisfactory because the delay was not caused by a legitimate law enforcement purpose and the government did not act diligently to minimize the delay.

Because the two arguments incorporate separate standards the government must satisfy, Hart's attorney separately argues each standard. In order to clearly identify the two arguments, Hart creates point-headings from the intermediate conclusions (the favorable rule of law, when applied to the client facts, results in an intermediate conclusion). Each intermediate conclusion compels the ultimate conclusion. Thus, the template for the entire fact-centered argument looks like this:

> **I.**  *Ultimate Conclusion*: The government's explanation was not satisfactory.
>
> A.  *1ˢᵗ Intermediate Conclusion*: The government failed to store the wiretap tapes in a manner that would protect them from any possibility of tampering.
>
> 1.  *Favorable Rule of Law*: A satisfactory explanation requires that the government's pre-sealing procedures protect the tapes from any possibility of tampering.
>
> 2.  *Proof and Explanation of the Favorable Rule of Law*:
>
> Case 1:  *Diana*—proves & explains favorable rule & distinguishable facts.
> Case 2:  *Mora*—proves & explains favorable rule & distinguishable facts.
> Case 3:  *Johnson*—use as tangential case to bolster argument.
>
> 3.  *Favorable Application of the Rule of Law to the Client*:
>
> (a)  The complete lack of security measures did not safeguard the tapes.
> (b)  Due to lack of security measures, tapes may well have been compromised.

4. *Restate Conclusion*: Because the government's pre-sealing procedures did not protect the tapes from any possibility of tampering, the explanation is not "satisfactory."

B. *2nd Intermediate Conclusion*: The government failed to act with reasonable diligence.

1. *Favorable Rule of Law*: A satisfactory explanation requires that the government act with reasonable diligence.

*Sub-rule*: Reasonable diligence exists only when the delay is caused by a legitimate law enforcement purpose and the government acts with diligence to minimize the delay.

2. *Proof and Explanation of the Favorable Rule of Law*:

Case 1: *Gigante*: proves & explains favorable rule and illustrates how a mistake is not a satisfactory explanation.

Case 2: *Vazquez*—proves & explains favorable rule & distinguishable facts.

3. *Favorable Application of the Rule of Law to the Client*:

(a) A mistake is not a legitimate law enforcement purpose.
(b) Agent Friday failed to act with diligence:
(i) when she lost the tapes; and
(ii) when she failed to locate the missing tapes in a timely manner.

C. *Restating the conclusion*: The government did not provide a satisfactory explanation because it both failed to store the tapes in a manner that would protect them from any possibility of tampering and failed to act with reasonable diligence to minimize the delay.

**EXERCISE 1**

Review the fact-centered argument for Sample Brief B that is illustrated in Appendix C (Motion to Quash). Draft a template of the fact-centered argument, separately noting: (1) the ultimate conclusion; (2) the favorable rule or rules of law formulated by the advocate; (3) the case used to prove and explain the favorable rule or rules of law; and (4) the factual premises (intermediate conclusions) that lead to the ultimate conclusion.

## II ▶ *DRAFTING THE ARGUMENT*

Once you have a clear template of the argument, you will simply fill in the argument construct with the details that illustrate and prove why each of your rules of law and premises are sound.

### A. *Roadmap Paragraphs*

#### 1. *Overview Paragraph*

In an argument with two or more issues, an overview paragraph provides the adjudicator with the framework of your argument. It identifies your ultimate conclusion about how the original rule of law applies to the client's factual situation and the required elements that will be discussed in the argument itself. Thus, the overview paragraph simply provides the basic roadmap of the argument itself, as follows:

| | |
|---|---|
| The government has failed to provide the statutorily-mandated "satisfactory explanation" in this case. A satisfactory explanation requires both that the government's pre-filing procedures ensured the tapes' integrity, *United States v. Johnson*, 696 F.2d 115 (D.C. Cir. 1976), and that it acted with reasonable diligence to obtain the required judicial safeguard. *United States v. Gigante*, 538 F.2d 502, 505 (2d Cir. 1976). The government has not satisfied either prerequisite of a "satisfactory explanation." | 1. Ultimate conclusion. 2. Two favorable standards the govt. must satisfy—the favorable rules of law. 3. Govt. fails to satisfy either standard. |

## 2.  Thesis Paragraph

In a fact-centered argument of any complexity, introduce each issue with a thesis paragraph that contains the essential components of your argument *for that issue*. The essential components of your argument should already be contained in your outline of that argument. Therefore, you need only convert your outline into narrative form, identifying: (1) the favorable rule or rules of law; (2) a summary of your proof/explanation of the favorable rule of law; (3) a summary of the basic factual premises that will lead to your intermediate conclusion; and (4) the ultimate conclusion. The following paragraph introduces the second fact-centered issue in the sample wiretap brief illustrated in Appendix D:

| | |
|---|---|
| Even when the government stores tapes in a manner that protects their integrity, its explanation is not "satisfactory" unless it acts with reasonable diligence to obtain a judicial seal. *United States v. Vazquez*, 605 F.2d 1269 (2d Cir. 1979). Governmental mistake, even innocent mistake, does not constitute reasonable diligence. *United States v. Gigante*, 538 F.2d 502, 505 (2d Cir. 1976). The government acts with reasonable diligence only when the delay is caused by legitimate law enforcement purposes and the government diligently acts to minimize the delay in obtaining the judicial seal. Here, the delay was caused by no legitimate law enforcement purpose. Moreover, the government's initial mistake in losing the tapes in the first place is exacerbated by its failure to minimize the delay. It was the government's own inattention and neglect that caused the two-month sealing delay. The government's carelessness and neglect does not rise to the level of reasonable diligence. | 1. Favorable rule.<br><br>2. Summary of the proof/explanation of the favorable rule.<br>3. Summary of factual premises that lead to intermediate conclusion.<br><br>4. Conclusion. |

## B.  Rule Explanation

The body of your argument should follow the template you created. Thus, just as in an office memo, the argument follows a deductive writing pattern, explaining the rule of law before applying the law to the client's facts. However, unlike your discussions in an office memo, your goal is to emphasize the favorable components of the law and to de-emphasize any unfavorable information. Thus, when proving and explaining the law, begin with a thesis sentence that identifies the favorable rule the case embodies. The favorable rule provides the context for the favorable case facts, holding, and/or rationale you will highlight within the paragraph or paragraphs that discuss that case.

## 1.   Favorable Result Cases

Ideally, after reading your discussion of an important precedent case, the adjudicator should be persuaded that your client's facts are at least as compelling as the fact pattern in the precedent case. Therefore, your goal is to emphasize every case fact that is less desirable and/or comparable to your client's factual situation and to de-emphasize unfavorable information. How might you achieve such a goal?

### (a)   Begin with a Favorable Thesis Sentence

The thesis sentence should highlight the favorable rule of law the case illustrates. As you draft the thesis sentence, consider how your client's factual situation would fare under the rule of law expressed in the thesis sentence. Ideally, the rule of law expressed in the thesis sentence should, when applied to your client, compel a favorable outcome.

For example, within the sample wiretap brief in Appendix D, Hart's attorney discusses the *Gigante* case in the second factual issue. The *Gigante* court's holding was favorable—the court held that the government's explanation was not satisfactory. Therefore, Hart's attorney begins the *Gigante* case discussion with a rule of law that both captures the court's holding and compels a favorable result for Hart:

> Inattention to governmental files does not constitute reasonable diligence.

### (b)   Highlight Favorable Facts

Following the thesis sentence, elaborate on favorable facts and reasoning by highlighting and flaunting every favorable aspect of the case. Do not summarize favorable facts or language by burying such favorable information within run-on sentences or dependent clauses. Instead, highlight favorable information by describing in great detail every favorable fact and favorable rationale. In addition, if there is a fact within the case that is less desirable than in your client's situation, you can emphasize the favorable distinction by incorporating it into the statement of the court's holding. The impression you want to make is this: "Even though X fact existed, the court still held in a favorable manner."

For example, consider again the *Gigante* case discussion within the federal wiretap brief. The *Gigante* court's holding was favorable because, in that case, the court held that the government's explanation was not satisfactory. If possible, Hart's attorney wants to emphasize facts that make the government in *Gigante* appear even more cautious than in the client's situation—if the government lost when they were even more cautious than the government in Hart's situation, then Hart should prevail as well. In *Gigante*, the tapes were stored in a locked cabinet under agency seal, a highly favorable fact because it makes the government appear very cautious. Therefore, the favorable factual distinction is highlighted by incorporating it in the statement of the court's holding:

> Even though the tapes had been stored in a locked cabinet under agency seal prior to receiving judicial attention, the court held that the government failed to provide a satisfactory explanation for its sealing delay. *Id.* at 505.

### (c)  Highlight Favorable Rationale

As with favorable facts, highlight any language within the case that supports your client's position. Selectively quoting favorable language is a wonderful way to emphasize favorable rationale. At the same time, you do not want your case discussion to be a string of quotes. Therefore, carefully select the most favorable, and important, language to quote. Again using the *Gigante* case discussion for purposes of illustration, Hart's attorney emphasizes favorable policy concerns expressed within the case:

> The court reasoned that the government's "explanation" for its mistake was "no explanation whatsoever." *Id.* at 504. Mere mistake does not constitute reasonable diligence, even with a change in personnel. In so holding, the court emphasized the importance of the immediate sealing requirement as "an integral part of this statutory scheme." *Id.* at 505. The court cautioned that "[m]aintenance of the integrity of such evidence is part and parcel of the Congressional plan to 'limit the use of intercept procedures to those situations clearly calling for the employment of this extraordinary investigative device.'" [cite]

Selective quote: "no explanation whatsoever."

Selectively quotes policy statements that support a high standard for the government to satisfy.

### (d)  De-emphasize Unfavorable Information

As you emphasize the favorable components of a case, also strive to de-emphasize unfavorable components. If the court's holding is favorable to your client, then de-emphasize the case facts that are more compelling than your client's factual situation. You want to convince the adjudicator that your client's situation is at least as strong as the precedent case; therefore, de-emphasize any facts that might be the basis of an unfavorable comparison. De-emphasize unfavorable information by burying that information within the middle of the paragraph or within a dependent clause within the middle of a sentence. For example, although the *Gigante* court's holding is favorable and there are favorable facts within that case, there is also an unfavorable distinction. In *Gigante*, the government delayed sealing the tapes for over a year. That delay makes the government appear even more careless than the government in the client's situation, where the government delayed only two months. Thus, Hart's attorney de-emphasizes that unfavorable distinction by burying the fact within the middle of the case discussion:

| | |
|---|---|
| Inattention to governmental files does not constitute reasonable diligence. In *Gigante*, the government's only explanation for its delay in obtaining a judicial seal was that the agent in charge of the files left the government's employ. The new agent was unaware the tapes had not received a judicial seal until one year later. 538 F.2d at 504. Even though the tapes had been stored in a locked cabinet under agency seal prior to receiving judicial attention, the court held that the government failed to provide a satisfactory explanation for its sealing delay. *Id.* at 505. The court reasoned that the government's "explanation" for its mistake was "no explanation whatsoever." *Id.* at 504. Mere mistake does not constitute reasonable diligence, even with a change in personnel. In so holding, the court emphasized the importance of the immediate sealing requirement as "an integral part of this statutory scheme." *Id.* at 505. The court cautioned that "[m]aintenance of the integrity of such evidence is part and parcel of the Congressional plan to 'limit the use of intercept procedures to those situations clearly calling for the employment of this extraordinary investigative device.'" *Id.* (citing *United States v. Giordano*, 416 U.S. 505, 527 (1974)). | Favorable rule. Favorable facts. <br><br> *Unfavorable fact buried here.* Favorable factual distinction. <br><br><br><br> Favorable rationale. |

## 2.   *Unfavorable Result Cases*

The same persuasive strategies described above are also used in describing cases that have unfavorable results. However, when addressing a case with an unfavorable result, the goal is to make the case appear distinguishable from, rather than similar to, your client's situation. Therefore, your goal is to emphasize every case fact that is distinguishable from your client's factual situation and to de-emphasize unfavorable information, including facts that are similar to your client's situation. As with favorable result cases, you will achieve that goal by incorporating a favorable rule of law into the thesis sentence, highlighting favorable facts and rationale, and de-emphasizing unfavorable information.

### (a)   *Begin With a Favorable Thesis Sentence*

In order to distinguish a case on its facts, you must construe the court's holding narrowly enough so that it is dependent on the distinguishable facts. By making the court's holding dependent upon the distinguishable facts, you can easily illustrate how the result would be different under your client's fact pattern. Therefore, as you draft the thesis sentence, consider how your client's factual situation would fare under the rule of law expressed in the thesis sentence. Ideally, the rule of law expressed in the thesis sentence, when applied to your client, should compel a *different* outcome. One way of accomplishing that goal is to weave distinguishable facts into your thesis sentence, thereby making the rule of law dependent on the distinguishable facts.

For example, recall the *Mora* case in the federal wiretap brief illustrated in Appendix D. The *Mora* case has an unfavorable holding—the *Mora* court held that the government had a satisfactory explanation for its sealing delay. Because the holding is unfavorable, Hart's attorney wants to highlight the case facts that are distinguishable from the client's factual situation. Thus, the thesis sentence highlights distinguishable facts and makes them integral to the rule of law the case expresses:

> The government can adequately safeguard the integrity of wiretap tapes only by instituting strict security procedures, such as guarding the tapes or locking them within a locked vault.

Within the second fact-centered argument, the thesis sentence introducing the *Vazquez* case does not incorporate specific facts. Nevertheless, it expresses a rule of law that, when applied to the government in Hart's case, would compel a different result than in *Vazquez*:

> A government's explanation is "satisfactory" only when the delay is caused by legitimate law enforcement purposes and the government diligently acts to minimize the sealing delay.

### (b) Emphasize Favorable Facts

When a court's holding is not favorable, your goal is to convince the adjudicator that your client's situation is distinguishable enough to merit a different outcome. Therefore, emphasize every case fact that is distinguishable from your client's factual situation, and de-emphasize every case fact that is similar to your client's factual situation.

For purposes of illustration, consider again the *Vazquez* case. In *Vazquez*, the court held that the government's explanation was satisfactory. Nevertheless, the facts are easily distinguishable because in *Vazquez*, the delay was caused by a legitimate law enforcement purpose. Therefore, when describing the case, Hart's attorney parades in great detail all of the facts that reflect how the delay was caused by a legitimate law enforcement purpose. The fact that the tapes were in Spanish, requiring translators, further seems to make the delay appear more reasonable, particularly when the agents worked "around the clock" to transcribe the tapes. Therefore, these facts are also highlighted.

| | |
|---|---|
| A government's explanation is "satisfactory" only when the delay is caused by legitimate law enforcement purposes and the government diligently acts to minimize the sealing delay. For example, in *Vazquez*, the government's delay in obtaining a judicial seal was caused by its difficulty in transcribing the tapes. Most of the conversations on the 200 tapes were in Spanish, requiring translation. Even with the limited equipment, a limited number of Spanish-speaking agents, and a lack of sufficient personnel to handle the scope of the investigation, the government nevertheless worked to minimize the sealing delay. Working around the clock, the government submitted the tapes for sealing after a delay of only one to two weeks. 605 F.2d at 1274. | Emphasizes distinctions:<br><br><br><br>—200 tapes<br>—Spanish<br>—Limited # of agents to translate<br><br>—Worked around the clock<br>—Only 1 to 2 week delay |

### (c)  Highlight Favorable Rationale

### (i)  Highlight Court's Emphasis on Distinguishable Facts

When dealing with an unfavorable result case, highlight the rationale that emphasizes the distinguishable facts within the case. As with favorable result cases, selectively quoting favorable language is a wonderful way to emphasize favorable rationale. Again using *Vazquez* for purposes of illustration, Hart's attorney highlights that part of the court's rationale that emphasized distinguishable facts. Thus, following the statement of the case facts, Hart's attorney describes the court's holding and rationale:

| | |
|---|---|
| The court accepted the government's explanation as "satisfactory," noting the government's legitimate law enforcement purposes and its diligence in attempting to produce the tapes as quickly as possible. *Id.* at 1279. The court emphasized that government personnel worked diligently *around the clock* to comply with the statute, as well as using strict security measures to ensure their integrity. | Holding linked to distinguishable facts. Rationale linked to distinguishable facts. |

### (ii)  Highlight Favorable Policy and Dicta

Favorable policy statements and dicta within a case can enhance the persuasive appeal of an unfavorable result case. Policy statements and dicta are persuasive when they can be used to argue that the result should be different in your client's case. Again using the *Vazquez* case for purposes of illustration, the *Vazquez* court warned of the danger of delays caused by governmental carelessness and mistakes. The government's careless behavior in Hart's situation is precisely the type of danger with which the *Vazquez* court was concerned. Moreover, the policy discussion is so well-written and favorable, Hart's attorney elects to quote the full policy statement. To reinforce the connection between the policy statement and the government's carelessness in Hart's case, Hart's attorney uses the persuasive writing style strategy of "context and juxtaposition" as a transition between the rule explanation and rule application sections of the argument. (Persuasive writing style strategies are discussed in Chapter 19.) The excerpt below follows the discussion of the *Vazquez* case facts and holding:

| | |
|---|---|
| The court emphasized that government personnel worked diligently *around the clock* to comply with the statute (as well as using strict security measures to ensure their integrity). Even then, the court cautioned the government about its one to two week delays: | *Rationale*: Emphasis on favorable distinctions. |
| However, in law as in life, today's satisfactory explanation may very well be tomorrow's lame excuse. As the federal and state case law in this area grows, the failure to foresee and where possible, prevent sealing delays becomes less justifiable, as law enforcement officials must be expected to learn from their own experiences and those of others. . . . It is our role to exclude from evidence tapes not sealed in conformance with the law, and we are aware that by faithfully performing this statutory duty we encourage law enforcement officers to perform their duties in an equally rigorous manner. | Quotes favorable policy statement that warns of danger and also encourages the government to be rigorous. |
| *Id.* at 1280. | |
| Tomorrow has arrived. And the government's "lame excuse" does not even approach the level of rigor and diligence required by the statute. . . . (rule application section follows) | *Rule Application*: Policy serves as link to first factual premise. |

 **EXERCISE 2**

Review the *Diana* case discussion that is contained within the first fact-centered argument for the federal wiretap problem illustrated in Appendix D. The first fact-centered argument argues that the government failed to store the tapes in a manner that protected the tapes from any possibility of tampering. As you review the *Diana* case discussion, identify how Hart's attorney emphasizes: (1) the favorable rule of law the case illustrates; (2) the favorable facts within the *Diana* case; and (3) favorable rationale.

## C.  Favorable Rule Application

This section of the argument explores and proves why the client must prevail when the favorable law is applied to the client's factual situation. The favorable rule or rules of law you formulated from the cases guide this part of the argument as you illustrate how the law, when applied to the client, inexorably leads to the intermediate conclusions that compel the ultimate conclusion.

Each paragraph or group of paragraphs that prove a factual premise should follow a deductive writing pattern. First clearly state the factual premise in a thesis sentence and then prove why the premise is sound in the remainder of the paragraph or group of paragraphs. To prove a factual premise: (1) elaborate on each and every client fact that illustrates and proves the factual premise; (2) make concrete, favorable analogies and distinctions to the case law whenever their use can help prove the premise; and (3) explain the factual and legal significance of the facts and analogies.

Again using the federal wiretap brief in Appendix D for purposes of illustration, the favorable rule of law Hart's attorney articulates for the second argument is: A satisfactory explanation requires reasonable diligence. Hart's attorney narrowed that broad rule into a favorable sub-rule: Reasonable diligence requires that the delay be caused by a legitimate law enforcement purpose and that the government work diligently to minimize the delay. Thus, Hart's favorable rule of law requires the government to comply with two requirements: (1) legitimate law enforcement purpose; and (2) minimize the delay.

When these two requirements are applied to Hart, they lead to the following two factual premises: (1) the government's delay was not caused by a legitimate law enforcement purpose; and (2) the government did not work diligently to minimize the delay. As Hart's attorney structures the argument, the attorney takes each premise and proves it by elaborating on client facts, making favorable comparisons to and distinctions from the precedent cases, and explaining the legal significance of the comparisons.

The following paragraph illustrates the argument for the first factual premise:

| | |
|---|---|
| Tomorrow has arrived. And the government's "lame excuse" does not even approach the level of rigor and diligence required by the statute. In vivid contrast to the government's one- to two-week delay in *Vazquez* caused by a legitimate law enforcement purpose, the government's only explanation for its two-*month* delay in the present case is that it made a "mistake" and lost the box of tapes in the confusion of an office move. As the *Gigante* court aptly noted, the government's mistake is "no excuse whatsoever." | *Premise:* Not diligent because no law enforce. purpose—instead, a mistake. Favorable distinction—2 weeks vs. 2 mos. Favorable quote applied to client. |

| | |
|---|---|
| In fact, the government's lack of diligence far exceeds the level of carelessness in *Gigante*. Unlike the agent in *Gigante*, who left the government's employ, Agent Friday assumed full responsibility for the government's evidence from the time the government obtained the tapes to the time she finally stumbled upon them. In fact, this case was Agent Friday's *only* responsibility during that time period. | Significance of favorable distinction.<br><br>Favorable distinction illustrated with facts. |

## EXERCISE 3

Review the rule application paragraphs for the first fact-centered argument in the federal wiretap problem illustrated in Appendix D. The first fact-centered argument argues that the government failed to store the tapes in a manner that protected the tapes from any possibility of tampering. For each of the four rule application paragraphs within that argument, identify: (1) the factual premise of each paragraph; (2) the client facts used to prove the factual premise; (3) the favorable analogies to and distinctions from the precedent cases; and (4) the factual and legal significance of client facts and analogies.

# 24

# ADDRESSING UNFAVORABLE LAW AND ARGUMENTS

## I   ETHICAL AND PRAGMATIC CONSIDERATIONS

As you evaluate the cases you might incorporate into a persuasive argument, you will face varying degrees of favorable and unfavorable case law. If you conclude that a case is not highly favorable to your client's interests, then you have some decisions to make. Should you omit any mention of the case in your argument? Should you disclose the case? If you disclose the case, should you attempt to emphasize the favorable components of the case or directly attack the case as unsound?

### A.   Ethical Considerations

First, consider the forum in which you are presenting your argument and the ethical rules that govern your conduct. For example, when you are presenting arguments before a court, you are ethically obligated to disclose certain adverse case law. Virtually every state has adopted a code of professional responsibility, most of which incorporate either the 1969 Model Code of Professional Responsibility or the 1983 Model Rules of Professional Conduct. If the adverse law has not been disclosed by opposing counsel, these codes require attorneys to inform courts of adverse mandatory law that is "directly adverse" to their client's legal position.[1] Moreover, although advocates can make a "good faith argument for an extension, modification, or reversal of existing law," both codes forbid advocates from advancing legal theories or arguments that are "frivolous" or "unwarranted under existing law."[2] An advocate who violates

---

[1] Model Code of Professional Responsibility, DR 7-106(B)(1); Model Rules of Professional Conduct, Rule 3.3(a)(3).

[2] Model Code of Professional Responsibility, DR 7-102(A)(2); Model Rules of Professional Conduct, Rule 3.1.

these rules of conduct can be censured, suspended, or even disbarred. There-fore, although there is still room for advocates to advance zealously the inter-ests of their clients, you must also be aware that all attorneys have an ethical obligation of integrity, honesty, and good faith.

## B.  *Pragmatic Considerations*

You are not ethically required to disclose unfavorable precedent if the precedent is distinguishable from the client's factual situation. Precedent that is factually distinguishable from a client's situation is not considered "directly adverse" to a client's legal position. You are also not ethically required to dis-close adverse precedent that is not mandatory precedent. For example, you may be arguing a case of first impression in your jurisdiction and find that courts in some jurisdictions have adopted your favorable interpretation of the law while courts in other jurisdictions have adopted an unfavorable interpreta-tion. You would not be ethically obligated to discuss the persuasive authority cases that are not favorable to your position.

However, even when you are not ethically compelled to disclose an unfa-vorable case or argument, you may decide to disclose and rebut the unfavor-able law anyway. Sometimes, disclosing unfavorable law will best promote your client's interests. For example, an unfavorable case may be so important in the jurisdiction in which you are practicing law that you might damage your credibility by failing to disclose the case. As another example, your opposing counsel's entire argument may rest on a line of unfavorable persuasive author-ity cases. Under such circumstances, you would want to attack directly the un-sound reasoning of such cases. When you are not ethically required to disclose unfavorable law, consider: (1) whether disclosure is necessary to maintain your credibility with the court or other adjudicator; and (2) whether your disclosure and skillful advocacy can minimize the damage from your opponent's poten-tial disclosure of the unfavorable law.

As you assess these pragmatic considerations, consider the following fac-tors:

---

✔   Relative importance of the case in the controlling jurisdiction;

✔   Likelihood the opposing counsel will disclose and rely on the case; and

✔   Relative degree of harm the unfavorable law presents.

If it is likely that opposing counsel will rely on the case, and you can easily minimize its potential damage by distinguishing the case or by attacking its reasoning, then you would likely want to disclose the case in your own argument. You would prefer that the adjudicator first consider the unfavorable law within the context of your own skillful presentation rather than within the confines of your opponent's argument. If, however, an unfavorable case is fairly damaging and it is questionable whether your opponent will rely on the case, you may well decide to omit any references to the adverse law. Instead, you may elect to anticipate and subtly rebut the damaging case through anticipatory rebuttal.

## II ▸ OPEN REBUTTAL

### A. Openly Rebutting Opponent's Potential Arguments

#### 1. Pre-Drafting Strategy

When you are responding to an opponent's argument, you will of course know the arguments your opponent has made and will want to rebut those arguments. You do not want an adjudicator to consider only your opponent's interpretation of the law. However, for ethical or pragmatic reasons, you may also decide to rebut unfavorable interpretations of the law even when your opposing counsel has not yet raised the adverse law. To anticipate your opponent's arguments, figuratively place yourself in your opponent's shoes. As you evaluate a statute or group of cases, consider not just your own favorable arguments but the arguments your opponent is likely to make from the same statute or group of cases. Assuming the role of your opponent, consider every argument you might make to win the case. Still playing the role of your opponent, make note of the following concerns:

1. With a statute, the *statutory language and/or its legislative history* that support the opponent's argument;

2. *Language in a case* that supports the opponent's argument (both favorable and unfavorable cases may have language that supports the opponent);

3. *Factual distinctions and comparisons* from precedent cases that support the opponent;

4.   Any *policy* reasons that support your opponent's argument;

5.   Any *prudential concerns* the opponent could advance (e.g., courts' reluctance to "open the floodgates" of litigation); and

6.   Using *common sense*, any other facts and arguments you think would favor the opponent, even if not directly addressed in a case or statute.

With respect to each potential opposing argument, consider your response. For example, if there is statutory language that favors the opposing party, is there other statutory language that favors your client? If not, does your interpretation more closely serve the legislative purposes? If there is language or facts from a precedent case that favors your opponent, is there competing language or facts that minimizes or undercuts the adverse impact of such language? If policy considerations favor the opposing party, are there competing policy concerns that favor your client's argument?

## 2.   Drafting Strategy

Chapter 20 discusses how to outline and structure a law-centered argument based primarily on statutory interpretation. Chapter 21 discusses how to outline and structure a law-centered argument based primarily on case law. Chapter 23 discusses how to outline and structure a fact-centered argument. These favorable argument constructs remain intact whether or not you also elect to rebut openly your opponent's interpretation of the law. You will simply weave the open rebuttal into your own favorable arguments by first affirming your favorable position relating to a specific idea and then attacking the opponent's position.

As an example, consider Sample Brief A in Appendix C. The arguments in that brief are discussed and illustrated at length in Chapter 20. Recall that the issue in Sample Brief A is whether individual employees are subject to liability under Title VII. In that brief, the defendant's attorney argues that Title VII does not impose liability on individual employees, but instead restricts liability to employers. In advancing that argument, the attorney makes several arguments. In the first argument, the attorney argues that the plain language of the statute itself restricts liability to employers. Directly following that favorable argument, the defendant's attorney openly criticizes any opposing interpretation of the statutory language (i.e., the opponent's argument). Next, the attorney argues that the statutory scheme as a whole supports the defendant's favorable interpretation. Directly following that favorable argument, the attorney argues why the statutory scheme is inconsistent with the opponent's argument. The attorney next argues how the legislative history supports the client's position, and so on.

## B.  Direct Rebuttal of Adverse Case Law

For ethical or pragmatic reasons, you may decide to rebut an adverse case or group of cases upon which your opponent has or will rely. When directly rebutting an adverse case, minimize the impact of the adverse case by saving the direct rebuttal until the end of the argument. It is far more persuasive to argue the client's position first, so that the adjudicator is already persuaded of the soundness of the client's position before considering the unfavorable law. An opposing argument loses much of its persuasive appeal when the adjudicator is already viewing the problem from the client's favorable perspective before reading the unfavorable argument. Moreover, by arguing the favorable law first, you provide an adjudicator with a favorable conceptual framework from which to consider the adverse law. When convincing an adjudicator to reject an unfavorable case, you can either attack the unfavorable court's reasoning or argue that the unfavorable case is no longer "good law."

### 1.  Attack the Unfavorable Court's Reasoning

The examples in Chapter 20 illustrate how an advocate attacks an opponent's *position*. When attacking a specific court's reasoning, however, the focus will be on the faulty reasoning within the unfavorable case itself. For example, you might argue how the unfavorable case would produce an inequitable and unfair result to the parties (the *equities* argument from Chapter 20). You might also argue how the unfavorable case would have negative public policy ramifications (the *public policy* argument from Chapter 20). You might also argue how the unfavorable case would negatively impact the functioning of the court system (the *prudential concerns* argument from Chapter 20). If the source of the law is statutory, you might also argue how the court ignored the plain language of a statute or failed to consider the statutory scheme as a whole (the *plain language* and *statutory scheme* arguments from Chapter 20).

The following example builds on the Title VII problem (Sample Brief A in Appendix C). Title VII prohibits employers from discriminating against employees on the basis of their sex, among other protected classifications. The statute defines the term "employer" to include "any agent" of the employer. The term "agent" lends itself to an argument based on the statute's language. Prior to 1991, when Title VII was amended, some attorneys argued that the term "agent" merely incorporated *respondeat superior* liability into the statute, with the employer thereby liable for the acts of its agents. Other attorneys argued that the term "agent" made supervisory employees liable. However, prior to 1991 the conflicting interpretations had little practical effect on the outcome because plaintiffs could recover only injunctive relief, reinstatement or hiring, or up to two years of back-pay.[3] These remedies are available only against an employer, not individual employees.

In 1991, Congress amended Title VII to allow plaintiffs to recover compensatory and punitive damages.[4] The expanded remedies intensified the debate. Following the amendment, some attorneys argued that, by expanding the available remedies, Congress also expanded the group of potential defendants to include individual employees who were supervisors. They argued that the term "agent," together with the expanded remedies available to plaintiff, made certain supervisory employees personally liable for both compensatory and punitive damages. Other attorneys argued that when Congress amended Title VII in 1991, it intended only to increase the monetary award plaintiffs could recover. These attorneys argued that the amendments did not also expand the class of potential defendants from employers to supervisory employees. They argued that the term "agent" merely incorporated *respondeat superior* liability into the statute, with the employer thereby liable in compensatory and punitive damages for the acts of its agents.

Sample Brief A in Appendix C illustrates the defendant's arguments. For purposes of this present discussion, however, assume that the defendant decides to attack an unfavorable case directly—the *Jendusa* case. Assume that the defendant is arguing the case before a federal district court in Illinois. The *Jendusa* case is also a federal district court case within Illinois. Because the *Jendusa* case is not a higher level court, it is not binding on another federal trial court judge. Nevertheless, it is certainly persuasive and the defendant therefore elects to attack directly the *Jendusa* case.

---

[3] 42 U.S.C. § 2000e-5(g) (1994).
[4] 42 U.S.C. § 1981a (1994).

| | |
|---|---|
| In *Jendusa,* the court ignored the overwhelming evidence that Congress did not intend to expand liability under Title VII to individual employees. 868 F. Supp. at 1016. | *Premise*: Court incorrectly interpreted the law by ignoring legislative intent. |
| Instead, the *Jendusa* court took a single isolated reference in the Committee Reports and misinterpreted it. The *Jendusa* court reasoned that Congress must have envisioned individual liability because the Committee Reports cite *Zabkowicz* as one example of why the 1991 Amendments were necessary. In citing *Zabkowicz*, the Committee Reports note that the "corporate employer and its officers" had violated Title VII. *Id.* From that isolated reference to an employer's "officers," the *Jendusa* court leapt to the faulty conclusion that Congress must have intended to make individuals liable. | *Proof*: Court misinterpreted isolated reference in legislative history. |
| The *Jendusa* court's reasoning has two flaws. First, the court failed to recognize that in *Zabkowicz*, the supervisory employees were liable in their official capacity only, not in their individual capacity. The plaintiff in that case recovered only back-pay. Second, the Congressional lament in citing *Zabkowicz* was the *paucity* of the award (only two months back-pay), not the limited *scope* of the award. *Hudson*, 873 F. Supp at 136. In other words, Congress was concerned that individuals were not able to recover fair compensation for their injuries, not that they were restricted to seeking damages from employers. | Openly identifies two flaws within the court's reasoning. |

## 2.   *Argue that the Unfavorable Case is No Longer "Good Law"*

Another way to attack an adverse case is to argue that the precedent is no longer "good law." If the adverse case is older than the favorable case you want the adjudicator to follow, you might argue that the older case no longer reflects present policy, and/or that it has been implicitly overruled by more recent case law. To illustrate this type of argument, consider the Fifth Amendment problem discussed and illustrated in Chapter 21 (Sample Brief B in Appendix C). In that hypothetical problem, the government is prosecuting the defendant, Mr. Browne, for unlawful distribution of drugs. The government has issued a subpoena to obtain Mr. Browne's personal diary. The government contends that the diary contains entries that reflect Mr. Browne's illegal drug activities. Rather than turning over the diary to the government, Browne's attorney has filed a Motion to Quash the subpoena. Browne's attorney argues that Mr. Browne's personal diary is protected by the Fifth Amendment of the United States Constitution. The Fifth Amendment protects people from self-incrimination. However, the language is vague and general, leaving courts to resolve specific issues as to the Amendment's meaning. The Amendment states that: "No person . . . shall be compelled in any criminal case to be a witness against himself. . . ." U.S. Const. amend. V.

Browne's attorney argues that the Fifth Amendment should be broadly construed to protect persons from incriminating themselves with their written documents as well as their oral testimony. Browne has a good Supreme Court case that has adopted this position—the *Boyd* case. However, this Supreme Court case is an old case and its holding has been eroded over the years. As Chapter 21 discussed and illustrated, Browne's attorney attempted to convince the court that more recent Supreme Court cases (*Fisher* and *Doe*) had not overruled *Boyd*. In attempting to convince the court of that argument, Browne narrowly interpreted the holdings in *Fisher* and *Doe* so as to preserve the earlier *Boyd* case.

For present purposes, however, let us consider the government's argument. The government's attorney would argue that the Fifth Amendment should be narrowly construed to protect persons from incriminating themselves only with their *oral* testimony. The government would argue that the Fifth Amendment does not also protect persons from incriminating themselves with their *written* documents. Thus, the government would argue that the holdings in *Fisher* and *Doe* should be broadly construed, implicitly overruling the early *Boyd* case. The government would attempt to convince the court to ignore the early *Boyd* case as no longer "good law," as follows:

> As recent Supreme Court opinions make abundantly clear, an individual's personal papers are not protected by the Fifth Amendment. *Baltimore City Dept. of Social Services v. Bouknight*, 493 U.S. 549 (1990); *United States v. Doe*, 465 U.S. 605 (1984); *Fisher v. United States*, 425 U.S. 391 (1976). As Justice O'Connor observed in her concurring opinion in *Doe*:
>
> > [T]he Fifth Amendment provides absolutely no protection for the contents of private papers of any kind. The notion that the Fifth Amendment protects the privacy of papers originated in *Boyd v. United States*, 116 U.S. 616, 630 (1886), but our decision in *Fisher v. United States*, 425 U.S. 391 (1976), sounded the death knell for *Boyd*.
>
> 465 U.S. at 618 (O'Connor concurring). In *Bouknight*, writing the majority opinion of the Court, Justice O'Connor affirmed that the Fifth Amendment's protection "applies only when the accused is compelled to make a *testimonial* communication that is incriminating." 493 U.S. at 554. With a majority of the justices joining Justice O'Connor in the majority opinion, the Supreme Court has effectively overruled any Fifth Amendment protection that *Boyd* once offered the contents of private papers.

*Premise*: Recent cases overrule *Boyd*.

*Proof*: Concurring opinion in *Doe-Fisher* sounded the "death knell" for *Boyd*.

Most recent case: clarified the narrow protection of the 5th Amendment.

Therefore, *Boyd* is no longer "good law."

## ◆ III  *ANTICIPATORY REBUTTAL*

After evaluating relevant ethical and pragmatic considerations, suppose you decide not to rebut openly an adverse case or an unfavorable argument your opponent might make. Deciding not to rebut unfavorable law does not mean that you should simply ignore the adverse law or argument. There is always the risk that opposing counsel may well artfully advance the argument you have chosen to ignore. If you have not anticipated your opposing counsel's argument and taken steps to minimize the damaging nature of that argument, the adjudicator will consider the argument for the first time while reading your opponent's very persuasive argument. To avoid this result, effective advocates weave into their own arguments indirect suggestions and innuendos that anticipate and subtly rebut an opponent's argument. This strategy is called "anticipatory rebuttal."

Anticipatory rebuttal protects an advocate from either consequence of the calculated risk not to rebut an adverse case or argument directly. Should your opponent ultimately advance the unfavorable argument, you will have defused the persuasive impact of that adverse argument by subtly anticipating and rebutting it within the body of your own argument. (In the event an opponent does directly address an adverse argument you have anticipated and indirectly rebutted, you will usually have the opportunity to rebut the opponent's argument directly in a reply brief.)[5] On the other hand, should opposing counsel fail to address the adverse argument, you will not have unnecessarily educated opposing counsel.

You can use anticipatory rebuttal to anticipate and rebut a single unfavorable fact, an entire unfavorable case, or a single part of a case that may otherwise be favorable. Therefore, you can weave anticipatory rebuttal into any part of an argument, from the introductory paragraph, through the factual statement, through the body of the argument itself.

## A.  Pre-Drafting Strategy for Anticipatory Rebuttal

How might you anticipate and plan an anticipatory rebuttal strategy? Prior to drafting the argument, you will have already considered the opponent's arguments by figuratively placing yourself in your opponent's shoes. Assuming the role of your opponent, you will have considered every argument the opponent might make to win the case. You will also have considered your responses to such arguments. In Part II, we evaluated how you would rebut directly such unfavorable arguments. The pre-drafting strategy does not change when you elect not to rebut a case or argument directly.

For example, recall the residential burglary problem illustrated in Sample Memo A in Appendix A. Assume for the moment that you are a prosecutor for the State of Illinois and want to convict a defendant of residential burglary. The defendant broke into someone's garage, which had been semi-converted into a carriage house for the resident's college-age son. You face the following problem: no court in Illinois has directly addressed whether a garage could ever be a residence, or "dwelling," for purposes of the residential burglary statute. You want to convict the defendant under the *residential* burglary statute rather than the standard burglary statute because of the increased criminal sanctions for residential burglary.

---

[5] If the relevant rules of court or other proceeding do not permit you to file a responsive brief, that procedural limitation would affect how you calculate the risk of omitting any direct rebuttal of an adverse argument.

You have the following three cases: (1) *McIntyre*—the court held that an attached, enclosed porch was a dwelling under the statute; (2) *Thomas*—the court held that a garage used only for parking a car was not a dwelling under the statute; and (3) *Benge*—the court held that a weekend get-a-way cottage in the country was a dwelling under the statute. You plan on openly addressing *McIntrye* because of its favorable holding and language. You also decide to address *Thomas* openly because it is an important case in the jurisdiction and you can easily distinguish it. However, *Benge* is more problematic. Although the case has a favorable result, there is potentially damaging legislative history described in that opinion implying that garages can never be dwellings. Therefore, assume that you decide not to mention *Benge* directly. Instead, you decide to anticipate your opponent's potential use of that case, and subtly lay the groundwork to minimize its damaging language should your opponent ultimately rely on the case. Your pre-drafting notes might look something like this:

| <u>My Argument</u> | <u>Opponent's Response</u> |
|---|---|
| 1. *McIntyre* & *Thomas* illustrate that the *use* of a structure is the most important predictor of whether a structure is a dwelling (not the physical structure itself).<br><br>2. But courts were not concerned with the physical structure itself, but with *activities within* the structure—<br><br>*McIntyre*—court stresses "these activities make the porch a living quarters"<br><br>*Thomas*—court states that the garage "at least in these circumstances" is not a dwelling—implication is that a garage *could* be a dwelling under other circumstances—i.e., with the appropriate use | 1. But look at the case facts: bottom line—the *McIntyre's* attached porch was a dwelling; the garage in *Thomas* was not a dwelling; and *Thomas* is the only "garage" case in Illinois.<br><br><br><br><br><br><br><br><br><br><br><br><br><br><br><br><br><br>2. You're emphasizing "use" too much and ignoring the structure itself—look at the legislative history—*Benge* court notes that when |

3. Wait a minute—this quote is consistent with my premise—the Senator was concerned with use and the threat to human life; most garages are not occupied—that's why he made the statement; but he couldn't have meant a garage would *never* be a dwelling because of its technical label as a garage. That would produce an absurd result:

Absurd result = a garage converted into a carriage house with an occupant who resides there for 365 days a year could never be a dwelling—while a burglary of a vacant home would always be a dwelling—contradicts legislative concern with threat to human life.

the legislature amended the statute, Senator Sangmeister states: "people should not be prosecuted for breaking `into unoccupied buildings such as garages'"—therefore, garages were not intended to be dwellings under the statute.

## B. Drafting Strategy

After carefully considering your opponent's arguments and your rebuttal to each argument, you are ready to weave anticipatory rebuttal into the argument itself. Depending on the adverse law you are rebutting, anticipatory rebuttal can be as subtle as a single adjective, or sweep through an entire argument. Again assuming the role of a prosecutor in the above example, your pre-drafting strategy notes reflect a potential adverse argument opposing counsel may raise and your rebuttal to that argument. Your rebuttal focuses on the legislative concern for protecting human life, resulting in the *use* of a structure as the critical factor (Pre-Drafting Note #3). However, you have decided not to include within your argument the Senator's statement itself, or your "absurd result" rebuttal to your opponent's argument. Each of these arguments would either tip your hand or appear defensive. The following example illustrates the way in which you might anticipate and rebut the opponent's potential use of

*Benge.* The following example paragraph would be inserted following favorable case discussions of *McIntyre* and *Thomas.*

| | |
|---|---|
| In each case, the courts applied the statutory definition of "dwelling" in a manner consistent with the statute's legislative purpose. In *McIntyre*, a porch occupied and used for living-type activities constituted a "dwelling" under the residential burglary statute. There, the burglary of a porch that was frequently occupied for living-type activities risked injury to human life, a risk associated with the burglary of a dwelling. | Favorable Premise.<br><br>Emphasizes holding based on "type of use."<br>Links the holding to favorable statutory purpose. |
| In contrast, burglary of the unoccupied garage in *Thomas* created no risk to human life greater than in a typical burglary of any unoccupied structure. | Links the holding to favorable statutory purpose. |

The above paragraph very subtly lays a foundation that would undermine an opponent's potential argument that the legislature intended that no garage could ever be a dwelling. It also advances the advocate's own theory of the case.

## EXERCISE 1

Consider again the fact pattern and legal arguments that support the federal wiretap brief (Sample Brief in Appendix D). For purposes of this exercise, assume that you represent Hart and that the matter is before a district court judge within the District of Columbia. Further assume that, prior to drafting a brief attempting to suppress the wiretap evidence, you find a precedent case in which the court held the government's explanation for its sealing delay was "satisfactory." That case, *United States v. Elsinore,* was decided in 1970 by the United States Court of Appeals for the District of Columbia. In that case, the court accepted the government's explanation as satisfactory, even though the government's pre-sealing procedures were inadequate to protect the tapes from any possibility of tampering. However, the court stated: "Where, as here, the government has proven through reliable expert testimony that the tapes were not in fact tampered with prior to sealing, the defendant was not prejudiced by the sealing delay. Therefore, the government's explanation for the sealing delay is satisfactory and the tapes were properly admitted into evidence."

During your research, assume that you discover another case arising out of the District of Columbia. In *United States v. Wilmore*, the United States Court of Appeals for the District of Columbia held that the government's explanation was not satisfactory. That case was decided in 1990. In *Wilmore*, the court held that the government's pre-sealing procedures were inadequate to protect the tapes from any possibility of tampering. However, unlike the *Elsinore* court, the *Wilmore* court declined to allow the government to produce expert testimony to prove that the tapes had not in fact been altered during the sealing delay. The court observed: "In recent years, technological advances have made forgery virtually impossible to detect. Alterations are likely to go undetected because a highly skilled forensic examiner who is an expert in the field of audio technology, using the most sophisticated equipment available today, can take months to establish with reasonable certainty that a tape has been falsified. This court declines to open the door to such lengthy and costly proceedings that might in themselves be inconclusive." In *Wilmore*, the court did not address the earlier *Elsinore* decision.

A.   Under these circumstances, would you have an ethical obligation to discuss the unfavorable *Elsinore* decision? Why or why not?

B.   Assume that you decide to address the *Elsinore* decision. Draft a paragraph that addresses both the *Wilmore* and *Elsinore* cases.

# TRIAL & APPELLATE COURT BRIEFS

 **I** *OVERVIEW OF A BRIEF*

*Pre-Trial Briefs*: A brief is a generic term that refers to any written argument submitted to a court. Some briefs are filed with a trial court judge prior to trial. This type of brief usually accompanies a "motion" requesting the court to grant the client relief in some manner. For example, upon receiving a Complaint, a defendant's attorney might file a "Motion to Dismiss," requesting the court to dismiss the lawsuit against the client. Motions are typically very short and to the point. They ask the judge to grant the client specific relief and may also include the bottom-line reasons the client is entitled to the relief requested. Because attorneys do not want the judge to rule on the motion before having an opportunity to argue its merits, they often file written arguments with the motion that are generically referred to as briefs. In fact, they are often technically labeled as "Memorandum in Support of" or "Memorandum in Opposition to" the motion. Both parties have an opportunity to file a written argument, so long as they comply with the time and space constraints imposed by the court.

*Trial Briefs*: Other trial court briefs are filed during or following the trial. For example, sometimes attorneys try their cases before a trial court judge rather than a jury. Following the trial, the trial court judge sometimes asks the attorneys to submit written briefs that address specific issues raised during the trial. This type of brief is referred to as a "Post-Trial Brief."

*Appellate Court Briefs*: Other briefs are filed when a case is appealed from a trial court to an appellate court. In an appellate court brief, the losing party appeals the lower court judgment. That party is called the "appellant" or "petitioner;" the other party is referred to as the "appellee" or "respondent." In an appellate court brief, the appellant argues why the lower court erred with respect to very specific points that become the issues on appeal.

Chapter 19 discusses common persuasive writing style strategies that enhance the appeal of any persuasive argument. Chapters 20 through 24 discuss the different argument constructs and strategies involved in both law-centered and fact-centered arguments. The previous chapters pertain to persuasive arguments in general, whether or not the persuasive argument assumes the form of a brief filed before a court. When such arguments appear in a brief, however, they must also comply with specialized rules adopted by the court.

# II  *STRUCTURE OF A TRIAL COURT BRIEF*

Before filing a brief before a trial court, check the local court rules to determine whether you must comply with any special rules of court. For example, local court rules often specify that briefs can not exceed a certain number of pages and must comply with certain font and margin requirements. Other court rules might require briefs of a certain length to contain a Table of Contents and a Table of Authorities. These components of a brief are required in all appellate court briefs and are discussed below in Part 3. Most trial court briefs, however, contain the following sections: (1) an Introduction; (2) a Statement of Facts; and (3) an Argument.

## A.  *Introduction*

If the trial court brief is lengthy enough to merit a summary of the argument, the brief begins with an Introduction section. In the Introduction, the advocate states why the client is entitled to a favorable judgment and summarizes the most compelling reasons that support the advocate's conclusion. The trial court briefs illustrated in Appendix C each contain a persuasive Introduction section that summarizes the argument.

## B.  *Statement of Facts*

In the Statement of Facts, the advocate attempts to convey a persuasive story of the underlying facts that relate to the argument. In the Statement of Facts, the advocate seeks to persuade the judge while also appearing fair and ethical. Chapter 26 discusses the strategies involved in crafting persuasive factual statements.

## C.  *Argument*

The Argument is the heart of the brief, where the advocate argues why the client should prevail. Thus, in a law-centered argument, the advocate argues why the law should be interpreted in a manner favorable to the client. In a fact-centered argument, the advocate argues why the law should be applied to the client's factual situation in a manner that compels a favorable judgment. These argument constructs are discussed at length in Chapters 20 through 24. Whatever argument construct you follow, in a multi-issue brief you would use point-headings to provide the court with persuasive roadmaps of the argument. Persuasive point-headings are discussed more fully in Chapter 27.

For a lengthy brief, the Argument may end with a short section entitled "Conclusion." For a shorter brief, the Argument may end with a simple prayer for relief: "Accordingly, plaintiff respectfully requests that this Court grant the Plaintiff's Motion to Dismiss and for such other and further relief as this Court deems proper."

##  STRUCTURE OF AN APPELLATE COURT BRIEF

Appellate courts have specialized rules with which attorneys must comply. Many appellate courts have specialized clerical rules that govern the typeface used in the brief, the margins, the size of the pages, and even the color of the pages. Other rules govern the mandatory components of the brief and the order in which they must be presented. Most courts also limit the number of pages within the brief. Before filing an appellate court brief, you must carefully review and then comply with the specialized rules that govern briefs filed before that court. Failure to comply with the rules of court could result in dismissal of an appeal.

Although different courts of appeal have specific rules with which attorneys must comply, most appellate courts require appellants to include the following components in their briefs:

### A. Cover Page

The cover page identifies for the court important identifying information about the case. Such identifying information includes the court in which the brief is being filed, the parties names, the party filing the brief, the docket number, and the names and addresses of the attorneys of record. If the pertinent court rules specify how you must prepare the cover page, you must comply with those rules exactly. However, the cover page for the brief illustrated in Appendix D is an example of a typical cover page.

## B.  Table of Contents

The Table of Contents describes each section of the brief and the page number on which each section begins. It is a map of the entire argument. Therefore, for purposes of clarity, separately identify each issue and sub-issue contained within the Argument. As you identify the issues, frame each issue as a declarative statement of the conclusion you want the court to adopt. Avoid identifying the issues generically (e.g., Argument I), or stating the issues in question form. Take a look at the brief in Appendix D to view a typical Table of Contents and the manner in which the issues are identified. For obvious reasons, wait to draft the Table of Contents until after you have finalized the brief itself. Any last minute changes reflected in the brief must be duly noted in the Table of Contents as well.

## C.  Table of Authorities

As the name suggests, the Table of Authorities identifies the authority cited within the brief. Usually, all of the cases are cited first, arranged alphabetically by the level of court. The list of cases is followed by a list of relevant statutes and constitutional authorities, followed by any secondary sources you may have cited in the brief. Next to each authority, you must include all of the page numbers on which the authority is cited within the brief. Thus, if you cite to an authority four separate times through-out the brief, you must include the page number of each reference. However, if you cite a particular case or other authority so frequently through-out the brief that page citations would be almost meaningless, you may use the term "passim" to replace page numbers. The Latin term "passim" denotes that the case is cited "everywhere" within the brief. Be careful not to use this term unless you can confidently state that the authority is truly used "everywhere" within the brief.[1] The sample brief in Appendix D contains a typical Table of Authorities.

As with the Table of Contents, wait to draft the Table of Authorities until after you have finalized your brief. It is very important that the page numbers and other references be accurate and complete. Appellate court judges often refer to the table to locate the citation to a specific authority or to refer to the specific places in the brief where the authority is cited.[2] First impressions are important: incorrect page references or any other inaccuracy can result in a loss of credibility. You certainly do not want the judges to question your competence and credibility before they even begin to read your argument.

---

[1] Nancy L. Schultz & Louis J. Sirico, Jr., *Legal Writing and Other Lawyering Skills* 285 (3rd ed. Matthew Bender 1998).

[2] Ruggero J. Aldisert, *Winning on Appeal: Better Briefs and Oral Argument* 100 (Rev. 1st ed. NITA 1996).

## D.  Statement of Jurisdiction

An appellate court must not only have subject matter jurisdiction to resolve the matter but have jurisdiction to hear an appeal at a particular point in time. In federal court, although there are specific, narrow exceptions, the appellant must appeal from a final appealable order. In state court, the appellant's ability to appeal an order is also restricted by state appellate court rules. Because the court can not consider the substantive merits of your argument without jurisdiction, the Statement of Jurisdiction is often included as a separate component of the brief.

## E.  Statement of the Issues

The Statement of the Issues is also commonly called the Questions Presented. The Statement of the Issues is an extremely important part of the brief because it frames the issues the court has been asked to resolve. Careful consideration should be given to the issues you want the court to address and how you might frame the issues in a manner that is both favorable to your client and also fair and ethical. Chapter 28 discusses and illustrates this section of the brief.

## F.  Constitutional and Statutory Provisions

This section identifies the text of relevant constitutional or statutory provisions that are critical to the court's disposition of the issues on appeal. This section might also contain any court rules that are at issue on appeal. However, if a statutory or other provision is not critical to the issues under consideration, do not include the text of that provision in this section. Instead, simply refer to it in the Table of Authorities. Assuming the constitutional, statutory or other provision is at issue on appeal, you may either quote the text of that provision or refer the court to the appendix in which the provision is reproduced. If the text is relatively short, quote the text of that provision within this section of that brief. If the provision is relatively lengthy, but only a specific part of that provision is at issue on appeal, quote only the part that is at issue. If the entire provision is at issue and it is lengthy and relatively complex, you might instead simply refer the court to the appendix in which the provision is reproduced.

## G.  Preliminary Statement

The Preliminary Statement briefly explains the procedural posture of the appeal by describing the order or judgment from which the party appealed and the relevant procedural events related to the appeal. The Preliminary Statement is sometimes called the "Proceedings Below" or "Nature of the Proceedings

Below." To add to the confusion, some courts call the Preliminary Statement the "Statement of the Case," and label what is referred to in this book as the Statement of the Case, as the "Statement of Facts."[3] However, by whatever label, this section simply explains why the appeal is before the court. Again, refer to Appendix D to review a typical Preliminary Statement.

## H.  Statement of the Case

The Statement of the Case tells the relevant factual story underlying the controversy. This section of the brief is described more fully in Chapter 26.

## I.  Summary of the Argument

The federal rules of appellate procedure require each brief to contain a Summary of the Argument that precedes the formal argument itself.[4] This section of the brief is extremely important because it is the judges' first opportunity to review the most important aspects of your argument. Chapter 27 discusses this section of the brief in greater detail.

## J.  The Argument

As its title suggests, the Argument section of the brief contains a complete articulation of the attorney's arguments. Thus, in a law-centered argument, the advocate argues why the law should be interpreted in a manner favorable to the client. In a fact-centered argument, the advocate argues why the law should be applied to the client's factual situation in a manner that compels a favorable judgment. These argument constructs are discussed at length in Chapters 20 through 24. Whatever argument construct you follow, in a multi-issue brief you would use point-headings to provide the court with persuasive roadmaps of the argument. Persuasive point-headings are discussed more fully in Chapter 27.

## K.  Conclusion

In most cases, the conclusion should be a very brief, succinct statement of the exact relief the attorney is requesting. For example, a brief commonly concludes with a simple statement such as:

---

[3] Richard K. Neumann, Jr., *Legal Reasoning and Legal Writing: Structure, Strategy & Style* 382 (4th ed. Aspen L. & Bus. 2001).

[4] Fed. R. App. P. 28(a)(5).

For the foregoing reasons, appellant requests the Court to reverse the judgment of the district court and to remand these proceedings with a direction to enter judgment in its favor.

Although the above illustration is the most common type of conclusion, some attorneys also include a brief recapitulation of the reasons why their client is entitled to the requested relief. Such brief summaries might be appropriate if the brief is unusually complex and lengthy. However, such recapitulations of the grounds for relief are not usually necessary. If they are included, they should not exceed a few sentences.

# 26

# TRIAL & APPELLATE COURT BRIEFS: THE FACTUAL STATEMENT

 **I** *PRE-DRAFTING CONSIDERATIONS*

## A. Working with the Record

Before drafting a factual statement, you must work with the available record. The record is not just restricted to transcripts of testimony but also includes affidavits, pleadings, prior court orders, and documents that were introduced into evidence. For example, if you were to draft a motion for summary judgment, you would work with pleadings, deposition testimony, documents and responses to interrogatories. If you were to draft an appellate court or a post-trial brief, you would also work with the trial court record that contains the testimony of witnesses and the documents entered into evidence during the trial. Working with the record can be intimidating because it involves examining numerous pleadings, documents and testimony that can span hundreds or even thousands of pages. Nevertheless, it is very important that you not only have a solid grasp of the factual record but that you accurately incorporate the relevant facts into your brief.

As you review the record, you may find it helpful to keep a checklist of the facts you are seeking. First, as discussed more fully below, look for facts that will help you advance your theory of the case. Second, as you review the record, keep in mind that the factual statement must include every legally significant fact that will appear in your argument. Legally significant facts include unfavorable as well as favorable facts. Third, look for any basic background facts that will help provide context for the factual story you will be telling. Finally, look for emotionally appealing facts that might appeal to the court's sense of fairness or equities.

---

*Checklist*:

1.  Facts that support your *theory of the case*.

2.  Facts that are *legally significant*, including both favorable and unfavorable facts.

3.  Facts that provide *context* for the story.

4.  Facts that have *emotional appeal*.

---

Every statement of fact contained within a brief must arise from the record. In fact, you will be required to support every factual statement you make in the brief with a citation to the record. Therefore, as you review the record to identify the facts you will include within your brief, carefully note the pages from which you have extracted factual information. For a voluminous record, you might also wish to create a page-by-page summary of the record as you read the record for the first time. The summary will prove useful later as you refer back to the record to prepare your factual statement and argument.

## B.  Ethical Considerations

### 1.  Legally Significant Facts

As you review the record, keep in mind that the factual statement must include every legally significant fact that will appear in your argument. Legally significant facts include unfavorable as well as favorable facts. Rules of professional conduct prohibit every attorney from "knowingly" making a "false statement of law or fact" to a court.[1] False statements not only include misrepresentations of the facts themselves but misrepresentations by *omission*. Therefore, should an attorney fail to include relevant adverse facts within a factual statement, the attorney not only risks losing the trust of the court but also risks sanctions.

### 2.  Factual Inferences

False statements of fact also include *inferences* that are stated as fact. Although you might properly include an inference of a witness that appears in

---

[1] *See, e.g.*, ABA Model Code Prof. Resp. DR 7-102(A)(5); ABA Model R. Prof. Conduct 3.3(a)(1).

the trial record, you must not state your own inferences as if they were facts.[2] For example, in the federal wiretap problem illustrated in Appendix D, Agent Friday testified that she sealed the box of tapes, while the janitor testified that the box was open when he found the tapes. These statements are facts that would properly be included in the factual statement of the defendant's brief. However, the following statement would be an impermissible inference from such testimony: "It is entirely possibly that an unknown person opened the box of tapes at some point during the two-month time period in which they were missing." Although this is a permissible inference from the facts, it is not a fact itself. Therefore, although it would be permissible for the defendant's attorney to argue this inference within the argument itself, it has no place within the factual statement. (Even in the argument, however, it must be clear that the attorney's conclusion is an inference from facts and not a fact itself.) Your review of the record will help you avoid stating inferences as fact. If a "fact" does not appear in the record itself, it is not a fact.

## ◆ II ▸ *DRAFTING FACTUAL STATEMENTS*

The factual statement in a trial court brief is commonly called a "Statement of Facts." In appellate court briefs, the factual statement is commonly called the "Statement of the Case." To confuse matters further, some appellate courts use the term "Statement of the Case" to refer to the "Preliminary Statement" of the procedural history of the case, reserving the term "Statement of Facts" for the statement of the factual story itself. To avoid confusion, this book uses the term "factual statement" to refer to the section of the brief that conveys the underlying factual story of the case.

As you draft the factual statement, keep in mind the dual purposes of the factual statement: (1) to inform the court of all legally significant facts; and (2) to persuade. You have a duty to the court to fairly and accurately inform the court of all facts that are legally significant, including unfavorable facts. At the same time, the factual statement is an ideal place to begin *subtly* painting a picture that portrays the client's position in an appealing, favorable light. Thus, you will want to emphasize facts that support your theory of the case and that have emotional appeal. This is a delicate balancing act. It will likely require many rewrites to produce a factual statement that is straight-forward and fair as well as subtly persuasive. However, the time you invest in drafting a persuasive factual statement is well worth the investment. As one federal appellate court judge observed: "[T]he statement of facts has tremendous significance to

---

[2] *See, e.g.*, *In re Greenberg*, 104 A.2d 46 (N.J. 1954) (holding that an attorney improperly stated a factual inference as a fact).

the outcome of the appeal. Cases turn far more frequently on their facts than they do the law."[3]

As you consider how to begin to persuade the court through your artful presentation of the factual story, consider the following guidelines. First, create an appealing story that emphasizes people rather than a detached commentary. Second, tell the story in a manner that emphasizes your theory of the case and highlights the favorable facts. Third, de-emphasize and neutralize the unfavorable facts. Fourth, organize the factual story for clarity and persuasive appeal. Finally, edit your factual story to ensure that it is accurate, supported by references to the record, and does not inadvertently include any argument or factual inferences.

## A. *Creating an Appealing Story*

People are captivated by other people's stories and how they experienced factual events. Stop and think for a moment about the real life stories that have affected you most strongly. It is probably safe to assume that most of us do not have a vivid recollection of detached commentaries about the economic forecast. However, we may recall a story about a family who was affected by the economy. We might not be personally moved by a news statistic that a mudslide killed hundreds of people in a country in another continent, but we would likely be moved by a story about specific people whose lives were tragically affected by that event.

A lawsuit is, on one level, a clash of competing stories. Like people everywhere, a judge will be drawn to the better story. A good story is one that focuses on people and portrays the story from the sympathetic perspective of the client. To read a story from the client's perspective, the reader must be able to sense what it must have been like to be there as the story unfolded. In other words, the reader must sense somehow what the people in the story must have heard, seen, tasted, smelled, felt and believed. These facts have emotional appeal and draw the reader into the story.

As an example, consider the Fifth Amendment problem illustrated in Sample Brief B in Appendix C. In that problem, the defendant, Mr. Browne, seeks to prevent the government from obtaining his diary and using incriminating statements within the diary to prosecute him for selling drugs. The defendant's theory of the case is that, because diaries are extremely personal and private, they are deserving of protection under the Fifth Amendment. With that in mind, consider the persuasive appeal of Example 1 below:

---

[3] Ruggero J. Aldisert, *Winning on Appeal: Better Briefs and Oral Argument* 155 (Rev. 1st ed. NITA 1996).

---

*Example 1:*

    Defendant's diary contains his private daily thoughts and reflections on the vicissitudes of life. Defendant's diary reflects his romantic life (Diary at 15) and his mother's death (Diary at 21) in addition to descriptions of his illegal drug trafficking. (Diary at 9, 27.)

---

Were you moved by the above story? Did the story leave you with a strong desire to protect the defendant from the government? Notice how the statements focus on the "diary," not on Mr. Browne. Even Mr. Browne's name is lost within the generic reference to the "defendant." Moreover, after reading the story, you still do not have a sense of who Mr. Browne is or why the diary was so important to him. Now consider the alternative factual statement in Example 2 below:

---

*Example 2:*

    Mr. Browne's diary contains his most private daily thoughts and reflections on the vicissitudes of life. Mr. Browne's diary is replete with his personal reflections about his romantic life, chronicling the highs and lows of the intimate relationship he has had with his girlfriend of four years. (*See, e.g.,* Diary at 15.) Following the death of his mother, Mr. Browne used his diary as an outlet to express his innermost feelings of grief and regrets. (Diary at 7, 21.) Mr. Browne poignantly notes that: " I am consumed with grief. I never had the chance to say good-bye. I never had the chance to say I was sorry—for not being the son she wanted me to be, and for a million other things." (Diary at 21.) Mr. Browne also voiced in his diary his feelings about the progress of his psychotherapy, lamenting: "Will this therapy ever end? Sometimes it all seems too hopeless. Every time we peel off a layer of pain, a deeper layer is revealed." (Diary at 4.) Although the diary contained incriminating statements regarding use of a boat for illegal drug distribution, Mr. Browne also used his diary as an outlet to express his personal despair over his drug addiction. (Diary at 9, 27.) Finally, Mr. Browne expressed private thoughts in his diary that he was not ready to share "with anyone, including Ms. Jones," his psychotherapist. (Diary at 5.)

---

The second illustration personalizes Mr. Browne and provides the reader with insight into who he is and the personal demons with which he struggled. The reader is left with the impression that the diary is not some impersonal object but a tangible expression of someone's deepest feelings and fears. As a result, this story has a better chance of motivating a judge to want to protect the diary from compelled public disclosure.

## B.  Emphasize Favorable Facts that Advance the Theory of the Case

### 1.  Pre-Drafting Strategy

As you consider how to incorporate the factual record into a compelling factual statement, carefully consider your over-all strategy and theory of the case. Chapters 20 through 24 discuss the argument strategies involved in crafting a winning argument for different types of law-centered and fact-centered arguments. These argument strategies reflect the various ways in which courts can be persuaded to adopt favorable positions. When the issue before a court involves a factual determination, you must consider how the various argument strategies interrelate with the factual record. The factual record must not only support your legal argument but should dovetail into that argument: the facts and law, viewed together, should make the court *want* to grant your client the relief you seek. Therefore, a well-crafted factual statement should artfully advance the theory of the case.

As an example, consider the federal wiretap problem that is the basis of the sample brief in Appendix D. In that brief, Hart's attorney argues that wiretap tapes must be suppressed because the government failed to provide a "satisfactory explanation" for its delay in obtaining the safeguard of a judicial seal. Hart's attorney argues that the court must adopt a two-prong legal standard that would require the government to prove: (1) that its pre-sealing procedures protected the tapes from any possibility of tampering; and (2) that it acted with reasonable diligence to minimize the sealing delay. When framing these favorable rules of law, Hart's attorney considered the factual record before the court. The fact that the government lost the tapes for two months motivated the attorney to argue that the court adopt the first prong of the legal standard—under that standard, the government can not prevail. In addition, the government's carelessness in handling the tapes prompted Hart's adoption of the second prong of the legal standard. A careless mistake that is not remedied for two months would likely not satisfy the "reasonable diligence" standard.

## 2.   Drafting Strategy: Highlight Favorable Facts

When drafting a factual statement, the facts should artfully advance your theory of the case. This is a challenge, indeed, because the factual statement does not contain legal argument or inferences from the facts. Moreover, the factual statement must include all of the facts that are described in the argument itself, both favorable and unfavorable. Nevertheless, as you draft your factual statement, focus on your theory of the case and consider how the facts support that theme. Facts that support the theme can be highlighted by prominently displaying all of their descriptive details. Therefore, instead of summarily dispensing with a favorable fact, parade out all of the details. If there is a statement within the transcript that graphically illustrates a favorable fact, then quote that statement within the factual story. Also consider how you might use the persuasive writing style strategies discussed in Chapter 19 to highlight favorable facts.

Again using the federal wiretap problem for purposes of illustration, Hart's attorney advances two themes. The first theme concerns the precautionary measures the government must take to protect wiretap evidence from tampering. To advance this theory, Hart's attorney wants to highlights facts reflecting the potential for tampering during the two month period in which the government can not account for the tapes' whereabouts. How compellingly does the following factual statement advance this theme?

---

**Example 1:**

. . . Agent Friday also testified that she labeled and sealed the box of tapes. (R. at 10.) The tapes were located in a supply room on Nov. 8, 2000. When the box of tapes was found, there was no label on the box of tapes and the box was not sealed. (R. at 14.)

---

In Example 1 above, the facts relating to this theme are present, but not highlighted. The above statement is a rather summary description of the relevant facts that advance Hart's theory of the case. Now consider the persuasive appeal of the following alternative factual statement in Example 2:

***Example 2:***

... Agent Friday also testified that she placed a label on the box indicating that the box was to be transported to the courthouse. (R. at
10.) In contrast, the building janitor testified that no label appeared
on the box of tapes. (R. at 14.) The government can not explain this
factual discrepancy. (R. at 15.) Finally, although Agent Friday testified that she sealed the box of tapes (R. at 10), the building janitor
testified that the box of tapes "was open. You could look right in and
see what was inside." (R. at 14.)


. . .


... The government speculates that the tapes sat exposed in an open
box in the unlocked office supply room for over two months. (R. at
15.) The exposed tapes sat in the busy supply room amidst note
pads, pencils, office supplies and party decorations, open to the
5,000 occupants of the building who frequent the room for coffee
and office supplies. (R. at 14.)

What makes this second factual statement more persuasive? Instead of
summarizing the evidence, Hart's attorney highlights the favorable facts by
drawing out their details. For example, the fact that the box of tapes was found
in an open office supply room appeals to the judge's concern that the tapes'
integrity may well have been compromised. Therefore, Hart's attorney highlights the underlying facts that support the vulnerable nature of the supply
room by noting the number of people who have access to that room, and the
various and sundry reasons why people would have occasion to visit the supply room. Hart's attorney also highlights the discrepancy between Agent Friday's testimony and that of the building janitor. Hart emphasizes the janitor's
favorable testimony by quoting the janitor: "You could look right in and see
the tapes." By highlighting facts that support this theory of the case, Hart's attorney appeals to the judge's concern about introducing tainted evidence at
trial that may well be used to convict the defendant.

Also note the persuasive writing style strategies used in the above statement.
How does Hart's attorney use the strategy of "juxtaposition" to illustrate in-
consistencies in the government's stories? What verbs and adjectives does Hart
use to appeal to the judge's concern that the tapes' integrity may have been
compromised?

Consider now the second legal theory Hart's attorney advances in the argument itself—that a "satisfactory explanation" requires the government to act with "reasonable diligence." To advance this theme, Hart's attorney wants to highlight facts that reflect carelessness and ineptitude, parading in great detail all of the precautionary steps Agent Friday failed to take and her ineptitude in locating the missing tapes. How effectively does the following factual statement advance that theme?

---

***Example 1:***

   On September 7, 2000, Agent Friday removed the tapes from the surveillance van and placed them in the bureau office, requesting that they be transported to the courthouse for sealing the next day. On September 8, 2000, the Bureau moved offices. On October 10, 2000 Agent Friday called the courthouse to inquire whether the tapes had been sealed. (R. at 12.) That telephone call alerted Agent Friday for the first time that the tapes were missing. Following the telephone call, Agent Friday testified that she undertook an intensive search of the office building and personally called the movers. (R. at 12.) On November 8, 2000, Agent Friday found the tapes in the office supply room. (R. at 13.)

---

The factual statement illustrated in Example 1 above certainly informs the court of the facts underlying the two-month sealing delay. However, it does not advance Hart's theme or portray the government's actions as careless. Of course, Hart's attorney can not state that the government was careless in the factual statement. Carelessness is a conclusion Hart's attorney wants the judges to draw from reading the facts, but, as a conclusion, it is not a fact itself. In the following illustration, note the persuasive strategies Hart's attorney uses to highlight the favorable facts that advance the theme:

*Example 2:*

For more than a month after the Bureau moved offices, Agent Friday never telephoned or appeared at the courthouse to ensure the tapes arrived for sealing. (R. at 11.) Agent Friday never asked the court clerk to confirm whether a judge had sealed the tapes. (R. at 11.) And, despite the fact that Agent Friday had no responsibilities other than this case during this entire time period, Agent Friday did not make a single attempt to locate her only evidence in this case. (R. at 12.)

It was not until October 10, 2000 that Agent Friday finally called the courthouse to inquire whether the tapes had been sealed. (R. at 12.) It was not until then that Agent Friday began searching for the missing tapes. Although Agent Friday testified that she undertook an intensive search of the office building and personally called the movers, (R. at 12), nearly a month elapsed before Agent Friday was able to locate the tapes. It was not until November 8, 2000, that Agent Friday finally stumbled upon the missing tapes while looking for party decorations. (R. at 13.)

. . .

In the second illustration, Hart's attorney highlights the favorable facts by describing them in detail. Hart's attorney also uses several persuasive writing style strategies discussed in Chapter 19. For example, Hart's attorney uses the active voice to link Agent Friday with her careless actions. The attorney also uses strong verbs, adverbs and adjectives to create a sense of incompetence: "*never* telephoned or appeared," "*single* attempt," "*only* evidence," "*not until* . . . that Agent Friday *finally* called," "Agent Friday *finally* stumbled," and "*party decorations.*"

## C.  De-emphasize Unfavorable Facts

As discussed earlier, advocates have an ethical duty to inform the court of unfavorable facts that are legally significant. This ethical duty has a pragmatic counterpart. An attorney who fails to disclose unfavorable facts risks losing the trust and respect of the court. Moreover, you will likely be able to portray an adverse fact in a more favorable light than your opposing counsel. The treatment of unfavorable facts presents an interesting challenge. How might you incorporate unfavorable facts into a factual story without portraying the client in an adverse light?

There are several ways to de-emphasize unfavorable facts. First, you can neutralize the negative impact of the fact by juxtaposing that fact next to favorable information. The juxtaposition of a negative with a positive fact is often introduced with terms such as "although," "even though," "despite." These terms signal that contrasting facts will be introduced. When juxtaposing unfavorable with favorable information in two or more sentences, the word "however" similarly signals that a contrasting fact will be introduced. Consider the following sentence excerpted from the federal wiretap brief in Appendix D. This sentence concedes Agent Friday's testimony that she undertook an intensive search of the office while juxtaposing it with the favorable fact that the search, nevertheless, took one month to complete.

> Although Agent Friday testified that she undertook an intensive search of the office building and personally called the movers (R. at 12), nearly a month elapsed before Agent Friday was able to locate the tapes.

Another way to de-emphasize an unfavorable fact is to bury the fact within the middle of a paragraph or sentence. Readers tend to pay the least attention to the information in the middle of a paragraph. In addition, rather than parading out the details of unfavorable facts, treat the unfavorable facts in a more summary fashion. However, when doing so, be careful to ensure that you have not summarized the unfavorable information to such an extent that the court would not recognize the fact that you dealt with the unfavorable information. You do not want to leave the impression that you are hiding important information from the court. Finally, you can de-emphasize unfavorable facts by using such persuasive writing strategies as the passive voice and non-action verbs to distance your client from unfavorable conduct (or to distance the opponent from favorable conduct). (Persuasive writing style strategies are discussed in Chapter 19.)

As an example, consider the excerpted factual statement from the Fifth Amendment problem that was illustrated in Section A above. That paragraph contained the unfavorable admission that Mr. Browne referred to illegal drug operations in his diary. In the sentence below, notice how the unfavorable admission is juxtaposed next to a favorable statement. Review again the excerpted paragraph in Section A to see how the statement is also buried within the middle of the paragraph.

> Although the diary contained incriminating statements regarding use of a boat for illegal drug distribution, Mr. Browne also used his diary as an outlet to express his personal despair over his drug addiction. (Diary at 9, 27.)

## D. Organize the Facts to Present a Compelling Story

### 1. Emphasize Favorable Facts

#### (a) Front-load Favorable Facts

A reader's attention span is at its greatest during the first few paragraphs.[4] Therefore, consider highlighting the favorable facts that advance your theory of the case by emphasizing such facts within the first few paragraphs of the factual statement. Of course, if it does not make logical sense to do so, do not blindly place such facts at the beginning of your factual statement. However, your story will be more persuasive if you can emphasize favorable facts that advance your theme *before* you acknowledge unfavorable facts that detract from your theme.

#### (b) End with Favorable Facts

Although readers pay the most attention at the beginning, some experts contend that "they remember longest the material at the end."[5] Because that information is the last thing the reader reads, it tends to linger in the mind. Therefore, end the factual statement with a compelling fact or facts that will create a favorable impression in the reader's mind. For example, in the federal wiretap brief, the factual statement ends with this lingering image that advances Hart's theme:

---

[4] Richard K. Neumann, Jr., *Legal Reasoning and Legal Writing: Structure, Strategy, and Style* 348 (4th ed. Aspen L. & Pub. 2001); Linda H. Edwards, *Legal Writing: Process, Analysis & Organization* 346 (2d ed. Aspen L. & Pub. 1999).

[5] Linda H. Edwards, *Legal Writing: Process, Analysis & Organization* 347 (2d ed. Aspen L. & Pub. 1999).

> The exposed tapes sat in the busy storage room amidst note pads, pencils, office supplies and party decorations, open to the 5,000 occupants of the building who frequent the room for coffee and office supplies. (R. at 14.)

### 2. *Providing Context within the Story: Chronological Order*

Readers need to understand the context of a story before they can absorb its details. Therefore, make sure you include contextual information at the beginning of the factual statement so that the court can appreciate the story that follows. In addition, if the story relates events that unfolded over a time sequence, readers can best follow such stories when they are presented in chronological order. Therefore, this method can be a clear and effective means of telling the story. Review again the Statement of the Case within the federal wiretap brief in Appendix D. Notice how the facts are presented chronologically, with favorable facts emphasizing the theories of the case woven into the chronological presentation.

### 3. *Issue Grouping*

Some facts do not lend themselves to an unfolding story. For example, the facts concerning the content of a personal diary do not lend themselves to a story of unfolding chronological events. Instead, they concern an object and whether that object merits the protection of the Fifth Amendment. Such facts should be grouped together according to the common issue to which they relate. The Statement of Facts in the Fifth Amendment brief illustrates this approach (Sample Brief B in Appendix C). Often, advocates combine both approaches by telling the story in chronological fashion while, within the chronology, grouping certain facts together that relate to common issues.

 **EXERCISE 1**

Draft a factual statement for the brief previously assigned by your professor.

# 27

# TRIAL & APPELLATE COURT BRIEFS: THE ARGUMENT

Chapters 20 through 24 discuss in detail how to formulate, outline and draft law-centered and fact-centered arguments. When incorporating such arguments into a trial or appellate court brief, you will need to add a few additional components to the argument. First, you will use persuasive point-headings to lead the court through your argument. In addition, you will incorporate into your argument an Introduction (trial court briefs) or Summary of the Argument (appellate court briefs). Finally, if you are drafting an appellate court brief, you will also draft a Statement of the Issues, which is discussed in Chapter 28, and comply with the technical requirements described in Chapter 25.

## ◆ I ◆ PERSUASIVE POINT-HEADINGS

Point-headings serve two purposes in a brief: (1) they serve as visual signposts that lend clarity to the argument; and (2) they serve a persuasive purpose. To satisfy both goals, point-headings should state the ultimate and intermediate conclusions you want the court to reach, and should state these conclusions as clearly and succinctly as possible. Thus, each issue you will address should be introduced by a major point-heading. Within each issue, introduce individual components of the issue (if any), with minor point-headings. If the discussion of a particular sub-issue within an issue requires the development of two or more arguments, you might also include point-headings to lead the court through those arguments as well. Point-headings follow this format:

---

1<sup>ST</sup> MAJOR POINT-HEADING

　　A.　*1<sup>st</sup> Sub-Heading*
　　B.　*2<sup>nd</sup> Sub-Heading*

　　　　1.　1<sup>st</sup> Secondary Sub-Heading (if applicable)
　　　　2.　2<sup>nd</sup> Secondary Sub-Heading (if applicable)

II.　2<sup>ND</sup> MAJOR POINT-HEADING

---

Do not include an "A" if there is no "B," or a "1" if there is no "2." Instead, simply include the argument within an umbrella point-heading that captures the argument.

If you sketched the outline of your argument before drafting the argument, your outline will also help you create the point-headings for your argument. When you outlined your argument, you noted the ultimate conclusion you wanted the court to reach and the intermediate conclusions that logically lead to the ultimate conclusion. As an example, Chapter 23 discussed how to outline and draft a fact-centered argument. In that chapter, the federal wiretap brief that appears in Appendix D was used to illustrate the process of outlining such an argument. Thus, in Chapter 23, we sketched the following template for that argument:

---

I.　　*Ultimate Conclusion*: The government's explanation was not satisfactory.

A.　　*1<sup>st</sup> Intermediate Conclusion*: The government failed to store the wiretap tapes in a manner that would protect them from any possibility of tampering.

　　　1.　*Favorable Rule of Law*: A satisfactory explanation requires that the government's pre-sealing procedures protect the tapes from any possibility of tampering.

　　　2.　*Proof and Explanation of the Favorable Rule of Law*:

　　　　　Case 1:　*United States v. Diana*—proves & explains favorable rule & favorable facts.

---

Case 2:   *United States v. Mora*—proves & explains favorable rule & favorable facts.

Case 3:   *United States v. Johnson*—use as tangential case to bolster argument.

2.   *Favorable Application of the Rule of Law to the Client*:

(a)   The complete lack of security measures did not safeguard the tapes.

(b)   Due to lack of security measures, tapes may well have been compromised.

4.   *Restate Conclusion*: Because the government's pre-sealing procedures did not protect the tapes from any possibility of tampering, the explanation is not "satisfactory."

B.   *2nd Intermediate Conclusion*: The government failed to act with reasonable diligence.

1.   *Favorable Rule of Law*: A satisfactory explanation requires that the government also act with reasonable diligence.

*Sub-rule*: Reasonable diligence exists only when the delay is caused by a legitimate law enforcement purpose and the government acts with diligence to minimize the delay.

2.   *Proof and Explanation of the Favorable Rule of Law*:

Case 1:   *United States v. Gigante*: proves & explains favorable rule and illustrates how a mistake is not a satisfactory explanation.

Case 2:   *United States v. Vazquez*—proves & explains favorable rule and facts.

3.   *Favorable Application of the Rule of Law to the Client*:

(a)   A mistake is not a legitimate law enforcement purpose.

(b)   Agent Friday failed to act with diligence:
(i)   When she lost the tapes; and
(ii)   When she failed to locate the missing tapes in a timely manner.

> C.  *Restating the conclusion*: The government did not provide a satisfactory explanation because it both failed to store the tapes in a manner that would protect them from any possibility of tampering and failed to act with reasonable diligence to minimize the delay.

To draft persuasive point-headings for this fact-centered argument, the ultimate and intermediate conclusions from this outline are simply converted into point-headings. For example, the ultimate and intermediate conclusions set forth in the above outline are as follows:

> I.  *Ultimate Conclusion*: The government's explanation was not satisfactory.
>
> A.  *1ˢᵗ Intermediate Conclusion*: The government failed to store the wiretap tapes in a manner that would protect them from any possibility of tampering.
>
> B.  *2ⁿᵈ Intermediate Conclusion*: The government failed to act with reasonable diligence.

After identifying the separate components of the argument to be introduced with point-headings, next consider your language. Each point-heading should be a clear, affirmative statement that identifies the conclusion you want the court to reach. Do not dilute the persuasive appeal of the point-heading by making the statement a request, or by stating the rule as your "opinion" rather than as a statement of affirmative truth. Using the federal wiretap brief problem for purposes of illustration, the ultimate conclusion from the initial outline is simply rephrased to add clarity and persuasive appeal. Thus, the ultimate conclusion is more persuasively stated as:

> *Correct:*
>
> II.  THE GOVERNMENT FAILED TO PROVIDE A "SATISFACTORY EXPLANATION" FOR ITS TWO-MONTH DELAY IN SEALING THE WIRETAP TAPES.

In the above example, the conclusion was clarified by adding the underlying context for the issue. The advocate also enhanced the persuasive appeal of the desired conclusion by using the active voice and a strong verb ("failed") to link the government with unfavorable conduct ("its delay"). Consider how much less effective that point-heading would be if it was phrased as an opinion rather than a conclusion:

---

*Incorrect:*

II.    THE DEFENDANT ARGUES THAT THE GOVERNMENT FAIL-
       ED TO PROVIDE A "SATISFACTORY EXPLANATION" FOR ITS
       DELAY IN SEALING THE WIRETAP TAPES.

---

Finally, point-headings that are too wordy and that contain too much information are also less effective. Consider how much less effective the point-heading would be if it were diluted with too much information:

---

*Incorrect:*

II.    THE GOVERNMENT FAILED TO PROVIDE A "SATISFACTORY
       EXPLANATION" FOR ITS DELAY IN OBTAINING A JUDICIAL
       SEAL OF THE WIRETAP TAPES WHEN IT LOST THE TAPES IN
       AN OFFICE MOVE AND DID NOT SUBMIT THEM FOR SEAL-
       ING UNTIL TWO MONTHS LATER WHEN IT FOUND THEM IN
       A SUPPLY ROOM.

---

 **EXERCISE 1**

Draft persuasive point-headings for the trial or appellate court brief your professor has previously assigned.

# ◆ II ◆ *SUMMARY OF ARGUMENT*

## A.  *Importance of the Summary of Argument*

All appellate and many trial court briefs contain a separate section that summarizes the most compelling components of the argument. Because it is a self-contained section outside of the Argument itself, this section is different from the overview and thesis paragraphs that might appear within the body of the argument itself. In an appellate court brief, the Summary of the Argument follows the Statement of Facts (often called the Statement of the Case). Therefore, the Summary of the Argument is sandwiched between the factual statement and the fully articulated argument. You may wish to review the sample brief in Appendix D to familiarize yourself with this section of the brief. A trial court brief of any length usually incorporates a summary of a similar nature, although it is called an "Introduction." An Introduction precedes both the Statement of Facts and the Argument itself. Sample Briefs A and B in Appendix C contain separate Introduction sections that precede the Statement of Facts. Whether drafting an argument summary for an appellate or trial court brief, the essential goals and components are the same. For purposes of brevity, this chapter generically refers to both the "Introduction" and the "Summary of Argument" as the "Summary of the Argument."

The importance of the Summary of Argument can not be overstated. It provides a critical persuasive roadmap of the argument that will follow. You can not even begin to persuade a court to agree with the myriad reasons and details that support an argument unless the court first understands the broad parameters of that argument. Providing context in persuasive writing is particularly important in brief writing because of the intended audience. The typical judge is very busy, handling hundreds of cases that may range from a sophisticated anti-trust problem to a simple negligence claim. As one judge writes:

> Judges "tend to be very busy. As a result, they have highly selective reading habits. They need and expect to know what a given case is about, and the opening of the summary of argument should tell them immediately. . . . The introduction of your summary . . . must let the reader know in a few sentences the scope, theme, content and outcome of the brief. It sets the stage for the discussion to follow. It dispatches your argument to the reader at once in succinct, concise and minimal terms. It describes the equitable heart of the [argument]. It sets forth the brief's strongest point—the argument . . . [in a manner] most calculated to persuade the court to your point of view. . . . If you are un-

able to write a cogent, succinct, encompassing introduction, you probably do not have a solid grasp of the subject matter."[1]

The Summary of Argument, or Introduction, is also important because it is often the first part of the argument the judge reads. Consider this statement from Judge James L. Robertson of the Mississippi Supreme Court:

> I think the most important part of the brief is the Summary of the Argument. I invariably read it first. It is almost like the opening statement in a trial. From clear and plausible argument summary, I often get an inclination to affirm or reverse that rises almost to the dignity of a (psychologically) rebuttable presumption. I do not mean to denigrate the importance of a fully developed and technically sound argument. But I read the subsequent argument in a "show me" frame of mind, testing whether it confirms my impression from the summary of the argument.[2]

## B. Drafting a Summary of Argument

The Summary of Argument should seize the court's attention by clearly describing: (1) the result you want the court to reach; and (2) the very best and most cogent reasons that would *compel* any reasonable person to agree with your conclusion. In doing so, the argument summary also provides the court with the legal framework of your argument.

Drafting an argument summary requires an intimate familiarity with the nuances of your argument. Therefore, wait to draft your Summary of Argument until after you have already drafted and polished the body of your argument and have incorporated point-headings into the argument. Because point-headings embody the basic roadmap of your argument, the Summary of Argument should incorporate the substance of your point-headings, with enough "filler" for the court to understand why such conclusions are sound. Because your point-headings should reflect your theory of the case, your theme should also be evident from reading the Summary of Argument.

Again we will use the federal wiretap brief for purposes of illustration. (Sample brief in Appendix D). Recall that the brief contains both a law-centered and a fact-centered argument. Therefore, the Introduction section incorporates both arguments, as follows:

---

[1] Ruggero J. Aldisert, *Winning on Appeal: Better Briefs and Oral Argument* 176 (Rev. 1st ed. NITA 1996).

[2] Ruggero J. Aldisert, *supra* n. 1 at 175–76 (quoting Robertson, *From the Bench: Reality on Appeal*, 17 Litig. 3, 5 (Fall 1990)).

The evidence obtained by the government from a wiretap on Mr. Hart's home telephone is inadmissible at trial because the government failed to comply with the requirements of the wiretap statute. The wiretap statute requires the government to safeguard the tapes by immediately "sealing" them or by providing a "satisfactory explanation" for its failure to do so. 18 U.S.C. § 2518 (8)(a) (1994). In this case, the government failed to comply with its statutory obligation. After intercepting private telephone conversations from Mr. Hart's home telephone, the government failed to surrender the tapes immediately to a judge who could have protected their integrity with a judicial seal. The government also failed to provide a "satisfactory explanation" for its failure to seek immediate judicial protection. A "satisfactory explanation" requires the government to satisfy two standards.

*Ultimate Conclusion.*

*Statutory context for issue.*

*States how the ultimate conclusion logically follows from the statute.*

First, a "satisfactory explanation" requires the government to prove that its pre-sealing procedures protected the tapes from any possibility of tampering. Congress enacted the immediate sealing requirement as an external safeguard to ensure that the integrity of wiretap tapes would remain inviolate. Therefore, when the government fails to protect the integrity of the tapes by immediately obtaining the protection of a judicial seal, its alternative explanation must ensure a similar level of protection. Here, the government wholly failed to provide any level of protection for its sensitive evidence. Instead, the wiretap tapes sat exposed in an open box in a busy, unlocked supply room for over two months. The box sat exposed and available for any one of the 5,000 occupants of the building, or any visitor to the storage room, to tamper with the tapes.

*Identifies the 1ˢᵗ favorable standard. Summarizes the policy reasons why this standard is proper (the law-centered arg.).*

*Summarizes why the government failed to satisfy this standard (the fact-centered arg.)*

Second, a "satisfactory explanation" requires that the government act with reasonable diligence to minimize the sealing delay. Again, the government's conduct falls far short of this standard. The sealing delay was caused by a mistake, a mistake that was not only foreseeable but easily preventable. Although the government knew that its bureau offices would be moving the following day, Agent Friday failed to take any precautions to ensure that the tapes would be safely delivered to the courthouse for sealing. Instead, she dropped the tapes into a box identical to the thousands of moving boxes used to move office files and supplies. To compound that initial

*Identifies the 2ⁿᵈ favorable standard.*

*Summarizes why the government failed to satisfy this standard:*

*(1) A foreseeable mistake.*

*(2) Mistake com-*

carelessness, Agent Friday delayed over a month before she placed a single telephone call to ensure that the tapes had arrived at the courthouse for sealing. Upon finding the tapes were missing, it took Agent Friday almost another full month to locate the tapes, despite the fact that she ultimately found them in an open box in a busy supply room. The government's lengthy delay in obtaining the protection of a judicial seal violates the mandatory provisions of the federal Wiretap Act.

pounded by carelessness after the move.

(3) Mistake compounded by the length of time it took to locate the missing tapes.

## EXERCISE 2

Draft an Introduction or Summary of Argument for the trial or appellate court brief your professor has previously assigned.

# 28

# APPELLATE COURT BRIEFS: SCOPE OF REVIEW & STATEMENT OF THE ISSUES

##  I  THE STANDARD OF REVIEW ON APPEAL

Appellate courts review different types of questions under different standards of review. Standards of review range from the extremely deferential standard accorded to facts found by juries to no deference at all accorded to questions of law adopted by lower courts. Therefore, it is important to know the appropriate standard of review that governs each issue on appeal. The lens through which the appellate court will be examining each issue will affect the way in which you frame your issues and argument; your arguments must show why, under the appropriate standard of review, your client should prevail.

### A.  Different Standards of Review

#### 1.  Questions of Law

Questions of law are simply law-centered issues that concern the meaning of a rule of law itself, without regard to specific facts. An appellate court resolves questions of law under a "de novo" standard of review. Under the de novo standard of review, the appellate court does not have to defer to the lower court's interpretation of what a rule of law means; instead, the appellate court is free to substitute its own judgment for that of the trial court.

For example, the federal wiretap problem illustrated in Appendix D contains the following question of law: What legal standard must the government satisfy to provide a "satisfactory explanation" for a sealing delay under the federal wiretap statute? In that problem, the trial court determined that the government provides a satisfactory explanation when it produces credible expert testimony that the tapes were not in fact altered during the sealing delay. On review, an appellate court is free to substitute its own judgment about the appropriate legal standard. Thus, for example, the appellate court would be free to conclude that a "satisfactory explanation" requires the government to prove that its pre-sealing procedures protected the tapes from any *possibility* of tampering.

## 2.   Questions of Facts

Facts are simply the historical and narrative accounts of "what happened" that were introduced into evidence during trial. A factual finding is simply the fact-finder's interpretation of that evidence. Pure factual findings are decided without reference to the law itself. For example, did the government lose the wiretap tapes? Where did the government find the missing tapes? On what date? Was the box sealed or open? Did Agent Friday originally seal the box?

### (a)   Factual Questions Resolved by a Jury

Factual questions resolved by a jury provide appellate courts with a very limited scope of review. These questions fall at the opposite end of the spectrum from questions of law, in which the appellate court is free to substitute its own judgment for that of the lower court. An appellate court will not disturb a jury's factual findings unless there is no evidence at all from which the jury could arrive at that finding. Thus, an appellate court will generally not disturb a jury's factual findings unless it is unsupported by any evidence. The deference accorded to jury verdicts stems in part from the parties' constitutional right to a trial by jury.

### (b)   Factual Questions Resolved by a Trial Court

Factual questions resolved by a trial court are accorded slightly less deference than questions resolved by a jury. When reviewing a factual question resolved by a trial court judge, the appellate court reviews the judge's determinations under a "clearly erroneous" standard of review. In other words, the appellate court will not disturb that finding unless it concludes that the judge's decision was clearly erroneous. The "clearly erroneous" standard has been defined by the United States Supreme Court to mean that an appellate court "can upset a finding of fact, even when supported by some evidence, but only if the court has 'the definite and firm conviction that a mistake has been committed.'"[1]

### 3.  *Mixed Questions of Fact and Law: Ultimate Facts*

Often, the fact-finder must determine whether the facts satisfy a certain standard under the law. Therefore, when arriving at an ultimate factual conclusion, the fact-finder must consider both the underlying historical facts that were introduced into evidence and the legal standard from which the facts should be evaluated. The resulting determination is called an ultimate factual conclusion.

Mixed questions of fact and law present interesting challenges for the appellate court. The appellate court may not disturb the basic *fact* component of the ultimate factual conclusion unless the fact-finder's determination was either not support by any evidence (in the case of a jury determination), or "clearly erroneous" (in the case of a trial judge's determination). However, an appellate court may review the *law* component of the ultimate factual conclusion "de novo." In other words, the appellate court is free to substitute its own judgment when interpreting the meaning of a rule of law. Thus, the standard of review becomes complex, with part of the findings subject to a "clearly erroneous" standard and part of the findings subject to "de novo" review.

### 4.  *Questions Within the Trial Court's Discretion*

The "abuse of discretion" standard is applied to matters that are within the trial court's discretion. For example, some statutes or court rules provide judges with the discretion to consider certain factors when resolving an issue. Under some statutes, judges have the discretion to award attorneys' fees. A trial court judge also has discretion over many matters of procedure. An appellate court might find an abuse of discretion when it finds the lower court's judgment to be "arbitrary, fanciful or unreasonable" or when "no reasonable [person] would take the view adopted by the trial court."[2]

However, the "abuse of discretion" standard is somewhat difficult to define, in part because the scope of review depends on the breadth of the discretionary power conferred on the trial judge. If a trial judge has broad discretionary

---

[1] Ruggero J. Aldisert, *Winning on Appeal: Better Briefs and Oral Argument* 63 (Rev. 1ˢᵗ ed. NITA 1996) (quoting *United States v. United States Gypsum Co.*, 333 U.S. 364, 395 (1948)).

[2] Ruggero J. Aldisert, *Winning on Appeal: Better Briefs and Oral Argument* 69 (Rev. 1ˢᵗ ed. NITA 1996) (quoting *Delno v. Market Street Ry.*, 124 F.2d 965, 967 (9ᵗʰ Cir. 1942)).

power to decide an issue, the corresponding scope of review should reflect that broad discretionary power. However, if the trial judge has more limited discretion, the scope of review should also reflect that more limited power.[3] Therefore, if you are appealing a trial court's use of discretion, you should research other cases involving the same or similar uses of discretion in order to gain a clearer idea of the deference the appellate court is likely to accord the trial judge.

 ## II   STATEMENT OF THE ISSUES

All appellate court briefs contain a section that describes the issues the appellate court is being asked to resolve on appeal. In some courts, this section is called the "Statement of the Issues." In other courts, this section is called the "Questions Presented" or the "Issues Presented for Review." By whatever label, your statement of the issues should accomplish two purposes. First, it should clearly inform the court of the question or questions it has been asked to resolve. When clearly identifying each issue, the issues should correspond exactly to the arguments you will address in the body of your argument. If you will address one issue in your argument, draft only one issue. If you will address two issues in your argument, draft two issues.

Second, each issue statement should very subtly persuade the court as to the merit of your position. Therefore, if possible, appeal to the court's sense of equities and fairness by framing each issue so that your position appears equitable and fair (and, by implication, your opponent's position appears inequitable and unfair). For a fact-centered issue, incorporate the critical facts that are at the core of your theory of the case. The court should be able to know from reading each issue statement exactly what you intend to prove. As Judge Sol Wachter advised:

> The issues should be stated in such a way that the court will know immediately what you intend to prove. "The Defendant Was Denied Due Process" could lead anywhere; "The Defendant Was Denied Due Process When the Court Refused To Allow Him To Call Any Witnesses" lets everyone know where you are going.[4]

Successfully accomplishing these two goals will require significant thought and revision. Before drafting your issue, review the court rules to determine if

---

[3] Ruggero J. Aldisert, *supra* n. 2 at 68–72.

[4] Ruggero J. Aldisert, *supra* n. 3 at 121 (quoting New York's Chief Judge Sol Wachter).

they address whether issues must be stated in a question form, or whether they can be stated in a declarative sentence. If you have a choice, it is more persuasive to state the issue in a declarative sentence that describes your desired conclusion than to ask a question. Thus, in the above example, Judge Wachter identified the issue as a declarative statement: "The defendant was denied due process when the court refused to allow him to call any witnesses." However, some courts require the interrogatory form. As a question, the same issue would be drafted as follows: "Did the court deny the defendant due process when the court refused to allow him to call any witnesses?" When drafting an appellate brief for class, you should follow your professor's instructions. When drafting an appellate brief for a moot court competition, follow the rules of that competition.

## 1. Law-Centered Issues

It is challenging to achieve the fine balance between divulging too little information and too much. As an example, consider the federal wiretap brief in Appendix D. In that argument, the defendant seeks to convince the court that the lower court erred when it interpreted the statutory requirement that the government provide a "satisfactory explanation" for its sealing delays. Consider the following issue statement:

---

**Example 1:**

Did the district court err in defining the statutory term "satisfactory explanation"?

---

The first example is neither clear nor persuasive. It simply does not provide enough information for the appellate court to know what you intend to prove. Now consider whether the following example is any improvement.

---

*Example 2:*

Did the district court err in finding that, as part of its "satisfactory explanation" for a two-month sealing delay, the government need not prove that it sealed the tapes and placed them in a locked cabinet, and/or maintained a chain of custody, and/or placed them under guard, to prove that its pre-sealing procedures afforded the same level of protection as an immediate judicial seal would have provided, thereby protecting the wiretap evidence from any possibility of tampering during the sealing delay?

---

The second example does identify for the court the issue on appeal. However, it is weighed down by unnecessary details that obscure the heart of the issue. When the unnecessary factual details are eliminated, the issue looks like this:

---

*Example 3:*

Did the district court err in finding that, as part of the government's "satisfactory explanation" for its two-month delay in obtaining a judicial seal of wiretap evidence, the government need not prove that its pre-sealing procedures protected the tapes from any possibility of tampering, thereby affording the same level of protection as an immediate judicial seal would have provided?

---

In the third example, Hart's attorney identifies the exact issue on appeal. In addition, the advocate appeals to the court's desire to promote the policy underlying the statute by noting that the level of protection Hart seeks is the same level of protection he would have received under the statute if the government had obtained an immediate judicial seal. Hart's attorney also appeals to the court's sense of fairness and equities by noting that the government caused a two-month sealing delay and that the standard Hart seeks will protect the evidence "from any possibility of tampering."

Assuming the relevant appellate court rules allow attorneys to frame issues in declarative sentences, the same issue could be stated as follows:

> ### *Example 3 in a declarative sentence:*
>
> The district court erred as a matter of law in finding that, as part of the government's "satisfactory explanation" for its two-month delay in obtaining a judicial seal of wiretap evidence, the government need not prove that its pre-sealing procedures protected the wiretap evidence from any possibility of tampering during the delay, thereby affording the same level of protection as an immediate judicial seal would have provided.

## 2.  Fact-Centered Issues

A well-drafted fact-centered issue should not only identify the exact issue before the court, but make the court *want* to decide the issue in your favor. To inspire the court to decide the issue in your favor, incorporate into the question the critical facts that are at the core of your theory of the case.

Again using the federal wiretap brief in Appendix D as an example, Hart's attorney argues that the government failed to provide a "satisfactory explanation" for its sealing delay. Consider the appeal of the following example:

> Did the district court err in finding that the government provided a "satisfactory explanation" for its sealing delay when the government lost the tapes for two months, only to find the tapes in an open box in an office supply room, and the government can neither account for the tapes' whereabouts for the two month period in which they were missing or explain why the box of tapes had been opened?

In the above example, Hart's attorney weaves into the question the critical facts that support the theories of the case. Thus, the attorney highlights the possibility that the tapes could have been altered during the two-month sealing delay by noting that the tapes sat in an "open box in an office supply room." Hart's attorney concludes the question with the highly favorable fact that the government can not account for the tapes' whereabouts or "explain why the box of tapes had been opened." The attorney subtly portrays the government as careless by emphasizing that the government lost the tapes for two months and can not account for the tapes' whereabouts.

## EXERCISE 1

Draft a Statement of the Issues for a brief assigned by your professor.

## EXERCISE 2

Review Sample Brief B in Appendix C. Assume the district court held that personal papers are not protected from compelled disclosure by the Fifth Amendment. Assume that the defendant was ultimately convicted and now appeals the district court's order denying the motion to quash the subpoena. Draft a Statement of the Issue on behalf of the defendant.

# 29

# ORAL ARGUMENTS

An oral argument serves several purposes. First and foremost, the oral argument provides judges with an opportunity to voice their concerns about the issues in a case by asking questions. Thus, the oral argument is more like a Socratic dialogue than an oral presentation and you should be prepared to respond to questions and to be interrupted. As you respond to the judges' questions, your goal is to persuade them to decide the case in your favor. Thus, your responses to questions should demonstrate how your legal position satisfies the judges' concerns. An oral argument is also an opportunity for advocates to help the judges focus on the most important, fundamental aspects of their written argument while also reinforcing the theme, or theory of the case. Therefore, you should also arrive at the oral argument with a solid grasp of the few critical points you want to convey to the judges.

 ## I   PREPARATION FOR THE ORAL ARGUMENT

### A.   Preparing an Outline of the Argument

By the time you begin preparing for an oral argument, you will have already drafted and filed your written brief and studied the brief of the opposing counsel. Therefore, you should already be very familiar with what it is you want the court to do and what you have to prove to win. You should also know how many points you must prove to win and whether they are mutually independent or dependent. Your written brief should also reflect the major premises that help prove your ultimate conclusions and the supporting proof for each issue. The supporting proof may consist of statutory construction, public policy, equities, legislative purpose and/or interpretation of case precedent. In a fact-centered argument, your supporting proof would also include argument about how the law favorably affects the client's facts.

You will not recite every detail of your written argument in your oral argument. You will be allotted only a limited amount of time to argue the merits of your case and you can expect to be interrupted with numerous questions from the bench. Therefore, your goal is to distill from the detailed arguments reflected in your written brief, the very essence of your case and to communicate the most fundamental points you will need to make to win. As you consider which arguments are most important, take a step back from your brief for a moment and consider your theory of the case and why the judges should rule in your favor. Then consider which two or three points are the pivotal points you want to emphasize in the argument. Consider which points best promote and emphasize your theory of the case.

## 1.  The Detailed Outline

From these fundamental points, create an outline of your argument. Avoid the temptation to draft a speech. An oral argument is a forum in which judges ask probing questions that reflect their concerns about the different legal positions being argued. An oral argument is more like a conversation than a rehearsed speech. Therefore, you will not have the opportunity to deliver a speech without interruption. Moreover, having a prepared speech would interfere with your ability to respond to the judges' questions and to move back and forth between your argument and your responses to questions. Instead, working from the conclusion you want the court to reach, create an outline of the most important points that support the conclusion. Begin with the strongest argument first, and then the second strongest argument, and so on.

Irrespective of the ultimate length of the outline you actually bring with you to the podium at the oral argument, begin by drafting a relatively extensive "thinking" outline that will allow you to think through your arguments. For each issue, draft the most important points that support the conclusion. Under each point, bullet-point the most persuasive reasons why that point is sound. Next to each supporting reason, make note of the most important cases and references to the record that illustrate why that reason is sound. As you create a fairly extensive initial outline, consider how your main points and your supporting proof support your theory of the case. In the oral argument itself, you will want to weave your theme into the argument as well-placed "sound bytes." Thus, the major points and supporting proof should be designed to allow you to highlight your theme during the oral argument.

## 2.  The Condensed Outline

After drafting a "thinking" outline, you will want to condense that outline into something more workable for the oral argument itself. Many advocates prefer to approach the podium with an outline of no more than a single-page that simply lays out the roadmap of their argument. A single-page outline avoids the problem of having to riffle back and forth between pages when responding to questions from the bench. With that said, if the thought of working from a single-page outline seems terrifying to you, then you might want to make your outline a bit more extensive. Whether a single-page or a couple of pages, the outline you bring with you to the podium should capture only the essential points you want to make in the argument. To make it easier for you to refer to your outline during the oral argument, use a large type-set that is easy for you to read at a glance. You may also wish to use wide margins on your outline so that you can include within the margins supporting data for each point. For example, you can include within the margins the names and citations of a few important authorities and critical pages from the record. Such an outline will provide you with a roadmap of the important points you want to make at oral argument.

### 3.  Preparing for "Hot" and "Cold" Courts

As you consider the length and complexity of your outline, also think about the judges themselves and their level of preparation for the argument. Some courts are known as "hot" benches, meaning that the judges have meticulously reviewed the briefs in advance of the argument and interrupt frequently to engage counsel in extended dialogue. With a hot court, a longer outline might prove to be distracting. In addition, as you field numerous questions from the bench, a lengthy outline increases the likelihood that you might forget a critical point you wanted to make during the argument. During the heat of the moment, two or three critical points will stand out on a single-page outline but may become lost within a more extensive outline.

On the other hand, some courts are known as "cold" courts. In a cold court, the judges have not carefully reviewed the briefs in advance and will usually not be prepared with a list of questions to ask the advocates. Therefore, the judges can be expected to listen fairly impassively with infrequent interruptions. With a cold court, you may wish to bring with you to the podium a more extended outline. Without the distraction of numerous questions, the extended outline may help you ensure that you make all of the points you want to make. With a cold court, you may not even use all of your allotted argument time.

In a moot court competition, you probably will not know in advance whether your judges will be "hot" or "cold." Therefore, you need to be prepared for either possibility. You may wish to prepare and bring with you to the podium two outlines. The first outline would be an abbreviated one or two-page outline that would be easier to use if you are engaged in a lively debate.

The second outline would be a more extensive outline to which you could refer if the judges are more impassive.

## B.    *Outlining Your Responses to Questions*

Judges ask different kinds of questions during oral argument. Some questions are merely neutral requests for information. For example, a judge may ask you to supply the name of a case, or to identify where in the record certain testimony might be found. A judge might also ask you to identify the appropriate standard of review. Know the standard of review for each issue before you arrive at the courthouse for oral argument. Unless the standard of review is at issue in the case, your thorough preparation should allow you to respond easily to such questions for information and clarification. Another type of question is the openly friendly question designed to help you promote your argument. These questions are sometimes called "softball" questions. For example, a judge might agree with your position and, through questioning, be trying to convince other judges on the panel of the merits of your position. Again, your thorough preparation of your own argument should allow you to respond easily to such questions. Other types of questions, however, are more challenging and require careful strategic thinking before the argument itself.

### 1.    *Positional Questions*

One type of question for which you should prepare in advance are "positional" questions. Sometimes judges ask questions designed to force attorneys to "draw their line in the sand." Not unlike a law school professor in a Socratic classroom, judges sometimes test how far attorneys are willing to travel down the slippery slopes of their arguments. A judge might describe a worst case scenario that could follow from your proposed position and ask you whether you would advocate your position even under those extreme circumstances. A judge might attempt to probe how firmly you are committed to the position described in your brief, and to discover whether you are willing to concede part of that position.

To prepare for this type of questioning, carefully consider the ultimate conclusion you want the court to adopt. You identified and argued in your written brief the major points that lead to the desired conclusion. Now consider whether you can concede or modify any of these points without losing the ultimate argument. It may be that, although you would prefer that the court adopt a particular legal standard, your client might also be able to prevail under another standard that is not quite as favorable. However, there are always points you absolutely can not concede and still prevail. On a sheet of paper, make a note of each of the points of your argument and how much you are willing to concede from your original positions. To help you identify the types of positional questions a judge might ask, review your opponent's brief. What are your opponent's positions? Are there any intermediate positions that lie somewhere between the two positions articulated by you and your opposing counsel? If your opponent has raised a "slippery slopes" argument that cautions the court about the "parade of horribles" that will result from adopting your position, be prepared to respond to questions that ask you to identify how far down the slippery slopes you are asking the court to slide.

As an example, consider the federal wiretap brief that is illustrated in Appendix D. In that hypothetical problem, Mr. Hart's attorney seeks to suppress wiretap evidence, arguing that because the government failed to obtain the protection of an immediate judicial seal of such evidence, its pre-sealing procedures must provide the same level of protection as an immediate judicial seal. The trial court disagreed, holding that the government could satisfy the statute if it produced credible expert testimony that the tapes were not altered during the sealing delay. Mr. Hart's attorney asks the appellate court to reverse the trial court. In preparing for the oral argument, Mr. Hart's attorney would be prepared to answer questions about their position. Thus, the attorney might draft the following question and answer in preparing for the argument:

> _Possible Question_: What if the government's expert testimony is conclusive that the tapes were not tampered with during the delay? Wouldn't that testimony allay your concerns about tainted evidence being used to convict a person?
>
> _Response_: No, your Honor. As the District of Columbia Circuit Court of Appeals stated in _United States v. Johnson_, modern technology makes it difficult, if not <u>impossible</u>, to detect whether tampering has in fact occurred. Experts simply can not provide the requisite level of proof that would ensure that tapes have not been tainted.

### 2.  Questions that Probe the Weaknesses in Your Theory

The other type of question for which you should be fully prepared to address in oral argument are oppositional questions that probe the weaknesses in your position. For example, judges might be concerned with potential adverse policy or equity ramifications should they adopt your position, or by whether mandatory case precedent allows them to adopt your position, or by whether a statutory scheme supports your position. These are the core type of questions that will be critical to your success at oral argument. Inexperienced advocates make the mistake of not preparing for these types of questions in advance. As a result, they waste the judges' time and patience by circuitous responses that do not really address the judges' concerns. Rather than taking thirty seconds to respond to the question, the advocate may have wasted several minutes of valuable argument time.

To anticipate these types of questions, carefully review your opponent's brief and any direct rebuttal in your own brief. You should be prepared to respond to each unfavorable argument raised in your opponent's brief. For each unfavorable argument you identify, draft an outline of your response. Do not outline a response that would take several minutes to express in all of its myriad supporting details. Instead, front-load your answer. Begin with your answer to the question itself, such as "yes, your Honor," or "no, your Honor," or "I respectfully disagree, your Honor." Then follow the conclusion with the one or two best reasons that support your conclusion.

Again using the federal wiretap problem for purposes of illustration, Mr. Hart's attorney should be prepared for questions reflecting the judges' concern about allowing guilty people to avoid punishment:

---

*Possible Question*: Under your theory, guilty parties will avoid punishment simply because the government's pre-sealing procedures were not fail-safe in every respect. In other words, I am concerned that culpable parties would go free even though the government could produce expert testimony that, almost to a 100% certainty, the tapes were not tampered with during the sealing delay. Isn't this too high a cost for us to pay?

*Response*: No, your Honor. It is true that a guilty person may avoid punishment under this standard. However, it is equally true that under the standard advocated by the government, an innocent person might be imprisoned for a crime he did not commit. As a society, that cost is too high, particularly when it is through the government's own careless procedures that the tapes were not properly sealed. Compelling the government to safeguard its own evidence would encourage the government to act more carefully in the future.

---

After you have drafted your proposed responses to various questions, then condense the questions and answers into a brief outline with bullet-points that identify the crux of your responses. This step will encourage you not to try and read from your extensive outline as you respond to questions. Like the delivery of your argument itself, your responses to questions should be a conversation with judges rather than a dry recitation of your notes. Moreover, the very process of drafting responses and then condensing the responses into a brief outline will help cement your understanding of the issues. Ideally, you should be so well-prepared during the oral argument that you will not need to refer to your outline of questions and responses.

## C. Preparing a Notebook for the Argument

You will not want to approach the podium armed only with a single-page outline because you may need to refer to important cases or parts of the record when you respond to the judges' questions. On the other hand, you do not want to approach the podium armed with a pile of loose papers or index cards. They not only look unprofessional, but can also be distracting as you sift through pages or index cards trying to find an answer to a judge's question. For similar reasons, avoid bringing a yellow legal pad to the podium with you. Flipping through the pages can not only be visually distracting but can also create auditory interference from the microphone.

Instead, prepare a notebook to bring with you to the argument. Many attorneys prefer to use a three-ring binder with tabs that easily identify the components of the notebook. Other attorneys prefer to use a folder. Using a binder or folder, you would include the outline of your argument under one tab, together with an outline of your responses to the most important questions you anticipate the court will ask. Other tabs may be reserved for supporting data, such as a summary of the most important cases in the argument. For each case, include the case name, the court that decided the case, the year the case was decided, the holding, and any relevant facts and rationale. If a precedent case was decided by the court before whom you are arguing, you would also note the panel of judges that decided the earlier case; the judges may ask for that information. You might also want to include in another section of the notebook any critical testimony from the record, together with references to the pages in the record.

## D. Rehearsing Your Argument

You should never arrive at the courthouse without having first gone through at least one dry-run of your argument. As a practicing lawyer, you would ask other members of your law firm to help prepare you for the argument. In a moot court competition, if the rules of your moot court competition allow, ask other law students or professors to review the briefs in advance of your dry-run and to come prepared to ask you tough questions. A practice session will help you spot any holes in your argument and identify questions to which you will need to refine your answers. Your colleagues may well have additional questions or avenues of inquiry that had not occurred to you while preparing for the argument. A practice session is a wonderful opportunity to work out some of the loop-holes in your argument and to polish your responses and your delivery. To make the session successful, encourage your colleagues to give you constructive criticism. Although it can be difficult to receive criticism, it is far better that you hear it from friendly colleagues than allow your mistakes to potentially affect the outcome of the case.

## E.  Final Details

### 1.  Updating the Law

Often, there is a significant time lapse between the date the brief is filed and the date of the oral argument. Therefore, before the oral argument, update your research to ensure that each of the cases you have relied on are still "good law." Also check to see whether there is any recent case that may affect the argument itself. If so, you must let the court and opposing counsel know of the recent development in the law. If possible, notify the court and opposing counsel of the new law prior to the date of the argument so that the judges are not distracted with reading and absorbing new law during your argument.

### 2.  Observing an Argument

If possible, prior to the date of your argument visit the courtroom in which you will argue, preferably with the panel of judges before whom you will argue. Use this opportunity to acquaint yourself with the courtroom itself, noting where the attorneys are seated, the location of the podium and microphone, and how attorneys are notified that their time has expired. If the panel of judges is the same panel before whom you will argue, also get a sense of the type of questioning you can expect, and the kinds of arguments and behavior that appeal or do not appeal to the judges. If you can not visit the courtroom in advance, arrive early for your argument and listen to other oral arguments. In a moot court competition, you will likely not have the opportunity to listen to other students' arguments. However, you may find it helpful to pay an advance visit to the room in which you will be arguing. At the very least, you can familiarize yourself with the lay-out of the room. That advance familiarity will help alleviate any pre-argument anxiety. In addition, if your school has an intra-school moot court competition involving upper-level students, attend the final rounds of the competition. If your school is near a courthouse that has appellate court arguments, you might also consider visiting the courthouse to observe the arguments.

## II ◆ THE ORAL ARGUMENT

### A. Setting of the Argument

Although a specific circuit may have twenty or more judges who sit on the appellate bench within that circuit, most appellate court arguments are heard by a panel of three judges from that circuit. Moot court competitions also commonly have panels of three judges. There are two counsel tables within the courtroom. Each counsel table is designated for attorneys who represent the appellant or the appellee. Thus, as counsel for the appellant, you would sit at the table designated for the appellant. Attorneys address the judges from behind the podium. The judges sit facing the attorneys and the podium.

You will usually be sitting at the appropriate counsel table when the judges enter the room. A bailiff will announce the entry of the judges. Rise when the judges enter the room and remain standing until after all of the judges have been seated and the chief judge asks you to be seated. The chief judge will ask you if you are ready to proceed. When asked, stand up and announce that you are "ready, your Honor."

The court allots each party a designated amount of time within which to argue. Because the appellant is the moving party, the appellant's attorney argues first. The appellant may, and should, reserve time for rebuttal. Any time reserved for rebuttal is subtracted from the time allotted to the opening argument. Thus, if the appellant has been allotted fifteen (15) minutes to argue, the appellant might reserve three (3) minutes for rebuttal, leaving twelve (12) minutes for the opening argument. After the appellant's counsel argues and sits down, the appellee's attorney then stands up and approaches the podium to deliver the argument of the appellee. The appellee can not reserve time for rebuttal. In an appellate courtroom, the time is electronically monitored. In a federal courtroom, an amber button lights up to warn the advocate that two minutes remain in the argument. A red button lights up to signal that time has expired. In moot court competitions, a time-keeper typically uses flash cards to signal the interim warnings and the expiration of time.

In a moot court competition, two team members often represent each party, each of whom argues separate issues. In such a competition, the appellants argue in succession before the appellees argue. The appellant's team will have picked in advance the team member who will deliver the rebuttal. That team member delivers the rebuttal after both of the attorneys for the appellee have argued.

## B.   The Structure of the Argument

### 1.   Introduction

After you have arrived at the podium, wait for the chief judge to let you know that the judges are ready for you to begin. Begin the argument by using the formal language used in all appellate arguments: "May it please the Court." Then state your name and the party you represent. If you are the appellant, tell the judges how much time you are reserving for rebuttal.

After stating your name, identify the issue on appeal in a manner that artfully captures your theme, or theory of the case. Your statement of the issue should favorably frame your argument and make the court *want* to decide the appeal in your favor. Therefore, prior to the argument, carefully consider your theme and the issue or issues on appeal. What is at the heart of your appeal? Why should the court rule in your favor? What facts or policy favorably advance your theme? Because the way you frame the issue or issues is so important, spend some time drafting and then revising your preliminary statement to ensure that it has maximum persuasive appeal. After crafting a favorable statement, include the exact language of that statement in your outline.

As an example, consider again the federal wiretap brief that is illustrated in Appendix D. In that hypothetical problem, Mr. Hart's theme, or theory of the case, is that the government acted carelessly and that its haphazard pre-sealing procedures failed to protect the wiretap evidence from tampering. These themes are illustrated in the following introduction:

> May it please the Court. My name is Sandra Saunders and I represent the appellant, Mr. James Hart. We ask the Court to reserve three minutes for rebuttal. After obtaining wiretap tapes on which the government relied to convict Mr. Hart, the government lost this sensitive wiretap evidence for a period of two months. The government can not account for the tapes' whereabouts for the two-month period in which they were missing; nor can the government explain why the box of tapes, which had presumably been sealed, was found open in an office supply room, vulnerable to the 5,000 occupants of the building and their visitors. Under these facts, the government's explanation for its sealing delay was not "satisfactory" under the federal wiretap statute.

## 2. Roadmap of the Argument

As former Wisconsin Chief Justice Judge Nathan S. Heffernan advises: "At the outset tell the judges what you are going to tell them, tell them, and if it appears necessary, tell them what you told them."[1] Just as with any written argument, it is important to provide the judges with a roadmap of your argument before presenting the argument itself. The roadmap should outline the two or three most important points you will make during the argument. The roadmap illustrated below would follow Ms. Saunders' introduction that is illustrated in the preceding example:

> The government's explanation for its own delay in sealing the tapes is not satisfactory for two reasons. First, its pre-sealing procedures failed to safeguard the tapes from tampering because the government can not account for the tapes' whereabouts for the two month period in which they were missing. Second, the government's explanation is also not satisfactory because it failed to act with diligence in minimizing the sealing delay. The delay was caused by an easily preventable mistake and was exacerbated by the government's carelessness and inattention to its own files.

## 3. Factual Statement

Advocates generally do not want to waste their limited argument time by providing the court with a detailed recitation of the factual statement that is already included with the written briefs. Usually, judges will have already read the briefs and will be familiar with the facts. If the judges have made it clear that they have read the briefs or you know that the court generally reads the briefs in advance, you can assume that the judges are familiar with the facts. Do not spend precious argument time reciting a formal statement of the facts. Instead, weave into the argument itself the critical facts that support your theme and help develop your issues.

However, if you are not sure whether the judges have read the briefs, you should be prepared to provide a brief factual summary for the court. There are two schools of thought regarding how to handle this issue. Some advocates prefer simply to ask the court whether the judges would like to hear a brief summary of the facts. For example: "Would your Honors like for me to sum-

---

[1] Ruggero J. Aldisert, *Winning on Appeal: Better Briefs and Oral Arguments* 305 (Rev. 1st ed. NITA 1996).

marize the relevant facts?" Other advocates believe that it is better practice not to ask a direct question, reasoning that the judges might be offended by a question that suggests the judges may not be familiar with the underlying facts. Instead, they prefer to give the court the opportunity to waive the reading of the facts without asking a direct question. Thus, they state: "I will briefly summarize the facts." After making that statement, they pause and give the judges the opportunity to waive the factual statement should they wish to do so. Whichever method you choose, should you provide a factual summary, make sure that it is very brief and promotes your theory of the case. As the attorney for the appellee, you will not need to restate the facts already provided by the appellant's counsel. However, the appellant's attorney will have framed the facts in a manner that advances the appellant's theme. Therefore, as the attorney for the appellee, you should be prepared to emphasize those few critically important facts that further your theory of the case.

### 4.   Presentation of the Argument

Following a favorable statement of the issue or issues on appeal, a roadmap of your argument, and the few facts that illustrate your theory of the case, you are ready to present the argument itself. Your outline should identify the arguments you plan to make, beginning with your strongest argument. As you state your first argument, front-load the argument by beginning with the major premise that proves your point. If necessary, then continue by identifying a point or two that illustrates why your premise is sound. Avoid the details and nuances of the argument that are already described in great detail in your written brief. Through questioning, the judges will let you know which points they want to explore in greater detail.

### 5.   Conclusion

When you are alerted that two minutes remain in your argument, if possible, try to begin leading to a concise, persuasive summary of why the court should rule in your favor. Ideally, you should save the last minute for a persuasive recap of your argument. If you finish your argument before time has expired, simply thank the court and sit down. If you have not finished your concluding statement when time has expired, stop and ask the court for permission to conclude your statement. If you are granted permission, your comments should not extend beyond 15 to 20 seconds, or you will risk incurring the wrath of the judges.[2]

---

[2] Ruggero J. Aldisert, *supra* n. 1 at 325.

With a "hot" bench, sometimes time expires while the advocate is in the middle of a response to a question from the bench. Should that happen to you, do not presume that you can continue your response, and then state your conclusion, following the expiration of your allotted time. Instead, when you are notified that time has expired, stop in the middle of your response and ask for the court's permission to briefly conclude. Very briefly complete your response to the question and state your conclusion. Again, your comments should not extend beyond a few seconds.

## C. Responding to Questions

One of the most common complaints judges make against attorneys at oral argument is the failure to provide honest and direct responses to questions. When an attorney attempts to evade a question or fails to acknowledge important aspects of the argument, the attorney loses credibility with the court and risks the ire of the judges. With thorough preparation before the argument, you should be prepared to answer clearly and honestly any question asked of you during the argument. Of course, you can not provide an effective response if you do not understand the question itself. It can be difficult to listen carefully when you are standing behind the podium attempting to respond to a seemingly endless stream of questions. It is all too easy to stop listening after the judge begins asking the question and begin preparing a response.

Instead, listen carefully to the entire question before considering your response. Before responding to any question, take a deep breath and pause to replay the question in your mind. What exactly has the judge asked of you? Also consider the type of question the judge has asked. Is the question merely seeking information, requiring only a brief response? Is the question one designed to hear your position on an issue? Does the question ask for a concession? Or is the question a "softball" designed to help you promote your argument and convince other judges on the bench? The judges will not begrudge your taking the time to reflect on the question before responding, particularly because your response is likely to be clearer and more concise following a thoughtful pause. If you are not sure that you understand what the judge has asked of you, ask for clarification. It is far better to ask the judge to repeat the question than to take the court's time responding to a question that was not asked.

When you have been asked a question, you must answer it at that time, not later. Do not tell the judges you will respond to the question later in your presentation. You are there at the request of the court to respond to the judges' concerns. There is nothing more important than responding to a judge's question at the very moment the judge's curiosity has been piqued. Begin your response by stating your conclusion, and then provide the most important reason or reasons why your conclusion is sound. Wait for further questions from the bench before delving into the details of your reasoning. If further questions are not forthcoming, return to your argument.

Should you begin to be barraged with hostile questioning about one of your positions, consider the importance of the position. If the point is not necessary for you to prevail, and you suspect that the court will not become convinced of the merits of your position on that point, move on to other parts of your argument. You do not want to spend an inordinate amount of argument time rebutting a non-critical point of your argument. However, if the point is critical to the success of your argument, you must face the hostile barrage of questions and respond to the best of your ability. Again, with thorough preparation prior to the argument, such questions should not be a surprise.

There may be times when a judge asks you a question to which you do not know the answer. Under such circumstances, do not try to bluff the court. When a court discovers through further questioning that an advocate has been bluffing, the advocate loses significant credibility with the court. Moreover, the advocate's integrity has then been brought into question. Instead, simply acknowledge that you do not know the answer and will be pleased to supply the court with a supplemental response later.

## D.   Appearance and Delivery

### 1.   Dress

When appearing before a court, dress conservatively and professionally. In a courtroom setting, conservative suits are appropriate attire that signal your respect for the court and the significance of the occasion.

### 2.   Maintain Eye Contact

The oral argument should ideally be a conversation between you and the judges. As you would in ordinary conversation, maintain eye contact with the judges and communicate with them rather than attempting to read from your written notes. This is another reason why an extensive outline can hinder your effectiveness at oral argument. An extensive outline can encourage you to read from the outline rather than talking with the judges.

### 3. *Body Language*

As you stand behind the podium, try not to engage in mannerisms that will distract the judges from listening to what you have to say. Therefore, stay behind the podium and refrain from restlessly moving about or gesturing wildly with your hands. Of course, it is also important to appear natural. If you normally use your hands to gesture when you speak, then do so, but in moderation, so that your gestures do not detract from the force of what you are saying. At the opposite end of the spectrum, avoid the tendency to clutch the podium with clenched fists. During practice sessions before the argument, practice arguing behind a podium with your hands lightly resting on the podium.

### 4. *Voice*

Your goal during the oral argument is to speak clearly and firmly, exhibiting confidence in your position. Speak loudly and clearly enough for the judges to hear you without straining. As you practice for the oral argument, consider how you speak when you are nervous. Some people tend to speak too quickly, making it difficult for the listener to follow their statements. If this is your tendency, practice speaking very slowly, almost excruciatingly slowly, clearly enunciating every word. By slowing down your speech pattern during practice, your speech should achieve the proper balance with the added adrenalin the oral argument will provide. If, on the other hand, your tendency is to speak very softly and timidly when you are nervous, over-compensate for these tendencies during practice. During practice sessions, practice speaking loudly and with authority.

### 5. *Demeanor*

Your goal is to appear earnest and convinced of the soundness of your position, while also showing respect for the judges. Your demeanor should be one of "respectful equality. Don't be disturbed or pushed around simply because a judge disagrees with your position. Stand your ground firmly but with courtesy and dignity."[3] At the opposite end of the spectrum, resist the impulse to show any irritation, either verbally or with your body language. At times, judges ask questions that, to the attorneys, seem irrelevant or off-track. Answer the question respectfully and then move back to your argument. Your demeanor should also show respect for the opposing party. Although you will attack the soundness of the opponent's legal positions, do not attack the opposing counsel or the opposing party personally. Finally, your manner of speech should reflect the seriousness of the occasion. Do not use slang or rhetoric.

---

[3] Judge Aldisert, *supra* n. 1 at 324.

## 6.   *References*

Refer to the judges as a group as "Your Honors" or "the Court." Refer to a specific judge as "Your Honor" or "Justice [last name]." Refer to other attorneys as "counsel for the appellee" or "opposing counsel." Refer to the parties by their last name, such as "Mr." or "Mrs." so-and-so, or "Dr." so-and-so.

# 30

# DEMAND & SETTLEMENT LETTERS

Attorneys commonly transmit letters to opposing counsel seeking to assert clients' rights and settle legal disputes. In a demand letter, the advocate demands that another party comply with a legal requirement (e.g., pay money due under a lease agreement), or that the other party cease from engaging in certain behavior (e.g., landlord refusing to make repairs). Demand letters precede lawsuits, and are often settled without a resulting lawsuit. Settlement letters, on the other hand, have the goal of inducing an opposing party to settle a dispute by offering or accepting a sum of money that constitutes a compromise.

 **I ACHIEVING THE PROPER TONE**

Before drafting a demand or settlement letter, carefully consider the tone you want to achieve. Inexperienced lawyers make two common mistakes when writing letters to opposing counsel. Out of a desire to appear reasonable and fair, some lawyers make the mistake of unwittingly portraying their client in an unfavorable light. For example, they might state that they can "understand" how the opponent would feel justified in believing that the client acted in bad faith. Make no mistake: carelessly written words can come back to haunt an attorney. It is not necessary to placate the opposing counsel in order to maintain a positive working relationship. At the other end of the spectrum, some advocates believe that a legal dispute is all-out war, and that "all is fair in love and war." The tone of such a letter is hostile and belligerent. Such letters also do not serve the client's interests because they are not likely to have the desired effect of encouraging a positive resolution of the dispute.

Effective advocates achieve a balance between the two extremes. Advocates are most effective when they affirmatively and clearly state their clients' position, yet do so in a manner that is respectful and professional. The goal of any demand or settlement letter is to persuade the opposing party to give your client a desirable result. The most effective way to achieve that goal is to convince the opponent that your client's position is legally sound, and to do so in a manner that does not anger or belittle the opposing party. No one wants to compromise or concede when they are angry or feel belittled.

For purposes of illustration, consider the hypothetical problem that is the basis of the client advisory letter in Appendix B, and of Exercise 1 in this chapter. In that problem, Mr. Johnson was injured when he slipped and fell on an icy sidewalk outside his apartment complex. Mr. Johnson seeks damages from his landlord, claiming that the landlord should have shoveled the walkways to prevent such accidents. Johnson's attorney faces the following problem: there are only a few cases that have evaluated whether a landlord has a duty to shovel common walkways and they are very old. In those older cases, the courts did not impose such a duty on landlords. However, recent cases within the jurisdiction have eroded the broad protections landlords previously enjoyed, and have held landlords responsible for taking precautionary measures to prevent reasonably foreseeable injuries. Unfortunately, none of the recent cases has addressed whether landlords have a duty to keep walkways clear of snow and ice. Therefore, despite the shift in policy, the older cases are still "good law."

Johnson's attorney recognizes that the only viable recourse within the judicial system is at the appellate court level. Trial court judges are compelled to follow the rulings of higher level courts within the jurisdiction. Because the appellate process would be lengthy and expensive, Mr. Johnson has authorized his attorney to explore settlement possibilities. Given this background, compare the persuasive appeal of the following three examples.

---

### Example 1:

I concede that it is true that early Missouri courts have not imposed a duty upon landlords to shovel the snow from common walkways. However, these decisions are more than thirty years old and I respectfully request that you consider the policy implications from more recent decisions. Under these more recent decisions, I hope that you understand that we are justified in asking that your client be held responsible for my client's injuries.

---

In Example 1, Johnson's attorney tries so hard to appear accommodating and fair that she ultimately appears defensive and unsure of her legal position.

The language "I concede" and "it is true" appears defensive and weak. In conjunction with that defensive language, other language in the letter appears unduly deferential: "I hope you understand that we are justified;" "I respectfully request that you consider." This letter would not encourage anyone to settle the dispute. Now consider the tone of Example 2:

---

*Example 2:*

   Your client is liable for Mr. Johnson's injuries. As you well know, recent Missouri Supreme Court decisions impose a broad duty on landlords to keep sidewalks free from snow and ice. Your client's blatant disregard for my client's safety has caused him injuries from which he will never fully recover. My client is justifiably angry and ready to take your client all the way to the Supreme Court if necessary.

---

In Example 2, Johnson's attorney tries so hard to be a strong advocate that she ultimately appears strident and accusatory. The language "[a]s you well know" implicitly accuses the opposing counsel of acting in bad faith. The language "blatant disregard for my client's safety" is also insulting and would only incite the landlord to remain firmly entrenched in defending his legal position. The language suggesting that the client is ready to "take your client all the way to the Supreme Court if necessary" is so extreme as to appear hyperbolic. Most attorneys would not take such a "threat" seriously. This letter would likewise not encourage anyone to want to settle the dispute. Now consider the tone of Example 3:

---

*Example 3:*

   Your client is liable in negligence for Mr. Johnson's injuries. Recent Missouri Supreme Court opinions impose a broad duty on landlords to keep sidewalks free from snow and ice. By failing to keep the sidewalk free from snow and ice, your client breached its duty of care owed to Mr. Johnson. This breach of duty was the proximate cause of his injuries.

---

In Example 3, the attorney strikes the right balance between defensiveness and stridency. She appears professional and cordial while also clearly affirming the client's legal position.

## II  FORMAT AND CONTENT

Letters to opposing counsel differ in length and complexity depending upon a number of factors, including the legal issue in dispute, the procedural posture of the litigation, the relative strength of the client's legal position, and the personalities and relationship of the attorneys themselves. In the early stages of litigation, while the facts are still unfolding, an advocate might elect to disclose very little information to opposing counsel. Disclosing information might force the client into factual or legal positions that may ultimately prove to be unfavorable as the factual investigation unfolds. On the other hand, a strong factual and legal position might make a lengthier, detailed argument very appealing. The personalities and relationship of the attorneys also play a role. Some attorneys are more successful in negotiating settlements verbally and prefer to express in person or over the telephone the reasons why the proposed settlement is fair. Other attorneys are more successful with the luxury of time and reflection that a letter provides—time to deliberate over the arguments and to select their language with care. Therefore, a determination as to how much, or how little, information to include in a demand or settlement letter is a decision you will make on a case-by-case basis as you practice law.

Although there are many variables that affect the length and complexity of a settlement letter, such letters also share certain common characteristics. Both demand and settlement letters incorporate the persuasive writing style techniques discussed in Chapter 19. Settlement letters emphasize favorable law and follow the persuasive argument paradigms discussed in Chapters 20–24. However, unless you are *responding* to an opponent's argument, you generally would not directly rebut unfavorable law in an adversarial letter. Advocates generally emphasize only favorable law and do not attempt to address and distinguish unfavorable law.

The adversarial letter follows the same deductive pattern typical of office memoranda and other persuasive arguments. Such letters begin with an introductory paragraph that summarizes the purpose of the letter, followed by the favorable facts that support the advocate's position, followed by the favorable law that supports the advocate's position, and concluding with a statement of demands or an offer of settlement.

### A.  Introductory Paragraphs

In addition to setting the over-all tone of the letter, the introductory paragraph serves the following purposes: (1) it identifies the attorney's representative capacity, if the attorney's representation has not already been established;

(2) it briefly states the client's demands or offer of settlement or response to such demands; and (3) it confirms in writing that the letter is the subject of confidential settlement negotiations and can not be used as evidence during trial. Under the federal rules of evidence and state evidentiary rules, settlement communications can not be used as evidence during trial. Of course, you would not want a confidential letter you have written to be introduced into evidence by the opposing party. Therefore, attorneys protect their confidential communications with a written statement confirming the confidential nature of the letter. The following example of an introductory paragraph is excerpted from Sample Letter A in Appendix E. In that problem, the McLeans are seeking damages arising out of the drowning death of their child.

> I represent Mr. and Mrs. McLean in the lawsuit they have recently filed against your clients in which they seek damages for the death of their young child. They are understandably anxious to seek full recovery under the law following the drowning death of their child in your client's man-made pond. However, to avoid protracted litigation, my clients are willing to allow me to explore settlement possibilities. My clients have authorized me to make the following offer: they will agree to dismiss this suit if your clients remit payment in the sum of $1,500,000. This offer will remain open until 5:00 p.m. on December 1, 2001. This letter is intended as a confidential settlement communication pursuant to Rule 408 of the Federal Rules of Evidence and Rule 1-14.1 of the Florida Evidence Code. As such, it will not be admissible in the above proceeding, or any other proceeding, for any purpose.

## B.  *Factual Support*

The length of a factual statement may be very brief or rather lengthy, depending upon the complexity of the facts in dispute and the factual context of the letter. Consider, for example, a settlement letter designed to persuade an opposing party to settle a lawsuit following extensive pre-trial discovery. Because the facts have already been fully disclosed during the discovery process, you might incorporate a significant number of relevant, favorable facts designed to convince the opposing counsel that your client will ultimately prevail in the lawsuit. On the other hand, if you were to draft a settlement letter in the early stages of a lawsuit, you might incorporate fewer facts into the letter. In the early stages of a lawsuit, you would typically not be in possession of all relevant facts or have a final trial strategy. Therefore, to avoid making factual misstatements, or "tipping your hand" about a trial strategy that is still uncertain, you might incorporate only a few favorable facts.

Whether the factual statement is lengthy or brief, include only those favorable facts that support your client's legal position. The purpose of an adversarial letter is to *persuade*. Because unfavorable facts do not serve the purpose of persuasion, they are typically not disclosed in demand and settlement letters. Unfavorable facts might be disclosed only when the opposing counsel is clearly aware of, and emphasizing, the unfavorable facts and the advocate can persuasively and easily argue why such facts are not legally significant. Consider the factual statement in Sample Letter A in Appendix E. In that problem, the attorney emphasizes highly favorable facts that support her theory of the case—that the landowners simply did not take reasonable precautions to avoid a foreseeable injury. The following factual statement is excerpted from that letter:

> As you are aware, on September 3, 2001, my client's young son drowned in the Hurt's pond. Although your clients knew that young children enjoyed feeding the ducks on their pond, they left town for the holiday weekend, leaving the gate to the pond unlocked, and the dock in a state of disrepair. Their actions in leaving this attractive nuisance accessible to young children is even more troublesome in light of the fact that they knew the dock was dangerous and in need of repair. Yet they had delayed the long-needed repairs. Mikey McLean drowned in the Hurt's pond after the dock collapsed from under his slight weight.

In the above factual statement, the attorney uses several persuasive writing style strategies to enhance the persuasive appeal of the factual story. First, she uses the strategy of "juxtaposition' discussed in Chapter 19 to juxtapose facts that make the Hurts appear to be very careless. Thus, she juxtaposes the Hurt's knowledge of trespassing children ("although your clients knew that young children . . .") with the fact that they nevertheless left town without taking precautions to protect trespassing children from their pond ("they left town for the holiday weekend, leaving the gate to the pond unlocked . . ."). The attorney also juxtaposes the Hurt's knowledge of the decaying dock with the fact that they had delayed repairing the dock ("Yet they had delayed . . ."). The attorney also uses the active voice to connect the Hurts with their careless actions: "they left town;" and "they knew the dock was dangerous;" and "they had delayed."

## C.  Legal Support—Explain the Law and Then Apply it to the Client Facts

The extent and nature of the legal support for your demand or settlement offer will vary depending upon how brief or detailed you decide to make the letter. In a simple demand letter you would not include any legal support at all. For example, in a demand letter demanding that a tenant pay back-rent due and owing under a lease, the landlord's attorney would support the demands by simply pointing out the applicable provisions of the lease. In such a letter, supporting case law would be unnecessary and distracting.

On the other hand, sometimes advocates seek to persuade opposing counsel by presenting a summary of all of the favorable law that supports their client. Again, when deciding how much information to disclose, it is critical to consider carefully each statement you make in the argument. Often during the litigation process, attorneys discover new factual information that affects their overall trial strategy. Thus, in presenting favorable law, it is important not to frame the resolution of the issue in a manner that could later foreclose other strategic decisions. In the following example, the advocate emphasizes the favorable law and facts in a summary fashion that is unlikely to foreclose later shifts in strategy. Again, the following example is excerpted from Sample Letter A in Appendix E:

| | |
|---|---|
| Under Florida law, the Hurts are liable for Mikey McLean's death under the doctrine of attractive nuisance. For almost forty years, a long line of Florida courts has consistently held landowners liable for the injuries sustained by child trespassers when the landowners leave a dangerous condition on their property and have reason to believe that children attracted to the dangerous condition will trespass onto the property. *See, e.g., Ansin v. Thurston*, 98 So. 2d 87 (Fla. Dist. Ct. App. 1957); *Samson v. O'Hara*, 239 So. 2d 151 (Fla. Dist. Ct. App. 1970). | The favorable conclusion.<br><br>Case law supports McLean's conclusion.<br><br>Citations to two favorable cases. |
| Here, the combination of the Hurt's dilapidated dock, the man-made pond, and the ducks that swam in the pond was dangerous and yet inviting and attractive to small children. The Hurts both knew that the dock was dilapidated and dangerous, and knew that children from the neighboring elementary school trespassed onto their dock to feed the ducks. Yet they left this attractive nuisance open and accessible to children while they left town for the long holiday weekend. | Case law favorably applied to the most favorable client facts. |

## D.  Conclusion

In the conclusion, it is important to clearly: (1) restate the demand or offer; (2) impose a specific time limit on the availability of the demand or offer; and (3) state the consequences should the opposing counsel fail to respond within the stated time. The following paragraph is excerpted from Sample Letter A in Appendix E:

| | |
|---|---|
| The Hurt's liability under Florida law is clear. If this case is tried, the jury will not be focused on liability, but on the amount of damages to award the parents of their only child—a six-year-old son. After evaluating Florida law, I think you will agree that our $1,500,000 settlement offer is more than reasonable. | 1. Restates conclusion and settlement offer. |
| Our offer remains open until 5:00 p.m. on December 1, 2001. If I do not hear from you by then, I will be in touch with you to schedule depositions. | 2. Time frame.<br>3. Consequences. |

## EXERCISE 1

Review the sample client advisory letter in Appendix B. Assume that you have forwarded that advisory letter to Mr. and Mrs. Johnson, your clients. After considering your recommendations, the Johnsons have decided to attempt to settle the dispute with their landlord, preferably without litigation. You have asked a more junior attorney in the law office to draft a settlement letter to the landlord's attorney. The junior attorney has submitted a draft settlement letter for your review and comment.

When reviewing the draft settlement letter, consider the following:

1.  Practical Consequences:

(a)  Does the opposing counsel know what he is supposed to do?

(b)  Does the opposing counsel know the practical consequences of his response or failure to respond?

2.  Clarity:

    (a)  Does the introductory paragraph:

         (i)   Contain a clear offer?

         (ii)  Clarify that this letter is a confidential settlement communication?

    (b)  Does the letter contain a clear factual statement?

    (c)  Does the letter contain a clear thesis paragraph?

    (d)  Does the letter contain legal and factual support for the client's argument?

3.  Persuasive Appeal:

    (a)  Does the letter use anticipatory rebuttal or direct rebuttal? Which would be a more persuasive strategy?

    (b)  Does the letter affirm the client's position or defend against the opponent's argument?

    (c)  Is the tone persuasive or neutral?

## Draft Settlement Letter for Review and Comment

Charlotte Turley, Esq.
105 S. Central Ave.
St. Louis, MO 63105

April 15, 2001

John D. Meyers, Esq.
201 N. Bemiston
St. Louis, MO 63105

Re: Johnson v. Apartment Management Corp.

Dear Mr. Meyers:

I met last night with my clients, tenants of Apartment Management Corp. Although my clients are anxious to press their claims, they would like to settle this dispute.

As you are aware, on December 18, 2000, Mr. Johnson slipped and fell on an icy patch on the sidewalk at your client's apartment complex. On December 18th, the sidewalk was icy and dangerous. Your client disclaims any responsibility to shovel the sidewalk or to salt the sidewalk.

Mr. Johnson's medical bills total $20,000.00 in actual out-of-pocket expenses. Moreover, Mr. Johnson is unable to continue his employment duties as a liquor driver. These duties require him to unload, lift and carry heavy boxes. Doctors estimate he will not be able to return to work for three months. His lost wages total $6,000.00.

It is true that earlier Missouri court decisions have not imposed a duty upon landlords to shovel the snow from common walkways. These courts have reasoned that landlords have no duty to keep an apartment building's "common premises" safe from temporary hazards such as snow. *See, e.g.*, Maschoff v. Koedding, 439 S.W.2d 234 (Mo. Ct. App. 1969). Such earlier courts justify this rule by noting that the duty to remove snow "would subject the landlord to an unreasonable burden of vigilance and care. . . ." Id. at 236. However, it is important to note that this decision is twenty-six years old.

More recently, in Jackson v. Ray Kruse Const. Co., 708 S.W.2d 664 (Mo. banc 1986), the Supreme Court imposed a duty on a landlord to place speed bumps in the parking lot of an apartment building. In Jackson, the plaintiff child was injured on the parking lot of the landlord's apartment complex when a speeding bicycle struck her. Id. at 666. By so holding, the court extended the burden of a landlord's duty to keep common areas safe from foreseeable injuries beyond the scope of earlier court decisions. "As strongly emphasized in recent cases," the landlord owes a duty to its tenants to make common areas of leased premises reasonably safe. Id. The dissenting justice recognized this trend, noting that the court modified the law in order to compensate the injured plaintiff. The dissenting justice noted: "It must be obvious to those who care that the majority is bent on making the need for compensation the overwhelming function of the law of torts in Missouri." Id. at 671.

The landlord, in Jackson, had "reasonable notice" of the dangerous condition. Testimony established that safety bumps were standard safety devices used in parking lots to slow the speed of vehicles. Id. at 666. Thus, even though the landlord had no actual knowledge of the danger of speeding bicycles, the jury found that the landlord had "notice of a condition which required the installation of speed bumps." Id. at 667.

A more recent Supreme Court decision reflects this Missouri trend to protect tenants' rights, even at the expense of the supposedly "well recognized" legal principles set out in older cases. In Aaron v. Havens, 758 S.W.2d 446, 448 (Mo. banc 1988), the court held that a jury could find a landlord has the duty to relocate the position of a fire escape to make it impossible for criminal intruders to use the fire escape to break in to a tenant's apartment. Again, the dissenting justices reflect the changes in the law by expressing their concern at the Court's continued willingness to impose such duties on landlords. Id. at 450.

It is true that the recent Missouri Supreme Court cases did not have the opportunity to address whether the older "temporary hazard" cases are still valid in this State. Under the broad language and shifts in policy reflected in the most recent Supreme Court opinions, it is arguable that your client owed Mr. Johnson a duty to keep the sidewalk free from ice. Your client reasonably should have foreseen that a tenant would slip and fall on an icy sidewalk that is a common part of the premises. By failing to do so, your client breached its duty to Mr. Johnson under the law. In fact, the duty your client has assumed is less burdensome than the duties the Supreme Court imposed on the landlords in each of these recent cases. Also, the danger in our case is more obvious and known than the dangers presented in Jackson and Aaron. In point of fact, public and private schools in the City of St. Louis closed for two days. In contrast, in each of the recent cases, the landlords had no actual knowledge of the existing dangerous conditions.

After you have had an opportunity to digest and consider this letter, please give me a call and let me know whether you wish to settle this litigation. I will wait to hear from you.

Very truly yours,

Charlotte Turley

 **EXERCISE 2**

Review the draft settlement letter in Exercise 1, and the sample client advisory letter in Appendix B. Redraft the letter in Exercise 1 to make it persuasive.

# Appendix A

## Sample Memo A:
## One-Issue Office Memorandum

### MEMORANDUM

To:     Chief of Felony Prosecutions
From:   Assistant Prosecutor
Re:     Gerry Arnold case—Residential Burglary Prosecution
Date:   August 28, 2001

### QUESTION PRESENTED

Is a detached garage a "living quarters" in which the owners "actually reside" under Illinois' Residential Burglary Statute, when it has been converted into a retreat for the owners' college-age son, who uses it on a weekly basis as a get-a-way and sleeps there half the year, although the retreat does not have plumbing facilities?

### SHORT ANSWER

Yes. A detached garage used as a retreat and seasonal sleeping place is a "living quarters" under the statute. The owner frequently and regularly uses the garage for residential activities associated with a living quarters. The garage is furnished to reflect that use.

### STATEMENT OF FACTS

On August 20, 2001, Defendant, Gerry Arnold, broke into Carl and Rita Stripe's two-car detached garage and removed some of their personal property. The State has charged Arnold under the Residential Burglary Statute. Arnold's attorney has moved to dismiss the charge, contending that the Stripe's ga-

---

The *Question Presented* identifies:
1. the rule of law;
2. element of the law that presents the issue; and 3. critical facts that frame the issue.
The *Short Answer*:

1. answers the question; and
2. briefly explains the answer.

This ¶ provides context by describing the foundational facts.

435

rage is not a "dwelling" within which the Stripes "reside," as required by the statute.

The garage is located approximately thirty feet behind the Stripe home. The Stripes have converted two-thirds of the garage into quarters for the couple's college-age son, Michael Stripe, to use as a get-a-way. They have walled-off that section of the garage from the section that stores the family car. The converted section of the garage has a window and a locked door.

Michael spends two to three evenings a week and his free time on weekends in the get-a-way, writing and listening to music and watching television. In addition, Michael is the lead singer of a band, R.E.N., that plays once a month in clubs around town. The band practices in the garage on Sunday mornings and stores some of their equipment there. During the summer and fall when his parents are in town, Michael sleeps in the garage on a futon in a loft area. When his parents travel to Florida during the winter and spring, Michael sleeps in the house.

The garage is equipped to accommodate Michael's interests. In addition to the futon, the garage contains an expensive sound system, a portable five-inch television, and a mini-refrigerator. The garage has electricity and a space heater, but no running water or heat.

### DISCUSSION

The Stripe garage is a dwelling under Illinois' Residential Burglary Statute (the "Statute"). To prosecute Arnold successfully under the Statute, the State must prove that Arnold "knowingly and without authority enter[ed] the *dwelling place* of another." 720 Ill. Comp. Stat. § 5/19-3 (1993) (emphasis added). There is no real dispute that Arnold "knowingly" entered the Stripe's garage or that his entry was "without authority." Whether the garage is a "dwelling place" is more problematic. The Statute defines a dwelling as "a house, apartment, mobile home, trailer or *other living quarters* in which . . . the owners or occupants *actually reside*. . . ." 720 Ill. Comp. Stat. § 5/2-6(b) (1993) (emphasis added). This memorandum addresses whether the Stripe garage is a "living quarters" in which Michael Stripe "actually resides."

The Stripe's garage is a "living quarters" in which Michael Stripe "actually resides." When determining whether a struc-

---

*The remaining paragraphs relate the legally significant facts, grouped by issue (i.e., physical characteristics of the garage, type of use, frequency of use and evidence of use.)*

*Note that details of the arrest are not included in the factual story because they are not relevant to the dwelling issue.*

*Overview paragraph*:
1. Conclusion.
2. Elements of the rule of law.
3. Dispenses with non-issues.
4. Identifies the issue as defined by statute.

*Thesis paragraph*:
1. Conclusion.

ture is a living quarters, courts evaluate the type of activities for which the owners use the structure, as well as the frequency of those activities and physical evidence of those activities. A structure is considered a dwelling when the owners frequently use the structure for activities that occur in a living quarters, and the furnishings reflect that use. *People v. McIntyre*, 578 N.E.2d 314 (Ill. App. Ct. 1991). Although a structure's attachment to the main residence is also relevant, physical attachment to the primary residence is not necessary. *See People v. Thomas*, 561 N.E.2d 57 (Ill. 1990). Therefore, a structure used as an extension of the home's living quarters may be a dwelling even though it is not physically connected to the primary residence. Because Michael Stripe frequently and regularly uses the Stripe garage as a living quarters, it satisfies the statutory definition of "dwelling."

An enclosed, attached porch frequently used as part of the home's living quarters is a dwelling under the residential burglary statute. In *People v. McIntyre*, the owners used an attached, screened porch for "sitting, eating and cooking." 578 N.E.2d at 315. They ate most of their meals on the porch in the summer and cooked meals there four or five times a week in the winter. The owners furnished the porch with wrought-iron furniture and a barbecue grill that reflected its use. The porch was enclosed, locked, and attached to the home. The court held that, under these facts, the porch was a "living quarters" under the Statute. *Id.*

The court reasoned that the owners used the porch as part of their living quarters by engaging in such activities as "sitting, eating, and cooking." *Id.* In addition, the owners regularly used the porch in this manner and furnished the porch with furniture and a grill that reflected such use. The court also observed that the porch was enclosed and attached to the house, indicating that the porch's physical attachment to the house was a relevant factor. However, the court emphasized that it was the activities of "sitting, eating, and cooking" that "make the porch part of the living quarters of the house." *Id.*

On the other hand, where a structure is attached, but used only for commercial, rather than residential activities, it is not a living quarters. *People v. Thomas*, 561 N.E.2d 57 (Ill. 1990). In *Thomas*, a garage was attached to a multi-unit apartment building. All of the garages and apartment units shared the same roof. The owner used the garage to park her car and to store large quantities of perfume for a commercial business. The court held that the attached garage, "at least in this in-

---

2. Relevant factors.

3. Synthesized rule of law from cases.

4. Brief application of factors to client situation.

*Rule Explanation—Case 1*:
1. Formulated rule of law from case 1.
2. Relevant case facts.

3. Holding.

4. Rationale reflecting how the court evaluated each relevant factor.

*Rule Explanation—Case 2*:
1. Formulated rule of law from case 2.

2. Relevant case facts.

3. Holding.

stance," was not a living quarters. *Id.* at 58.

The court implicitly reasoned that a garage used only to store products for sale in a commercial business is not a living quarters, even when attached to the owner's apartment building. However, the court left open the possibility that a garage could, given the appropriate use as a living quarters, constitute a dwelling under the Statute. The court reasoned that "an attached garage is not *necessarily* a 'dwelling' within the meaning of the residential burglary statute." *Id.* (emphasis added). That language implies that a garage, appropriately used as a residence or living quarters, could be a dwelling under the statute. *See also*, *People v. Silva*, 628 N.E.2d 948, 953 (Ill. App. Ct. 1993) (noting that *Thomas* left open the possibility for a garage to be a dwelling under the statute).

4. Rationale reflecting how the court evaluated the relevant factor.

Like the porch in *McIntyre*, Michael Stripe used the Stripe's garage for activities commonly associated with a living quarters. Like the activities of "sitting, eating and cooking" in *McIntyre*, Michael Stripe's use of the garage for playing and listening to music, watching television, and eating snacks are uses commonly associated with a living quarters. In addition, Michael Stripe's use of the garage as a sleeping quarters during the summer and fall only strengthens the argument that the garage is a dwelling under the Statute. Unlike the *McIntyre* activities of barbecuing, eating, and sitting, which can occur outside of a dwelling, sleeping is an activity uniquely associated with a living quarters. Moreover, Michael Stripe's use of the garage is clearly distinguishable from *Thomas*, where the owner used the garage only for storage purposes.

*Rule Application Factor 1: Use*
1. Conclusion.
2. Favorable elaboration of how client facts under this factor support the attorney's conclusion.
3. Concrete analogies to cases 1 & 2 to support the argument.

In addition, like the owners in *McIntyre*, Michael Stripe furnished the garage in a manner that reflects its use as a living quarters. Like the grill and wrought-iron furniture in *McIntyre*, Michael Stripe's sound system, small t.v., mini-refrigerator, and futon reflect that he uses the garage for activities typically associated with a living quarters. Again, the furnishings are a far cry from the garage in *Thomas*, which housed only the owner's car and boxes of commercial products for sale.

*Rule Application Factor 1(a): Evidence of Use*

Facts & analogies explored for subfactor.

Finally, the frequency of Michael's use of the garage as a living quarters is also similar to the use of the porch in *McIntyre*. Michael spends at least two to three evenings a week and his spare time on weekends in his get-a-way. During the summer and fall, he sleeps there seven nights a week. Michael's

*Rule Application Factor 1(b): Frequency of Use*

Facts & analogies

regular and frequent use far exceeds the owner's limited, occasional use of the garage in *Thomas* to retrieve her car or perfume products from storage. In fact, in August when the garage was burglarized, Michael's frequency of use even exceeded that of the owners in *McIntyre*, who used the porch only four to five times a week.

Defendant may argue that, despite Michael Stripe's frequent use of the garage for activities associated with a living quarters, the garage's physical detachment from the Stripe's home prevents it from being a "living quarters" in which the owners "reside." Under this theory, the defendant would argue that the garage, standing alone, is not a living quarters in which anyone resides. The garage has no running water, bathroom facilities or heat. Thus, the garage's status as a dwelling is dependent upon whether it can reasonably be viewed as an extension of the Stripe family's living quarters within the home itself. The defendant would argue that the fact that the *McIntyre* porch was physically attached to the family's home was essential to the court's holding. Only because it was physically attached to the home could the porch reasonably be viewed as an extension of the family's living quarters. In contrast, the Stripe's garage stands thirty feet away from their residence.

While having some merit, this argument should fail. Although the *McIntyre* court did note that the porch was physically "attached and enclosed," it concluded that it was the owners' "activities" and *use* of the porch that made the porch "part of the living quarters of the house." 578 N.E.2d at 314. Thus, the court implied that the activities for which the porch was used were more important than the porch's attachment to the home. Moreover, the fact that the porch was separated from the utility room of the owners' home by a door with "three locks" lends less significance to the attached/detached distinction. The presence of three locks implies that the porch area was not an open part of the main residence, but was instead physically separate from the main residence. Like the physically separate porch in *McIntyre*, the Stripe garage is used as an extension of the Stripe family's living quarters.

*People v. Thomas* lends further support to this conclusion. In *Thomas*, the court minimized the importance of the garage's physical attachment to the main residence while emphasizing the garage's use. The court reasoned that "[a] garage, at least in this instance, *whether attached to the various living units or not*, cannot be deemed a residence or living

explored for "frequency" subfactor.

*Opposing Argument #1*:
1. Identifies and explores an opposing argument resulting from a factual distinction between an earlier case and the Stripe situation.

2. Writer's conclusion re: validity of the opp. argument.
3. Arguments that support attorney's conclusion.

Note how the writer uses deductive reasoning to create an argument based on the fact that the porch was locked.

Note how the writer uses exact language from the earlier cases to support the writer's quarters." 561 N.E.2d at 58 (emphasis added). By that statement, the court implied that the garage's physical attachment to the owner's home was not important. That statement, together with the court's earlier definition of a dwelling as a structure used as a "living quarters," implies that a detached garage used as a living quarters would be a dwelling under the statute. Therefore, the fact that the Stripe's garage is physically detached from their residence does not deprive it of its status as a "living quarters" in which the owners "actually reside."

> 4. Conclusion repeated for lengthy analysis.

Defendant might also argue that the legislative history suggests that the legislators did not intend for the statute to cover structures such as garages. As the court noted in *People v. Silva*, 629 N.E.2d 948 (Ill. App. Ct. 1993), the legislature amended the statute in 1986 to clarify and narrow the meaning of the term "dwelling." The court quoted the following statement of Senator Sangmeister made during legislative hearings: "It was even brought to our attention by the Illinois Supreme Court in a number of cases that . . . there should be a better definition to the dwelling house. We are having people prosecuted for residential burglary for breaking into . . . unoccupied buildings *such as garages*." *Id*. at 951(emphasis added).

> *Opposing Argument #2*:
> 1. Identifies & discusses a 2nd opposing argument.

This argument lacks merit. The *Silva* court noted that "[t]he residential burglary statute is designed to protect the 'privacy and sanctity of the home,' with a view toward the 'greater danger and potential for serious harm from burglary of a home as opposed to burglary of a business.'" 629 N.E.2d at 951, *quoting*, *People v. Edgesto*, 611 N.E.2d 49 (Ill. App. Ct. 1993). Senator Sangmeister's concern that people are being prosecuted for breaking into "unoccupied buildings" is consistent with the general legislative purpose to deter residential burglary because of its potential for serious harm. An occupied garage used as a living quarters invokes the same legislative concerns for the sanctity of the home and the increased risk of harm that results from an invasion of that home. Moreover, the Illinois Supreme Court decided the *Thomas* case only a few years after the amendment. In *Thomas*, the court suggested that a garage used as a living quarters would be a dwelling under the statute.

> 2. Writer's conclusion re: validity of opposing arg.
> 3. Arguments that support the conclusion.

> Again, the attorney uses deductive reasoning—noting the significance of the dates of the *Thomas* decision and the legisl. amendment.

conclusions.

In conclusion, the Stripe's garage is a living quarters in which Michael Stripe resides for purposes of prosecuting Arnold under the Statute. Not only does Michael Stripe use the garage for residential activities, he uses it frequently and regularly.

Brief conclusion.

*Sample Memo B*
*One-Issue Office Memorandum*

*Citations Purposefully Omitted from this Memo: Subject of
Exercises, Chapter 17*

## MEMORANDUM

To:     Senior Attorney
From:    Junior Attorney
Date:    October 1, 2001
Re:     Chester Tate

### QUESTION PRESENTED

Does a defendant have a viable defense under Illinois' Aggravated Kidnapping Statute that he did not "secretly" confine another under the statute, when he confined a victim in the victim's home in front of a large picture window visible to neighbors and passers-by and made no effort to conceal the victim, although he failed to answer the telephone or doorbell?

### SHORT ANSWER

Yes, a defendant has a viable defense that he did not secretly confine another under the statute. The defendant selected a visible location near a public area from which witnesses were likely to view the confinement, and made no effort to conceal the victim in a less visible location. In view of the location's visibility to potential witnesses, the fact that the defendant failed to answer the telephone or doorbell should not make the confinement "secret."

### STATEMENT OF FACTS

On September 19, 2001, Mr. Tate tied Mr. Campbell to a chair in Mr. Campbell's living room and shot him in the shoulder. The State has charged Mr. Tate with assault and aggravated kidnapping. This office has agreed to represent Mr. Tate.

Mr. Tate and Mr. Campbell have been friends for a number of years, and Mr. Tate has frequently been a visitor at Mr. Campbell's home. In early September, 2001 Mr. Tate and Mr. Campbell argued about a loan Mr. Tate had made to Mr. Campbell that had not been repaid. After that argument, Mr. Campbell and Mr. Tate did not see or speak to each other until September 19th. At 1:30 p.m. on

September 19th, Mr. Tate arrived unexpectedly at Mr. Campbell's home. When he arrived, the two friends talked for several minutes on the front porch. After talking for several minutes, they decided that they would let bygones be bygones, and walked into the house to have a beer.

After they entered the house, Mr. Campbell noticed the strong smell of alcohol on Mr. Tate's breath and suggested that it would not be a good idea to have a drink. Mr. Tate became upset, and the two friends began quarreling again. The argument escalated and Mr. Tate put his arm around Mr. Campbell's neck in what Mr. Campbell described as a "headlock." Mr. Tate then put the nose of a gun he carried with him into Mr. Campbell's side and ordered Mr. Campbell to seat himself in a living room chair. Mr. Tate then tied Mr. Campbell's hands behind him and his feet to the chair. At some point during their argument, Mr. Tate shot Mr. Campbell in the shoulder while he was tied to the chair.

At approximately 4:00 p.m. that afternoon, Ms. Marva Stewart arrived at Mr. Campbell's home to meet with Mr. Campbell regarding some interior design work he had engaged her to perform. She rang the doorbell repeatedly. When there was no answer, she walked around to the back of the house, thinking that Mr. Campbell might be in his back yard gardening. When she did not find him there, she knocked on the back door repeatedly. When there was no answer, she returned to the front of the home, where she saw Mr. Campbell's car sitting by the curb. Thinking that he must be home, she tried calling him from her car telephone. When, after repeated rings, there was no answer, she assumed that he must be sleeping and left. She made no attempt to look into the windows of the home.

Because of his intoxicated state, Mr. Tate does not recall how long he stayed with Mr. Campbell in his living room. However, he does recall hearing the telephone ring and the doorbell chime. He did not answer the telephone or open the door. Mr. Tate also recalls the living room lamp switching on from an automatic timer. (The timer is set to go on at 7:30 p.m.) A friend of Mr. Campbell's discovered him at 9:00 that evening blindfolded, gagged, bleeding from a gunshot wound to the right shoulder, and bound to a chair in his living room.

Mr. Campbell's home is a large, renovated, two-story brownstone. The first floor is primarily a glass picture window (a large, uninterrupted pane of glass), with a small amount of brick surrounding the entrance and providing support at the exterior wall of the home. The picture window is not tinted or coated in any way to affect its transparency. The second floor is primarily brick with two windows facing the street. The lot on which the home is situated is level, and the front door to the home is only two steps up from the sidewalk that leads to the home. The front door is solid wood with no window. The home sits back only twenty feet from the street. The street in front of Mr. Campbell's home is classified by the police as "moderately traveled" and is open to both commercial and residential traffic.

Ms. Gretchen Kraus, Mr. Campbell's neighbor directly across the street, has stated to police that she saw Mr. Tate arrive at Mr. Campbell's home in the early afternoon of September 19th. She observed Mr. Campbell greet Mr. Tate with a smile and a handshake. Although she did not actually see the two men enter the home, she did see them on the small, concrete, two-step "porch" together. She assumed that the two men were going to enter Mr. Campbell's home. Ms. Kraus is able to see into Mr. Campbell's living room from her porch; in particular, during daylight, she is able to see figures and movement, and at night, when the living room lights are on, she is able to make out the activities within the room more clearly. However, she did not attempt to see into Mr. Campbell's living room on the afternoon or evening of September 19th.

## DISCUSSION

For the State to prosecute Mr. Tate for aggravated kidnapping, it must prove that Mr. Tate "knowingly . . . and secretly confined another against his will . . . while armed with a dangerous weapon." There is no real dispute that Mr. Tate "confined another against his will . . . while armed with a dangerous weapon" because Mr. Tate tied Mr. Campbell to a chair and shot him with a gun. While the "knowingly" requirement may be an issue due to Mr. Tate's apparent intoxication, this memorandum focuses only on whether Mr. Tate's actions satisfy the "secretly" requirement.

Illinois courts have defined "secretly" to mean "concealed; hidden; not made public; . . . kept from the knowledge or notice of persons liable to be affected by the act." When considering whether a confinement is secret, courts evaluate the visibility of the location of the confinement, as evidenced by its proximity to a public area and by whether there were, or could have been, witnesses, and the defendant's attempts to conceal the victim from the knowledge of others. When a defendant confines the victim in a location clearly visible to witnesses, and makes no attempt to conceal the victim, the confinement is not secret. Because Mr. Tate confined Mr. Campbell in front of a large window visible to potential witnesses, and did not attempt to conceal Mr. Campbell from the knowledge of others, the confinement was not secret.

When the defendant confines the victim in a location close to a public area that is visible to potential witnesses, and makes no attempt to conceal the victim, the confinement is not secret. In *Lamkey*, the defendant confined the victim in the vestibule of an apartment building that had commercial space on the first floor. The vestibule was two steps up from one of Chicago's busiest streets and was separated from the sidewalk by a glass door. From within the vestibule, the victim was able to see cars and passersby. Moreover, a passing motorist witnessed and interrupted the assault. On these facts, the court held that the confinement was not "secret" and overturned the defendant's conviction. The court reasoned that the attempted assault occurred "within public view . . . in an area clearly visible to anyone walking or driving down the street." Moreover, the court found it significant that the defendant made no attempt to conceal the victim by moving her to a more concealed location within the building.

On the other hand, when the defendant attempts to conceal the confinement by moving the victim to a location not visible to potential witnesses, the confinement is secret. In *Franzen*, the defendant met the victim at a bar parking lot, where he knocked the victim unconscious and dragged her thirty feet into a field behind a fence. He then dragged her an additional 130 feet into the field, where sorghum plants were high enough to conceal them. In fact, a bouncer from the bar was unable to observe the victim from the bar's parking lot. Under these facts, the court held that the defendant's confinement was "secret." The court reasoned that the defendant successfully attempted to conceal the victim by dragging her 160 feet into a dark field that was not visible to "anyone who might have wandered out into the parking lot."

Like *Lamkey* and unlike *Franzen*, Mr. Tate confined Mr. Campbell in a visible location close to a public area. The living room in which Mr. Tate confined Mr. Campbell is visible through a large picture window that runs the length of the living room. Moreover, the living room is close to a public area, being only twenty feet and two steps up from a moderately traveled commercial and residential street. Although the living room is not as close to or as public an area as the vestibule in *Lamkey*, which was only two steps up from a busy street, the picture window is significantly larger than the glass door in *Lamkey*. Therefore, Campbell's living room is arguably as visible as the vestibule in *Lamkey*. In any event, the living room is far removed from the dark field in *Franzen*, in which the tall sorghum plants and fence concealed the victim from any potential witness who might have wandered out into the parking lot 160 feet away.

The possibility of witnesses further demonstrates the visibility of the location of Mr. Campbell's confinement. Mr. Campbell's neighbor is able to see figures and movement within Mr. Campbell's living room during the day and is able to see much more clearly into the living room at night. Moreover, like the motorist in *Lamkey*, passersby would have seen Mr. Campbell had they looked in the window, especially after 7:30 p.m., when the light automatically switched on inside the room.

The State may argue that the mere possibility of witnesses to the confinement does not negate secrecy. However, the fact that no one actually looked in Mr. Campbell's window does not undermine the argument that the confinement was not secret. In *Lamkey*, the court held that the confinement was not secret in part because the confinement was "in an area clearly visible to anyone walking or driving down the street." Moreover, in *Franzen*, the court held that the confinement was secret, in part, because the victim was concealed from "anyone who might have wandered out into the parking lot." *Lamkey* and *Franzen* imply that it is the *possibility* of a witness viewing the confinement that is important rather than the happenstance of an actual witness.

Like the defendant in *Lamkey* and unlike the defendant in *Franzen*, Mr. Tate did not attempt to move Mr. Campbell to a more concealed location. Like the *Lamkey* defendant's failure to move the victim to his upstairs apartment, Mr. Tate did not attempt to move Mr. Campbell to an upstairs bedroom where the home is mainly brick or to a more concealed room on the first floor. Mr. Tate even failed to close the curtains of the living room window or unplug the automatic light. This conduct contrasts with the defendant's actions in *Franzen*, who twice moved the victim deeper into the sorghum field.

However, confinement also is secret when the defendant confines the victim in a location not visible to the public and successfully attempts to conceal the victim from the knowledge of potential witnesses. In *People v. Enoch*, witnesses saw the defendant and the victim walking together toward and within 100 feet of the victim's apartment. Later that night, the victim's boyfriend arrived at her apartment and unsuccessfully tried to determine if the victim was home. He rang the doorbell several times, checked the victim's place of work to see if she was still there, and called her on the telephone. The defendant failed to answer the telephone or doorbell, and the victim's boyfriend assumed she was not at home. Later, the boyfriend looked through the apartment windows, but could not see the victim inside the bedroom of her apartment.

Under these facts, the court held that the defendant's confinement of the victim was secret. The bedroom of the victim's apartment was not visible to the public and, by refusing to answer the doorbell or telephone, the defendant acted to conceal the victim further. Moreover, the court reasoned that the defendant's actions in concealing the victim successfully kept her confinement from the knowledge of any potential witnesses. No one knew the victim was home until after the defendant left her premises.

The State will surely compare *Enoch* to our case, arguing that each defendant confined the victim in the relative privacy of the victim's own home, and that each defendant attempted to further conceal the confinement by refusing to answer the telephone or doorbell. However, *Enoch* is distinguishable. Although both defendants failed to answer the telephone or doorbell, Mr. Tate did not conceal Mr. Campbell from the knowledge of others. First, unlike the basement apartment in *Enoch*, Mr. Tate confined Mr. Campbell in a visible location. Had anyone actually looked through Mr. Campbell's picture window, they would have seen him confined in the living room. Therefore, despite Mr. Tate's failure to answer the doorbell or telephone, the visibility of the location made it possible for a witness to view the confinement. In contrast, the boyfriend in Enoch was unable to see her by looking through the apartment windows.

Second, the defense can argue that both Mr. Campbell's neighbor and his interior designer actually knew that Mr. Campbell was home. The neighbor saw Mr. Tate and Mr. Campbell on the porch of Mr. Campbell's house. Because they were next to each other and on the front porch, the neighbor believed that "they were going to enter the home." In contrast, witnesses in *Enoch* saw the defendant and the victim together from 100 feet away from the victim's apartment. Because of the distance that remained to the apartment, and because the apartment was in a mixed residential and commercial area with many possible destinations for the two, these witnesses did not know the defendant and the victim were in the victim's apartment.

Although Mr. Tate failed to answer when the interior decorator rang the doorbell or called on the telephone, Ms. Stewart assumed Mr. Campbell was home because Mr. Campbell's car was parked in front of his home. In contrast, in *Enoch*, the victim's boyfriend assumed that the victim was not at home and attempted to locate her elsewhere.

Accordingly, Mr. Tate has a viable defense that the confinement was not secret. He confined Mr. Campbell in a location close to a public area and visible to potential witnesses. Additionally, he did not conceal Mr. Campbell from the knowledge of others.

## Sample Memo C:
## One-Issue Office Memorandum Illustrating
## Format Option 3

### MEMORANDUM

To:      Chief of Felony Prosecutions
From:    Assistant Prosecutor
Re:      Gerry Arnold case—Residential Burglary Prosecution
Date:    August 28, 2001

### QUESTION PRESENTED

Is a detached garage a "living quarters" in which the owners "actually reside" under Illinois' Residential Burglary Statute, when the owners' college-age son uses it several days a week and on weekends as a get-a-way retreat and sleeps there half the year?

*The Question Presented identifies:*
*1. the rule of law;*
*2. element of the law that presents the issue; and 3. critical facts that frame the issue.*

### SHORT ANSWER

Yes. A detached garage used as a retreat and seasonal sleeping place is a "living quarters" under the statute. The owner frequently and regularly uses the garage for residential activities associated with a living quarters. The garage is furnished to reflect that use.

*The Short Answer:*
*1. answers the question; and*
*2. briefly explains the answer.*

### STATEMENT OF FACTS

On August 20, 2001, Defendant, Gerry Arnold, burglarized Carl and Rita Stripe's two-car detached garage. The State has charged Arnold under the Residential Burglary Statute. Arnold's attorney has moved to dismiss the charge, contending that the Stripe's garage is not a "dwelling" within which the Stripes "reside," as required by the statute.

*This ¶ describes the procedural context of the case.*

The garage is located approximately thirty feet behind the Stripe home. The Stripes have converted two-thirds of the garage into quarters for the couple's college-age son, Michael Stripe, to use as a get-a-way. They have walled-off that section of the garage from the section that stores the family car. The converted section of the garage has a window and a locked door.

*The remaining paragraphs tell the factual story of the case as it relates to the issue: whether the Stripe's garage is a dwelling.*

Michael spends two to three evenings a week and his free time on weekends in the get-a-way, writing and listening to music and watching television. In addition, Michael is the lead singer of a band, R.E.N., that plays once a month in clubs around town. The band practices in the garage on Sunday mornings and stores some of their equipment there. During the summer and fall when his parents are in town, Michael sleeps in the garage on a futon in a loft area. When his parents travel to Florida during the winter and spring, Michael sleeps in the house.

The garage is equipped to accommodate Michael's interests. In addition to the futon, the garage contains an expensive sound system, a portable five-inch television, and a mini-refrigerator. The garage has electricity and a space heater, but no running water or heat.

Thus, details of Arnold's arrest are not included because they are not relevant to the dwelling issue.

## DISCUSSION

The Stripe garage is a dwelling under Illinois' Residential Burglary Statute (the "Statute"). To prosecute Arnold successfully under the Statute, the State must prove that Arnold "knowingly and without authority enter[ed] the *dwelling place* of another." 720 Ill. Comp. Stat. § 5/19-3 (1993) (emphasis added). There is no real dispute that Arnold "knowingly" entered the Stripes' garage or that his entry was "without authority." Whether the garage is a "dwelling place" is more problematic. The Statute defines a dwelling as "a house, apartment, mobile home, trailer or *other living quarters* in which . . . the owners or occupants *actually reside. . . .*" 720 Ill. Comp. Stat. § 5/2-6(b) (1993) (emphasis added). This memorandum addresses whether the Stripe garage is a "living quarters" in which Michael Stripe "actually resides."

*Overview paragraph*:
1. Conclusion.
2. Elements of the rule of law.

3. Dispenses with non-issues.

4. Identifies the issue as defined by statute.

The Stripe's garage is a "living quarters" in which Michael Stripe "actually resides." When determining whether a structure is a living quarters, courts evaluate the type of activities for which the owners use the structure, as well as the physical evidence of those activities and the frequency of such activities. A structure is considered a dwelling when the owners frequently use the structure for activities that occur in a living quarters, and the furnishings reflect that use. Although a structure's attachment to the main residence is also relevant, physical attachment to the primary residence is not necessary. Therefore, a structure used as an extension of the home's living quarters may be a dwelling even though it is not physically connected to the primary residence. Because Michael Stripe

*Thesis paragraph*:
1. Conclusion.

2. Relevant factors.

3. Synthesized rule of law from cases.

4. Brief applica-

frequently and regularly uses the Stripe garage as a living quarters, it satisfies the statutory definition of "dwelling."

### A. Type of Use.

The owners must use a structure for activities associated with a living quarters for the structure to be classified as a dwelling. *People v. McIntyre*, 578 N.E.2d 314, 315 (Ill. App. Ct. 1991). In *McIntyre*, the owners used a screened porch for "sitting, eating and cooking." They ate their meals on the porch in the summer and cooked meals there during the winter. *Id.* The court held that the porch was a "living quarters" under the Statute, reasoning that the owners' use of the porch for "sitting, eating and cooking" made it "part of the living quarters" of their home. *Id.*

In contrast, where a structure is used only for commercial activities, it is not a dwelling. *People v. Thomas*, 561 N.E.2d 57, 58 (Ill. 1990). In *Thomas*, the owner used her portion of the garage of a multi-unit apartment building to store large quantities of perfume for a commercial business. The court held that the attached garage, "at least in this instance," was not a dwelling because it was not used as a "living quarters." *Id.* at 58. However, the court left open the possibility that a garage could, given the appropriate use as a living quarters, constitute a dwelling under the Statute.

The court reasoned that "an attached garage is not *necessarily* a 'dwelling' within the meaning of the residential burglary statute." *Id.* (emphasis added). That language implies that a garage, appropriately used as a residence or living quarters, could be a dwelling under the statute. *See also*, *People v. Silva*, 628 N.E.2d 948, 953 (Ill. App. Ct. 1993)(noting that *Thomas* left open the possibility for a garage to be a dwelling under the statute).

Like the owners in *McIntyre*, Michael Stripe used the Stripe's garage for activities commonly associated with a living quarters. Like the activities of "sitting, eating and cooking" in *McIntyre*, Michael Stripe's use of the garage for playing and listening to music, watching television, and eating snacks are uses commonly associated with a living quarters. In addition, Michael Stripe's use of the garage as a sleeping quarters during the summer and fall only strengthens the argument that the garage is a dwelling under the Statute. Unlike

---

tion of factors to client situation.

*Rule Explanation—Factor 1*:

Case 1—facts & rationale that relate to "type of use" factor.

Case 2—facts & rationale that relate to "type of use" factor.

Case 2 discussion continued. Note how a case of secondary importance is used parenthetically to lend further support for the writer's interp. of Case 2.

*Rule Application—Factor 1*
1. Thesis for Factor.
2. Client facts that prove the thesis.

3. Analogies to

the *McIntyre* activities of barbecuing, eating and sitting, which can occur outside of a dwelling, sleeping is an activity uniquely associated with a living quarters. Moreover, Michael Stripe's use of the garage is clearly distinguishable from *Thomas*, where the owner used the garage only for storage purposes.

The furnishings in a structure can serve as evidence of its use as a living quarters. In *McIntyre*, the owners furnished their porch with wrought-iron furniture and a barbecue grill that reflected their use of the porch for "sitting, eating and cooking." 578 N.E.2d at 315. Similarly, Michael Stripe's sound system, small television, mini-refrigerator, and futon reflect that he uses the garage for activities associated with a living quarters.

An occupant must not only use a structure as part of the living quarters of the home, but use it for those purposes on a frequent and regular basis. In *McIntyre*, the owners ate most of their meals on the porch in the summer and cooked meals there four or five times a week in the winter. 578 N.E.2d at 315. In contrast, the owner in *Thomas* presumably used the garage only on those limited occasions on which she delivered perfume to be stored and moved the perfume to a location where it would be sold. 561 N.E.2d at 58.

The frequency of Michael's use of the garage is similar to that in *McIntyre* and exceeds that in *Thomas*. Michael spends at least two to three evenings a week and his spare time on weekends in his get-a-way. Moreover, during the summer and fall, he sleeps there seven nights a week. Michael's regular and frequent use of the garage far exceeds the limited, occasional use of the garage in *Thomas*. In fact, when the garage was burglarized in August, Michael's frequency of use even exceeded that of the owners in *McIntyre*, who only used the porch four to five times a week

B. Proximity to Primary Residence.

The proximity of the structure to the primary residence is also a relevant factor. In *McIntyre*, for example, when holding that the porch was part of the home's living quarters, the court

*McIntyre* and *Thomas* to further support the thesis.

*Factor 1(a)—*
*Evidence of Use.*
Facts in *McIntyre* case AND application to Stripe garage.
Because this is a minor sub-factor that does not require extensive discussion, the rule explanation & rule application are combined into a single paragraph.

*Rule Explanation:*
*Factor 1(b)—*
*Frequency of Use.*
Facts in the *McIntyre* and *Thomas* cases that relate to frequency of use.

*Rule Application:*
*Factor 1(b)—*
*Frequency of Use.*
1. Thesis

2. Client facts that support the thesis.

3. Analogies to cases that lend further support to the thesis.

*Rule Explanation:*
*Factor 2—*

Rationale in *McIntyre & Tho-*

observed that "the porch is attached and enclosed. . . ." 578 N.E.2d at 314. However, this factor does not seem to be as important as the manner in which the owners use the structure. For example, in *Thomas*, the court minimized the importance of the garage's physical attachment to the residence. The court reasoned that "[a] garage, at least in this instance, *whether attached to the various living units or not*, cannot be deemed a residence or living quarters." 561 N.E.2d at 58 (emphasis added). By that statement, the court implied that the garage's physical attachment to the owner's home was not as important as its use.

Nevertheless, the defendant may argue that, despite Michael Stripe's frequent use of the garage for activities associated with a living quarters, the garage's physical detachment from the Stripe's home prevents it from being a "living quarters" in which the owners "reside." Under this theory, the defendant would argue that the garage, standing alone, is not a living quarters in which anyone resides. The garage has no running water, bathroom facilities or heat. Thus, the garage's status as a dwelling is dependent upon whether it can reasonably be viewed as an extension of the Stripe family's living quarters within the home itself. The defendant would argue that the fact that the *McIntyre* porch was physically attached to the family's home was essential to the court's holding. Only because it was physically attached to the home could the porch reasonably be viewed as an extension of the family's living quarters. In contrast, the Stripe's garage stands thirty feet away from their residence.

While having some merit, this argument should fail. Although the *McIntyre* court did note that the porch was physically "attached and enclosed," it concluded that it was the owners' "activities" and *use* of the porch that made the porch "part of the living quarters of the house." 578 N.E.2d at 314. Thus, the court implied that the activities for which the porch was used were more important than the porch's attachment to the home. Moreover, the fact that the porch was separated from the utility room of the owners' home by a door with "three locks" lends less significance to the attached/detached distinction. The presence of three locks implies that the porch area was not an open part of the main residence, but was instead physically separate from the main residence. Like the physically separate porch in *McIntyre*, the Stripe garage is used as an extension of the Stripe family's living quarters.

*mas* that explains "proximity" factor.

*Rule Application: Factor 2—*
1. Thesis for opposing argument #1.
2. Explores the basis of the opposing argument.

3. Writer's conclusion re: validity of opposing argument.
4. Explores *McIntyre* case to illustrate the writer's point.

Defendant might also argue that the legislative history suggests that the legislators did not intend for the statute to cover structures such as garages. As the court noted in *People v. Silva*, 629 N.E.2d 948 (Ill. App. Ct. 1993), the legislature amended the statute in 1986 to clarify and narrow the meaning of the term "dwelling." The court quoted the following statement of Senator Sangmeister made during legislative hearings: "It was even brought to our attention by the Illinois Supreme Court in a number of cases that . . . there should be a better definition to the dwelling house. We are having people prosecuted for residential burglary for breaking into. . . . unoccupied buildings *such as garages*." *Id*. at 951(emphasis added).

This argument lacks merit. The *Silva* court noted that "[t]he residential burglary statute is designed to protect the 'privacy and sanctity of the home,' with a view toward the 'greater danger and potential for serious harm from burglary of a home as opposed to burglary of a business.'" 629 N.E.2d at 951, *quoting*, *People v. Edgesto*, 611 N.E.2d 49 (Ill. App. Ct. 1993). Senator Sangmeister's concern that people are being prosecuted for breaking into "unoccupied buildings" is consistent with the general legislative purpose to deter residential burglary because of its potential for serious harm. An occupied garage used as a living quarters invokes the same legislative concerns for the sanctity of the home and the increased risk of harm that results from an invasion of that home. Moreover, the Illinois Supreme Court decided the *Thomas* case only a few years after the amendment. In *Thomas*, the court suggested that a garage used as a living quarters would be a dwelling under the statute.

In conclusion, the Stripe's garage is a living quarters in which Michael Stripe resides for purposes of prosecuting Arnold under the Statute. Not only does Michael Stripe use the garage for residential activities, he uses it frequently and regularly. The fact that the garage is not attached to the primary residence does not deprive it of its status as a living quarters.

*2nd opposing argument for Factor 2:*
1. Thesis for opposing arg.
2. Explores the basis of the opposing argument.

3. Writer's conclusion re: validity of that argument.

4. Arguments that support the conclusion.

Brief conclusion.

## *Sample Memo D:*
## *Multi-Issue Office Memorandum*

### MEMORANDUM

To:      Senior Attorney
From:    Junior Attorney
Date:    October 15, 2001
Re:      Allison McLean—Potential Litigation under the Attractive Nuisance
         Doctrine

### QUESTIONS PRESENTED

Does our client have a valid claim against landowners under Florida's attractive nuisance doctrine, which requires proof that: (a) the landowners could reasonably foresee the presence of trespassing children on their property, (b) the property contained a hidden danger, and (c) the landowners failed to exercise reasonable care to protect the child from injury?

A.  Is the presence of trespassing children reasonably foreseeable when the property is located next to an elementary school, a pond on the property contains inner-tubes, ducks, and fish, and the landowners had previously discovered school children trespassing?

B.  Is a dock a hidden danger to a six-year-old child when it is covered by moss and algae, provides the only means of access to the pond, and is so deteriorated that it collapsed under the weight of the child?

C.  Do landowners fail to exercise reasonable care to protect children from foreseeable injury when they do not lock the gate to the property, repair the dock, or post warning signs of the deteriorating condition of the dock, although they erected a chain link fence around the property and posted a "Do Not Climb Fence" sign on the fence?

### SHORT ANSWER

Yes, our client has a strong claim against the landowners for injuries sustained by her child under the doctrine of attractive nuisance.

A.  First, her child's presence on the property was reasonably foreseeable because the landowners' property is both visible and accessible from an area that young children frequent, it contains objects or conditions that attract children, and the landowners had previously discovered school children trespassing on their property.

B.    Second, the deteriorating dock was a hidden danger because a six-year-old child is too young to appreciate its dangerous condition.

C.    Finally, the landowners failed to exercise reasonable care to protect trespassing children from the danger of the dock because the burden of taking reasonable precautionary measures was slight when compared to the risk of harm to foreseeable child trespassers.

## STATEMENT OF FACTS

On Sunday, September 3, 2001, six-year-old Mikey McLean drowned in a pond on Fred and Thelma Hurt's property when their dock collapsed out from under him. Mikey's parents, Mr. and Ms. McLean, have retained this firm to represent them in potential litigation against the Hurts.

The Hurt's property contains a man-made pond, which they have stocked with fish and ducks. Approximately twenty years ago, they installed a dock that extends about one foot above and fifteen feet over the pond. Because of the rocky shoreline, the dock is the only means of access to the pond. The Hurt's children, and now their grandchildren, fish in the pond, feed the ducks, and play on inner-tubes the Hurts leave in the pond.

Ten years ago the Reed Elementary School was built on property adjacent to the Hurt's property. After the school was built, the Hurts erected an inexpensive chain-link fence around their property. The fence installer attempted to persuade the Hurts to build a privacy fence around their property, informing them that the four foot high chain-link fence would not keep out school children. However, the Hurts declined to purchase the more expensive privacy fence. Instead, they posted a "No Trespassing" sign on the fence.

It became common practice for elementary school students to feed the ducks through the chain-link fence. The Hurts have not objected to this practice. However, when two of Mikey's classmates climbed the fence to feed the ducks that were swimming in the pond, the Hurts told the children that they "should get back to school." Mikey observed this incident. After that incident, some of the older students began to dare each other to climb the fence without getting caught. Apparently to prevent the students from climbing the fence, in May, 1998, the Hurts removed the "No Trespassing" sign and replaced it with a "Do Not Climb Fence" sign.

On Monday of Labor Day weekend, Mikey and two classmates decided to visit the ducks. The Hurts were out of town for the Labor Day weekend. Due to the warning sign, Mikey and his friends knew that they should not climb the fence. Instead, they entered the property through an unlocked gate. Mikey's two friends ran across the dock and dove into the pond to swim and play on the inner-tubes. Mikey followed them onto the dock. Because he could not swim well, he decided to stay on the dock and toss bread crumbs to the ducks in the pond. While he was standing on the dock, it collapsed out from under him. Mikey fell into ten feet of water and drowned.

On the day of the fatal accident, the Hurt's wooden dock was decaying and rotting. However, the decay was partially hidden by a green shiny coating of moss and algae growing on the dock. The Hurts claim that they had planned to replace the dock, but postponed the repairs until the winter months.

## DISCUSSION

The McLeans have a strong negligence claim against the Hurts under Florida's common law doctrine of attractive nuisance. In determining whether a landowner is liable for injuries to a child trespasser under the attractive nuisance doctrine, Florida courts require the plaintiff to prove that: (1) the child's presence on the property was reasonably foreseeable; (2) the condition that injured the child trespasser was a hidden danger, or "trap;" and (3) the landowner failed to exercise reasonable care to protect foreseeable child trespassers from the hidden danger. All three issues merit discussion.

### A.   Trespassing Children Were Foreseeable.

When evaluating the foreseeability of trespass, courts consider such factors as the property's visibility and accessibility to young children, its attractiveness to children, and the landowners' knowledge of previous trespass. The Hurts should have reasonably foreseen Mikey's presence on their property. The Hurt's pond, ducks, and inner-tubes are conditions both visible and attractive to the young children who attend an elementary school adjacent to their property. Moreover, they had knowledge that young elementary school children had previously trespassed on their property.

It is foreseeable that children will trespass on property when the property is attractive and alluring to children and the landowner has actual knowledge that children have previously trespassed on the property. *Ansin v. Thurston*, 98 So. 2d 87, 88 (Fla. Dist. Ct. App. 1957). In *Ansin*, the defendant's property contained an artificial pond with white sand banks, a floating dock, and a raft. *Id.* at 88. A child drowned in the pond after playing on the raft. The court upheld a jury's finding that the presence of child trespassers was reasonably foreseeable, holding that it was "certain that children would be attracted to such a place. . . ." *Id.* The court reasoned that the pond was both visible and accessible to children, as it was close to well-traveled streets and homes. Moreover, the property was seven blocks from an elementary school. Finally, the owner knew that children had used the pond for swimming. *Id. See also Allen v. William P. McDonald Corp.*, 42 So. 2d 706, 707 (Fla. 1949) (holding that white sand banks adjacent to a pond were sufficiently alluring and attractive to children to entice them to trespass).

As in *Ansin*, Mikey was a foreseeable child trespasser. Like the pond in *Ansin*, the Hurt's pond, ducks, and fish were appealing lures that attracted children to the Hurt's property. Moreover, like the raft in *Ansin*, the Hurt's innertubes are characteristic water toys that invite children to jump into the pond to play. In addition, the pond was visible and accessible to the young children who attended the adjacent elementary school. In fact, its close proximity to a school that requires the presence of children on a daily basis makes trespass even more foreseeable than in *Ansin*, where the property was seven blocks from an elementary school. Finally, like the landowner in *Ansin*, the Hurts knew that children were trespassing on their property. The Hurts actually observed children climbing the fence to feed the ducks. Accordingly, Mikey was a foreseeable child trespasser on the Hurt's property.

B.    The Dock Was a Hidden Danger.

The Hurt's dock is a hidden danger. When evaluating whether a condition is a hidden danger, or trap, courts consider the inherent dangerousness of the condition and the age of the injured child. A condition constitutes a hidden danger, or trap, if its dangerous condition would be hidden to a child because of the child's age and immaturity. *Ansin*, 98 So. 2d at 88. In addition, the dangerous condition that injures the child must have a connection with the object that initially attracts the child onto the property, such that the two conditions jointly contribute to the child's injury. *Starling v. Saha*, 451 So. 2d 516, 518–19 (Fla. Dist. Ct. App. 1984). The dangerous condition of the Hurt's dock would be hidden to a six-year-old child, who would lack the maturity and the experience to recognize that the existence of moss and algae on the wooden dock contribute to structural decay. Moreover, the ducks that initially attracted Mikey to trespass acted in concert with the dock and water to contribute jointly to Mikey's death, as Mikey had to walk onto the dock to feed the ducks.

1.   <u>The Dock Was Inherently Dangerous to a Young Child</u>.

When a dangerous condition is hidden to a child because of the child's age and immaturity, it constitutes a hidden danger, or trap. In *Ansin*, the defendant's pond contained a floating wooden dock that extended into the water about twelve-feet, well over a child's head. A make-shift raft that was "prone to tip" floated in the water at the end of the dock. A nine-year-old child drowned in the pond after playing on the tipsy raft. *Id.* at 88. The court held that the pond, floating dock, and tipsy raft combined to constitute a hidden trap. The court observed that the tipsy raft floated in water of a depth well over the child's head. The court reasoned that a nine-year-old boy could not be expected to recognize its danger. *Id. See also Allen*, 42 So. 2d at 707 (holding that a two-and-a-half-year-old child could not be expected to recognize the danger presented by steep sandy banks that led into water ten feet deep).

Like the dock and raft in *Ansin*, the Hurt's dock was a hidden danger, or trap. In fact, the deceptive safety of the Hurts' dock made it inherently more hidden, and therefore dangerous, to a child trespasser than the raft in *Ansin*. A wooden, anchored dock has a seemingly solid foundation. Children simply do not expect that the "ground" might collapse out from under them. It is precisely because of its illusion of safety that Mikey stayed on the dock. Mikey knew that he did not swim well and deliberately stayed out of the water on a seemingly solid foundation. To a child who does not swim well, the dock promised a safety that it did not deliver. In contrast, a child is more likely to foresee the danger that one might fall off of a raft that floats on the water, particularly the "visibly tipsy raft" in *Ansin*. The child in *Ansin* deliberately risked the danger of the water by jumping from a floating dock onto a floating raft. In short, the floating dock and raft were less dangerous because their danger was more obvious.

Moreover, Mikey's age is also more compelling than in *Ansin*. Mikey was only six years old, three years younger than the nine-year-old child in *Ansin*. A six-year-old child is far less likely to anticipate that a seemingly solid foundation would collapse out from under his weight than a nine-year-old child would be expected to anticipate that he might fall off of a tipsy raft. Moreover, no six-year-old child would possess the experience and the maturity to appreciate that moss and algae were likely to cover structural decay. In fact, to a six-year-old child, the moss and algae covering the Hurt's dock would serve only to hide the dangerous condition of the deteriorating wood. Certainly, Mikey's two classmates, who walked across the dock to jump into the pond, did not appreciate the danger. Having observed his friends walk across the dock, Mikey would be even less likely to appreciate the dock's hidden danger.

2. The Attractive Condition and Hidden Danger Jointly Contributed to Mikey's Injury.

Florida courts also require that the dangerous condition that injures a child have a connection with the object that initially attracts the child onto the property, such that the two conditions jointly contribute to the child's injury. *Starling v. Saha*, 451 So. 2d at 518–19. The Hurts might argue that the requisite connection does not exist in the present case. They would argue that it was the ducks that lured Mikey onto their property, while the combination of the dock and water injured him. To support that argument, the Hurts would rely on older Florida cases that narrowly construe this requirement. *See Johnson v. Bathey*, 376 So. 2d 848 (Fla. 1979) (holding no cause of action when child was not even aware of existence of condition that injured him until after he had trespassed onto the property); *Newby v. West Palm Beach Water Co.*, 47 So. 2d 527 (Fla. 1950) (holding no cause of action when child was lured to reservoir by spray reflecting rainbows in the air, but drowned by falling into the water).

The Hurt's argument should fail. More recent appellate court cases have broadly construed this requirement, narrowly restricting the older cases to their facts. For example, in *Starling*, a child was lured to the defendant's pool by the prospect of swimming. While swimming, the child became caught and held under water by the suction of an underwater hose and drowned. 451 So. 2d at 517. The court held that the plaintiff satisfied the requirement that the condition that lured the child onto the land also acted to injure the child. *Id.* at 518–19. The court reasoned that it would not interpret *Johnson v. Bathey* "so literally that we abolish application of the attractive nuisance doctrine to concealed dangers operating in connection with conditions or other objects on property, which jointly contribute to the child's injury." *Id.* The court pointed out that the combined effect of the hose that held the child under water and the water in the pond drowned the child. *Id.* at 518.

In a more recent case, a Florida appellate court stretched *Bathey* and *Newby* even further. In *Mueller v. South Fla. Water Mgmt. Dist.*, a sixteen-year-old boy trespassed onto the defendant's property to ride on the defendant's dirt-bike path. 620 So. 2d 789 (Fla. Dist. Ct. App. 1993). While riding his dirt-bike, he was injured by a concealed guardrail that stretched across the path. *Id.* at 790. Presumably, the child was not aware of the guardrail when he entered the defendant's property. Despite that fact, the court held that the plaintiff satisfied the requirement that the condition that lured the child onto the land also acted to injure the child. *Id.* at 791. *Cf. Bathey*, 376 So. 2d at 849. Following *Starling*, the court reasoned that the steel guardrail was "an integral part of the dirt-bike path, the condition which lured [the child] onto the premises." 620 So. 2d at 791.

Under *Starling* and *Mueller*, the Hurt's dock, ducks, and water all combined to lure Mikey onto the Hurts' property and to injure him. Mikey was lured onto the Hurt's property by the prospect of feeding the ducks that swam in the Hurt's pond. In order to gain access to the ducks swimming in the pond, Mikey was compelled to walk over the Hurt's dock. (The dock provided the only access to the water.) When the dock collapsed, Mikey was thrown into the pond and drowned. The combination of the ducks, dock, and water jointly contributed to Mikey's death. Accordingly, the Hurt's dock, combined with the ducks and water, constituted a hidden danger, or trap.

C.    The Hurts Failed to Exercise Reasonable Care.

In evaluating whether a landowner has exercised reasonable care to protect trespassing children from hidden dangerous conditions, courts balance the likelihood of child trespassers and the degree of danger posed by the hidden condition against the burden imposed on the landowner to protect child trespassers from harm and the preventive measures the landowner has taken. As the likelihood of child trespassers and resulting harm increases, the burden imposed on a landowner to protect child trespassers from harm also increases. *Howard v. Atlantic Coast R.R. Co.*, 231 F.2d 592, 594 (5th Cir. 1956); *Samson v. O'Hara*, 239 So. 2d 151, 152 (Fla. Dist. Ct. App. 1970). Here, it was easily foreseeable that children would trespass on the Hurt's dock while the Hurts were out of town and that the dangerous condition of the dock would seriously injure a trespassing child. Because the Hurts could have easily prevented Mikey's death by taking such minimal protective measures as locking the gate or posting a sign warning of the dock's condition, they failed to exercise reasonable care to protect Mikey from harm.

When landowners know of a dangerous condition on their property and fail to take minimal measures to protect foreseeable child trespassers from the risk of serious harm, the landowners have failed to exercise reasonable care. In *Samson*, an eighteen-month-old child drowned in a neighbor's swimming pool after being attracted to it by the sound of a hose running into the water. Although the defendants had built an enclosure around the pool, they left open a door in the pool enclosure. While the defendants were not at home, the child wandered through the door and fell into the pool. 239 So. 2d at 152. On these facts, the court held that a jury could find that the defendants failed to exercise reasonable care to protect the child from harm. The court reasoned that a jury should weigh the foreseeability of a child trespassing onto the defendants' pool area against the "ease of guarding against injury. . . ." *Id.* Implicit in the court's opinion was the suggestion that a jury could reasonably find that the risk of harm to a child far outweighs the burden of locking a gate.

Like the defendants in *Samson*, the Hurts failed to take even minimal precautionary measures to protect foreseeable child trespassers from a dangerous condition that posed a serious risk of harm. As in *Samson*, the Hurts built a fence around their property. However, as the court implied in *Samson*, by leaving the gate unlocked they negated the protective effect of the fence. The burden of locking the gate instead of merely closing it was small compared to the danger of serious injury. Thus, locking a gate to enclose a swimming and fishing hole is a simple precaution that a reasonable person would have taken under any circumstances. Moreover, the duty to take this simple precaution is enhanced when, as here, the Hurts were out of town for the long holiday weekend. Leaving a gate unlocked over a long holiday weekend was an open invitation for disaster.

When a landowner has knowledge that children trespass on the property, and the degree of danger is great, the landowner exercises reasonable care by repeatedly investigating to determine whether its precautionary measures were effective and by making repeated new efforts to keep child trespassers away. In *Howard*, the defendant railroad covered abandoned wells on its property by closing them with boards and nailing them shut. 231 F.2d at 593. The railroad also posted "No Trespassing" signs on its property. Despite these precautions, an employee of the railroad discovered boys swimming naked in an abandoned well. The employee verbally ordered the boys to leave and then replaced the boards and nailed them shut. When these efforts proved to be ineffective, the defendant cut down the bushes around the well, reasoning that the boys would be deterred from swimming naked without the bushes for cover. The defendant's employee then went back to the well to determine whether the latest efforts to deter trespassing had been successful. When the defendant's employee again found boys swimming in the well, he told them they would not be allowed to swim there anymore. The defendant then ordered a bulldozer to fill up the well with dirt. Before the bulldozer could do so, the plaintiff's child drowned in the well. *Id*. The court held that the well did not present a hidden, unusual danger. *Id*. at 595. However, in dictum, the court indicated that the defendant had exercised reasonable care to keep the child trespassers away. The court reasoned that the defendant had repeatedly and persistently attempted to deter the children from trespassing. The court concluded that a landowner is not required to ensure the success of its efforts. *Id*.

The Hurt's attempts to deter children from trespassing on their property fall far short of the repeated and persistent efforts of the railroad company in *Howard*. The Hurt's efforts to prevent harm to trespassing children consisted of: (1) installing an inexpensive chain link fence the installer warned them would not keep out trespassing children; (2) posting a "No Trespassing" sign and replacing it with a "Do Not Climb Fence" sign; and (3) verbally admonishing previous trespassers to "get back to school." These efforts do not rise to the level of reasonable care, particularly in light of the minimal steps the Hurts could have taken to prevent harm.

The Hurt's precautionary measures were ineffective and not reasonably calculated to prevent harm to trespassing children. As the fence installer warned, the Hurt's four foot chain link fence was not designed to, nor was it effective in, preventing children from entering their property. As the Hurts observed, school children regularly climbed the fence. The Hurt's failure to improve the quality of their fence, or to replace it, contrasts with the railroad company's repeated efforts to board up the abandoned well after discovering trespassers. Even if the Hurt's fence could be considered a safety precaution, their failure to lock the gate while they were out of town for the long holiday weekend wholly negates its effectiveness as a preventive device.

Moreover, the Hurt's written and verbal warnings were also ineffective and meaningless. Their failure to lock the gate while they were out of town renders their "Do Not Climb Fence" sign meaningless as a preventive device. Mikey and his friends understood the literal meaning of the "Do Not Climb Fence" sign and, therefore, looked for an open gate. By entering the property through an unlocked gate, Mikey and his friends did not disobey any written warning posted by the Hurts. Nor did their entry into the property violate any verbal warning. On prior occasions, the Hurts had warned children only not to climb the fence and to "get back to school." Mikey could reasonably have interpreted the verbal warning to "get back to school" in a literal sense rather than as a statement of the Hurt's desire for the children to leave their property. Their vague verbal warnings stand in stark contrast to the railroad company's specific and repeated warnings in *Howard* that the children were not allowed to swim in the well and were not allowed to trespass on the railroad company's property.

Moreover, with minimal expense and inconvenience, the Hurts could easily have protected children from the serious risk of harm posed by the decaying dock and water. First, the Hurts admit that they knew the dock was decaying and needed to be replaced. However, they wanted to wait until winter to make the necessary repairs, presumably out of a desire to use the dock throughout the summer months. By repairing the dock during the summer, the Hurts would not have incurred any additional expenses beyond that which they had already planned to incur. At most, the Hurts would have been inconvenienced by the loss of their dock for part of the summer. When weighing the serious risk of injury posed by the dock against the Hurt's inconvenience, a trier of fact should find that the Hurts had a duty to replace the dock when it needed to be repaired. Even if a trier of fact would find that the Hurts were reasonable in delaying repairs, reasonable precaution required them to post a sign warning that the dock was dangerous. By failing to do so, children were not aware of the dock's hidden danger. Accordingly, the Hurts failed to exercise reasonable care to protect child trespassers from serious injury.

## CONCLUSION

The McLeans have a strong claim against the Hurts under the attractive nuisance doctrine. First, Mikey McLean was a foreseeable trespasser on the Hurt's property. Second, the deteriorating dock was a hidden, dangerous trap to a six-year-old child and acted in concert with the water and ducks to harm Mikey. Third, the Hurts failed to exercise reasonable care to prevent injury to a trespassing child.

## *Sample Client Advisory Letter*

Charlotte Turley, Esq.
105 S. Central Ave.
St. Louis, MO 63105
January 5, 2001

Mr. & Mrs. Johnson
234 N. Bemiston
St. Louis, MO 63105

Confidential Attorney/Client Communication

Re: Dispute with Apartment Management Corp.

Dear Mr. & Mrs. Johnson,

As you requested, I have analyzed the viability of a legal claim against your landlord to recover for the injuries you suffered when you fell on an icy sidewalk at your apartment complex. This letter summarizes the facts as I understand them and my analysis of Missouri law concerning a landlord's duty to keep common walkways free from snow and ice. Our legal option is to sue your landlord for negligence. Unfortunately, we face significant legal hurdles in recovering damages against your landlord.

Under the facts as I understand them, on December 18, 2000, Mr. Johnson slipped and fell on an icy patch of the sidewalk that leads to several different apartments at your apartment complex. You advised me that the sidewalk was icy and that the landlord had not shoveled the walkway or placed any salt on the sidewalk. You have discussed the incident with your landlord and he has denied all responsibility for your accident. Your landlord claims that if the tenants wish to have walkways free from snow and ice, they are welcome to shovel the walkways themselves. The landlord insists that he has never agreed to assume that responsibility. However, because the landlord mowed the lawn in the summer, you assumed that he would also shovel the common sidewalks in the winter. I have examined your lease and it does not address which party is responsible for keeping the common walkways safe from weather hazards.

You have also provided me with medical bills that reflect extensive injuries to Mr. Johnson's ankle. These injuries unfortunately prevent you from being able to continue your duties as a liquor delivery truck driver. These duties require you to unload, lift and carry heavy boxes. At present, your medical bills are about $10,000.00. You do not have medical insurance and would like to know whether the law can require your landlord's insurance company to pay your medical bills and compensate you for your lost wages. You estimate your medical damages will be $20,000.00.

Although we have a legitimate cause of action, we face significant legal hurdles to recovery of damages. Our legal option is to sue your landlord for negligence. We would argue that your landlord was "negligent" by breaking his duty to keep the common premises safe from your foreseeable injuries.

Under the law of "negligence," you cannot recover compensation for even the severe injuries you suffered unless the law first finds that your landlord violated some "duty" he owed you under the law. The courts impose a duty on landlords to keep an apartment building's "common" areas safe from permanent hazards. Although the walkway is part of the "common" area, unfortunately, Missouri courts have distinguished cases where the danger in the common areas is caused by a temporary weather hazard, such as snow. When the danger is caused by snow, courts have not imposed a duty upon landlords to shovel the snow from common walkways. Courts justify this rule by noting that the duty to remove snow would "subject the landlord to an unreasonable burden of vigilance and care."

A trend in landlord/tenant court decisions does offer a ray of hope. The last reported Missouri opinion that decided the issue of snow removal is over thirty years old. Even in that thirty-two year old decision, the court noted that the more "modern" rule adopted in other states imposed a duty on landlords to shovel snow from their common walkways. We could argue that more recent Missouri Supreme Court opinions reflect this State's willingness to follow a national trend to protect tenants' rights to a greater degree than they have been protected in the past. The Missouri Supreme Court has implied that landlords have a broad duty to keep common areas safe from all dangers of which the landlords have "reasonable notice."

Fifteen years ago, the Missouri Supreme Court imposed a "duty" on a landlord to place speed bumps in the parking lot of an apartment building. In this case, a child was injured on the parking lot of the landlord's apartment complex when a speeding bicycle struck her. The Supreme Court affirmed a jury verdict for the child, finding that the landlord should have taken the precaution of installing speed bumps on the parking lot. The court reasoned that, "as strongly emphasized in recent cases," the landlord owes a duty to its tenants to make common areas of leased property reasonably safe. A couple of years later, the Missouri Supreme Court found that a landlord had a duty to relocate the fire escape on an apartment building so that criminal intruders could not use the fire escape to break into a tenant's apartment.

Under the broad language and shifts in policy reflected in the more recent Supreme Court opinions, we could argue that the landlord owed you a duty to keep the sidewalk free from ice because the landlord had "reasonable notice" of the danger. The landlord had actual notice that snowy and icy conditions existed, as public and private schools in the City of St. Louis were closed for two days prior to your injury. Given the known snow and ice conditions, the landlord arguably had "reasonable notice" that a tenant might slip and fall on the icy sidewalk. Under this argument, by failing to keep the sidewalk safe, the landlord breached his duty to you under the law. If a court were to adopt this interpretation of the law, the law would permit you to recover damages for injuries you suffered as a result of the landlord's breach of duty.

Unfortunately, these recent Missouri Supreme Court cases did not address whether the older "temporary hazard" cases involving snowy conditions are still valid in this State. The court did not address that issue because the hazards involved in the recent cases were permanent hazards, not temporary conditions. Therefore, the Missouri Supreme Court did not have to decide whether the earlier cases involving temporary hazards were still good law. In short, despite a policy trend that favors tenants, and broad policy language that favors us, the latest Supreme Court decisions do not explicitly reject any of the older cases that protect landlords from liability for injuries from temporary conditions such as snow. Because the older cases are the only higher level court cases that address the landlord's responsibility to protect against temporary hazards, the trial court will probably follow these older cases. (A trial court judge has to follow the law announced by higher level courts.) Realistically, our best chance to prevail in such a lawsuit would be before a higher court, most likely the Missouri Supreme Court.

In sum, Missouri law does not provide us with a promising opportunity to succeed at the trial court level. I do believe we have a reasonable chance of succeeding at a higher court level. However, that option will likely take a number of years and involve significant legal fees. In light of the present state of the law in Missouri, and your desire to resolve this dispute quickly, I recommend that we contact the landlord to negotiate the best possible settlement under the circumstances. Although the landlord may not be willing to offer you money that would fully compensate you for your medical bills and lost wages, the landlord may be willing to settle this dispute to avoid lengthy litigation.

After you have had an opportunity to digest and consider this letter, please give me a call and let me know the course of action you want me to pursue. I will wait to hear from you before I take any further action.

Very truly yours,

Charlotte Turley

## Sample Brief A:
## Title VII Brief

DEFENDANT'S MEMORANDUM IN SUPPORT OF
MOTION TO DISMISS

INTRODUCTION

Defendant, Ronald Crane, respectfully requests that this Court issue an order dismissing Plaintiff's complaint pursuant to Fed. R. Civ. P. 12(b)(6) for failure to state a claim upon which relief can be granted. Defendant is entitled to an order dismissing Plaintiff's complaint because he cannot provide the relief Plaintiff seeks. Plaintiff seeks from Mr. Crane in his individual capacity compensatory and punitive damages under Title VII and the 1991 Amendments to Title VII. However, those statutes apply only to employers, not to individuals in their individual capacities. Because Plaintiff is suing Mr. Crane in his individual capacity and because Mr. Crane does not qualify as an employer under the statutes, he cannot provide the relief Plaintiff seeks.

The plain language of Title VII defines "employer" so as to provide exclusive employer liability and, therefore, to exclude individuals in their individual capacities. Moreover, the remedies available under Title VII are remedies that only employers, and not individuals in their individual capacities, can provide. When Congress amended Title VII in 1991, they merely strengthened the remedies available to victims of Title VII violations by adding the potential for compensatory and punitive damages; Congress did not expand the class of defendants against whom victims could proceed. Thus, they preserved Title VII's provision of exclusive employer liability. Finally, as intended by Congress, exclusive employer liability sufficiently achieves the dual goals of those statutes: to deter discrimination and to compensate victims of discrimination. Realizing that individuals face deterrents outside of the statutes, Congress excluded them from liability to ensure that employers vigilantly police their workplaces and workforces. Accordingly, Mr. Crane is entitled to an order dismissing Plaintiff's complaint for failure to state a claim upon which relief can be granted.

## STATEMENT OF FACTS

Plaintiff has filed a complaint seeking from Mr. Crane in his individual capacity compensatory and punitive damages for alleged violations of Title VII. In her complaint, Plaintiff claims that Mr. Crane made a series of unwanted sexual advances toward her while she worked for him at Digicom, Inc. Additionally, Plaintiff claims Defendant threatened to retaliate against her for rejecting his unwanted sexual advances. Finally, Plaintiff claims Defendant, in fact, did retaliate against her by sabotaging her professionally, namely by claiming she had made unwanted sexual advances toward him and by rescheduling a meeting at which Plaintiff was to speak and not informing her, thus ensuring that she missed the meeting, and then firing her.

## ARGUMENT

I.    THE PLAIN LANGUAGE OF TITLE VII REFLECTS THAT CONGRESS ENVISIONED EXCLUSIVE EMPLOYER LIABILITY FOR VIOLATIONS OF TITLE VII.

Defendant, Mr. Crane, is entitled to an order dismissing Plaintiff's complaint because the plain language of Title VII reflects that Congress envisioned exclusive employer liability for violations of Title VII. First, Title VII defines "employer" so as to provide for exclusive employer liability and, therefore, to exclude individuals in their individual capacities. Second, the remedies available under Title VII are remedies that only employers, and not individuals in their individual capacities, can provide. Therefore, Mr. Crane is not liable to Plaintiff for compensatory or punitive damages under Title VII.

   A.    *Title VII's Definition of "Employer" Provides for Exclusive Employer Liability for Violations of Title VII.*

When prohibiting employers from discriminating against their employees, Title VII narrowly defines employer as "a person engaged in an industry affecting commerce who has fifteen or more employees . . . and any agent of such a person. . . ." 42 U.S.C. § 2000e(b) (1994). By defining employer as a "person . . . who has fifteen or more employees . . . and any agent of such a person," Congress codified its intention to exclude individuals in their individual capacities from liability for violations of Title VII. First, individuals in their individual capacities do not qualify as "person[s] . . . who ha[ve] fifteen or more employees." Individuals do not have employees, employers do.

Second, interpreting the statutory language to include individuals in their individual capacities would produce an absurd result. The conjunctive term "and" links the term "any agent" to the phrase "person . . . who has fifteen or more employees." Thus, as an "agent" of an employer, an individual employee's liability would depend on whether the employer employed fifteen or more employees. Individuals who are "agents" of employers with fewer than fifteen employees would be exempt from liability—as an agent of an employer with fewer than fifteen employees, they would fall within the statutory exemption. In contrast, individuals who are "agents" of employers with fifteen or more employees would be liable in their individual capacities. Because their employer would not fall within the exemption, they would similarly not be exempt. Congress could not have intended this result. *Hudson v. Soft Sheen Prods.*, 873 F. Supp. 132, 135 n.2 (N.D. Ill. 1995).

Finally, reading individual liability into the statute would thwart Congress' goal of shielding small entities with limited resources from the cost of litigating Title VII claims. "Congress' explicit limitation of the definition of 'employer' to 'a person engaged in an industry affecting commerce who has 15 or more employees' suggests an intent to protect those with limited resources from liability." *Haltek v. Village of Park Forest*, 864 F. Supp. 802, 805 (N.D. Ill. 1994). "If Congress decided to protect small entities with limited resources from liability, it is inconceivable that Congress intended to allow civil liability to run against individual employees." *Miller v. Maxwell's Int'l, Inc.*, 991 F.2d 583, 586 (9th Cir. 1993).

Thus, the "any agent" language merely incorporates respondeat superior into the statute and ensures that employers are liable for the discriminatory acts of their employees acting in their official capacities. *See id.* at 586 ("The obvious purpose of this [agent] provision was to incorporate respondeat superior liability into the statute.") (quoting *Padway v. Palches*, 655 F.2d 965, 968 (9th Cir. 1982)). Even the courts that have found individuals liable under Title VII have found them liable only in their official capacities, not in their individual capacities. *See id.* ("Many of the courts that purportedly have found individual liability under that statutes actually have held individuals liable in their *official* capacities and not in their individual capacities.").

B. *The Remedies Available under Title VII Confirm that Congress Intended Exclusive Employer Liability for Violations of Title VII.*

Moreover, the remedies available under Title VII confirm that Congress intended the "any agent" language merely to incorporate respondeat superior into the statute. Title VII originally allowed successful plaintiffs to recover only injunctive relief, reinstatement or hiring, or up to two years of back pay. 42 U.S.C. § 2000e-5(g) (1994). These remedies are "'damages [that] an employer, not an individual would generally provide. . . .'" *Hudson*, 873 F. Supp.

at 134 (quoting *Weiss v. Coca-Cola Bottling Co.*, 772 F. Supp. 407, 411 (N.D. Ill. 1991)). For example, "'individual defendants cannot be held liable for back pay.'" *Miller*, 991 F.2d at 585 (quoting *Padway*, 665 F.2d at 968). Had Congress intended individuals to be liable in their individual capacities for violations of Title VII, it would have included in Title VII a remedy that individuals could provide. By failing to do so, Congress indicated it intended exclusive employer liability for violations of Title VII.

II.   WITH THE 1991 AMENDMENTS, CONGRESS EXPANDED THE SCOPE OF REMEDIES WHILE PRESERVING THE CLASS OF DEFENDANTS AGAINST WHOM VICTIMS OF TITLE VII VIOLATIONS COULD PROCEED.

The 1991 Amendments to Title VII preserved Title VII's provision of exclusive employer liability. In amending Title VII in 1991, Congress expanded the scope of remedies available to victims of Title VII violations. *See* H. R. Rep. No. 40, 102nd Cong., 1st Sess., pt. 1 (1991) (the purpose of the amendments to Title VII is "to strengthen existing remedies to provide more effective deterrence and ensure compensation commensurate with the harm suffered . . ."). However, Congress specifically did not expand the class of defendants against whom victims could proceed. Instead, Congress codified this intent by leaving unaltered Title VII's definition of employer, by enacting damages caps based on the number of "employees" a respondent has, and by focusing on *employer* payment of damages and on *employer* deterrence in the legislative history to the 1991 Amendments. Therefore, Mr. Crane is not liable to Plaintiff for compensatory and punitive damages under Title VII.

A.   *In the 1991 Amendments, Congress Preserved Title VII's Provision of Exclusive Employer Liability.*

In enacting the 1991 Amendments to Title VII, Congress expanded the scope of remedies available to victims of a Title VII violations. However, Congress did not expand the class of defendants against whom victims could proceed. Instead, Congress left unaltered Title VII's definition of employer and preserved the exclusion of employers with fewer than fifteen employees. *See* 42 U.S.C. § 1981a(b)(3) (1991). Had Congress intended to expand the class of defendants to include individuals in their individual capacities, it would have done so explicitly. "Congress must have been aware that the majority of jurisdictions interpreted . . . Title VII to exclude individual liability. Congress would not have expected to change the law with silence." *Hudson*, 873 F. Supp. at 136.

B.   *§ 1981a's Damage Caps Make Sense Only in the Context of Exclusive Employer Liability.*

The elaborate liability scheme of the 1991 Amendments confirms that Congress intended to preserve Title VII's provision of exclusive employer liability. In expanding the scope of remedies available to victims of Title VII violations to include compensatory and punitive damages, Congress also carefully limited the damages to which an employer could be subjected depending upon the number of employees employed by the employer. For example, on the low end, Congress subjected an employer who employs between fourteen and 101 employees to no more than $50,000 in compensatory and punitive damages. 42 U.S.C. § 1981a(b)(3)(A) (1994). On the high end, Congress subjected an employer who employs more than 500 employees to no more than $300,000 in compensatory and punitive damages. *Id.* § 1981a(b)(3)(D). Congress' failure to include a damage cap for individuals reflects that it did not contemplate individual liability for compensatory and punitive damages under the Amendments. *See Hudson*, 873 F. Supp. at 135 ("[I]f Congress had envisioned individual liability under Title VII for compensatory and punitive damages, it would have included *individuals* in this litany of limitations . . .") (quoting *Miller*, 991 F.2d at 588 n.2).

Moreover, reading individual liability into the statute would mean that individuals would be subjected either to unlimited liability or to liability that depends upon the size of the employer for whom they work. Neither of these alternatives makes sense. First, subjecting employees to unlimited individual liability is simply inconsistent with Congress' careful efforts to prescribe the parameters of employer liability. "It is unreasonable to think that Congress would protect small entities from the costs associated with litigating discrimination claims and limit the available compensatory and punitive damages based on the size of the . . . employer, but subject an individual supervisory employee to unlimited liability." *Haltek*, 864 F. Supp. at 805. This result would cavalierly subject individuals to the vagaries of juries while protecting employer liability. Such a result would not only be manifestly unfair to individual employees but would thwart Congress' carefully calibrated scheme of damages.

Second, imposing individual liability depending upon the size of the employer for whom the individual works is equally as nonsensical and unfair. Under this scenario, individuals who work for an employer with fewer than fifteen employees would not be subject to liability at all, while individuals who work for employers with fifteen or more employees would be subject to liability. In other words, it would create an incentive for potential violators of Title

VII to work for small employers to ensure that they could escape liability. Congress could not have intended this result. *Hudson*, 873 F. Supp. at 135.

Moreover, the damage caps reflect an employer's ability to pay, not an individual's ability to pay. In enacting the damage caps, Congress carefully calibrated the caps to consider an employer's ability to pay and the amount necessary to "punish" the offending employer, i.e., "to make it hurt." Thus, the calibrated damages caps reflect Congress' intention not to bankrupt an employer or punish an employer beyond the amount necessary to "make it hurt." Imposing an employer's damages cap on its individual employees would create unfair results that Congress could not possibly have intended. The calibrated damage caps do not similarly reflect an individual's ability to pay or the amount necessary to "punish" an individual. An individual who works for a large company does not necessarily have the ability to pay up to $300,000 in compensatory and punitive damages for violating Title VII, nor is that amount necessary to punish the individual. In fact, that penalty would easily bankrupt many employees and would thwart the legislative intent to avoid that prospect. Thus, the damages caps make sense only in the context of exclusive employer liability.

### C.  The Legislative History to § 1981a Reflects that Congress Intended Exclusive Employer Liability.

The legislative history to the 1991 Amendments also confirms that Congress intended only to expand the scope of remedies available, not to expand the class of defendants against whom victims of Title VII violations could proceed. None of the Committee Reports, including the House Reports on the 1991 Amendments and the Senate Reports on the precursor bill to the 1991 Amendments, even mention individual liability. *See Hudson*, 873 F. Supp. at 136 (detailing the failure of the legislative history to mention individual liability). Instead, the legislative history is replete with references to *employer* compensation and the possibility of *employer* deterrence. For example, Congress focused on the need for employers to compensate wronged employees. The House Reports reflect Congress' intent to prevent "employers who intentionally discriminate [from avoiding] any meaningful liability." H.R. Rep. No. 41, 102nd Cong., 1st Sess., pt. 2, at 4 (1991). The Senate Reports addressed the need to make "employers liable for all losses—economic or otherwise—[that] are incurred as a consequence of prohibited discrimination." *Id.* at 5.

The legislative concern with deterrence also focused on employers, not on individual employees. The Senate Reports noted that employers must provide "punitive damages . . . in cases of intentional discrimination if the employer acted with 'malice'. . . ." *Id.* The reports also observed that employer liability "will serve as a necessary deterrent to future acts of discrimination . . ." *Id.* Even the suggested mechanisms for deterrence are restricted to mechanisms an employer might implement, not an individual. Congress hoped to "encourage employers to design and implement complaint structures [that] encourage victims to come forward by overcoming fear of retaliation and fear of loss of privacy. . . . Data suggests that employers do indeed implement measures to interrupt and prevent employment discrimination when they perceive that there is increased liability." *Id.* at 18 (statement of Dr. Klein).

Moreover, the vocal dissenters to the Amendment failed to mention individual liability in their complaints. Had they considered individual liability even a remote possibility, they would have objected.

> [T]he dissenters supplied exhaustive, thoughtful, and even caustic responses to the Amendments. On such issues as the cost of business, number of litigants, and remuneration of lawyers, [Congress] apparently thought of every conceivable negative outcome and shouted it from the rooftops . . . [H]ad they considered individual liability a conceivable outcome, they would also have considered it a negative one and denounced it in a similar fashion. Yet they never mentioned it.

*Hudson*, 837 F. Supp. at 138.

III. EXCLUSIVE EMPLOYER LIABILITY SUFFICIENTLY ACHIEVES TITLE VII'S GOALS OF COMPENSATION AND DETERRENCE.

Finally, exclusive employer liability sufficiently achieves Title VII's goals. Title VII's two main goals are "to compensate the victims of discrimination . . . and to deter discrimination in the future." *Hudson*, 873 F. Supp. at 135–36. Exclusive employer liability achieves those goals because the expansion of remedies in the 1991 Amendments ensures adequate compensation, because the expansion of remedies encourages and ensures that employers will police their workplaces and their workforces, and because individuals already face effective deterrents aside from individual liability.

The 1991 Amendments to Title VII ensure that victims of discrimination will be adequately compensated. In enacting the 1991 Amendments to Title VII, Congress expanded the scope of remedies available to victims of Title VII violations to include compensatory and punitive damages. Congress enacted this expansion out of recognition that Title VII often failed adequately to compensate victims of Title VII violations. *See* H.R. Rep., 102nd Cong., 1st Sess., pt. 1 (1991). By making employers liable for damages, Congress recognized that employers, not individuals, are best able to provide the necessary compensation.

Additionally, restricting liability to employers, as Congress intended, adequately serves the deterrent purpose of the 1991 Amendments. By imposing liability on employers, Congress ensured that employers would police their workplaces and workforces. "A company that risks liability for the discriminatory acts of its agents will police its employees and institute disciplinary measures to deter discriminatory acts." *Haltek*, 864 F. Supp. at 805–06. No employer would permit its employees to violate Title VII when the employer is liable for the Title VII violation. "An employer that has incurred civil damages because one of its employees believes he can violate Title VII with impunity will quickly correct that employee's erroneous belief." *Miller*, 991 F. 2d at 586.

Moreover, individuals face deterrents outside of Title VII that promote the Congressional goal of deterring future discrimination. For example, individuals face both professional and social sanctions in the form of demotion or firing and disapproval. They face "a loss of employment status, defense fees, and social approval." *Hudson*, 873 F. Supp. at 136. In addition, any conduct that violates Title VII also subjects an individual to civil liability for, among other things, assault, battery, and intentional infliction of emotional distress, or criminal liability for criminal sexual assault. Thus, individual liability under Title VII is unnecessary. It would be redundant as a deterrent and would unfairly expose individuals to double or triple punishment.

It may be that imposing individual liability in addition to employer liability would ensure adequate compensation and provide an added deterrent for individual behavior. However, Congress did not provide for individual liability in enacting Title VII and the 1991 Amendments to Title VII. It is not the role of the judiciary to expand the statute in pursuit of "some vague, aspirational broad intent. Congress had lofty goals but provided limited means for reaching those goals. Individual liability was not one of them." *Hudson*, 873 F. Supp. at 136.

For the foregoing reasons, Defendant, Mr. Crane, respectfully requests that this Court grant Defendant's motion to dismiss Plaintiff's complaint for failure to state a claim upon which relief can be granted.

## *Sample Brief B:*
## *Fifth Amendment Brief*

<u>DEFENDANT'S MEMORANDUM IN SUPPORT OF MOTION TO
QUASH THE SUBPOENA OF DEFENDANT'S DIARY</u>

<u>INTRODUCTION</u>

Defendant, Mr. Browne, seeks to quash the government's subpoena of the personal contents of his diary because its contents are protected by the Fifth Amendment to the United States Constitution. The Supreme Court has long held that the Fifth Amendment protects personal papers as well as oral testimony. *Boyd v. United States*, 116 U.S. 616 (1886). Although business documents do not fall within the privilege, the Supreme Court has carefully preserved *Boyd*'s protection of private, personal papers. *United States v. Doe*, 465 U.S. 605 (1984); *Fisher v. United States*, 425 U.S. 391 (1976). Because the contents of Mr. Browne's diary are private, personal papers subject to the protection of the Fifth Amendment, the Government can not subpoena their disclosure.

<u>STATEMENT OF FACTS</u>

After charging Defendant with unlawful distribution of marijuana in violation of 21 U.S.C. § 841 (1994), the government served Mr. Browne with a subpoena requesting that he produce certain documents, including his personal diary. (Subpoena of 12/1/94.) Mr. Browne objects on the grounds that the Fifth Amendment protects his diary from compelled disclosure.

Mr. Browne's diary contains his most private daily thoughts and reflections on the vicissitudes of life. Mr. Browne's diary is replete with his personal reflections about his romantic life, chronicling the highs and lows of the intimate relationship he has had with his girlfriend of four years. (*See, e.g.*, Diary at 15.) Following the death of his mother, Mr. Browne used his diary as an outlet to express his innermost feelings of grief and regrets. (Diary at 7, 21.) Mr. Browne poignantly notes that: "I am consumed with grief. I never had the chance to say good-bye. I never had the chance to say I was sorry—for not being the son she wanted me to be, and for a million other things." (Diary at 21.) Mr. Browne also voiced in his diary his feelings about the progress of his psychotherapy, lamenting: "Will this therapy ever end? Sometimes it all seems too hopeless. Every time we peel off a layer of pain, a deeper layer is revealed." (Diary at 4.) Although the diary contained incriminating statements regarding use of a boat for illegal drug distribution, Mr. Browne also used his diary as an outlet to express his personal despair over his drug addiction. (Diary at 9, 27.) Finally, Mr. Browne expressed private thoughts in his diary that he was not ready to share "with anyone, including Ms. Jones," his psycho-therapist. (Diary at 5.)

## ARGUMENT

I.   THE FIFTH AMENDMENT'S PRIVILEGE AGAINST COMPULSORY SELF-INCRIMINATION PROTECTS PERSONAL PAPERS.

The Fifth Amendment grants a privilege against self-incrimination, stating that: "No person . . . shall be compelled in any criminal case to be a witness against himself. . . ." U.S. Const. amend. V. This privilege against compulsory self-incrimination derives from the Fifth Amendment's "'respect [for] a private inner sanctum of individual feeling and thought' . . . that necessarily includes an individual's papers." *Bellis v. United States*, 417 U.S. 85, 91 (1974) (quoting *Murphy v. Waterfront Comm'n of Harbor*, 378 U.S. 52, 55 (1964)). Accordingly, the Supreme Court has long held that the privilege protects personal papers as well as oral testimony. *Boyd v. United States*, 116 U.S. 616 (1886). Although business documents do not fall within that "private inner sanctum," *see United States v. Doe*, 465 U.S. 605 (1984); *Fisher v. United States*, 425 U.S. 391 (1976), the Supreme Court has carefully preserved *Boyd*'s protection of personal papers. Moreover, the courts in this district have recognized that *Boyd* continues to protect personal papers. *See In re Grand Jury Subpoena*, 144 F.R.D. 357 (D. Minn. 1992), *rev'd on other grounds sub nom., United States v. Spano*, 21 F.3d 326 (8th Cir. 1994).

The privilege against compulsory self-incrimination derives from the Fifth Amendment's "'respect [for] a private inner sanctum of individual feeling and thought' . . . that necessarily includes an individual's papers." *Bellis*, 417 U.S. at 91. In particular, it recognizes that "compelling self-accusation . . . would be both cruel and unjust." *Boyd*, 116 U.S. at 629. While the privilege may at times protect the guilty, the Supreme Court has admonished that "the evils of compelling self-disclosure transcends any difficulties . . . in the detection and prosecution of crime." *United States v. White*, 322 U.S. 694, 698 (1944). These evils include subjecting people to "iniquitous methods of prosecution," *id.*, betraying "the inviolability of the human personality," risking encroachment on the basic liberties of all citizens, and undermining the adversarial system. *Murphy*, 378 U.S. at 55. Accordingly, the Fifth Amendment proscribes invasion into "the privacies of life." *Boyd*, 116 U.S. at 630.

Personal papers are part of "the privacies of life." Failure to protect personal papers would thwart their development, thus inhibiting creativity and suppressing expression. Moreover, failure to protect personal documents would adversely affect the innocent as well as the guilty. *Boyd*, 116 U.S. at 629. Finally, failing to protect personal documents would create an artificial distinction between an individual's oral testimony and writings, even if the two are substantively identical. The Fifth Amendment does not contemplate such an anomalous result.

Accordingly, the Supreme Court has long held that the Fifth Amendment protects personal papers as well as oral testimony. *Boyd*, 116 U.S. at 633. In *Boyd*, the Court equated seizing a person's documents as evidence against him with compelling that person to be a witness against himself: "And we have been unable to perceive that the seizure of a man's private books and papers to be used in evidence against him is substantially different from compelling him to be a witness against himself." *Id.* Additionally, the Court admonished that "any forcible and compulsory extortion of a man's own testimony or of his private papers . . . is within the condemnation of [the Fifth Amendment]," *id.* at 630, and "contrary to the principals of a free government." *Id.* at 635–36.

Since *Boyd*, the Supreme Court has reiterated *Boyd's* protection of personal papers. For example, in *Bellis*, the Supreme Court acknowledged that "[i]t has long been established . . . that the Fifth Amendment . . . protects an individual from compelled production of his personal papers." 417 U.S. at 87. And, in *White*, the Supreme Court observed that it is the Fifth Amendment's "historic function [to protect an individual] from compulsory incrimination through his own testimony or personal records." 322 U.S. at 701. In each of these cases, the Supreme Court could not have been clearer; the Fifth Amendment protects individuals from the compelled production of their personal papers.

Although the Supreme Court recently concluded that *Boyd* does not protect *business* documents, it has preserved *Boyd's* protection of personal papers. *See Doe*, 465 U.S. at 610; *Fisher*, 425 U.S. at 403. In *Fisher*, the Court held that the Fifth Amendment does not protect the contents of tax records prepared by the defendant's accountant. *Id.* at 393. The Court based this holding on the fact that business documents do not implicate the privacy interests of personal papers: "special problems of privacy [that] might be presented by subpoena of a personal diary are not involved here." *Id.* at 407 n.7. Additionally, the Court preserved *Boyd's* protection of personal papers by emphasizing that "[w]hether the Fifth Amendment would shield the taxpayer from producing his own tax records . . . is a question not involved here; for the papers demanded here are not his 'private papers.'" *Id.* at 414.

Similarly, *Doe* preserved *Boyd's* protection of personal papers. In *Doe*, the Court held that the Fifth Amendment did not protect the contents of business records in the possession of the owner of a sole proprietorship. *Doe*, 465 U.S.

at 617. However, the *Doe* Court preserved *Boyd*'s protection of personal papers by premising its holding on the corporate nature of the documents. The Court carefully noted that "each of the documents sought here pertained to [the defendant's] business." *Id.* at 610 n.7.

Justice O'Connor's solitary *Doe* concurrence that "the Fifth Amendment provides absolutely no protection for the contents of private papers of any kind," *id.* at 618 (O'Connor, J., concurring), in no way undermines *Doe*'s preservation of *Boyd*'s protection of personal papers. First, no other Justice agreed with her broad statement; thus, it is merely the dicta of a solitary justice. Second, in a powerful partial concurrence, Justice Marshall, joined by Justice Brennan, chided Justice O'Connor and expressly reaffirmed *Boyd*'s protection for personal papers:

> This case presented nothing remotely close to the question that Justice O'Connor eagerly poses and answers. . . . Were it true that the Court's opinion stands for [that] proposition . . . I would assuredly dissent.

*Id.* at 618–19 (Marshall, J., concurring in part and dissenting in part).[1]

Finally, although the Eighth Circuit has not had occasion to address the issue, the courts in this district recognize that *Boyd* continues to protect personal papers. In 1992, the district court could not have been clearer: "An individual may refuse to comply with a subpoena duces tecum seeking personal records by asserting the Fifth Amendment's privilege." *In re Grand Jury Subpoena*, 144 F.R.D. 357, 361 (D. Minn. 1992). Therefore, this Court should follow the Supreme Court and the courts in this district in recognizing that *Boyd* continues to protect personal papers.

II.   DEFENDANT'S DIARY IS A PERSONAL PAPER ENTITLED TO FIFTH AMENDMENT PROTECTION FROM COMPELLED DISCLOSURE.

Mr. Browne's diary is the quintessential personal paper entitled to Fifth Amendment protection. Privileged personal papers are those papers in which the defendant has a legitimate expectation of privacy. *Bellis*, 417 U.S. at 87–88. Because of the deeply personal and private nature of diaries, diaries are "a fortiori" the kind of intimate personal recordings that are protected under the Fifth Amendment. *Fisher*, 425 U.S. at 426 (Brennan, J., concurring). More-

---

[1] The Court in *Baltimore Dep't of Social Servs. v. Bouknight*, 493 U.S. 549 (1990), also preserved *Boyd*'s protection of personal papers. *Bouknight* did not involve the production of documents of any sort, but instead the production of a child in a noncriminal case. Because *Bouknight* did not involve the privacy interests present in *Boyd*, *Bouknight* is inapt.

over, when an individual records his private thoughts and affairs in a diary, it is protected from disclosure by the Fifth Amendment, even if the diary also contains sporadic references to business matters. A personal paper becomes a business record that is not entitled to Fifth Amendment protection only if it is the type of document normally used to record business transactions, and the actual entries in the document list business transactions. *United States v. Mason*, 869 F.2d 414, 416 (8th Cir. 1989). Here, Mr. Browne's diary recorded his most intimate and private thoughts and reflections on life. Mr. Browne legitimately expected that these intimate recordings would remain private. Therefore, the diary is protected from compelled disclosure by the Fifth Amendment to the United States Constitution.

As the Eighth Circuit recognized in *Mason*, disclosure of certain intimate papers might "break the heart of our sense of privacy." *Mason*, 869 F.2d at 416. The compelled disclosure of documents used to record and list business transactions are not such intimate documents. In *Mason*, the defendants recorded in day-timers the detailed daily business activities of their marijuana operation. The defendants recorded in the day-timers such items as the "rate of growth of the marijuana plants, the expected costs of completing the project, the expenses incurred, and the formula by which profits would be distributed." *Id.* The Eighth Circuit appropriately held that these business journals were more like the business records in *Doe* than personal diaries. A day-timer is the type of document normally used to record business transactions. Moreover, the daily entries recorded actual business transactions. *Id.*

In contrast to the day-timers in *Mason*, a personal diary is not the type of document used to record business transactions but a deeply personal record of one's most intimate reflections. Nor does Mr. Browne use his diary for the purpose of recording business transactions. Instead, Mr. Browne's diary is replete with his personal reflections regarding his relationship with his girlfriend and the joys and the sorrows of their relationship (*see, e.g.*, Diary at 15), his relationship with his mother and his attempts to deal with her death (*see, e.g.*, Diary at 7, 21), the slow progress of his psychotherapy (*see, e.g.*, Diary at 27), and anxiety about his career. (*See, e.g.*, Diary at 15.) Additionally, throughout his diary, Mr. Browne refers to feelings of helplessness because of his addiction and to his deep desire for a sense of control over the problem. (*See, e.g.*, Diary at 7, 21, and 28.) Finally, Mr. Browne laments that his innermost feelings are so private that he can not "share" his life with anyone, including his psychotherapist.

Mr. Browne's sporadic, incriminating references to his potential involvement in drug distribution do not rise to the level of "listing business transactions." In contrast to the day-timers in *Mason*, in which the defendants routinely recorded such business details as profits and expenses, Mr. Browne's incriminating statements lack the type of detail and frequency of detail recorded in business journals. Instead, Mr. Browne's sporadic references to involvement in drug distribution include thoughts that he was "scared" when he took the boat, (Diary at 9) and his fear that his girlfriend will discover his activities (Diary at 14). Such entries do not remotely resemble the day-to-day records of the operations and financial condition of a "sophisticated marijuana growing facility," as did the day-timers in *Mason*.

## CONCLUSION

A diary is the quintessential personal paper that strikes at the very heart of our sense of privacy. Because Mr. Browne uses his diary for the purpose of recording his most intimate thoughts and feelings, it is protected from compelled disclosure by the Fifth Amendment. Therefore, Defendant respectfully requests that this Court enter an order quashing the government's subpoena of Mr. Browne's personal diary.

**Appendix D**

*Sample Appellate Court Brief*
*Federal Wiretap Problem*

UNITED STATES COURT OF APPEALS
FOR THE TWELFTH CIRCUIT[1]

---

No. 99-769

---

UNITED STATES OF AMERICA,

Plaintiff-Appellee,

v.

JAMES HART,

Defendant-Appellant.

BRIEF FOR APPELLANT

---

[1] This is a mythical circuit.

## TABLE OF CONTENTS

## TABLE OF AUTHORITIES

### UNITED STATES SUPREME COURT CASES

### UNITED STATES COURT OF APPEALS CASES

### STATUTES

### LEGISLATIVE HISTORY

## STATEMENT OF JURISDICTION

This Court has jurisdiction over this appeal pursuant to 28 U.S.C. § 1291 (1993).

## STATEMENT OF THE ISSUES

I.   Did the District Court err in finding that, as part of the government's "satisfactory explanation" for its two-month delay in obtaining a judicial seal of wiretap evidence, the government need not prove that its pre-sealing procedures protected the tapes from any possibility of tampering, thereby affording the same level of protection as an immediate judicial seal would have provided?

II.  Did the District Court err in finding that the government provided a "satisfactory explanation" for its sealing delay when the government lost the tapes for two months, only to find the tapes in an open box in an office supply room, and the government can neither account for the tapes' whereabouts for the two month period in which they were missing or explain why the box of tapes had been opened?

## STATUTE INVOLVED

18 U.S.C. § 2518 (8)(a) (2000) provides as follows:

(8) (a) The contents of any wire, oral, or electronic communication intercepted by any means authorized by this chapter shall, if possible, be recorded on tape or wire or other comparable device. The recording of the contents of any wire, oral, or electronic communication under this subsection shall be done in such way as will protect the recording from editing or other alterations. Immediately upon the expiration of the period of the order, or extensions thereof, such recordings shall be made available to the judge issuing such order and sealed under his directions. Custody of the recordings shall be wherever the judge orders. They shall not be destroyed except upon an order of the issuing or denying judge and in any event shall be kept for ten years. Duplicate recordings may be made for use or disclosure pursuant to the provisions of subsections (1) and (2) of section 2517 of this chapter for investigations. The presence of the seal provided for by this subsection, or a satisfactory explanation for the absence thereof, shall be a prerequisite for the use or disclosure of the contents of any wire, oral, or electronic

communication or evidence derived therefrom under subsection (3) of section 2517.

## PRELIMINARY STATEMENT

The defendant, Mr. James Hart, appeals from a conviction under 18 U.S.C. § 371 (2000). Before trial, Mr. Hart moved to suppress the government's sole evidence against him on the ground that the government failed to comply with the mandatory requirements of the federal wiretap statute. 18 U.S.C. § 2518 (8)(a) (2000). The government had failed to obtain an immediate judicial seal of the wiretap evidence. Mr. Hart alleged that the government failed to provide a "satisfactory explanation" for its sealing delay, as required by 18 U.S.C. § 2518 (8)(a) (2000). The District Court denied that motion and later convicted Mr. Hart of violating 18 U.S.C. § 371 (2000). Mr. Hart appeals the lower court's denial of his motion to suppress the wiretap evidence and the conviction based on that evidence. The opinion of the District Court is unreported and appears in the Transcript of Record (R. 22–26).

## STATEMENT OF THE CASE

Defendant, Mr. James Hart, is an accountant for many small businesses, including Oak Hill Dry Cleaning. (R. at 5.) Oak Hill Dry Cleaning is owned by individuals the government believes to be members of the Desperado crime syndicate. On August 11, 2000, the lower court granted authorization to intercept Mr. Hart's home telephone for a period not to exceed thirty (30) days.

On September 6th and 7th, the government obtained the tapes it later used as the sole evidence of Mr. Hart's culpability. (R. at 9.) On September 7, 2000, Agent T. Friday removed the tapes from the surveillance van parked near Mr. Hart's home and took them to the investigating bureau's office. (R. at 10.) Although Agent Friday was aware that the Bureau was moving offices the next day, she dropped the tapes in a plain cardboard box identical to the thousands of cardboard boxes used for the move. (R. at 10.) Agent Friday also testified that she placed a label on the box indicating that the box was to be transported to the courthouse. (R. at 10.) In contrast, the building janitor testified that no label appeared on the box of tapes. (R. at 14.) The government can not explain this factual discrepancy. (R. at 15.) Finally, although Agent Friday testified that she sealed the box of tapes (R. at 10.), the building janitor testified that the box of tapes "was open. You could look right in and see what was inside." (R. at 14.)

For more than a month after the Bureau moved offices, Agent Friday never telephoned or appeared at the courthouse to ensure the tapes arrived for sealing. (R. at 11.) Agent Friday never asked the court clerk to confirm whether a judge had sealed the tapes. (R. at 11.) And, despite the fact that Agent Friday had no responsibilities other than this case during this entire time period, Agent Friday did not make a single attempt to locate her only evidence in this case. (R. at 12.)

It was not until October 10, 2000 that Agent Friday finally called the courthouse to inquire whether the tapes had been sealed. (R. at 12.) It was not until then that Agent Friday began searching for the missing tapes. Although Agent Friday testified that she undertook an intensive search of the office building and personally called the movers (R. at 12), nearly a month elapsed before Agent Friday was able to locate the tapes. It was not until November 8, 2000, that Agent Friday finally stumbled upon the missing tapes while looking for party decorations. (R. at 13.) The government speculates that the tapes sat exposed in an open box in the unlocked office supply room for over two months. (R. at 13.) The exposed tapes sat in the busy supply room amidst note pads, pencils, office supplies and party decorations, open to the 5,000 occupants of the building who frequent the room for coffee and office supplies. (R. at 14.)

## SUMMARY OF ARGUMENT

The evidence obtained by the government from a wiretap on Mr. Hart's home telephone is inadmissible at trial because the government failed to comply with the requirements of the wiretap statute. The District Court therefore erred in denying Mr. Hart's motion to suppress the wiretap evidence. The wiretap statute requires the government to safeguard the tapes by immediately obtaining a judicial seal or by providing a "satisfactory explanation" for its failure to do so. 18 U.S.C. § 2518 (8)(a) (2000). In this case, the government failed to comply with its statutory obligation. After intercepting private telephone conversations from Mr. Hart's home telephone, the government failed to surrender the tapes immediately to a judge, who could have protected the tapes' integrity with a judicial seal. The government also failed to provide a "satisfactory explanation" for its failure to seek immediate judicial protection.

A "satisfactory explanation" requires that the government satisfy two standards. First, a "satisfactory explanation" requires the government to prove that its pre-sealing procedures protected the tapes from any possibility of tampering. Congress enacted the immediate sealing requirement as an external safeguard to ensure that the integrity of wiretap tapes would remain inviolate.

Therefore, when the government fails to protect the integrity of the tapes by immediately obtaining the protection of a judicial seal, its alternative explanation must ensure a similar level of protection. With today's modern technology, tapes can easily be altered without detection by even skilled experts. Thus, requiring the government to prove that its pre-sealing procedures protected the tapes from any possibility of tampering is the only effective means of protecting the integrity of wiretap evidence. Here, the government wholly failed to provide any level of protection to its sensitive evidence. Instead, the wiretap tapes sat exposed in an open box in a busy, unlocked storage room for over two months. The box sat exposed, available to any one of the 5,000 occupants of the building, or any visitor to the storage room, who might be tempted to tamper with the tapes.

Second, a "satisfactory explanation" requires that the government act with reasonable diligence to minimize the sealing delay. Again, the government's conduct falls far short of this standard. The sealing delay was caused by a mistake, a mistake that was not only foreseeable but easily preventable. Although the government knew that its bureau offices would be moving the following day, Agent Friday failed to take any precautions to ensure that the tapes would be safely delivered to the courthouse for sealing. Instead, she dropped the tapes into a box identical to the thousands of moving boxes used to move office files and supplies. To compound that initial carelessness, Agent Friday delayed over a month before she placed a single telephone call to ensure that the tapes had arrived at the courthouse for sealing. Upon finding the tapes were missing, it took Agent Friday almost another full month to locate the tapes, despite the fact that she ultimately found them in an open box in an office supply room. The government's lengthy delay in obtaining the protection of a judicial seal violates the mandatory provisions of Title III, 18 U.S.C. § 2518(8)(a).

## ARGUMENT

I.    AS PART OF ITS "SATISFACTORY EXPLANATION" THE GOVERNMENT MUST PROVE THAT ITS PRE-SEALING PROCEDURES PROTECTED THE WIRETAP TAPES FROM ANY POSSIBILITY OF TAMPERING.

Title III states in no uncertain terms: "The presence of the seal as provided for by this subsection [an immediate seal], or a satisfactory explanation for the absence thereof, shall be a *prerequisite* for the use or disclosure" of the tapes. 18 U.S.C. § 2518(8)(a) (2000) (emphasis added). In this issue of first impression, the plain language of Title III requires that the government comply with one of two procedures as a "prerequisite" to introducing wiretap tapes into evidence during trial. Concerned with the abuse of electronic surveillance techniques, Congress enacted the first prerequisite, the immediate sealing requirement, as an external safeguard to ensure that the integrity of wiretap tapes would remain inviolate. When the government fails to protect the integrity of the tapes by immediately obtaining a judicial seal, the government's alternative satisfactory explanation must ensure a similar level of protection. Whether the government satisfies the legislative requirement of obtaining an immediate seal, or takes the scenic route to obtain the seal, the government must prove that its *procedures* protected the integrity of the tapes. Without such a safeguard, the statutory protective device of immediate judicial supervision would be rendered meaningless. *United States v. Johnson*, 696 F.2d 115 (D.C. Cir. 1981). Accordingly, the district court erred in failing to require the government to prove that its pre-sealing procedures protected the tapes from any possibility of tampering. As a pure question of law, this issue is subject to de novo review.

When Congress enacted Title III, it sought to ensure that the purity of the gathered evidence would remain unsullied. This purpose is clearly reflected in the statutory language itself. Section (8)(a) provides that interceptions of conversations must be accomplished "in such way as will protect the recording from editing or other alterations." 18 U.S.C. § 2518(8)(a). The Congressional intent expressed in that language could not be clearer. Congress enacted Title III to protect the integrity of evidence that might be used as evidence in a criminal trial. *See also United States v. Sklaroff*, 506 F.2d 837, 840 (5th Cir. 1975) (the purpose of § 2518(8)(a) "is to safeguard the recordings from editing or alteration").

The legislative history also reflects this clear and unequivocal Congressional purpose. "Preservation of the integrity of tape recordings was unquestionably a fundamental concern of the drafters of Title III." *United States v. Gigante*, 538 F.2d 502, 505 (2d Cir. 1976). When Congress enacted Title III's detailed restrictions on electronic surveillance, it "intended to ensure 'careful judicial scrutiny throughout' the process of intercepting and utilization of such evidence." *Gigante*, 538 F.2d at 505 (quoting *United States v. Marion*, 535 F.2d 697, 698 (2d Cir. 1976)). The Senate Reports noted that, because of the "widespread use and abuse of electronic surveillance techniques," Congress enacted this statute to "safeguard the identity, physical integrity, and contents of the recordings to assure their admissibility in evidence." S. Rep. No. 1097, 90th Cong., 2d Sess. 2193 (1968), *reprinted in* 1968 U.S.Code Cong. & Admin. News 2193.

Maintenance of the integrity of such evidence is an integral part of the Congressional plan to "limit the use of intercept procedures to those situations clearly calling for the employment of this extraordinary investigative device." *United States v. Giordano*, 416 U.S. 505, 527 (1974). Thus, § 2518 plays a "central role in the statutory scheme." *Giordano*, 416 U.S. at 528. *See also, United States v. Chavez*, 416 U.S. 562 (1974); *United States v. Diana*, 605 F.2d 1307, 1312 (4th Cir. 1979) (Section 2518 "is a central or functional safeguard in Title III's scheme to prevent abuses. . . .'") (quoting *United States v. Chun*, 503 F.2d 533, 542 (9th Cir.1974)). "Clearly all of the carefully planned strictures on the conduct of electronic surveillance, e. g., the "minimization" requirement of § 2518(5), would be unavailing if no reliable records existed of the conversations which were, in fact, overheard." *Gigante*, 538 F.2d at 505.

By requiring the immediate sealing of wiretap evidence, Congress sought to protect the purity of that evidence. After sealing, the records become "confidential court records," and can not be unsealed without a court order. S.Rep. 1097, 90th Cong., 2d Sess. 2193 (1968), *reprinted in* 1968 U.S. Code Cong. & Ad. News 2193. The statutory requirement of judicial supervision therefore creates a procedural assumption of integrity because the judicial seal ensures the tapes were handled in a manner that precludes any possibility of tampering. *United States v. Johnson*, 696 F.2d 115, 123 (D.C. Cir. 1981). Thus, the immediate sealing requirement serves as an external, procedural safeguard against tampering.

Only procedural safeguards can ensure that the integrity of sensitive wiretap evidence remains inviolate. Procedural safeguards are necessary because tape-recorded evidence is highly vulnerable to tampering and is cost-prohibitive to prove. In fact, with modern technology, it is often impossible to detect. *Johnson*, 696 F.2d at 124.

> Tapes that are made for use in criminal investigations can be falsified, even by relatively unskilled persons, in ways that are superficially convincing. . . . Such alterations, moreover, are likely to go undetected because a highly skilled forensic examiner who is an expert in the fields of tape recording, signal analysis, and speech communication, using the best available analysis equipment, can take weeks and even months to establish with reasonable certainty the fact that a tape has been falsified. The advantage, in terms of effort, time and cost is clearly with the forger.

*Id.*

Congress carefully incorporated external safeguards within the statute to avoid the costly, time-consuming and inconclusive expert inquiries that inevitably result from fact-finding expeditions. *Id.* By proving it held the tapes in a manner that ensures their integrity remained inviolate, the government's satisfactory explanation not only affords the level of protection of an immediate seal but avoids the problems Congress sought to avoid.

Finally, fairness mandates that the government bear this burden. "Inasmuch as a need for a 'satisfactory explanation' only arises when those in charge of the wiretap operation fail to do their homework and to present the tapes for immediate sealing, any doubts about the integrity of the evidence should be laid at law enforcement's doorstep." *United States v. Mora*, 821 F.2d 860, 868 (1ˢᵗ Cir. 1987). Therefore, the District Court committed reversible error by declining to compel the government to prove that its procedures safeguarded its evidence from any possibility of tampering.

II.  THE GOVERNMENT FAILED TO PROVIDE A "SATISFACTORY EXPLAN-ATION" FOR ITS TWO-MONTH DELAY IN SEALING THE WIRETAP TAPES.

The government has failed to provide the statutorily-mandated "satisfactory explanation" in this case. A satisfactory explanation requires both that the government's pre-filing procedures ensured the tapes' integrity, *United States v. Johnson*, 696 F.2d 115 (D.C. Cir. 1976), and that it acted with reasonable diligence to obtain the required judicial safeguard. *United States v. Gigante*, 538 F.2d 502, 505 (2d Cir. 1976). These standards are necessary to implement the procedural safeguards reflected in § 2518(8)(a). As the United States Supreme Court cautioned, "Congress intended to require suppression where there is failure to satisfy any of those statutory requirements that directly and substantially implement the congressional intention to limit the use of intercept procedures. . . ."*United States v. Giordano*, 416 U.S. 505, 527 (1974). Here, the government has not satisfied either prerequisite of a "satisfactory explanation." Therefore, the district court erred in refusing to suppress the wiretap evidence.

A.  *The Government Failed to Store the Tapes in a Manner That Protected Them From Any Possibility of Tampering.*

When the government fails to obtain an immediate judicial seal, it must store the tapes in a manner that ensures their integrity. Mere governmental knowledge of the tapes' whereabouts does not even begin to rise to the level of protection required. Instead, the government ensures the tapes' integrity by placing its *own* physical seal on the tapes, *United States v. Diana*, 605 F.2d 1307 (4th Cir. 1979), and by limiting access to the tapes to authorized personnel, either by appointing a custodian to guard the tapes, and/or by placing the tapes in a limited access vault. *United States v. Mora*, 821 F.2d 860, 868 (1st Cir. 1987). Here, the government failed to take any such precautions to secure the tapes' integrity. In fact, the government not only has no idea where the tapes were stored during the two-month period in which they were lost, but has no explanation for why the box was found open and without an identifying seal. The government's failure to secure the tapes' integrity falls far short of the required satisfactory explanation.

Only by instituting procedures that preclude any possibility the tapes might be compromised can the government satisfactorily explain its sealing delay. For example, the government can ensure the integrity of tapes by placing its own seal on the tapes. *United States v. Diana*, 605 F.2d 1307 (4th Cir. 1979). A physical seal, if broken, provides a visual warning that someone has attempted to tamper with the evidence. In *Diana*, the government initialed and affixed seals to each of the envelopes containing wiretap evidence. An FBI agent ensured that each of the envelopes had a piece of Scotch tape over at least one of his initials placed on the back of the envelope. "The purpose of this procedure was that if anyone would attempt to get inside the envelope, not only would they tear the envelope . . . they [would] break the seal where my initials were. . . . I felt there was [no] way anyone could break that seal without me seeing it. . . ." *Id.* at 1315–16. Under these facts, the court held that the government's precautions were "satisfactory." *Id.* at 1316. The court reasoned that the government's precautions ensured that the tapes' integrity remained inviolate. Even with these procedures, the court admonished the government "to be more careful in the future," noting that its "opinion should not be read as a license to disregard the sealing requirement." *Id.*

The government can adequately safeguard the integrity of wiretap tapes by instituting strict security procedures, such as guarding the tapes or locking them within a locked vault. In *Mora*, the government designated a Massachusetts State Policeman as custodian of the tapes. The trooper placed the tapes in a cardboard box, closed the box, and signed it. He then sealed the box within a plastic bag. The trooper originally kept the bag at a listening post, which was staffed and guarded twenty-four hours a day. After two weeks, he removed the tapes and placed them in a locked vault that was accessible only to limited, authorized personnel. The vault was equipped with an alarm system. 821 F.2d at 862. Under these facts, the court could not find "any scintilla of evidence" that the tapes could have been tampered with, even after "scour[ing] the record, searching in vain for any intimation that the content of the tapes was compromised." *Id.* at 869. *See also United States v. Johnson*, 696 F.2d 115 (D.C. Cir. 1976) (tapes stored in a locked vault with access limited to authorized personnel).

In stark contrast to the government's strict security measures in *Diana*, *Mora*, and *Johnson*, the government in the present case took absolutely no precautions to secure the tapes in a manner that ensured their integrity would remain inviolate. Unlike the government precautions in *Diana*, the government not only failed to secure the individual tapes in protective envelopes, but Agent Friday may have failed to take even the most elementary precaution of sealing the box itself so that casual observers could not gain access to this sensitive evidence. Although Agent Friday testified that she sealed the box (R. at 10.), the building janitor testified the box "was open. You could look right in and see what was inside." (R. at 14.) The government has not explained this factual discrepancy. If indeed Agent Friday never sealed the box itself, then the box containing the government's sensitive evidence was left open to public view for a period of two months. The entire group of tapes purportedly sat, exposed, in an open box in an unlocked storage room amidst party decorations and office supplies. The tapes sat in that open box for over two months. In vivid contrast to the locked vaults with limited access in *Mora* and *Johnson*, the storage room was unlocked and easily accessible to the 5,000 occupants of the building who had reason to frequent this room for coffee, office supplies, and party decorations.

If, however, Agent Friday did seal and label the box, as she testified, then the fact that it was later found, open and without a label, raises the troubling possibility that the security of the tapes was in fact compromised. In *Diana*, *Mora*, and *Johnson*, because of the government's strict security procedures, after "scouring" the record, the courts found that there was no intimation or "scintilla of evidence" that the tapes could possibly have been compromised. In glaring contrast, the government in the present case has not and cannot explain why the box of tapes was later found open and without a label. This factual discrepancy raises the ominous possibility that an unidentified individual opened the box and tampered with the tapes. In fact, any one of the 5,000 occupants of the building, or any visitor to the office supply room, could have removed the tapes from their box and tampered with them. Having failed to obtain an immediate judicial seal, the external safeguard against tampering, the government wholly failed to ensure that the tapes' integrity remained inviolate during its two month delay. The government's total failure to explain the tapes' whereabouts during its two month delay does not rise to the level of a "satisfactory explanation." Accordingly, the district court erred in refusing to suppress the tapes.

### B.    *The Government Failed to Act With Reasonable Diligence.*

Even when the government stores tapes in a manner that protects their integrity, its explanation is not "satisfactory" unless it acts with reasonable diligence to obtain a judicial seal. *United States v. Vazquez*, 605 F.2d 1269 (2d Cir. 1979). Governmental mistake, even innocent mistake, does not constitute reasonable diligence. *United States v. Gigante*, 538 F.2d 502, 505 (2d Cir. 1976). The government acts with reasonable diligence only when the delay is caused by legitimate law enforcement purposes and the government diligently acts to minimize the delay in obtaining the judicial seal. Here, the delay was caused by no legitimate law enforcement purpose. Moreover, the government's initial mistake in losing the tapes in the first place is exacerbated by its failure to minimize the delay. It was the government's own inattention and neglect that caused the two-month sealing delay. The government's carelessness and neglect does not rise to the level of reasonable diligence.

Inattention to governmental files does not constitute reasonable diligence. In *Gigante*, the government's only explanation for its delay in obtaining a judicial seal was that the agent in charge of the files left the government's employ. The new agent was unaware the tapes had not received a judicial seal until one year later. 538 F.2d at 504. Even though the tapes had been stored in a locked cabinet under agency seal prior to receiving judicial attention, the court held that the government failed to provide a satisfactory explanation for its sealing delay. *Id.* at 505.

The court reasoned that the government's "explanation" for its mistake was "no explanation whatsoever." *Id.* at 504. Mere mistake does not constitute reasonable diligence, even with a change in personnel. In so holding, the court emphasized the importance of the immediate sealing requirement as "an integral part of this statutory scheme." *Id.* at 505. The court cautioned that "[m]aintenance of the integrity of such evidence is part and parcel of the Congressional plan to `limit the use of intercept procedures to those situations clearly calling for the employment of this extraordinary investigative device.'" *Id.* (citing *United States v. Giordano*, 416 U.S. 505, 527 (1974)).

A government's explanation is "satisfactory" only when the delay is caused by legitimate law enforcement purposes and the government diligently acts to minimize the sealing delay. For example, in *Vazquez*, the government's delay in obtaining a judicial seal was caused by its difficulty in transcribing the tapes. Most of the conversations on the 200 tapes were in Spanish, requiring translation. Even with the limited equipment, a limited number of Spanish-speaking agents, and a lack of sufficient personnel to handle the scope of the investigation, the government nevertheless worked to minimize the sealing delay. Working around the clock, the government submitted the tapes for sealing after a delay of only one to two weeks. 605 F.2d at 1274. The court accepted the government's explanation as "satisfactory," noting the government's legitimate law enforcement purposes and its diligence in attempting to produce the tapes as quickly as possible. *Id.* at 1279. The court emphasized that government personnel worked diligently *around the clock* to comply with the statute (as well as using strict security measures to ensure their integrity). Even then, the court cautioned the government about its one to two week delays:

> However, in law as in life, today's satisfactory explanation may very well be tomorrow's lame excuse. As the federal and state case law in this area grows, the failure to foresee and where possible, prevent sealing delays becomes less justifiable, as law enforcement officials must be expected to learn from their own experiences and those of others. . . . It is our role to exclude from evidence tapes not sealed in conformance with the law, and we are aware that by faithfully performing this statutory duty we encourage law enforcement officers to perform their duties in an equally rigorous manner.

*Id.* at 1280.

Tomorrow has arrived. And the government's "lame excuse" does not even approach the level of rigor and diligence required by the statute. In vivid contrast to the government's one- to two-week delay in *Vazquez* caused by a legitimate law enforcement purpose, the government's only explanation for its two-*month* delay in the present case is that it made a "mistake" and lost the box of tapes in the confusion of an office move. As the *Gigante* court aptly noted, the government's mistake is "no excuse whatsoever." In fact, the government's lack of diligence far exceeds the level of carelessness in *Gigante*. Unlike the agent in *Gigante*, who left the government's employ, Agent Friday assumed full responsibility for the government's evidence from the time the government obtained the tapes to the time she finally stumbled upon them. In fact, this case was Agent Friday's *only* responsibility during that time period.

Agent Friday failed to act with reasonable diligence in losing the tapes in the first place. Agent Friday was well aware that the 5,000 occupants of the building were moving the next day. However, she failed to take the extra precautions required in anticipation of such a move. Notably, Agent Friday failed to place the tapes in a secured, locked, and labeled file cabinet that would survive the move to the new building. Nor did she appoint a custodian to personally transport this sensitive evidence to the courthouse. Instead, she dropped the tapes in a box identical to the thousands of boxes used to move office supplies. And, although Agent Friday testified that she sealed the box (R. at 10.), the box was open when discovered two months later. If the box of tapes was not later opened by an unknown individual, then Agent Friday failed to take even the most elementary precaution of sealing the box itself so that tapes could not be inadvertently tossed out of the box during the chaos of the move (or intentionally removed by any one of thousands of persons who had access to the open box). Finally, if the label Agent Friday testified that she placed on the box was not somehow removed from the box, the only alternative explanation for its absence is that Agent Friday never labeled the box in the first place. Any such failure to label the box would only exacerbate her lack of diligence in tossing the tapes into an open box identical to thousands of moving boxes.

Agent Friday also failed to act with diligence in locating the lost tapes. Despite her knowledge of the office move, Agent Friday waited a full month before taking even the elementary precaution of placing a telephone call to ensure that the government's critical evidence arrived at the courthouse. Not until October 10, 2000, did Agent Friday finally call the courthouse to inquire whether the tapes had been sealed. It was not until after that telephone call that Agent Friday begin searching for the missing tapes, and it was not until nearly a month later when, on November 8, 2000, Agent Friday finally stumbled upon the missing tapes while looking for party decorations. (R. at 12.) The government speculates that the tapes sat exposed in an open box in the unlocked storage room for over two months. (R. at 12.) This highly sensitive evidence sat, openly exposed, in a busy storage room amidst note pads, pencils, office supplies and party decorations, open to the 5,000 occupants of the building who frequent the room for coffee and office supplies.

## CONCLUSION

Because the government neither acted with reasonable diligence to minimize its two-month sealing delay, nor protected the tapes from any possibility of tampering, Defendant requests that the judgment of the District Court be reversed and remanded with instructions to the District Court to grant Defendant's motion to suppress the wiretap tapes.

Respectfully submitted,

DATED: _____        _____
Attorney for Defendant/Appellant

## CERTIFICATE OF SERVICE

I, _____, do hereby certify that I have this date served a true and correct copy of the Appellant's Brief upon counsel for the Appellee by placing a true and correct copy of the Appellant's Brief in the United States mail, with sufficient postage affixed, and addressed as follows:

William Schultz, Esq.
125 Sonoma Blvd.
Crichton, [State]

Dated this _____ day of _____, 2002.

_____
Attorney for Defendant/Appellant

## Sample Settlement Letter

CERTIFIED MAIL
RETURN RECEIPT REQUESTED

November 15, 2001

Ms. Liza Capshaw
2811 Windemere
Ft. Lauderdale, FL

### CONFIDENTIAL SETTLEMENT COMMUNICATION

Re: <u>McLean v. Hurt</u>

Dear Ms. Capshaw:

I represent Mr. and Mrs. McLean in the lawsuit they have recently filed against your clients in which they seek damages for the death of their young child. They are understandably anxious to seek full recovery under the law following the drowning death of their child in your client's man-made pond. However, to avoid protracted litigation, my clients are willing to allow me to explore settlement possibilities. My clients have authorized me to make the following offer: they will agree to dismiss this suit if your clients remit payment in the sum of $1,500,000. This offer will remain open until 5:00 p.m. on December 1, 2001. This letter is intended as a confidential settlement communication pursuant to Rule 408 of the Federal Rules of Evidence and Rule 1-14.1 of the Florida Evidence Code. As such, it will not be admissible in the above proceeding, or any other proceeding, for any purpose.

As you are probably aware, on September 3, 2001, my client's young son drowned in the Hurt's pond. Although your clients knew that young children enjoyed feeding the ducks on their pond, they left town for the holiday weekend, leaving the gate to the pond unlocked, and the dock in a state of disrepair.

Their actions in leaving this attractive nuisance accessible to young children is even more troublesome in light of the fact that they knew the dock was dangerous and in need of repair. Yet they had delayed the long-needed repairs. Mikey McLean drowned in the Hurt's pond after the dock collapsed under his slight weight.

Under Florida law, the Hurts are liable for Mikey McLean's death under the doctrine of attractive nuisance. For over forty years, a long line of Florida courts have consistently held landowners liable for the injuries sustained by child trespassers when the landowners leave a dangerous condition on their property and have reason to believe that children attracted to the dangerous condition will trespass onto the property. *See, e.g., Ansin v. Thurston*, 98 So.2d 87 (Fla. Dist. Ct. App. 1957); *Samson v. O'Hara*, 239 So.2d 151 (Fla. Dist. Ct. App. 1970).

Here, the combination of the Hurt's dilapidated dock, the man-made pond, and the ducks that swam in the pond, was dangerous and yet inviting and attractive to small children. The Hurts both knew the dock was dilapidated and dangerous, and knew that children from the neighboring elementary school trespassed onto their dock to feed the ducks. Yet they left this attractive nuisance open and accessible to children while they left town for the long holiday weekend.

The Hurt's liability under Florida law is clear. If this case is tried, the jury will not be focused on liability, but on the amount of damages to award the parents of their only child—a six-year-old son. After evaluating Florida law, I think you will agree that our $1,500,000 settlement offer is more than reasonable.

Our offer remains open until 5:00 p.m. on December 1, 2001. If I do not hear from you by then, I will be in touch with you to schedule depositions.

Sincerely,

Beth Manning

## *Sample Demand Letter*

July 20, 2002

CERTIFIED MAIL
RETURN RECEIPT REQUESTED

The Bancroft Corporation
c/o Thomas Jones, President
1128 Madison Avenue, Suite 120
New York, New York 2002

Dear Mr. Jones,

This firm represents Suartez and Associates (the "Landlord"). The Bancroft Corporation (the "Tenant"), is in default of its obligations under a Lease Agreement by and between the Landlord and Tenant, dated April 10, 2002 (the "Lease"). Rent is due and owing for the months of June and July 2002 in the amount of Fifteen Thousand Two Hundred Sixty-Five Dollars and Fifty-Eight Cents ($15,265.58) per month, as required under Paragraph 4 of the Lease, together with late charges in the amount of One Thousand Three Hundred Fifty-Six Dollars and Fifty Cents ($1,356.50), required pursuant to paragraph 15(c) of the Lease.

If Tenant does not pay to Landlord the sum of Thirty-One Thousand Eight Hundred Eighty-Seven Dollars and Sixty-Six Cents ($31,887.66) by 5:00 p.m. on July 28, 2002, the Landlord intends to exercise its rights and remedies under the Lease. These rights and remedies include, but are not limited to, terminating the Lease, instituting suit for recovery of possession of the leased premises, and recovering all damages incurred by the Landlord as a result of this default, including legal fees.

Sincerely,

Joseph Litton

cc: [client]

MEMORANDUM

To:         Junior Attorney
From:     Senior Attorney
Date:      September 1, 2001
Re:         Jeffrey Bing matter


Yesterday I met with Jeffrey Bing, who is incarcerated in the Cook County jail. Chicago police have arrested Mr. Bing and charged him with the murder of John Geller, who was apparently a friend of his. Mr. Bing has retained our office to defend him on these charges. After reviewing the police file and meeting with Mr. Bing, I think we have enough preliminary information for you to begin researching a possible defense.

As you may have seen on the news over the past few days, Mr. Bing shot Mr. Geller at close range while they were on a camping trip. As the friends were completing a day-long hike, Mr. Bing stated that he wanted to take a rest break, even though they were only about five minutes from the lodge where they were staying. Mr. Bing complained that he was winded. As they sat down in a meadow, a third friend, Mr. Newton, began goading Mr. Bing about a weekend Mr. Bing had recently spent in New York with Mr. Geller's former girlfriend, Jill Jacoby. Until that point, Mr. Geller was not aware that Mr. Bing was seeing his former girlfriend, much less traveling with her. (Apparently Mr. Bing had lied to Mr. Geller, telling him that his traveling companion was a woman Mr. Geller had never met.)

In Mr. Newton's statement to the police, he stated that when Mr. Geller discovered that Mr. Bing was seeing his former girlfriend and that he had lied to him, he "went berserk." He pounced on Mr. Bing, threw him on his back, and began beating our client's face with his fists. Mr. Bing apologized several times, but Mr. Geller did not stop the beating. After a minute or two, Mr. Newton tried to stop the fight by shouting at Mr. Geller to "calm down." Mr. Geller replied: "Stay out of this. My fight's with Jeff." Mr. Newton then began to physically lift Mr. Geller off of Mr. Bing. While Mr. Newton was in the process of separating the two men, Mr. Geller whipped out a hunting knife and slashed Mr. Newton in the arm. Mr. Newton jumped back and then shouted: "Man, I've never seen him like this before. I'm going to run for help." When Mr. Newton left the scene, the other two men were circling each other, with Mr. Geller brandishing a knife.

After Mr. Newton left the scene, Mr. Geller again attempted to charge and tackle Mr. Bing. When Mr. Geller was about twenty feet from our client, Mr. Bing reached down into his open knapsack and took out a gun that he carried with him when hiking in the wilderness. Mr. Bing began waving the gun at Mr. Geller in an effort to keep Mr. Geller away from him. For about five minutes, the two men continued to circle each other. Each time Mr. Geller charged our client, Mr. Bing waved the gun at him. By waving the gun, Mr. Bing managed to keep Mr. Geller about ten feet away from him. During this time, Mr. Bing pleaded with his friend to "give it up" and to "calm down." However, Mr. Geller kept shouting at him that he would "kill you for this." Finally, Mr. Bing yelled: "I don't want to have to shoot you, but I will if you don't stop." Mr. Geller replied that "only one of us is going to walk out of here alive." With that threat, Mr. Geller again charged towards Mr. Bing. When he was between five to ten feet away, Mr. Bing shot him, pulling the trigger once. Our client claims that he didn't want to kill Mr. Geller, but that he feared for his life.

A few other random facts: Our client is 5' 11" and weighs 175 pounds. Mr. Geller was 6' and weighed 190 pounds at the time of his death. Mr. Newton is 5' 11" and weighs 180 pounds. Mr. Geller was a member of the cross-country track team in college (four years ago). Our client is not athletic. By the way, following the incident the police searched our client's backpack. They discovered reading materials, bird guides, binoculars, and miscellaneous clothing, but no rope, cooking utensils or other potential weapons.

At this preliminary stage, I believe our client may have a defense under Illinois' self-defense statute. A summer law clerk has found and copied the self-defense statute for you. Please review the statute and determine which of the two sentences is relevant to our client's situation. Then outline the elements of the relevant sentence and identify any issues the statute poses for our client.

720 Ill. Comp. Stat. 5/7-1—Use of force in defense of person.

A person is justified in the use of force against another when and to the extent that he reasonably believes that such conduct is necessary to defend himself or another against such other's imminent use of unlawful force. However, he is justified in the use of force which is intended

or likely to cause death or great bodily harm only if he reasonably believes that such force is necessary to prevent imminent death or great
bodily harm to himself or another, or the commission of a forcible felony.

## PEOPLE v. S.M.
### 93 Ill. App. 3d 105, 48 Ill. Dec. 690, 416 N.E.2d 1212 (1981)

**PRIOR HISTORY:** APPEAL from the Circuit Court of Cook County; the HON. JOSE VASQUEZ, Judge, presiding.
**DISPOSITION:** Reversed and remanded.
**COUNSEL:** James A. Stamos, of Chicago, for appellant.
Bernard Carey, State's Attorney, of Chicago (Marcia B. Orr, Myra J. Brown, and Thomas A. Gibbons, Assistant State's Attorneys, of counsel), for the People.
**JUDGES:** MR. JUSTICE JIGANTI delivered the opinion of the court. ROMITI, P. J., AND JOHNSON, J., concur.

**OPINION BY:** JIGANTI

**OPINION:** On April 28, 1978, the minor respondent, then 14 years old, shot and killed two teenage boys and wounded two others in the parking lot of the high school which the boys attended. A petition for adjudication of wardship was filed charging him with the murder of Michael Truppa and Robert Paulish, with aggravated battery upon Michael Gale and Russell Peterson, and with unlawful use of a weapon. Prior to trial the respondent pleaded guilty to unlawful use of a weapon. Following trial he was adjudged delinquent for the commission of two counts of voluntary manslaughter and two counts of aggravated battery. A dispositional hearing was conducted and the respondent was committed to the Illinois Department of Corrections. He appeals, contending that (1) the State failed to prove beyond a reasonable doubt that he was not acting in self-defense; and (2) the trial court's dispositional order was contrary to the weight of the evidence or an abuse of discretion.

The State called 12 occurrence witnesses, all of whom were students at the high school at the time of the occurrence. The respondent also testified concerning the incident.

On the night in question there was a dance at the high school. The respondent did not attend the dance. Rather, he invited Barbara Siemasko, Sue Pederson, and Mark Keifer to his home. The four youths ate pizza and watched television until 9 p.m.

At about 9 p.m., the respondent told his friends that he had seen many raccoons at the DesPlaines River that afternoon. He asked Keifer whether he wanted to hunt the raccoons. Keifer stated that he did not want to go because he had a track meet the following day. After some discussion Keifer agreed to go along. The respondent then obtained a gun from his room. He strapped it on with a holster and covered it with a jacket.

The four youths left the respondent's house at approximately 9:45 p.m. They walked to Keifer's house where the respondent and Keifer went inside to look for a flashlight to use while hunting. The boys then walked the girls to the high school so that the girls could call their relatives for a ride home.

The victims did not attend the high school dance either. Preceding the incident they played games at a bowling alley, drank beer in the Forest Preserves, and stopped to eat at a fast food restaurant. They then drove to the high school parking lot, apparently to see if any of their friends were there.

According to the State's witnesses, the respondent arrived at the high school at approximately 10 p.m. The dance was almost over. He stood on the sidewalk east of the school auditorium near the southern end of the parking lot, talking to a group of high school students. A little while later a station wagon carrying the victims drove past to the end of the parking lot and turned around. After turning around, the station wagon proceeded back toward where the respondent was talking to the other youths. Some of the State's witnesses testified that the station wagon was headed directly for the respondent at a steady rate of speed. Other witnesses testified that the station wagon would not have hit the respondent or the other youths even if it had not stopped. The respondent yelled "whoa, mother-fucker" or something similar.

Keifer, Siemasko, Pederson and four other high school students testified that after the car stopped the respondent apologized for the remark he had made. . . .

Gale got out of the station wagon and approached the respondent. The respondent backed away. Gale followed after him. Then the respondent pulled out his gun. Some of the witnesses saw him waving the gun in the air. Other witnesses stated that he cocked the pistol and pointed it at Gale. Gale yelled that the respondent had a gun. While this was occurring Truppa and another youth, Rick Johnson, got out of the station wagon. Some of the witnesses heard the onlookers yelling for Gale to leave the respondent alone.

The respondent continued to back up further into the parking lot. The lot was fenced in. Gale and Truppa followed him. After a while Paulish and Peterson joined Gale and Truppa. The respondent continued to retreat from the four boys but they pursued him. He was walking or running backwards. The other boys threw things at the respondent but missed hitting him. The objects thrown included a flattened tin can and a piece of asphalt. As he backed away the respondent was yelling for Gale, Peterson, Truppa and Paulish to "stay away." The respondent's back was to the parking lot fence. He was facing Truppa, Peterson, Gale and Paulish. They formed a semicircle around him.

The defendant broke through the semicircle and started to run away from the four boys. Four witnesses heard the respondent yell "go get help." These four ran into the school to tell a teacher.

Gale, Johnson, and the respondent each testified that the respondent next fired a shot into the air. Peterson did not hear a warning shot. Peterson, Truppa, Gale and Paulish continued to advance upon the respondent.

. . . .

Peterson testified that he, Paulish, Truppa and Gale were jogging after the respondent. The respondent said, "I got a gun, I'll shoot." Peterson heard four or five shots in rapid succession. He was hit once in the left arm. At the time he was shot, Peterson was "about 10, 15 feet" from the respondent.

. . . .

At the time of the incident Truppa and Paulish were 16 years old. Gale and Peterson were 15 years old. The respondent was 14 years old. Gale had been on the wrestling team for two years. He was also on the football team as were Truppa and Paulish. Gale, Truppa, Paulish and Peterson had known each other for many years. They were not acquainted with the respondent except that they had seen him around the high school. The respondent did not know any of the victims prior to this incident, except that Gale had once helped the gym teacher show the respondent's gym class how to wrestle.

. . . .

It is not disputed that the respondent properly raised the issue of self-defense. Therefore, the dispositive issue is whether the State disproved beyond a reasonable doubt the respondent's claim of self-defense. People v. Woods (1980), 81 Ill. 2d 537, 410 N.E.2d 866; People v. Shipp (1977), 52 Ill. App. 3d 470, 367 N.E.2d 966.

A person is justified in the use of deadly force when that person "reasonably believes that such force is necessary to prevent imminent death or great bodily harm to himself. . . ." (ILL. REV. STAT. 1977, ch. 38, par. 7–1.) As stated in People v. Motuzas (1933), 352 Ill. 340, 346, 185 N.E. 614, 617, "one who is deliberately assaulted in a manner to make him reasonably apprehensive" that he will suffer great bodily harm "has the right, under the law, to deliberately kill his assailant if it reasonably appears that such act was necessary, or apparently so, in order to save himself from great bodily harm."

Whether a person has acted in self-defense depends upon the surrounding facts and circumstances and is a question for the trier of fact. (People v. Woods). However, this court must carefully review the evidence and has the duty to reverse a conviction where the record leaves us with a grave and substantial doubt of the guilt of the accused. People v. Lewellen (1969), 43 Ill. 2d 74, 250 N.E.2d 651; People v. Goodman (1979), 77 Ill. App. 3d 569, 396 N.E.2d 274.

Where the fact-finder concludes that the accused subjectively believed that the use of deadly force was necessary but that this subjective belief was unreasonable, then the proper verdict is voluntary manslaughter. (People v. Lockett (1980), 82 Ill. 2d 546, 413 N.E.2d 378.) If that subjective belief is found to be reasonable, then the accused should be acquitted on the ground that he acted in self-defense. (People v. Lockett.) In view of the fact that the respondent here was convicted of voluntary manslaughter, it is clear that the fact-finder concluded that the respondent subjectively believed that deadly force was necessary to prevent imminent death or great bodily harm to himself. Therefore, we need only consider whether the State has proved beyond a reasonable doubt that the respondent's belief was unreasonable.

The evidence, even when viewed in the light most favorable to the State, shows that the respondent tried to avoid a confrontation. He apologized for swearing and immediately retreated. Gale, who the respondent knew was a wrestler, pursued him. It appears from the evidence that the respondent apprehended that he would have trouble with Gale when he saw Gale get out of the car and advance toward him. Motivated by this apprehension the respondent showed that he was armed. That his fears were well founded is borne out by the appearance and conduct of Gale's three companions and by the fact that the boys were in no way discouraged by the respondent's gun. The respondent made repeated efforts to flee. At no time did he stand his ground or advance toward the other boys. Even after the four boys cornered the respondent and threw things at him, he did not shoot. Rather, he tried again to run away and called for the onlookers to get help. When the other boys continued to pursue him, the respondent fired a warning shot or made a verbal warning. According to the evidence the four boys continued to advance on the respondent even as they were shot.

Truppa, Peterson, Paulish and Gale were older than the respondent. Gale was on the wrestling team and played on the football team with Truppa and Paulish. All four boys had been drinking. The respondent was outnumbered 4 to 1. Under these circumstances we cannot say that the respondent's belief that he was in immediate danger of death or great bodily harm was unreasonable.

. . . .

We believe that the evidence failed to prove beyond a reasonable doubt that the respondent did not act in self-defense. We therefore dismiss the judgment of the circuit court which adjudged the respondent delinquent for the commission of two counts of voluntary manslaughter and two counts of aggravated battery. The trial court's dispositional order committing the respondent to the Illinois Department of Corrections is vacated. The cause is remanded for dispositional hearing on the judgment of delinquency for the unlawful use of a weapon.

Reversed and remanded.

# MEMORANDUM

To:      Junior Attorney
From:   Senior Attorney
Date:    September 15, 2001
Re:      Jeffrey Bing: Self-Defense Plea


Thank you for your evaluation of Illinois' self-defense statute and *People v. S.M.* I have met again with our client and want to provide you with the additional information I received during that meeting.

Mr. Bing and Mr. Geller became friends when they attended college together. Although they have been extremely close friends for six years, they had a volatile relationship. It is well known among their circle of friends that Mr. Geller has an explosive temper. During college, the two fought frequently, with two or three of their arguments escalating into fist fights. The fights were violent enough that they emerged with swollen knuckles and bloodied noses. During one of the fights, Mr. Bing also sustained a black eye. However, Mr. Bing always managed to stop the fights before either one of them became more seriously hurt, by apologizing and/or by pleading with Mr. Geller to calm down. Since their graduation from college four years ago, Mr. Bing and Mr. Geller have refrained from any physical fighting. However, a year ago, Mr. Geller got into a violent argument with his roommate. During that fight, Mr. Bing and Mr. Newton were able to pull Mr. Geller away from his roommate after a couple of minutes. However, the roommate sustained a broken rib, black eye, and numerous bruises.

In addition to this new factual information, I want to direct your attention to two additional cases interpreting the self-defense statute that a summer law clerk has discovered: *People v. Shipp*, 367 N.E.2d 966 (Ill. App. Ct. 1977); *People v. Moore*, 357 N.E.2d 566 (Ill. App. Ct. 1976).

## PEOPLE v. SHIPP
52 Ill. App. 3d 470, 10 Ill. Dec. 357, 367 N.E.2d 966 (1977)

**SUBSEQUENT HISTORY:** Rehearing denied October 12, 1977.

**PRIOR HISTORY:** APPEAL from the Circuit Court of Stephenson County; the HON. EVERETT E. LAUGHLIN, Judge, presiding.

**DISPOSITION:** Judgment reversed.

**COUNSEL:** Ralph Ruebner, Peter B. Nolte, and Rosetta Hillary, all of State Appellate Defender's Office, of Elgin, for appellant.

William E. Sisler, State's Attorney, of Freeport (Phyllis J. Perko and Martin Moltz, both of Illinois State's Attorneys Association, of counsel), for the People.

**JUDGES:** MR. PRESIDING JUSTICE RECHENMACHER delivered the opinion of the court. SEIDENFELD and NASH, JJ., concur.

**OPINION BY:** RECHENMACHER

**OPINION:** Defendant was charged with the offenses of murder, voluntary manslaughter, and unlawful use of weapons. After a jury trial, she was acquitted of murder and unlawful use of weapons, but convicted of voluntary manslaughter. She appeals contending that the State failed to prove beyond a reasonable doubt that she could not reasonably have believed that her action in shooting the decedent, Robert Shipp, five times with a .38 caliber revolver, was necessary in order to prevent her death or the infliction of great bodily harm upon her. Under the bizarre facts in this case, we conclude that she is correct in this contention.

For the most part, the facts are undisputed. The decedent, whom defendant had known since she was a young girl, had been convicted of voluntary manslaughter in 1952 for killing his first wife, and sentenced to 10 to 20 years in the penitentiary. In 1962, the decedent was released on parole and defendant entered into a "business relationship" with him, by working as prostitute, while he served as her pimp. In 1965, defendant determined to give up prostitution. The decedent reacted by going to defendant's parents' home (where defendant had been staying) and breaking in. There, he cursed the defendant, pulled out a gun, and shot her in the left shoulder. Defendant's mother attempted to intervene, and the decedent told her to "shut up, or else I'll kill you, too." He then shot defendant again, this time in her hip, and dragged her from the bedroom, in spite of the courageous efforts of defendant's mother to stop him. As defendant struggled, the decedent shot her a third time in the face. Somehow, she managed to escape and ran out of her mother's house and up the street as decedent continued to fire at her, hitting her again, twice.

She ran into a tavern and locked herself in the restroom. The decedent followed and attempted to get the restroom door open. He was unsuccessful and fired two shots through the door. These shots missed defendant, who had "pinned herself" against the wall. The police arrived and arrested the decedent, who subsequently pleaded guilty to a charge of attempted murder, and received a sentence of 8 to 15 years in the penitentiary.

Strangely, this incident did not end defendant's relationship with the decedent. In fact, defendant corresponded with the decedent and visited him regularly while he was serving his sentence for attempting to murder her. After the decedent was released in 1972, he and the defendant began living together, and the two were married the following year.

Not surprisingly, their marital relationship was less than idyllic. On a number of occasions the decedent became violent during arguments and beat the defendant, and on one occasion, the defendant had to be hospitalized with a broken rib, as the result of such an incident. The defendant subsequently suffered a nervous breakdown and obtained a divorce from the decedent in August of 1975.

According to the defendant's trial testimony, the decedent continued to harass her after their divorce, forcing her to engage in sexual activity, and threatening her; several times, he "pulled a gun out." After one incident, the defendant swore out a warrant against the decedent for trespass, but later dropped the charges because she "cared so much" for him. On October 31, 1975, the decedent attempted to force the defendant to go home with him and hit her in the forehead, causing a scar, when she resisted. The defendant stated that she then went to see her attorney, who obtained a court order restraining the decedent from harassing, annoying or talking to her. In spite of all of this, the defendant and the decedent were together on January 20, 1976, and had dinner at a restaurant. There they got into an argument and refused to pay for dinner. After the police arrived there was a scuffle, during which the defendant was observed trying to kick the decedent, and was seen to push him toward a cigarette machine. The decedent was arrested for disorderly conduct, aggravated battery, and resisting arrest.

On January 23, the defendant encountered the decedent at a local V.F.W. bar. When two other patrons began fighting, the defendant went outside and the decedent followed her. There the two argued and the decedent produced a knife and threatened to "cut" the defendant's face "where nobody would be able to recognize [her]." He told her that he'd "just cut [her] throat and go back to the penitentiary." He grabbed the defendant by one arm and began forcing her into his car. Fortunately, the police arrived and arrested the decedent for assault.

About 10 days later, on the evening of February 3, 1976, the defendant shot and killed the decedent. At 8:30 p.m. she had again gone to the V.F.W. bar. Before going inside she checked to make certain that the decedent's car was not in the parking lot. However, after entering the V.F.W., she saw the decedent sitting at the end of the bar. Defendant nonetheless remained, talking to a number of other women who were present. Then, on a sudden impulse, she propositioned Selmon Hall, a friend of the decedent's, for prostitution, in spite of the fact that the decedent had told her that he would kill her if he ever caught her with another man. Her testimony was that she had "made up her mind that she was going to show [the decedent] that she could be with somebody if she wanted to."

The defendant and Hall left the V.F.W., went to the home of Jeff Manning, and went upstairs to a bedroom. Shortly afterward, the decedent appeared at the downstairs door where he was confronted by Manning. Manning told the decedent that he shouldn't come in since "she [defendant] didn't want to be bothered no more." Manning said that the decedent was drinking from a pint bottle of gin, seemed angry, and spoke for the most part in a loud voice; however, the decedent replied, "Jeff, I'm your friend. I ain't going to cause no trouble." The decedent then pushed past Manning and went upstairs to the room where the defendant and Hall were.

When the decedent entered the room, Hall became so terrified that he attempted to crawl underneath the bed. Since Hall was, apparently, a large man, this effort was not successful and Hall testified at trial that the decedent told him "I'll take care of you and I'll take care of [the defendant]." A statement which Hall had given police was used by the prosecutor in an attempt to impeach Hall. According to that statement, Hall had told police that the decedent had said, "I'll take care of you and then I'll talk to her," but Hall said that this was not correct.

After the decedent had assaulted the defendant on January 23, 1976, the defendant obtained a revolver which she kept in her purse. The defendant had placed this weapon on the dresser. When decedent entered the room, the defendant "got hysterical," and began reciting the terms of the court order to the decedent. The decedent said, "I want to talk to you, man," and began edging toward her; he had one hand in his coat pocket. The defendant picked up the revolver, cocked it, pointed it at the decedent, and told him, "Please don't come any closer." The decedent continued to advance and the defendant began backing up. The decedent said, "If you want to shoot me, go ahead and shoot." The defendant told him not to take his hand out of his coat, since she thought that he had a weapon of some sort. The decedent did not move his hand, but continued his advance toward the defendant. The defendant backed up until she was in the corner of the room. When the decedent was within six feet of her, she "knew then that [she] had to shoot him," or else decedent "would take that gun away" from her and "beat and shoot her." She testified that, "I remember pulling the trigger, and he kept coming, so I kept shooting. I couldn't stop." . . . Death was caused by "acute heart failure." . . .

However, the dispositive question here is whether the State disproved the defendant's claim of self-defense, beyond a reasonable doubt. . . .

Where a claim of self-defense is presented in a murder case, evidence of the violent disposition of the deceased, or threats directed at the defendant by the deceased, have probative value in establishing that the defendant reasonably believed that the employment of force likely to cause death or great bodily harm was necessary to prevent the killing or infliction of great bodily harm upon the defendant. (People v. Stombaugh (1972), 52 Ill. 2d 130.) Here, the evidence of the decedent's violent disposition and prior threats could hardly have been stronger. Not only had the decedent been convicted of killing his first wife, and of attempting to murder the defendant, but he had brutally assaulted the defendant on a number of other occasions. He had made numerous threats against her life, including a chillingly calculated statement on January 23, 1976, as he held her at knife-point, that he would simply cut her throat and then go to the penitentiary. Against this backdrop, the decedent's threat to kill the defendant if he ever caught her with another man was highly credible. Although the defendant's action in leaving the V.F.W. with Selmon Hall was thus extremely irrational, unless viewed as a calculated effort to lure decedent to his death (a theory which the jury evidently rejected), there can be no question, not only that (as the jury found) the defendant actually feared death or great bodily harm when decedent entered the bedroom and confronted her and Hall, in his view, "flagrante delicto," but also, that such fear was highly reasonable, under the circumstances.

Other evidence amplified this conclusion. The defendant heard the decedent "scuffle" with Manning, as he pushed his way into the house. The decedent threatened to "take care of" Hall, after entering the bedroom, and Hall stated that the decedent said he would "take care of" the defendant, as well, though this testimony was contradicted by an earlier statement which he gave to the police. The decedent, who weighed 190 pounds, continued to advance upon the defendant, even after she told him to stop. Though the State has emphasized that no weapon was found on the decedent's person, that fact is not dispositive in the context of this case, since the defendant did not know whether or not decedent had a weapon and the decedent had the ability to inflict great bodily harm upon the defendant, even without a weapon (see People v. Reeves (1977), 47 Ill. App. 3d 406), and it is the defendant's perception of the danger, and not the actual peril, which was dispositive. (People v. Limas (1977), 45 Ill. App. 3d 643.) The stark terror manifested by Hall, who had known the decedent for six years, provided further evidence that the defendant's fear was reasonable. In sum, it is clear from the record that the defendant's belief that deadly force was necessary to protect herself from death or great bodily harm, was justified under the circumstances.

. . . .

After a review of all of the record, we are left with a grave doubt as to the defendant's guilt. It is therefore our duty to reverse the judgment of the circuit court of Stephenson County.

Judgment reversed.

## PEOPLE v. MOORE
### 43 Ill. App. 3d 521, 2 Ill. Dec. 399, 357 N.E.2d 566 (1976)

**PRIOR HISTORY:** APPEAL from the Circuit Court of Cook County; the HON. NATHAN KAPLAN, Judge, presiding.

**DISPOSITION:** Judgment affirmed.

**COUNSEL:** David C. Thomas and Kathleen J. Hittle, both of Chicago, for appellant.

Bernard Carey, State's Attorney, of Chicago (Laurence J. Bolon, Joan S. Cherry, and R. Burke Kinnaird, Assistant State's Attorneys, of counsel), for the People.

**JUDGES:** MR. JUSTICE McNAMARA delivered the opinion of the court. MEJDA, P.J., and McGLOON, J., concur.


**OPINION BY:** McNAMARA

**OPINION:** Defendant, James Moore, was charged with voluntary manslaughter. A jury in the circuit court of Cook County found him guilty of that crime and the court sentenced him to one to three years. On appeal defendant contends that the trial court erroneously refused to give a certain instruction to the jury, and that he was not proved guilty of the crime beyond a reasonable doubt.

On August 26, 1973, Phillip Taylor was shot and killed in the alley behind defendant's home in the City of Chicago. Defendant admits that he shot the decedent, but claims that he acted in self-defense. Up until a few minutes before the shooting occurred, the facts are substantially uncontroverted.

Decedent lived with his sister and Robert King. On the evening in question, decedent and Robert King had been drinking beer. At about 8 p.m., the two men were looking for John King, Robert's brother. When they were unable to locate John, they drove down the alley and met Neil Huff and defendant, who lived a few doors from John. The four men purchased some beer and returned to the alley. Defendant watched while the other three men played cards for about two hours on the hood of Robert King's auto. The decedent and one of the other card players began to argue and, when defendant intervened, the decedent told him to mind his own business.

Shortly after that argument, defendant stated that he had a gun. The decedent bet him that he did not have it with him. Defendant insisted that he did, but did not produce the weapon. Decedent then began to quarrel with defendant about a fight the pair had engaged in several years before. The decedent claimed that defendant had struck him over the head with a baseball bat, and he threatened to beat up the defendant. When the quarrel subsided, defendant left to get more beer. The others continued to play cards.

At about 10:30 p.m., defendant returned with the beer. He and decedent quarrelled again about the brand of beer defendant had purchased. Defendant joined the card game for a few hands, but then went into his house for his gun. He returned with the gun handle protruding slightly from his pocket.

Defendant and decedent engaged in another argument. The decedent, 5 feet 10 inches and weighing 187 pounds, pushed defendant, 5 feet 5 inches and 120 pounds, up against the garage, and told defendant that he would beat him. At this point, contradictory testimony was adduced.

Robert King testified for the State that he did not see the decedent strike defendant. The witness pinned decedent's arms to his sides and held him against a fence. Robert King succeeded in dragging the decedent about 15 feet westward down the alley and away from defendant. Robert King further testified that the decedent broke away from him and started walking toward defendant saying he was going to whip him. When decedent was four or five feet from defendant, the latter shot him. In his statement to the police, Robert King stated that the decedent was running toward defendant. He explained at trial that it could have appeared that defendant was running. When the decedent fell to the ground, defendant ran away. The witness summoned the police.

John King testified that at approximately 10:30 p.m. defendant's wife came to his house to ask him to break up a fight in the alley. She said that defendant had a gun. Hearing a shot, the witness, his wife, and defendant's wife ran out. Defendant's wife ran home, while John King and his wife proceeded directly to the alley. As he entered the alley on the east side of the garage, John King saw defendant standing two or three steps from the alley. Defendant was holding a gun with his right hand as he ejected a shell with the left hand. John King told the defendant to take the gun and go upstairs. Defendant refused, replying profanely that he would shoot the decedent if the latter came near him. From that vantage point John was unable to see decedent. He entered the alley and saw his brother holding the decedent. When the decedent broke loose from Robert, the witness attempted unsuccessfully to grab him. His wife Jean also tried to grab decedent but was unable to get a firm grip on him. Decedent ran toward defendant who was standing in the east gangway. Defendant shot decedent and immediately left the scene.

. . . .

Defendant testified that seven years before the shooting he had cut his right wrist so severely that he was unable to grip items or make a fist. Since the injury he wore a wrist band.

. . . .

Jean King testified for the State in rebuttal that during the previous two years she had ridden on a motorcycle with defendant. On each occasion, defendant had been driving.

John King testified in rebuttal that he had seen defendant drive a motorcycle one month prior to the shooting. The witness had also worked on vehicles with defendant within two weeks of the shooting. The work which they performed was of the type that required the use of both hands. John King further testified that as he approached the defendant in the gangway he told defendant if he took the gun into the house that the deceased probably would go home. Defendant refused. He told King that he would shoot the decedent if he came near him.

We initially shall consider the issue of whether the State failed to prove defendant guilty of voluntary manslaughter beyond a reasonable doubt. Defendant asserts that the evidence adduced at trial supported his theory of self-defense.

Illinois statute defines self-defense in pertinent part as follows:

> A person is justified in the use of force against another when and to the extent that he reasonably believes that such conduct is necessary to defend himself or another against such other's imminent use of unlawful force. However, he is justified in the use of force which is intended or likely to cause death or great bodily harm only if he reasonably believes that such force is necessary to prevent imminent death or great bodily harm to himself or another,. . . . (ILL. REV. STAT. 1973, ch. 38, par. 7–1.)

One does not have to retreat from a place where he has a right to be. However, the nonaggressor may use force likely to cause death or serious bodily harm only if he reasonably believes that the imminently threatened force has placed him in danger of death or great bodily harm. (People v. Williams (1974), 57 Ill. 2d 239, 311 N.E.2d 681.) The State bears the burden of proving the defendant guilty beyond a reasonable doubt as to the issue of self-defense and all the elements of the offense charged. (People v. Williams). The test in determining self-defense is one of reasonableness. (People v. Johnson (1954), 2 Ill. 2d 165, 117 N.E.2d 91.) Whether the facts and circumstances would induce a reasonable apprehension of serious bodily harm is a question of fact for a jury to determine in light of defendant's perception of the situation at the time he employed deadly force against his aggressor. People v. Kelly (1975), 24 Ill. App. 3d 1018, 322 N.E.2d 527.

In our judgment, the jury was justified in holding that defendant was unreasonable in his anticipation of death or serious bodily harm and that, therefore, his employment of deadly force was not justified and he was guilty of voluntary manslaughter.

The decedent was an unarmed man, surrounded by persons who had endeavored, although unsuccessfully, to end the argument. Decedent also faced what he knew was a loaded gun. Moreover, the testimony of John King, which was apparently accepted by the jury, is crucial. He testified that he entered the alley just after the first shot was fired. He saw defendant in the east gangway ejecting a shell. At that time, King's brother was holding the decedent some 50 feet away. King told defendant to take his gun and go upstairs. Defendant refused and stated his intention to shoot and kill the decedent if he came near him. Defendant's statement was not the remark of a person possessed of a reasonable belief that he was in imminent danger of suffering serious harm. Rather it amounted to a threat to use unneeded deadly force, and demonstrated a readiness for an encounter with the decedent.

Defendant maintains that his considerably smaller size, his crippled right hand, the decedent's use of physical force against him, and the failure of the others to restrain the decedent provided the requisite justification for his use of deadly force in self-defense.

The significance of the difference in size between the two men is diminished considerably by the facts that defendant was armed, and that the decedent was unarmed and was aware that defendant was carrying a loaded gun. As to defendant's crippled right hand, the State introduced considerable evidence that defendant had full use of the hand right up to the time of the shooting. Considering the evidence the State adduced in opposition to defendant's claim that he could not use the hand, the jury had ample grounds to conclude that defendant was not incapacitated as a result of his prior hand injury.

The testimony was in dispute as to whether the decedent had struck defendant prior to the shooting. Robert King testified that the decedent had merely shoved defendant, and stated that he did not see decedent strike defendant. Defendant, his wife, and Neil Huff all testified that the decedent twisted defendant's arm, struck him several times, and knocked him down. The jury had the opportunity to view the demeanor of the witnesses and to weigh their testimony. It was for the jury to determine which witnesses were telling the truth. (People v. Horton (1954), 4 Ill. 2d 176, 122 N.E.2d 214). The defendant, however, points out that it was not necessary for him to have suffered a beating before it would be reasonable for him to believe that decedent would inflict serious bodily harm upon him. (People v. Dowdy (1974), 21 Ill. App. 3d 821, 316 N.E.2d 33). Whether or not the jury concluded that the decedent had struck defendant, it remained within their province, as they did, to determine that deadly force was unjustifiable under these circumstances.

. . . .

For the reasons stated, the judgment of the circuit court of Cook County is affirmed.

Judgment affirmed.

# MEMORANDUM

To:      Junior Attorney
From:    Senior Attorney
Date:    Date of Assignment
Re:      Chester Tate—Attempted Murder Charge

I have read the memorandum prepared by another associate in our firm analyzing whether we have a tenable argument that Mr. Tate did not kidnap Mr. Campbell. I have now learned that the State has decided to charge Mr. Tate with attempted murder as well, due to his having shot Mr. Campbell during the incident in question. We may have a viable defense to attempted murder based on intoxication. In other words, we might argue that Mr. Tate was so intoxicated at the time he shot Mr. Campbell that he could not form the requisite intent to attempt murder. I have discovered the following facts relevant to Mr. Tate's intoxication.

As the October 1st office memorandum notes, Mr. Campbell met Mr. Tate in front of his house on the afternoon of September 19th as Mr. Campbell exited his car. Although the two had quarreled a few weeks earlier and had not seen or spoken to each other since, Mr. Campbell greeted Mr. Tate with a hand-shake. On the front porch of Mr. Campbell's home, the two friends talked for a few minutes, decided that they would let bygones be bygones, and walked into the house to have a beer. However, after they entered the house, Mr. Campbell noticed the strong smell of alcohol on Mr. Tate's breath and suggested that it would not be a good idea to have a drink. Mr. Tate got upset and accused Mr. Campbell of not being fun anymore.

The argument escalated and Mr. Tate firmly put his arm around Mr. Campbell's neck in what Mr. Campbell described as a "headlock." Mr. Tate then put the nose of a gun he carried with him into Mr. Campbell's side and ordered Mr. Campbell to seat himself in a living room chair. Mr. Tate then tied Mr. Campbell's hands and feet to the chair. Throughout Mr. Tate's binding of Mr.

Campbell's hands and his feet, Mr. Tate mumbled to himself. Although the mumblings were audible to Mr. Campbell, he could not understand their content. Mr. Tate appeared steady throughout his binding of Mr. Campbell, i.e., he did not stagger and did not struggle with knotting the bindings.

After binding Mr. Campbell's hands and feet, Mr. Tate poured himself several vodka and orange juice drinks from Mr. Campbell's bar and began to rant about his unhappiness with the turn their relationship had taken. Mr. Campbell had difficulty understanding Mr. Tate's ranting, which he described as disjointed and illogical to the point of being nonsensical. Mr. Campbell stated that he recalls Mr. Tate mumbling tearfully that no one wants to be his friend and that he has been picked last for every Little League team this year. When Mr. Campbell tried to reason with him, Mr. Tate became exasperated, gagged Mr. Campbell by stuffing a handkerchief into his mouth, and blindfolded him. Throughout the time Mr. Campbell was bound to the chair and gagged and blindfolded, Mr. Tate continued alternatively to rant and to sit silently near Mr. Campbell. After one particular rant during which Mr. Tate seemed to become increasingly enraged, Mr. Campbell heard a gun shot simultaneous with feeling a searing pain in his right shoulder and the warmth of blood trickling down his side.

Although Mr. Campbell was unable to observe Mr. Tate because of the blindfold, he did hear Mr. Tate preparing more drinks for himself. Mr. Campbell determined from the amount of vodka missing from his bar that Mr. Tate's drinks were comprised of large amounts of vodka and only a small amount of orange juice. In fact, during the entire ordeal, Mr. Tate appears to have drunk the equivalent of at least ten drinks. The police estimate that Mr. Tate left Mr. Campbell's house sometime between 7:30 pm and 9:00 pm.

Police arrested Mr. Tate at his home just after midnight on the morning of the 20th. Although they did not test his blood alcohol level, the arresting officers indicated that Mr. Tate reeked of alcohol, sweat, and vomit. In addition, they found two separate piles of Mr. Tate's vomit in Mr. Tate's front yard. Apparently, Mr. Tate vomited after stumbling home from Mr. Campbell's house that evening.

Mr. Tate recalls little of the afternoon of the 19th. He started drinking vodka screwdrivers with his lunch. He had 4–6 screwdrivers before heading over to Mr. Campbell's. He did not go to Mr. Campbell's with the intention of harming Mr. Campbell. Instead, he went over with the intention of rescuing their friendship. He recalls meeting Mr. Campbell in front of his house, talking with him briefly on the porch, and then accompanying Mr. Campbell into the home to have a beer. When Mr. Campbell withdrew the offer for beer, Mr. Tate admits to having "lost it" and to pulling a gun on Mr. Campbell and to binding him to a chair in his living room. Angry and agitated, he then drank three tumblers of vodka to calm his nerves. He recalls nothing after that. He does not recall ranting at Mr. Campbell. He does not recall shooting Mr. Campbell. He does not recall leaving Mr. Campbell's home. He does not recall returning to his home.

Finally, I am certain that we can hire an expert witness who will testify that the amount of alcohol Mr. Tate consumed would have resulted in his having a blood alcohol level of at least .3 during the ordeal, especially during the time the shooting occurred.

In light of the facts regarding Mr. Tate's alcohol consumption, please review the attached cases a summer law clerk found and assess how they affect the viability of our defense to attempted murder. In addition, please consider the statutes provide below.

720 Ill. Comp. Stat. 5/8-4 (1993):
**8-4. Attempt.**
§ 8-4. Attempt. (a) Elements of the Offense. A person commits an attempt when, with intent to commit a specific offense, he does any act which constitutes a substantial step toward the commission of that offense.

720 Ill. Comp. Stat. 5/6-3 (1993):
**6-3. Intoxicated or drugged condition.**
§ 6-3. Intoxicated or drugged condition.
A person who is in an intoxicated or drugged condition is criminally responsible for conduct unless such condition either:

(a) Is so extreme as to suspend the power of reason and render him incapable of forming a specific intent which is an element of the offense; or . . .

## PEOPLE v. OLSON
96 Ill. App. 3d 193, 51 Ill. Dec. 603, 420 N.E.2d 1161 (1981)

**PRIOR HISTORY:** APPEAL from the Circuit Court of Boone County; the HON. JOHN C. LAYNG, Judge, presiding.

**DISPOSITION:** Reversed and remanded.

**COUNSEL:** Mary Robinson and Manuel Serritos, both of State Appellate Defender's Office, of Elgin, for appellant.

John Maville, State's Attorney, of Belvidere (Phyllis J. Perko and Martin P. Moltz, both of State's Attorneys Appellate Service Commission, of counsel), for the People.

**JUDGES:** MR. JUSTICE LINDBERG delivered the opinion of the court. SEIDENFELD, P. J., and VAN DEUSEN, J., concur.


**OPINION BY:** LINDBERG

**OPINION:** Defendant, Olaf Olson, was convicted after a jury trial in Boone County of attempted murder, armed violence, reckless driving, attempting to elude an officer and two traffic offenses. He was sentenced to concurrent terms of 27 years for attempted murder, 10 years for armed violence, 3 months for reckless driving, 30 days for attempting to elude an officer and fined $100 for each of the two traffic offenses. From the convictions for armed violence and attempted murder, defendant appeals. ILL. REV. STAT. 1977, ch. 38, pars. 8-4(a), 9-1(a), 33A-2.

At approximately 1 p.m. on March 27, 1979, defendant Olson was observed by Illinois State Trooper Ken Kaas sitting in an automobile parked along Genoa Road near Rockford in such a way as to partially block the entrance to the Northwest Tollway. Kaas approached the automobile and asked Olson to pull over to the shoulder. Olson, who was slumped toward the passenger side of the front seat, took one look at the trooper and accelerated the car, ran through a red light and proceeded northbound on Genoa Road. Kaas gave chase. He testified that the speed of defendant's car exceeded 80 miles per hour and that the vehicle often strayed into the southbound lanes forcing oncoming traffic to swerve in order to avoid collision. Defendant ran a stop sign in an effort to turn onto Route 20, and then continued eastbound on that road.

Defendant stopped his car on Route 20, and Kaas pulled up behind. Kaas observed a long-barreled gun extending from the window of defendant's car from which a shot was fired in his direction. Olson again fled with Kaas in close pursuit.

The chase ended when Olson's car swerved in front of Kaas' vehicle, crossed the westbound lanes and hit an embankment on the north side of the road. Kaas testified that Olson fired a shot from his car and the trooper returned the fire. Defendant got out of his car, took another shot in the direction of Kaas and then staggered toward the trooper with his gun extended. Kaas fired several rounds at Olson who finally fell to the ground. He was hospitalized at about 3 p.m. A blood test taken at the time of admittance to the hospital showed blood alcohol content of .34 percent.

Subsequent inspection of the car yielded a bottle of whiskey and several items which were later identified as belonging to Tim and Matilda Breitbach, whose trailer home near Galena, Illinois, had been robbed earlier on the same day. The Breitbachs testified that two men in a car fitting the description of that owned by defendant had come to their farm about 9 o'clock on the morning of March 27 and had asked directions to the Galena Territories. Returning from work later in the evening, the Breitbachs discovered that their trailer had been ransacked and several things stolen, including a shotgun. There were bullet holes in the windshield, cab door and hood of a truck parked outside. Although no fingerprints were recovered, the shotgun retrieved from defendant Olson was identified as belonging to the Breitbachs, and a spent cartridge found near the truck was matched to the shotgun.

Donald Greenshaw, work release director for Boone County, testified that on March 27, 1979, Olson was employed at Barnes Auto Body Shop in Belvidere pursuant to a work release program, the conditions of which required that inmates such as Olson go directly from jail to work. They could go nowhere else without special permission. On March 27, 1979, no such permission had been given Olson.

A fellow employee at Barnes Auto Body Shop, Jack Cooper, testified that on the day of the incident defendant arrived at work at about 12:30 p.m. "pretty drunk." Olson asked Cooper whether he still had his job, then mumbled that he wanted to call his girlfriend. Because of his drunken condition, Olson was unable to dial the telephone number. Cooper placed the call and handed him the phone. Olson left shortly thereafter.

I

Defendant's first contention on appeal is that the evidence of his intoxication precluded a finding that he had the requisite intent to sustain a charge of attempted murder or armed violence.

Both of these crimes require a showing of specific intent (People v. Trinkle (1977), 68 Ill. 2d 198, 369 N.E.2d 888; ILL. REV. STAT. 1979, ch. 38, par. 33A-2), and are therefore subject to the defense of intoxication. (People v. Harkey (1979), 69 Ill. App. 3d 94, 386 N.E.2d 1151; People v. Remon (1976), 40 Ill. App. 3d 337, 352 N.E.2d 374.) However, voluntary intoxication may negate the element of intent only when it is so extreme as to entirely suspend the defendant's power of reason, i.e., his ability to act knowingly. People v. Mikel (1979), 73 Ill. App. 3d 21, 391 N.E.2d 550; People v. Fleming (1976), 42 Ill. App. 3d 1, 355 N.E.2d 345.

Defendant called two doctors to testify as to his state of mind at the time of the incident. The first, Dr. Carl Hamann, who had earlier been appointed by the court to determine Olson's competency to stand trial, stated that the American Medical Association standards on alcohol levels in the blood provide that an amount of .3 to .4 percent alcohol is "definitely sufficient to cause death. . . . and .5 is almost invariably fatal." At .3 to .35 percent levels, the person "would usually be stuporous and would have difficulty comprehending what they saw or heard." Dr. Hamann speculated that at the time of the incident two hours before the blood test was administered, Olson's blood alcohol level would have been in the neighborhood of .4 percent. However, even at the lower level of .34 percent recorded two hours later, a person's ability to distinguish right from wrong would be "seriously impaired" and his power to reason would be "practically" suspended. At .4 percent, the person would be "very near comatose, near coma in a very stuporous position, and extremely difficult to think and reason or have any mental functioning except reflex actions." Dr. Hamann emphasized that certain routine physical actions might still be performed by persons with this amount of alcohol in the blood, but that such actions would be more indicative of reflex than intent. This would account, he said, for a person's ability to drive a car (although not well), get to one's place of work, or even shoot a gun if threatened. Dr. Hamann stated that Olson had a history of fighting and a deep-seated belief that others imposed upon and took advantage of him. When asked whether these characteristics affected his ability to form an intent to do something, he replied that it would likely make his reaction automatic.

The second medical witness, Dr. J. G. Graybill, testified that with a blood alcohol level of .34 percent it was "highly questionable" whether a person could form a judgment as to what is right and wrong, and that such a person's power to reason would be limited to "impulsive action" which Dr. Graybill distinguished from reasoning ability or judgment. The following colloquy between defense counsel and Dr. Graybill ensued:

"Q. Would this person with this .34 percent of alcohol in his blood stream know what he was doing?
A. To some degree he might, but he might not know why he is doing it.
Q. Could he form any intent as to a physical act with the .34 percent alcohol in his blood stream?
A. To form an intent requires reasoning and it requires judgment.
I would think this man's reasoning and judgment would be so far impaired that he could not intend—form an intent to commit a certain act. He might commit an act, but I would think it would be more of an instinctive type of thing or fright reaction, or perhaps a reflex action.
There is some stimuli he has viewed as threatening to him."

For its part, the State offered no medical testimony to refute that given by the two defense witnesses. Instead, the State argues that despite the evidence of blood alcohol levels, intent was shown by Olson's flight upon first seeing Officer Kaas, an act which it characterized as "a reasoned reaction from an individual who knew he was in trouble (because his car was filled with stolen items) and who thought that a quick escape would constitute his best chance of avoiding an unpleasant encounter with the authorities." The State also points to defendant's ability to drive an automobile in excess of 80 miles per hour, and to shoot a weapon with such accuracy as to hit the grillwork of Officer Kaas' car as further evidence that defendant's intoxication was not so extreme as to entirely suspend his power of reason.

Although we have been unable to find a case where the objective, medical evidence of intoxication was more compelling, neither are we aware of any legal threshold with respect to blood alcohol levels beyond which a presumption of suspended reason is said to arise. Despite considerable development in psychiatric research and changes in medical and legal attitudes toward alcoholism, the law with regard to the effect of voluntary intoxication upon criminal responsibility has shown little tendency to change or develop. (See Annot., 8 A.L.R.3d

1236 (1966).) Under present law, the focus of our inquiry cannot be limited to whether the defendant was intoxicated, but whether in light of all the evidence surrounding his actions Olson had the requisite mental state. (<u>People v. Huggy</u> (1974), 19 Ill. App. 3d 247, 311 N.E.2d 355.) A jury is not required to accept the conclusions of a psychiatrist with respect to this issue. (<u>People v. Goodwin</u> (1980), 83 Ill. App. 3d 203, 403 N.E.2d 1051.) Rather, the weight to be given any testimony relating to the mental state of the defendant is peculiarly within the province of the jury (<u>People v. Fleming</u> (1976), 42 Ill. App. 3d 1, 355 N.E.2d 345), and where the evidence admits of two inferences, a reviewing court will not substitute its judgment unless the jury's decision is inherently impossible or unreasonable. (<u>People v. Jones</u> (1978), 67 Ill. App. 3d 477, 384 N.E.2d 523.) Although the question is a close one, we hold that despite defendant's intoxication, there was other evidence sufficient for the jury to find that Olson's power of reason was not entirely suspended.

## II

Defendant next assigns as error the trial court's admission, over continuing objection, of evidence that Olson had earlier on the day of the incident committed a burglary near Galena, Illinois, and that he was on parole and work release at the time.

Both parties recognize the general rule that evidence of other crimes is inadmissible to show criminal tendency or disposition, but will in proper circumstances be allowed for the purpose of demonstrating motive, intent, identity, absence of mistake, or *modus operandi.* (<u>People v. McDonald</u> (1975), 62 Ill. 2d 448, 343 N.E.2d 489.) They also acknowledge that even where such evidence is offered for a proper purpose, the court must balance its relevance against its tendency to inflame and prejudice the jury. (<u>People v. Copeland</u> (1978), 66 Ill. App. 3d 556, 384 N.E.2d 391.) It is defendant's contention that the evidence here was neither offered for a proper purpose, nor was its relevance to the crimes for which Olson was being prosecuted nearly as great as the prejudice and hostility toward the defendant which its admission may have aroused in the jury. The State replies that the evidence was important to show motive, *i.e.*, to explain why the defendant responded as he did to his encounter with a policeman. The State would also justify this evidence in light of Olson's intoxication defense, in that it tends to show that his reaction to Officer Kaas was a reasoned act, in view of the burglary, work release and parole violations, rather than merely a reflexive response, as defendant contended.

Particularly in view of Olson's vigorous intoxication defense, we agree with the State that the introduction of some evidence of other offenses to show motive was proper here. (People v. Parker (1976), 35 Ill. App. 3d 870, 343 N.E.2d 52.) The more important question, however, is whether too much evidence was admitted. Five of the 15 State's witnesses either described the shambles left by the robber of the Breitbach home or commented on the evidence found in and around the house. The Breitbachs themselves described to the jury in graphic detail how the house had been "torn apart," the refrigerator tipped over and many items stolen. Mr. Breitbach and Detective Don Trost both testified with regard to damage to a truck parked outside from shotgun blasts. In addition, two other State's witnesses testified that Olson was on parole and that he had violated the conditions of his work release on the day of the incident.

In sum, a substantial amount of evidence was introduced which tended to prove the commission of another crime and the violation of the conditions of defendant's parole and work release, despite the fact that defendant was then being tried for none of these offenses. The State has cited People v. Witherspoon (1963), 27 Ill. 2d 483, 190 N.E.2d 281, wherein our supreme court held that evidence of warrants issued for the arrest of a defendant for previous crimes was admissible to establish a motive for the subsequent killing of a police officer who had attempted to arrest the defendant. Yet, unlike Witherspoon, the State here was not content to introduce just the warrants but went so far as to prove, through the testimony of seven witnesses, all the details of the other alleged offenses. The putative purpose of all this evidence was merely to show motive. Yet, such cumulation of inflammatory evidence of other offenses on an issue which was only peripheral to the crimes for which defendant was being tried demonstrates an insensitivity by the trial court to the need of balancing the probative value of each piece of evidence against its potential prejudice to the defendant. (People v. Reimnitz (1979), 72 Ill. App. 3d 761, 391 N.E.2d 380.) At some point, the cumulation of evidence here clearly became such as could "overpersuade the jurors and cause them to convict the defendant as an 'evil person' worthy of punishment rather than because he is guilty of the crime charged. [Citations.]" (People v. Butler (1978), 63 Ill. App. 3d 132, 139, 379 N.E.2d 703, 708.) We are therefore compelled to reverse and remand this case for a new trial in which the introduction and use of any evidence of other offenses will be more circumscribed.

Because of our disposition of the evidentiary issue, we need not address defendant's final contention that attempted murder is here a lesser included offense of armed violence.

Reversed and remanded.

## PEOPLE v. BRUMFIELD
72 Ill. App. 3d 107, 28 Ill. Dec. 422, 390 N.E.2d 589 (1979)

**PRIOR HISTORY:** APPEAL from the Circuit Court of Madison County; the HON. HORACE L. CALVO, Judge, presiding.

**DISPOSITION:** Reversed and remanded.

**COUNSEL:** Helen D. Moorman, Assistant Public Defender, of Edwardsville, for appellant. Nicholas G. Byron, State's Attorney, of Edwardsville (Raymond F. Buckley, Jr., and Bruce D. Irish, both of State's Attorneys Appellate Service Commission, of counsel), for the People.

**JUDGES:** MR. PRESIDING JUSTICE GEORGE J. MORAN delivered the opinion of the court. KARNS and KASSERMAN, JJ., concur.


**OPINION BY:** MORAN


**OPINION:** Defendant, Clarence Brumfield, appeals from a judgment of the circuit court of Madison County entered on a jury verdict finding him guilty of two counts of rape. He was sentenced to concurrent terms of 30 to 60 years imprisonment. While defendant has made numerous assignments of error, our disposition of this case makes it necessary to consider only those questions concerning the trial court's elimination of defendant's defense of involuntary intoxication and other matters which may arise on a subsequent retrial of this case.

Before proceeding to the principal question raised in this appeal, it is necessary to review certain matters which may arise in a subsequent retrial of this case. On the fourth day of the trial, with the State having presented all of its evidence except the testimony of defendant's mother, defendant moved for mistrial on the basis of a violation of his sixth amendment right to a public trial. Defendant argued that his mother, who testified only as to his age, his brother-in-law and a friend had been excluded from the courtroom by the State through the use of groundless subpoenas. It was further pointed out that these individuals had not been included on the State's list of potential witnesses to be called in the trial. The State argued that the defendant was not denied a public trial because no members of the public had been excluded, that defendant's mother was in fact on defendant's list of witnesses to be called during the trial, and that defense counsel had retaliated by excluding a number of potential State witnesses from the court room by use of the same procedure employed by the State. At the time the court heard arguments on defendant's motion, both parties had released all witnesses in question from their subpoenas.

These facts do not constitute the general indiscriminate exclusion of the public from the trial of a criminal case which is necessary for a defendant to be denied his constitutional right to a public trial. (People v. Frisco (1972), 4 Ill. App. 3d 1034, 283 N.E.2d 277.) However, we regard such tactics as misconduct by both the prosecution and the defense counsel and upon retrial such misuse of the subpoena power shall not be repeated.

A further matter relates to the State's violation of court ordered discovery. On December 17, 1976, the trial court granted defendant's discovery motion and ordered that all motions be answered in 10 days. Subsequently, defendant's motion for substitution of judge was granted, a hearing determining defendant's fitness to stand trial was heard, defendant's motion for continuance to complete a psychiatric examination to determine defendant's sanity at the time of the offense was denied, and that same psychiatric examination was performed on March 7, 1977. Jury selection began on the same day. During conference in chambers, conducted between periods of *voir dire*, defendant requested the State to provide relevant medical reports and the result of blood and hair tests. In addition, defendant objected to the list of 18 witnesses the State intended to call for trial which was tendered the following morning and which included names of people not listed in the police reports defendant had previously been supplied. Defendant requested that sanctions be imposed excluding the testimony of those witnesses not listed in the police reports but included on the State's list of witnesses to be called for trial. The State indicated to the court that additional witnesses not listed in the police reports included hospital personnel and police officers from the crime laboratory who were previously known to defense counsel. Responding to the lengthy delay in answering discovery, the State commented that defendant was equally negligent by failing to request sanctions at an earlier time. Noting that it had not been informed as to when the State had actually obtained its discovery information, the court ordered the State to supply the defendant with the medical reports and blood and hair test results requested. It additionally indicated that defendant would have an opportunity to interview any surprise witnesses called by the State prior to their testimony. During trial, four witnesses not listed by the State on its list of witnesses submitted to the defendant on March 8, 1977, were allowed to testify for the State. Police reports having not been included in the record on appeal, it is unclear if defendant received notice that these witnesses would be called. Defendant now contends that he did not receive a fair trial when the State was allowed to call those witnesses not on the list first tendered to the defendant after the trial had begun.

The troublesome aspect of this issue is the apparent "bad faith" on the part of the State. The State supplied the list of 18 witnesses to the defendant on March 8, 1977, when *voir dire* was taking place, almost three months after the court had ordered it to comply with discovery. It is inconceivable that the State was still unaware that four witnesses not on the list would testify the following day. In addition, the State refused to furnish requested medical reports and hair and blood samples until after the trial had commenced.

Although the trial prosecutor explained that she had only recent involvement in the proceedings, this does not excuse the State from its duty to make good faith efforts to comply with discovery orders. (ILL. REV. STAT. 1975, ch. 110A, par. 412(d), (f), (g).) We trust that because of the present status of this case these errors will not recur upon retrial.

We now turn to the critical question in this appeal. During the second day of the trial proceedings and while *voir dire* examination was being conducted, the State filed a written motion *in limine* requesting the trial court to instruct the defendant to refrain from any mention during the trial of defendant's intoxicated state or drugged condition prior to the alleged offense without first obtaining permission from the court outside the presence of the jury. The State's premise was that defendant's intoxicated or drugged condition, whether voluntary or involuntary, was not a valid defense to rape. Therefore, any reference to the condition would prejudice the State's case by conveying a misconception of the law to the jury and serve to raise sympathy for the defendant even if the court were to sustain an objection and instruct the jury to disregard such material.

During the hearing on the motion, the defendant argued that involuntary intoxication was a defense to rape and there would be evidence introduced at trial to support this defense. In the offer of proof made by defense counsel, it was asserted that defendant smoked marijuana on the night in question which, unbeknown to defendant, contained a strong intoxicating drug ("angel dust"). When he subsequently consumed alcohol voluntarily, the combined effects of these drugs led to defendant's involuntary acts. At the conclusion of argument, the trial court allowed the motion, noting that it was "the feeling of the court that either voluntary or involuntary use of drugs is not a defense of the crime of rape." Thus the trial court struck a defense before any evidence was heard.

Our Criminal Code of 1961 provides for the following affirmative defense of intoxicated or drugged condition:

> "A person who is in an intoxicated or drugged condition is criminally responsible for conduct unless such condition either:
> (a) Negatives the existence of a mental state which is an element of the offense; or
> (b) Is involuntarily produced and deprives him of substantial capacity either to appreciate the criminality of his conduct or to conform his conduct to the requirements of law." ILL. REV. STAT. 1977, ch. 38, par. 6-3.

Since rape is a crime of general intent (People v. Hunter (1973), 14 Ill. App. 3d 879, 303 N.E.2d 482), voluntary intoxication set out above in section 6-3(a) is clearly not a defense to such a charge. However, an involuntarily produced intoxicated or drugged condition which conforms to the requirements of section 6-3(b) relieves an individual of criminal responsibility for the commission of any crime. The trial court's order precluding any evidence of involuntary intoxication or drugged condition was accordingly in error.

Conceding in this appeal that involuntary intoxication is a defense to the charge of rape, the State now maintains that the trial court's order, though based on faulty reasoning, was actually correct. The State argues that the trial court properly excluded consideration of the defense of involuntary intoxication since the defendant's offer of proof was not sufficient to establish this defense. Citing People v. Walker (1975), 33 Ill. App. 3d 681, 338 N.E.2d 449, it is argued that involuntary intoxication must be accompanied by some outside influence operating on the will of the intoxicated defendant. In Walker the defendant testified that approximately one week prior to the shooting for which he was charged he obtained some pills from his brother to alleviate a stomachache. On the evening in question, defendant took two more of the pills from the jar where they were kept in his brother's house and later consumed some beer and wine. Defendant claimed that his subsequent conduct was involuntary since his brother had not told him that the pills contained the tranquilizing drug Seconal which, mixed with alcohol, could have the effect of intensifying his intoxication and reducing his control over his impulses. The court noted from the defendant's testimony that no one was present when he took the pills and that there was no evidence that fraud or force had been used to induce him to take the pills. Addressing the question of whether the defendant's testimony supported the defense of involuntary intoxication, the court stated:

"[I]nvoluntary drunkenness must be caused by trick, artifice or forced. While the present statute refers only to 'Intoxicated or Drugged Condition' which is 'involuntarily produced' with reference to the means of inducing such involuntary intoxication, it is distinguished in the statute from voluntary intoxication and seemingly, therefore, must be accompanied by some outside influence operating on the will of the intoxicated defendant." (33 Ill. App. 3d 681, 689.)

Ruling that the defendant's ignorance of the Seconal contained in the pills which he voluntarily took did not constitute evidence of involuntary intoxication, the court upheld the trial judge's refusal to instruct the jury on the defense of involuntary intoxication.

Both parties have provided forceful arguments for the application or inapplication of the <u>Walker</u> decision to this case. However, we believe these arguments only exemplify the fundamental error which has permeated this entire case. As noted previously, it was error for the trial court to preclude evidence of involuntary intoxication or drugged condition since such evidence may provide a defense to the crime of rape. While the defendant may have been obliged to respond to inquiries by the State with defenses he sought to establish, there was certainly no obligation on the part of the defendant to prove that he had sufficient evidence to establish that defense prior to trial. Once the defendant asserted a legally viable defense in response to the State's discovery motion, the State and the trial court were without authority to question the propriety of that defense prior to trial. Both parties and the trial court proceeded upon the faulty assumption that the defendant's offer of proof governed the efficacy of the defense of involuntary intoxication. However, the content of the offer of proof is irrelevant to the disposition of this issue. When the trial court judged and disallowed evidence of involuntary intoxication on the basis of this offer of proof, reversible error was committed.

While we believe for the above reasons that the holding in <u>Walker</u> has no application to this case, we note that in that case the defendant was allowed to introduce evidence of intoxication to the jury. In this case the trial court precluded the opportunity to establish the defense. The motion *in limine* filed by the State in this case was in substance a motion to strike an entire defense. Granting such a motion and thereby preventing the defendant from presenting evidence on an available defense not only distorts the traditional application of motions *in limine*, but likewise raises serious constitutional questions relating to an accused's right to present a defense. U.S. Const., amends. VI and XIV; Ill. Const. 1970, art. I, § 2.

A motion *in limine* should be used with caution, particularly in criminal cases. When used in the manner of its application in this case, it has the potential to deprive a criminal defendant of his day in court. That a defendant may have a tenuous defense is an insufficient justification for prohibiting him from trying to establish that defense. Nor should a party ordinarily be required to try a case or defense twice— once outside the jury's presence to satisfy the trial court of its sufficiency and then again before the jury. Whether the defendant will be able to substantiate his defense sufficiently to generate a jury question cannot be known until the evidence is in, but a defendant has the right to present his defense at trial. The trial court's order granting the State's motion *in limine* before the admission of any evidence deprived the defendant of his fundamental right to defend himself in a criminal trial. Summary judgments are allowed on rare occasions in civil cases, but never in criminal cases.

For the foregoing reasons the judgment of the circuit court of Madison County is reversed, and this cause is remanded for a new trial.

Reversed and remanded with directions.

## PEOPLE v. AGUIRRE
30 Ill. App. 3d 854, 334 N.E.2d 123 (1975)

**PRIOR HISTORY:** APPEAL from the Circuit Court of De Kalb County; the HON. CARL A. SWANSON, JR., Judge, presiding.
**DISPOSITION:** Judgment affirmed.
**COUNSEL:** Ralph Ruebner and Phyllis J. Perko, both of State Appellate Defender's Office, of Elgin, for appellant. James M. Carr, State's Attorney, of Sycamore (James W. Jerz and Edward N. Morris, both of Illinois State's Attorneys Association, of counsel), for the People.
**JUDGES:** MR. JUSTICE THOMAS J. MORAN delivered the opinion of the court. RECHENMACHER, P. J., and DIXON, J., concur.

**OPINION BY:** MORAN

**OPINION:** Defendant was charged in a 13-count indictment with attempted murder, aggravated battery, aggravated assault, and disorderly conduct. After a bench trial, he was found guilty of two counts of aggravated battery against two police officers, one count of aggravated assault against a police officer, and disorderly conduct. He was sentenced to concurrent prison terms of 1 to 3 and 1 to 5 years for aggravated battery, and fined $100 for disorderly conduct. He was not sentenced for the lesser included offense of aggravated assault.

On appeal, defendant asserts that he was not proven guilty of aggravated battery beyond a reasonable doubt, and that the trial court abused its discretion by denying the defendant probation.

Evidence reveals that at approximately 10 p.m. on the evening of January 19, 1973, the defendant consumed 1½ capsules of a substance which contained an undetermined amount of lysergic acid diethylamide, commonly known as LSD, and also drank four small glasses of wine. He appeared normal at this time. At approximately midnight, defendant, along with his brother and a friend, arrived on the campus of Northern Illinois University, and were escorted by defendant's sister to a room of the dormitory in which she lived. There, joined by five other young women, the defendant and the others drank an undetermined quantity of alcoholic beverages and smoked an undetermined amount of marijuana.

In the room, defendant first reclined on the floor and mumbled to himself. Later he moved to position on the top bunk-bed where he removed his shirt and shoes. Everyone else in the room remained fully clothed. A witness characterized defendants' [*sic*] speech as mumbled and said that he could not be understood but she attributed her lack of understanding to the fact that she was "high" on wine and marijuana. Defendant's removal of his shirt was thought by another witness to be due to the fact that the room was "quite warm." At one point, the defendant's [*sic*] jumped off the top bunk and stated that he wanted to make love to all the women in the room. At another point, he was observed laughing while he looked at himself in the bathroom mirror.

The defendant and the others left to attend an "after set" party in the basement of another dormitory. Upon entering the lobby of that building, defendant communicated with certain unknown individuals and hostile words were exchanged. Defendant's attitude at this time was characterized as loud, obnoxious and provoking.

Some time after 2 a.m. on January 20, 1973, Northern Illinois University police officers Lawson and Phifer, on duty and in uniform, observed defendant nude in a skylight leading to the roof of the dormitory. They grabbed defendant and a struggle ensued during which defendant gained control of Lawson's service revolver by ripping it through the stitching of the hip holster. Defendant fired the revolver a number of times. Phifer was struck in the head by ricochetting bullet fragments and defendant's knee was struck by either a direct hit or by ricochetting fragments.

As soon as the shooting stopped, Lawson grabbed the defendant; the latter bit the officer on the arm and chest. Phifer rejoined the struggle, struck the defendant four or five times in the face, and radioed for assistance. Defendant continued to struggle with the officers until he was subdued by the shackling of his hands and feet and thereafter he continued to thrash about violently. His facial expression was described as one of anger or belligerence and as denoting an intoxicated stupor.

Concerned that defendant was not alone, the officers twice asked him who was with him. Defendant replied, "My mother," and "You know Richard Nixon." His words and general attitude were described by a third officer as incoherent and sarcastic.

Shortly thereafter, defendant was transported to the hospital for treatment of his wounds. The doctor who attended him described defendant's behavior as agitated, hostile, aggressive, sarcastic and flippant. The doctor also stated that he believed the defendant was suffering from delusions, a belief based upon the fact that defendant answered "Rumplestilskin" when asked his name. Defendant was vulgar and spit. The doctor noted that defendant's behavior was not rational and that his responses were not communications.

After indictment, in answer to the State's discovery motion, the defendant notified the State that he intended to "assert the affirmative defense of lack of mental state necessary to commit the offenses enumerated in the indictment." See ILL. REV. STAT. 1971, ch. 38, §§ 6-3 and 6-4.

At trial, a psychiatrist called by defendant was asked a hypothetical question based upon defendant's version of the facts. The doctor answered that, in his professional opinion, the person described did not have the conscious purpose or objective to cause bodily harm to the two officers. His opinion was based upon the fact that the person came into the period of bizarre, totally incoherent behavior from a period of normal behavior and remained "crazy" up to the end of the narrative. The doctor labeled this person temporarily psychotic, and noted that the time of the occurrence was a cold winter's night and a nude man trying to climb through a skylight was not responding to reality. The doctor was more impressed with evidence of the person's "craziness" than with what he took, but noted that it appeared the person had taken a substantial amount of LSD which causes time and space to become distorted and the brain to become disrupted.

The trial court found that the evidence left a reasonable doubt as to the defendant's ability to form the requisite mental state for attempt murder but found that the evidence demonstrated beyond a reasonable doubt that the defendant was able to form the requisite mental state for the crime of aggravated battery.

The aggravated battery indictments charged defendant with intentionally committing batteries upon officers Lawson and Phifer. For the State to prove that the defendant acted intentionally, it must introduce evidence which demonstrates beyond a reasonable doubt that the defendant's conscious purpose or objective was to commit a battery upon the officers. (ILL. REV. STAT. 1971, ch. 38, § 4-4). Ordinarily, the requisite mental state can be inferred from the character of the act. But once a defendant has introduced evidence to show that a drugged condition negated the existence of the requisite mental state and such evidence raises a reasonable doubt, the State must then overcome the affirmative defense by proving, beyond a reasonable doubt, the existence of the requisite mental state. (ILL. REV. STAT. 1971, ch. 38, § 3-2(b); People

v. Redmond, 59 Ill.2d 328 (1974); LaFave & Scott, Handbook on Criminal Law ch. 1, § 8, at 48 (1972).) This can be accomplished by expert testimony or by evidence of lucid periods before, during or after the voluntary act.

It is undisputed that defendant's evidence was sufficient to raise a reasonable doubt as to his ability to form the requisite mental state for the crime of aggravated battery, but there remains the question of whether the State's evidence was sufficient to rebut defendant's evidence and proved beyond a reasonable doubt the nonexistence of the affirmative defense. In a bench trial, it is for the trial court to determine the credibility of the witnesses and to make a finding of fact as to whether the guilt of the accused has been established. We will not set aside the trial court's judgment unless the proof is so unsatisfactory that it gives rise to a reasonable doubt of guilt. People v. Walcher, 42 Ill.2d 159, 165 (1969); People v. Smith, 26 Ill. App. 3d 1062, 1065 (1975); People v. Behning, 130 Ill. App. 2d 536, 540 (1970).

In order for voluntary intoxication or a drugged condition to be a legal excuse, the condition must be so extreme as to suspend all reason and make impossible the existence of the mental state which is an element of the crime. (People v. Walcher, 42 Ill.2d 159, 163 (1969); People v. Gonzales, 40 Ill.2d 233, 241 (1968); People v. Hicks, 35 Ill.2d 390, 397 (1966); People v. Winters, 29 Ill.2d 74, 80–81 (1963); People v. Strader, 23 Ill.2d 13, 21 (1961); People v. Cochran, 313 Ill. 508, 518 (1924); People v. Fuller, 17 Ill. App. 3d 1005, 1007 (1974); People v. Wicker, 4 Ill. App. 3d 990, 996 (1972).) The question is not whether the defendant was intoxicated or drugged but whether the evidence demonstrates beyond a reasonable doubt that, in spite of his altered consciousness, he could have formulated the requisite mental state for the crime charged. See People v. Huggy, 19 Ill. App. 3d 247, 252 (1974); People v. Davis, 6 Ill. App. 3d 622 (1972).

The evidence presented by the State reveals that prior to the altercation the defendant was able to control his desires, restraining himself from attempting to "make love to all [or any] of the women in the room," and again, refraining from engaging in a physical struggle with the unknown individual in the dormitory lobby.

While after the altercation defendant asserted he was in company with his mother and Richard Nixon, and later, that he was Rumplestilskin, the trial court need not have accepted these as delusions or manifestations of irrationality. The evidence presented by the State reveals that these apparently nonresponsive answers were given in a manner that denoted sarcasm and flippancy. Such answers would then evidence a basic understanding of the questions and a capacity to give a sarcastic response.

The State's evidence demonstrates beyond a reasonable doubt that both before and after the altercation defendant had lucid periods during which his reasoning power functioned, that the defendant's apparently irrational behavior was, upon analysis, the outward manifestation of an arrogant, sarcastic, and provoking personality, and not the actions of a person whose power to reason had been totally suspended. We therefore find that the State's evidence demonstrates beyond a reasonable doubt that defendant's intoxicated and drugged condition did not suspend all of his power to reason and that he could have formulated a conscious purpose or objective to commit a battery upon the officers. Cf. People v. Redmond.

Defendant next maintains that he was not proven guilty of aggravated battery beyond a reasonable doubt in that his unrebutted evidence proved him to be insane at the time of the offense. Defendant did not raise the defense of insanity at trial. The record expressly demonstrates that the defendant's theory of the case at trial was predicated upon the affirmative defense of an intoxicated and drugged condition and not upon the affirmative defense of insanity. The issue concerning an affirmative defense cannot be raised for the first time on appeal. (People v. Abrams, 48 Ill.2d 446, 458 (1971).) We, therefore, do not consider this issue.

Defendant contends that the trial court abused its discretion in denying his request for probation, and that he should be granted probation by this court. Attacking two officers of the law is a serious offense, and the use of a firearm during commission of such offense significantly aggravates the cause. A sentence of probation would deprecate the seriousness of the offense and would be inconsistent with the ends of justice. Under the circumstances here, the trial court did not abuse its discretion by denying probation and entering the minimum sentence for each offense.

Judgment affirmed.

## PEOPLE v. PACE
34 Ill. App. 3d 440, 339 N.E.2d 785 (1975)

**PRIOR HISTORY:** APPEAL from the Circuit Court of Cook County; the HON. ROBERT J. DOWNING, Judge, presiding.

**DISPOSITION:** Affirmed as modified, in part. Mittimus amended.

**COUNSEL:** Paul Bradley and Margaret Maxwell, both of State Appellate Defender's Office, of Chicago, for appellant.

Bernard Carey, State's Attorney, of Chicago (Laurence J. Bolon, Linda Ann Miller, and Iris E. Sholder, Assistant State's Attorneys, of counsel), for the People.

**JUDGES:** MR. PRESIDING JUSTICE BARRETT delivered the opinion of the court. DRUCKER and SULLIVAN, JJ., concur.

**OPINION BY:** BARRETT

**OPINION:** Brian Pace and Robert Montgomery were indicted for attempt murder in violation of section 8-4 of the Criminal Code (ILL. REV. STAT. 1969, ch. 38, § 8-4) and aggravated battery in violation of section 12-4(b)(1) of the Criminal Code (ILL. REV. STAT. 1969, ch. 38, § 12-4(b)(1)) of Justo Rivera and Angel Rivera. Both defendants were released on bail. On October 26, 1970, defendants were in court when their case was reached for trial. At that time defendants' motion to suppress identification was denied. A panel of 50 veniremen was then brought into the courtroom and sworn to answer questions as to their qualification to act as jurors. The venire was given an initial orientation, the indictment was read, and defendants were introduced to the prospective jurors. A list of prospective witnesses was read to the veniremen and, after the judge gave further orientation and admonitions, he adjourned the case until the following morning.

The next morning when court reconvened, defendant Pace failed to appear. On inquiry, Montgomery advised the court that from his conversation with Pace the previous night he believed that Pace had left and was not going to return. The trial court denied the motion of defense counsel to withdraw as counsel for Pace and a later motion for severance and a continuance and ruled that the trial had already begun and would proceed without Pace. Defendant was then tried *in absentia.*

The jury returned a verdict of guilty against Pace of attempt murder and aggravated battery of Justo Rivera and aggravated battery of Angel Rivera. After having postponed sentencing in hopes of securing Pace's presence, the court, on December 10, 1970, pronounced a sentence of

8 to 20 years on the count of attempt murder of Justo Rivera, and 5 to 10 years on the count of aggravated battery of Angel Rivera, the terms to run consecutively. The court imposed this sentence upon the defendant's return to Chicago in 1972.

Defendant raises three issues on appeal: whether he was deprived of due process of law for being tried *in absentia* where he voluntarily absented himself from the courtroom after the veniremen were sworn to answer questions, the indictment and a list of possible witnesses was read and the veniremen were given their orientation and admonitions; whether the evidence showed that he was so intoxicated that he could not have formulated the specific intent required to commit the offenses and therefore was not proven guilty beyond a reasonable doubt; whether his consecutive sentence of 5 to 10 years for aggravated battery and 8 to 20 years for attempt murder should be reduced in accordance with the sentencing provisions of the Illinois Unified Code of Corrections.

The evidence introduced at trial showed that on the Sunday afternoon of August 10, 1969, Justo Rivera, his wife, their children and Luis Pagan, another child, went to Lincoln Park to play baseball. They took sporting equipment with them, including several mitts, a ball and a bat. Two men approached the family, one of whom was later identified as Robert Montgomery, asked Justo Rivera if they could play. Mr. Rivera told him no and Montgomery walked a short distance away. Defendant at that point proceeded to argue with Justo Rivera, swearing, and threatening to kill him. While Justo Rivera bent over to pick up some of the equipment, Montgomery grabbed and held him from behind, permitting defendant to punch Rivera. Eleven-year old Angel Rivera grabbed the baseball bat and began hitting his father's attackers on the back and the legs. Defendant stopped hitting Justo Rivera and ran after Angel whom he then kicked in the stomach and hit with the bat. As Justo Rivera, who was still being held by Montgomery, tried to get up and help his son, Pace turned and began to strike Justo Rivera several times with the bat. Luis Pagan found a police canine unit and toured the park with the officer until they found the defendants, whom Pagan identified as the assailants. Pace and Montgomery were placed under arrest and were subsequently identified by others who had witnessed the incident. Justo Rivera was taken to the hospital where he remained unconscious for five days. Angel Rivera was permitted to go home after receiving stitches for his facial wounds. The Rivera family subsequently moved back to Puerto Rico, but returned to Chicago for the trial.

James O'Kennard testified that he was in Lincoln Park on August 10, 1969, and that he observed defendant hitting a child with a baseball bat and later saw defendant hit Justo Rivera five times on the head with a bat while being held by Montgomery. He said that he suspected that defendant was under some form of sedation.

Gerald Stevens testified that he observed defendant hitting both Angel and Justo Rivera and that he did not see any aggressive moves on the part of the Rivera family to provoke the attack. He stated that defendant did not appear to be intoxicated or under the influence of drugs because he did not stagger.

Dennis McQuen testified for the defendant that he attended a rock music festival with defendant and Montgomery in Lincoln Park on August 10, 1969, and that they joined three young women with whom they drank some wine. Though the number varied, there were usually at least nine people sitting in a circle sharing numerous quart bottles of wine. He felt defendant was drunk when he left the group because he was no longer well coordinated and seemed very happy.

Robert Montgomery testified that he and defendant sat with some people and drank wine over a period of four or five hours. He estimated that defendant consumed about two quarts of wine. He has no recollection of any of the events between the time he left the group and when he was stopped by the police.

Morgan Lloyd, the arresting officer, testified that on August 10, 1969, he spoke with Luis Pagan about the incident and then proceeded to search for the defendants. He arrested the defendants after they had been identified by Pagan. He said he subsequently spoke with Mr. O'Kennard, Mr. Stevens and the Rivera family.

*Opinion*

The first issue raised on appeal is whether defendant was deprived of due process of law for being tried *in absentia* where he voluntarily absented himself from the courtroom after the veniremen were sworn to answer questions, the indictment and a list of witnesses was read and the veniremen were given their orientation and admonitions. A defendant in a criminal case has a constitutional right to be present at all stages of his trial. (People v. Mallett, 30 Ill.2d 136, 195 N.E.2d 687.) However, a defendant may not prevent his trial by voluntarily absenting himself therefrom, and a defendant in a criminal case who has been released on bail has a duty to present himself in court. (<u>People v. Steenbergen</u>, 31 Ill.2d 615, 203 N.E.2d 404.) It has long been held that where a defendant is at liberty on bail and voluntarily absents himself from his trial after it has begun, he waives the right to be present and the court can proceed without him. <u>Diaz v. United States</u>, 223 U.S. 442, 56 L.Ed. 500.

Defendant, in arguing that he has absented himself before his trial began, asks this court to rely on the holding of <u>People v. Davis</u>, 39 Ill. 2d 325, 235 N.E.2d 634. In that case our Supreme Court in reversing defendant's conviction, stated that it would be a deprivation of defendant's constitutional rights to be tried *in absentia* where he fails at any time to appear in court for his trial by jury.

The circumstances surrounding the trial in the instant case cannot be compared to those found in <u>Davis</u>. Here, defendant was present in the courtroom on October 26, 1970, at which time his attorney answered that defendants were ready to proceed to trial. Defendants' motion to suppress identification and the testimony relating thereto of three witnesses was heard. After this motion was denied a jury venire was brought into the courtroom. The veniremen were sworn to answer questions as to their qualifications and a preliminary orientation as to their duties was given by the court. The defendants were introduced to the jury, the indictments and a list of possible witnesses was read. After further orientation and admonitions the court recessed until the following morning at which time the selection of the jury commenced. Defendant failed to present himself to the court at that time and the trial continued without him.

Though <u>Davis</u> sets the outer parameter in determining that a defendant may not be tried *in absentia* where he fails to present himself at any time in court, we are guided by the language in <u>Hopt v. Utah</u>, 110 U.S. 574, 28 L.Ed. 262, in determining at what stage of a judicial proceeding a defendant's subsequent absence from the courtroom becomes a waiver of his right to be present at his trial. The United States Supreme Court in <u>Hopt</u> stated that:

> For every purpose, therefore, involved in the requirement that the defendant shall be personally present at the trial, where the indictment is for a felony, the trial commences *at least* from the time when the work of empanelling a jury begins.

Based upon this proposition, we find that the judicial proceedings of October 26, 1970, were indeed the work of empaneling the jury, and marked the beginning of defendant's trial. To hold otherwise would permit defendant to frustrate and impede the judicial process by monopolizing the time of both the court and the venire and then profit from his own wrong by voluntarily absenting himself. We have previously stated that although this court is loath to proceed with court hearings in defendant's absence, we cannot encourage defendants to treat their court appearances as discretionary. (<u>People v. Stubbs</u>, 25 Ill. App. 3d 181, 323 N.E.2d 26.) Defendant was not deprived of due process of law where he volutarily [*sic*] absented himself after his trial had begun, and the court proceeded to continue the trial without him.

Defendant argues that his absence from trial was not an effective waiver because it was not an intentional relinquishment or abandonment of a known right or privilege under <u>Johnson v. Zerbst</u>, 304 U.S. 458, 82 L.Ed. 1461, 58 S.Ct. 1019. We find that the recent United States Supreme Court decision in <u>Taylor v. United States</u>, 414 U.S. 17, 38 L.Ed.2d 174, 94 S.Ct. 194, where defendant failed to return to the afternoon session of his trial, is dispositive of this issue. In finding that Taylor voluntarily absented himself, the trial court relied on the testimony of defendant's wife that she and defendant separated after the morning session, that defendant had not appeared ill, and that she has not heard from him since. The Supreme Court, in rejecting the application of <u>Johnson v. Zerbst</u> to the circumstances in <u>Taylor</u>, held that "[i]t seems equally incredible to us, as it did to the Court of Appeals, 'that a defendant who flees from a courtroom in the midst of a trial—where judge, jury, witnesses and lawyers are present and ready to continue—would not know that as a consequence the trial could continue in his absence.'" 414 U.S. 17, 20, 38 L.Ed.2d 174, 178.

In considering the circumstances of the instant case, such as defendant's presence throughout the proceedings on October 26, 1970, his knowledge that the five members of the Rivera family who had moved back to Puerto Rico were now in the courtroom ready to testify against him, and the statement of the codefendant Montgomery that from his conversations with defendant, he did not believe that defendant was going to return, we can only conclude that defendant knowingly and voluntarily waived his right to be present at the continuation of his trial the following day.

In his second issue on appeal defendant contends that his consumption of alcohol made him incapable of forming an intent to commit murder and aggravated battery, and that since the State failed to prove the intent to commit these offenses beyond a reasonable doubt, the conviction must be reversed.

The legislature has provided that where an individual voluntarily consumes alcohol he is criminally responsible for his conduct unless such condition negatives the existence of a mental state which is an element of the offense. (ILL. REV. STAT. 1969, ch. 38, par. 6-3(a).) To negative the specific intent required for defendant's offenses, and thus be a legal excuse, defendant's condition of intoxication must be so extreme as to suspend all reason. (People v. Rose, 124 Ill.App.2d 447, 259 N.E.2d 393.) The evidence in this case falls short of this requirement. Merely being "drunk" or "intoxicated" is no defense. (People v. Williams, 14 Ill. App. 3d 789, 303 N.E.2d 585.) Therefore, we believe that defendant's condition did not negative the required specific intent and that the evidence supports the jury's findings of guilt beyond a reasonable doubt. Defendant's conviction will not be reversed.

In his third issue on appeal, defendant contends that his consecutive sentence of 5–10 years for aggravated battery and 8–20 years for attempt murder be reduced in accordance with the sentencing provisions of the ILLINOIS UNIFIED CODE OF CORRECTIONS which became effective on January 1, 1973.

The Code in section 8-2-4 provides that:

> Prosecution for any violation of law occurring prior to the effective date of this Act is not affected or abated by this Act. If the offense being prosecuted has not reached the sentencing stage or a final adjudication, then for purposes of sentencing the sentences under this Act apply if they are less than under the prior law upon which the prosecution was commenced. ILL. REV. STAT. 1973, ch. 38, § 1008-2-4.

Under the classification of offenses of the Code, the offense of aggravated battery is a Class 3 felony. (ILL. REV. STAT. 1973, ch. 38, par. 12-4(d).) Section 5-8-1(c)(4) of the Code provides that for a Class 3 felony the minimum sentence "shall not be greater than one-third of the maximum term set in that case by the court." ILL. REV. STAT. 1973, ch. 38, § 1005-8-1(c)(4).

This court finds that since no final adjudication of this matter has been reached (People v. Harvey, 53 Ill.2d 585, 294 N.E.2d 269), that defendant's sentence must be modified in accordance with the above provisions. We therefore reduce defendant's minimum sentence for aggravated battery to three years and four months.

Defendant was sentenced to a term of 8 to 20 years on the charge of attempt murder. Under the UNIFIED CODE OF CORRECTIONS, attempt murder is a Class 1 felony (ILL. REV. STAT. 1973, ch. 38, par. 8-4 (c)(1)), which requires a minimum term of four years "unless the court, having regard to the nature and circumstances of the offense and the history and character of the defendant, sets a higher minimum term." (ILL. REV. STAT. 1973, ch. 38, par. 1005-8-1(c)(2).) Since the term imposed is allowable under the Code, we will not disturb the sentence imposed by the trial court.

Defendant asks this court to modify his sentence for attempt murder so that it may run concurrently, rather than consecutively, with his sentence for aggravated battery. Section 5-8-4 of the ILLINOIS UNIFIED CODE OF CORRECTIONS provides that:

> (b) The Court shall not impose a consecutive sentence unless, having regard to the nature and circumstances of the offense and the history and character of the defendant, it is of the opinion that such a term is required to protect the public from further criminal conduct by the defendant, the basis for which the court may set forth in the record.

We find that though the record demonstrates defendant's act to have indeed been a brutal one, a consecutive sentence is not required to protect the public from any further criminal conduct by the defendant. Therefore, we believe that the sentence for aggravated battery should run concurrently with the sentence for attempt murder.

For the reasons stated herein, the judgment of conviction for attempt murder is affirmed. The judgment of conviction for aggravated battery is also affirmed, with the sentence reduced as stated; and this cause is remanded for correction of the *mittimus* to reflect concurrent sentencing.

Affirmed, as modified, in part.

Mittimus amended.

## PEOPLE v. BRADNEY
170 Ill. App. 3d 839, 121 Ill. Dec. 306, 525 N.E.2d 112 (1988)

**SUBSEQUENT HISTORY:** Rehearing Denied July 19, 1988.

**PRIOR HISTORY:** Appeal from the Circuit Court of Calhoun County; the HON. CECIL J. BURROWS, Judge, presiding.

**DISPOSITION:** Judgment affirmed and cause remanded with directions.

**COUNSEL:** Daniel D. Yuhas and Arden J. Lang, both of State Appellate Defender's Office, of Springfield, for appellants.

Charles H. Burch, State's Attorney, of Hardin (Kenneth R. Boyle, Robert J. Biderman, and Gwendolyn W. Klingler, all of State's Attorneys Appellate Prosecutor's Office, of counsel), for the People.

**JUDGES:** JUSTICE KNECHT delivered the opinion of the court. LUND, J., concurs. JUSTICE MCCULLOUGH, concurring in part and dissenting in part.

**OPINION BY:** KNECHT

**OPINION:** Following a bench trial, the defendants, Bruce C. Bradney (Bruce) and Linda Bradney (Linda), were convicted of residential burglary (ILL. REV. STAT. 1985, ch. 38, par. 19-3) and theft over $300 (ILL. REV. STAT. 1985, ch. 38, par. 16-1). They appeal, contending: (1) evidence concerning the recovery of various items of stolen property from Linda Bradney's automobile should have been suppressed because the stolen property was not seized pursuant to a search warrant or as part of a valid inventory search; (2) the State did not disprove their affirmative defense of voluntary intoxication beyond a reasonable doubt; (3) the results of electrophoretic analysis of dried bloodstains found at the scene of the offenses and in Linda Bradney's automobile were improperly admitted; (4) the State did not establish an adequate foundation for testimony concerning the frequency of blood characteristics in the general population; (5) the State did not establish a proper chain of custody for blood specimens drawn from the defendants; (6) in imposing sentence, the circuit court did not give proper consideration to various mitigating factors; and (7) they are each entitled to 592 days of sentence credit for the time they were incarcerated after their arrests and prior to being sentenced for the present offenses.

The victims of the offenses of which the Bradneys were convicted were Ralph and Genevieve Moses, who reside in a rural area of Calhoun County near Golden Eagle. Upon returning home at approximately 8:30 p.m. on the evening of June 8, 1985, after spending the afternoon and early evening in Alton, the Moses discovered their home had been burglarized. On the following day, Ralph Moses talked with neighbors and discovered that during the previous afternoon, an unfamiliar brown automobile had been seen on both the Moses' property and on the nearby property of Marvin Gelber. It was determined that automobile belonged to Linda Bradney. On the basis of this information, Linda's automobile was seized in Alton on June 10, 1985. Discovered in Linda's automobile was personal property which had been stolen from the Moses' residence. Marvin Gelber made an in-court identification of the Bradneys as the occupants of the unfamiliar brown vehicle. The above evidence, together with evidence supporting an inference bloodstains found in the Moses' residence on the evening of the burglary may have consisted of Bruce's blood, constituted the principal links in the chain of circumstantial evidence which the State presented in support of the charges against the Bradneys. Additional evidence pertinent to the issues presented for review will be set out in relevant portions of this opinion.

## I. *Search of Automobile*

As a preliminary matter, we note in determining whether the circuit court properly ruled upon the Bradneys' motion to suppress evidence, we may consider evidence presented at their trial, in addition to that presented at the hearing on their motion to suppress. (People v. Braden (1966), 34 Ill. 2d 516, 216 N.E.2d 808.) In view of our decision with respect to this issue, the evidence introduced at the Bradneys' bench trial is of greater relevance than that introduced at the hearing on their motion to suppress evidence.

At Bradneys' bench trial, Mary Ellen Freidel testified she is related by marriage to the Moses, and lives about a half-mile down the road from the Moses' residence. On June 8, 1985, she and two of her small children left their home at about 4:30 p.m., in order to go to church in Grafton. On their way to Grafton they passed the Moses' residence and noticed a car backed into the Moses' driveway. The car was parked at a point closer to the Moses' residence than guests of the Moses normally park. The back of the car was open. Freidel described the automobile as "a small, brown, older model car." Upon hearing of the burglary of the Moses' residence on the following morning, Freidel supplied Genevieve Moses with information concerning the vehicle which she had seen in their driveway on the previous afternoon.

On cross-examination, Freidel stated she did not immediately call the police when she saw the car in the Moses' driveway because she at first thought it belonged to one of the Moses' grown children. She acknowledged the brown car could have been in the Moses' driveway for some reason other than the burglary, and the burglary of the Moses' residence could have occurred before or after she saw the brown car in the Moses' driveway.

Marvin Gelber, a resident of Creve Coeur, Missouri, testified he owns a farm about 1½ miles from the Moses' residence. Gelber was at his farm on the afternoon of June 8, 1985. At approximately 3:45 or 4 p.m. on that afternoon, one of his workmen called Gelber's attention to the presence of strangers on his property. Gelber proceeded to the entrance of his farm, where there is a small, white four-room house which was at that time unoccupied. There he saw a light brown two-door Pinto hatchback automobile. Also present were a white woman with straight dishwater-blond hair and a white man with a small thin mustache. Gelber inquired what they were doing there, and they replied they wanted to rent the white house. Gelber stated the house was not for rent and said there was no "for rent" sign, but the couple insisted they wanted to rent the white house. Gelber thought this was odd, and jotted down the license plate number of the brown automobile as it was backing up. On the following day, Gelber informed Ralph Moses of the previous day's incident involving the strangers on his property, and also provided Moses with the license plate number of the brown Pinto automobile which had been on his property on the previous day. Gelber made an in-court identification of the Bradneys as the strangers he had seen on his property on the afternoon of June 8, 1985.

Ralph Moses testified that on the day following the burglary of his residence—June 9, 1985—he was informed Mary Ellen Freidel had seen a car in the Moses' driveway between 4:30 and 5 p.m. on the previous day. He subsequently talked with Freidel. He also talked with Gelber, and Gelber gave him the license number of the brown car he had seen on his property on the previous day. After obtaining the license plate number from Gelber, Moses called the Calhoun County sheriff's department and requested a check be run on that number.

Calhoun County sheriff Richard Meyer testified the license plate number which Gelber wrote down and which Moses relayed to the sheriff's department was for a vehicle registered in the name of Linda Bradney. On June 10, 1985, Meyer turned that information over to the

Alton police department because the "[license] plate number come back [*sic*] to Alton area."

Detective Sergeant Raymond H. Galloway of the Alton police department testified on the basis of information the Bradneys were wanted by the Calhoun County and Madison County sheriff's departments, he, on June 10, 1985, issued a dispatch to the effect the Bradneys were to be arrested. The Bradneys were arrested on the same day, and their Ford Pinto automobile was towed to the Alton police department.

Sergeant Don Lovell of the Alton police department testified that on June 10, 1985, he received information from Sergeant Galloway the police were seeking a brown Pinto hatchback automobile, and Bruce and Linda Bradney were being sought with reference to that automobile. Lovell kept the Bradneys' automobile under surveillance for a brief period of time, observed the Bradneys enter the vehicle, and followed the Bradneys for several blocks. He was preparing to stop the Bradneys when they pulled over.

When the Bradneys exited their vehicle, Sergeant Lovell placed them under arrest. He transported Linda to the police station, and another officer transported Bruce Bradney to the station. Linda Bradney's automobile was towed to the police station and secured in the basement garage.

Mary Ellen Freidel further testified that on June 10, 1985, Trooper Thomas Jacobs transported her to the Alton police department, where she identified a vehicle which she saw in the police garage as that which she had seen at the Moses' residence on the afternoon of June 8, 1985.

Sheriff Meyer stated he was present while items were removed from the Bradneys' vehicle at the Alton police department. He thought Ralph Moses identified items as they were removed from the vehicle.

Ralph Moses testified that on June 10, 1985, he was summoned to the Alton police department, where he was met by Sheriff Meyer, Sergeant Galloway, and another officer with whom he was not familiar. At the police department, Moses saw a brown Ford hatchback automobile bearing the license number which Gelber had provided him. While Moses was at the police department, the brown Pinto hatchback was searched by Galloway, assisted by an individual whom Moses did not know. Among the items discovered in the automobile were cameras, jewelry boxes, and binoculars which were among the items missing from the Moses' residence. The car also contained items which did not belong to the Moses.

On cross-examination, Moses testified before Linda Bradney's automobile was opened, one could see duffel bags and a suitcase, which were closed, through the glass. As items were removed from the car's hatchback, Moses looked at them and identified some items as being his.

Trooper Thomas F. Jacobs of the Illinois State Police stated that on June 10, 1985, he transported Mary Freidel and her small daughter to the Alton police station to enable them to identify a vehicle which the Alton police department had impounded. The impounded automobile was a light brown 1975 Ford Pinto. Freidel identified that vehicle in Jacobs' presence. Jacobs personally viewed the vehicle and observed one suitcase and two bags in the vehicle's back compartment. These articles were still in the vehicle when Mary Freidel identified it. Jacobs further testified that after Freidel identified the vehicle, Ralph Moses looked into the automobile's back glass, hesitated a moment, saw a brown suitcase in the back of the vehicle, and said, "Hey, that looks like my suitcase." Sergeant Galloway opened the vehicle so Moses could get a better look at it, and Moses said, "That's my suitcase." Galloway then opened a bag, and a camera was immediately exposed. Ralph Moses said, "[There's] my camera."

Sergeant Galloway testified that when Linda Bradney's vehicle was brought to the police department, he, Sergeant Lovell, Sheriff Meyer, and Officer Hickman were present. Mary Freidel and her daughter arrived later. Galloway was present when the Freidels examined Linda Bradney's car and identified it. According to Galloway, Linda Bradney's vehicle was a hatchback, and one could see into the large rear back window very plainly. Ralph Moses looked into the vehicle's rear window and said, "[That] looks like my suitcase." At that time, Moses was not able to see any of the items inside the suitcase. Galloway then proceeded to open the suitcase and duffel bags which were in the rear section of Linda Bradney's vehicle. Upon Galloway opening one of the duffel bags, Moses stated, "[That's] my camera." Galloway then took the articles found in Linda Bradney's automobile to an investigation room, where he "inventoried the items out on the table." Galloway removed the suitcase and duffel bags from Linda's vehicle because, "I had merchandise taken from the Calhoun County burglary."

Elmer Hickman, a patrolman with the Alton police department, testified he accompanied Linda Bradney's vehicle from the location of its seizure to the Alton station. When he turned the vehicle over to Sergeant Galloway in the basement of the police station, it contained suitcases, duffel bags and other items.

On August 9 and 13, 1985, Bruce and Linda Bradney filed motions to exclude evidence, in which they alleged their constitutional rights under the United States and Illinois Constitutions were violated by a wrongful seizure of their persons and Linda's automobile. At the hearing on these motions, the State contended the Bradneys were properly arrested and Linda's automobile was properly seized on the basis of probable cause to believe the Bradneys were guilty of residential burglary. The State further argued Linda Bradney's automobile was searched as a result of an inventory of the vehicle and pursuant to a lawful arrest. The Bradneys' attorneys argued the removal of items from Linda's automobile constituted an illegal search and seizure as opposed to a valid inventory search. They further argued (1) the search of Linda Bradney's automobile was not incident to an arrest, (2) no exigent circumstances which would have justified a warrantless search, such as the imminent destruction of evidence, were present, and (3) the plain view doctrine was inapplicable because there was no way of knowing what was in the duffel bags until the contents thereof were examined.

In its order denying the Bradneys' motions to exclude evidence concerning the items found in Linda's automobile, the circuit court found a search and inventory of the vehicle was performed without the benefit of a search warrant. The court further found two duffel bags and a suitcase were in plain view through the hatchback window of Linda's automobile, and Sergeant Galloway indicated Ralph Moses spotted a suitcase which Moses thought belonged to him. Relying on the facts the Bradneys were properly arrested for burglaries in Calhoun and Madison Counties, and two duffel bags containing unknown articles together with a suitcase at least tentatively identified by a victim were visible in the back of Linda Bradney's automobile, the court concluded the police had reasonable grounds to believe Linda's vehicle contained the fruits of a burglary committed in Calhoun County. Relying on <u>United States v. Ross</u> (1982), 456 U.S. 798, 72 L. Ed. 2d 572, 102 S. Ct. 2157, the court held the fact the stolen property was recovered from containers was immaterial. The court further held the fact the search was not conducted immediately upon seizure of Linda's automobile was of no consequence in view of the Supreme Court's decision in <u>United States v.</u>

Johns (1985), 469 U.S. 478, 83 L. Ed. 2d 890, 105 S. Ct. 881. Also, the court held Linda's automobile was properly searched as a result of an inventory of the items contained in the vehicle.

On July 15 and 16, 1986, Bruce and Linda filed motions for reconsideration of the circuit court's decision with respect to the admissibility of evidence concerning the items found in Linda's automobile. The basis for this motion was some of the law enforcement officers who testified for the State in the present case testified at a Madison County trial involving the Bradneys to the effect no inventory search of Linda's automobile was performed at the Alton police department on June 10, 1985. At a hearing on these motions, the State's and the Bradneys' arguments centered on the question of whether the June 10, 1985, search of Linda's automobile was a valid inventory search. The court denied these motions, holding an inventory search of Linda's vehicle was performed on June 10, 1985. The court also noted, with respect to its ruling on the Bradneys' previous motions to exclude evidence, "the inventory rationale was not the only reason for not suppressing the seizure," and found "the arresting officers had information which would lead them to reasonably believe that [Linda's] vehicle was transporting contraband."

The arguments of both the Bradneys and the State as to the question of whether the circuit court should have suppressed evidence stolen property was discovered during the search of Linda's automobile concentrate on the issue of whether the items stolen from the Moses' residence were discovered during a valid inventory search of Linda's vehicle. Additionally, the State contends Linda's automobile was properly seized, since at the time the automobile was impounded, the Bradneys were suspects in residential burglaries. The State also argues a search warrant for the Bradneys' automobile could not have been obtained since it was not certain it contained stolen items (the burglary having occurred two days earlier), and the police thus could not have stated with specificity the items for which they would be searching. In their reply argument, the Bradneys contend the Moses could easily have described the items missing from their home with sufficient specificity to enable them to be listed on a valid search warrant.

Although the focus was on the issue of whether the police performed a proper inventory search of Linda's vehicle, we believe the question of whether the police had probable cause to believe Linda's vehicle contained stolen property was sufficiently presented in the circuit court proceedings to enable us to consider that issue on appeal. We conclude the police properly searched Linda's automobile on the basis of probable cause to believe it contained stolen property. Therefore, we need not consider whether the police performed a valid inventory search of Linda's vehicle. Also, since the Bradneys did not in their opening brief assert the initial seizure of Linda's vehicle violated their constitutional rights, we need not consider whether the police acted properly in seizing Linda's vehicle before it was towed to the Alton police station. See 107 Ill. 2d R. 341(e)(7) (points not argued in appellant's opening brief are waived).

Observation of that which is in plain view does not constitute a search. (People v. Davis (1965), 33 Ill. 2d 134, 210 N.E.2d 530.) The viewing of items contained in an automobile from a location at which the person observing the objects has a lawful right to be is not a search of the vehicle. (People v. Exum (1943), 382 Ill. 204, 47 N.E.2d 56.

Probable cause for a search exists where, on the basis of all known circumstances, "there is a fair probability that contraband or other evidence of a crime will be found in a particular place." (Illinois v. Gates (1983), 462 U.S. 213, 238, 76 L. Ed. 2d 527, 548, 103 S. Ct. 2317, 2332.) Once the police have probable cause to believe an automobile contains contraband or stolen property, they may search any containers found in areas of the vehicle which they have probable cause to believe may contain contraband or stolen property. (United States v. Ross (1982), 456 U.S. 798, 72 L. Ed. 2d 572, 102 S. Ct. 2157; United States v. Caroline (D.C. Cir. 1986), 791 F.2d 197.) Some Federal courts have limited the Ross decision to the extent police may not search an entire vehicle if they have probable cause to believe only a specific container within the vehicle holds contraband and have no basis for believing a search of other areas of the vehicle may turn up contraband. In such situations, a warrant is required in order to search the suspect container. (E.g., United States v. Williams (D.C. Cir. 1987), 822 F.2d 1174; United States v. Mazzone (7th Cir. 1986), 782 F.2d 757, cert. denied (1986), 479 U.S. 838, 93 L. Ed. 2d 84, 107 S. Ct. 141.) If the police have probable cause to believe an area of an automobile contains contraband or stolen property, the fact they focus their search on a specific container or containers found within that area is of no consequence. McKinney v. State (1987), 184 Ga. App. 607, 362 S.E.2d 65.

A search of a properly seized automobile premised on probable cause to believe it contains contraband need not occur immediately upon seizure of the vehicle. Rather, the police may remove the automobile from the scene of its seizure and search it and closed containers found therein at a different location. <u>United States v. Johns</u> (1985), 469 U.S. 478, 83 L. Ed. 2d 890, 105 S. Ct. 881; <u>United States v. Weber</u> (11th Cir. 1987), 808 F.2d 1422.

In the present case, Mary Freidel identified Linda Bradney's automobile as the vehicle which she saw at the Moses' residence on the day it was burglarized. Additionally, law enforcement officers were aware Marvin Gelber had on the day of the burglary seen the same vehicle on his property, which is located near the Moses' residence, under highly suspicious circumstances.

Ralph Moses did not testify he identified a suitcase in Linda Bradney's automobile as belonging to him before the vehicle was searched. Nevertheless, both Detective Galloway and Trooper Jacobs testified Ralph Moses (while looking into Linda Bradney's automobile from a vantage point at which he had a lawful right to be) made a statement to the effect, "[That] looks like my suitcase" before the police searched the vehicle. The circuit court specifically relied upon this uncontroverted facet of Sergeant Galloway's testimony in holding the police had reasonable grounds to believe Linda Bradney's automobile contained fruits of a crime prior to searching it. This portion of Sergeant Galloway's testimony is corroborated by the testimony of Trooper Jacobs of the Illinois State Police. Trooper Jacobs' only role in the investigation of the burglary of the Moses' residence was to transport Mary Freidel and her daughter from their Calhoun County home to the Alton police department and back, so they could view Linda Bradney's vehicle at a time when the Calhoun County sheriff's department was apparently shorthanded. Thus Jacobs was for practical purposes an unbiased and impartial witness to the events leading up to the search of Linda Bradney's automobile.

Because Ralph Moses tentatively identified a suitcase in Linda Bradney's automobile as belonging to him and the vehicle had been seen in proximity to the time and place of the burglary of the Moses' residence, the police had probable cause to believe property stolen from the Moses' residence was located throughout Linda's automobile and to search any containers which they found in the vehicle, including the duffel bags in which property stolen from the Moses' residence was discovered (see <u>Mazzone</u>, 782 F.2d 757 (police who observed what they believed were drugs being handed to occupants of van and car had probable cause to believe searches of all areas of those vehicles might turn up additional drugs, drug paraphernalia or proceeds of other drug sales)). For the above reasons, we hold the circuit court properly denied the Bradneys' motions to suppress the evidence property stolen from the Moses' residence was found in Linda Bradney's automobile.

## II. *Voluntary Intoxication*

At the Bradneys' trial, Bruce Bradney testified he began using alcohol at the age of 16. He failed ninth grade because of alcohol usage. As a teenager, he used alcohol as often as he could get people to supply it. Bruce also outlined his drug usage, which began with the inhalation of Benzedrine in 1957 while in the military. At that time Bruce discovered by swallowing inhalers he could consume large quantities of alcohol over a two- to three-day period. When stationed in Germany he took Preludin, a drug which was then legal and cost 35 cents for 20 pills. He stated Preludin is a derivative of Benzedrine and is a powerful amphetamine. While in the ambulance service at Fort Dix he had ample supplies of alcohol and received amphetamines from the Army hospital. At that time Bruce "started soaking them [nasal inhalers] down and injecting them into [his] arms." As a result Bruce has practically no circulatory system left. During his military service, Bruce suffered from memory loss following overindulgence in alcohol and drugs. He has experimented with heroine, cocaine and morphine.

Bruce further testified that on May 29, 1985, he was released from Menard Correctional Center, and Linda drove him to Alton. En route they stopped at a bar near the prison and had "a couple of drinks and bought a six-pack of bottles." From that date through June 8, 1985, Bruce drank and consumed alcohol on a daily basis. At first he only intended to celebrate his release from prison with Linda and their landlady in Alton. However, on the morning following his release, he discovered Linda had just been denied early release from parole. As a result, the couple would have to remain in Madison County instead of moving to Iron Mountain, Missouri, in order to start a new life as they had planned. In Madison County, "people . . . were not particularly happy with us to begin with . . . I knew that it would be just a matter of time before they would find some reason to throw me in jail like they did before. The more I thought about it the more I drank. The more I drank the more I wanted some pills."

Bruce also injected drugs during the period between his release from prison and June 8, 1985, and his house and Linda's car were full of used syringes. Bruce had no memory concerning where he was or what he did on June 8, 1985. Bruce had $500 upon his release from prison, but upon his arrest had only $8 or $9, and Linda had $13.

Linda testified she began drinking at the age of 12 and as a child became intoxicated two to three times per week. She "did uppers and downers" during that time. She first began experiencing blackouts or memory losses as a result of intoxication while a teenager. As an adult she could "drink two or three quarts of Mad Dog 20/20 [Mogan David 40-proof wine]." She further stated she could drink "up to a case and half of beer by [herself]." She drank heavily when she was depressed.

Linda stated that on May 29, 1985, she drove to Menard Correctional Center to pick up Bruce. She brought two six-packs of beer with her, and they stopped on the way home to buy Mad Dog wine. From then until June 8, 1985, she consumed alcohol in the form of Southern Comfort, Mad Dog wine, beer, gin, and rum, and became intoxicated on a daily basis. She also consumed Placidyl and Valium pills during the same period. Linda stated she has no present memory of what happened on June 8, 1985.

On cross-examination, Linda stated she remembered last consuming drugs and alcohol on May 30, 1985. When asked whether she recalled consuming any drugs or alcohol after that date, she replied, "[Only] my apartment when I woke up is nothing but beer cans and empty wine bottles."

The Bradneys also presented an evidentiary deposition of Dr. Robert Carroll, a physician specializing in neuropsychiatry. Approximately 10% to 20% of Dr. Carroll's practice is devoted to alcohol and drug treatment.

Carroll testified as to the effects of alcohol and Valium on the human mind and body. He was then asked hypothetical questions concerning a hypothetical man possessing Bruce's characteristics, who had consumed the amount of alcohol Bruce claimed to have consumed during the 10-day period preceding and including June 8, 1985. When asked whether, at the tail end of such a drinking spree, the hypothetical man's ability to reason would be impaired, Carroll responded:

> "I would say that his ability to reason would be impaired, although, all functions of, all brain functions, may not be impaired; for instance, he may be able to walk, talk, communicate with others, drive a car, appear conscience [*sic*]. Other brain functions, personality functions could be impaired such as judgment, emotion, level of provocation, value system, inhibitions [*sic*]."

Carroll was next questioned concerning a hypothetical woman who consumed the amount of alcohol and drugs Linda claimed to have consumed during the 10-day period preceding and including June 8, 1985. Carroll implied his answers would be similar to those he gave for the hypothetical man having Bruce's characteristics. The following dialogue then occurred:

"Q. . . . [Could] this hypothetical woman distinguish between what's right and what's wrong?

A. It's quite likely that the function would and could be impaired. I mentioned a hypothetical man that not only would and could [*sic*] her own inhabitions [*sic*] and her own value system be impaired, but also her awareness of and/or her appreciation and, and her taking into account of other people's and society's value systems be impaired. In other words, the consequences of her acts and her appreciation could be (inaudible); and the likewise (inaudible) at that level of chemical effect on her nervous system to do such a thing."

The Bradneys contend as a result of their voluntary intoxication on June 8, 1985, they were unable to form the requisite intent to burglarize the Moses' residence, and the State did not present sufficient evidence to rebut the evidence of voluntary intoxication which they presented. The Bradneys place particular reliance on the testimony of Dr. Carroll, which they contend establishes they were so drugged and intoxicated on the date in question they were incapable of forming a mental intent to commit residential burglary and theft. They also rely on their own testimony as to their prior history of alcohol and drug addiction and their testimony that beginning May 29, 1985, they began drinking and taking drugs on a daily basis until June 10, 1985. They also note they both testified they suffered from memory loss for about the first 10 days of June 1985.

The State contends the Bradneys' actions on the date of the burglary of the Moses' residence are inconsistent with a conclusion their ability to reason was totally suspended when they burglarized the Moses' residence. The State notes the Bradneys were able to quickly formulate an alibi for their presence on Gelber's property and backed up Linda's automobile close to a stranger's house and opened its hatchback.

Voluntary intoxication which negates the existence of a mental state which is an element of a crime is an affirmative defense. In order to constitute an affirmative defense, voluntary intoxication must be so extreme as to suspend all powers of reason. There are many levels of intoxication through which an individual may pass before he or she reaches the level of being incapable of the formation of the intent to commit a crime. If the evidence is sufficient to raise this affirmative defense, the State has the burden of rebutting it beyond a reasonable doubt by proving the defendant was aware of his actions at the time of the offense. (People v. Gutknecht (1984), 121 Ill. App. 3d 839, 460 N.E.2d 60.) The weight to be accorded testimony relating to the affirmative defense of voluntary intoxication is peculiarly within the province of the trier of fact. People v. Fleming (1976), 42 Ill. App. 3d 1, 355 N.E.2d 345.

In determining whether a defendant was so intoxicated his or her powers of reason were totally suspended, the trier of fact is not obligated to rely on the testimony of experts to the exclusion of other evidence relevant to the defendant's mental state. Rather, the trier of fact may consider the opinions of experts together with all of the other evidence relevant to the defendant's mental state at the time of the offense and reject the expert testimony if it deems the other evidence more probative. See People v. Ehrich (1988), 165 Ill. App. 3d 1060, 1068, 519 N.E.2d 1137, 1142; People v. Jones (1977), 56 Ill. App. 3d 600, 371 N.E.2d 1150.

Dr. Carroll did not testify the powers of reason of the hypothetical persons possessing the Bradneys' characteristics would have been totally suspended as a result of their ingestion of drugs and alcohol in the quantities which the Bradneys stated they consumed during the 10-day period preceding and including June 8, 1985. Rather, Dr. Carroll stated the powers of reason of the hypothetical persons would be impaired. Thus, Dr. Carroll's testimony does not directly support a conclusion the Bradneys' powers of reason were totally suspended when they burglarized the Moses' residence.

There is ample circumstantial evidence on the basis of which the circuit court could have discounted the Bradneys' testimony and the expert testimony which they presented concerning their degree of intoxication when they burglarized the Moses' residence and concluded their powers of reason were not totally suspended on that date. In order to burglarize the Moses' residence, it was necessary for the Bradneys to drive from their home in Alton and either cross a river on a ferry or travel a circuitous alternate route in order to arrive at the Moses' residence in the southern part of Calhoun County. They backed Linda's automobile into the Moses' driveway, most likely in order to facilitate the task of carrying stolen goods from the house or to avoid the possibility of anyone seeing them removing stolen property. They gained entry to the Moses' residence through a basement window, and there is some evidence one or both of the Bradneys wore gloves in order to avoid leaving fingerprints in the Moses' home. Additionally, they were able to quickly formulate an alibi when they were discovered on Marvin Gelber's farm. This evidence is simply inconsistent with the proposition the Bradneys' powers of reason were totally suspended on the day they burglarized the Moses' residence. It provides a sufficient basis for the circuit court's implicit finding the State disproved the Bradneys' affirmative defense of voluntary intoxication beyond a reasonable doubt.

### III. *Electrophoretic Analysis of Dried Bloodstains*

The Bradneys assert the circuit court erred in admitting the results of electrophoretic analysis of dried bloodstains found in the Moses' residence and in Linda Bradney's automobile following the burglary of the Moses' residence. The Bradneys concede electrophoretic analysis of fresh blood is generally accepted in the scientific community. However, they assert electrophoretic analysis of dried blood, which may have been exposed to any of a number of contaminants, is less reliable than electrophoretic analysis of fresh blood. They argue the State did not present evidence electrophoretic analysis of dried blood has gained general acceptance in the scientific community. They further assert the alleged error in admission of results of electrophoretic analysis of dried bloodstains could not have been harmless, since the bloodstains found in the Moses' home were the only physical evidence placing Bruce Bradney at the scene of the burglary.

The State first asserts the results of electrophoretic analysis of dried bloodstains which was presented at the Bradneys' trial did not specifically identify Bruce as the person who burglarized the Moses' residence, but instead only established Bruce could not be excluded as the burglar. The State also asserts the results of electrophoretic analysis of dried bloodstains were corroborated by the fact Bruce had a cut on one of his fingers when arrested. The State notes the circuit court stated the blood analysis testimony was not necessary in order for it to reach its decision, and argues admission of results of electrophoretic analysis of the dried bloodstains, if error, did not prejudice the Bradneys, since strong nonscientific evidence linked them to the crimes of which they were convicted.

Dennis Aubuchon, a forensic serologist with the Illinois Department of Law Enforcement, testified with regard to the electrophoretic analysis of the dried bloodstains found in the Moses' home and in Linda Bradney's automobile following the burglary of the Moses' residence. According to Aubuchon:

> . . . [Electrophoresis] is a method of separating blood proteins present in human blood and categorizing them according to the various phototypes present in the systems that we are testing for. Simply put, it's a method of typing other than ABO. It's a method of breaking down the blood group further. It's a technique whereby we can determine whether or not a person has a different, in this case, ESD type or PGM type. Those standards are [esterase-D (ESD)] and Phosphoglucomutase [PGM], proteins present in human blood; and they are typeable and distinguishable from each other on the basis of my tests.
>
> . . . .
>
> . . . [PGM] exists in different molecular forms; in other words, the different molecular forms would all perform the same function in the human body; but they would be detectable as being different in different people or belonging to several common types similar to the ABO groups. You could have PGM1, PGM21, PGM2, being the most common types. . . .
>
> . . . .
>
> There are rare ones, too; but we generally deal with these three. . . . The main thing to understand is that there are three common types that you would see by staining a particular plate, taking pictures of the plate and then reading the results after they've been incubated.

Testing for different types of ESD enzymes is also one of the electrophoretic techniques of blood analysis. The ESD test is run at the same time as the PGM test but is developed and read separately from the PGM test.

Aubuchon first began performing electrophoretic tests of blood in 1975, and there has never been a dispute concerning the accuracy of this technique as applied to liquid blood. In discussing the reliability of electrophoretic analysis of dried bloodstains, Aubuchon stated:

In all the cases I've worked on, literally hundreds, I've never found any discrepancies that would lead me to believe that it would be unethical or unreliable to use [electrophoresis]. To the contrary, I've many many times have resolved questions using these systems. I've always been able to look at my results and feel they were clear cut, and I have never had any problems with the system.

The only problem, if I do see a particular band or pattern that isn't, doesn't make sense, simply inconclusive [*sic*]. I don't bother deciding why. It is true that eventually blood will break down, and you won't get any—the enzymes will simply degrade. You won't detect them. So the analyst has to use his individual experience to decide when these are readable, when the results are reliable and when not, etc.

. . . I've used this for many years, and there are times when blood is decomposed. The case in front of me is not one of those times.

On cross-examination, Aubuchon acknowledged he had no way of knowing whether the dried blood found in Linda Bradney's automobile and in the Moses' home had been contaminated before he tested it.

On examination by the court, Aubuchon testified as follows with respect to the decision in <u>People v. Young</u> (1986), 425 Mich. 470, 391 N.W.2d 270, where the court held admission of results of electrophoretic analysis of dried bloodstains was reversible error when considered in the view of the closely balanced evidence:

. . . I read the decision. . . . There was no objection on the use of electrophoresis in fresh liquid blood standards. The objection was in, which I have been asked about here, well how do you know what this dried blood has been subjected to. How do you know that it wasn't contaminated. How do you know that it hadn't degraded partially, and this was the objection; and I don't know that it hasn't. All I can go by is that am I looking at a logical type here. Do my readings make sense to me, and there's no reason for me to believe that, say, a type 1, would decompose into a type 21. It would decompose, but it would decompose into something from my experience that is unreadable, undetectable and eventually going into something that's eventually dust.

I have never seen a type disintegrate into another readable type.

Aubuchon's tests revealed the blood found in both Linda's automobile and the Moses' residence, as well as the blood contained in samples obtained from Linda and Bruce, was ABO type O. Also, both Linda and Bruce have PGM type 1 blood. However, further testing revealed Bruce's blood is ESD type 21, while Linda's blood is ESD type 1. The blood discovered in the Moses' home was ESD type 21. Thus, that blood could have come from Bruce but not from Linda. Aubuchon was unable to exclude either Linda or Bruce as the person whose blood was found in Linda's automobile. Aubuchon further testified American Red Cross statistics indicate the combination of characteristics present in Bruce's blood and in the blood found in the Moses' residence—ABO type O, PGM type 1, ESD type 21—occurs in approximately 5.4% of the Caucasian population of the United States.

Scientific opinions relevant to factual issues must be premised on principles which have gained general acceptance in the scientific community in order to be admissible. People v. Harbold (1984), 124 Ill. App. 3d 363, 464 N.E.2d 734; see People v. Baynes (1981), 88 Ill. 2d 225, 430 N.E.2d 1070.

At least four previous Illinois decisions have considered the admissibility of the results of electrophoretic analysis of dried substances. In the first of these decisions, People v. LaSumba (1980), 92 Ill. App. 3d 621, 414 N.E.2d 1318, cert. denied (1981), 454 U.S. 849, 70 L. Ed. 2d 138, 102 S. Ct. 170, the forensic scientist who analyzed dried bloodstains testified she had performed electrophoretic tests thousands of times. She stated in performing the tests, she kept in mind the fact there might be some difficulty in typing aged bloodstains and performed the ESD test several times until she obtained a clear result.

The defendant contended electrophoretic analysis of dried bloodstains is unreliable. In support of this contention, the defendant introduced a journal article indicating the accuracy of electrophoresis is subject to doubt when it is performed on aged bloodstains. Additionally, the defendant presented the testimony of two experts who questioned the reliability of electrophoretic analysis of dried bloodstains. However, one expert had never performed electrophoretic tests, and the other had not performed the tests for some time. This court affirmed the circuit court's denial of the defendant's motion to exclude testimony concerning the results of electrophoretic analysis of dried bloodstains.

In <u>People v. Harbold</u> (1984), 124 Ill. App. 3d 363, 464 N.E.2d 734, the court did not hold electrophoretic analysis of dried bloodstains unreliable as a matter of law, but concluded the record and the case law presented unanswered questions concerning the scientific acceptance of the technique. The appellate court's reversal of the defendant's conviction was premised on trial errors other than admission of results of electrophoretic analysis of dried bloodstains.

This court likewise held in <u>People v. Redman</u> (1985), 135 Ill. App. 3d 534, 481 N.E.2d 1272, electrophoretic analysis of a dried semen stain was not unreliable as a matter of law. In <u>Redman</u>, there was no objection to the foundation for the testimony of the State's expert witness concerning the results of electrophoretic analysis of the semen stain, and any objections to the foundation for that testimony were therefore waived.

The most recent Illinois decision to consider the admissibility of results of electrophoretic analysis of dried bloodstains is <u>People v. Partee</u> (1987), 157 Ill. App. 3d 231, 511 N.E.2d 1165. Relying in part on a South Dakota case (<u>State v. Dirk</u> (S.D. 1985), 364 N.W.2d 117), the court held electrophoretic analysis is generally accepted by forensic scientists as a reliable method of detecting genetic markers in blood, and results of tests using this technique are therefore admissible. The court noted concerns aging and possible contamination of bloodstains may create false readings have been recognized by forensic scientists in evaluating the results of electrophoretic analysis of dried bloodstains, and these variables are a factor considered by forensic scientists in detecting genetic markers in dried bloodstains.

The previous Illinois decisions which have considered the admissibility of results of electrophoretic analysis of dried substances make it clear this investigative technique is not unreliable as a matter of law. None of these decisions have imposed a requirement the State establish the reliability of this technique through the testimony of impartial expert witnesses who are not employed by law enforcement agencies. In the absence of the presentation of expert opinion supporting the defendants' position electrophoretic analysis of dried bloodstains is unreliable as a matter of law, such as that presented in <u>People v. Young</u> (1986), 425 Mich. 470, 391 N.W.2d 270, we decline to impose such a burden on the State. To the extent the cases from other jurisdictions on which the Bradneys rely (<u>Young</u>, 425 Mich 470, 391 N.W.2d 270; <u>People v. Brown</u> (1985), 40 Cal. 3d 512, 726 P.2d 516, 230 Cal. Rptr. 834) impose such a requirement, we decline to follow those decisions.

In the present case, Dennis Aubuchon implied contamination or deterioration of a blood specimen does not alter the ESD or PGM enzyme discovered in the specimen. Rather, contamination or deterioration produces a substance in which neither of these enzymes are clearly detectable. The Bradneys presented no evidence which contradicted this facet of Aubuchon's testimony.

The testimony presented in this case, as well as previous decisions of Illinois courts, establish electrophoretic analysis of dried bloodstains is generally accepted in the scientific community, is not unreliable as a matter of law, and the enzymes detectable in dried blood are not altered as a result of contamination or deterioration. For these reasons, we hold the circuit court did not err in admitting Dennis Aubuchon's testimony as to the results of electrophoretic analysis of the dried bloodstains found in the Moses' residence and in Linda Bradney's automobile.

## IV. *Blood Characteristics Frequency*

The Bradneys assert the circuit court improperly permitted Dennis Aubuchon to testify as to the probability the bloodstains found in the Moses' residence consisted of Bruce's blood, since Aubuchon did not positively identify the source of the statistics on which this statement was premised, and the statistics were not admitted into evidence.

The State argues statistics such as those on which Aubuchon based his testimony are highly reliable, since they are used for such purposes as determining blood types in connection with blood transfusions. The State also argues the probative value of this evidence far outweighed any prejudice to Bruce Bradney, given the strong nonscientific evidence linking him to the crimes with which he was charged.

Aubuchon testified the statistics concerning the frequencies of blood characteristics on which he relied were gathered by the American Red Cross. He later stated the statistics were in a scientific paper which he "would have to go and actually dig . . . up [in order to] tell you exactly where it came from." According to Aubuchon, the statistics were gathered from the "broadest base that we could get from a reliable source." He stated such statistics should be a "rough guideline" and implied they may contain a .2% margin of error.

As noted by the Bradneys, the admissibility of expert opinion is conditioned upon the laying of a proper foundation for the opinion, and the facts on which an expert opinion is premised must generally be introduced into evidence. (People v. Driver (1978), 62 Ill. App. 3d 847, 379 N.E.2d 840.) Experts may, however, premise their testimony on information and opinions obtained from the reading of standard publications in their fields, and the cases do not impose a requirement experts name the publications on which their opinions are premised. (See Carter v. State (1851), 2 Ind. 617; State v. Baldwin (1886), 36 Kan. 1, 12 P. 318.) Also, experts may testify concerning the general opinion of a profession as to a certain matter. See 6 J. Wigmore, Evidence § 1694, at 12–13 (Chadbourn rev. ed. 1976).

Blood characteristic frequency statistics for the general population in the United States are a matter as to which there is a general consensus of opinion in both the medical and forensic science professions. Aubuchon testified the statistics on which he relied were derived from American Red Cross studies involving large numbers of blood specimens taken from the population of the United States. (This court denied a motion by the Bradneys to supplement the record with a letter from the American Red Cross, not introduced into evidence at trial, which purportedly establishes the Red Cross was not the source of the blood characteristic frequency statistics on which Aubuchon relied.) In view of the general consensus of medical and forensic science opinion as to this matter and the failure of the Bradneys to present at trial any evidence contradicting the relevant portion of Aubuchon's testimony, we hold Aubuchon's failure to name the publication which contains the statistics on which he relied did not preclude the admission of his testimony relating to the frequency of blood characteristics.

### V. *Chain of Custody*

The Bradneys contend the State did not establish a proper chain of custody for the blood samples taken from them for comparison with blood discovered in the Moses' home and in Linda Bradney's automobile. The Bradneys assert the blood samples were not properly marked and identified, and the State failed to call a witness (Michael Brown) who came into contact with Linda's blood samples. Furthermore, they contend the State's evidence does not sufficiently exclude the possibility the blood samples were naturally altered before testing due to environmental conditions such as weather, heat or humidity.

The State contends the Bradneys' blood samples could not have been tampered with, because once they left the possession of Sheriff Meyer, they were in the custody of a crime laboratory in Fairview

Heights. The State further contends the transportation of the blood samples to the crime laboratory in insulated containers excluded any possibility they were altered as a result of environmental factors. The State also notes in order to establish a sufficient chain of custody, it is not necessary every person in the chain testify. The State contends it established a proper chain of custody by presenting evidence the Bradneys' blood specimens were drawn at a medical facility, were personally transported by Sheriff Meyer to a scientific laboratory, and were tested at that laboratory.

In their reply argument, the Bradneys maintain the State's contention the containers in which their blood samples were transported were designed to protect the samples during transportation has no support in the record. Also, the Bradneys assert the State did not refute the testimony of its own witnesses that blood deteriorates if unrefrigerated or unpreserved. Finally, the Bradneys assert the State did not rationalize the fact their blood samples were improperly marked.

At the Bradneys' trial, Rosalind Angel, a laboratory technician at the Calhoun County Medical Center, testified she drew blood specimens from Bruce Bradney on September 27, 1985. Angel placed the samples of Bruce's blood in hematocrit tubes. Her normal practice is to seal the ends of such tubes with clay. The tubes are so thin they cannot be labeled. According to Angel, blood specimens need not be refrigerated, but exposure to heat can cause the components of blood specimens to change.

Sheriff Meyer testified he personally accompanied Bruce and Linda Bradney to medical facilities for the purpose of obtaining blood specimens from them. He stated the blood specimens of both defendants were drawn in his presence and handed to him. On both occasions, Meyer tagged the blood as evidence. Meyer transported the tubes containing the Bradneys' blood samples to the crime laboratory in a small insulated styrofoam case containing slots which fit the tubes holding the blood samples. Meyer believed he handed Linda's blood specimens to Dennis Aubuchon when he arrived at the Fairview Heights Crime Laboratory. However, there were other personnel at the crime laboratory when Meyer was there. Also, Meyer made several subsequent trips to the crime laboratory, and "dealt with [Aubuchon] throughout the course of this coming and going." Aubuchon also returned the blood specimens to Meyer.

The Bradneys introduced into evidence a document indicating Aubuchon received Linda's blood specimens from forensic scientist Michael Brown.

Evidence which is of such a nature as to be easily susceptible to alteration, tampering or contamination may not be admitted unless the proponent of the evidence establishes a chain of custody sufficient to render it improbable the original evidence has been exchanged with other evidence, contaminated or tampered with. (People v. Cole (1975), 29 Ill. App. 3d 369, 329 N.E.2d 880.) Establishment of a sufficient chain of custody does not require every person involved in the chain to testify; nor need the State exclude all possibilities the evidence may have been subject to tampering. (People v. Winters (1981), 97 Ill. App. 3d 288, 422 N.E.2d 972, *cert. denied* (1982), 455 U.S. 923, 71 L. Ed. 2d 464, 102 S. Ct. 1282.) The fact persons other than those who testified at trial had access to the area where evidence was stored does not require a holding the State failed to establish a sufficient chain of custody. (See People v. Harper (1962), 26 Ill. 2d 85, 185 N.E.2d 865, *cert. denied* (1963), 372 U.S. 966, 10 L. Ed. 2d 130, 83 S. Ct. 1092.) The abuse of discretion standard governs review of circuit court decisions to admit evidence over chain of custody objections. People v. Irpino (1984), 122 Ill. App. 3d 767, 461 N.E.2d 999.

There is no basis for the Bradneys' contention the circuit court abused its discretion in admitting evidence of the results of the tests of their blood because their blood samples may have been altered due to climatic factors or because the samples were improperly labeled and identified. It may be inferred from Rosalind Angel's testimony blood samples do not deteriorate unless exposed to extreme heat, and Sheriff Meyer testified he transported the Bradneys' blood samples to the crime laboratory in an insulated styrofoam container. In view of the Bradneys' failure to present any contrary evidence, the circuit court could properly have found on the basis of this testimony the Bradneys' blood specimens were not exposed to conditions which could have altered components.

As for the identification of the Bradneys' blood samples, Angel testified the tubes containing the samples were too small to label, and Sheriff Meyer stated he tagged the blood specimens as evidence. From this testimony, the trier of fact could reasonably have concluded Meyer adequately labeled the styrofoam containers which held the tubes containing the Bradneys' blood samples.

Sheriff Meyer's testimony he handed Linda's blood specimens to Aubuchon rather than Michael Brown and the State's failure to call Brown as a witness did not preclude admission of the results of the tests of Linda's blood specimens. Sheriff Meyer's frequent trips to the crime laboratory, frequent contacts with Aubuchon, and the approximately 13 months elapsed between the time the blood specimens were obtained and the date of trial provide an adequate explanation for Sheriff Meyer's possible confusion as to the person to whom he handed Linda's blood specimens. If Meyer did, in fact, hand Linda's blood samples to Brown, the State's failure to call Brown as a witness did not in itself preclude the circuit court from concluding the State established a proper chain of custody for Linda's blood samples.

Neither of the two cases on which the Bradneys rely in support of their contention the State did not establish a proper chain of custody for their blood specimens supports their position. In People v. Brown (1972), 3 Ill. App. 3d 879, 279 N.E.2d 382, a whiskey bottle was the sole item of evidence offered in support of an illegal transportation of alcohol charge. The arresting officer placed the bottle in his locker shortly after the defendant's arrest, where it remained until the time of the defendant's trial. The arresting officer did not tag the bottle or seal it. Other persons may have had access to it between the time of the defendant's arrest and trial. Therefore, the appellate court held the bottle was improperly admitted into evidence. In the present case, by contrast, the blood specimens were tagged and taken to a crime laboratory immediately after they were drawn.

In People v. Anthony (1963), 28 Ill. 2d 65, 68–69, 190 N.E.2d 837, 839, the court held the State established a proper chain of custody for a substance containing heroin. Anthony supports the State's position to a much greater extent than the Bradneys', for there the court held the State's failure to call as a witness a crime laboratory employee to whom the arresting officer handed a bag containing the heroin-based substance did not provide a basis for holding a proper chain of custody was not established.

The State established a sufficient *prima facie* chain of custody for the blood samples obtained from the Bradneys. Absent evidence of possible tampering with the blood samples or evidence the samples were in fact altered as a result of climatic or environmental factors, the circuit court did not abuse its discretion in admitting into evidence the results of the tests of those samples.

## VI. *Alleged Abuse of Discretion in Sentencing*

At the Bradneys' sentencing hearing, Linda testified she had no present recollection of the burglary of the Moses' residence because at that time she and Bruce were high on drugs and alcohol. She further stated she considered herself addicted to both chemicals and alcohol and had in the past been under psychiatric care for mental problems. Linda also testified stated she was remorseful for any harm or grief she had caused with respect to the burglary of the Moses' residence.

Linda's presentence report and the certified records of prior convictions introduced at trial disclose the following prior convictions:

| DATE | OFFENSE | LOCATION | SENTENCE |
|------|---------|----------|----------|
| 3/7/81 | Theft under $300 | Wood River, IL | $130 fine and costs |
| 3/11/82 | Indecent liberties with a child (5 counts); Aggravated incest (1 count) | Madison County, IL | 5-year concurrent terms of imprisonment on each count |
| 6/10/85 | Residential burglary | Godfrey, IL | 10 years' imprisonment |

Bruce Bradney testified he is 46 years old and in poor health. He suffers from asthma and emphysema. He has recently undergone eye surgery and is legally blind in his right eye. His left eye permanently contains particles of a foreign substance. He further stated his kidney and spleen have been surgically removed. He has been addicted to drugs and alcohol since he was a teenager but thought he had overcome his addiction.

Bruce further testified he has no recollection of committing a residential burglary in Calhoun County and has no recollection of the time period during which the Moses' residence was burglarized. However, he remembered the day he was released from prison because: "I didn't drink anything or have any drugs and no intentions of it." Later, after Linda was denied early release from parole he thought:

I am free to leave the state. I have a job at another place. We have a place to live in another state and we can't go. We're stuck right here.

. . . .

Right back in the same place, same drugs.

Bruce's presentence report and the records of prior convictions introduced at trial reveal the following prior offenses:

| DATE | OFFENSE | LOCATION | SENTENCE |
|------|---------|----------|----------|
| 1/1/59 | Intoxication | Alton, IL | Unspecified fine |
| 4/21/59 | Carrying a concealed weapon | Alton, IL | Unspecified fine |
| 9/8/60 | Destruction of property | Alton, IL | Unspecified fine |
| 9/23/60 | Intoxication | Alton, IL | Unspecified fine |
| 4/13/61 | Intoxication | Alton, IL | Unspecified fine |
| 3/26/65 | Armed robbery | Miami, FL | 15 years' imprisonment |
| 2/27/78 | Theft over $ 300 | Jersey County, IL | 2 years' imprisonment |
| 7/24/80 | Retail theft | Alton, IL | Unspecified fine |
| 9/10/81 | Aggravated battery of a child (2 counts) | Madison County, IL | 7-year concurrent terms of imprisonment on each count |
| 12/14/84 | Battery | Alton, IL | Returned to prison as parole violator |
| 6/10/85 | Residential burglary | Godfrey, IL | 15 years' imprisonment |

At the conclusion of the sentencing hearing, the court sentenced both Bruce and Linda Bradney to extended terms of 25 years' imprisonment for residential burglary and terms of imprisonment of three years for theft over $300.

The Bradneys contend in sentencing them, the circuit court did not give sufficient consideration to various mitigating factors, including their alcohol and drug dependency and their entry of the Moses' residence when the Moses were not at home. Furthermore, the Bradneys note they were not armed during the commission of the burglary of the Moses' residence, and they have no history of violence. They also point out they did not flee when approached by Gelber while on his property and provoked no violence when Gelber discovered them. They also assert their prior criminal records are misleading because the residential burglary in Godfrey of which they were convicted occurred within a few hours of the burglary of the Moses' residence, and both offenses arose out of their heavy drug and alcohol usage during the period preceding June 8, 1985. Additionally, they argue Linda's other Class 1 felonies were of a different nature than residential burglary and involved actions not likely to recur, because Linda's parental rights were terminated as a result of those convictions. Also, they observe Bruce had no Class 1 felony convictions within the 10 years preceding the present offenses, other than the conviction of the residential burglary which took place in Godfrey. They conclude by stating nothing in their behavior mandates sentences 10 years above the statutory minimum for residential burglary on the basis of the threat which they pose to the people of Illinois.

The State argues two of the aggravating factors necessary to support extended terms are present in this case: (1) the offenses were committed against persons 60 years of age or older and (2) both of the Bradneys had previously been convicted of the same class or greater felony within the past 10 years. The State further contends (1) the circuit court may be presumed to have considered all mitigating evidence offered by the Bradneys, even though the court did not specifically refer to it, and (2) because of other contrary evidence, the circuit court was not obligated to accept at face value the evidence which the Bradneys offered in mitigation. Finally, the State observes in sentencing the Bradneys, the circuit court did not completely ignore the possibility of rehabilitation, for they were sentenced to five years less than the maximum extended term for residential burglary and their rehabilitative potential is limited given their poor educational background and prior criminal records.

We need not consider whether the circuit court improperly relied on the ages of the Moses as an aggravating factor, for it is undisputed both Bruce and Linda Bradney were convicted of Class 1 felonies within the 10 years preceding their burglary of the Moses' residence, which was also a Class 1 felony. (ILL. REV. STAT. 1985, ch. 38, par. 19-3(b).) That factor alone was a proper basis for imposition of extended-term sentences on the Bradneys. ILL. REV. STAT. 1985, ch. 38, par. 1005-5-3.2(b)(1).

On review, the circuit court is presumed to have considered evidence offered in mitigation, unless there is some statement in the record, other than the sentence imposed, which indicates the court did not consider such evidence. (People v. Fugitt (1980), 87 Ill. App. 3d 1044, 409 N.E.2d 537.) In the present case, the record contains no statements which would support a conclusion the circuit court did not consider all of the evidence which the Bradneys offered in mitigation.

Although the circuit court must consider all testimony offered in mitigation, it is not obligated to believe such testimony if there is other evidence which undercuts its veracity. (People v. Matzker (1983), 115 Ill. App. 3d 70, 450 N.E.2d 395.) In this case, the circumstances surrounding the burglary of the Moses' residence reflect it was a well-planned crime, and the Bradneys were not so much under the influence of alcohol or drugs they could not appreciate the gravity of their wrongful acts. For instance, the Bradneys purposefully drove from their Alton residence to an isolated area of Calhoun County in order to commit the burglary and were quickly able to come up with an excuse for their being on Marvin Gelber's farm. (See discussion of the Bradneys' defense of voluntary intoxication.) Therefore, the circuit court would have been justified in disbelieving the Bradneys' claims their burglary and theft of property from the Moses' residence were attributable to their alcoholism and drug addiction and instead considering those offenses were well planned crimes when imposing sentence on them.

A sentence imposed on a criminal defendant is not subject to reversal on appeal unless it represents a clear abuse of the circuit court's discretion. (People v. Cox (1980), 82 Ill. 2d 268, 412 N.E.2d 541.) It is manifest the circuit court did not abuse its discretion in imposing sentence on Bruce Bradney. Bruce's prior criminal record represents a virtually unbroken string of rather serious offenses dating back to 1965. None of the punishments imposed for these offenses caused Bruce to refrain from engaging in subsequent criminal activities. Thus, with respect to Bruce, the circuit court's emphasis on the objective of protecting society from the offender was well founded.

In view of Bruce Bradney's history of serious offenses, the facts he was not armed when he burglarized the Moses' residence, has no history of violence, and none of his offenses during the 10 years preceding the offenses committed against the Moses (other than the burglary committed in Godfrey on the same day) were Class 1 felonies are of no consequence. Bruce's committing the residential burglary in Godfrey during the same period of purported intoxication as the burglary of the Moses' residence is also of no significance. As the State's Attorney indicated during argument at the Bradneys' sentencing hearing, a holding a prior offense is to be regarded as less of a factor in aggravation for sentencing purposes simply because it allegedly occurred during the same period of intoxication as the offense for which sentence is being imposed would in many cases have the practical effect of merging the two offenses for purposes of sentencing. We decline to engraft such a rule onto the sentencing statutes.

Most of what we have just said with regard to the matters argued in mitigation also applies to the sentences imposed upon Linda Bradney. None of these factors require us to hold Linda's sentences were an abuse of discretion. It is true Linda's record of prior offenses is less extensive than is Bruce's. However, Linda committed three rather serious offenses—the present residential burglary and theft and the residential burglary in Godfrey—while on parole as a result of previously being found guilty of serious offenses. Linda's convictions of aggravated incest and indecent liberties with a child did result from offenses of a different nature from that of residential burglary and theft, but her participation in the burglary and theft of property from the Moses' residence indicates an inability on her part to abide by the norms of socially acceptable conduct. The circuit court could therefore have reasonably concluded fairly lengthy sentences are necessary in order to protect the public from further criminal activity on the part of Linda. Although we may not have imposed upon Linda the same sentences which the circuit court imposed, we cannot say the sentences which the circuit court imposed on her represented a manifest abuse of the court's discretion.

### VII. Credit for Time Served Prior to Sentencing

The Bradneys were arrested for the burglary and theft of property from the Moses' residence on June 11, 1985. On January 27, 1986, they were sentenced by the Madison County circuit court to 15 years' imprisonment for the residential burglary which they committed in Godfrey. (Contrary to the Bradneys' contentions, certified copies of their convictions of the residential burglary in Godfrey, including statements of the sentences imposed, are included in the record of the present case.) The Bradneys were sentenced for the present offenses on January 23, 1987. Their mittimuses do not reflect any sentence credit for time served prior to sentencing. However, in a letter to Linda dated March 10, 1987, Judge Burrows stated she was entitled to credit for time served awaiting trial.

The Bradneys contend they are entitled to credit on their sentences for the entire period of time between the date of their arrests for the present offenses and the date they were sentenced for these offenses. They therefore request we remand this cause for issuance of amended mittimuses reflecting they are each entitled to 592 days' credit on their sentences.

The State concedes the Bradneys are entitled to 231 days' sentence credit for time spent in custody between their arrest on the present charges and their January 27, 1986, sentencing for the residential burglary which they committed in Godfrey. However, the State argues the Bradneys are not entitled to credit on their sentences for time spent in custody after they were sentenced for the Godfrey residential burglary, since the time they have spent in prison after that date represents time served on an unrelated offense.

Individuals sentenced to prison are generally entitled to one day of credit on their prison sentence for each day spent in custody as a result of the offense for which they were sentenced to prison prior to their arrival at a Department of Corrections facility. (ILL. REV. STAT. 1985, ch. 38, pars. 1005-8-7(a), (b); 1003-6-3(a)(2).) Sentences imposed on a defendant who is already serving a sentence for a prior offense may be either concurrent with or consecutive to the sentence imposed for the previous offense. Sentences run concurrently unless otherwise specified by the court. (ILL. REV. STAT. 1985, ch. 38, par. 1005-8-4(a).) In the present case, the Bradneys' mittimuses do not indicate whether their sentences are to be served concurrently with or consecutive to unexpired sentences imposed with respect to prior offenses. Thus, the Bradneys' sentences for the burglary and theft of property from the Moses' residence must be deemed to run concurrently with any prior unexpired sentences.

On facts similar to those here present, the Fifth District of this court has recently concluded a defendant who is serving a sentence for a previous offense and fails to post bond while awaiting trial or sentencing on a second charge is entitled to credit on the sentence for the second offense for the period of incarceration between the date he or she was charged with the second offense and the date sentence was imposed for that offense. The rationale for this holding is even if the defendant were not serving a sentence for the first offense, he or she would still be subject to detention as a result of his or her failure to post bond with respect to the second charge. Thus in such situations, the defendant is incarcerated as a result of both offenses prior to being sentenced for the second offense. People v. Higgerson (1987), 157 Ill. App. 3d 564, 510 N.E.2d 574; People v. Powell (1987), 160 Ill. App. 3d 689, 513 N.E.2d 1162.

People v. Krankel (1985), 131 Ill. App. 3d 887, 476 N.E.2d 777, on which the State principally relies, is factually distinguishable from the case at bar. There, the defendant was sentenced to a prison term which was to be served consecutively to sentences for prior offenses. This court held the defendant was not entitled to credit on the sentence for the second offense for time spent in jail awaiting trial for that offense which was credited to the sentences for the prior offenses. In the present case, by contrast, the Bradneys' sentences are to run concurrently with their sentences for the Godfrey residential burglary. Thus there is no danger they will receive unintended double credit for time spent in custody if they receive sentence credit for all of the time they spent in custody after they were arrested but before they were sentenced for the present offenses.

Because the Bradneys at no time posted bond with respect to the charges stemming from the burglary and theft of property from the Moses' residence, they would have been subject to detention on those charges during the period subsequent to June 27, 1986, even if they had not been sentenced to prison on that date for the residential burglary which they committed in Godfrey. Since at all relevant times prior to being sentenced for the burglary and theft of property from the Moses' residence the Bradneys were subject to detention as a result of those offenses, we hold the Bradneys are each entitled to 592 days' credit on both of their sentences for time served prior to sentencing.

The convictions of defendants Bruce and Linda Bradney are affirmed. These causes are remanded to the circuit court with directions to issue amended mittimuses reflecting both Bruce and Linda Bradney are entitled to 592 days' credit for time served prior to sentencing on their sentences for both residential burglary and theft over $300.

Affirmed and remanded with directions. . . .

## PEOPLE v. LePRETRE

1990 Ill. App. LEXIS 473, 196 Ill. App. 3d 111, 142 Ill. Dec. 578, 552
N.E.2d 1319 (1990)

**PRIOR HISTORY:** Appeal from the Circuit Court of Woodford
County; the HON. RICHARD M. BANER, Judge, presiding.

**DISPOSITION:** Judgment affirmed.

**COUNSEL:** Daniel D. Yuhas and Arden J. Lang, both of State Appellate Defender's Office, of Springfield, for appellant.

John B. Huschen, State's Attorney, of Eureka (Kenneth R. Boyle,
Robert J. Biderman, and David E. Mannchen, all of State's Attorneys
Appellate Prosecutor's Office, of counsel), for the People.

**JUDGES:** JUSTICE LUND delivered the opinion of the court. SPITZ and
McCULLOUGH, JJ., concur.

**OPINION BY:** LUND

**OPINION:** On April 21, 1989, following a jury trial in the circuit court
of Woodford County, defendant Brian LePretre was convicted of committing the offense of attempt (murder). (ILL. REV. STAT. 1987, ch. 38,
pars. 8-4, 9-1.) He was subsequently sentenced to the minimum six-
year prison term. He now appeals, alleging (1) he was not proved guilty
beyond a reasonable doubt; (2) the court improperly refused his tendered jury instructions; (3) he received ineffective assistance of counsel; (4) the court erred by refusing to allow him to recall a witness; and
(5) the court's post-trial comments indicate the court should have
granted defendant's post-trial motion. We affirm.

On January 5, 1989, defendant was charged in the circuit court of
Woodford County with committing the offense of attempt (murder). (ILL.
REV. STAT. 1987, ch. 38, pars. 8-4, 9-1.) The information alleged defendant performed a substantial step toward the commission of murder, in
that he knowingly thrust a knife toward Bernard Remmert with the intent to kill him. Defendant raised the affirmative defense of voluntary
intoxication. The jury trial commenced on April 19, 1989.

The State's first witness was Bill Myers, under-sheriff of Woodford
County. He stated he interviewed defendant on January 5, after defendant's arrest for the instant offense. After waiving his *Miranda* rights,
defendant told Myers that his sister and brother-in-law, Michelle and
Daniel Schirer, picked him up on December 31 around 7:30 p.m., and
they went to a bar in Metamora for a New Year's Eve party. While there,
he had six to eight drinks of Jack Daniels and Coke. He also had one

glass of champagne at midnight and two puffs from a marijuana cigarette. At approximately 2 a.m., they left the bar and returned home.

Defendant told Myers that the Schirers then dropped him off at his
residence. However, he was not feeling well and decided to walk
around for awhile. At this time, he thought it was around 2:30 a.m. He
walked around for a couple hours. Around 5 a.m., he was at the north
end of Remmert Funeral Home parking lot and he saw Bernard Remmert. Defendant knew who Remmert was, though he had not seen him
or spoken to him for several years. Defendant walked through the
parking lot and later returned. He chatted with Remmert for awhile, and
Remmert invited him in for some coffee.

They entered the funeral home and went to Remmert's office, where
Remmert began making coffee. Defendant then jumped Remmert and
put his left arm around Remmert's chest and neck area. Defendant
pulled a knife out of his coat pocket with his right hand, and they struggled. The next thing defendant remembered was that he was lying on
the floor, with Remmert on top of him.

After they calmed down, Remmert let defendant up. They talked
about the attack and drank coffee. Defendant could not remember why
he attacked Remmert or the actual attack. Remmert then let defendant
go home. Upon his return, defendant told his parents about the attack,
but failed to mention the knife.

Myers recovered the knife from the scene. The blade had been broken during the fight. The knife had a four-inch body and a three-inch
blade. On cross-examination, Myers acknowledged that defendant was
always cooperative, never indicated he had an intent to kill Remmert,
and could not remember any of the incident after he took the knife from
his pocket.

Bernard Remmert testified that at 5 a.m. on January 1 he was at his
funeral home, having just picked up a body from a nursing home. As he
exited the hearse, he could hear someone walking in the alley behind
him. As he entered the funeral home, Remmert waved a greeting at the
person, who continued through the parking lot, heading south. After
entering, Remmert proceeded to turn up the heat, and thought the person might be his tenant who lives in the house to the north. He thought
this tenant might have overindulged in partying the night before and
was now walking it off. He decided to invite him in and offer him a cup
of coffee.

Remmert stepped outside, where it was still dark, and invited the person in for coffee. After they entered the building and the bright light, Remmert noticed the person was not the tenant. In response to Remmert's question, the person explained he was a Roanoke boy and his name was Brian LePretre. Remmert asked him if he was the son of Nancy and Armand, who are good friends of his. When defendant responded affirmatively, Remmert felt more comfortable. As they walked to his office, they discussed the fact that defendant had been in the military service in Germany and was discharged last April.

Once they entered the office, Remmert went to the coffee pot to make the coffee. Defendant was walking behind him. Defendant suddenly jumped on Remmert's back and got an arm lock, using his right arm, on Remmert's neck.

The arm was under Remmert's chin and across his neck. Remmert was having trouble breathing.

The next thing Remmert knew, defendant started bringing his left arm down and, out of reflex, Remmert lifted his arm up to block it. Defendant's arm crossed Remmert's and, for the first time, Remmert saw the knife. The point of the knife pricked Remmert's shirt several times and cut a tear in his coat, but he was not injured. The knife was poised over his heart, and defendant was applying a lot of pressure. They wrestled around the room, breaking furniture and banging into the wall. Defendant kept pressing with the knife. Eventually, after several minutes, Remmert was able to shove defendant to the ground.

Remmert climbed on top of defendant and picked up the knife, which was now broken. Defendant then began saying he was sorry and that he did not know what he was doing. Remmert helped defendant up and seated him on the couch. Remmert asked defendant why he attempted to kill him. Defendant repeatedly stated, "I don't know." Defendant said he was sorry and asked Remmert to not call the sheriff. Defendant explained he had never done anything like this before.

They then had a cup of coffee and talked. Remmert indicated he would not call the sheriff and stated that defendant should get inhouse help. He let defendant go home. When he told his wife what happened, she insisted that he call the sheriff. He then called defendant's parents.

Remmert explained that other than various scratches, bruises and a banged-up ankle, he suffered no injuries. He did not believe defendant was intoxicated or high on anything. He denied telling defendant's mother that he thought defendant was high. He explained that he asked her if defendant was possibly on drugs or drank a lot. The State then rested.

Defendant's first witnesses were his sister and brother-in-law, Michelle and Daniel Schirer. They picked defendant up around 7:30 p.m., and arrived at the bar around 8 p.m. While there, Daniel drank screwdrivers, Michelle drank some beers and some sodas, and defendant drank Jack Daniels and Coke. They estimated defendant drank three to four drinks per hour. They all had some champagne at midnight. They stayed at the bar until around 3:45 a.m., and arrived at defendant's parents' house around 4 a.m.

They were both of the opinion defendant was intoxicated when they dropped him off. Daniel based his opinion on the fact defendant seldom drank, the amount he drank, and the fact his eyes were glazed. Michelle based her opinion on the amount defendant drank, his lack of drinking experience, his gayer and happier mood, and the fact he vomited on his parents' driveway when he exited the car.

However, neither observed that defendant had any trouble walking. They both acknowledged defendant danced some, and they did not observe him the entire evening. Michelle also admitted that, after vomiting, defendant responded to her question asking if he was alright.

Stan Schertz testified that he was also at the party with defendant. He left between 2 and 3 a.m. He was the designated driver of his group, so he drank only one glass of champagne. He estimated defendant consumed three to four mixed drinks per hour. It was his opinion, based on defendant's staggering walk and stuttering speech, that defendant was drunk when Schertz left.

Defendant's mother testified that, on January 1, Remmert told her that defendant was inebriated or high on something. She explained that Remmert never said that was his opinion, but she got the opinion from their conversation that it was. She also observed vomit in her driveway that morning.

Defendant testified he is 22 years old and currently lives with his parents. At the party, he drank Jack Daniels and Coke and one glass of champagne. He does not remember how many mixed drinks he drank. He also had two puffs on a marijuana cigarette. They left the bar around 2 a.m. and arrived home around 2:30 a.m. Once he got home, he threw up on the driveway. At that point, he decided to walk uptown to get some air. As he walked, he went through the funeral home parking lot and said hello to Remmert. He later turned around and went back to the parking lot. Remmert came outside and asked if he would like a cup of coffee.

They, then, went to the office. Prior to this, defendant did not know Remmert. As Remmert was working on the coffee machine, defendant remembered bringing his left arm up. Defendant is right-handed. The next thing he remembered is that he was on the ground, with Remmert in control of him. Then, they sat on the couch and Remmert asked why it happened. Defendant told Remmert he did not know, and that there was no reason for it. Defendant apologized repeatedly. Remmert stated he would not press charges, but would call defendant's parents. At that time, the defendant went home.

On January 5, defendant spoke with Deputy Myers. However, he denied telling Myers any of the details of the fight, or that it took place at 5 a.m. Defendant believed he was intoxicated and stated he did not go into the funeral home intending to kill Remmert.

On cross-examination, he explained he could not remember how many mixed drinks he had. When he told Myers he had six to eight drinks, he only guessed. He does not remember eating a sandwich or hearing last call, but he does remember arriving home. He also remembers carrying the knife with him that night. He remembers walking around town, including several of the places that he passed.

Dr. Robert Chapman was qualified as an expert in the field of psychiatry and forensic psychiatry. He interviewed defendant on February 13, 1989. Prior to his examination of defendant, Chapman interviewed his sister and reviewed various reports, including a psychiatric examination from the Veterans Administration Hospital. Chapman related what defendant told him about the night in question. It correlated with defendant's testimony, except that Chapman remembered defendant specifically saying he consumed six to eight drinks during the evening. His examination showed defendant was free of any major mental disorder or defect. He made three diagnoses concerning defendant's status at the time of the offense. First, he believed defendant was suffering from acute alcohol-abuse syndrome, also known as alcohol intoxication. Defendant was also suffering alcohol blackout. The third diagnosis was that of episodic discontrol, which has also been referred to as intermittent explosive disorder or an isolated explosive disorder. It was Chapman's opinion that defendant was not suffering from a mental disease at the time of the offense. It was also his opinion that defendant's intoxication was such that it interfered with his power of reason.

On cross-examination, Chapman admitted that much of the information he relied on in forming the opinion came from defendant and his sister and, if the information was incorrect, it could affect his opinion. The defense rested.

Remmert testified, on rebuttal, that defendant was walking fine the entire time. When they spoke, defendant always answered responsively. He never noticed any slurred or stuttered speech, and he never smelled any alcohol on defendant's breath. Defendant never staggered or supported himself.

Defendant was found guilty of the charge. He was eventually sentenced to the minimum six years' imprisonment. Defendant now appeals.

Defendant initially argues he was not proved guilty beyond a reasonable doubt. He observes he raised the affirmative defense of voluntary intoxication. (ILL. REV. STAT. 1987, ch. 38, par. 6-3.) He notes that when an affirmative defense is raised by the pleadings or the evidence, the State has a burden of proving the defendant guilty beyond a reasonable doubt as to that issue, together with all the other elements of the defense. (People v. Smith (1978), 71 Ill. 2d 95, 105, 374 N.E.2d 472, 476.) He does not believe the State has done so.

In order to constitute an affirmative defense, voluntary intoxication must be so extreme as to suspend all reason. (People v. Bradney (1988), 170 Ill. App. 3d 839, 855, 525 N.E.2d 112, 122.) Merely being drunk or intoxicated is insufficient to create the defense. (People v. White (1977), 67 Ill. 2d 107, 119, 365 N.E.2d 337, 343.) The question is not whether the defendant was intoxicated, but whether the evidence demonstrates beyond a reasonable doubt that the defendant could have formed the requisite mental state for the crime charged. (People v. Aguirre (1975), 30 Ill. App. 3d 854, 857–58, 334 N.E.2d 123, 127.) There are many levels of intoxication through which an individual may pass before he reaches the level of being unable to form the intent to act. (Bradney, 170 Ill. App. 3d at 855, 525 N.E.2d at 122.) The weight to be accorded testimony relating to this defense is peculiarly within the province of the trier of fact. <u>Bradney</u>, 170 Ill. App. 3d at 855, 525 N.E.2d at 122.

When a defendant raises a challenge to the sufficiency of the evidence, it is not the function of this court to retry the defendant. (<u>People v. Collins</u> (1985), 106 Ill. 2d 237, 261, 478 N.E.2d 267, 277.) The relevant question is whether, if after viewing the evidence in the light most favorable to the prosecution, any rational trier of fact could not have found the essential elements of the crime beyond a reasonable doubt. <u>Jackson v. Virginia</u> 443 U.S. 307, 319, 61 L. Ed. 2d 560, 573, 99 S. Ct. 2781, 2789; <u>Collins</u>, 106 Ill. 2d at 261, 478 N.E.2d at 277.

Defendant believes the evidence establishes that he did not have the requisite intent. He points to the testimony of those at the party, which established he drank three to four drinks per hour. They are also of the opinion that he was intoxicated. This is borne out by his being unsure of the time that he left the bar, not being sure the number of drinks he consumed, and vomiting in the driveway. He also observes he blacked out totally during the attack and that it was a totally irrational, violent act. He finally rests on the expert testimony of Dr. Chapman, who stated his opinion that defendant did not possess the required intent.

In determining whether a defendant was so intoxicated that his powers of reason were totally suspended, the trier of fact is not obligated to rely on the testimony of experts to the exclusion of other evidence relevant to the defendant's mental state. Rather, the trier of fact may consider the opinion of experts, together with all of the other evidence relevant to the defendant's mental state at the time of the offense, and reject the expert testimony if it deems the other evidence more probative. <u>Bradney</u>, 170 Ill. App. 3d at 855, 525 N.E.2d at 122.

In the present case, the evidence, considered in the light most favorable to the State, establishes that the defendant drank six to eight mixed drinks over an eight-hour period. While his companions opined he was intoxicated, they were unable to point to many factors other than the amount he drank. These assessments were based on conduct from one hour to three hours prior to the time of the attack. Thus, the jury could have found that if defendant had been intoxicated, he may have sobered up. Further, defendant's sister stated he responded appropriately to her question after he vomited. Defendant was able to relate where he walked and what places he passed. When he met Remmert, they were able to carry on a normal conversation. Defendant was able to explain his military background and answer other questions.

Remmert observed no slurring of speech or staggering of his walk. Once the episode was over, defendant was again able to carry a conversation and then walk home. Admittedly, defendant said he blacked out during the attack but, due to his rational conduct both before and after the episode, the jury could reasonably have disregarded this testimony. Similarly, the jury could have disregarded Dr. Chapman's opinion, since it was based, in good part, on statements of defendant and his sister, and does not conform to the other evidence.

We acknowledge that, due to the unexplainable irrational conduct, this case is factually close. However, it is in just such cases that the opportunity for the jury to observe and to evaluate the witnesses is so valuable. We cannot say that, based on the recited evidence, no rational trier of fact could have found defendant guilty beyond a reasonable doubt. The evidence is sufficient.

Defendant next contends the court erred in refusing to submit his proffered instructions on the offense of reckless conduct (ILL. REV. STAT. 1987, ch. 38, par. 12-5), which he maintains is an included offense of attempt (murder).

Initially, the court had accepted the instruction over the State's objection. However, later, prior to the closing argument, the State sought to give instructions on aggravated battery (ILL. REV. STAT. 1987, ch. 38, par. 12-4), asserting this is also an included offense. Defendant objected, and a recess for research purposes was taken. After the recess, the court concluded, based on People v. Primmer (1983), 111 Ill. App. 3d 1046, 444 N.E.2d 829, that reckless conduct is not an included offense of attempt (murder) and, reversing its earlier decision, denied defendant's proffered reckless conduct instructions.

A defendant is entitled, under certain circumstances, to have the jury instructed as to an offense less serious than that with which the defendant is charged. (People v. Roberts (1989), 189 Ill. App. 3d 66, 72, 544 N.E.2d 1340, 1345.) The purpose of such a rule is to give the jury a third option by permitting it, if it deems the defendant not guilty of the charged offense but reluctant to completely acquit him, an opportunity to find the defendant guilty of a lesser offense, if the jury finds the proof of the lesser offense strong enough to convict. (People v. Bryant (1986), 113 Ill. 2d 497, 502, 499 N.E.2d 413, 415.) An included offense instruction is only proper when the charged offense requires the jury to find an element which is not required for conviction of the lesser offense (People v. Cramer (1981), 85 Ill. 2d 92, 100, 421 N.E.2d 189, 192), or, stated in another way, an included offense is an offense which contains some, but not all, of the elements of the greater offense and contains no element not included in the greater. People v. Traufler (1987), 152 Ill. App. 3d 987, 990, 505 N.E.2d 21, 23.

However, as our supreme court has observed, in something of an understatement, the grounds for determining whether a particular offense is included in another are not always clear. (Bryant, 113 Ill. 2d at 502, 499 N.E.2d at 415.) Section 2-9 of the Criminal Code of 1961 (Code) provides the following definition:

> 'Included offense' means an offense which
>
> (a) Is established by proof of the same or less than all of the facts or a less culpable mental state (or both), than that which is required to establish the commission of the offense charged. (ILL. REV. STAT. 1987, ch. 38, par. 2-9.)

The supreme court has recognized that this definition does not explain which of the following is determinative in deciding if a particular offense is an included offense of another: (1) the abstract statutory definition of the greater crime; (2) the greater crime as it is alleged in the indictment or other charging instrument; or (3) the greater crime as its necessary elements are proved at trial. (People v. Mays (1982), 91 Ill. 2d 251, 255, 437 N.E.2d 633, 635.) The courts have recognized that either review of the abstract charge, or review of the offenses as charged, is an appropriate means to be used. People v. Bratton (1989), 178 Ill. App. 3d 718, 727, 533 N.E.2d 572, 578; Traufler, 152 Ill. App. 3d at 991, 505 N.E.2d at 23–24.

Defendant acknowledges that this court previously answered the question of whether reckless conduct is an included offense of attempt (murder) in Primmer. There, the court stated:

> The offense of reckless conduct in shooting at David Farris was not an included offense of the attempt to murder David Farris because the reckless conduct charge, which defendant deems an included offense, required an endangering of the safety of Farris while the attempted murder charge had no such element. (Primmer, 111 Ill. App. 3d at 1053, 444 N.E.2d at 834.)

Similar conclusions have been reached by other courts. See People v. Smith (1980), 90 Ill. App. 3d 83, 86, 412 N.E.2d 1102, 1105; People v. Coleman (1985), 131 Ill. App. 3d 76, 80, 475 N.E.2d 565, 568.

Defendant argues that Primmer was decided prior to the supreme court's decisions in People v. Dace (1984), 104 Ill. 2d 96, 470 N.E.2d 993, and Bryant. He believes these cases require a different conclusion.

In Dace and Bryant, the court looked to the evidence proved at trial and the language contained in the charging instrument. Thus, in Bryant, the court held that criminal damage to property is an included offense of attempt (burglary), where the indictment alleged that the substantial step toward the burglary was breaking of a window, and the evidence adduced at trial would have supported a criminal damage conviction. The court concluded it was not necessary to have all the elements of the included offense contained in the charge, as long as the charging instrument sets out the main outline of the lesser offense for which an instruction is sought. (Bryant, 113 Ill. 2d at 505, 499 N.E.2d at 416–17.) Accordingly, Bryant seems to conclude that included offense instructions should be given when the elements in the included offense are, in a broad sense, included in the offense charged, and the evidence that develops at trial proves the included offense. Roberts, 189 Ill. App. 3d at 74, 544 N.E.2d at 1346.

However, we need not determine if Bryant changes the Primmer holding because, even if Bryant does apply, it is apparent defendant is not entitled to the proffered instruction. The court, in Bryant, observing that restrictions upon the use of included instructions do exist, stated:

There are several notable limits on the operation of the included-offense doctrine, however. For example, because a defendant's instruction on a lesser offense is appropriate 'if the evidence would permit a jury rationally to find him guilty of the lesser offense and acquit him of the greater.' (Keeble v. United States (1973), 412 U.S. 205, 208, 36 L. Ed. 2d 844, 847, 93 S. Ct. 1993, 1995), the evidence presented in a particular case might rationally preclude the use of an instruction on a lesser offense. (See Hopper v. Evans (1982), 456 U.S. 605, 612–13, 72 L. Ed. 2d 367, 373–74, 102 S. Ct. 2049, 2053–54; People v. Perez (1985), 108 Ill. 2d 70, 81–83; People v. Mitchell (1984), 105 Ill. 2d 1, 14.) Moreover, an included-offense instruction "'is only proper where the charged greater offense requires the jury to find a disputed factual element which is not required for conviction of the lesser-included offense.'" (<u>People v. Cramer</u> (1981), 85 Ill. 2d 92, 100, quoting <u>Sansone v. United States</u> (1965), 380 U.S. 343, 349–50, 13 L. Ed. 2d 882, 887–88, 85 S. Ct. 1004, 1009.) Thus, instructions on less serious offenses are not required in every case." <u>Bryant</u>, 113 Ill. 2d at 507, 499 N.E.2d at 417–18.

Defendant asserts the evidence in this case would support a reckless conduct conviction. A person is guilty of this offense if he harms or endangers the safety of another, and he recklessly performs the acts which did so. (ILL. REV. STAT. 1987, ch. 38, par. 12-5.) Defendant submits that the reckless act in this case was his becoming intoxicated at the bar, and it was due to this intoxication that the attack occurred.

Section 4-6 of the Code provides that a person acts recklessly when he consciously disregards a *substantial* and unjustifiable risk that a result will follow. (ILL. REV. STAT. 1987, ch. 38, par. 4-6.) This clearly connotes a certain sense of foreseeability that the result will occur from the conduct. We do not believe this is such a situation. The evidence establishes that between one and two hours after defendant ceased drinking, he suddenly attacked and attempted to kill a man defendant hardly knew and who had offered defendant some assistance. It would be difficult to conclude that defendant, as he was becoming intoxicated, was consciously disregarding the risk that he would subsequently, due to the drinking, attack with a knife and attempt to kill another for no apparent reason. While it could be argued that it is conceivable that something like this would occur, we note the definition requires a substantial risk. This is not such a risk.

Defendant can cite no cases where the alleged reckless act is so distant or attenuated from the harm to the victim, or where the resulting harm was due to such an unlikely outcome of the reckless act. To hold as defendant suggests would seem to require that in any case where a perpetrator's intoxication can be related to the actual harmful conduct, irregardless of the remoteness or the unlikelihood, his conduct can be viewed as reckless. We believe this is neither the scope nor intent of section 4-6. Defendant's intoxication is properly addressed to his affirmative defense. We, therefore, hold that, under the circumstances of this case, the evidence would not support a reckless conduct conviction. Accordingly, since the evidence would not permit a jury to rationally find defendant guilty of that offense, his offered instructions were properly refused.

Defendant next contends he received ineffective assistance of counsel, since his counsel objected to the State's included-offense instructions alleging aggravated battery.

The United States Supreme Court in Strickland v. Washington (1984), 466 U.S. 668, 80 L. Ed. 2d 674, 104 S. Ct. 2052, formulated a two-part test for evaluating whether a claim of ineffective assistance of counsel rises to the level of a constitutional deprivation. Defendant must first demonstrate that counsel's performance was deficient. (People v. Owens (1989), 129 Ill. 2d 303, 309, 544 N.E.2d 276, 278.) Defendant must also prove that his counsel's deficient performance substantially prejudiced his defense. (Owens, 129 Ill. 2d at 309, 544 N.E.2d at 278.) To meet this second test, a defendant must show a reasonable probability that "but for counsel's unprofessional errors, the result of the proceeding would have been different." Strickland, 466 U.S. at 694, 80 L. Ed. 2d at 698, 104 S. Ct. at 2068.

Defendant observes that courts have held that aggravated battery can be an included offense of attempt (murder). (See People v. Gvojic (1987), 160 Ill. App. 3d 1065, 513 N.E.2d 1083; People v. Cross (1980), 84 Ill. App. 3d 868, 406 N.E.2d 66.) Therefore, defendant maintains that counsel was mistaken in objecting to the instructions, and this conduct falls below the level of professionalism required. He also believes he was prejudiced by this conduct because, since the case is closely balanced, the jury might have chosen the "third option" and convicted him of the lesser charge, while acquitting him of the greater.

However, a review of the record establishes that counsel was not acting under a mistaken belief. Rather, he forcefully argued that the evidence presented would not support an aggravated battery charge. To properly evaluate counsel's conduct, it is necessary to be aware of the procedural background.

As noted earlier, at the jury instruction conference the court accepted, over the State's objection, defendant's reckless conduct instructions. Later, prior to closing argument, the State sought to have the questioned instructions accepted. Defense counsel objected, and a recess was taken. Upon the court's return, it reversed its earlier decision and refused defendant's reckless conduct instructions. At this point, the State withdrew its aggravated battery instructions, while defense counsel, to no avail, sought to have the court reconsider its reckless conduct ruling.

Thus, it is clear that counsel's objections were based on trial strategy. At the time he made the objections, the jury was to be instructed on attempt (murder), a Class X felony (ILL. REV. STAT. 1987, ch. 38, par. 8-4(c)), and reckless conduct, a Class A misdemeanor (ILL. REV. STAT. 1987, ch. 38, par. 12-5(b)). This is sound strategy. It was not until after he had argued forcefully against the aggravated battery instructions (a Class 3 felony (ILL. REV. STAT. 1987, ch. 38, par. 12-4(e))) that the reckless conduct instructions were removed. By then, it was too late, since this position had been taken. It could be argued that counsel should not have objected at all. After all, having two included charges is better than none. However, his desire was to ensure that the only in-cluded charge was a misdeamnor [*sic*] and not a felony. Since counsel is continually subject to criticism in hindsight for strategies which may not have been successful, judicial scrutiny of counsel's performance must be highly deferential. (Strickland, 466 U.S. at 689, 80 L. Ed. 2d at 694, 104 S. Ct. at 2065.) Courts presume that counsel's performance falls within the wide range of professionally competent assistance. (Owens, 129 Ill. 2d at 309, 544 N.E.2d at 278.) To overcome this pre-sumption, the defendant must prove that his counsel's representation fell below an objective standard of reasonableness. (Strickland, 466 U.S. at 694, 80 L. Ed. 2d at 698, 104 S. Ct. at 2068.) We have no doubt that other counsel may have proceeded differently. However, this is true of every case. Counsel's strategy was sound and is definitely within the range of acceptable representation.

Defendant argues, in the alternative, that the court should have *sua sponte* given the aggravated battery instructions. Defendant failed to in-clude this assertion in his post-trial motion, and it is, therefore, waived. People v. Tannenbaum (1980), 82 Ill. 2d 177, 181, 415 N.E.2d 1027, 1029.

Defendant next maintains the court erred by refusing to allow him to recall a witness. After Schertz testified and was excused, defendant made a request to recall him. This was done while it was still defen-dant's case in chief. In an offer of proof, Schertz testified that he ob-served defendant drink champagne out of a party horn and break plas-tic glasses against his head. Schertz explained that he remembered this after he left the stand and brought it to defense counsel's attention. The court declined to let him be recalled.

It is well settled that the decision of whether to allow recall of a wit-ness is left to the sound discretion of the trial court. (People v. Harris (1979), 74 Ill. 2d 472, 477, 386 N.E.2d 60, 62; People v. Smith (1986),

149 Ill. App. 3d 145, 152, 500 N.E.2d 605, 610.) This ruling will not be reversed, absent a clear abuse of discretion. <u>Smith</u>, 149 Ill. App. 3d at 152, 500 N.E.2d at 610.

The offered testimony is simply further evidence of defendant's intoxication. This is merely cumulative, since there already existed substantial evidence on this point. Further, the testimony dealt with defendant's level of intoxication at midnight, which is over five hours prior to the incident. Thus, it is of marginal probative value concerning defendant's state of mind at the time of the offense. We find no abuse of discretion.

Lastly, defendant insists the trial court erred by failing to grant his post-trial motion. At the sentencing hearing, the court found, in mitigation, that defendant did not contemplate that his conduct could cause or threaten serious physical harm to another. (See ILL. REV. STAT. 1987, ch. 38, par. 1005-5-3.1(a)(2).) Defendant notes that to be found guilty of attempt (murder), it is essential that he be found to have intended to kill Remmert. He maintains the court's finding is contrary to the presence of such an intent and is tantamount to an acquittal. Therefore, he insists the court erred by not granting defendant's post-trial motion.

This question has already been resolved by <u>People v. Hendricks</u> (1986), 145 Ill. App. 3d 71, 495 N.E.2d 85, *aff'd* (December 21, 1988), No. 63803, *rehearing granted* (1989). There, in refusing to impose the death penalty, the trial judge observed he was not convinced beyond a reasonable doubt of defendant's guilt. An argument identical to the present one was made by Hendricks' defense counsel. The reviewing courts observed that the court had already denied the motions for directed verdict, alleging the sufficiency of the evidence, and that the trial court specifically stated the evidence was sufficient to convict. The courts held the comments were made in the context of sentencing and were not a comment on the sufficiency of the evidence.

Similarly, in the present case, it is clear the comments are solely made in the sentencing context. The court specifically made this clear when it stated:

"So, with regard to Factor No. 2 as to sentencing only, Court would conclude independent of the jury's conclusion, particularly given the fact there is no particular burden on these findings, that the Defendant did not contemplate that his criminal conduct would cause or threaten serious physical harm to another."

Further, the court earlier denied motions for directed verdicts, and later denied the post-trial motion which specifically raised the question of the sufficiency of the evidence. Thus, pursuant to <u>Hendricks</u>, there is no error.

Affirmed.

# INDEX

[References are to text pages and to appendices.]

[References are to text pages and to appendices.]

[References are to text pages and to appendices.]

[References are to text pages and to appendices.]

# S

# T

[References are to text pages and to appendices.]

# V